The Presidents Were Here

The Presidents Were Here

A State-by-State Historical Guide

Ralph Gary

McFarland & Company, Inc., Publishers
Jefferson, North Carolina, and London

The present work is a reprint of the illustrated case bound edition of The Presidents Were Here: A State-by-State Historical Guide, *first published in 2008 by McFarland.*

All photographs are by the author.

Library of Congress Cataloguing-in-Publication Data

Gary, Ralph, 1940–
The presidents were here : a state-by-state historical guide / Ralph Gary.
p. cm.
Includes bibliographical references and index.

ISBN 978-0-7864-7715-9
softcover : acid free paper ∞

1. Presidents— United States— Homes and haunts— Guidebooks. 2. Historic sites— United States— Guidebooks. 3. United States— Guidebooks. I. Title.
E176.1.G28 2013 973.09'9 — dc22 2008030426

British Library cataloguing data are available

On the cover: *clockwise from top left* Christ Church, Alexandria; Grand Tetons; Virginia capitol; The Old House Chamber

Manufactured in the United States of America

McFarland & Company, Inc., Publishers
Box 611, Jefferson, North Carolina 28640
www.mcfarlandpub.com

To my best friends:
The loveliest woman I know, my wife Judy.
The bravest and most admirable man I know, Bob Byrd.
And the wisest man I know, Loyce Gary, now in his tenth decade.

Acknowledgments

Of course a book like this could not be developed without help from many who live in historic areas and make a lifetime's study of various historical sites and structures. In particular I express thanks and appreciation to those who have supplied information and been of great support to me throughout the last ten years of this project developing Lincoln and other presidential material: Frank Williams, Chairman of the Lincoln Forum and Chief Justice of the Rhode Island Supreme Court, and Harold Holzer, Vice Chairman of the Forum. Both are noted historians, prolific authors, and on the Abraham Lincoln Bicentennial Commission. Also Ron Keller and Paul Gleason of Lincoln College, John Waugh, another noted historian and prolific author, Richard Sloan of the New York Lincoln Group, many in Springfield and the Lincoln home, and many other of the Lincoln Forum members with their incredible knowledge of Lincoln and presidential sites.

Several have taken many hours to review my manuscript related to their particular areas of expertise to make suggestions and modifications. These include those listed above; Trenton Historical Society; Sally Lane, Carson City historian at the State Library; Guy L. Rocha; Albemarle Historical Library; Margaret O'Bryant; Patricia Gochenour of Winchester, Virginia; John Pierce at the James Monroe Museum in Fredericksburg; many others in Fredericksburg including Paula Felder; Jane Conner of Stafford County; Don Pfanz at the National Historic Park in Fredericksburg; Andrew Jackson O'Shaughnessy and others at Monticello; Paul O'Neil at the Baltimore Civil War Museum; and others in many states who received samples related to their areas. Also thanks to Mark Greenough, supervisor and historian at the Capitol in Richmond for his unique knowledge about that area.

I am especially grateful to Richard Hart, Wayne Temple, Nicky Stratton, the director of Looking for Lincoln Coalition, and many others in Springfield, including many at the State Library and Lincoln historic site.

Others who have gone out of their way to aid in this project include: Brad Hoch in Gettysburg for his knowledge of Lincoln in Pennsylvania; Philip Stone of Bridgewater College; Chris Calkins of Petersburg; Eileen Morales, curator of the Bainbridge House in Princeton; Arizona History Librarian Donald H. Langlois; Julie Northrip, Park Ranger, Ft. Smith National Historic Site; Dick Rice at the Sam Houston Museum; Joe Lojeski at the Augusta Historical Society; Gorden Cotton, Vicksburg Museum and Historical Society; Groton School historian Doug Brown; Dedham, Massachusetts, historian Bob Hanson; Petersburg, Dulany Ward; Sandy Allen, historian at Salem, Oregon; Ranger Doug Halsey, Ft. Vancouver; Surratt Society and Joan Chaconas, Washington D.C.; Richmond, Petersburg, Lexington, Louisville, Cincinnati, Columbus, Cleveland, and countless numbers of park rangers and historians, docents and local historians in countless numbers of places who led me in the right direction with many sources of material, published and unpublished.

Many libraries with their research assistants were especially helpful in developing this material, including libraries in Independence, Missouri, Fredericksburg, Leesville, Orange, Alexandria, Vancouver, Seattle, Dallas, New York City, Augusta, Atlanta, San Francisco, Los Angeles, Las Vegas, Billings, Helena, Chicago Historical Society, Nashville City Library, Tennessee State Library, and many other historical societies and state and local libraries in all states visited.

Table of Contents

PREFACE

This book identifies and describes sites with historical ties to American presidents. Ranging from long- and short-term residences to speech locales and even the locations of overnight stays, this state-by-state survey employs inclusion criteria that are admittedly broad. But this inclusiveness is entirely by design; the author's intentions were to document any site of potential interest to either the researcher or the casual fan of history.

While no such compilation can ever be absolutely comprehensive — documentation for overnight visits might have been lost, for instance, or gone unrecorded — this volume is based on decades of travel and research in library collections, historical sites and societies, and government sources. Academic historians, authors of local histories, and even tour guides were consulted in an effort to obtain and verify information. The coverage falls primarily within the following categories:

- Birthplaces and boyhood homes, including those where the exact site is in question
- Other places of residence during their lives
- Presidential retreats and recreation spots
- Churches and marriage sites
- Sites of historic speeches and other historic events
- Hotels and visitation sites
- Battlefield sites, military headquarters and wartime sites for wartime presidents
- Work sites before their presidency, including business and government service
- Retirement homes
- Sites of alleged scandalous behavior
- Attempted and actual assassination sites
- Death sites, including those which are lesser known
- Schools attended or where they visited their children
- Military training sites for presidents who served in the military
- Many other interesting sites discovered along the way

Both familiar and little known, marked and unmarked sites from every state, some barely known even to locals, are described.

Conflicting information and questions are resolved where possible, based on available information. Many presidents stayed at many sites in their lifetimes and made multiple visits to multiple areas. The amazing thing is not that we know of so many, but that we do not know of more.

The Confederate president, **Jefferson Davis**, and Texas president, **Sam Houston**, are included; these significant historical figures were each a president of a national entity situated within the present United States.

Readers are requested to send additions and modifications to the author in care of the publisher so that the information can be as complete and accurate as possible for future editions.

Those structures or sites highlighted with an asterisk (*) are open and accessible to the public, at least some of the time.

Introduction: Presidents of the United States

1. **George Washington**, born 1732, died 1799, served 1789–97: But for "The Father of Our Country," commander of the Colonial military forces, president of the Constitutional Convention, and "The Indispensable Man," the Colonies probably would not have maintained their army, won their independence and then forged or maintained a lasting federal union.

2. **John Adams**, born 1735, died 1826, served 1797–1801: A major leader in the Congress before and during the Revolution, minister to France, Great Britain, and the Netherlands, he was the father of John Quincy Adams.

3. **Thomas Jefferson**, born 1743, died 1826, served 1801–09: He wrote his own epitaph to emphasize his proudest achievements, "Author of the Declaration of Independence, Statute of Virginia for Religious Freedom, and Father of the University of Virginia."

4. **James Madison**, born 1751, died 1836, served 1809–17: "The Father of the Constitution" led the nation into the War of 1812, the "Second War for Independence."

5. **James Monroe**, born 1758, died 1831, served 1817–25: Like his predecessors, he served in the Continental Congress and was also governor of Virginia, minister to France and Great Britain, and a senator, and once held two simultaneous cabinet posts.

6. **John Quincy Adams**, born 1767, died 1848, served 1825–29: Among the nation's most intelligent presidents, he served a number of diplomatic and political posts, is rated the best secretary of state, and only president to be elected to the House after leaving office.

7. **Andrew Jackson**, born 1767, died 1845, served 1829–37: This member of both houses of Congress and a major general won the important Battle of New Orleans, and helped to win Florida and much of Alabama, Georgia, and Mississippi from the Indians, Spain, and Britain by his aggressive military actions. He was the first log cabin president.

8. **Martin Van Buren**, born 1782, died 1862, served 1837–41: The first president born after the Declaration of Independence, he was governor of New York, secretary of state, and the last sitting vice president elected president until George H.W. Bush, 152 years later.

9. **William Henry Harrison**, born 1773, died 1841, served 1841: The major general, senator, representative, and territorial governor of Indiana had 48 grandchildren, 106 great-grandchildren, and died a month after his inauguration. He was the first Whig elected and the first president to die in office

10. **John Tyler**, born 1790, died 1862, served 1841–45: His refusal to become only an "acting president" after Harrison died set a continuing precedent. He served as governor of

Virginia, and was in the House, Senate, and Confederate Congress. One of his fifteen children survived World War II.

11. **James K. Polk**, born 1795, died 1849, served 1845–49: This governor of Tennessee, speaker of the U.S. House, and possibly one of the more underrated presidents, injured his health by overwork and died a few months after leaving office.

12. **Zachary Taylor,** born 1784, died 1850, served 1849–50: This major general served on the frontier and gained prominence during the Mexican War, held no prior political office, and never voted in any election, including his own. He was the second and last Whig, both of whom died in office.

13. **Millard Fillmore**, born 1800, died 1874, served 1850–53: One of the least well known presidents, he served four terms in the House, was the first comptroller of New York, and vice president.

14. **Franklin Pierce**, born 1804, died 1869, served 1853–57: His only army rank was as brigadier general during the Mexican War. He served in the House and Senate before winning election as a compromise candidate because he supported the Compromise of 1850. He was defeated later for the same reason, along with his support for the disastrous Kansas-Nebraska Act. He was one of three presidents (with Lincoln and Coolidge) greatly affected by a young son's death after election.

15. **James Buchanan**, born 1791, died 1868, served 1857–61: He was one of the most prepared presidents, serving in the House and Senate and as secretary of state and minister to Great Britain, but one of the poorest rated.

16. **Abraham Lincoln,** born 1809, died 1865, served 1861–65: Known as the best president, he preserved the country during its worst crisis, served in the House, was elected five times to the Illinois Legislature, then lost twice for the Senate. He was the first of four assassinated presidents.

17. **Andrew Johnson**, born 1808, died 1875, served 1865–69: In Congress and governor of Tennessee before and during the Civil War, he returned to the Senate after leaving office, having been impeached and saved by one vote from conviction and removal.

18. **Ulysses S. Grant**, born 1822, died 1885, served 1869–77: The commanding general of Union forces during the Civil War became rich, lost it all, died poor, but wrote what is considered one of history's best military memoirs, providing a fortune for his survivors.

19. **Rutherford B. Hayes**, born 1822, died 1893, served 1877–81: The governor of Ohio and former House member was declared winner on March 2, two days before Grant's term ended. After losing the popular vote by 51 to 48 percent, he won the disputed electoral vote by one when a special commission voted down party lines to award him three contested states.

20. **James A. Garfield**, born 1831, died 1881, served 1881: The second assassinated president had been a major general and was in the House and Senate.

21. **Chester A. Arthur**, born 1829, died 1886, served 1881–85: The former spoilsman or federal job broker held no elected office prior to becoming vice president at the request of a political boss, and succeeded Garfield.

22. **Grover Cleveland**, born 1837, died 1908, served 1885–89: He was also the 24th president, governor of New York, and the first Democrat elected after the Civil War.

23. **Benjamin Harrison**, born 1833, died 1901, served 1889–93: The grandson of the ninth president, this brigadier general and senator won the electoral vote after losing the popular vote to Cleveland.

24. **Grover Cleveland**, served 1893–7: He was also the 22nd president and won the popular vote three times.

25. **William McKinley**, born 1843, died 1901, served 1897–1901: The third assassinated president presided over the Spanish-American War; he had been governor of Ohio and in the House.

26. **Theodore Roosevelt**, born 1858, died 1919, served 1901–09: Our youngest president made one of the worst presidential mistakes by declaring on the night of his second election that he would not run again when he probably would have been successful. He then spent his second term as a "lame duck" and much of his remaining life trying to win the office back; he might have done it in 1920 had he lived. One of the strongest presidents, he has his image on Mount Rushmore and won the Nobel Prize.

27. **William Howard Taft**, born 1857, died 1930, served 1909–13: Governor of the Philippines and secretary of war, he was the only president also to be chief justice and swore in Coolidge and Hoover.

28. **Woodrow Wilson**, born 1856, died 1924, served 1913–21: The former governor of New Jersey and most honored man in the world at the end of World War I could not convince Congress to pass his vision of the League of Nations, suffered a stroke trying to sell it the public, and ended his life an invalid. He was the first since the 17th president to not have been born in or elected from Ohio or New York.

29. **Warren Harding**, born 1865, died 1923, served 1921–23: Maybe our worst president, he had been in the Senate, and lived down to his own low expectations.

30. **Calvin Coolidge**, born 1872, died 1933, served 1923–29: The former governor of Massachusetts was maybe the most reticent president. His wife liked to tell of when someone told him that she had bet she could get him to say more than two words, and he responded, "You lose." After he died, someone asked, "How could you tell?"

31. **Herbert Hoover**, born 1874, died 1964, served 1929–33: This self-made millionaire and world's greatest mining engineer was orphaned at eight, led besieged citizens in China during the 1900 Boxer Rebellion, and left business at age 40 at the beginning of World War I to devote his life to public service. He directed food relief during and after World Wars I and II, saving maybe hundreds of millions from starvation, but was blamed by many for the Great Depression during his term. He donated his government salaries, including presidential, to charity and paid his own expenses.

32. **Franklin Delano Roosevelt**, born 1882, died 1945, served 1933–45: The only four-term president generally is rated number two or three overall for his leadership during the Great Depression and World War II. He was confined by polio in 1921 to a wheelchair, and could not walk after that time, and barely missed assassination in 1933. He led the country, 18th in military power at the start of World War II to number one status militarily and economically, where it has remained ever since.

33. **Harry S. Truman**, born 1884, died 1972, served 1945–53: The former senator is generally thought to have successfully filled the place of his predecessor by presiding over the end of and recovery from World War II, the Marshall Plan, and the Korean War.

34. **Dwight David Eisenhower**, born 1890, died 1969, served 1953–61: The five-star general had commanded Allied European forces during World War II.

35. **John F. Kennedy**, born 1917, died 1963, served 1961–3: Like the two presidents who followed, he was a representative and senator and was the youngest elected president and the fourth to be assassinated, at the height of his popularity.

36. **Lyndon B. Johnson**, born 1908, died 1973, served 1963–9: One of the most powerful senators in history gave up a probable third presidential term mostly because of the endless military stalemate in Vietnam. Like his successor he reached the highest acclaim and soon fell in approval rating and effectiveness.

37. **Richard M. Nixon**, born 1913, died 1994, served 1969–74: He resigned in disgrace after being overwhelmingly reelected less than two years before.

38. **Gerald R. Ford**, born 1913, died 2007, served 1974–77: The only president not elected even as vice president, had been in the House and was the victim of two assassination

attempts in 17 days. He joined John Adams and Ronald Reagan as the longest-lived presidents.

39. **Jimmy Carter**, born 1924, served 1977–81: The only Deep South president since the Civil War, and the only one to walk in his inaugural parade from the Capitol to the White House, had been governor of Georgia and later won the Nobel Prize.

40. **Ronald W. Reagan**, born 1911, died 2004, served 1981–9: The nation's oldest president went from a Hollywood movie career to the governor's office in California.

41. **George H.W. Bush**, born 1924, served 1989–93: The former representative and CIA director was only the second two-term vice president to move directly to the White House and also to see a son elected president, was born on the same extended street as the other's (John Adams) home.

42. **Bill Clinton**, born 1946, served 1993–2001: The nation's youngest ever governor and, after leaving office, husband of a senator from New York, was the second president to be impeached.

43. **George W. Bush**, born 1946, served 2001–: This governor of Texas was, like John Quincy Adams, one of only two sons of a president to be elected. They both lost the popular vote to a Tennessean, but were elected by the electoral vote.

Jefferson Davis, born 1808, died 1889: A Mexican War hero, he served as president of the Confederate States 1861–5, after serving as a representative, senator, and strong secretary of war. He was captured fleeing after the Civil War and kept in prison without being charged at Fort Monroe for two years.

Sam Houston, born 1793, died 1863: He was president of Texas 1836–8 and 1841–4. He had been governor of Tennessee, but resigned soon after his marriage, left his wife, and fled to Oklahoma to live with the Indians. He later led the Texas army to victory, securing Texas independence, leading to the Mexican War and U.S. acquisition of much of the Southwest and West. He was later a senator and was removed as governor of Texas for failing to support the Confederate government. The largest city in the country named after an individual bears his name, which was the first word spoken on the moon: "Houston, the Eagle has landed."

A STATE-BY-STATE HISTORICAL GUIDE

ALABAMA

JACKSON FORTS • **Jackson** built a series of forts during several military campaigns as follows:

Fort Deposit was a supply post built in 1813 at the influx of Thompson's Creek with the Tennessee River in today's Decatur. **Jackson** was here on his way to and from his military campaigns.

Fort Lashley was erected in 1813 in the present city of Talladega.

Fort Strother, a major Indian campaign site built in 1813, was the site of two mutinies quelled by **Jackson's** controversial iron will and determination. Seventeen-year-old John Wood was executed for disobeying an order. He left his post with permission, but did not return fast enough when ordered and challenged an officer. Several others tried to leave, feeling that their enlistments were up, and broke into supplies, resulting in their trial and execution. The log fort was one-half mile south of Henry Neely Dam on the Coosa River in St. Clair County, now about 20 miles south of Gadsden on Alabama 77. After the Indian battle 13 miles east at the Creek village of Talluschathes or Tallushatchee when a number a Creeks were killed, **Jackson** noticed a ten-month-old Indian boy not taken by the remaining squaws, who actually wanted to kill him. He took him to his tent, dissolved brown sugar in water and coaxed him to drink. He probably was sympathetic to the youngster who, like himself, was a helpless orphan at an early age due to war. He raised the boy as his son only to grieve greatly when he died as a teenager.

Ft. Crawford was erected in 1818, a mile from Brewton across Murder Creek in Escambia County, north of the Conecuh River. **Jackson** used it for a supply post and defensive position against marauding Indians. When the Creeks began to surrender, he met with them here and told them that they must stay north of this position or be considered still at war.

Fort Williams, built in 1814 just prior to the Battle of Horseshoe Bend, a few miles west of his victory at Talladega, was six miles southwest of Fayetteville, and is now under Lay Lake.

BIRMINGHAM • **Theodore Roosevelt** visited in 1905, and **Franklin D. Roosevelt** spoke from his railroad car at the train station in 1933. **Hayes** toured the town in 1891, when he was met by 20,000 at the Union Station, toured Lakeview Park and the Highlands before a reception at the Caldwell House that was on 22nd Street at the train tracks. In 1921 **Harding** honored the city on its 50th anniversary by laying a cornerstone for the Masonic Temple and spoke at First Methodist and Woodrow Wilson Park.

DECATUR • In 1863 **Grant** met for a conference in what is now the Rhea-McEntire House* on the shoreline of Wheeler Lake. Both sides used this at various times as war headquarters. **B. Harrison** stayed in the Tavern Hotel at Grant and Sixth, burned in 1923. **A. Johnson** traveled through in 1823, and **Van Buren** attended the opening of the Old State Bank* at 925 Bank St. in 1833. It is the oldest standing bank in Alabama and served as a Union hospital

DEMOPOLIS • **Davis** was entertained at Bluff Hall,* on North Commissioners Avenue.

FLORENCE • **Jackson** visited his plantation on the Tennessee River at Melton's Bluff, where he owned 50 slaves. He is believed to have stopped at Pope's Tavern,* 203 Heritage Drive.

**Designates a site open to the public.*

Horseshoe Bend National Military Park • **Jackson** led the Tennessee militia and United States forces to a victory over the Creek Nation on March 27, 1814, ending their threat to settlers during the War of 1812. Young **Houston** was hit with a jagged-point arrow, leaving a large wound. He drew his sword, ordered a man nearby to pull it out, and then passed out when it was. **Jackson** witnessed part of what had happened and ordered **Houston** to the rear, but Houston disobeyed and went into the fight again, drawing the attention, confidence, and friendship of **Jackson**, later his political mentor.

The Indians were forced behind a stronghold. **Jackson** called for volunteers to storm the key point. No one stepped forward until injured Ensign **Houston** seized a musket, ordered and led a charge, again being hit with a barbed arrow in the right shoulder. He almost died, was taken to Fort Williams, and two months later to New Orleans for an operation, but was lamed for life. The site is now a well-marked park about 50 miles northeast of Montgomery on Route 49.

Huntsville • **Jackson** joined his cavalry at Ditto's Landing near U.S. 29, east on Hobbs Island Road on the Tennessee. In May 1814, he organized his troops on the square and his army passed through on the way back from Horseshoe Bend. He was then hosted at the oldest mansion in Alabama, the Pope Home at 403 Echols. **Monroe** was entertained in 1819 at the NW corner of Franklin and Gates in Constitution Hall Park about 301 Madison. **Garfield** was on the same site as presiding officer in a Civil War court martial. In 1960 **Eisenhower** came here on the way to inspect George Marshall Space Flight Center and participated in the unveiling of a bust of his World War II commander. **Kennedy** visited in 1963. **Nixon** spoke in a downtown park in 1975.

Marion • **Houston** married in 1840 at the Lea House,* 318 Green. He had met 20-year-old Margaret on a trip to Mobile and convinced her to come to Texas to get married. When he met what he thought was her boat in Galveston, her mother only got off and informed him that her daughter "is at home where she should be, and ... the ceremony will be performed in my own home in Marion."

Mobile • **Jackson** used Fort Conde,* 150 S. Royal at Church Street, in his military operations against Pensacola and New Orleans. The fort has been reconstructed at one-third the actual size. To the south he strengthened Fort Bowyer about where Fort Morgan* was later built, to prevent British capture of Mobile, denying them a foothold on the Gulf Coast and a path to New Orleans. The British and Spanish did not consider Mobile to be covered in the treaty ending the War of 1812 or the Louisiana Purchase, and probably would have used it to strengthen their territorial claims. He organized forces here before and after his attack on Pensacola.

The Battle House, SE corner of Royal and St. Francis, was the scene of several presidential visits, before and after the antebellum hotel was destroyed and built back in the early 20th century. **Jackson** had his headquarters on the spot later visited by **Davis** and **Fillmore. TR** saw the ruins in 1905, and **Wilson** ate in the restored hotel. **TR** also made a speech around the corner at Bienville Square. Other visits have included **Hayes** and **Garfield** at Oakleigh,* 350 Oakleigh Place, and **Fillmore** at the Sixth Mobile Theatre, Royal and St. Michael.

Grant came from New Orleans in 1880 to the depot on Governor Street to be a guest at several locations. Most greeting him were said to be colored. He attended a banquet at City Hall, Market and Royal, another at his lodgings, the Battle House, court room at the Customs House across the street, the Manassas Club on another corner at this location, and the Cotton Exchange on the NW corner of Commerce and St. Frances.

Van Buren stayed at the Mansion House and saw a play at the Corinthian Theater on April 6, 1842. **Polk** passed through and stopped at the head of Dauphin Street. **TR** dedicated the Masonic Temple on St. Joseph in 1902. **Wilson** made a famous speech at the Lyric Theater on Joachim Street on the east side between Condi and Government. The theater and long fought-over marker are no longer there. This was the first time that an American president renounced expansionism, saying that the United States would not seek another foot of territory by conquest and implied that Europe should keep its hands off this hemisphere. **Nixon** came through the Bankhead Tunnel on Government Street in 1971 to the International Trade Center and Parliament House Hotel, where various events were planned.

Montgomery • After the Battle of Horseshoe Bend, **Jackson** rebuilt a 1714 French fort, renaming it Fort Jackson.* It is now restored as a state park 17 miles north off Route 231, probably on the route used by the explorer DeSoto in 1540.

While here he received the surprise surrender of the famed Indian war leader, Red Eagle, or William Weatherford, who wandered in. **Jackson** had told the Creeks that unless Red Eagle was tried as a prisoner, the war and killing would continue. Half-white Weatherford decided he could not prevail and voluntarily and defiantly came in. Even though he had led the Fort Mims massacre and committed many atrocities, **Jackson** was impressed with his bravery shown here and felt that the Indians would listen to the hostile chief who was paroled and went to his people to convince them to surrender.

General Pinckney relieved **Jackson** several weeks later; he returned to Nashville only to soon learn that he had been named a major general in the U.S. army and put back in command. (He got **William Henry Harrison's** rank when he resigned.) He then returned to Ft. Jackson to demand that all chiefs meet him there to discuss surrender. When they did in August 1814, **Jackson** demanded and got 23 million acres, or three-fifths of Alabama and one-fifth of Georgia. Much was from tribes not at war and above the terms authorized by the government, but he considered it war reparations. This Treaty of Fort Jackson ended the Indian uprising and opened the area to settlement. **Jackson** waited here for supplies and moved on to New Orleans. Later, when the Treaty of Ghent ending the War of 1812 conflicted with these terms, **Jackson** ignored the latter treaty and upheld his own with its harsher consequences for the Indians. In 1814 he visited nearby Prattville's "historic treasure," Buena Vista, at 641 CR 4.

The first and only president of the Confederacy, **Davis**, moved in 1861 to the SW corner of Bibb and Lee Streets in Montgomery, then the Confederate capital. The home, known as the first Confederate White House,* is now located at Washington and Union, across from the Confederate Capitol,* still the State Capitol. **Davis** was inaugurated at a spot marked on the front Capitol steps, where he gave his inaugural address; he then spoke to the legislature inside.

Davis first lived at the Exchange Hotel, NW corner of Commerce and Montgomery, before moving into the White House, met with his cabinet, and spoke to the citizens from the balcony on the Commerce Street side. He worked at the government building, Market and Commerce, and dined at the Exchange throughout his time in the city. He stayed here again in 1886 on a grand tour where he was greeted by well-wishers and spoke of the Civil War as "that war which Christianity alone approved — a holy war for defense." **Davis's** pew is marked inside St. John's Episcopal on the NE corner of Madison and Perry. He was a frequent visitor to the Murphey House at Bibb and Coosa, later Union headquarters. In April 1886, he laid the cornerstone for the Confederate Monument on the north lawn.

TR, Houston, Reagan, and **Cleveland** also spoke at the Capitol, **TR** at the **Davis** inaugural site. Union veteran **McKinley** was given a Confederate medal when he spoke at the same spot in 1898. He also spoke at Tuskegee Institute, as did **FDR** in 1940 when he met George Washington Carver. **Pierce** is reported at Court Street Methodist. The **Bushes,** lifetime members of the Bass Anglers Sportsmanship Society, liked to fish in a 55-acre bass pond at the Alabama River in nearby Prattville called the "President's Lake."

MOORESVILLE • **Andrew Johnson** worked as a tailor in 1825 at a shop at the SW corner of Piney and Martin while lodging at the adjacent McNeill House. **McKinley** attended the Church of Christ on Piney Street in 1863 where **Garfield** preached. **Garfield's** pulpit and Bible are here.

STEPHENSON • Union General William S. Rosecrans was headquartered in the "Little Brick House"* at the base of a mountain here when he was joined by his successor, **Grant**, and General **Garfield**. The accessible ruins are in the National Register of Historic Places.

TUSKEGEE • Scientist George Washington Carver taught at the Institute, and Booker T. Washington lived on campus at "The Oaks,"* 1212 Old Montgomery Road, from 1900 until 1915, visited by **TR** (1903), **Coolidge** (1923), **FDR** (1938), and **Bush** (1981). **TR** also visited antebellum Grey Columns* at 399 Old Montgomery Road near the university.

Alaska

ANCHORAGE • Most presidents since **Eisenhower** have visited the Chateau at Elmendorf Air Base at the end of North C Street. **Nixon** met Japanese Emperor Hirohito here. **Kennedy, Johnson,** and **Ford** stayed at the Hilton or its predecessor at 500 W. Third.

George H.W. Bush told his audience on February 22, 1989, he recognized that presidents going to the Far East landed at Elmendorf. He thought that 45 degrees below zero was not too bad, but 60 below "took a lot out of a feller." **George W. Bush** addressed soldiers here on November 14, 2005, on the way west.

JUNEAU • **Harding** came to Alaska Territory in 1923 with **Hoover** during his last journey in life before dying unexpectedly in San Francisco. They visited the Capitol on Fourth between Seward and Main and the Governor's Mansion at 716 Calhoun. His ship landed at Metlakatla, and he was warmly greeted at eight ports, plus Anchorage, Nenanat, and Fairbanks. They stayed at the railroad's Curry Hotel near the entrance to Denali National Park near Talkeetna and Curry, and Hotel Norvale in Fairbanks, 522 Second Street. His pew at the old church in Sitka is marked, and he laid the cornerstone of the Masonic Temple in Ketchikan. The Curry burned in 1971 and was rebuilt as the Hotel McKinley.

Arizona

PAGE • **Theodore Roosevelt** visited Rainbow Bridge on March 18, 1911, where he swam underneath and spend a long period at night gazing at the formation in moonlight. This is now accessible from WahWeep Marina on the north side of the Glen Canyon Dam. He also visited the Grand Canyon and wrote that he hoped Congress would make it a national park. He had been to the canyon in 1903 also as was Clinton on September 18, 1996.

PHOENIX • **McKinley** came in 1901 to visit the Territorial Capitol at Washington and 17th Streets and stayed at the Adams Hotel at Adams and Central for a reception and speech. **TR** visited the Capitol in 1911 and dedicated the nearby Roosevelt Dam. **Truman** spoke from his train at the Phoenix Station on September 24, 1948, at 10:45 P.M. He apologized for being late, but said he felt no one else could have gotten in if he had been sooner.

In 1936 **Kennedy's** parents sent him to the Jay 6 Ranch outside of Benson, owned by John Speiden, so that he could build up his fragile body. He had been sickly in England and hoped to soon go to Harvard with his older brother, who also came here. The young men herded cattle, repaired wire fences, and built an adobe house that the owner called "the house that Jack built." In January 1945, **Kennedy** came to recover from war injuries at the isolated Castle Hot Springs Hotel, seven miles northwest of Lake Pleasant and about 50 miles north of downtown Phoenix. (It is west of Interstate 17, exit 223, on a dirt road north of Route 74.) **Ford** and **TR** also stayed here. The hotel later burned and has been vacant for years. After about three months, he moved to the Arizona Biltmore,* 25th and E. Missouri, and then the Camelback Inn* on Lincoln Drive, where he learned that **FDR** died. **George W. Bush** spoke here on Nov. 28, 2005.

Nixon honeymooned at the Westward Ho Motel on North Central and W. Fillmore in 1940. **Reagan** visited the St. Thomas the Apostle Church, 2312 E. Campbell Ave., in 1973.

PRESCOTT • In 1928–9, **Nixon** came to a private sanitarium at 937 Apache where his brother with TB and mother stayed.

SCOTTSDALE • Reagan stayed with his wife's parents at 24 Biltmore in 1952 and later.

ARKANSAS

FAYETTEVILLE • What has been called the greatest football game in the state's history was between the number one and two ranked Texas Longhorns and Arkansas Razorbacks in 1969 at Razorback Stadium. **Nixon** attended with Congressman **George H.W. Bush**. The Longhorns fumbled as **Nixon** entered. The president beamed and gave the "V" sign as the thought the yelling was for him. **Bush** later presented the Presidential Medal of Freedom to founder of Wal-Mart Samuel Walton in nearby Bentonville at the headquarters in 1992.

Clinton lived eight miles west on Route 16 when he wrote a letter to a frequent burglar and hung it over the fireplace explaining that he had nothing in the home but junk. It did not convince the thief, who came back and took several items including his "Daddy's" World War I military sword and his prized sax. After campaigning all over the area in a losing bid for Congress, he was married to Hillary Rodham at his home, 930 California Boulevard,* where they lived from 1975 until 1976 when he was on the law faculty at the University of Arkansas. They had seen the house when he was taking her back to the airport after a visit, and he bought it for her as a surprise. When her parents arrived for the wedding and found that they were too poor to buy a wedding dress, the bride and her mother hurried out to the only store still open to pick one off the rack. His offices were in Waterman Hall, Maple and Garland, rooms 206 and 302, and he attended the First Baptist Church* at 10 E. Dickson.

FORT SMITH • **Taylor** was assigned at Cantonment Belknap, off Garrison Avenue one mile from Fort Smith, to command the army of observation for the annexation of Texas. The old 1838 commissary building is the Commissary Museum* on Garrison near the bridge. He may have attended church on the post between Fourth and Fifth Avenues and lived from 1841 to 1845 on the north side of Garrison at 13th Street behind the present Catholic Church where the Sisters of Mercy Convent now is as shown on the marker. Part of his house is believed to be a chimney of the Immaculate Conception Church, although the National Park Service is not sure and has almost nothing related to his time here. His home burned in 1875, and the "Taylor chimney" is marked. **Kennedy** visited the fort on October 29, 1961, when he got a deed to ten acres of the original fort site, and visited again in September 1963.

Ford visited St. Edward's Mercy Medical Center on August 10, 1975.

HOPE • **William Jefferson Clinton** was born on August 19, 1946, at the Julia Chester Hospital on Main between Ninth and Tenth. His father had died the previous May on the way to take his wife back to Chicago, where he was looking for a house, and the future president was named for him, William Jefferson Blythe IV. The 29-year-old father had four previous wives and several children that Bill's mother did not find out about until her son became president. Mrs. Blythe lived with her newborn son until he was four at the home of her parents at 117 S. Hervey* with no indoor plumbing. In 1950 she married abusive, alcoholic Roger Clinton and moved to 321 E. Thirteenth* until 1953; Bill liked to play cowboy in the yard. He felt that his stepfather loved his family, but liquor sent him out of control. One night Roger fired a shot at his wife, who grabbed Bill, who then ran and called the police.

The future president went to First Baptist Church on South Main at Fourth, kindergarten behind 509 Stores (now a vacant lot), where he broke his leg jumping a rope, and school at 500 S. Spruce. He has been pictured at the graves of his parents at Rosehill Cemetery* on North Hazel, Bus. Rte. 29 off Interstate 30, exit 31. The graves are enclosed within a small fence on the north side about 80 yards east of the street. His grandfather operated a neighborhood grocery across the street. **Clinton** is also pictured at the old train station at South Main and Division in downtown, now the visitor center,* where maps are available to the area Clinton sites.

Hot Springs • The **Clintons** moved to 1011 Park Avenue in 1954 until 1961, after living a short time in a rented home outside of town, and then at 213 Scully. He enjoying taking care of the grounds on Park Avenue notwithstanding bees, hornets, tarantulas, an occasional rattlesnake and all, as this was one of the few activities that he could do with his "Daddy." He went to a private school at 583 West Grand Avenue in the second grade since his mother did not think he was ready for a large public school, getting bad conduct marks because he kept yelling out answers without being recognized. He attended public school at 200 Ramble, where his sixth-grade teacher predicted that his mouth would make him governor or get him in big trouble when he grew up. A church is now on the site.

His high school was at Orange and 125 Oak, where he was drum major. In 1961, 15-year-old Bill Blythe took the last name of his stepfather. The year before, during one of the senior Clinton's alcoholic abusive periods with his wife, Bill harshly warned him to never harm his mother again. He went to Park Place Baptist, 721 Park Place, even though his parents seldom attended. When he and a close friend were waiting on the stairs of the baptistery to be baptized in shoulder-high water, a nervous woman being baptized before them panicked; her foot shot straight up and got caught on the window dividing the water from the choir and she began wildly splashing everywhere. Bill wrote that the two boys were in stitches from laughing so hard, and figured that if Jesus had this much sense of humor, being a Christian was not going to be so tough. His Order of DeMolay met at the Masonic Temple at 311 W. Grand, and he bowled at 3917 Central. His favorite places to hang out and eat were 510 Park and 314 and 505 Albert Pike. He was active in the State Democratic Convention at the Civic Center, feeling that the Party came alive after Ford pardoned Nixon.

Kennedy spoke at the Arlington Hotel, Central and Fountain, in September 1963 (where **Clinton** had his proms), and **Truman** visited the Park Hotel in 1941 at 211 Hot Springs Mountain Drive. As a reserve office he was frequently given checkups at the Army and Navy Hospital. **Kennedy** also visited Governor Orval Faubus at St. Joseph's Hospital. **TR, Hoover, FDR, Eisenhower,** and **LBJ** were also at the Hot Springs. **TR** spoke at Oaklawn Park in 1910 at the State Fair, visited in 1936 by **FDR**.

Little Rock • **Taylor** was given a rousing reception here on the way to Fort Smith in 1841. **Grant** passed through in 1879 and stayed at the Markham Hotel, 517 W. Markham. He came back in 1880 and stayed at the Capital Hotel,* 111 W. Markham near the Old Capitol* at 300 W. Markham, where he was entertained during both visits. In 1880 a group of women set up their chairs on the Main Street parade route with their backs to his procession to show their disdain for the former Union commander. He was honored in the hotel's Concordia Hall. **Clinton** announced for the presidency and gave his victory speeches from there.

The first president to visit while in office was **Benjamin Harrison** in 1891 when all downtown buildings were decorated in his honor.

Theodore Roosevelt and **Taft** visited the Old Capitol in 1905 and 1909. **Roosevelt** made a major speech in Old City Park after a Main Street parade and visited Fort Logan Roots. **Taft** has the honor of making the shortest visit. He stepped off the train on October 24, 1909, to make a brief speech, then left. **Wilson** visited his sister at 606 W. Third in 1886, a site now a parking lot, and frequently visited Augusta Presbyterian,* Third and Walnut, where his brother-in-law was pastor. **FDR** visited Sen. Joe Robinson at 2122 S. Broadway in 1936 after arriving at the Missouri-Pacific Depot. **Truman** visited Robinson's widow there in 1949 and attended a reception at the Hotel Marion, 200 W. Markham, where the Peabody now stands. **Reagan** spent the night there on Nov. 2, 1984. **Truman** met his old army buddies at the Robinson Auditorium on Markham and Dr. Hyman Rosenblum on Kenyon Street. On June 11, 1949, he filled War Memorial Stadium* to dedicate War Memorial Park.

Eisenhower stopped at Adams Field and MacArthur Park on September 2, 1952. **Carter** opened his campaign on November 12, 1975, with an announcement in Little Rock. **Reagan** visited the Capitol in 1984 and stayed at the Arkansas Excelsior House, 3 State House Plaza. His one-night stay for him and the staff was $25,000, including his order of ginger ale and jelly beans.

Clinton served as Arkansas Attorney General at the Justice Building, 1500 W. Seventh, and lived in the 10,000-square–foot Governor's Mansion* at 1800 Center Street in 1979 at age 32, the nation's youngest governor. He was re–elected every year, except one, through 1990. He introduced his running mate, Al Gore, on the lawn in 1992. He served in the State Capitol,* Woodlane and Capitol, from 1979 to 1981 and 1983 to 1992. He first lived from 1977 to 1979 in a 980-square–foot home at 5419 L Street, 816 Midland, out of office from 1981 to 1983 after Chelsea was born at Arkansas Baptist Hospital, and with his mother in 1980 at 405 Bayside. He was impressed hearing evangelist Rev. Billy Graham at War Memorial Stadium* as a boy in 1958 and as governor in 1988. Between terms as governor he worked at a law firm at 2200 Worthen Bank Building, Capital and Center. His home church was Immanuel Baptist at 1000 Bishop Street, and he retained membership while president. He sometimes attended his wife and daughter's church, First United Methodist, 723 Center Street.

He ran for president from his headquarters, 112 W. Third, and voted at the Dunbar Recreation Center,* 1001 W. 16th. A reception was then held for him at Concordia Hall, 305½ W. Markham. After election he hosted an economic conference at the Robinson Center,* Markham and Broadway. His favorite restaurant was Doe's, 1023 W. Markham, although he frequently stopped at McDonald's at 701 Broadway. He loved to shop at Andina's Coffee Shop at 400 President Clinton Ave. and golfed at Rebsamen Golf Course,* 3400 Rebsamen Park Drive.

In November 2004, former presidents **Carter** and **Bush** with the incumbent, **George W. Bush,** dedicated his presidential library* at the end of President Clinton Ave., a continuation of Markham. The museum sells a guided tour map of Clinton sites in Little Rock.

TEXARKANA • In 1964 **Johnson** dedicated a memorial to **Kennedy** on State Line Avenue at the post office* where he had spoken in 1960. **Carter** later appeared on a stage here in 1980, crossing the state line on the stage where bands changed from the "Arkansas Fight Song" to "The Yellow Rose of Texas."

WASHINGTON • **Houston** (1834), Davy Crockett, and other famous frontiersmen stopped at a tavern that no longer exists, but was probably at the site of the First Baptist Church now, on this important stop on the Southwest Trail.

CALIFORNIA

BAKERSFIELD • In between their stays in Odessa and Midland, Texas, the **Bushes** lived on Water Street while the senior Bush worked at Dresser Industries, 1435 S. Union Avenue.

EUREKA • In 1854 **Grant** was stationed at isolated Fort Humboldt, now a state historic park* (U.S. 101, 3431 Fort Avenue). He came from Fort Vancouver, Washington. There was little to do either place, and he became depressed because he was so far from his family. He evidently drank more than he should have, was arrested, and threatened with court-martial if he did not resign. Friends urged him to stay, believing that he could be acquitted, but he resigned and returned to his family in Missouri. Actually the facts are clouded, and his reason for resignation is debated, but he had not seen his family for two years and desperately wanted to be with them.

LOS ANGELES AREA • **Hayes** (1878) and **Benjamin Harrison** (1891) both stayed in the Green House (Webster Hotel) on Columbia Street in Pasadena. **Hayes** was at the St. Elmo on Main Street in 1880 in L.A. **Theodore Roosevelt** stopped off in 1903 to see Garfield's widow at 1001 Buena Vista and attended a reception at the Raymond Hotel, both also in Pasadena. He stayed at Los Angeles's Westminster Hotel, 342 S. Main, in 1903. **Wilson** stayed at the Alexander, 501 S. Spring, in 1919. **FDR** spoke at the Memorial Coliseum in 1935 and stayed at the Coronado.

Kennedy's official address was the Millennium Biltmore Hotel downtown, 506 S. Grand Street at Fifth, during the 1960 Democratic Convention. **FDR, Truman, Carter,** and **Reagan** also were guests. The Music Room (now the lobby) was **Kennedy's** official headquarters. Here he and his brother decided on **Johnson** as his running mate, and **LBJ** was so informed at the hotel. **Kennedy** was also reported at the El Royale Apartments at 450 N. Rossmore Avenue and the Rossmore House two doors away, 522 N. Rossmore, room 301. They were nominated and accepted at the Los Angeles Memorial Sports Arena, 3939 S. Figueroa.

Kennedy tried to restore his health and get away from his father, who was insisting that he run for Congress, in 1945 when he came here via a ranch in Arizona. He stayed in the Beverly Hills Hilton, 9876 Wilshire, and went to Sam Spiegel's and Gary Cooper's while making a play for actress Olivia De Havilland. He also stayed with agent Charles Feldman and met many other stars including Marylyn Monroe, a client and neighbor. He met many stars at Frank Sinatra's home, 320 Carolwood, and stayed with Bing Crosby in 1962 at 10050 Camarillo in Toluca Lake. He had planned to stay with Sinatra then, but aides convinced him that the singer's Mafia ties would hurt the president's image. The failure of **Kennedy's** brother-in-law, actor Peter Lawford, to convince the president otherwise ended Sinatra's friendship with Lawford. Marilyn Monroe reportedly met **Kennedy** in bungalows at the Beverly Hills Hotel, 9641 Sunset Blvd., and at her home at 12305 Fifth Helana Drive off Carmelina Street, near San Vicente Blvd., where she died in August 1962. In the area is the home of **Nixon**, 901 N. Bundy, rented in 1961, where he wrote *Six Crises.* Lawford's beach house was at 625 Palisades Beach Road, the Pacific Coast Highway beneath the Santa Monica Bluffs. FBI Director J. Edgar Hoover supposedly had wiretaps of **Kennedy** and Monroe making love there. The house, once owned by movie mogul Louis B. Mayer, was loaned to **Kennedy** for the Western White House. Here the president was pictured in his swimsuit in *Life Magazine* in August 1962 after being mobbed trying to go for a private swim. Officially the president was at the Beverly Hilton, but he came here to relax by the pool and be entertained when his sister Pat Lawford was away. Lawford was said to throw lavish parties for the president with his show business friends and wild women, including Marilyn.

Nixon lived in many locations in the area, as follows:

He was born in 1913 in Yorba Linda at 18001 Yorba Linda Boulevard,* now the grounds of his presidential museum.* **Carter, Ford, Reagan, George H.W. Bush,** and **Clinton** were photographed together here at his funeral.

The family moved to 7926 (present number) S. Palmer in East Whittier from 1922 until 1924. His father ran a gas station and grocery on East Whittier Boulevard between Whittier and LaHabra and then on E. Whittier opposite Russell.

He went to the Friends Church on School Street from 1913 until 1922 and then to a church at 15911 E. Whittier Boulevard near Russell Street from 1922 to 1942, in Whittier, where he played the piano and taught Sunday school.

Later the family lived at 15844 East Whittier and ran a grocery next door. From 1928 until 1929 **Nixon** lived in Prescott, Arizona, and returned to Whittier in 1930 at 1104 Santa Gertrudes Road. In 1942 he was at 1400 E. Whittier.

He went to Fullerton High School, 201 East Chapman Avenue in Fullerton, and then transferred to Whittier High at 9401 Painter in his junior year. He was president of his class at Whittier College, and practiced law here after graduating from Duke Law School. He met his future wife in an amateur theater group and married her in 1940 in the Presidential Suite of the Mission Inn, 3649 Seventh Street in Riverside, with a reception in the Spanish Art Gallery.

Nixon's wedding party was received at his father's home, 6799 Worsham, and Nixon moved to 12336 East Beverly. After the war **Nixon** lived at 13217 East Walnut, 14033 Honeysuckle Lane, and 15257 Anaconda. From 1945 until 1960 his home was at 1461 Amalfi Drive, David Niven's "Pink House," where actress Whoopi Goldberg married and lived. The "Checkers" speech, which drew the largest audience in TV history to that time, was at the NBC studio, a block from Hollywood and Vine.

Nixon moved to the Gaylord Apartments on Wilshire in February 1961 while the girls stayed in Washington to finish school. When the family arrived they stayed at a leased home in Brentwood at 901 N. Bundy (mentioned earlier), and then moved to 410 Martin Lane in Beverly Hills. After he lost his bid for governor in 1962 he made his "You-won't-have-Nixon-to-kick-around-any-more" speech in the Cadoro Room at the Beverly Hilton Hotel, 9876 Wilshire Blvd. After his 1968 election he lived at 14033 Honeysuckle Lane in South Whittier. His Western White House, La Casa

Pacifica, was on the ocean at 4100 Calle Isabella off Del Presidente Avenue, San Clemente, south of Los Angeles off I-5 and directly northwest of adjoining Camp Pendleton. **FDR** had visited the mansion in 1935. The **Nixon** family returned here after he left office until 1980, and then he lived in New York and New Jersey for the rest of his life.

In 1948, **FDR**'s son James confronted **Truman** at the Ambassador Hotel, 3400 Wilshire (destroyed), during the election campaign, with the president jabbing the younger man in the chest, saying, "Your father asked me to do this job. I didn't want it ... and if your father knew what you are doing to me, he would turn over in his grave." In 1952 **Nixon** stayed there during the campaign when he wrote his "Checkers speech," and on election night. He stayed election night in 1960 in the Royal Suite. (Robert Kennedy was assassinated in the kitchen in 1968.)

Reagan came to Hollywood in 1937 and took a screen test, starting his movie career. He stayed at the Hollywood Plaza, 1637 Vine, now a retirement home, then lived at 6650 Franklin (where Mickey Rooney, George C. Scott, Julie Harris, and Gene Hackman have also lived) and then 1128 Cory after he married movie star Jane Wyman. Their marriage took place at Wee Kirk o' the Heather Chapel at Forest Lawn Memorial Park* in Glendale in 1940. After a short time they moved to 1326 Londonderry View, Jane's apartment, and then 9137 Cordell Drive until about the time they divorced in 1948. He joined Hollywood Christian Church, 1717 N. Grammercy Place, in 1940 and was a member until 1989. His American Legion Post until the presidency was at 2035 Highland with Gene Autry, Clark Gable, and many other stars.

After the divorce he moved back to the Londonderry View apartment, then lived at 939–943 Hilgard in 1949 and later at 333 Beverly Glen in the Holmby Hills section of Beverly Hills. He was president of the Screen Actors Guilt from 1947 through 1952. He was asked to help a young actress named Nancy Davis; that led to their marriage at the Little Brown Church in the Valley* at 4418 Coldwater Canyon, Studio City, in 1952. Afterwards they lived on Beverly Glen, 1258 Amalfi Drive in Pacific Palisades from 1953 until 1956, and then 1669 San Onofre Drive, where they continued to live until the inauguration in 1981. In the early 1960s he filmed *Death Valley Days* in a studio at 650 Bronson, just south of Paramount Studios. After retirement wealthy friends bought 668 St. Cloud, not far from TV star Johnny Carson at 400 St. Cloud. The address was 666, but Nancy insisted that it be changed since the number is the "Sign of the Beast" in the New Testament book of Revelation. They regularly attended Bel Air Presbyterian in Bel Air, near their last home, where they still lived when he died in 2004 as the oldest-lived president. (Unlike earlier years, no part of the home can now be seen from the street.)

His post-presidential offices were at the Fox Plaza, 2121 Avenue of the Stars. Bruce Willis's character in *Die Hard* tried to rescue fictional hostages on the 33rd and 34th floors. **Reagan's** Presidential Library* and burial place are at 40 Presidential Drive in Simi Valley, where **George Bush, Carter, Ford,** and **Nixon** attended the opening with **Reagan.**

MONTEREY • **Hoover** proposed to his wife by telegram on the way to New York from London and stopped off to meet her in her home at 302 Pacific Street, where they were married. That same day they left for San Francisco, and the next for China. About two years later they lived at 600 Martin. **B. Harrison** and **TR** both stayed at a predecessor of the Hotel del Monte on CA 1, where **McKinley** later was received. In May 1901, **McKinley** addressed veterans at nearby Pacific Grove and took the still popular 17-Mile Drive.

PALO ALTO • **Hoover** came here at age 17, without a high school education. He did not pass the easy first entrance exams in the first Stanford University class of 1895, but was allowed to enter because of his impression of eagerness, general intelligence, and firm character. The youngest and maybe poorest student at the young university both greatly benefited himself and his school with his engineering degree that made him rich and famous. He had first lived at room 38 in Encina Hall and then Romero Hall. Once, in Yosemite Park, he got word that he had a summer job, but he could not report, as he had no money for train fare. So he walked the 80 miles. Within 20 years he was a millionaire and recognized as the world's outstanding mining engineer.

As a shortstop and manager of the freshman baseball team he was reluctantly sent to demand 25 cents from an elderly, dignified, bearded gentlemen who came in without paying. The others were afraid to ask. He found out it was former President **Benjamin Harrison. Hoover** was sent to perform the same task later when industrialist

Andrew Carnegie did not pay. The concert that he sponsored with Ignacy Paderewski lost $400, and they were not able to pay his $2000 fee. The artist waived the loss. Twenty-five years later when **Hoover** was being honored in Poland by the same pianist, then prime minister, for saving tens of thousands from starvation, Hoover mentioned the incident, and the country felt it had been adequately repaid.

In 1907 he arranged for the construction of a cottage at 623 Mirada. He later lived at various places around the world in various capacities, and returned to the safety of California after frantically searching for his sons during the bombing of London at the beginning of World War I. They were found calmly on the roof watching German zeppelins rain bombs. They rented many different homes between 1914 and 1920 in this area, including 61 Salvatierra, 774 Dolores, 747 Santa Ynez, 262 Kingsley, 612 Alvarado, 575 Salvatierra, 775 Santa Inez, and 14 Cabrillo. In fact it is said that they lived in dozens of countries and hundreds of homes. They designed a new home in 1920, now known as the Lou Henry Hoover House, 612 Miranda, that Mrs. Hoover oversaw while her husband served in various government duties in Washington and Europe. This was their principal residence from June 1920 until she died in 1944. They returned after leaving the presidency in 1933, and he lived here off and on into 1950s, when the house was given to Stanford University, where it is now the home of the president.

T. Roosevelt spoke at the university in 1903 as part of an extensive speech-making tour including Barstow, Redlands, San Bernardino, Riverside (Mission Inn, 3649 Seventh), Pasadena, Oxnard, Santa Barbara, San Luis Obispo, San Jose, USC at Berkeley, the dock in Oakland, Modesto, Truckee, Redding, and other towns in each area. **Kennedy** attended graduate business school in the winter of 1940–1 and lived at the President Hotel and 624 Mayfield.

RANCHO MIRAGE AREA • **Ford** and **Ike** visited the Walter Annenberg Estate at Annenberg Circle, 39000 Bob Hope Dr. **Ford** died as the oldest ex-president in history on December 26, 2006, at his home in the Thunderbird Estates, 70612 Highway 111. He had been visited here by **George W. Bush**. During his last few years he rarely left except to attend St. Margaret's Episcopal Church in nearby Palm Desert, 47535 Highway 74. **Nixon** dedicated the Eisenhower Medical Center on Nov. 27, 1971, later visited by **Ford**. At least two presidents played golf nearby in Palm Springs. **Eisenhower** made a hole-in-one at the Seven Lake Country Club in 1968, and **Ford** made two at different times at the Tamarisk Club.

SACRAMENTO • **Reagan** lived in the palatial California Governor's Mansion,* 1526 H Street, upon becoming governor in 1967. It had been the home to twelve prior governors after having been built for a partner in the Central Pacific Railroad, but was now close to the noisy corner of 16th and H Streets, lacked privacy, and was thought to be a firetrap. So the family moved to 1341 45th Street, which served as their home for his two terms.

Many presidents have visited the Capitol* beginning with **Harrison** in 1891. **Theodore Roosevelt** was photographed on the east side. **Taft** was there in 1909, and **LBJ** spoke from the steps in 1964. **FDR** passed through at the train station in 1938, but did not appear in public. An attempted assassination of **Ford** took place almost adjacent at the Senator Hotel, 1121 L Street in 1976. The building has been converted to other uses. As the president was getting into his limo, he responded to the enthusiastic crowd by stepping across the street to Capitol Park to shake hands when a young woman fired several shots at him. A famous photograph shows her pinned against the prominent tree still near the street.

SAN BERNARDINO • **B. Harrison** (1891) and **Taft** (1909) visited before **Lyndon Johnson** worked for an unethical lawyer for several months at 491 West Fifth Street and also operated the elevator. **Johnson** had, in effect, run away from home and knew the lawyer had left Texas under suspicious circumstances. The man had promised that he could get the 16-year-old high school graduate admitted to the Nevada and California Bars although the standards were such that this was almost impossible.

SAN DIEGO • One of the country's most beautiful and famous hotels is the historic Hotel del Coronado at 1500 Orange, on the beach. It has hosted **Benjamin Harrison, McKinley, Taft, FDR, Carter, Nixon,** and **Reagan. Wilson** (1919) and **George H.W. Bush** (1992) have stayed in the Grant Hotel on 326 Broadway. **Carter** was stationed at the Naval Base at Broadway and Harbor Drive in 1950. **JFK** was at the State College on Fairmont and Montezuma and Hall Field Marine Depot on Harbor and Lindberg Field, June 6, 1963.

SAN FRANCISCO • As a favorable magazine article, "A Calm View of a Calm Man," was being read to **Harding**, the president died in room 8064 at the Palace Hotel,* SW corner of Market and New Montgomery, on August 2, 1923. It was maybe his good fortune to die when he did, as the scandals of his administration could not have remained hidden much longer. He said it was his friends, not his enemies, that did him in. **Hoover** was traveling with him. At death he was much loved, but no president ever suffered such a loss of reputation in so short a time. Rumors of murder or suicide circulated, but are discounted by historians. Within months scandals long simmering beneath his "normalcy" were revealed that could have led to impeachment, although it is not believed that **Harding** himself was involved in the many crooked shenanigans. His widow took no chances and burned everything of his that she could find in the White House and back home in Marion before she died a year later. This reminded many historians of Robert Lincoln's suspected burning, going on at about the same time, of his father's correspondence and papers. Regardless of rumors and writings to the contrary, **Harding** apparently died of a heart attack. Prior to that evening, **Harding** arrived at the Ferry Building and went to Letterman Hospital at the Presidio and reviewed troops. **Hoover** and General Pershing acted as honorary pallbearers and are pictured with the casket as the body was placed on a train to leave town. Vice President **Coolidge** had been in town about a year before.

Hayes, B. Harrison, McKinley, TR, Taft, FDR, Truman, Eisenhower, Kennedy (in 1946 when he worked as a journalist), and **George H.W. Bush** were also guests of the Palace. **Grant's** farewell dinner was one of the lavish events held there. The hotel was rebuilt after the 1906 earthquake. The rebuilt City Hall near Van Ness has hosted **Taft, Wilson,** and others.

Hoover lived at 1901 Pacific in 1912 and 1913. In 1975 **Ford** was the victim of an attempted assassination in front of the St. Francis,* 450 Powell, west side of Union Square. **Taft, Wilson, Reagan, Eisenhower,** and **Truman** (1951, 1955) also stayed there. The Fairmont,* 950 Mason, claims to be the most famous hotel in the City by the Bay and has hosted nine presidents since opening in 1907, every president since **Taft**, but only **Taft, Truman, Kennedy,** and **Ford** are listed in the official history of the hotel. **Kennedy** was across the Street at the Mark Hopkins* in 1943. **Carter and Ford** debated on national TV at the Palace of Fine Arts Theater, Baker and Marina, in 1976. **Eisenhower, Nixon,** and **Bush** were at the Cow Palace in 1964.

TR's 1903 visit was one of the most celebrated. He arrived at the Third Street and Townsend Depot on May 12 for an enormous parade led by Gen. Arthur McArthur down Van Ness and Market. He spoke at the Palace and the YMCA at Mason and Ellis, where he burned their mortgage in the auditorium. He visited the Cliff House,* same site as the present one at the end of Geary Street, and Golden Gate Park,* where he broke ground for a statue of McKinley. He also dedicated the Dewey Monument on Union Square* where **McKinley** had turned the first spade of dirt in 1901 and spoke at the Hall of the Native Sons of the West at 1044 Stockton.

McKinley visited his niece at 1578 Fell, still standing, where a local resident let him use his chair that **Washington** had used visiting Joshua Ward in Salem, Massachusetts. **Grant** previously used it at the Palace. **FDR** was nominated for vice president at the Civic Auditorium in 1920, now the Bill Graham Auditorium, 99 Grove Street in Civic Center Plaza. **Clinton** spoke there April 14, 2007. **Hoover** was in town in 1932 the day he was defeated by **FDR**, who came in 1938. **Truman** attended the opening sessions of the United Nations after Germany's surrender in 1945. The opening sessions were in the Civic Opera House and Veterans Memorial Building* on Van Ness facing City Hall. **Nixon** and **Reagan** were both at the Sheridan Palace, 639 Market.

SANTA BARBARA • Governor **Reagan** bought Rancho del Cielo in his last year in office, 1974, located in the Santa Ynez Mountains east of Santa Barbara and spent much of his presidency there. It is on Pennsylvania Avenue off Dos Vista Road. **George H.W. Bush,** Queen Elizabeth II, Russia Premier Gorbachev, and many other heads of state visited.

YOSEMITE NATIONAL PARK • **TR** visited in May 1903, when many photographs were taken of him at Glacier Point and in the Big Trees and Mariposa Groves, including by the Grizzly Giant and Wawona Tree. **FDR** toured in 1938, and **Taft** stayed in the Wawona, Glacier Point, and Sentinel Hotels in 1909.

Colorado

Central City Area • On May 7, 1873, **Grant** came through Black Hawk and stayed at the Teller Hotel on Eureka Street. His path from the stage stop was paved with solid silver bricks, each claimed to weigh over 100 pounds. He was presented with a half interest in a Clear Creek County mine. This was one of several trips to the area, and he stayed in the Teller more than once, including July 1880, on the way via the Fall River Road from Denver to Georgetown, Idaho Springs, and elsewhere. **Taft** opened the Gunnison Dam at Glenwood Springs in 1909; **TR** had stayed in the Hotel Colorado here in 1905.

Colorado Springs • **Grant** stayed at nearby Manitou for a month after his 1880 world tour and spent the night in here in 1873. The Broadmoor Hotel has long been a favorite with presidents including **Hoover, FDR, Nixon, Eisenhower,** and **Reagan. George W. Bush** was here with a group of friends for a collective fortieth birthday party. The morning after a loud celebration, he was quiet at breakfast and then announced to his wife when he returned home, "It's easy to say, 'I quit,' but this time I mean it." And he did, ending his drinking problem, a moment he described as one of the two "defining moments" of his life. (See Kennebunkport, Maine.) Many presidents have been to Falcon Stadium at the Air Force Academy including **Nixon** (1969), **Kennedy** (1963), and **Reagan** (1984). **Taft** was at the Garden of the Gods in 1909.

Denver • **Grant** was in town several times and visited nearby towns and mines. In 1868 he attended a party with Generals Sherman and Sheridan at 16th and Champa, the Shaffenburg home, and attended the Lawrence Street Methodist Church with his family. In 1870 **Grant** attended a reception, bowing and shaking hands, at the Grand Central, SW corner of Lawrence and 17th. He came again in 1873, going to Golden, and visited other towns shown in this chapter. In 1880 he was in and out of town for eight days, going also to Leadville, Gunnison City, Sagauche, Trinidad (Ruffenburg Hotel, later known as the U.S. Hotel), and Pueblo, each with tremendous public demonstrations. The next president to visit was **B. Harrison**, who addressed Sunday school children, and visited Glenwood Springs (First Presbyterian at 1016 Cooper), Colorado Springs, Leadville, Salado, Cañon City, and Pueblo.

TR was in town several times and spoke in front of the Capitol on May 4, 1903, as he had in 1900 on a 21,209-mile campaign tour of 673 speeches. His 1901 hunting party killed 14 cougars in the state. At a dinner in Glenwood Springs at the Hotel Colorado, 526 Pine, some of his unsophisticated companions did not know which fork to use. He instructed, "Get a good knife and fork, boys, and stay by them." **Grant** and **TR** stayed at the Windsor Hotel, 18901 Larimer. **Taft** spoke at Denver University on October 3, 1911. The story is not thought to be true that **Taft** had to be pried out of his bathtub when he stayed later. He dedicated the Air Force Golf Course where he played, and that was later named for him.

Mamie Doud grew up at 750 Lafayette and married **Eisenhower** there; they later used it as a presidential retreat. The family worshipped at Corona Presbyterian at 1208 E. Eighth Avenue about two blocks from the Doud house. He also laid the cornerstone of the Rose Memorial Hospital at 4567 Ninth Avenue. He also attended the Central Presbyterian, 1660 Sherman.

Seventeen presidents, all except Coolidge since **Theodore Roosevelt** in 1905, have been to the 1892 Brown Palace Hotel at 17th and Broadway. **TR** returned after a hunting trip to be greeted here with 2000 pink carnations, 1000 roses, and carloads of apple blossoms as the orchestra played "In the Good Old Summer Time." **Taft** stayed during a 15-hour trip to the capital in 1911. **Wilson** stayed before his speech on the League of Nations in 1919. **Harding** came in 1923, and **Hoover** visited as guest of **Eisenhower** in 1954. **Ike's** 1952 campaign headquarters were set up on the eighth floor, and he was here often before, during, and after his presidency. **JFK** and **LBJ** came in 1960, before office. **Truman** was here to raise funds for his presidential library in 1955, and **Carter** came in 1995 to sell his books. **Nixon** was here twice, 1954 and 1968, as were **FDR,** who hosted two political receptions in 1932 and 1935, and **Clinton** in 1996 and 1997. **Ford** came three times. **G.H.W. Bush** was there in

1982, and **G.W. Bush** came at least three times: August 2001, June 2004, and November 2005.

Following **Ike's** heart attack in 1955 at the Doud house, he was admitted to the Fitzsimmons Army Medical Center in Aurora, where he had had an appendectomy in 1923. This is now University Medical Center. The eighth floor suite where he recovered retains its design. Lowry Air Force Base, SE Sixth and Quebec, was **Ike's** summer White House from 1955 to 1958.

FDR spoke in town in 1932, and he visited the hospital and Capitol in 1936. He spoke from his train at the station in 1932. **Truman** spoke at the Capitol in 1947 and 1948, as did **Harrison** in 1891 and **Taft** in 1909. **Truman** was cheered in a parade down Seventh and also spoke at Fitzsimmons Army Hospital. **Clinton** welcomed Pope Paul II at Stapleton Airport and went to church on Capitol Hill at St. John's Episcopal at 14th. The pastor was also from Arkansas.

LEADVILLE • **Grant** visited this then second largest city in Colorado with his wife and oldest son on July 22, 1880, at the invitation of area Union veterans. He had to leave the train about a quarter of a mile from the foot of Third Street at the Boulevard Crossing. Between here and Cañon City, the train stopped many times for the locals to come out and shake his hand. The official greeting committee seemed annoyed at this, but the general insisted that he see everyone and shook hands with all of the 500 who greeted him at Buena Vista. The greeting at the crossing is still stated as "one of the most gaudy and numerical pageantries that has ever been witnessed in Colorado" with over 100 bonfires, half a dozen bands along Chestnut, Harrison, Spruce, and Sixth, and arches on Harrison at Chestnut and Third. Due to a severe cold he could only speak briefly from a platform in front of his hotel, the Clarendon on the NE corner of Harrison and Third, adjacent to the south of the then highly decorated Tabor Opera House.* The hotel site is a gas station. His son, Ulysses Jr., had a mine here.

He visited several mines the next day, but refused to go down the Morning Star Mine's questionable buckets. Later he was honored at the Sixth Street City Hall, Union Veterans Hall, and at a banquet at the Clarendon, where he met several who fought with him at his first battle, Belmont. He stated that he enjoyed this best of all, just chatting with veterans without having to make much of a speech. Champagne "flowed freely" except for the general, who only had coffee. After many toasts, Grant reminded everyone that he was not a speech maker, but had made several speeches this day including the concluding remarks here. The group stayed until July 27, probably going to Soda Springs, the race track, and the Mount Massive Hotel. They were also guests for a presentation at the Tabor before leaving for Salado, Aspen, Alamosa, and Denver.

B. Harrison briefly spoke on May 11, 1891, from the balcony of the Tabor Grand Hotel during his one-and-a-quarter-hour visit. He was given a large silver brick, briefly saw two mines and some of the shaft houses, and then left at the Rio Grande Station. The hotel later became the Vendome, but is now an office building on the NW corner of Harrison and Seventh.

VAIL • Ford fell in love with the area in 1968 and bought a condo in the lodge in 1970. Upon becoming president, he felt he had to move and bought a $300,000 lot and built a house in 1983 in nearby Beaver Creek, where he also had an office until the end of his life. This remained the "Winter White House." As vice president, he was once stranded on the Vail gondola for eight anxious minutes. He generally bought his own lift tickets for the ski life, and while president in 1975 while waving to crowds, he was grazed by an oncoming lift chair. He was hospitalized here several times and helped build the gardens and Gerald Ford Amphitheatre.

CONNECTICUT

ASHFORD • **Washington** had to stay two nights in Perkins Tavern, "not a good one," in early November 1789. His horses were fatigued because of poor roads, but mainly he stayed an extra night as it was "contrary to law and disagreeable to the People of the State to travel on the Sabbath day."

He went to a meetinghouse nearby and heard "lame discourses."

DANBURY • **Washington** visited Col. Joseph Platt Cooke at 342 Main Street, torn down in 1972. In 1930, **Kennedy** had his appendix out in the hospital at 24 Hospital Ave.

EASTFORD • **Washington** was claimed to be at Eastford House, now the General Lyon Inn* on CT 198, that still has the desk where he wrote letters in 1789, although the present building apparently dates to the 1840s.

FAIRFIELD • **Washington** traveled through Greenwich, Stamford, Norwalk, Fairfield, Stratford, Darby, Milford, West Haven, New Haven, Wallingford, Mansfield, Middletown, Berlin, and Hartford in late 1789. Here he was at the Sun Tavern, now Penfield's (private), on the Green, April 11, 1776, and October 16, 1789. **Jefferson** ate at Buckley's on the Green, June 7, 1784.

GAYLORDSVILLE • **Washington** stopped to eat and rest on September 20, 1780, under a large oak tree, marked on Gaylord Road on the south side of the Newton Road intersection.

GREENWICH • **George H.W. Bush** lived at 11 Stanwich Road from 1925 to 1931 and 15 Grove Lane from 1931 to 1937 and went to school until age 12 at the Greenwich County Day School on Old Church Road between Interstate 95 and Route 15. He met Barbara Pierce at Round Hill Country Club. He and **George W.** attended family funerals, including that of patriarch Sen. Prescott Bush, at the family church, Christ Episcopal, 254 E. Putnam, and in the Putnam Cemetery. They all played tennis at the Field Club on Lake Avenue.

GROTON • **Jackson** stayed at the Bailey House, 108 Thames, in 1833. **Carter** was stationed at the Naval Base here in 1948 and 1951–2. He sometimes conducted services at the Chapel on the Thames on Shark Blvd.

GUILDFORD • **Jefferson** and **Madison** stayed at Stone's Inn on the Green, June 11, 1791.

HARTFORD • **Washington's** headquarters were here on September 20, 1780, when he first met with French General Rochambeau in the Old State House,* 800 Main. Many presidents have been there including **Jackson, Van Buren, Grant, TR, Eisenhower, Carter, Ford,** and **George H.W. Bush. Jefferson** and **Madison** stayed two nights at Bunch of Grapes Tavern (Bull's) opposite north of the Courthouse on their 1791 New England journey. **Washington** stayed there in 1789 and walked the town. **Monroe** stayed at Morgan's Coffee House in 1817.

Lincoln spoke March 5, 1860, at Old City Hall, then 85 Market Street, now a parking lot near the Old State House, on the west side of Market between Central Row and Talcott Streets. He spent the night at 81 Trumbull Street, in mid–block on the west side between Pearl and Jewell Streets, also a parking lot. Neither site is marked. He visited Brown and Gross Bookstore, Main and Asylum, with his later Navy secretary, Gideon Welles.

All presidents from **John Adams** to **Lincoln** with exception of **Polk** are claimed to have visited the George Catlin House, 17 Hurlburt. **Grant** visited Mark Twain at 351 Farmington.* The first president to ride in an automobile was **Theodore Roosevelt** down Asylum Street.

LEBANON • **Washington** used the homestead of Jonathan Trumbull,* West Town Street on the Green just northwest of Route 87, to hold strategy sessions during the Revolutionary War. He also used a stable* next door and a smaller dependency now called "The War Office"* on the Green or Common. The Council of Safety of Connecticut is claimed to have met here 1200 times during the war with **Washington, Adams,** and Benjamin Franklin at times. **Washington** and **Jefferson** both visited later in 1789. **Jefferson** may have stopped in 1784 when he came through town. **Washington** was also at William Williams' home.

LITCHFIELD • **Washington** and his staff traveled through this beautiful little town at least six times in 1780–1 during the Revolution. At times, including September 23, 1780, his headquarters were in the Oliver Wolcott Sr. house, 89 South Street, four houses south of St. Anthony's Church on the east side of South Street, just north of Wolcott Street. He was also at the Elisha Sheldon Inn, 73 North Street, at least twice. Nine-year-old Elihu Hubbard Smith's home is still at 74 North, across the street from Sheldon's. He proudly brought over a basket of apples for the general on one occasion, but was then embarrassed twice. First he only had his shabby mid–week clothes to wear. Then when he got to the tavern, Washington was gone, and he was confronted by, he thought, Alexander Hamilton. Washington's aide found out that he had studied Latin and then humiliated him with his deficiencies. But when **Washington** and Knox arrived they so warmly thanked him and bade farewell to the "little prince" that he forgot his embarrassment.

Washington was also at Benjamin Tallmadge's, at 47 North, where Col. Tallmadge, an aide to Washington, gave the general a farewell dinner on August 20, 1783. Benjamin Franklin's illegitimate son, William, was the British governor of New Jersey when the Revolution started and remained a British supporter, even after being held as a hostage and jailed at Tallmadge's.

Taft came when Chief Justice to the Tapping Reeve House, 82 South Street, in 1930 as president of a preservation committee. This is called the first law school in America. It graduated over 100 members of Congress and two vice presidents, including Aaron Burr.

Marlborough • **Washington** and **Monroe** visited Marlborough Tavern in 1789, CT 2 and 66.

Middletown • **Washington** visited Fuller's Tavern on Berlin in 1789 for breakfast. **Hayes** was educated at Wesleyan College and stayed in South College Hall on High Street. While **Wilson** taught history and politics at Wesleyan University Memorial Chapel on Church Street, he lived at 106 High Street from 1888 to 1890 and later with his wife and three daughters on Liberty Street, off Cleveland Lane. They went nearby to First Congregational, Pleasant at Crescent.

Milford • In 1789 **Washington** stayed at Andrew Clark's Tavern, 46 W. River. According to a maybe questionable story, here he ordered bread and milk and was given a pewter spoon. When he requested a silver one, he was told they could not afford it, so he gave the owner a shilling and told them to go to the nearest clergyman who no doubt would have a silver one. **Clinton** stayed in a beach house at Trumbull Beach while at Yale, 1970 until 1973.

New Haven • **Washington's** headquarters on April 11, 1775, were at Isaac Beer's, where the New Haven House now is, on the north side of George between Temple and College. He stayed at the Hubbard House at the junction of Church and George. He and **John Adams** were also here in 1789. **Washington** then attended Trinity Episcopal on the Green at the NW corner of Temple and Chapel, and White Haven Congregational next door to where the first church was located. The preacher surprised all by not mentioning Washington's presence and just preaching to the children. **Jackson** and **Van Buren** outdid him in 1833 by visiting these two in addition to the Methodist church on the NW corner of Elm and Temple. **Jefferson** visited the president of Yale at his house, 37 Hillhouse. **Monroe** stayed at Butler's Hotel on Church Street after being honored with a parade during his 1817 visit. He also visited Eli Whitney's factory and Trinity Church.

On February 28, 1860, **Lincoln** stopped at the Chapel Street Station, two blocks east of the Public Square at Fleet, Chapel, Crown, and Union Streets, on the way to Providence. On March 6, 1860, he went to J.F. Babcock's, 92 Olive, and then was escorted by 1000 headed by the New Haven Band to Union Hall at 75 Union, producing "the wildest scene of enthusiasm and excitement that has been in New Haven for years." After his speeches here and in Meridian's Town Hall, he was entertained at Babcock's again. The newspaper lamented, "It is a shame to New Haven that we have, as yet, no Hall that can accommodate a tithe of those who would attend" to hear "the eloquent champion of Freedom."

Taft became a popular law professor at Yale University after his presidency and lived at the Taft Hotel, 265 College, in 1913, 367 Prospect Street (1913–17), 70 Grove (1918–9), 113 Whitney Avenue (1920–1), and then 60 York Square (1921). All homes are gone. Earlier while a student he had stayed at 64 High in 1874 and 1875. He attended Battel Chapel on the Yale Campus and later First Unitarian Universalistic Society, 608 Whitney, for the eight years he was on the Yale faculty. He and **TR** attended Harvard-Yale games at the stadium.

Three consecutive presidents went to Yale beginning with **George H.W. Bush** from 1945 until 1948. **Ford** also went to the law school, York and Wall, living at 268 Dwight (1939–40) and 100 Howe (1940–41). As captain of the baseball team he met Babe Ruth on the pitcher's mound during a special presentation a few weeks before the Bambino's death. At that time the baseball legend gave his original autobiographical manuscript to the university. **Bush** and his wife lived on Chapel Street and then 281 Edwards Street when **George W.** was born July 6, 1946, at the New Haven Hospital. In 1946 they had an apartment at 37 Hillhouse Avenue next to the Yale president, who asked the Bushes to please remove **W.'s** diapers from the line when he expected important company. **Bush** worked at the Yale Sterling Memorial Library* at 120 High where **Clinton** met fellow student Hillary Rodham. After they both stared at each other for a long time, she came over and said, "If you're going to be staring at me and I'm going to be staring back, I think we should at least know each other. I'm Hillary Rodham. What's your name?" **Clinton** said that he could not respond because he forgot. He lived at 21 Edgewood from 1970 until 1973. **Truman** lectured at the school for three days in 1958.

New London • **Washington** stayed in the Shaw Mansion,* 11 Blinham, on April 9, 1776, as he traveled to New York. This is now the home of the New London Historical Society. **Monroe** as president stayed in General Huntington's home, still at the NW corner of Huntington and Broad, and visited Forts Trumbull and Griswold on opposite sides of the Thames; these forts had held out against traitor Benedict Arnold.

Lincoln signed an autograph book when stopped on March 8 and 10, 1860, at the depot on the same site as now. The chairman of the Republican Town Committee found him walking around Main Street after missing him and took him to eat at the City Hotel close to about what is now the SW corner of State and Eugene O'Neil Drive. Both the original street and hotel are gone. While **Lincoln** ate, the chairman brought in prominent Republicans to meet the westerner.

New Milford • **Kennedy** lived in North House at Canterbury School from 1930 until an appendicitis attack in 1931. The school is above the town on a hill at 101 Aspetuck.

Norwich • **Washington** was "frequently" at the Leffingwell Inn,* 348 Washington Street, SR 2, 32, and 169, to discuss military affairs with Colonel Leffingwell. His headquarters were here on April 8, 1776. He was at the Teel House on the Parade, General Jedidiah Huntington's (private) at 223 E. Town Street, and Samuel Huntington's (private) at 11 Huntington Lane. **Jackson** visited the Unca Indian burial grounds at the corner of Washington and Sachem Streets in 1833 and laid the cornerstone for monument to a chief. **Lincoln** spoke at the Town Hall on March 9, 1860, and "was listened to with unflagging attention." He received visitors and had discussions with the rival factions at the Wauregan Hotel, Main, Union and Broadway.

Old Lyme • **Washington's** headquarters on April 10, 1776, were in John MacCurdy's House.* **Wilson** vacationed at Boxwood House in 1905 and at 96 Lyme in 1909. He dedicated the Congregational Church in 1910 at the SW corner of Ferry Road and Lyme. He vacationed several years and stayed at boarding houses of a Miss Thibetts in 1905.

Stafford Springs • **Adams** came here several times to springs now in Hyde Park on Spring Street in back of the library.

Stamford • **Washington** was at Webb's Tavern at Main and Bank on October 16, 1789. Martha probably stayed here on the way to join her husband at Cambridge in 1775.

Wallingford • **Washington** had tea at Squire Stanley's on the corner of the Choate campus in 1789. From 1931 to 1935, **Kennedy** went to Choate School, now Choate Rosemary Hall, North Main at Christian. He stayed in Choate House in 1931–2, moved to East College, and then to the West Wing. He was so scrawny that he was called "rat face," finished 64 out of 112, but was a popular "cut-up" and still was voted "most likely to succeed," even though his accomplishments were less than outstanding. The coveted highest school award went to the most serious, studious student who exemplified the school's ideals. He was almost expelled, but his friends mounted a campaign and one biography suggests that he rigged the election. The fact that his father had given a newfangled sound system and swimming pool to the school did not hurt his popularity.

Wethersfield • **Washington** visited the Silas Deane House* at 203 Main in 1775 and returned to meet with Comte de Rochambeau on May 21–22, 1781, at the Joseph Webb House,* 211 Main. He attended services on May 20 at the First Church of Christ across the street from Webb's. This momentous meeting marked the implementation of the Franco-American alliance with actual field operations and resulted in the decisive siege and victory at Yorktown, Virginia.

This town, the oldest English settlement in Connecticut, was about halfway between Washington's headquarters at New Windsor, New York, and French ally Rochambeau's in Newport. In mid–1781 the commanders learned that the French Admiral de Grasse was definitely sailing north from the Caribbean to cooperate with the allies. Now **Washington** wanted cooperation to lead an offensive against New York City, and suggested that Virginia be considered only to relieve pressure on Lafayette if the British sent forces from New York there. Washington felt that a march to Virginia would be a waste of time since the British would be rescued by their fleet. Rochambeau argued that with the French fleet holding off the British ships, Cornwallis and his men at Yorktown would be trapped, assuming he was headed there and would be there when the French fleet arrived. If Washington had held to his plan to operate against the main British force in New York and not agreed to march south, possibly the French would have given up as the Revolution was taking too long, costing too much, and looking hopeless. Congress might have tried to negotiate their best deal. Later the Colonial commander agreed with his French counterpart, joined forces to march north of New York City, feinted toward the city, and then moved to Virginia to save the Revolution.

WINDSOR • **Washington** and **Adams** visited the Ellsworth House,* 778 Palisado, in 1789.

WOODSTOCK • The Bowen House* (Roseland Cottage) at 556 Route 169, on the Common, hosted **Grant, Hayes, Benjamin Harrison,** and **McKinley**.

DELAWARE

CLAYMONT • **Washington** lodged several times, including before the Battle of Brandywine, at the Robinson House,* NE intersection of Routes 13 and 92, 1 Naamans Road, the road from Baltimore to Philadelphia.

DOVER • Various presidents no doubt have passed through this capital of Delaware. **George H.W. Bush** spoke at the Old Capitol* on the Green during his first campaign. **George W.** campaigned then for his father and later for himself here.

NEW CASTLE • A marker at Packet Alley leading to the wharf notes that **Jefferson, Houston,** and many others followed this path. This should also include all early Virginia presidents and **Jackson**, who walked through the town on the way to a northern tour in 1833. He was impressed with a sign over the street echoing his famous toast: "The Union, It Must Be Preserved."

Washington was a wedding guest at Governor Nicholas Van Dyke's* at the NE corner of Fourth and Delaware on April 30, 1784, also known as the Amstel House. According to the chief justice, he kissed the bride, the daughter of the governor, and then all the rest of the girls, "as was his wont." He was at the Gilpin House Inn, 210 Delaware in 1774. The presidents saw the old Capitol, now the Courthouse,* dating from 1732 and adjacent 1709 Episcopal Church.

Christiana, just northwest, hosted **Washington** at the Shannon Hotel, NE corner of Delaware 7 where the road turns south in the main crossroads and the Old Baltimore Pike, and at Christiana Inn on the SW corner. He also crossed the Christiana Bridge several times at SR 7 on the edge of town. His diary shows that he had an accident here in September 1787.

NEWARK AREA • **Washington's** diary and **Jefferson's** Memo Book show that they were at the Buck Tavern, 11 miles south of Newark on the south side of the Chesapeake and Delaware Canal on SR 71 and 896, and the Red Lion Inn at the junction of Routes 7 and 71 in Red Lion, various times from 1780 to 1790. It is now a post office. **Jefferson** (and probably **Washington** and **Madison**) also stayed at the Middletown Hotel or Witherspoon's Inn,* still near the southwest corner of Main (Rte. 299) and Broad at the center of nearby Middletown.

WILMINGTON • **Washington** passed through many times. His diary (Sept. 4, 1774) mentions that he arrived at the ferry at the foot of Fourth Street, near the Old Swedes Church. He visited Anthony Wayne's headquarters just northwest of the Market Street Bridge over Brandywine Creek, at Joseph Tatnall's,* 1803 N. Market. This is behind the Lea-Derickson House, a mill house built in 1770. They came before the Battle of Brandywine, and **Washington** stopped here many times from 1777 to 1786 to see his friend and met with Generals Lafayette, Greene, and Wayne at the Hale-Byrnes House* on September 3, 1777, between the Battles at Cooch's Bridge and Brandywine. The home is on White Clay Creek on

Stanton-Christiana Road just north of the Route 4 junction, north of exit 4 off I-95, southwest of town, and south of Stanton. Washington ordered cannon placed in front of the house to guard against the British approach.

Colonial troops encamped at Brandywine Park south of the creek at Lovering and Broom Street where **Washington** visited. His headquarters from August 25 until September 8, 1777, just before Brandywine, were at the NW corner of 303 West and Third. The tablet marks the high location where he saw the surrounding area. The site of a famous old tavern, Sign of the Ship (or O'Flinn's) is marked at the SE corner of Market and Third. It hosted **Washington, John Adams, Jefferson**, and many others. In 1786 **Washington** visited John Dickinson, Eighth and Market.

Madison attended a scientific meeting at the Old Academy on Market between Eighth and Ninth, where Benjamin Franklin experimented with electricity. **John Quincy Adams** visited nearby Brandywine Springs at an upscale resort in Mill Spring Hundred that burned in 1852. **Polk** rode in an open carriage up French Street, turned at the Brandywine River and then rode down Market. He had dinner in town before he left on a steamer for Philadelphia. **Fillmore** also took a steamer from here on May 12, 1851, after visiting the Town Hall* and the nearby Indian Queen Hotel at 500 Market. The Old Town Hall* is open next to the Heritage Center at 504 Market. On June 10, 1848, **Lincoln**, dubbed by the press here as "The Lone Star of Illinois," made what they called "an eloquent and patriotic speech" to a Whig meeting from the balcony of the Athenaeum at the Fourth Street Market House, on the east side of the building, at the west side of Market.

Johnson, Grant, and Sec. of State Seward passed through in 1866, and **Johnson** made a speech from the railcar. **FDR** made a speech at the same site in 1936. **McKinley** also spoke there. The site is now the Amtrak Station between French and Front Streets, a block south of Martin Luther King Jr. **Grant** returned in 1873 to visit several factories in the area and attend a banquet in Institute Hall, Market and Eighth.

FDR attended the 1937 wedding of his son FDR Jr. at nearby Christ Church in Greenville. The reception was at the bride's parents,' Owl's Nest on Kennett Pike. He was back in 1938 to receive Swedish Crown Princess Louise at Fort Christina State Park* near the Old Swedes Church* when the Swedish Monument was dedicated.

Eisenhower walked through crowds in Rodney Square* in the center of downtown on Market Street when he campaigned in 1952. **LBJ** spoke from the steps of the library* at about the same place. **Nixon** spoke on the west side of the square, and **Carter** spent two hours at the same location at a fundraiser in 1978 in the Gold Room of the DuPont Hotel.* **George H.W. Bush** and **Ford** were also at the hotel. In one of **Kennedy's** last official acts, he stood in the middle of I-95 at exit 9, Marsh Road, toward the Pennsylvania border to dedicate the superhighway, now named for him. **Ford** spoke in 1974 at the Delaware Park Race Track on Rte. 7. **Clinton** campaigned in Rockford Park* in northern Wilmington in 1992.

Those mentioned would have seen the Old Swedes Church,* c. 1698, at the east end of Sixth and Seventh Streets at Church Street, west of Christina's Creek, claimed the oldest Protestant church in the United States. I found no record that they attended, but both **Roosevelts** and **Cleveland** did visit the church and also the Tatnall House mentioned above.

District of Columbia

The federal city of Washington, D.C., was created in the 1790s after Congress approved an agreement by two of President **Washington's** cabinet members, also the leaders of their political parties. Alexander Hamilton and **Jefferson** agreed that the federal government would share the Revolutionary War debts of the states and the capital city of the new nation would be located near the Potomac River, moving from New York City to Philadelphia for ten years. **Washington** was pleased since he believed that the commerce of the nation would flow west up the river. The fact that his home was a few miles downstream did not displease him either. New York lost the capital status in 1790, and Philadelphia would lose it again when this new city was ready in about a decade. Both cities tried to lure the government back, and problems in creating a new city out of rural farms almost caused Congress to change its mind. But the government and President **Adams** moved here shortly after **Washington** died late in the old century. The first president did not occupy any of the federal buildings, but he planned and surveyed the sites and visited inns and private homes in the new federal town, some still there. (Note that all addresses shown in this chapter are N.W. unless otherwise noted.)

The White House

The White House, 1600 Pennsylvania Avenue, has been the residence of all presidents beginning with **John Adams**, who moved in on November 2, 1800. (Secretary of State John Marshall, later chief justice, lived there for a time as the mansion was being completed.) Construction started in 1792, when **Washington** drove the stakes that sited it; he measured it at various stages, and inspected it nearly finished, walking the floors. When he inspected the house in March 1797, he was given a 16-gun salute, the only ceremony he attended there. He and others felt that the house would get larger through the years, but the basic house is still the same although many expansions were later planned.

There have been many periods of remodeling, and the interior has been reconstructed twice, beginning in 1815 and in the late 1940s. The British burned out the insides in 1814 after the **Madisons** hurriedly stripped the contents. It even seemed then that the capital city would be moved to the interior of the country. The rebuilding took four years, although **Monroe** moved in in October 1818 before completion. Since the original external

The most famous and historic house in America is the White House, where all presidents have lived except Washington, who walked the foundations. Great decisions were made; Cleveland was married; Harrison and Taylor died; and many children have married, died, and been born.

walls were largely used, this was six less years than the original structure had taken to build, but it was weaker, requiring the interior to be fully rebuilt in the late 1940s. The 1817 repainting of the 1815 whitewash covered the burns, cracks, patches, and scars and gave rise to the name "White House," although it had been called that in **Jefferson's** day. The outer walls remain the same as those supervised by **Washington**.

At other times it was suggested and planned to move the residence to another location in the city, particularly under **B. Harrison, McKinley,** and **Theodore Roosevelt.** But the capital city remained on the Potomac, and the president's house stayed where it still is, greatly renovated and expanded by the west wing offices in 1902 and later. At that time, it more fully became the president's home with offices in the wings. All presidents refurbished and changed the interior in some way. The major exterior changes were **Jackson's** north portico and **Truman's** south balcony. **TR's** irrepressible daughter Alice said the house in her day was furnished "late Grant, early Pullman." **Coolidge** turned the attic, where **Lincoln** and **TR** romped with their sons and their friends, into a livable third floor. **TR** liked to run obstacle courses with his sons in the halls, play hide and seek, and almost knocked himself out running into a post playing in the dark.

Lincoln attended his sons' "theatre performance" there as they dressed in Mary's old clothes. **Truman** added the controversial balcony on the south side in 1948 and determined then that more was needed than patch-ups and cheap renovations. The house was falling in. The second floor of the White House began to sag dangerously, and **Truman** had to move out of his bedroom. Then while the **Trumans** lived in the Blair House, the White House interior was gutted and reconstructed back to the original design. Unfortunately much of the interior that might have been saved was used as a landfill. Some of the bricks were used to build the greenhouse at Mt. Vernon. Now it is our most historical residence, full of art treasures and memories of historical events and famous families who have endeared themselves to the nation. Its history and the anecdotes of its residents fill books with great events and human interest revelations.

It had taken **Adams** five days to get to the new capital from Philadelphia after he got lost in the wilderness. The house had no privy, and water had to be hauled five blocks. Abigail Adams referred to it as a barn, and hung her washing in the East Room. **Van Buren's** laundry also hung somewhere inside and once caught fire. Senator Henry Clay and others passing by rushed in to help, but the president met them in the entrance to tell them everything was under control. Clay, who ran for president for about twenty years, assured him that even though they wanted him out, they did not want him burnt out.

The house was built in a wagon-rutted field of weeds with piles of stone and rubble. But **Adams** wrote his wife, "I pray heaven to bestow the best of blessings on this house and all that shall hereafter inhabit it. May none but honest and wise men ever rule under this roof." His wife arrived in time for them to mourn the death of their son Charles, who died of depression and drink. About the only art there was the Stuart painting of **Washington**, still here after being rescued from the British by Dolley Madison. (Some said then that our now maybe most familiar view of **Washington**, in fact, did not look like him.)

It was for generations the largest house in America. **Jefferson** thought it big enough for a Pope, two emperors, and a Grand Lama. Presidents married and died inside, and presidential children have been born (Esther **Cleveland**), married (many), and died (Willie **Lincoln**).

In spite of claims that **Adams** and **Jefferson** were now not speaking to one another, they dined together on the first News Year's Day after **Adams** moved in. It was the people's house as well as the president's residence. The first birth in the home was that of **Jefferson's** grandson in 1806, unless you count a slave or two born to **Jefferson's** "servants."

The first of many weddings was that of **Monroe's** daughter, probably also the least publicized and celebrated. Widower **Van Buren** moved in with his four bachelor sons in 1837. This was the first time that the five had lived together since his wife died, since the youngest child was raised as an infant by relatives. Dolley **Madison** then got to work and brought a young female relative intent on attracting the eye of one of the sons; she did, resulting in a South Carolina wedding. Other White House weddings included **John Quincy Adams**' son and the daughters of **Tyler, Grant, Theodore Roosevelt, Wilson, Lyndon Johnson,** and **Nixon**.

Tyler's wife died in the home. She moved in in very poor health and appeared at virtually no functions except the wedding of her daughter there. Fifty-four-year-old **Tyler** then robbed the cradle before leaving office, marrying a 24-year-old, with whom he had seven more children to add to the seven that he already had. **Polk** virtually worked himself to death after being the first sitting president photographed, and that was in the state dining room. (**John Quincy Adams** was the first former president to have his image photographically preserved.) **Polk** was the first president to spend all of his time here rather than spend summers elsewhere and died three months after leaving office. **Arthur** refused to move in until Mrs. Garfield had recovered from the shock of her husband's assassination, and then, appalled at the condition of the furniture, ordered everything sold or auctioned off, including a pair of **Lincoln's** trousers.

By the 1860s it was still better known as the President's House or Executive Mansion, but known as the "White House" long before the Civil War. The name "White House," used for years, became official under **Theodore Roosevelt**, who first used the name on his stationary. At the time of the Civil War it was still the largest house in the country, but served several functions so that only part of the second floor was used as living space or "home" for the family. At any time until the mid–20th century just about anyone could just walk in and see the president. For years presidents kept the noon hour open for the public to drop in and shake the presidential hand until **Hoover** had enough, complaining that he had to waste "a whole hour every day shaking hands with 1,000 to 1,200 people."

The first floor was the "State Floor" for public rooms, with all devoted to state purposes except the family dining room. The presidential offices were on the second for many years. The visitors' exit today, under **Jackson's** north portico, was the entrance for many years until **TR** added new offices. **Lincoln** sometimes conferred with overweight General Winfield Scott in the front to save the gouty Scott from having to climb the stairs. His last speech was out the window above, as John Wilkes Booth listened and swore, accurately, that it would be his last. **Andrew Johnson** stood here and told a group of supporters that Congress was trying to assassinate him and start another rebellion. This did not improve his popularity with the legislature branch.

The East Room started off as Abigail Adams' laundry and **Jefferson's** pantry but soon began to be used for large receptions where the president shook thousands of hands for long hours. **Madison** used part of the room for cabinet meetings, but it was mostly unfinished and undecorated until **Jackson** created the grand reception hall known as Jackson's Room, destroyed in the 1950 reconstruction. **Lincoln** was first in the room (as large as his Springfield house during his congressional term) for a reception with President **Polk**. Soldiers camped here during the early days of the Civil War. **Lincoln** was criticized for letting the boys use it as a playground, but it was so used by **TR** and **Taft's** sons, who skated there when their mothers weren't looking.

Lincoln lay in state here as thousands filed by the open coffin. The two prior presidents who had died in office, **William Henry Harrison** and **Taylor**, had also lain here in state, as did **Harding** and **FDR** later. Seven weddings occurred in the room, including those of Jessie **Wilson**, Nellie **Grant**, and Alice **Roosevelt**. Young **Franklin Roosevelt** arranged the train on Alice's gown. The haughty president's daughter crammed in 1000, including Nellie Grant, and returned in 1975 for Tricia **Nixon's** wedding in the Rose Garden, where young **Clinton** shook hands with **Kennedy** a few months before the assassination. Earlier **Franklin** had attended Alice's debut party here. **Cleveland** had his wedding reception here after marrying in the Blue Room. **Ford** was sworn in in the East Room, where his earlier nomination by **Nixon** was announced.

The Green Room, next to the East Room, was used as **Jefferson**'s bedroom, then his dining room where he ate his two meals: breakfast, and a generally stag dinner party at 4:00. **Madison** wrote the message leading to the War of 1812 in his office here and signed the declaration of war into law. In 1862 the body of Willie **Lincoln** was embalmed and his coffin stayed in the room during his East Room funeral. At noon the president watched over his favorite son behind locked doors.

The elliptical Blue Room was so named after **Jefferson** furnished it in that color. This is the reception room for all presidents where guests were routinely greeted for many years. It was **John Adams**' entrance, but now opposite the main entrance, in the center of the first floor on the south side facing the lawn. The **Madisons** made the White House the social center of the backwater town on Wednesday nights with their engaging socials held in the suite of rooms from the Blue Room to the State Dining Room, and Dolley became the town's first "hostess with the mostest." **Monroe** had greeted Lafayette in 1824; the French hero was renowned on two continents after being jailed during the French Revolution. He and his family were almost guillotined, but escaped only to be captured and held in prison in Austria. **Monroe**'s wife, with incredible audacity, brazened her way into the prison and, virtually single-handedly, secured the release of the family, who were permitted to leave the country. **John Quincy Adams**'s son was married in the room in 1828.

Jackson was considered the first "people's president." After his inauguration his people flooded "their house," coming in through windows as well as doors. They almost wrecked it, breaking china, overturning tables, brawling, and standing with muddy boots on the fancy chairs to get a good look at "Old Hickory." He was almost suffocated by the press of well-wishers until his aides fought through the masses and drew him out through the window here back to his hotel.

The Marine Band played here for several presidents, including **Pierce** and **Taylor**, while they circulated. Outside the windows was the portico where the **Grants** liked to sit and did not mind being seen. One of **Wilson's** daughters married the secretary of the treasury here; he was 26 years older, had been married before and had two children.

The **Clevelands** also married in the room in 1886 after the president marched his bride down the grand stairs and central hall while John Phillip Sousa conducted the Marine Band. The 49-year-old married a 21-year-old, and was the only president married in the house. When friends asked why he had never married, he told them he was waiting for his wife to grow up. He had been guardian for his partner Oscar Folsom's daughter and executor of his estate. When the rumors proved true that he was to marry, it was not Mrs. Folsom as thought, but the 21-year-old daughter. He won the popular vote three times, but the electoral only twice. When he lost his second campaign, his wife, in a huff, told the White House staff, "We'll be back four years from today." And they were. Their daughter Esther was the only presidential child born inside the house. Four of their children outlived the Watergate scandal of the 1970s. His widow was the first president's wife to remarry, surviving him 39 years to 1947.

On many occasions the reception line passed through to greet **Lincoln** at regular levees, generally Tuesdays and Saturdays, and then on to the larger East Room to mingle. It was also used for various other social events and receptions for diplomats. To reach the lawn on the south side, the family would step on the back porch going through a window in this room. The family watched parades from the south portico. It was here that **Lincoln** first met General **Grant**, who had just become only the third lieutenant general in the country's history. (The other two were **Washington**, late in life, and temporarily, Winfield Scott.)

McKinley organized hymn singing in the room. **FDR** brought his new bride, to see her uncle **Theodore Roosevelt** here and then told his fellow law clerks he was going to follow a career modeled after his Uncle Ted (legislature, assistant secretary of the Navy, governor, president), which he did. On January 20, 1945, he stood behind the doors on the south portico with **Truman**, and was inaugurated for the fourth time. **Truman's** balcony, added in 1947, shaded the windows, but was claimed (wrongfully) by many to ruin the historical look.

The Red Room, next to the State Dining Room, was used as a drawing room or family room by the **Lincolns** and contained the picture of Washington, now hanging in the East Room. The room was known for years as the Washington parlor, used as a family parlor and where all could be informally entertained after dinner. **John Adams** used it as his dining room. **Jefferson** changed it to a sitting room, and Dolley **Madison** turned it into an antechamber, decorated in yellow, where she and the president greeted guests. **Jackson** changed it from yellow to blue. **Polk** was modest and sometimes entered receptions here before dinner parties almost unnoticed. So Mrs. **Polk** got the idea of having the Marine Band play an old Scottish anthem, "Hail to the Chief." (Another version gives credit to Julia **Tyler**.) She liked to gather with friends to sing Methodist hymns around the piano that later Willie and Tad **Lincoln** took lessons on, and Willie liked to play. He was once scolded here by one of Mary's cousins for playing on the Sabbath. **Lincoln's** friend Ward Hill Lamon sometimes gave impromptu singing concerts for the president. **Lincoln** met President **Buchanan** on February 24, 1861, in the room, and gathered his cabinet after a dinner on March 28, 1861, to discuss the Ft. Sumter crisis. Mary **Lincoln** had her séances here, where **TR's** children later used their stilts.

March 4 was set in the Constitution for inauguration day as Benjamin Franklin noted that there would be fewer Sunday March 4ths than any other day. It was correctly supposed that no president-elect would want to be sworn in on Sunday. The Sunday problem happened first in 1821, but **Monroe** had just retained his office. **Hayes** was not declared winner in 1877 until March 2 after a disputed election that raised public tension. (He received the announcement on his train while traveling to Washington, hoping to be inaugurated.) Before the public ceremony on Monday, he had attended a large dinner party with President **Grant** and the Supreme Court in the White House on Saturday, March 3 (although some accounts show that this ceremony was on March 4). During the evening, they slipped into the Red Room, where he took the oath in private, the first to take it in the White House. The public did not know this, and he was sworn in again in a public ceremony on Monday. So it might be said the country had two presidents for a couple of days. Or it could be argued that **Grant's** term ended at noon Sunday, and the country could have been without a "sworn-in" president as it might have been at least in 1849 when Taylor waited until the Monday after the Sabbath. (David Rice Atchison, president pro tempore of the senate, claimed that the vacant office elevated him to the presidency for a day, but actually his term had also ended on March 3 when the senate session ended.) The Sunday date also occurred during the middle of **Wilson's**, **Reagan's**, and **Eisenhower's** terms. All were sworn in on Sunday in private, respectively in the Senate Chamber, the East Room, and the landing of the grand staircase.

The Family Dining Room was on the north side of the first floor, across from the Executive or State Dining Room on the southwest corner. **Jefferson** used the latter for his office and private world as he worked many hours alone. He kept his potted plants well tended in the room and trained a mockingbird to fly around and sing for him. Here he worked with Meriwether Lewis to plan and train him for the great expedition to the west. **Madison** began its use as the State Dining Room. **Polk** sat here with his cabinet for the first White House interior daguerreotype. The **Lincoln** boys used both dining rooms as a makeshift schoolroom before Willie died. **TR's** children repeatedly startled dinner guests by introducing their pets at unexpected moments. The famous journalist Jacob Riis was once having breakfast with the family when **Roosevelt** apologized for not being able to show a kangaroo rat. Young Kermit then produced it from his pocket and showed how it could jump all over the table. Many state dinners continue to center in the room, although the one **Ford** hosted for Elizabeth II during America's bicentennial was in the Rose Garden with the guests moving here as the president began the dancing with the queen to the tune of "The Lady is a Tramp."

The upstairs was the family living quarters as well as working space for the executive. The president's office, now the "Lincoln Bedroom," since the early days was above the Green Room, and the second office from the southeast corner. The tradition was begun by **John Quincy Adams** and **Jackson**, who had their office and cabinet room here. The area was so used until **TR** moved his cabinet offices to the West Wing Oval Office in 1902, and **Taft** established the presidential oval office there. **Lincoln** called this "the shop." There is no evidence that friends or relatives slept here, although Tad spent many hours at his father's side and feet after his brother died, would leap to hand him a pen when he started to write, and would go to sleep on the floor waiting to be carried to bed. Five-year-old **Franklin Roosevelt** met **Cleveland** here in 1887. **Cleveland** told him, "My little man, I have a strange wish for you. It is that you may never be president of the United States."

Lincoln began the Gettysburg Address and signed the Emancipation Proclamation in the room. The former was probably the country's (world's?) greatest speech, certainly the most quoted, and the latter has been called the greatest act of the nineteenth century. The **Trumans** converted the room to a bedroom known the Lincoln Bedroom ever since and furnished it with the large "state bed" ordered by Mary **Lincoln**. Though it is now known as the "Lincoln Bed," **Lincoln** himself during life probably did not use it, but it is believed he was embalmed on or near it when it was in the Prince of Wales Bedroom. Various presidents and their wives did sleep in it, including the **Theodore Roosevelts**, **Wilsons**, and **Coolidges**. Winston Churchill tried the bed and didn't like it, so he stayed in the Rose Room. **Truman** wrote in his diary that he slept in the Lincoln Bedroom, in "old Abe's bed," and found it quite comfortable. The **Hoovers** probably used it before having it moved from the president's bedroom back to the old Prince of Wales Bedroom across the hall. (**FDR's** aide Louis Howe used it in his room.) Willie **Lincoln** is sometimes said to have died in the bed, although this is also disputed, and his father spent many hours by the boy's side during his last illness. **Wilson** was confined to the bed as he recovered from a stroke late in his term. When hostile Senator Albert Fall told him that he was praying for him, **Wilson** had enough spunk left to ask, "Which way?"

Margaret Truman loved to entertain college

friends in the White House. One time she planned to sleep three in the big bed in the Lincoln bedroom. One of the butlers looked somewhat like **Lincoln**, and **Truman** arranged for him to dress up in white and appear at the door at midnight. The butler chickened out. In any event, the bed was so hard the girls couldn't sleep, talked most of the night, and ended up on the floor. **Truman**, as a joke, told his visiting mother, whose own mother had celebrated **Lincoln's** assassination, that she was to sleep in "**Lincoln's** bed." She would have none of it, and said she'd sleep on the floor. She had too many vivid memories of "**Lincoln's** men" ravaging her home in Missouri during the war. The house was not a good place for Margaret's other grandmother, either; she died here at age ninety-four.

The bedroom was a favorite study room for **Nixon**, who liked to turn up the fireplace heat in the winter and air conditioning in the summer. He handed his resignation to his secretary of state in the room. **Nixon** told ten-year-old John Kennedy Jr., as the boy sat on the bed in 1971, that if he made a wish on it, it would come true, according to a White House legend. Young John wrote the president that he had great luck the next day at school. The **Clintons** made headlines letting Hollywood famous sleep in the Lincoln bed during their administration.

In June 1939, George VI of England slept here; the room was then known as the Lincoln Study, since **Hoover** had used it as a study. The queen slept across the hall to the north in what was known as the Rose Bedroom, where Prime Minister Winston Churchill later stayed for several weeks just after the United States entered World War II, and returned several times during the war. Fortunately he and the president, both with super egos, learned to like each other. One early morning after **Roosevelt** got the inspiration for the name of the new world organization, he wheeled in to share the name "United Nations" when Churchill was emerging from his bath. The president apologized, but Churchill responded, "The Prime Minister of Great Britain had nothing to hide from the President of the United States." **Roosevelt's** aide, Harry Hopkins, lived in the room during World War II. The bedroom is now known as the Queen's Bedroom. **Jackson's** live-in portrait artist lived here during his administration. He was once copying a painting of **Jackson's** beloved, deceased wife when **Jackson** accidentally strolled in, saw the painting, and began crying so deeply that the artist had to remove it.

The next office adjacent to what is now the Lincoln Bedroom toward the center was the cabinet room, sometimes combined with the president's office and now called the Treaty Room. Presidents beginning with **Theodore Roosevelt** used it as a private study after the Executive Office Building and west wing were built and the presidents began to do office work there.

On the other side of the Lincoln Bedroom at the southeast corner was **Lincoln's** secretary's room where **Andrew Johnson** was finally able to get a telegraph put in. It later became **McKinley's** war room, where he received the latest developments on the Spanish American War including the battles of San Juan and Kettle Hill.

The room directly above the Blue Room is now called the Yellow Oval Room, the center room of the floor. **Pierce** read his daily Bible readings here and held a rare Sabbath Day conference with Stephen Douglas, **Davis**, John C. Breckenridge, and other senators just before the Kansas-Nebraska Bill was voted on, called the worst bill ever enacted and the first shot of the Civil War. No one expected this to become the great disaster of his administration, leading to renewal of the slavery controversy by theoretically allowing expansion of slavery. It had been thought to promote westward expansion and development. During **Lincoln's** occupancy, the room was used as a family sitting room or private parlor, and so used until the 1950s. Mrs. **Fillmore** began the library added to by Mary **Lincoln**, and it was so used until **Eisenhower** began using it as a formal entertaining area. **Lincoln** liked to read a chapter in the Bible while the family gathered for breakfast. His boys had school here briefly. **Andrew Johnson** was here when a runner from the Capitol came to inform him that he was acquitted in the trial following his impeachment.

This was the first **Roosevelt** family's favorite room. They put up their Christmas stockings here, and **Benjamin Harrison** donned a Santa Claus suit for his grandchildren. **Theodore Roosevelt** once made a prediction here before the **Tafts**. He pretended to be clairvoyant and said he saw a man weighing 300 pounds with something hanging over his head; was it the presidency or the chief justiceship? Mrs. Taft said, "Make it the presidency." **Taft** said, "Make it the chief justiceship." Both had asked for what they wanted. Both eventually got it. (**John Quincy Adams** was also appointed to the Supreme Court, but turned it down.) Mrs. **Taft** pushed her husband into a job that he did not want to fulfill her lifetime ambition to live here. But then she suffered a stroke soon after moving in so that she could not enjoy it. **Harding** played poker here several times a week with his cronies and freely served liquor even though Prohibition was law.

Franklin Roosevelt and George VI spent several hours talking in the room discussing the coming war. Early in the morning the president patted the king on the knee and said, "Young man, it's time you went to bed." The king said later that he wished his ministers had talked to him like that. This was the most important room of **FDR's** presidency. Here he ate, studied, worked, held meetings, including his first cabinet meeting, and ceremoniously made his cocktails. The first council of war was held here on December 7, 1941. On January 1, 1942, the president, Churchill, a Soviet Union representative, and others signed a twenty-six-nation agreement against the Axis powers. When Lincoln biographer Carl Sandburg visited he asked **Roosevelt** which window **Lincoln** used to see smoke from Confederate cannon. The president did not know, so they wandered from room to room until they got to the window here and Sandburg became silent and stared. The president did not wish to break the mood, and began to shuffle papers until Sandburg announced that this was the window; he "felt it." **Roosevelt's** map room was two floors directly below in the basement. The Truman Balcony is outside. It was near the south side on September 11, 1994, that small airplane with a suicide pilot crashed into a magnolia tree, still there, planted by **Jackson**. The **Clintons** were then staying at the Blair House.

Monroe established the state bedroom west of the oval room, made into separate rooms about 1850. **FDR** slept in the room, worked, generally propped up in bed, and received visitors. Most presidents have slept in the bedrooms, generally the second bedroom, immediately to the west of the oval room, with family members sleeping in rooms across the hall facing north in one of several guest bedrooms overlooking Pennsylvania Avenue. Across the hall from the oval room over the north door, **Lincoln** made speeches to listeners outside. Mary Lincoln stayed there after the assassination, as she would not go back to her prior rooms. The **Theodore Roosevelt** boys slept in various rooms along the north side and roller-skated down the hall.

The largest bedroom was the suite at the northwest end known as the Prince of Wales Bedroom, named after the 19-year-old royal guest here shortly before the **Lincolns** arrived. He later was King Edward VII of England. This was actually **Buchanan's** bedroom, but when Edward visited, there was no suitable guest room; so the president slept on a sofa in the hall or in his office. **Jackson's** secretary, Andrew Jackson Donalson, lived in this and adjoining rooms, across the hall from **Jackson**, and four of Donalson's children were born here. **Jackson's** slave nurse stayed in the corner room and took care of the children. The **Lincolns** may have used the room in October 1861, during redecorations elsewhere. **William Henry Harrison**, the **McKinleys**, and **Clevelands** used it for their bedrooms, with others depositing various family members here or using it for other purposes. **Cleveland's** second daughter was born here. His first daughter, "Baby" Ruth, was so popular that later a candy bar was named after her. At least that's what baseball hero Babe Ruth was told when he sued the company for using his name.

Most presidents used the bedroom directly opposite on the south side, beginning with **John Adams. TR** had the big ("Lincoln") bed moved out of this, daughter Alice's room, to his bedroom so he could sleep in it as it was thought to have been **Lincoln's** bed. Invalid Ida **McKinley** stayed here most of the time and knitted 3500 pairs of slippers for charity. **Wilson** also used the great bed in his bedroom across the hall from the Prince of Wales Room beginning in his second marriage. He had met a friend of a staff member visiting the White House several months after his wife's death, and married her at 1308 20th Street, a little over a year after his wife died. Here he lay for months recovering from his stroke. His wife brought papers to him and someone initialed them. It is believed that his wife may have acted as president during this time as she was the only one to have access to the president.

Willie **Lincoln's** death here devastated the family and further imbalanced **Lincoln's** fragile wife. He was the only presidential child to die in the mansion, although Teddy Jr. and Archie **Roosevelt** almost did. Some sources say **Lincoln** spent days alone in the room. When Archie began to recover, his brothers smuggled his pony up to his bedroom.

At the northeast corner of the second floor was another bedroom, part of the Prince of Wales Suite, and now the President's Dining Room. It was **Andrew Johnson's** living room and has been a dining room since the **Kennedys**. The **Clevelands**, **McKinleys**, and Alice **Roosevelt** slept in this area. **Lincoln** and Tad may have slept in this room much or all of the time after Willie died.

Since the early 1800s the north lawn adjacent to Pennsylvania Avenue was enclosed by a fence appearing about the same as the one now. A similar fence enclosed Lafayette Park across the street and was later moved to be a border between Evergreen and the National Cemetery in Gettysburg. The statue of Jefferson, now in the Capitol Rotunda, once stood in front of the house where the current fountain is. Near the south lawn toward the Washington Monument site until the late 1800s was marshland that opened into the putrid Washington Canal, where Constitution Avenue later was built. The **Lincolns** hosted traditional Easter egg rollings on the lawn.

During the Civil War interior paths crisscrossed the grounds and were used by **Lincoln** to wander over to the State Department on the east side and the Navy and War Departments on the west. Here he played with Tad and nightly came to the War Department to examine and answer telegrams. He sometimes walked out early to Pennsylvania Avenue to get a paper. Young Quentin **Roosevelt**, after being scolded by his father **TR** because the gardener complained that his stilt-walking ruined the flowerbeds, remarked that it did his father no good to be president since he didn't control anybody. When a reporter tried to get inside information from Quentin, the boy said of the president, "I see him sometimes, but I know nothing of his family life."

The roof was a promenade, hidden from the public view, where various presidents and their families suntanned and watched the stars. **Grant** and his youngest son set up a telescope, and **Lyndon Johnson** at least once gave a Texas-style barbecue. Mrs. **Clinton** raised tomato plants there. The **Lincoln** sons pretended that this was a battleship, and Alice **Roosevelt** sneaked up to smoke her cigarettes since her father prohibited her from smoking "under" his roof. Smoking must not have done her much harm; she lived longer than any presidential child, to 96.

TR once shook his youngest son out of bed to berate him for the "double disgrace" of covering the eyes of the first ladies' pictures with spitballs, in "the house of the nation." Quentin said it really didn't matter because Charlie **Taft** had helped him, and it would soon be his house.

The Capitol Rotunda shows the Jefferson statue (center), which was on the White House lawn for 27 years beginning in 1847. Lincoln's sons climbed on it when it was where the fountain is now.

When **Coolidge**'s 16-year-old son died from a blister he got while playing tennis, the president felt that this was the price he paid for occupying the house and stated, "The power and glory of the presidency went with him." **Pierce** felt the same when he moved in after his son had been killed. Once when **Coolidge** was walking in front of the mansion, a senator asked facetiously, "I wonder who lives there." **Coolidge** answered, "Nobody, they just come and go."

The White House Area and West

The Executive Office Building now stands on the SE corner of G Street, 17th and Pennsylvania. **Washington** himself requested the spot, and insisted that it be used as such even though **John Adams** tried to get the government to move the site closer to the Capitol. The State Department, which had been there until 1829, was where secretaries of state served who later became presidents: **Madison**, **Monroe**, and **Quincy Adams**. During the Civil War era, the War Department was at the north end of the building with the Navy Department at the south end. **Davis** served in the building as secretary of war. It was just west of the White House and parallel in size and location to the Treasury Building to the east. The telegraph office here was the closest one to **Lincoln**, and he came almost daily for the latest news, often hand-in-hand with Tad. It is claimed that **Lincoln** spent more time here than any other place in **Washington** outside the White House. **Grant** occupied the secretary of war's office under **Johnson**.

The new "Old Executive Office Building," now the Eisenhower Executive Office Building, was constructed on the site from 1871 until 1888. **Grant** ordered it built, and the completion of the then largest office building in the world ended a long-time debate about moving the capital to somewhere in the middle of the country. Over the next century both **Roosevelts** served here as assistant secretary of the Navy, **Taft** as secretary of war, **Eisenhower** (1926, 1929–35) as aide to General MacArthur, and **Truman**, **Nixon**, **Johnson**, **Ford**, and **Bush** as vice presidents. **Nixon** and **Hoover** had offices in the building while president. It was considered an embarrassment for years, and almost torn down in the late 1950s. **Truman** said, "I don't want it torn down; I think it's the greatest monstrosity in America."

Lincoln missed General Winfield Scott at his residence (site), 1732 Pennsylvania, the first day he arrived in the capital, but saw him there many times later. **Madison**, **Monroe**, **John Quincy Adams**, and **Jackson** visited the Van Ness Mansion at 18th and C Streets, now the site of the Pan American Union Building.

Davis lived at 609 14th Street as a representative and moved to 14th between F and G Streets in late 1853 as secretary of war under **Pierce**. The **Pierces** had recently lost their remaining son and were very despondent. Mrs. **Pierce** stayed in her White House room for a year, but President **Pierce** came here often to see his friend. Jane **Pierce** at last emerged from her room to come to the Davises.' (Her dress in the Smithsonian First Ladies Collection is the only black one.) She grew very fond of **Davis's** young son and took him for carriage rides that seemed to restore her. Unfortunately the two-year-old died in June 1854 in the house, and **Pierce** attended the funeral there. **Davis** then moved for the rest of his term to the NE corner of 18th and G Streets, a three-story, 20-room house, a block west of the War Department. At other times, **Davis** lived at Mrs. Duvall's on Missouri near Four and a Half Street in late 1848, in Gadsby's and Willard's Hotels and in several boarding houses on Capitol Hill in 1848, G between 13th and 14th Streets in late 1857, on G between 17th and 18th, and 1736 "I" Street, where he last lived from 1859 to 1861 as the South seceded. (Dates and addresses differ in various sources.) **Davis** hosted a dinner there in 1860 with presidential candidate John C. Breckenridge and friends of rival candidates John Bell and Stephen Douglas. He tried to convince them that they should all drop out and concentrate on Horatio Seymour as the lone Democratic Party candidate to block Republican **Lincoln**. But Douglas would not agree, leading to a split Democratic vote, **Lincoln's** election, secession, and the Civil War.

General **Grant** set up after Lee's surrender in General Scott's old office at the SW corner of 17th and F Streets in a modest residential building. He received unofficial notification of his nomination for the presidency here in 1868. The Winder Building,* NW corner of F and 17th, served many functions including Army Headquarters. Secretary of War **Davis** used it in the 1850s. It has now been restored to its Civil War appearance and still functions as a government office building. **Lincoln**, who hated to wait in his office, often visited high Union commanders with offices here, including Generals Scott, McClellan, Halleck, and **Grant**, who later traveled back and forth to his secretary of war office across the street.

The Octagon House,* NE corner of New York

Madison lived in the Octagon House in D.C. after the British burned the White House. John Adams, Jefferson, and Jackson at least were entertained, and Washington watched it being built.

and 18th Streets, was used for about a year as President **Madison's** home after the British burned the White House. The prominent mansion, begun about 1798, is one of the oldest in the city. The prior owner entertained **Adams**, **Jefferson**, **Monroe**, and **Jackson**. **Washington** is said to have watched its construction and admired it. The British spared it because it had been the home of the French minister. The **Madisons** lived in the suite on the east side of the second floor. Here Dolley resumed her weekly entertainments, the president received first the news of the January 1815 victory in New Orleans, and then the news of the peace treaty signed in Europe the previous Christmas Eve. For a while it seemed that the federal city would not be rebuilt and the capital would be moved, but the victory and treaty changed this. The Treaty of Ghent was signed in the parlor, ending the War of 1812.

From 1815 to 1817 the **Madisons** moved to the corner house (1901) of the Seven Buildings, 1901–13 Pennsylvania, probably because the Octagon was too small. They continued to hold receptions, including the largest for General **Jackson** and his wife in late 1815, resulting in their house being known as the "House of 1000 Candles." The Buildings were the only houses left standing between the White House and Georgetown when the British left. **Polk** lived in number 1901 in 1826, and **Van Buren** lived there as vice president and continued as president for four days. Numbers 1907–09 still stand.

Monroe lived in a Federal townhouse at 2017 I Street* as **Madison's** secretary of war and while the White House was being restored during the first six months of his presidency. Ironically the building was leased to the British Legation in 1821. It is now a National Historic Site, much-altered, and known as the Washington Arts Club. **Madison** conferred with him here and is said to have ridden a horse in the front door and out the back to escape the British. **Madison** accompanied

Monroe to and from here to **Monroe's** first inauguration.

Madison had lived in the Six Buildings, 2107–17 Pennsylvania, for a short time as secretary of state. Prior to that the **Madisons** had lived in the White House with **Jefferson**. After returning to the city after the British burned it, **Madison** met with **Monroe** here. **Houston** lived at 2107 for a short time about where **Jackson** and his wife lived on the north side of I Street just east of 21st when he came as senator in 1823 with his friend John Eaton. Here they all took a liking to the innkeeper's daughter, Peggy O'Neal—John more than the others. **Jackson** encouraged Eaton to marry her in spite of her bad reputation, which surfaced when Eaton was later **Jackson's** secretary of war. The other wives of cabinet officials refused to call on Mrs. Eaton even after **Jackson** declared her "as chaste as a virgin." This created a major crisis in the administration not ended until the cabinet itself was reorganized.

Lincoln visited the Old Naval Observatory (site), south of E between 23rd and 25th Streets, and north of the Lincoln Memorial dedicated by **Harding** and Chief Justice **Taft**, visited by all subsequent presidents. "The Pathfinder of the Seas," Mathew Fontaine Maury, made many scientific discoveries at the Observatory. All presidents since **LBJ** have attended the Kennedy Center north of the Theodore Roosevelt Bridge.

Chief Justice John Marshall's house (private) still stands at 1801 F Street. Here he was visited by **Madison** and **Monroe**.

Distraught **Truman** heard his daughter sing in Constitution Hall just after his lifelong friend, schoolmate, and press secretary Charlie Ross died. Then a *Washington Post* critic wrote a less than flattering review, causing the president to write a widely publicized note, that he would punch him out if they ever met. They did, but he didn't, as they later became friends.

The current Renwick Gallery (Old Corcoran Art Gallery), at the NE corner of Pennsylvania and 17th Street, was built to house the art collection of financier William Corcoran. The building was taken over by the government and became the largest Civil War distribution center in the city for uniforms, tents, and equipage as the headquarters of Quartermaster General Montgomery Meigs' department. **Lincoln** called on Meigs once to slump in front of the fire and seek advice or solace saying, "The bottom is out of the tub."

Jackson's informal or kitchen cabinet, including **Van Buren**, met in the Blair House east of the Renwick. **Truman** and his family lived there, combined then with the Lee House, for the first three weeks of his administration while Mrs. **Roosevelt** moved out, and then from 1949 until 1952 during the extensive $5 million reconstruction of the White House interior. It was here that an assassination attempt was made on his life in 1950. As the president watched from the second floor, a secret serviceman and a would-be assassin were killed in the exchange of 32 shots on the street, some striking the house. (**Carter** pardoned the other assailant.)

While in the Blair House **Truman** entertained Princess Elizabeth. He stayed here in 1963 when he came for the **Kennedy** funeral and met with **Eisenhower** for about an hour in the front parlor. They had met for three other funerals since the 1952 election (George Marshall's, Sam Rayburn's, and Eleanor **Roosevelt's**), but now for the first time they seemed to have patched up their prior animosity provoked in the 1952 election. **Houston** played poker here while living with **Jackson** in the White House. **Johnson** rented the Lee House next door when he became president and before Mary **Lincoln** moved out of the White House. After waiting here a few days, he used a residence at 334 H Street. **Eisenhower, Kennedy, Truman, Reagan**, and **Clinton** stayed at the Blair House before their inaugurations. When **Reagan** was awakened at nine o'clock on inauguration morning and told he had two hours before the ceremony, he asked if that meant he had to get up. The National Park Service shows that **Lincoln** paid calls here. The **Clintons** were here when a small airplane tried to crash into the White House.

Lafayette Park

Lafayette Park,* on Pennsylvania Avenue opposite the White House, was the "President's Park," the center of early social life for the city as many prominent officials and citizens lived in the area around it. Pennsylvania Avenue did not come this far until the mid–1820s. **Jefferson** kept goats here, where his aggressive ram severely injured an adult and killed a child. **Fillmore** unveiled the **Jackson** statue in 1853 that the **Lincoln** children enjoyed climbing on, as they did **Jefferson's** statue on the White House lawn. **Lincoln's** sister-in-law wrote how **Lincoln** unburdened himself in front of the statue and pleaded for her not to go back to Illinois after Willie died. **Buchanan** had a habit of walking around the park after lunch. **Lincoln** crisscrossed the park going to General McClel-

Buildings on the west side of Lafayette Square include the Decatur House on the corner, visited by many, where Van Buren lived. It was called the lobby of the White House. John Quincy Adams and Monroe frequented. The adjacent house is where Pierce lived when he left the White House and Theodore Roosevelt lived as the White House was being renovated. He fell and broke his leg in front.

lan's house and other sites listed. **Grant** began a tradition of reviewing the inaugural parades in front of the White House facing the park.

The Decatur House,* 748 Jackson Place, on the street's SW corner, has been called the lobby of the White House and was home to many prominent people, including **Van Buren. Monroe** and **John Quincy Adams**, among others, visited. **Grant** stayed many times with a friend here, and **Reagan** founded the James Brady Foundation in 1982. Just south at 736 Lafayette (22 Jackson Place), the **Roosevelts** lived for four months in 1902 while the White House was being refurbished. **Theodore** fell in front and hurt (broke, in some accounts) his leg. He had also hurt it severely between Pittsfield and Lenox, Mass., when thrown 30 feet from a carriage when a trolley hit it, and he had to have an operation here. **Pierce** stayed here after leaving the White House.

The Hay-Adams Hotel covers the home site of **Lincoln's** secretary of the Navy at 1607 H Street, where the president frequently visited, and Secretary of State John Hay's later home at 1603, frequently visited by **TR.** Hay was close to **Lincoln** as a secretary and aide as well as **TR.** Hay had known **TR**'s father and visited frequently their New York home on 20th St.

St. John's Episcopal Church* and Parish House, 1525 H St., is known as the Church of the Presidents, where new presidents traditionally worship on inaugural day. All presidents beginning with **Madison** have come here, and it is unchanged from the Civil War period. **Madison, Monroe, Van Buren, William Henry Harrison, Tyler, Taylor, Pierce,** and **Arthur** were parishioners. **Madison** chose pew 54, Row 9, occupied by the next five presidents and a number of other presidents, including those who worship in the church today. **William Henry Harrison** occupied the pew and helped ladies into their carriages.

St. John's, opposite the White House, has been called the "Church of the Presidents" as all from Madison have attended.

Three weeks into his term, already tired and worn out, he told the rector that he planned to join. He then walked back to the White House in sleet and cold rain, caught pneumonia, and died a week later. (Actually this is one of the several times **Harrison** is described as having caught a cold or worse or further injuring his health. He possibly got it shopping nearby.) His funeral was in the church and attended by **Tyler** and **John Quincy Adams**.

Lincoln worshiped on February 25, 1861, accompanied by his secretary of state, William H. Seward, sitting in Seward's pew, number 65. (This is third back from the front on the middle right side.) The church claims that the burdened president often came to a back pew during afternoon prayer sessions. **Franklin Roosevelt** started his inaugural day here and usually worshipped in the church, but also liked the Baptist and Methodist churches. He hated to have tourists ogling at him in church, and stated, "I can do almost everything in the goldfish bowl of the president's life, but I'll be hanged if I can say my prayers in it." **Johnson** came the morning after **Kennedy's** assassination. The public is still welcome. **George W. Bush** liked to attend the early service and kneel to pray on his father's prayer cushion. **Carter**'s cushion is still in his pew.

Vermont Street runs into Lafayette Square just to the east. **Lincoln** generally took that route when he stayed in the Soldiers' Home. The Arlington Hotel stood on the SW corner with H Street and claimed that most presidents from **Buchanan** through **Taft** stayed there.

The Cutts-**Madison** House, marked at 1520 H Street, SE corner of Madison Place, was build by Dolley **Madison's** brother-in-law, and passed by debt to **Madison**, who had advanced money for its building. Dolley (often misspelled "Dolly," as on the marker here) moved in as she liquidated the **Madison** plantation home, and continued to live here until she died. (Her incompetent, spendthrift, spoiled son caused her great financial distress, necessitating the selling of the **Madison**

property and papers.) She was visited by many national leaders including **John Quincy Adams** and **Taylor**. Many came by to tell her they appreciated her saving the Washington portrait from the British. It became a custom to visit the White House on special occasions, such as News Year's Day, and then come here to see her. Senator Stephen Douglas's wife told Mary **Lincoln** that she had met her (and surely Abe) in her Aunt Dolley's home in 1848. During the Civil War it was General George B. McClellan's headquarters from November 1861 through March 1862. The general wrote in his memoirs that **Lincoln** had a "very close" association with him, and he "often came to my house, frequently late at night" to confer and get news. On November 13, 1861, the president, Seward, and Hay came across Lafayette Park to see the general. When they were informed that he was out, they waited; they heard him return after an hour and go directly upstairs. When the president asked if he knew they were there, he was informed that McClellan knew, but had gone to bed and they should come back another time.

McKinley frequently visited the Tayloe House (marked) at 21 Madison Place, south of Dolley's home so that it was called the "Little White House." Many presidents are claimed to have visited including all presidents between 1829 and 1868.

The four-story home of **Lincoln's** secretary of state was two lots (about 45 feet) north of Pennsylvania Ave. on the east side of Lafayette Park, at 17 Madison Place. **Lincoln** frequently met with Seward for warm companionship and relaxation felt with his former rival for the 1860 nomination. He spent more time with him than he did his own family in his first year in office so that Mary became resentful of this close relationship and these many evenings. His last time was April 9, 1865, when he comforted Seward, who had been severely injured in a carriage accident. Booth's henchman, Lewis Powell, tried to kill Seward in his bedroom on the night **Lincoln** was killed. The house was located almost adjacent to the street, in the yard of the present structure.

East of the White House to Ford's Theater

Madison lived from 1801 until he became president in 1809 at 1333–1335 F Street (destroyed), one of the most elegant residences in town, and had a reception here after his inauguration. Dolley's sister and her family moved in when the president moved to the White House. **Madison** came back a short time after the White House burned in 1814, conducted business, but moved to the Octagon House, as it was larger and more functional for the president. Later **John Quincy Adams** acquired the property as secretary of state and was here when elected president in 1824. (A poll of historians several years ago by American Heritage Magazine rated him the best secretary of state. Seward was second.) He had purchased the house as a political asset so that he could entertain in style, and it is said that his campaign was fought and won in his ballroom. One ball here for 900 people honored **Jackson**, his main rival, on the tenth anniversary of the Battle of New Orleans. **Adams** left the home at 7:30 A.M. to walk to the Capitol for his inauguration. After leaving the presidency, **Adams** leased the Potter House at Meridian Hill Park on 16th Street, then in the country at the edge of the city on Meridian Street. As was the case with his father, he did not get along with the new president, refused to attend his inauguration, and rode here alone from the White House as **Jackson** was being sworn in. From 1829 until 1834 **Adams** lived at 2400 16th Street and Crescent Place, between I and K Streets, less than two blocks north of President's Square, with his son John. When John died in 1834, **Adams** moved with the rest of the family back to 1333–1335 F Street, where he principally lived (off and on) for the rest of his life as a congressman.

While secretary of state under **Polk** from 1845 to 1849, **Buchanan** lived next to **Adams**, one door west at 1331 F Street, and entertained lavishly. Bachelor **Buchanan** lived for 16 years with Sen. William Rufus King; both were said to be somewhat effeminate, and were referred to as "she" and "the Siamese Twins." King was elected vice

Opposite, top: **Lincoln is said to have spent more time at the Old Soldiers' Home in Washington than anywhere else. Other presidents, including Buchanan, Hayes, and Arthur, also stayed here, where it was a little cooler in the summer.** ***Opposite, bottom:*** **Madison owned the Cutt's Mansion on Lafayette Square in D.C., where Lincoln met with General McClellan, or at least tried to: the general went to bed when he returned to find Lincoln waiting in the parlor. John Quincy Adams and Zachary Taylor, among others, visited Dolley Madison when she lived here.**

The building in the right center was the site of Secretary William Seward's home where Lincoln spent many hours visiting his close friend. Seward was the subject of an assassination attempt here the night Lincoln was shot.

president under **Pierce**, traveled to Cuba after the election for relief from tuberculosis, became the only elected official to be sworn in on foreign soil, and died before returning to Washington. Earlier the two may have lived at Rock Creek Church Road and Upshur. Before that **Buchanan** lived on the west side of 13th between E and F.

The Treasury Building, SW corner of 15th and Pennsylvania, was to be used by the president and cabinet during the Civil War in case Washington was invaded. It had been stocked with food and the doors were sandbagged. **Lincoln** reviewed troops and raised a flag over the south front at 15th and Pennsylvania. The Treasury Building was first placed here in the new city and was destroyed by an arson fire while **John Adams** was president. He helped pass the water buckets. It is said that President **Jackson** was tired of wrangling over where a newer building was to be built. So while out walking and listening to the arguments, he struck his cane in the ground and ordered it built there. This ruined the intended view from the Capitol to the White House, but saved other views of the mansion from having an executive complex in Lafayette Park or south ruining that vista. The much-quoted **Jackson** story is no doubt a myth as the Treasury has always been there. The suite used by the Treasury secretary has been restored to the time when **Lincoln** frequently came to visit. Down the hall is the **Andrew Johnson** Suite, used by him after the assassination until Mary **Lincoln** moved out. He held his first cabinet meeting on the afternoon of April 15, 1865, and was here until June 8. The northwest corner of the building was the secretary of state's office from 1820; **John Quincy Adams**, **Van Buren**, and **Buchanan** served here. **Grant's** first inaugural ball was here.

Around the corner near the NE corner of 15th and F Streets was the site of Rhodes Tavern from 1801 until 1984, visited by most presidents. British officers doused the candles in August 1814 as they ate inside so they could enjoy the sight of the White House burning. While it was the National Press Club from 1909 to 1915, **TR**, **Taft**, and **Wilson** visited. Around the corner, the Old Ebbitt Grill at 675 15th was visited by most presidents from **Grant** to **TR**. One block north at the NE corner of F and 14th Streets was Ebbitt's Hotel, where **Pierce** burst into a congressman's room one night in the middle of a snowstorm to exclaim, "Ah my dear friends! I am so tired of the shackles of Presidential life that I can scarcely endure it!" **McKinley** got his only exercise walking up and down in front of his residence in the hotel smoking his cigar, as his wife objected to the fumes. **Taft** stayed in 1890 and attended Grace Reformed Church at 1405 15th Street while president.

All presidents since **Truman** have made speeches and eaten at the Capital Hilton, 16th and K Streets. The only president to return as senator, **Andrew Johnson**, took up residency at the Imperial Hotel on E Street between 13th and 14th Streets in 1875, the same year that **Lincoln's** first vice president, Hannibal Hamlin, returned to the senate.

Lincoln attended Foundry Methodist, NE corner of G and 14th, with many of his cabinet members on January 18, 1863, when he was made a life director of the Missionary Society. **John Quincy Adams**, **Grant**, **Jackson**, **Madison**, **Andrew Johnson**, and **Polk** also attended on occasion. **Hayes** attended regularly from 1865 until 1881, although he never joined. After the church moved to 1500 16th, **Coolidge**, **McKinley**, **Truman**, **FDR**, and **Clinton** attended. **FDR** attended with Churchill in 1941, three weeks after Pearl Harbor.

Lincoln attended a funeral at the Epiphany Church,* north side of G Street between 13th and 14th. **Davis** considered this his church home from 1845 until 1861, and bought a pew although he was not very religious. His friend **Pierce** also attended. **Taft** lived at 1603 K while secretary of war, near 1323 K, where **Lincoln** frequently visited his crusty secretary of war, Stanton. The two grew close after both lost small children during the war. **Grant** attended a party here on the night before **Lincoln's** assassination and stood on the front steps to watch fireworks.

Lincoln frequented A. Stuntz's Fancy Store, a toy shop at 1207 New York Avenue, with his spoiled sons; it was known as their favorite place. **Coolidge** laid the cornerstone for the National Press Club, where 16 presidents have been card-carrying members, at 14th and F. Vice President **Truman** is pictured here playing the piano with movie star Lauren Bacall perched on top.

The **Lincolns** throughout the war attended New York Avenue Presbyterian,* New York and H. The president rented the same pew used by **Buchanan. Quincy Adams**, **Jackson**, **W. Harrison**, **Fillmore**, **Pierce**, **Buchanan**, **Andrew Johnson**, **Cleveland**, **TR**, **Taft**, **Hoover**, and **Eisenhower**, at least, attended. **Truman** laid the cornerstone of a modern, slightly larger church in 1951 with the help of prominent former pastor Peter Marshall's son. **Lincoln's** pew inside and hitching post outside remain. The church history claims that he had made all the necessary arrangements to join on the Easter Sunday following his assassination. **Quincy Adams** was a member, and there is a parlor with memorabilia of his as well as the **Lincolns**.'

Sometimes **John Quincy Adams** went to Second Presbyterian, where he was a trustee, in the triangle of H and New York Streets in the evening, and All Souls Unitarian at Sixth and D Streets in the morning. When he was president, this was his principal church. **Fillmore** also attended. The church later moved to 14th and L Streets, then 16th and Harvard Streets in 1924, and was church home for **Taft** at both of these locations. His funeral was at the latter.

Grover's Theater (site), is now the National Theater, 1321 Pennsylvania, formerly E Street. **Polk**'s inaugural ball was here. It is claimed that **Lincoln** attended this theater at least a hundred times. It was where he was when he received word of his second nomination and where he may have intended to come on his last night. Tad was here when his father was shot in nearby Ford's Theater.

Willard's,* 1401 Pennsylvania, was long the city's most famous and prominent hotel. In fact the hotel claims that all presidents from **Taylor** to **Coolidge** have been guests. The current building replaces the wartime structure where the **Lincolns** stayed before his inauguration. He met with the Peace Convention, presided over here by **Tyler.** President **Buchanan** called on his successor here to travel to the inauguration. Later the **Lincolns** attended concerts and lectures. **Fillmore** was living here as vice president when he was informed that **Taylor** had died and then moved back after leaving the presidency for what he planned to be a short time. Mrs. **Fillmore** was exposed to cold weather at **Pierce's** inaugural, got sick, and died in the hotel. The **Polks** moved in the day before his term ended, and he worked until

Lincoln, John Quincy Adams, and other presidents attended the New York Avenue Presbyterian Church, which claims that Lincoln had made arrangements to join on the next Sunday before he was assassinated. His hitching post ring is still on the curb, and his pew is inside.

early the next morning. He stumbled into bed at 2:00 A.M., but was awakened again at 6:00 to sign other documents. When **Lincoln** arrived before his inauguration, **Andrew Johnson** was living here. All presidents from **Hayes** through **Eisenhower** attended gridiron dinners here. **Clinton** stayed on the eve of his inauguration at the reconstructed hotel. **Taylor** stayed at the Mansion House, across the street on the NE corner, in 1826.

In 1864, an unrecognized general checked in and was given a small out-of-the-way room until the clerk noticed the not so unknown name, "U.S. **Grant** and son of Galena, Ill." (He had also stayed in 1852.) He had come to be named general-in-chief. As a new president, **Grant** liked to escape to the lobby and relax with his cigars, until he began to be noticed. He finally had to stop coming because he was harassed by so many in the lobby, or as he called them, "lobbyists." When **Johnson** returned as senator in 1875, he first stayed here as he had at times from 1857 to 1862. (He was the only former president elected to the Senate, and had lost two House elections after his term.) A friend commented that his quarters were not as spacious as those he once occupied further up the Street. **Johnson** agreed but declared, "They are more comfortable."

Wilson addressed the League to Enforce Peace in 1916 here. **Harding** stayed before his inauguration and used it to meet his mistress, Nan Britton. **Coolidge** lived in an $8-per-day suite with his family as vice president. (He had to stay for several days after **Harding** died to give Mrs. **Harding** time to burn most of his papers.) While here a fire alarm brought all to the lobby, but when the danger seemed past, they were still detained. **Coolidge** became impatient and started up the stairs when the fire marshal screamed at him, "Who do you think you are?" "The vice president," was yelled back. The marshal agreed for him to go ahead, then asked, "Vice president of what?" **Coolidge** answered back, "The United

States." The marshal then yelled for him to come back, saying, "I thought you were the hotel vice president." He was sworn in as president for the second time (after his father had done so in Vermont) at the hotel. While they were waiting for Mrs. **Harding** to leave as she culled, purged, burned, and carted off her husband's official papers, **Coolidge** was awakened by a shocked burglar who just happened to pick the president's room. The college student had overspent his vacation money. The president sat him down, lectured him, loaned him money, and sent him on his way.

Andrew Johnson lived at the Kirkwood House (site), in a room overlooking Pennsylvania Avenue at the NE corner with 12th Street, where Chief Justice Chase swore him in a few hours after **Lincoln** died. George Atzerodt, one of Booth's fellow conspirators, had taken a room nearby and was supposed to shoot the vice president when Lincoln was killed. Authorities were told about the strange man living near Johnson, went to his room, and found Booth's bankbook and other incriminating evidence. **Tyler** had stayed here when he left the White House.

Harvey's Restaurant was on the SE corner of Pennsylvania and 11th and served every president from **Grant** through **FDR**. **Lincoln** is said to have eaten his first catered public meal here in a party set up by Seward.

The **Lincolns** attended plays and operas during his congressional term and presidency at the Washington Theater or Carusi's Hall (site), NE corner of C and 11th Streets. Inaugural balls were held there for all presidents from **John Quincy Adams** (1825) through **Buchanan**, except **Pierce**, who canceled his because of the recent death of his son. C Street no longer extends to this location, now north of Constitution Avenue, and the Internal Revenue Building occupies the site, just south of Pennsylvania Avenue. One of **Polk**'s inaugural balls was at the National Theater. Multiple inaugural balls soon caught on. **George H.W. Bush** had 11, **Clinton** 13, but **George W.** cut back to eight. However, up to **Lyndon Johnson**, only **Washington** and **William Henry Harrison** had actually danced. When the strait-laced **Polks** arrived, all dancing and fun stopped until they left. **Houston** felt that **Polk** drank too much water.

When the Civil War began, **Johnson** lived on E Street between 13th and 14th Streets. **Garfield** bought a plain three-story house at 901 13th and I Streets, across from Franklin Square, in 1869 and lived there with his wife and five children until he was inaugurated in 1881.

Lincoln was assassinated at Ford's Theater, 511 10th Street, now restored to its appearance on April 14, 1865. The original walls still stand, except the rebuilt east side, with two original casement windows in the south bay, the pilasters, and the five arched doorways. **Lincoln** attended Ford's at least twelve times beginning in 1862, including February 10, 1865, with **Grant**, and had seen Booth perform there several times, including November 9, 1863, when he had heartily applauded the actor. Booth ignored a request from the president to meet him, saying he would rather have had the applause of a Negro.

Both **Lincolns** would have probably preferred to stay home that fatal night, but she knew how much he enjoyed the theater, and he hated to disappoint the expectant crowd. General **Grant** and nine or more others, including son Robert, turned down an invitation to attend. The presidential party, which arrived after the play had started, included Major Henry R. Rathbone and his fiancée, the daughter of Sen. Ira T. Harris. They had been picked up at the senator's house on H Street near 15th.

Booth crossed under the stage and out a side door, then went to an adjoining saloon on 10th before entering **Lincoln's** box to shoot him in the back of the head as he held his wife's hand. Rathbone was slashed while grabbing Booth as he attempted to jump to the stage 12 feet below, distracting him so that his fall was broken. His spur (now in the Naval Museum in Annapolis) caught one of the Treasury Guard flags draped on the box, now in the downstairs museum. Booth either broke his leg then, or when his horse fell crossing into Maryland.

The original door and couch are still in the presidential box, but the president's bloodstained chair (probably Rathbone's blood) is in the Henry Ford Museum in Dearborn, Michigan. The picture of George Washington in front is original. The museum in the basement contains most of the original weapons from the assassination plot, Booth's diary with pages mysteriously missing, clothes then worn by **Lincoln**, and other **Lincoln** material, although many items here in prior years are in storage in Harpers Ferry.

After being shot, **Lincoln** was carried to the Petersen House,* 516 10th Street, a rooming house across the street, since the ride to the White House would have been too dangerous. Mary waited in the front parlor sobbing hysterically as

government officials (including **Andrew Johnson** briefly) and friends watched and grieved. The president died at 7:22 A.M. on April 15. From that moment Mary formally mourned for the rest of her life. A few months earlier, Booth was a visitor to the same room, then occupied by an actor friend, and slept on the bed where **Lincoln** died. The building adjacent to the north also dates to this period. The furniture from the death room is in the Chicago Historical Society.

Between Ford's Theater and the Capitol Building

Harding attended Calvary Baptist at Eighth and H Streets, but on his first Sunday as president, he skipped to play golf, as noted in the newspapers.

The 1836 National Portrait Gallery, F and G Street between Seventh and Ninth Streets, was the Patent Office during the Civil War. **Lincoln** visited on April 10, 1848, and again February 19, 1849, to check on a constituent's application. As a congressman he brought his oldest son and his youngest as president. **Lincoln** raised a flag over the building on May 2, 1861, and was caught off guard by the crowd's insistence for a speech while visiting on February 22, 1864. He did a poor job in the eyes of his wife, who criticized him so severely in front of their guests that all conversation stopped between them as they were returning to the White House. Several inaugural balls were held here including **Lincoln's** on March 6, 1865, attended by, according to the *New York Times*, "5000 people in space prepared for 300." The ball and banquet were on the second floor overlooking Seventh Street in a room now known as the Lincoln Gallery, then the largest room in America, where the Declaration of Independence was displayed from 1841 until 1871. **Eisenhower** saved the building from becoming a parking lot in 1953.

Lincoln had 40 pictures taken at Alexander Gardner's Photographic Studio (site), 401 Seventh Street, NE corner of Seventh and D Streets, including his last four days before his death.

Treasury Secretary Salmon Chase lived on the NW corner of Sixth and E Streets where **Lincoln** came several times, including to Chase's daughter's wedding, when he stayed an unusually long time to compensate for his wife's absence. Mary **Lincoln** despised Kate and her father, who never ceased to run for president, as he believed himself better qualified than anyone else. Historian Doris Kearns Goodwin characterized the home as a rival court to help catapult Chase to the presidency in 1864. Chase's close friend, **Garfield**, lived here during the fall of 1862.

William Henry Harrison's inaugural ball was at the Washington Theater on Indiana Street, opposite Fifth Street. You might say this was his last dance, as he died a month later.

The Pension Building* between Fourth, Fifth, F, and G Streets was the site of inauguration balls for all presidents between **Cleveland** and **Taft**, **FDR**, and **Nixon** through **Clinton**. **George W. Bush** attended a nationally televised Christmas concert here in 2002.

John Quincy Adams worshipped at First Unitarian at D and Sixth that had the city's first church bell. On the first Christmas as president he attended St. Patrick's at 609 Tenth, where **Andrew Johnson** sometimes worshiped. On another occasion he went in unannounced and found it hard to get a seat. **Houston** went to the E Street Baptist between Sixth and Seventh, where he whittled animals during the service to give to children. He must have paid attention to the sermon because he wrote a summation to his wife every Sunday. **Taylor** heard **Polk** eulogized there in July 1849. **Grant** was the first president to attend a Jewish synagogue when he went to Adas Israel,* then at Sixth and G, now a museum.

On July 2, 1881, **Garfield** was shot as two of his sons, ages 15 and 17, were nearby, at the Baltimore and Potomac Railroad Station at the SW corner of Sixth and Constitution. **Hayes** had boarded his train here when he left Washington a few months before and barely escaped serious injury when his train collided with another near Baltimore. The National Gallery of Art, dedicated by **Franklin Roosevelt** in 1941, stands on the site. The station ran down the west side of 6th Street. The assassination spot would be now about at the west side of the central rotunda. The religious fanatic assassin was locked up in the "Washington Bastille" opposite 19th and C Street SE. **Garfield** lingered in the White House until early September, when he was taken to New Jersey, where he died. The assassin claimed that he had not killed the presi-

Opposite: **Ford's Theater was the site of probably the worst presidential tragedy, Lincoln's assassination.**

dent; the doctors did. This is possibly true; endless probing with non-sterile instruments and fingers failed to find the bullet, found after death in a place not particularly dangerous. Infections may have doomed him from the first. Secretary of War Robert Lincoln was nearby and rushed to the dying president's side. Robert was later nearby when **McKinley** was assassinated in Buffalo, and vowed never to attend another presidential function.

Lincoln came on his first day in town as president-elect to the studio and gallery of the world's first noted war photographer, Mathew Brady, 633 Pennsylvania, unfortunately not open to the public. This original building probably saw more famous Americans than any other building in the capital than the White House and Capitol. The photographs were done on the top floor under a skylight. Other famous Americans were immortalized on the site on or near here when it was painter Gilbert Stuart's studio in the early 1800s. Brady died in poverty after spending $100,000 to take 10,000 pictures that he hoped to sell to the government, but could not.

The **Lincolns** stayed at Brown's (Marble) Hotel (site), NW corner of Pennsylvania and Sixth, beginning December 2, 1847, when he first came to Congress. They arrived at the old train shed on the north side of Pennsylvania between First and Second. The hotel was also known as the Indian Queen for the swinging sign that bore a likeness of Pocahontas. "His Accidency," **Tyler**, was alternating between Brown's and his Williamsburg home; he was at the latter when notified of **Harrison's** death and was sworn in as president inside one of Brown's parlors two days later. He stayed later as a delegate to the Peace Conference trying to avert the Civil War. **Madison** had his second inaugural ball here. **Van Buren**, **Grant**, **Andrew Johnson**, and others also were guests. **Houston** lived here in 1824 as congressman when it was called O'Neale's, and returned in 1830 and 1832

Mathew Brady's Photography Studio (original in the center, but not open) probably saw more important men before the Civil War than any building in Washington other than the Capitol and the White House. Many presidents stayed at a hotel on the corner on the right.

with a group of Indians to air grievances before President **Jackson**. He stayed again in 1834, although he actually spent more time in the White House. When **Johnson** stayed there in 1873, it was known as the Metropolitan Hotel. **Jackson** was at a Jefferson Day Dinner here with **Van Buren** in 1830 when three famous toasts were made. **Jackson** began with, "Our Union: It must be preserved." Senator Robert Hayne rushed over to urge that "Federal" be inserted, and **Jackson** agreed he had intended it. This phrase became **Jackson's** trademark as the toast occurred during the Nullification Crisis when Vice President Calhoun and others were proposing the states could nullify a federal act. Calhoun rose and made the toast, "The Union, next to our liberty, the most dear." This would have been accepted, but then he began an unacceptable lecture to **Jackson. Van Buren** ended with an appropriate toast emphasizing the Union.

Pierce lived in Brown's as a newlywed and then moved to Third Street just north of the SW corner with Pennsylvania Ave., also his office. In 1832 while **Houston** was there, Representative William Stanbery charged him on the floor of the House with trying to get an illegal or fraudulent contract with the Indians. **Jackson** perceived this as an attack on him, and **Houston's** reputation would be ruined if he did not challenge. **Houston** confronted the congressman on the street nearby and beat him with his cane as Stanbery put a gun to his chest, discharging the powder, but not the ball. The House then charged the former congressman with assault against a member, although the legality of the charge was questioned. Stanbery later charged him in the local courts where the action should have been. **Houston** planned strategy in Brown's with **Polk**, another **Jackson** team member. On the floor of the House he was represented by Frances Scott Key, author of the National Anthem, who was too drunk to be effective. So **Houston** represented himself and made such an impression that he was re-established as a national figure and trusted friend of the president. **Jackson** loaned him money to get decent clothes, then sent him with official powers for a mission west of unknown purpose. First **Houston** met with Indians, probably to open up western migration, and wound up in Texas.

Lincoln attended a dinner in 1848 at the National Hotel (Gadsby's), then on the NE corner of Pennsylvania and Sixth. Gadsby also had a new hotel at the NW corner of Third where **Davis** stayed several months beginning December 1847. **Jackson, Van Buren, William Henry Harrison, Fillmore, Polk, Pierce**, and **Buchanan** also had lived in the hotel, as did **Davis** (1845), and **Houston** when he was first elected to the Senate. **Davis** started a fistfight in a public room with his fellow Mississippi senator in 1847. Senator **Jackson's** wife, Rachel, hated Washington so much that she rarely left her room. **Jackson** later waited here to be inaugurated, and had to flee back his first night as president, as happy but ill-mannered well-wishing mobs ransacked the president's house. He served his first week as president conducting business from inside. Feeble **W. Harrison** was so besieged here before his inauguration that he fled to his ancestral home in Virginia. Mrs. Tyler called on the **Polks** when they got to town before the inauguration to get them to move early to the White House, but they preferred to stay here. **Buchanan** and his nephew got sick here just before the inauguration, and it was thought that they had been poisoned. The nephew died, and it was later decided that this was due to bad sewers. Thus the illness was described for years as "**Buchanan's** mysterious sickness" or the "National Hotel Sickness." President-elect **Lincoln** was honored on February 28, 1861, with a private dinner. Booth's plot to kidnap **Lincoln** was planned for March 17, 1865, to take place elsewhere, but failed as **Lincoln** had come to Booth's residence to make a speech rather than be where the kidnappers had planned. He spoke from a balcony then and told the crowd that the end of the war was near as "we can see the bottom of the enemy's resources." Booth was able to mingle by the carriage and give "a demoniac expression of hatred" toward the president.

General **Grant** lived at 205 "I" Street much of the time from 1866 until 1869. The house had been a partial gift from rich admirers. **Grant** gave a $30,000 mortgage on the property and then quickly paid it off with part of a $105,000 testimonial check other rich friends raised knowing that he did not have the resources to pay for all of the social obligations that he would incur. (**Grant** also got a 5000-volume library from the citizens of Boston.) **Johnson** and **Hayes** attended a party here in 1866 as **Grant** demonstrated that the Civil War was over by also having former Confederate Vice President Alexander Stephens and radical Congressman Thaddeus Stevens. He received official notification here in 1868 of his nomination to be the then youngest elected president. When he was elected, several purchased the house for $65,000 and gave it to General William

T. Sherman. Before the war Stephen Douglas lived in such elegant style at number 201 that his house was known as "Mount Julep" because he was well known as a host. Vice President Breckinridge lived next door to the man he split the Democratic vote with in 1860. The connecting houses were hospitals during the war. The site is now part of I-395.

John Marshal Park, NW corner of Fourth and Pennsylvania, is the site of Chief Justice Marshall's rooming house, marked on Pennsylvania. **Quincy Adams** lived from 1818 until 1820 at the NW corner of Four-and-a-Half and F Streets at John Marshall Place. **Pierce** lived at the NE corner with C Street. Also nearby on Four-and-a-Half Street between C and Louisiana Avenue was First Presbyterian, attended by **Jackson**, **Polk**, **Pierce**, **Buchanan**, **Grant**, **Cleveland**, **Wilson**, and **Reagan**. **Pierce** came his first Sunday as president, one of the few places Mrs. Pierce attended. He walked when Mrs. Pierce did not go and sometimes walked to Ninth Street Presbyterian. **Lincoln** came to First Presbyterian with John Hay on August 6, 1863, but found the pastor was away. So they continued to the New York Street Presbyterian. Freemason's Hall on the SW corner with D Street is where inaugural balls for **Jackson** and **W. Harrison** were held. **Buchanan** lived at Four-and-a-Half Street between Pennsylvania and C Streets in 1821. **Polk** lived in the Elliott House on the north side of Pennsylvania between Third and Four-and-a-Half Streets from 1837 until elected in 1845. **Johnson** lived at 504 Pennsylvania in 1843.

Coolidge attended Metropolitan Methodist on the SW corner of C and John Marshall Place. **Grant** attended some after a disastrous first Sunday after his inauguration. He understood that the first pew had been reserved for him, and paraded with the family down the center aisle after the service had started. When he got to the front, he found the pew occupied, exchanged stares, then turned, and paraded out the back door. **McKinley** later occupied his pew, part of which survives in the present church at Nebraska and New Mexico Avenues.

Jackson Hall at 339 Pennsylvania was the site where **Lincoln** attended an inaugural ball for **Taylor**, on March 5, 1849, held to benefit the poor. He stayed until after three o'clock in the morning, then was unable to find his hat, and left bareheaded. Festivities for **Fillmore** and **Lincoln** were also here. **Buchanan** and **Polk** both lodged at Mrs. Peyton's, 501 Pennsylvania.

Andrew Johnson lived in the St. Charles Hotel, NE corner of Third and Pennsylvania, while in the senate. **Lincoln's** other vice president, Hannibal Hamlin, was a fellow boarder. **Jackson** and **Van Buren** lived there when it was called the New Capital Hotel.

TR served in the pre–Civil War west wing of City Hall,* Fourth and D, on the Civil Service Commission from 1889 until 1895. **Lincoln** served on a committee that met there. **Fillmore** lived in a house at 226 Third Street. Chief Justice Taney lived at 318 Indiana near the SE corner of D and Third, where **Lincoln** attended his funeral in 1864. **Davis** lived at Mrs. Potter's rooming house on the south side of Pennsylvania between Second and Third when he first came to Congress in 1845.

Pennsylvania Avenue, the city's main thoroughfare, is ceremonial avenue of the nation. Most presidents used this route to the Capitol for their inauguration, although **FDR** used Constitution Avenue. **Van Buren** and **Jackson** started the tradition of being present when the successor rode with the outgoing president, although **Jefferson** accompanied his best friend, **Madison**. **W. Harrison** rode his favorite horse to his inauguration. **Jackson** walked it. **Harding** was the first to ride in an automobile. Stephen Douglas rode with his friend and rival **Lincoln**. Many regiments in the Civil War made a march down the avenue past the White House their first order of business. **Lincoln** stood on the sidewalk in front of the White House to review parades; many presidents have followed suit. Also many took unaccompanied walks around the area until **Garfield** was assassinated in 1881. **Lincoln's** funeral procession, composed of 30,000 men, April 19, 1865, proceeded slowly along this route. The first real inaugural parade was **Grant's** although most presidents traveled up and down before and after the inaugural ceremonies. **Grant** liked to walk daily while in office from the White House to the Capitol and back. **Carter** walked the street from his inauguration to the White House, but security was so tight for **George W. Bush** in 2001 that he could not be seen by many at the curb (including me) in his fortress-like vehicle.

Many also traveled the avenue in death, including all presidents who died while in office except **FDR**, whose funeral procession was down Constitution Avenue. **Reagan**'s funeral also proceeded down Constitution. The Tiber Creek crossed Pennsylvania at Second Street until it was covered. Future senators **Davis** and William Allen were almost killed as they walked off a bridge about here into the creek on a dark night in 1837. **Jefferson** helped rescue a number of men caught in a flood at the site. The city's business center was generally dusty or muddy, and partially and badly paved with rough cobblestones, and was gaslit at night. **Tyler** was almost carried to death as his horse once panicked on the avenue and ran uncontrollably until the president was rescued. Since there was then no vice president, and some did not even accept **Tyler** as a president after he succeeded on **W.H. Harrison**'s death, the country was spared a crisis of succession.

The Baltimore and Ohio Station was on the NE corner of New Jersey between D and C Streets, at the Louisiana Street junction, and was used for 80 years by presidents from **Monroe** to **TR**. A corner of the present Union Station touches the site, now vacant. The depot was north of the present Robert Taft Memorial. **Lincoln** arrived secretly at 6:00 A.M. on February 23, 1861, after leaving his official party and family. Illinois Congressman Washburne surprised him, and drove him to Willard's Hotel. He used the station several times. His funeral train to Illinois left from here in April 1865, as did **McKinley's** in 1901. Maybe as many as 100,000 were here to welcome **Wilson** back from the 1918 Paris Peace Conference at Union Station, used by all presidents from **Wilson** through **Ford**, at least. It opened in 1907 to combine all railroad stations, as they all had separate depots. The **FDR's** coffin arrived and left from here.

Washington owned Lot 16, Square 634, marked by a stone in the middle of the west side of North Capitol between B and C between the Capitol and Union Station. On this lot he built two three-story townhouses just before he died.

North of the White House — Connecticut and Massachusetts Avenue Vicinity, N.W.

Washington dined with his friend General Uriah Forrest at Rosedale House in the 1790s. The home is still at 3501 Newark Street, back of the street in a park, almost across from Red Top, mentioned below. The back part dates to the 1730s and the front part is about 1793. **John Adams** stayed here when coming to view the new capital. **Cleveland** did not like the lack of privacy at the White House and lived part of his first term at Oak View or "Red Top" at 3542 Newark. He purchased it for $21,000, put in $10,000, and sold it for $140,000. The area is now named Cleveland Park, and the house has been destroyed. It was always ready for him whenever he could come, not just in the summer as other presidents had escaped out of town. In his second term he summered at Woodley, a Georgian-style house at 3000 Cathedral Avenue at the head of Woodley Street, now the Maret School. **Tyler, Buchanan,** and **Van Buren** had also lived there, as well as World War II General George Patton. **Davis** lived nearby in Redwood.

The Highlands was a mansion at the site of the present Washington Cathedral and was known by **Jefferson**, **Madison**, **Monroe**, and **John Quincy Adams**. The former home of the base commander at the Naval Observatory on Massachusetts and 34th at Observatory Place became the official vice president's home in 1974, first occupied during the **Carter** administration. **Bush** lived there, longer than he had in any other single residence in his then forty years of marriage. He is the only one to live here and the White House.

National Presbyterian or St. Andrew's is on Connecticut at 18th and N Streets. **Jackson** (pew 6), **Buchanan**, **Grant** (pew 69), **Cleveland** (pew 132), **Benjamin Harrison** (pew 43), **McKinley**, and **Truman** attended. **Eisenhower** (pew 41) was baptized here on February 1, 1953.

TR lived at 1215 19th Street or 1720 Jefferson Place, off Connecticut from 1889 until 1895 while on the Civil Service Commission. This was about one-tenth the size of his home in New York. He economized by not serving champagne. Later it was converted into an office building and sold in 1987 for a record $288 per square foot. It is still known as the Roosevelt Mansion. He returned in 1897 to fulfill his dream of being assistant secretary of the Navy and lived at 1810 N Street just opposite the British Embassy. As vice president he lived at the nearby home of his sister, 1733 N Street, and stayed there the first several days as president until Mrs. McKinley could leave the White House. His niece Eleanor said, "There was never a serious subject that came up while he was President that he didn't go to her home on N Street and discuss with her." He was here so much it was called the second or "little" White House.

Franklin Roosevelt also lived at 1733 N, still owned then by **Theodore's** sister, from 1913 until 1917, and walked the six blocks down Connecticut to his office. **Wilson**'s appointment of him, at 31 the youngest ever to fill the post held by the first **Roosevelt**, was a giant step in his road to the White House. The post was later held by

Theodore's son Ted, who ran for governor of New York and lost to Al Smith in 1924, allowing **Franklin** to win the office in 1928. Thus the path to the White House via positions in the New York Assembly, assistant Navy secretary's office, and governor's office, went to **Franklin** and not Ted. **Theodore** visited **Franklin** here several times and, in 1917, raced down several flights of stairs with young Franklin Jr. and John in his arms as their parents cringed, argued politics, and got the younger man's cooperation in arranging with the secretary of war for President **Wilson** to see the former president. **Theodore** had been strongly opposed to **Wilson**, but was now offering to be put back into the army to fight in Europe. **Franklin** arranged the meeting, but **Wilson** refused to allow the aging hero of San Juan Hill to serve in combat. This was the house that Lucy Mercer came to as Eleanor's social secretary, until Eleanor began to feel that there was something between Lucy and her husband after the move to R Street. Lucy was discharged, but the relationship between **Franklin** and Lucy heated up until discovered again by Eleanor in 1919. (See the entry on their residence in New York City.)

Later, from 1917 until 1920, the **FDR** family was at 2131 R Street, now the Malinese Embassy. The original structure is marked. In May 1919 a bomb exploded across the street at the home of Attorney General Palmer, killing an unknown anarchist and damaging the home. The **Roosevelts** were returning from a dinner party at the time and ran the last few steps to see if the children were all right. They found 11-year-old James looking out the window; he remembered all his life the tight hug his father gave him. But his mother just asked what he was doing up at this hour and told him to go to bed: "It was just a little bomb." For years if something exciting happened, the family would explain, "It was just a little bomb." They lived at 2121 Massachusetts in the 1920s.

TR's sharp-tongued daughter Alice lived at 2009 Massachusetts for nearly 50 years and died there in 1980. Several presidents including **Kennedy, Ford**, and **Nixon** came to tea. While in office **T. Roosevelt** once told author Owen Wister that he could be president or control Alice, but not both. Alice was famous for her irreverent imitation of Eleanor and for criticizing everyone, rich and famous, many times to their face. She even invited **Franklin** and Lucy Mercer here to encourage their affair at her first home at 18th and I Streets, where carousing buddy **Harding** played poker with her husband while Mrs. Harding tended bar during Prohibition. **TR** came here late in life to meet newsmen, Army and Navy officers, and politicians.

Taft lived at Five DuPont Circle in 1890 as Solicitor General. While secretary of war, he was at 1603 K Street, where he received news of his nomination. After his presidency, he served as co-chairman of the National War Labor Board and lived at 2029 Connecticut, SE corner of Wyoming. As Chief Justice in 1921, he bought 2215 Wyoming and 23rd, walked three miles to the Capitol, and died in the home in 1930. **Taft** and **Carter** both used the pulpit at the Metropolitan AME Church, 1518 M Street. **Harding** lived at 2314 Wyoming, 1915–21.

The mansion at 1500 Rhode Island served as the Imperial Russian Embassy for Count Arturo Cassini, his mistress, and their child. Their lavish parties just enhanced the scandal of their living together, but did not deter **McKinley** and **TR** from attending embassy dinners.

Garfield and **Lyndon Johnson** both attended the National City Christian Church at Five Thomas Circle. **Garfield's** assassin stalked him there for the three Sundays before his assassination. **Grant** was arrested for speeding his racehorse on M Street between 11th and 12th while president. He paid the fine and sent in a commendation for the police officer.

When he left the White House in 1921, **Wilson** retired to 2340 S Street,* where his wife remained for forty years after he died in 1924. Ten friends contributed $10,000 each to buy the five-story home, and Bernard Baruch later contributed another $10,000. **Wilson** tried to form a legal partnership, but was too incapacitated to perform any work. The National Trust for Historic Preservation keeps the home much as it was when the former president resided here.

In 1913 he laid the cornerstone for the Central Presbyterian at 16th and Irving, where he worshipped from then until his death. (**Cleveland** had worshipped at the site also.) **Wilson's** second marriage was at the home of his wife, 1308 20th. He is buried in the Washington National Cathedral,* Wisconsin, Massachusetts, and Woodley, the only president buried in the capital. **Wilson**'s tomb is inside on the right facing the front. **TR** had laid the foundation stone for the building in 1907. **Eisenhower**'s funeral was here, attended by **Truman** and **Nixon. Reagan's** was attended by the **Bushes, Ford, Carter**, and **Clinton. Ford**'s funeral on January 2, 2007, also involved these presidents, as did the memorial service for the

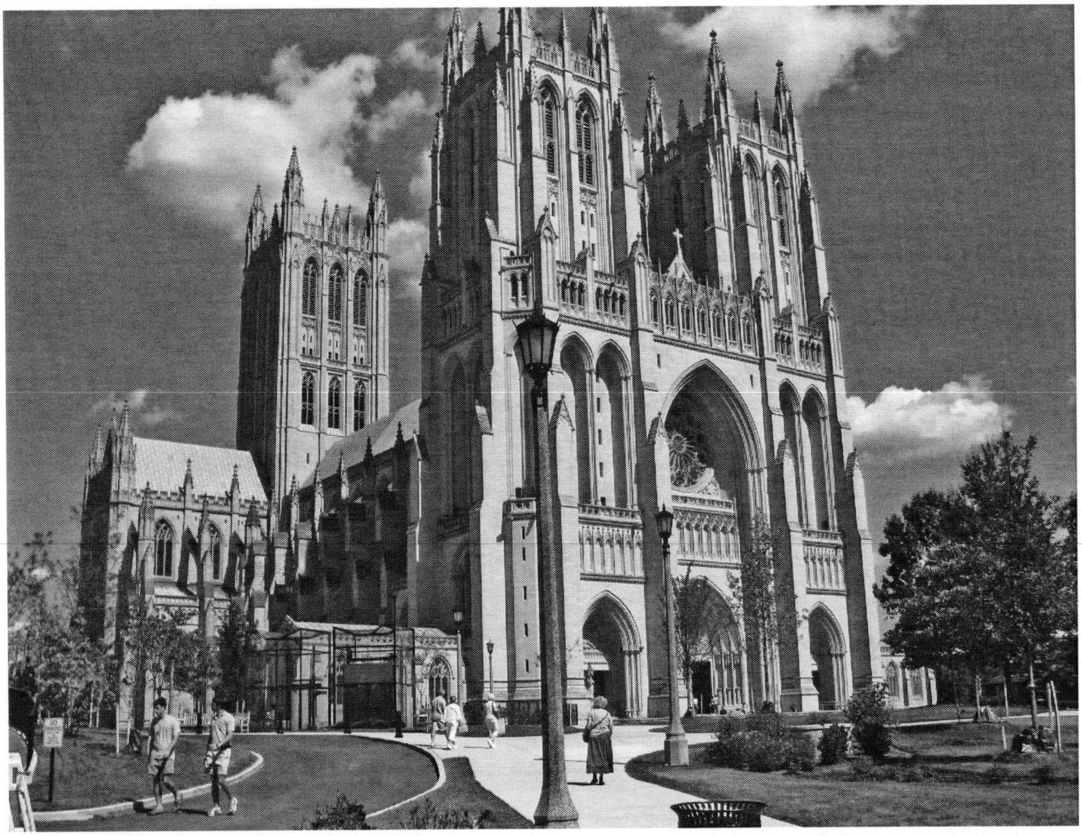

Many presidents have been to Washington Cathedral, where Wilson is buried. A stone on the grounds shows Washington's route north. Eisenhower's, Reagan's, and Ford's funerals here were attended by other presidents. Jefferson, Madison, Monroe, and John Quincy Adams visited a house on the site.

victims of the September 11, 2001, terrorist attacks. By his death at 93, **Ford** had become the longest-lived president. Braddock's Boulder on the grounds, marked with a plaque on the boulder in the trees to the right on the path to the church, marks General Braddock's and **Washington's** line of march to Ft. Duquesne in the 1750s. **George H.W. Bush** lived at times nearby at 5161 Palisade Lane from 1969 to 1976. He had previously lived at 4910 Hillbrook.

The Mayflower Hotel at 1127 Connecticut was completed in time for the inaugural ball for **Coolidge**. They stayed at 15 DuPont Circle while the White House was being renovated for six months in 1927. The 30-room mansion with 10 baths was known as the Patterson House, and today is the Washington Club. Here he welcomed Charles Lindbergh when he returned from his historic flight, and later Will Rogers. The **Franklin Roosevelts** stayed in rooms 776–781 at the Mayflower while waiting to move into the White House. **Truman** made the bold prediction from here that he would win in 1948, impersonated radio commentator H.V. Kaltenborn at a dinner the night before his second inauguration, and ate breakfast there the next morning. He met with **Kennedy** in 1960 to promise he would ease off on his attacks on the youthful presidential contender. FBI Director J. Edgar Hoover dined there almost every day. **Ike** started the tradition that the president addressed an annual interdenominational prayer breakfast here. **Johnson** stayed with his first Washington boss, Congressman Richard Kleberg, for several weeks after arriving in town in December 1931, and then moved to the Grace Dodge Hotel (destroyed) at 500 First, one block south of Union Station.

Hoover lived at 1628 16th in 1917 before moving to 2221 Massachusetts (the old **Adams** residence), and then to 1701 Massachusetts. From

1921 until 1929 he lived at 2300 S Street, near **Wilson**, while secretary of commerce until his inauguration. President-elect **Kennedy** used offices at the Brookings Institute, 1775 Massachusetts. **Ike** enjoyed breakfasts with Republican women at the Sulgrave Club, 1801 Massachusetts. The site of Joel Barlow's house, visited by **Jefferson, Madison,** and **Monroe**, is 2301 S.

FDR and his family regularly attended the St. Thomas Episcopal Church at 18th and Church Streets near DuPont Circle from 1913 until 1920, and also later as president. He was made vestryman after the end of World War I.

Truman lived at various locations:

Lafayette Hotel, 16th and I Streets, in 1928 and 1935;
3016 Tilden Gardens at 3000 Tilden at Connecticut and Sedgwick in 1935–6 and 1939. Ten-year-old Margaret felt hemmed in by the small space after living in the large, fourteen-room home in Independence;
Sedgwick Gardens, 3726 Connecticut Avenue, SW corner of Sedgwick in 1936;
The Carroll Arms, 301 First Street NE in 1937 (**Kennedy** had an apartment here);
The Warwick Apartments at 3051 Idaho Avenue in 1938;
3930 Connecticut in 1940;
4701 Connecticut and Chesapeake, street side second floor, from 1941 until he became president in 1945. He lived modestly in these four rooms for $120 a month, as he had no outside income.

The **Eisenhowers** lived off and on from 1926 until 1935 at the Wyoming Apartments, 2022 Columbia Road, SW corner of Connecticut near Rock Creek. In 1956 he watched as the cornerstone was laid for Saint Sophia Greek Orthodox Cathedral at Massachusetts at 36th Street. **Truman** laid the cornerstone at Washington Hebrew Congregation, Massachusetts at Macomb.

In 1941 and 1942 **Kennedy** lived at the Dorchester House 502, 2480 16th Street and the west side of 16th between Kalorama Road and Euclid Street. At this time he had an affair with the Dutch journalist Inga Arvad, a possible Nazi spy or sympathizer, who lived at 1600 Sixteenth. FBI Chief J. Edgar Hoover had wiretapped his apartments at this time attempting to find compromises in **Kennedy's** life, and did, resulting in a transfer to Charleston. He later lived at 1528 31st from 1947 until 1948 and at 1400 34th in 1949–50. He met Jackie at 2237 48th in 1952. His funeral was attended by **Johnson, Nixon, Truman,** and **Eisenhower** at St. Matthew's Cathedral* at the NW corner of Connecticut and Rhode Island.

Nixon lived at several sites including 4801 Tilden from 1951 until 1953 and 4308 Forest Lane in Wesley Heights while vice president. When **Ford** was a freshman congressman he lived at 2500 Q. **Johnson** spent a few days after his honeymoon here before moving to 1910 Kalorama Road for several months (and also in 1939–1940), and then to 3133 Connecticut from 1937 until 1939. He managed a playboy congressman's office, forcing all help to spend marathon days with no one working harder than himself. The Johnsons lived from 1943 to 1961 at 4921 30th Place and then at The Elms, 4040 52nd Street, from when he came to office after **Kennedy's** assassination until December 7. This was famous hostess Perle Mesta's old home.

Reagan was coming out of the Washington Hilton,* 1919 Connecticut, when he was shot at the T Street lower-level entry on March 30, 1981. As he approached the open car door he heard what sounded like firecrackers and was pushed into the car as it sped off. He moaned for a Secret Service man to get off him as he felt he had broken a rib, but by the time he got to the hospital, he had blood coming out his mouth. The fact that he almost died, having lost a lot of blood, was not publicly known at the time. He was taken to George Washington University Hospital at 901 23rd at Pennsylvania, where he told the waiting staff that he hoped they were Republicans and confessed to his wife that he forgot to duck. She then insisted that he never be in crowds again and wear a bulletproof vest under his sweaters.

Carter went to First Baptist Church* at 1328 16th Street, where he taught Sunday school every few weeks. This had been **Truman's** church, although a new building was dedicated in 1956. He once arrived unannounced and gave an impromptu commencement address to a Sunday school graduating class. **Clinton** attended there the night before his inauguration. He later bought nearby 3067 Whitehaven Lane for $2.85 million.

Griffin Stadium was between Fifth, W, and U Streets, and Georgia Ave. **Taft** threw out the first baseball in 1910. Presidents afterward attended games at one time or the other as the park hosted the Senators baseball team and Redskins football team until it closed in 1961. Mickey Mantle's April 17, 1953, shot was deemed the longest baseball hit of all time. All presidents from **Taft** through **Kennedy** threw out first pitches at most of the first games of the season. **Nixon** also threw out a pitch as vice president. **Johnson** sat next to **Kennedy** at that last year before the ball team then moved to the new D.C. Stadium. There **Johnson** and **Nixon** carried on the tradition until the team moved to Arlington, Texas, where **Ford** and the **Bushes** performed the act. **FDR** threw out more than anyone, but attended no game during World War II. **Truman** renewed the tradition a few weeks after Japan surrendered and was booed here the day after General MacArthur gave his famous farewell address to Congress in 1953. He threw out two pitches, one with each arm, on April 18, 1950.

The Washington Monument Area

The Washington Monument* was partially completed to about 154 feet when the Civil War started. When completed in 1884 it was the world's tallest building. **Washington** himself approved the central axis between the Capitol and White House, marked with a stone by **Jefferson**, still in place. But that spot is 360 feet east and 120 feet north as that intended site for the massive structure, still the tallest masonry object in the world, was too marshy.

The stone used to finish the monument did not quite match the prewar stone when **Arthur** finally dedicated the completed monument in 1885. Representative **Lincoln** took part in the dedication ceremonies on July 4, 1848, when **Polk** laid the cornerstone. In 1850, when President **Taylor** came to ceremonies there, he overexerted himself, and then died a few days later. In mid–1861 **Lincoln** asked his brother-in-law to guess at the width of the structure, then paced off the dimensions, and sat down by it to continue conversation. He attended the testing of experimental and new weapons in the area.

The Potomac flowed just west of the monument site, separated from the White House area by a foul-smelling and dirty canal where Constitution Avenue is today. The canal widened into the Potomac at about 17th Street, where President **John Quincy Adams** liked to skinny dip. Once someone stole his clothes, and he had to yell to passing boy to run to the White House for replacements. This was also the place where a woman reporter stood over his clothes until he, at last, granted a long sought-after interview while submerged. Many presidents walked the many paths through the Mall area and Washington Streets. **Arthur** frequently took midnight walks past the monument, and **TR** liked to ride around it late at night. **Kennedy** worked in the Naval Intelligence Office in 1941–2 at Constitution and 18th.

The original Smithsonian* building (The Castle) was completed in 1856 and dominated the Mall. **Lincoln** sat "with an impassive face" as the crowd in front of the building rose cheering on January 3, 1862, when Horace Greeley faced the president and proposed the end of slavery as "the one sole purpose for the War." The president handed out awards here on July 24, 1862, at a school program. An army officer once stormed into **Lincoln's** office with the head officer of the Smithsonian as prisoner with proof that the learned and respected Professor Joseph Henry was a spy. He had seen "red lights flashing from the roof at midnight signaling to the Secesh." **Lincoln** rose and said, "Now you're caught! What have you to say, Professor Henry, why sentence of death should not be immediately pronounced?" Then, smiling, he explained that he had been with Henry, "experimenting with army signals." **Garfield's** inaugural ball was in the new Smithsonian National Museum, now the Arts and Industries Building.*

Taft and **Harding** dedicated the Lincoln Memorial in 1922 with **Lincoln's** son Robert. Other presidential visits to the memorials west of the Washington Monument are numerous.

The United States Capitol Building

The Capitol's cornerstone was laid on September 18, 1793, by **Washington**, although no one knows where. The British burned the building during the War of 1812 after **Monroe** helped evacuate valuable items. The original shell is still underneath many additions and restorations.

The Capitol* is the inauguration site of most of the presidents, although at different locations. The east portico was used for most, with **Jackson's** as the first. Several preceding **Jackson** were sworn in inside, and **Monroe**'s was across the street. The west front has been used, beginning with **Reagan's** first. His second was to be there also, and actually took place three times: at the White House on Sunday, January 20; inside the Capitol Rotunda on the 21st, when the outside temperature was four degrees below zero; and then briefly outside on the steps. Of the almost 60 inaugural addresses, only the first by **Washington**, **Jefferson**, **Wilson**, and **FDR**, both of **Lincoln's**, and **Kennedy's** achieved distinction.

2

Virtually nothing of any of them was heard by more than a few, other than **Taft's** indoors, before **Harding** got an amplifier, **Coolidge** went on radio, **Hoover** made the movies, and **Truman** was seen by a few on television.

William Henry Harrison gave his 8,441-word speech on the east side in 1841, so long and in such bad weather that he caught or aggravated a cold and died of pneumonia a month later. He purposely exposed himself to bad weather to show his physical vitality as the oldest president to date. **Pierce** "affirmed" rather than swore, and delivered his address without notes. Also at the east steps, **Lincoln** gave his immortal second inaugural address urging that the nation's wounds be bound with "malice toward none, with charity for all." **TR** promised "a square deal for every man," as cousin **Franklin** listened a few feet away with his fiancée, **TR's** favorite niece. **FDR** told the nation, "The only thing we have to fear is fear itself," and promised a "new deal." And **Kennedy** admonished his listeners to ask not what their country could do for them as five presidents (himself, **Eisenhower** and **Truman**, and future presidents **Johnson** and **Nixon**) were photographed together for the first time. **Reagan's** disability and **Ford**'s temporary illness in 2001 prevented six presidents from gathering for an inauguration. Four were there then as in 2005, **Carter**, **Clinton**, and the **Bushes. Garfield's** mother was the first mother to see her son sworn in, as Mollie **Garfield** and Fanny **Hayes**, both fourteen, the only girl in each family with four brothers, held hands. Chief Justice **Taft** swore in **Coolidge** and **Hoover**.

The Old House of Representatives from 1807 until 1857, now Statuary Hall,* was the site of several presidents' service as congressmen: **Quincy Adams, Houston, Davis, Buchanan, Fillmore, Andrew Johnson, Lincoln, Pierce, Polk,** and **Tyler**. Markers in the floor note the location of their desks, a spot that served as their office as they had no other. The then wooden floors and ceilings produced a "whisper effect," limited now due to a steel ceiling installed after the representatives moved. Guides still demonstrate the effect at **Quincy Adams**' desk site, where sound bounces off the ceiling and is carried to another part of the room. **Lincoln** was present when **Adams** suffered a stroke on February 21, 1848. The former president served for seventeen years in the House, the only former president to return to the House, and died two days after his stroke in the Speaker's Room just through the doors from the chamber. **Adams** had won his bid for the presidency in the room when the House voted him in after no candidate received a majority in the 1824 election. He, **Madison Van Buren,** and **Fillmore** were sworn in as president here. The "Liberty" statue overlooking the front of the room and the figure of Muse Clio in the chariot at the rear are original. The House moved to their present chambers in 1857. **Reagan's** second inaugural luncheon was here in the old chamber.

Congressman **Lincoln** sometimes listened to debates in the Old Senate Chamber,* used as such from 1810 until 1859. **Houston, Davis, Buchanan, W. Harrison, A. Johnson, Pierce, Tyler, Van Buren,** and **Jackson** served here as senators, and **Quincy Adams** served downstairs in an earlier chamber. The picture of Washington, vice president's desk, shield, and eagle were in the chamber at the time. The Supreme Court met here for three-quarters of a century beginning in 1860, and **Taft** was sworn in as chief justice. **Jackson** was sworn in here at his second term when it was too cold outside. Vice presidents were sworn in also, including **Fillmore**.

The room below was the first part of the building completed, and served as chamber of both houses until the completion of the Senate chamber, where **Jefferson** presided in February 1801 to officially announce that he had tied with Aaron Burr in the presidential race. The writers of the Constitution did not foresee political parties and provided that every elector would get two votes for different candidates for president, intending that the runner-up would be vice president. But by 1796 parties had arisen with intended candidates for both offices rather than just the top job. So each elector voted twice, supposedly one vote for his candidate for president, and another for the party candidate for vice president, although all candidates were on the ballot for president. Thus both candidates of a party could each get the same number of votes for the president. In 1796 **Jefferson** and **John Adams** ran for different parties, but there was a revolt by Federalist leader Hamilton, who wanted Thomas Pinckney elected president rather than the intended candidate, **Adams**. Some Federalists voted for Democrat **Jefferson** rather than their own candidates, and **Jefferson** received

Opposite: **The U.S. Capitol was well known by all presidents. Washington laid the cornerstone.**

The Old House Chamber marks the spots where many future presidents served and had their desks, and where John Quincy Adams had his fatal stroke with Lincoln present.

the second most votes, making him vice president. In 1800, the Democratic (then called "Republican") candidates tied, and Burr refused to bow to the fact that **Jefferson** was intended for the presidency. The House then voted over and over without a majority until several Federalists abstained, giving **Jefferson** the presidency. He was then sworn in and gave his 1801 and 1805 inaugural addresses—his only public addresses during his eight-year term — there in the room, which is now part of the lower hallway, outside of the Old Supreme Court Chamber. The Constitution was then changed by the Twelfth Amendment to prevent this happening again by separate votes for the two offices.

The Old Supreme Court Chamber,* where the court met from 1810 until 1860, is the scene of **Lincoln's** admission to practice and his losing argument on March 7, 1849, of a case he had tried. The figures carved into the back wall are among the oldest in the Capitol, dating prior to the burning during the War of 1812. **John Adams** addressed Congress on November 22, 1800, in the narrow hall outside, the last president to speak in person to Congress before **Wilson**.

Congressman **Lincoln** frequented the Library of Congress and Supreme Court Library in the Capitol. The Library of Congress was across from the Old Senate Chamber, was destroyed by fire in 1851, and is now room S-230, not open to the public. He reportedly became friends with another lonely House member, his future vice president, **Andrew Johnson**.

Secretary of War **Davis** began a new construction, still being carried on when **Lincoln** was inaugurated. The statue of **Jefferson** now in the Rotunda was on the White House front lawn during **Lincoln's** term. **Polk** liked it after it had been in the Rotunda for several years, and had it moved in 1847 to the White House grounds, where it stayed twenty-seven years. The statue of **Jackson** at the Rotunda exit leading to the Old Senate Chamber was the approximate location of an attempt to assassinate him in 1835. Two pistols were fired pointblank; both misfired, but later were determined to be in perfect working order. By the second shot, the assailant was in more danger from **Jackson's** swinging cane. The current large paintings and some of the other artwork have been seen here by presidents since the 1840s.

On January 16, 1864, **Lincoln** heard his liberal reconstruction policies denounced by a popular lecturer who then endorsed his reelection. **Lincoln's** face is said to have dropped either from the thought of four more years or from the controversial speaker's endorsement itself. He also attended meetings in the House on February 2, 1864, and January 19, 1865, and other non-congressional meetings. He and **Johnson** stood to sing the "Battle Hymn of the Republic" there on January 29, 1865.

Taft was inaugurated in the House Chamber due to inclement weather. **Wilson** addressed a special session of Congress on April 7, 1913, the first time a president spoke directly to Congress since **John Adams**. All since **Wilson** have spoken in the House to joint sessions. **George H.W. Bush, Ford, Garfield, Hayes, Lyndon Johnson, Kennedy, McKinley**, and **Nixon** served in the new House Chamber. **Harding, B. Harrison**, both **Johnsons, Kennedy, Nixon** and **Truman** served in the new Senate Chamber, where **Arthur** was sworn in as vice president. **Lincoln** visited.

The opulent President's Room was designed for visiting presidents, and was first used to sign a bill into law by **Lincoln**. This is off the private lobby, on the north outside wall behind the northwest corner of the Senate Chamber. The mahogany table that he used is still in the room.

Lincoln was inaugurated on March 4, 1861, before 30,000 at the east entrance facing the large white seated statue of **Washington**, now prominent in the Smithsonian's Museum of American History. The impressive dome under construction caused the building to resemble a Roman ruin. The president insisted, while long-time rival Stephen Douglas held his hat, that the work continue even during the secession crisis so that the people would know "we intend the Union to go on." The Bible used is kept in the Rare Book and Special Collections Divisions of the Library of Congress.

The black-draped bier or catafalque built to hold **Lincoln's** coffin can be seen in the basement. In 1865, **Lincoln** became the first person to lie in state in the Rotunda. **Garfield, McKinley, Taft, Harding, Hoover, Kennedy, Eisenhower, Lyndon Johnson, Reagan**, and **Ford** have been likewise so honored since.

The Capitol Area

Washington stayed at Varnum's Hotel at the NE corner of New Jersey and C Street, S.E., as did **Jackson**. The boarding house was built in the 1790s and destroyed to make way for the Longworth Building in 1929. **Jefferson** lived there and walked to his inauguration as **Adams** was traveling back to Massachusetts. **Jefferson** went back for the first fifteen days of this term. At dinner, as president, he found all seats taken at the dinner table and no one willing to give one up for him. Finally a senator's wife offered, but he declined. A block away at Three B Street S.E. was **Arthur's** home and temporary White House, also displaced by the Longworth Building.

The Old Capitol Prison was on the SE corner of First and Maryland Avenue N.E., in front of the present Supreme Court Building. It was also known as the "Old Brick Capitol," built in 1815 for the temporary home of Congress after the British burned government buildings during the War of 1812. **W. Harrison** and **Tyler** served in Congress during this time. The tradition of outside inaugurals started on this site. **Monroe** was inaugurated, with **Madison** attending, on a platform or portico outside the building when it is said that Congress could not decide whose house to use. It is sometimes reported that **Monroe** spoke outside because House Speaker Henry Clay would not let him use that hall. He said the floor would not hold the number of people who would attend, but rumor had it that Clay was upset because **Monroe** would not name him secretary of state. After housing Congress for four years it became a boarding house for many prominent members of Congress including **Polk** and John C. Calhoun, who died there.

The first inaugural ball, **Madison's**, was in at Long's Inn on Carroll Row at about where the **Lincolns** later lived in a boarding house run by Mrs. Sprigg during his congressional term. **Lincoln's** residence is at the present site of the Library of Congress lawn, Jefferson Building, SE corner of East Capitol and 1st Streets, S.E. **Lincoln** stayed from late 1847 during his first and second sessions until the end of his term in 1849. The exact site is near the street just north of the northern steps of the Jefferson Building. As seen from old photographs, Pennsylvania Avenue intersected First where the Neptune Statue and fountain are now. Mrs. Sprigg's can be seen about one third of the block north. **Andrew Johnson** probably stayed in Carroll Row in the 1840s.

Arthur was so unhappy with the condition of the White House that he moved out to live in the second floor of Senator John P. Jones' residence at New Jersey and B Street, S.E., while the building was being renovated. As mentioned earlier, **Johnson** lived at the Dodge Hotel on Capitol Plaza while working on Capitol Hill during the latter days of the **Hoover** administration and the beginning of **FDR's** term. He, as well as **Garfield,** went to St. Marks at the NE corner of Fourth and A, S.E. **Johnson** came here with thirty bodyguards the Sunday after **Kennedy** was assassinated. From then on worshipers have been upset at dogs in churches in the capital, but these are necessary to sniff for bombs when presidents attend.

All presidents would have known the Sewall-Gallatin-Belmont House, one block from the Capitol, Maryland and One B, N.E., the oldest on Capitol Hill. Parts of a 1680 barn are said to be incorporated in it. The British tried to burn it in 1814 when they were fired on from inside.

East of the Capitol Building, S.E.

The Maples,* at 619 D Street, extending to 620 South Carolina Street, now known as Friendship House, once hosted **Washington**, who referred to it in his diary as a "fine house in the woods." **John Adams** moved nearby in November 1800, to Tunnicliff's City Hotel on the SW corner of Ninth and Pennsylvania before moving into the White House. The first record of any ball in the city was there. **Adams** came to the hotel at least twice before the capital moved from Philadelphia. **Washington's** diary showed that he ate at Tunnicliff's on October 18, 1798.

Adams, Jefferson, Madison, Monroe, and **John Quincy Adams** attended Christ Church, the first church in the city, at New Jersey and D, the foot of Capitol Hill. It later moved to 620 G Street, where **Quincy Adams** attended. The first real mansion in town was the 1794 Duddington House (destroyed), on the square between First and Second Streets SE at Duddington Place south of E Street, where the presidents from **Adams** to **Jackson** were entertained regularly. **Washington** had to convince the owner to move the intended house out of the middle of what would become New Jersey Street. The Marine Barracks at Eighth and I occupies the site selected by **Jefferson. Madison** and **Monroe** came here on the way to meet the British invasion in 1814.

To escape the pressures of his office, **Lincoln** visited the Navy Yards almost every week, coming in the Latrobe Gate at Eighth and M S.E., sometimes with his sons. Reviews were made with deep fascination of many new inventions and mechanical devices tested on the grounds. He received a 21-gun salute on April 26, 1862, as he boarded a French frigate, the first president to set foot on a French ship. He attended several funerals and viewed close friend Col. Elmer Ellsworth's body twice on May 24, 1861. Several structures he knew include Quarters "A," built about 1804, adjacent to the Latrobe Gate on the east side, and two structures down Ninth Street on the west side north of "N." The northernmost dates from 1801, and the Historical Center dates to the mid–1800s. A marker just east of the Naval Museum at the Commandant's Office relates **Lincoln's** visits with Admiral Dahlgren, a special favorite, and others.

Tyler and his party arrived here after the cannon exploded on the *Princeton* in February 1844, killing several cabinet members and his lady friend's father. The president's friendship with Julia Gardiner had been kept quiet since his wife had died a little over a year before. After the explosion, Julia fainted, and **Tyler** carried her ashore. She remembered later that she struggled so that both were almost knocked off the gangplank. The bodies of those killed were taken to the White House, where Julia stayed until her return home to New York. Shortly thereafter 24-year-old Julia married the 54-year-old widower president and added seven more children to his family of seven living children. (See Alexandria, Virginia, for details of the explosion.)

On March 14, 1797, **Washington** ate with Thomas Law and his wife, the granddaughter of Martha, at the NE corner of Sixth and N S.W. at what was then a steep bank of the Potomac. It is now north of Fort McNair where **Ike** went to the Army War College at P and Third.

Our first National Cemetery is the Congressional Cemetery, 1801 E Street at 18th and G S.E. **Lincoln** was on a congressional committee that conveyed **John Quincy Adams'** body here for burial in the presence of **Polk** and **Buchanan**. After about a week in the public vault, the body was taken to Boston. **W. Harrison** and **Taylor** were also temporarily buried in the same vault. This is northeast of two road extensions of G and 18th Streets. **Jackson** came with the body of Indian Chief Pushmataha, who is still buried here.

Lincoln led a cortege to the cemetery in 1864 when twenty-one women were buried after being killed in an explosion at the Washington Arsenal. This monument is just east of the G Street gate. A map is available at the entrance, 18th and G.

On June 6, 1966, Luci **Johnson** found her father more despondent than usual, worried that he had started World War III by bombing around North Viet Nam's capital. After a discussion, he ordered a car around midnight to St. Dominic's, 630 E, S.W., to spend the night praying that such was not the case. On another occasion he was criticized for taking communion at St. Mark's Episcopal, 118 Third S.E., when he was not a member of that faith.

The Northeast Section

To escape hot summers **Buchanan**, **Lincoln**, **Hayes**, and **Arthur** came to Anderson Cottage* at the Soldiers' Home, Rock Creek Church Road and Upshur Street, N.W., known as a summer White House. **Lincoln** is said to have spent about 30 percent of his presidency living at the cottage, where he made major decisions. In mid–2000, **Clinton** spoke in front to declare the building as the President Lincoln and Soldiers' Home National Monument. The cottage and adjacent main building have changed little since the Civil War.

Luci **Johnson** was the first president's daughter married in a church. This occurred in 1966 at the Basilica of the National Shrine of the Immaculate Conception, Michigan and Fourth N.E., the largest Roman Catholic Church in the country.

The museum at Walter Reed Army Medical Center, Georgia and 14th Street, N.E., displays **Lincoln** assassination artifacts including the bullet that killed him, part of his skull, and hair removed from the wound. Part of **Garfield**'s spinal column showing the path of the fatal bullet is also displayed, as is General Daniel Sickles' leg, lost at Gettysburg, and a vertebra of John Wilkes Booth. **Eisenhower** died at the Center in 1969.

The remains of Ft. Stevens* at 13th and Quakenbos are marked just south of Walter Reed Center off Highway 29 at Georgia Street. **Lincoln** rode here on July 11, 1864, to witness action when Confederates threatened the capital. A man near the president was wounded and soldiers "roughly ordered" him off the parapet. The next day **Lincoln** rode out again and was exposed to sharpshooters. Captain Oliver Wendell Holmes, the future Supreme Court justice, bragged later that he yelled, "Get down, you damned fool."

Georgetown (N.W.)

The North and South were united here in a well-traveled route crossing the Potomac to land at the foot of Wisconsin Street, used by the Virginia presidents and others. On August 12, 1776, **Washington** is claimed to have stayed at the Bowie-Sevier House (private) at 3124 Q, across from Tudor Place, on the way to rejoin his troops. The Forrest-Marbury House at 3350 M was used by **Washington** to determine the boundaries of the District. **Jefferson** and **Madison** dined there in September 1790, when they had gone up the river to Little Falls to survey locations for the capital. A marker on the present Ukraine Embassy notes that **Washington** was hosted there on March 29, 1791, in a famous dinner to celebrate land settlements making way for the new capital city. The Old Stone House, c. 1765, at 3051 M is believed to be the oldest house in the District. The story that **Washington** met here to help plan the city is probably not true, but all presidents would have noticed the prominent landmark. A marker at the end of the Key Bridge shows that **Washington** passed up 34th Street on the way to his inauguration in New York.

The Union Tavern, NE corner of 30th and M, played host to **Jefferson** on Christmas Day, 1799, and **John Adams** in 1800 while he waited for the White House to be finished. **Washington** noted in his diary that he dined there on February 8, 1798, and then went to Thomas Law's on Capitol Hill. He was here at other times, including a birthday ball on his last birthday in 1799. **Buchanan** and **Van Buren** both attended a June 1849 wedding at 3322 O Street, where Robert E. Lee visited his mother when she lived there.

Washington came to Georgetown numerous times to inspect the progress of the capital and president's house and stayed in Suter's Tavern (Fountain Inn). **Jefferson** was entertained there in February 1797. The inn is long gone, and the site is questionable. It was probably either on or within a block of Wisconsin Avenue, probably south of the M Street intersection. There is some speculation that it was on the west side of 31st, about two blocks south of the canal, at the NW corner of Copperthwaite, and some support for its being on the north side of the canal. **Washington** met here with surveyors, landowners, and commissioners on March 29, 1791, and afterward to work out agreements for the sale of land. **Adams** also stayed here, including when he came in 1792 to attend the laying of the cornerstone of the White House.

The 1796 City Tavern or Indian King at 3206–8 M, now a private club, also was known by the early presidents. **Adams** visited friends at Prospect House, 3508 Prospect. **John Quincy Adams** lived just east at 2618–20 K while in the Senate. This was the home of his sister from 1803 until 1807, now under the Whitehurst Freeway. **Washington** stayed there when it was the home of one of Martha's granddaughters and her husband, Thomas Peter.

Jefferson, Madison, and **Monroe** visited Uplands or Prospect Hill Farm, 1800 Foxall Road, west of the business district. **Quincy Adams** and prior presidents were frequent guests of Henry Foxhall at 2908 N. Madison probably met Dolley in the Dumbarton House on their flight when the British invaded in 1814. It is now at 2715 Q, across from where it was then.

Willie **Lincoln** was buried in the Carroll vault at Oak Hill Cemetery,* 30th and R, near the northwest corner, down a hill overlooking Rock Creek. **Lincoln** saw the original vaults here now when he visited and revisited; he may have opened the lid, and stood at the entrance to look inside. He attended a funeral service in the Oak Hill Gothic Chapel,* still near the entrance. Samuel **Davis, Jefferson's** two-year-old son, was buried nearby in 1854 with **Davis's** close friend, President **Pierce**, in attendance. Both sons are now with their fathers elsewhere. General-in-Chief Henry W. Halleck rented 3238 R, where **Lincoln** and **Grant** consulted with him. **Grant** used it as a "Summer White House."

Lincoln comforted wounded at the Methodist Episcopal, 3127 Dumbarton, when it served as an army hospital. He frequently visited Forrest Hall, 1262 Wisconsin, converted to a hospital, and attended a funeral service in 1861 at Holy Trinity, 3513 N, where **Kennedy** worshipped from 1947 until his death. **Hoover** attended a funeral at the church also. **Truman's** final dinner party as president was at Secretary of State Dean Acheson's home at 2805 P. He stayed at 3508 Prospect for a while during the White House renovation.

Kennedy lived in the area, including 2808 P in 1951, 3260 N in 1951–2, 3271 P in 1952–3, and 3321 Dent Place in 1953–4. He lived at Hickory Hill, 1147 Chain Bridge in McLean, Virginia, sold to his brother Robert after Jackie lost a baby in 1956. From 1957 until inaugurated, he lived at 3307 N, where he played football in the street. After his election he named the cabinet and had many impromptu front porch announcements, creating press corps traffic jams.

In 1948 the **Fords** moved to the Carlin Apartments at 2500 Q, where they lived until 1951. In the mid–1960s, **Clinton** went to Georgetown University, lived in Loyola Hall on the 35th Street entrance at N, room 225, and at 4513 Potomac. He attended the Georgetown Presbyterian, 3115 P, as there was no Baptist church nearby.

City Perimeter

All presidents from the early days have been familiar with Arlington House overlooking the capital and now known as the Custis-Lee Mansion* in Arlington National Cemetery. The Memorial to the Unknown Soldier is nearby, visited by all presidents since the dedication with **Taft, Harding, Coolidge,** and **Wilson** present. **Kennedy's** grave and eternal flame are below the hill in front. The home belonged to Robert E. Lee's father-in-law, George Washington Parke Custis, the grandson of Martha Washington from her earlier marriage; he was raised by **Washington. Houston** reportedly visited and tried to woo Mary Custis, but she told him that her heart belonged to a young underclassman at West Point. Lee married her in the parlor. Custis left the house to his daughter for life, and then to his oldest grandchild and namesake, Custis Lee. When the Lees were forced to move on May 16, 1861, they took as much of the **Washington** artifacts as they could. Some others were found and stored in the Patent Office. Others were lost. The family lost the house when it became legally necessary to pay the property tax in person, which was impossible for Mrs. Lee. The government then confiscated the property and converted it to a cemetery partly to prevent it from ever being inhabited by a Lee. **Lincoln** observed bodies there. **Taft** is buried up a path near the eastern side. His grave, Robert Lincoln's nearby, and those of the many military heroes are marked on maps available at the visitor center.

Opposite: **Lincoln attended a funeral service for his son Willie in this chapel in Georgetown's Oak Hill Cemetery and visited the grave behind the building. Jefferson Davis buried his son nearby with Pierce at his side.**

Fort Lincoln was located in what is now Fort Lincoln Cemetery,* just south of U.S. Highway Alt. 1, Bladensburg Pike, at the D.C. border with Maryland. A marker in front of the mausoleum at the top of the hill at the western edge notes the site of the Battle of Bladensburg, where **Madison** with **Monroe** witnessed the defeat in 1814 that allowed the British to enter and burn the capital. By some accounts **Madison** took over actual command and was under fire although **Lincoln** is generally considered the first in actual command and under fire at Ft. Stevens. **Lincoln** met the commander under the "Lincoln Oak," west of the Bladensburg dueling grounds (marked at 38th Street) where Commodore Stephen Decatur was killed in 1820. The remains of the oak are marked at the spring where **Lincoln** drank at the Old Spring House,* dating to 1683. All **Lincoln** sites and the fort are marked down the hill east of the mausoleum.

The remains of the Fort Foote, Maryland, Fort Foote Road and Park, are some of the best in the area. This is about three miles south of I-95/495, exit 3, on the east bank of the Potomac off Oxon Hill Road. **Lincoln** was here August 20, 1863. The fortification made nearby Fort Washington* obsolete since that old masonry fort could not hold up to the modern cannon fire. **Washington** selected that site in 1794 when he visited friends who lived there. Fort Washington is just to the south on Old Fort Road off Route 210 and is still an impressive sight from both sides of the river. **Lincoln** was there on October 19, 1861. In 1864 he was at Fort De Russey, Oregon and Military Roads.

FLORIDA

KEY BISCAYNE • **Nixon** used 500 and 516 Bay Lane, the home of his friend Bebe Rebozo, as his Southern White House. **Kennedy** visited him here after the 1960 election.

KEY WEST • **Grant** came here with General Philip Sheridan after the Civil War and paused under an arch in front of the Russell House on Duval Street. **Taft** came to Trumbo Point on his way to and from the Panama Canal in 1912. He was also at the mayor's home, now Fogarty 1875 Restaurant, facing Duval at Caroline. In 1939 **FDR** was driven down Overseas Highway from Miami to Key West. **Truman** spent eleven working vacations, 175 days, at the summer White House, 11 Front Street,* with various leaders. Here he planned the North American Treaty Organization (NATO) with Winston Churchill, swam (and once had his glasses knocked off by the surf), played poker and the piano, visited the enlisted men's barracks, walked the area, and listened to his daughter sing. He was photographed all over town, including in front of City Hall on Truman Street. **Eisenhower** recuperated from his 1956 heart attack here, at the Commandant's home, but reportedly refused to sleep in **Truman's** bed. So he slept down the street at 51 Front Street, the Surgeon's House. After leaving office, **Truman** vacationed at the Casa Marina Hotel,* 1500 Reynolds. **Kennedy** was at the summer White House in 1961 with Prime Minister Macmillan during the Bay of Pigs crisis. **Carter** celebrated New Year's Day 1996 in the dining room.

MIAMI • On February 15, 1933, President-elect **Franklin Roosevelt** was in an open car leaving the Amphitheater, Bayfront Park, Biscayne Boulevard between SE Second and Sixth Streets, when an assassination attempt was made. Chicago Mayor Anton Cermak and four others took the bullets meant for Roosevelt. As the car raced to Jackson Hospital, **FDR** remained calm, and holding Cermack, explained that **Theodore Roosevelt** had been wounded in a similar manner in 1912. The assassin was first tried and convicted for the assault on Cermack and his appeal was rejected. Then Cermack died, and the assassin was re-tried for murder with another conviction and rejected appeal. After all of this, he was then executed on March 20, thirty-three days after the attack.

Nixon made his political comeback when nominated in 1968 at the Miami Beach Convention Center at 1901 Convention Center Drive. Both parties held their national conventions there in

1972. **Reagan** visited Vizcaya Mansion* in 1987 with the Pope. Both **FDR** and **Eisenhower** stayed at the Biltmore, 1200 Anastasia, but by the time **Ike** was there it was part of a hospital. **FDR** also stayed at the Astor, 956 Washington. **Kennedy, Johnson, Ford** and **Carter** stayed in the Fontainebleau in Miami Beach at 4441 Collins, and **Johnson, Nixon** and **Reagan** stayed in the Deanville, 6701 Collins. Show business's "Rat Pack" called this home. The **Kennedys** saw the 1963 Orange Bowl game, and the **Clintons** saw their Arkansas Razorbacks win it in 1978. **George W. Bush** debated Democratic challenger Senator John Kerry at the University of Miami Convocation Center at 1245 Walsh on September 30, 2004.

ORLANDO • The senior **Bush** and **Clinton** "brought their unique combination of personal anecdotes and political observations" to the Orange County Convention Center* on May 27, 2007. **George W.** appeared with his brother, Governor Jeb Bush, at Tinker Field on October 30, 2004, and related that they both had the same political advisor, "Mother." He appeared at the Rita Carleton* in Grand Lakes in September 2006. **Clinton** appeared at nearby Patrick AFB on June 30, 1994, pledging to do everything possible to rid the world of terrorism.

In nearby Winter Park, **Arthur** used the depot in 1883, across now from the present station, and stayed at the Seminole Hotel at Chase and Osceola and at the home of Lewis Lawrence, 1300 Summerland. **Cleveland** stayed at the Seminole in 1889. **Coolidge** (1929), **FDR** (1936), and **Truman** visited Rollins College at 1000 Holt. On March 8, 1949, **Truman** landed at Orlando Air Force Base, dedicated the causeway over Lake Estelle, visited the college president at 208 N. Interlocken, and honored him in Knowles Memorial Chapel, where both got honorary degrees. **George H.W. Bush** visited Thom Rumberger, 1015 Greentree Dr., during his term.

In nearby Sanford, **Grant** (1880), **Arthur** (1883), **and Cleveland** (1889) stayed at the Hotel Sanford, now the library site, 1101 E. First. **Arthur** attended the Episcopal church at 410 S. Magnolia. **Taylor's** presence at Ft. Mellon is marked in Ft. Mellon Park, 600 E. First.

PALM BEACH • **Kennedy**'s father owned 1095 Ocean Drive, where **JFK** came many times through childhood, brought friends as a teenager, and convalesced at various times with various illnesses. In 1945 after World War II, father and son came to map out a strategy leading to the White House. The old man said later that he got his son into politics: "Jack did not want to do it; he did not feel he had the ability." But "demanded" probably is a better concept than "got into." He was here many times for vacations while president after his father suffered a debilitating stroke, and used the C. Michael Paul Villa, 601 N. County Road. While here he attended St. Edward's at 165 N. County Road and St. Mary's Hospital, 901 45th St. **Truman** stayed at 513 N. County Road (Ocean Ave.) in 1950, and **Wilson** stayed at the Flagler House,* Whitehall, Cocoanut Row and Whitehall Way, now a museum. **Harding** visited Royal Poinciana Chapel* at 60 Coconut Row, as did **Hoover**, who stayed at the Royal Poinciana (closed), marked by the Palm Beach Tower.

PENSACOLA • In November 1814, **Jackson** camped at the end of the present-day Jackson Street near the end of Zaragoza at the head of Bayou Chico. He had come to seize the Spanish town to protect the Gulf Coast during the War of 1812 and after the Treaty of Fort Jackson with the Indians, thus preventing the British from entering the continent here or by Mobile. This meant that the British would have to rely on themselves, not the Indians or Spanish, and left the British only a route through New Orleans, where **Jackson** then headed. He captured Spanish Pensacola again in May 1818, during the war against the Seminoles, by surrounding and forcing the surrender of Fort Barrancas* as he had in 1814. The actions taken against the Indians were of questionable legality in this foreign jurisdiction, and there is a question of how much of his preemptive action of invading foreign territory was intended by President Monroe. But **Jackson** stated that he would occupy Florida until Spain could provide military force to prevent criminal acts against the United States. The move succeeded in intimidating both the Indians and Spain, virtually ended Spanish presence, and led to peace and Spanish cession.

He was back here in 1821 as governor after the United States acquired Florida and stayed about eleven weeks. His appointment as governor caused him to resign his army commission as one of two major generals, easing a budget crunch with the government. A marker on Zaragoza Street shows the place where he received West Florida from Spain. Flags were exchanged on July 17 at the Old Spanish Government House on Plaza Ferdinand VII, S. Palafox Street between East Government and East Zaragoza. One of his first acts was to assemble Indian chiefs here to find out where they were and whether they intended to submit to United States authority.

Jackson, the first Territorial Governor, and his wife Rachel occupied the home then at the SE corner of Palafox and Intendencia. They went to Tivoli Theater on the SW corner of Zaragoza and Barracks, renamed Jacksonian Commonwealth Theater in his honor. Rachel complained of dancing there on Sundays. There was a dispute over the transfer of governmental power, so he locked up the Spanish governor at the calabozo, SW corner of Alcaniz and Intendencia. The **Jacksons** hated the town, job, and climate, but Rachel learned to appreciate a good Cuban cigar. The Spanish and British commanding officers' headquarters were still on Zaragoza between Jefferson and Tarragona, but **Jackson** would not use them. Archeological remains are marked just east of the Wentworth Museum on the east side of the square. **Theodore Roosevelt** was welcomed with his Rough Riders at Wright and Tarragona in 1898.

St. Augustine • **Cleveland, Grant, Harding,** and **TR** stayed at the Ponce de Leon Hotel on Cordova between King and Valencia. **Arthur** stayed four days at the Magnolia, where a park is still at St. George and Hypolita. Several presidents came to the resort of Green Cove Springs a few miles west, where **Arthur** and **Grant** stayed in the Old Magnolia Hotel, now apartments off Route 209 near Route 17, two miles north. **Cleveland** stayed in the Union Hotel, 1885–9.

St. Marks • General **Jackson** captured the Spanish Fort St. Marks* during the 1818 Seminole campaign and tried two British traders believed to be inciting and supplying the Indians. The trial of the traders resulted in a sentence of execution, but the court then lessened the punishments. **Jackson** ordered them executed anyway, touching off a potential international crisis. Regardless of the problems to the United States caused by the rash actions of **Jackson**, Spain saw that retaining a colony here was more trouble than it was worth, and agreed to cede the area to the Untied States in 1819. The remains of the fort are accessible on the western edge of town, south of U.S. 98 at the junction of the St. Marks and Waskulla Rivers.

Sarasota • Just before **George W. Bush** went into a second grade class at Emma T. Booker Elementary School, 2650 MLK Way, on September 11, 2001, he was informed at 9:02 that a plane had hit the North Tower of the World Trade Center. At 9:06 he was photographed being told about the South Tower. He left the classroom at 9:16 to make a brief statement before leaving at 9:33. He and the school were vulnerable, almost in the local airport landing pattern. He had stayed at the Colony Beach Resort, 1620 Gulf of Mexico Drive, Longboat Key, the night before and jogged four miles around a golf course. Reportedly, hijackers Mohamed Atta and another went to Saratoga on September 7, the day **Bush's** travel plans were announced, and ate at the Holiday Inn down the beach from **Bush's** hotel. On the morning of the eleventh, two Middle Eastern men posing as a news crew were denied access to the president in a possible assassination attempt. Apparently the same men made threatening gestures and derogatory shouts several times afterward.

Tampa • **Taylor** was stationed here with his family in 1837–1838 at Fort Brooke, SW corner of Platt and Franklin. **TR** came here in 1898 with his Rough Riders and encamped at the National Guard Armory on Howard Avenue. He was at the Tampa Bay Hotel, Plant Park between Lafayette and Cass on Kennedy Blvd., now occupied by the University of Tampa. To be with his wife, he had to leave each morning at 4:00 a.m. to travel the ten miles to his troop camp site to drill. He and **Cleveland** both visited the El Pasje at 1318½ Ninth Ave. **Kennedy** (1963) and **LBJ** (1960) visited the Courthouse, Madison and Pierce. **Hoover and Coolidge** were at the Renaissance Vinoy (formerly Stouffer) Resort,* 501 Fifth on Shell Isle on Tampa Bay in nearby St. Petersburg, in 1930 and other times.

GEORGIA

ATLANTA • During the War of 1812, **Jackson** is claimed to have been at Fort Peachtree at a spot marked on Ridgewood Road at Ridgewood Circle off Bolton Road, but I can find no documentation of this. **Benjamin Harrison** fought in the area Civil War battles. **Grant** came once, in 1865, and stayed at a boarding house that later became the Ivy Street Hospital. **Hayes** stayed in 1877 at the Washington Hall Hotel on the east side of Central opposite Wall Street. **Cleveland** stayed at 330 Peachtree S.W. at Porter Place and the Kimball House at the SW corner of Decatur and 33 Pryor in 1887. In 1895 he visited an exposition in Piedmont Park. **McKinley** and **Fillmore** were also at the Kimball House, although **Fillmore** (1854) stayed in the one later burned by General Sherman. **Wilson** practiced law for about a year beginning in 1882 at the SW corner of Alabama and Pryor, and then at 48 Marietta and Forsyth, marked, while living at 344 Peachtree Street. He then decided to teach and write and left to return home to Wilmington, North Carolina. In 1911 **TR**, **Taft**, and **Wilson** all visited a convention in town. **Taft** spoke in Alumni Hall, Courtland and Washington, in 1909. Visitors to the Capitol include **B. Harrison**, **McKinley**, **TR**, **Taft**, and **Nixon**. **Carter** worked here as governor and in the legislature.

The first Governor's Mansion was located on the SW corner of Peachtree and International Blvd., now the Westin Peachtree Plaza. Before demolition in 1933 it hosted **Hayes** and all presidents from **Cleveland** through **Taft**, including **Harrison**. A newer mansion was built on Prado that hosted all from **Coolidge** through **Eisenhower**.

Carter lived in the Grady Hotel, 210 Peachtree N.W., and later the Piedmont Hotel, 108 Peachtree, as state senator, and as governor at the Governor's Mansion, 391 West Paces Ferry Road. His church was the Northside Baptist, 3100 Northside Drive at Northside Parkway. His offices after the presidency were in the Carter Center, One Copenhill Avenue. Several presidents have visited Martin Luther King Jr.'s church, Ebenezer Baptist, at 407 Auburn, including **Carter** and **Nixon**. Both **Bushes**, **Carter**, and **Clinton** have also visited Dr. King's tomb and the Carter Center, and all, with their wives, attended Mrs. King's funeral in suburban Lithonia at the New Birth Baptist Church, 6400 Woodrow, on February 7, 2006.

AUGUSTA • When Augusta was the state capital, **Washington** was a guest for parts of four days at a spot still debated. The earlier claim and marker that he stayed with George Walton at 1320 Nelson in 1791, now known as Meadow Garden House Museum,* is not thought to be accurate in spite of historical markers and claims shown in several early histories. This house is variously dated before and after **Washington's** visit, but the current "Official Visitors Guide" shows it pre–1791. Evidently it was built between 1780 and 1790, and Walton is thought to have moved in in 1792. The president met Governor Edward Telfair at a spot marked on Route 56 and Louisville Road. He was also entertained with dinner and a later reception at the Telfair House, site marked on the NE corner at Broad Street at East Boundary. A large banquet was held at the Government House, probably Fourth and Reynolds, rather than the Old Government House* at 432 Telfair as claimed. The latter was apparently erected in 1801 although claimed by a marker and other sources to be the site of **Washington's** visit, but town records are questionable. **Fillmore** was received in 1854 in the Government House, probably then at 1958 Appling Harlem Way.

A marker off Bay Street on Fourth marks **Washington's** visit to the Richmond Academy, then a short distance east on Bay. He may have stayed next to the Academy at Mrs. Dixon's boarding house, but two sources show that his residence was on Broad Street. Still the historical society debates the location. He attended a ball there with between 60 and 70 well-dressed ladies, examined students, and was said to be impressed. The Academy housed the General Assembly, courts, and Masonic Lodge. He toured the battlefields and Revolutionary War sites, including the sites of Ft. Augusta/Ft Cornwallis, at the parking lot of St. Paul's Church, 605 Reynolds on the river. A later 20th century church replaces the

1750 structure that **Washington** probably entered.

He no doubt saw another battle site, Mackay Trading Post at 1822 Broad, once called "Georgia's most cherished shrine of liberty." An earlier historical marker related that in September 1780 a band of patriots attacked the building held by British troops. Just as they were about to surrender, reinforcements arrived and the patriots had to retreat, leaving twenty-nine wounded behind. Thirteen were claimed to have been hanged in the stairwell so their wounded commander could watch and the rest surrendered to the Indians to be tortured and killed. It is now believed that the current building, now known as the Ezekiel Harris House,* was later built on the site in 1797. The story that **Washington's** dog, Cornwallis, died while here and was buried with his grave marked does not seem to be true as historians and town histories cannot verify this. It is not mentioned in **Washington's** diary or later annotations.

Monroe visited in 1819 and was at the Globe and Planters Hotel, marked at the corner of 900 Jones and 100 McCartan, just east of the listed site at 945 Broad. He inspected the federal arsenal being built on the river, still at Walton Way and Katherine. **Grant** and **Davis** are also shown to have stayed at the hotel. After his nomination **Taft** spent a month at the Terrett Cottage on Milledge Road and the Telfair Hotel at the SW corner of Walton Way and Heard, frequented the Seven Gables Restaurant and the Bon Air Golf Club, and attended the Tabernacle Baptist Church* at 1223 Laney Walker. He honored black Americans at the Haines Institute and Shiloh Orphanage.

Wilson moved here when he was one year old, and lived in the 600 Block of Greene Street. He later moved to 419 Seventh Street* at Telfair, NW corner, where he lived from 1860 until 1870, longer than any other home during his life. His father was the pastor of First Presbyterian Church* at 642 Telfair Street where "Tommy," as Woodrow was called in his younger years, attended until they moved to Columbia, South Carolina. (Both Democratic presidents, **Cleveland** and **Wilson**, elected in the years between 1860 and 1932 dropped their first names and used their mother's maiden names, "Grover" and "Woodrow.") The home served as a Confederate hospital during the Civil War. Tommy saw **Davis** pass through under heavy guard in 1865 at the train station where the civic center now is located on Telfair between Seventh and Eighth. **Grant** came after peace, also in 1865.

Eisenhower enjoyed coming (47 times) to the Augusta National Golf Club, where "Mamie's Cottage" was built at 2604 Washington Road for his visits. In November 1965, he suffered a heart attack there, requiring several weeks in the hospital. He helped dedicate the cornerstone of Reid Memorial Presbyterian Church on Walton Way. While **Reagan** played golf here, a pickup truck crashed through the fence, threatening the president.

BRUNSWICK • Before it closed in 2004, the Cloister Hotel on Sea Island Drive south of Sea Island hosted **Coolidge** in 1928, **Bush** in 1945 for his honeymoon, **Eisenhower** in 1946 and **Ford** in 1974. A new hotel is in a different location. **George W. Bush** hosted the G-8 summit here in 2004.

COLUMBUS • **Polk** (1849) and **Fillmore** (1854) visited the St. Elmo Mansion at 2810 St. Elmo Drive, and **FDR** visited the Springer Opera House at First Ave. and Tenth Street in 1928.

IRWINVILLE • **Davis** was captured on May 8, 1865, at what is now Jefferson Davis Memorial State Park. He was in his wife's cloak, mistakenly grabbed in the dark, as 300 soldiers approached. He had just been reunited with his family, who had fled their home in Richmond. The government took the cloak and other relics later after a story ridiculing **Davis** circulated that he tried to escape in women's clothes. As seen in his Biloxi home, they do not appear to differ from men's clothing of the period, and the story of his "cowardly disguise" has little merit. A number of state historical markers show the escape route and explain that "he was held as a 'state prisoner,' his hopes for a new nation, in which each state would exercise without interference its cherished 'Constitutional rights,' forever dead." Wisconsin and Michigan Cavalry were both pursuing and unaware of each other's presence. As the rivals for the honor of capturing the enemy approached, two Michigan soldiers were killed as the Wisconsin unit fired blindly into camp. Yankee soldiers ate the breakfast prepared for the four Davis children (aged ten to ten months) and taunted them, singing, "We'll hang Jeff Davis from a sour apple tree."

MACON • After his capture, **Davis** was brought to the Lanier House, now the Lanier Plaza Hotel, marked on the north side of Mulberry Street between Second and Third. He came back in 1887 and made a speech on the still present bandstand at Central City Park, Riverside and Seventh.

PLAINS • **Carter**'s 1924 birthplace is now the Lillian G. Carter Nursing Center, then Wise Sanitarium, at 225 Hospital Street. He was the first president born in a hospital. His mother was a nurse there, and doctors convinced her that she could return to work two days quicker than if she had her baby at home. During his first few years he grew up where only the chimney exists today at the SW corner of South Bond and Moon Road, next to his future wife. He lived from age four in a cottage two and a half miles west off Highway 280 and Ga. 27, near a railroad flag stop called Archery. This is owned today by the National Park Service and open as the Carter Boyhood Farm* on the Old Plains Highway. The farmhouse had no indoor plumbing or electricity until after Jimmy was thirteen. A store run by the family is restored next door. Here the **Carters** raised crops, farm animals, and four children. Jimmy picked cotton with black employees and learned to hate racial injustice. His father placed a battery-operated radio in the window so the employees could listen to Joe Louis fights. After the black hero beat the German champion Max Schmeling prior to World War II, the crowd outside the home politely thanked Mr. Carter, silently walked back to their homes, shut the doors, and as the president relates, "All hell broke loose."

His church was Plains Baptist at Bond and Paschal Streets, across (west) from his old high school, now a museum and visitor center.* The church split in the 1970s and the **Carters** joined Maranatha Baptist,* north on Highway 45, Buena Vista Road, where he taught Sunday school into the 21st century. He was married in the Methodist church* at the SW corner of Thomas Street and 305 West Church, Highways 290 and 27. The young Navy officer returned as his father was dying of cancer, and noted that everyone in town seemed moved by his father's life, a man who had touched and bettered all in the community. **Carter** then decided that he was going nowhere and wanted to make something of his life. So he left the service to settle back here.

He first lived in public housing at the SE corner of Paschall and Thomas and also a short time in the Plains Bed and Breakfast just west of his brother Billy's service station on Church Street, west of Bond. Later the family, now including three sons, moved for five years to a house down the Old Plains Highway. The house is still standing, but the owners will not sell to the Park Service. It is run down and deserves its name, Haunted House, due to the appearance and stories related to it. In 1960 he moved to Woodlawn Drive, the only home he ever owned, now enclosed as a compound. His mother later lived in a still yellow house on South Bond directly east of the Highway 45 (Bottsford/Dawson Road) junction.

The driving tour begins at the visitor center, 300 N. Bond, with a good map including most the sites listed here, and covers his Peanut Warehouse* and family homes. The old Plains depot* on the west side of the business district has been restored as his 1976 headquarters.

ROME • **TR** came in 1910 to visit the Martha Berry School, 2277 Martha Berry Blvd., at Louisa Hall and the Colonial Administration Building. **Wilson** visited his aunt and uncle for several years at 709 Broad. He also stayed at 304 E. Fourth (1867–9), 205 E. Tenth (1875–82), 402 E. Third, and Six Coral Ave. As a young attorney he first saw his future first wife in the First Presbyterian Church, 101 E. Third, where, as president in 1914, he attended her funeral and burial at Myrtle Hill Cemetery on S. Broad. As governor of New Jersey he visited the Hope Building of Berry College, 2277 Martha Berry Blvd.

ROSWELL • **Theodore Roosevelt's** mother was born and married at Bullock Hall* just west of the town square, one block north of Highway 120 at Mimosa and Bullock. The president was photographed in front of the house in 1905 and made a speech on the Town Square.

SAVANNAH • **Washington** stayed four days in 1791 at the NW corner of Barnard and State on Telfair Square where the Telfair Museum* now stands. **Davis** was present at its dedication. The royal governor lived on the site before the Revolution, and was captured here by Colonial forces in January 1776. **Washington** was also entertained at 110 East Oglethorpe and several times at Brown's Coffee House near the City Hall on Bay Street. He ate with the Cincinnati Society and drank fifteen toasts at another gathering. The only landmark still surviving from the time that **Washington** would recognize is the Lachlan McIntosh House, now used as a law office at 110 E. Oglethorpe. He also was entertained at the Filature, on the south side of Bryan Street, just east of Reynolds Square. He danced, enjoyed the 96 ladies presented to him, but had to retire at 11:00

although the party lasted until 3:00 A.M. The next day he presented the "Washington guns" captured at Yorktown to Chatham's Artillery and toured the battlefield in town. The guns are now on the north side of Bay Street, opposite the courthouse at the head of Drayton Street. The marker shows that they thundered a welcome for **Polk**, **Monroe**, **Arthur**, **Davis**, **Cleveland**, **McKinley**, both **Roosevelts**, and **Taft**. **Fillmore** should also be included, but probably not **Grant**, although he was here in late 1865 and 1880. Some sources claim that one gun was given by **Washington** and one by Lafayette in 1825, but the marker shows both from **Washington**.

A fireworks show was given in **Washington's** honor on the bank of the river. Before leaving he attended Christ Church on Johnson Square. On the way out of town he received a parting salute at the Spring Hill British Redoubt, a center of fighting in 1779. General McIntosh gave **Washington** an account of the battle and showed him the sites. He had been dismissed earlier from **Washington's** command because of conflicts with fellow officers and a hot temper that resulted in the fatal duel with the first Declaration signer to die, Button Gwinnett, in 1777.

The first president visited the home and widow of General Nathanael Greene, ten miles north at Mulberry Grove, before and after staying in Savannah. Greene was his top subordinate who was to succeed the commander if needed, but he died of sunstroke at age forty-three here before **Washington's** visit. Later Eli Whitney would invent the cotton gin at the plantation, preserving slavery by making it somewhat profitable for several more decades. The old plantation, burned by Sherman's troops during the Civil War, is off U.S. 17 on the bank of the Savannah River, across from Isla Island. A marker on highway 17 notes the vicinity, but the ruins are inaccessible.

Monroe was entertained in the Scarbrough House* at the corner of Martin Luther King Jr. and Congress Streets and attended a dedication of the Independent Presbyterian Church in 1819. The present church is on the SW corner of Bull and Oglethorpe, just north of where it was in **Monroe's** and **Wilson's** time, at Hall and Bull. **Wilson** was here in the 1880s and went to Independent Presbyterian, which burned in 1889. He was married next door at the manse in 1885. **Fillmore** and **Polk** also attended the church. **Wilson** also attended Anderson Presbyterian on the NE corner of Barnard and Anderson and visited 143 Broad and 164 Hall Streets.

Monroe attended a reception at the Exchange and lodged at present-day 111 Martin Luther King Boulevard. He stayed here three days and was here when the steamboat *Dallas* set out for Europe, the first steamboat to do so, and was able to cruise on the ship up and down the river before it left. The whole town turned out for a large dinner in a pavilion on Johnson Square, just south of City Hall. **Polk** passed through on the way home after leaving office in 1849 and stayed at the Pulaski House, NW corner of Bull and Bryan at Johnson Square. He also attended the Episcopal church on Johnson Square and Independent Presbyterian. **Fillmore** stayed in the Pulaski House in 1854 and visited three churches in a single day.

At the end of General Sherman's 1864 march to the sea, his headquarters were in the Green-Meldrim House* at Bull and Harris on the west side of Madison Square. **Davis** dedicated Greene's Monument* in Johnson Square in 1886. The Comer House, where **Davis** was honored in 1886, is marked on the NE corner of Bull and Taylor. The marker notes that **Davis** "received tributes of respect and affection from the local citizenry, visiting military organizations ... [and] thousands of visitors." His statements, however, did little to settle the "lost cause." He stated:

> In 1776 the colonies acquired state sovereignty.... Is it a lost cause now? Never! Has Georgia lost the state sovereignty ... she won in 1776? No, a thousand times, no! Truth crushed to the earth will rise again. You may hold it down but it will rise again in its might, clothed in all the majesty and power that God gave it, and so the independence of these states, the constitution, liberty, state sovereignty, which they won in 1776 ... can never die.

Grant stayed at the Screven House, SE corner of Bull and Congress, in 1880, as did **Wilson** in 1885. **Arthur** suffered so much from his kidney problems while docked here on his yacht that a doctor had to be summoned, leading to the first diagnosis of his fatal Bright's disease. He visited a relative in 1883 at 125 W. Gordon Street at the SW corner with Bull Street and also visited 126 Liberty Street. **Cleveland** dedicated the Jasper Monument on **Washington's** Birthday in 1888 opposite Sherman's headquarters. **McKinley** and **Taft** visited the Gordon House at the NE corner of Bull and Oglethorpe Streets and the Green-Meldrim House on Macon, now the parish house of St. Johns Church. **FDR** was here for the city's 200th anniversary in 1944 to speak in Grayson Stadium, 1401 Victory. **Nixon** was the 19th president to visit the town.

SYLVANIA • **Washington's** 1791 route through the state was roughly U.S. 301 and 24, and he stayed about five miles north of here and several miles southeast, as shown on area markers.

WARM SPRINGS • **Franklin Roosevelt** used the "Little White House"* sixteen times during his presidency. It is two miles south on U.S. 27 Alt. and SR 85W. He first came here in 1924 to an old, run-down resort to test its warm buoyant water pools to aid his recovery from polio and was here 41 times. (Actually, between the 1924 and 1928 elections, he was away from his home and family 116 weeks out of 208. Eleanor was with him only two weeks on these excursions, but his secretary/mistress?/close companion, Missy LeHand, was away from him only six weeks.) After getting the disease he felt that he could be cured, and when he heard of a young man getting better by swimming in the warm waters here he felt that this was the place to be rehabilitated. He spent many months and got the idea of restoring the area for a resort, although few wanted to come to a place where a man with polio swam. Then he got the idea to develop it for invalids. Eleanor objected, thinking it would divert his mind from a return to his political career. This produced what has been called their only real argument, but he insisted and spent about two-thirds of his wealth in building up the facility.

Governor Al Smith convinced him to run for governor of New York in 1928 to keep his (Smith's) place safe in case he lost his presidential campaign. **Roosevelt** wanted several more years of exercise to regain his ability to walk, but consented to run upon the insistence of Smith and his own advisors, who convinced him that this was his opportunity for advancement. It is now believed that further therapy would not have allowed him to physically progress, and future events showed that this was the time for him to emerge politically. Much of Smith's persistence occurred via telephone while **Roosevelt** was here. Smith convinced him that he could spend most of his time here, while Smith controlled events in Albany. Thus it could be argued that **FDR**'s polio allowed a path to the presidency that would not have existed without it. Smith handed the opportunity to an unwilling candidate who was thought not to be a political threat and would passively hold the office under Smith's control.

The water and exercise produced no physical miracles, but did improve his emotional well-being, giving him a new life although the waters actually had no medicinal properties. He enjoyed riding horses and driving around the countryside talking to farmers and residents in a roadster preserved on site. For the first time he got to know people suffering from lack of electricity, low farm prices, fear of mortgage payments, and real poverty. He became more sympathetic to people in suffering beyond his own experience, enabling him to better relate to citizens when he became governor and then president.

During this period he stayed in several cottages, including McCarthy Cottage and Meriweather Inn, shown on the park map. The latter was behind the pool and burned in 1956. The old train depot where he arrived and departed is gone, with the town welcome center on site at the main intersection of Highways 27A, 85, and 41. It is claimed that he spent at least one night in the Hotel Warm Springs just up the street, east of the depot site on Ga. Highway 41.

In 1932, when he was governor of New York, he constructed a small wooden cottage,* returning often after his election to the presidency. He enjoyed swimming with other patients at the Warm Springs Foundation, especially the children. He last returned on March 30, 1945, and it is little changed from the day he died there on April 12, 1945, as his portrait was being painted. The unfinished painting is still in the room. Eleanor came from Washington, D.C., and spent about ten minutes alone in his bedroom after his death to reflect on her abrupt life change, the loss of her husband, and the fact that she had just learned that Lucy Mercer (Rutherford), his old mistress, had been with him when he died. According the historian Doris Kearns Goodwin, after his mother and personal secretary died, **Roosevelt** asked Eleanor to stay home and once again be close in their relationship. She could not do this, so the president developed a close relationship with his daughter, who renewed the relationship with Lucy.

One of his favorite places was Dowdell's Knob* in **FDR** State Park on Ga. 190. The barbecue grill (filled in) that he used is at the scenic overlook. Even though the setting was rustic, he preferred hot lunches with silver and a tablecloth. He was here with Lucy the day before he died. **Clinton**, **Kennedy**, and **Carter** spoke at the cottage during their campaigns.

WASHINGTON • **Davis** stayed in the Robertson House on the north side of the public square when fleeing at the end of the Civil War. This was also the Bank of Georgia Building, later known as the Heard Building. It has been destroyed and was where the Courthouse now is. **Davis** probably would have stayed in Robert Toomb's home,* 216 E. Robert Toombs Ave., Business Route 78, but his rival made a point of not being at home. (Confederate Vice President Alexander Stephens lived nearby and had a room there when he frequently visited.) Many former soldiers recognized the man said to still look like their president even though he probably did not feel like one as he had arrived exhausted and slept most of the afternoon and evening.

Yet another "last cabinet meeting" was held on May 4, 1865, shown in a marker at the southwest corner of the Courthouse, **Davis**' last official act as president. But this meeting with some officers and cabinet members was more to determine which direction each should flee and whether or not to dissolve the government. The Yankees had seemingly done a pretty good job of this by now. **Davis** just decided that he had no authority to dissolve a government set up by states and to just temporarily disband it for now to meet further west later. But this meeting in effect dissolved the Confederate government.

The street in front was the scene of a tearful goodbye to Navy Secretary Mallory, various soldiers, and others remaining behind as only a small escort went further. His wife and children had waited for him at the Dr. Fielding Ficklen home (private), marked at the SE corner of Alexander and Water, about a block south of the sites noted in the paragraph below. But they continued west before **Davis** arrived. All felt they were safer apart. Later that day he fled towards the army of his brother-in-law, Richard Taylor, not knowing that Zachary's son had surrendered. During the next few days he caught up with his family and was captured near Irwinville.

Thomas Woodrow Wilson as a small boy occasionally came with his preacher father when he preached in the summers at the Presbyterian church, marked on Robert Toombs Avenue west of the Toombs House, and stayed at Wisteria Hall,* now a bed and breakfast at 225 E. Robert Toombs across the street. Tommy helped his father in the church and organized a club in the garage with the symbol of the devil taken from a deviled ham ad.

HAWAII

HONOLULU • **Harding** stayed at the Beach Hotel in 1915 and **Taft** stopped on the way to and from the Philippines. All presidents have stopped here since **Franklin Roosevelt**. He came in July 1934 to honor the governor at Schofield Barracks and spent the night in the Royal Hawaiian Hotel, 2259 Kalakaua, fished for swordfish, dedicated the Ala Moana Park and planted a kukui tree just east of the Iolani Palace, noted with a plaque and still here. He was supposed to plant a kamani tree, but a Democratic women's organization strongly objected and evidently got the ordered tree switched at the last minute before anything could be done. He was back with the military leaders of the Pacific War on June 22, 1944. General MacArthur persuaded him to follow his plans rather than the admirals.' He drove around in an open touring car, seen by many, but the press did not report his presence until he was safely back home. **Nixon** was at the Royal Hawaiian in April 1952, as was **LBJ**.

Kennedy was at the Hawaiian Village Hotel, 2005 Kalia Road, on June 8, 1963. He passed from Pearl Harbor to Waikiki Beach in an open car before 300,000, many of whom got to shake his hand. This presidential openness somewhat ended with his assassination a few months later. **Truman** stopped off on his way to the Wake Island meeting with MacArthur in 1950 that led to the general's firing shortly thereafter. The president felt that it would be inappropriate to wear a lei, but changed his mind for his 1953 vacation. **Ike** was at a military camp in 1946 on Hilo Island. He spent four days in 1960 golfing and relaxing before a goodwill trip to Asia. This was the year after he signed Hawaii into the

Union, and 300,000 let him know they appreciated the act.

George H.W. Bush was assigned here for rest in 1944 and visited the National Cemetery and *Arizona* Memorial on December 7, 1991, when he told how he felt when he first flew to Pearl Harbor in 1944. In October 1990 he got a flowered lei at the airport on a political trip for a local candidate. **Ford** visited the memorials on Pearl Harbor Day in 1975. **Reagan** visited Easter services at St. Andrew's Cathedral and the Governor's Mansion in April 1984 and stayed at the Kahala Hilton, 5000 Kahala Ave., where he was photographed in the water. **Carter** was at the Nimitz Naval housing unit, 318 Sixth, in 1949–1950 and greeted crowds at the air base July 1, 1979. **Clinton** got more attention in his week here in July 1993 than **Truman** did for his month's vacation in 1953. **Clinton** gave an open invitation for a speech at the Hilton Hawaiian Village, and spoke on the beach to 20,000. In all **Clinton** made seven stops here as president, including on the way to Viet Nam, as the first president to visit the unified country.

LBJ stopped here seven times on the way to and from the Far East. His first trip was in February 1966, and he decided at the last minute to stay in the Royal Hawaiian. The hotel had to scramble to find rooms for all that were needed, including relocating their own guests. He later stayed at the estate of Henry Kaiser on Koko Head. **Nixon** came four times in office, including his 1972 trip to China, and preceding troop withdrawal from Vietnam in 1969 on the way to Midway Island. **George W.** met Pearl Harbor survivors and spoke at the *Arizona* and *Missouri* Battleships, as shown below.

The *Arizona* Memorial has been visited by the following: **JFK** (1963), **LBJ** (1968), **Nixon** (1972), **Ford** on the 30th anniversary of the end of World War II (1975), **Carter** (1977), **Reagan** (April 1984 and April 1986), **George H.W. Bush** (Oct. 1990, 1991), **Clinton** (July 1993, Nov. 1994, August 1995, Nov. 1996, Nov. 1998, twice in Sept. 1999), **George W. Bush** (October 23, 2003).

IDAHO

ARCO • This city was the first to be powered by atomic energy and received visits to the Energy Commission Building by **Truman** in 1948 and by **LBJ** (August 26, 1966). At nearby Carey **Truman** dedicated an airport: "To the boy who died for liberty so that this country might live." Newsmen laughed and informed him that the honoree was a girl.

BOISE • **B. Harrison** was the first president to visit when he spoke on May 8, 1891, at the old Capitol at the site of the new House section. He was also the first to plant a tree, marked on the lawn, and stayed at the Overland Hotel, Eighth and Main. **TR** paraded through on May 29, 1903, and stayed at the Idhana Hotel, NE corner of Main and Tenth. His parade took him by St. Margaret's Academy, with 100 scholars dressed in white, at First and Idaho. He is pictured on Jefferson Street in front of the Capitol, where he planted a sugar maple tree. **Taft** visited in 1911 and 1915, when he planted an Ohio Buckeye and came to Old City Hall at Eighth and Idaho. He spoke on Americanism and Bolshevism at the Boise High School Auditorium on June 2, 1920. The city claims that every president since **Hoover** has visited. **FDR** spoke at Capitol and Bannock on September 27, 1937. Kids were let out as he drove by every city school, and he spoke from his car at Seventh and Bannock. **Ike** launched his campaign in 1952 at the Western Governors Conference and visited the Capitol. On August 5, 1978, **Carter** stayed in suite 500 at the Rodeway Inn, Chinden and 29th, and vacationed at nearby Camp Indian Creek. He and **Nixon** spoke at the airport while campaigning. **Carter** spent three isolated days rafting the Middle Fork of the Salmon, boarded at the Harrah Ranch, slept on a sand bar, and paid his $7 fishing license fee.

Reagan spoke for Ford at the Rodeway Convention Center on October 29, 1976, accusing the Democrats of "charting the most dangerous course since Egyptians tried to take a short cut through the Red Sea." Vice President **Bush** scrambled for cover as secret service agents hurriedly arrested two men with guns outside the Chart House on October 30, 1982. **Bush** was thrown under a table and hovered over until it was learned that the two returning hunters did not know he was there. He then spoke at the Eight Street Market House and Civic Auditorium.

CALDWELL • **Hoover** spoke at the Memorial Park, from a stand at the Odd Fellows Temple, and saw a parade on Spring Ave. He also ate at the Warm Springs Ave. home of Max Mayfield.

IDAHO FALLS • **Truman** at age 78 seemed to take seriously the facetious question, "Will you run in 1964?" He stated anyone with brains would know and answered the expected question about an upcoming legalized gambling vote as he had been coached, that it was a local issue. But he then added that anyone for it was crazy since Nevada had been made "one of the blackest holes on the continent." He also reiterated about when he found out he was president, he wondered then if he was equal to the greats, **Jefferson, Wilson, FDR,** and **Jackson.**

POCATELLO • On May 25, 1903, **TR** was met two miles from town by Indians from Ft. Hall, and then spoke to 8000 at the stadium and from a platform at the high school after many celebrations. **Taft** spoke in the old high school in 1911. **TR** came back the next year to Old City Hall. **FDR** made a campaign stop on September 18, 1937. **Truman** came in 1948 and was said to be a frequent visitor. **LBJ** in 1966 outdrew **JFK's** numbers at the high school in 1960.

ILLINOIS

ALTON • **Lincoln** promoted Harrison for president on April 9, 1840, in Calvin Riley's Building at Market and Broadway. He came on September 22, 1842, to fight a duel with the state auditor of Illinois, James Shields, later a senator from three states and Civil War general. (He was not a very good general, but he did defeat Stonewall Jackson at Kernstown, Virginia.) Shields was upset at derogatory articles in a Springfield newspaper ridiculing him, supposedly written by **Lincoln,** and probably partly by Mary Todd with **Lincoln** taking the blame. Since dueling was illegal in Illinois they agreed to fight across the Mississippi River on Sunflower Island (also "Tow Head" or "Bloody Island"), now mostly under water. **Lincoln** had his choice of weapons, and first chose cow pies. Then the long-armed lawyer chose broadswords, and swung at a few branches out of Shield's reach. This prompted apologies, and the duel was called off. Afterwards the parties were hosted at the Old '76 Tavern at Front and Market Streets adjacent to the 1858 debate site. **Lincoln** was next back on October 2, 1849, to speak in front of the Presbyterian church then on Broadway and Market, across from City Hall.

The last of the great **Lincoln** and Douglas debates occurred October 15, 1858, on Broadway at the end of Market on a platform at the east side of the City Hall that burned in 1920. They traveled on the same steamer from Quincy to Douglas' headquarters at the Alton House a block south at Front and Alby, from which **Lincoln** was escorted by Republican leaders to the Franklin House,* 208 State. Lincoln and Douglas had both attended a reception in 1841. Mary and Robert joined and the family ate in a restaurant below their bedroom on the second floor facing State Street, where both buildings can be seen today.

FDR spoke from the train at the station 3400 College in 1936.

BLOOMINGTON • The David Davis Mansion,* Monroe and Davis Street, is an 1870 structure begun eight years after **Lincoln** appointed his old friend to the Supreme Court. **Lincoln** was often at a prior home on site. **Grant** visited in 1881. Davis could have decided the presidency in 1876 with his vote if he had not resigned his spot on the commission set up to determine who won. Democrats in the legislature selected him for the Senate, and he resigned to assume that role. But this backfired for the Democrats as

Davis' successor to the commission voted with the Republicans to select **Hayes** from contested electoral votes.

Lincoln spoke many times at Majors Hall, SW corner East and Front Streets, and gave his famous May 1856 "Lost Speech" at the first state convention of the Illinois Republican Party, said to boost **Lincoln** into the leadership of the new party, leading to his nomination. The McLean County Courthouse Museum,* at 200 N. Main, was built in 1903 on the site used by **Lincoln.** Prior courthouses at sites marked here burned or were destroyed in 1868 and 1900, destroying most county records, including **Lincoln's. Lincoln** acquired two lots in 1851 on the NW corner of McLean and Jefferson Streets and held them for more than four years.

Numbers 106 and 108 are all that remains of Phoenix Hall and Block on the south side of the square, 106–112 W. Washington. **Lincoln** made his last long political speech on April 10, 1860, at the Hall just west of 108. On April 8, 1859, only about forty people showed up to hear **Lincoln's** lecture on inventions, but he felt this was too few and canceled. On April 6, 1858, he was scheduled to give the lecture in Majors Hall, but moved to Centre Hall, at 113 N. Centre on the SE corner of Washington and Centre (now "Center"). **Lincoln's** friends Ward Hill Lamon, Leonard Swett, and others, had offices on the second floor of the Dr. Crothers Buildings on the corner at 116–118 West Washington Street and 111–113 N. Center. Close friend Swett lived at 63 Mulberry. Judge Davis believed that "Swett and William Herndon were his intimate personal and political friends" and knew "more detailed information" about **Lincoln** than anyone.

Lincoln stayed and spoke many times from the balcony at the Pike House, SE Corner of Monroe and Center, when it was called the Matteson House. He also stayed at 601 North Lee and the National Hotel at 105–111 West Front. He also used his friends' offices at the 1843 Miller-Davis Buildings, 101–103 North Main and 102–104 East Front.

CAIRO • President-elect **Taylor**'s boat was so delayed as he came by on the way to his inauguration that the large crowd saluted the wrong boat. By the time his came through at 3:00 A.M., the crowd was so incensed that they fired large guns to make sure he was awake.

Grant's headquarters in 1861 were at 609 Ohio, where he assembled forces awaiting orders. His commander, Frémont, had told him not to advance, but when the general was removed, **Grant** felt that he could act. From here he proceeded down river to attack Belmont, Missouri, after the Confederates occupied Columbus, Kentucky, across the river. This was **Grant's** first action in the Civil War. It was not a success, but the rare Union aggressive action led to greater glory. His family lived here part of the time on the second floor opposite his office, where Julia was appalled at his new bizarre whiskers and out-of-style new hat. He also stayed at the St. Charles Hotel at Ohio and Second. It burned in 1943. When the **Grants** returned from their world tour in 1880, they were hosted at Magnolia Manor,* 27th and Washington.

CHARLESTON • **Lincoln** stopped at nearby Wabash Point, about two miles northeast of the current town of Paradise, to see family friends and relatives when he traveled with his family in 1830 on the way to the Decatur area. The family later returned here and lived on three farms in the area before purchasing the Goosenest Prairie site where **Lincoln's** father died in 1851. **Lincoln** visited his father and stepmother sixteen times at the site now preserved as Lincoln Log Cabin State Historic Site,* eight miles south on the east side of Route 1668. The Sargent farm home and outbuildings were moved here from about a mile east of the small community of Hutton, approximately ten miles almost due east and about a mile to the north. **Lincoln** had visited his friends several times at that location.

When **Lincoln** had cases in town, he used the offices of Usher F. Linder at the northeast corner of the square. He stayed at times at the Capitol House or Johnson Tavern at the NE corner of Sixth and Monroe, his headquarters during the debate. He made speeches in 1840 and 1856 in Charleston on the north side of the railroad tracks, then at about 14th Street and Olive. The courthouse is the same site where **Lincoln** practiced. He also stayed at the Union House, on the NW corner of the square, Douglas' headquarters, and spoke at least once, January 31, 1861, at Mount and Hill Hall, SE corner of Fifth and Monroe.

The September 18, 1858, debate site is marked west of "E" Street at the eastern end of the fairgrounds on the west side of town, on the south side of State Avenue, State Highway 316. The speaker's platform faced east at a spot noted by a marker at the museum on site. **Lincoln** stayed with a friend who lived at 218 Jackson Street (private), where **Lincoln's** cousin Dennis Hanks had an earlier house. He visited his relatives on the 19th and spent the night with Dennis Hanks' son-in-law Augustus H. Chapman at 400 Jackson. **Lincoln** stayed with Chapman frequently here and from 1852 to 1857 at the corner of Eighth and Monroe.

Just before he left for Washington, **Lincoln** came on January 30, 1861, to see his stepmother and spent the night with Marshall, with whom he had been traveling, on the west side of Tenth Street, north of Harrison, where he received several hundred well-wishers. After breakfast at the home of Dennis Hanks, then on the west side of the square, **Lincoln** and Chapman rode to see **Lincoln's** stepmother, who was staying with her daughter since the chimney of her own cabin had fallen the day before. This home, the old Moore House,* is marked southwest of town, one mile north of the Lincoln cabin on the Lerna Road, out Fourth St., Highway 170. She broke down when he hugged her, telling him that she would never see him again, crying, "Abe, you are too good a man, and they will kill you." He held her hand and talked about the past most of the day before going to nearby Shiloh Cemetery and church where his father, Thomas, is buried, about a mile northwest of the site of the old cabin to the west and clearly marked. His stepmother did not go, in spite of a statement to that effect on a marker there, although they surely visited together before. Thomas's tombstone is of later date, although many others there then are still present. He spent the night with the Chapmans, and went to a reception at the Mount and Hill Hall, second floor. His stepmother again lamented the next morning that she felt that she would never see him again, as his enemies would assassinate him.

CHICAGO • Lt. **Davis** led a timber-cutting expedition in 1830 near the small village around Ft. Dearborn. They got lost and wandered for days without food and water. **Davis** stumbled to a spot on the river bank opposite the fort, probably where the Wrigley and Tribune Buildings are now, and attracted the attention of future general David Hunter at the fort, who paddled over to rescue him.

As of the early 21st century, Chicago has had 25 national political conventions. **Lincoln's** was the first. **Grant's** in 1868 was at the Crosby Opera House on Washington between State and Dearborn. After the Great Fire of 1871, the Republicans met in 1880, and both parties came in 1884, with all meetings at the Inter-State Exposition building, east side of Michigan, next to Lake Michigan at Adams, replaced by the Art Institute. In 1888 **Harrison** was nominated at the partially completed Civic Auditorium,* still on the NW corner of Michigan and Congress. It was built to be the largest, grandest, and most expensive theater in the world. **Cleveland** laid the cornerstone, and **TR** made his "Bull Moose" speech in 1912 when he was nominated by the Progressives. **FDR** (for vice president in 1920) and **JFK** spoke there during their campaigns.

In 1892 **Cleveland** and Adlai Stevenson were nominated at the "Wigwam" on Michigan between Madison and Washington, just before the roof caved in from heavy rains. **Cleveland's** New York delegation had expected it as they were patiently waiting to vote inside with their umbrellas open under some already bad leaks. In 1896 the Democrats met in the Chicago Coliseum, then at 63rd and Stoney Island in the Woodlawn Neighborhood. Then a new Coliseum was built at 16th and Wabash, west of today's Soldier Field, where the infamous Libby Prison from Richmond was reconstructed after the Civil War. Republicans met there in their conventions from 1904 through 1920. The Democrats met in the International Amphitheater at 43rd and Halsted south of downtown in 1952, 1956, and 1968, as did the Republicans in 1952 and 1960. In 1996 they met at the United Center on the site of the Chicago Stadium, 1800 W. Madison, which had hosted their convention in 1940 and both national party conventions in 1932 and 1944. Various candidates who had been and became presidents were at the meetings, spoke, politicked, and nominated others. **Harding** nominated **Taft** in 1912.

Lincoln spent at least 150 days in Chicago. Returning from Washington in 1848 he stayed at the Sherman House, NW corner of Clark and Randolph, now occupied by the State of Illinois Building. **Johnson** and **Grant** stayed at the hotel in 1866 on the way to visit **Lincoln's** grave. Frantic **Truman** finally found fellow Missouri senator Bennett Clark here in 1944, in a last-minute effort to get his drunken colleague to nominate him for vice president.

Lincoln spoke and presented cases many times at the County Courts Building, Clark, Randolph, LaSalle, and Washington, where a modern building now stands. On Oct. 6, 1848, he "enchanted the meeting" for two hours outside speaking in support for **Taylor**. After **Taylor** died, **Lincoln** returned to deliver a eulogy on July 25, 1850. An estimated 125,000 viewed **Lincoln's** body inside on May 1 and 2, 1865. Mary's 1875 insanity trial was here in a building constructed after the Great Fire destroyed most **Lincoln**-era structures.

Lincoln met fellow lawyers in the Metropolitan Hall, along the north side of Randolph between Wells and LaSalle, and the Metropolitan Hotel on the SW corner of Wells. He spoke there on February 28, 1857, and attended a minstrel show in March 1860. He tried many cases in the U.S. Circuit Court at the Saloon Building, SE corner of Clark and Lake, where most of his legal business in Chicago was. On February 28, 1857, he had the second picture of his life taken by Alexander Hesler, the famous "tousled hair" pose, at a studio then on the south side of Lake about midway between Clark and Dearborn. Before the railroads were built, **Lincoln** often arrived at the Frink and Walker Stage Line, located on the south side of Lake just west of Dearborn.

The Tremont House on the SE corner of Dearborn and Lake is the Chicago hotel most closely associated with **Lincoln**. In April 1854 he attended a meeting of Whigs and Democrats opposed to Douglas and spoke in 1856 to a Republican banquet, responding to a toast with: "The Union — the North will maintain it — the South will not depart therefrom." On July 9, 1858, he sat behind Douglas on the balcony facing Lake Street and responded there the next day, a pattern followed for the senatorial campaign. He brought his son Willie in June 1859 and Mary the next month. His 1860 campaign headquarters were later in the hotel during the Republican convention at the Wigwam on the south side of Lake and Market (now Wacker), across from the present Merchandise Mart. After he was nominated he brought Mary in November, when he met 6-feet-two-plus-inch vice president-elect Hannibal Hamlin, and hosted a large reception on the first floor.

Lincoln visited the publishers at the Chicago Tribune Building, east side of Clark between Randolph and Lake, a little south of mid-block. The Larmon Block, NE Clark and Washington, was the scene of the *Sand Bar* Case tried by **Lincoln** in March 1860. Leonard W. Volk made a life mask of **Lincoln** in March 1860 at his studio, SE corner of Washington and Dearborn, fifth floor. **Lincoln** saw two plays in July 1857 at North's Amphitheater, on the NW corner of Wells and Monroe. He used the Chicago and Galena Union Depot between Wells and Franklin several times and used the Union Depot on Van Buren just west of the Chicago River in November 1860, now across the river from the Sears Tower. His remains left from this depot in 1865.

On Nov. 23, 1860, **Lincoln**, Mary, and Hamlin visited the Post Office, Customs House and U.S. Court Building between Clark, Madison, Monroe and Dearborn, now the site of the First National Bank Building. The president-elect then surprised the awe-struck children at the Moody-Mission Sabbath School at North Market Hall, NW corner of Hubbard and Dearborn. Ebenezer Peck hosted **Lincoln**, Hamlin, and Senator Lyman Trumbull at Clark and Fullerton, where they discussed cabinet selection on November 24. The next day he attended the St. James Church,* SW corner of Huron and Wabash. Part of the original walls and most of the tower survived the Great Fire and are incorporated into the present building.

Johnson and **Grant** helped dedicate the Stephen Douglas Monument,* 635 E. Thirty-fifth and Lake Shore Drive, in 1866. **Grant** visited the city several times including a reunion of the Army of the Tennessee at the Palmer House, 17 E. Monroe, in 1879, and Potter Palmer's "Castle" in 1880 at 1350 Lake Shore Drive. He also visited 1145 S. Wabash (1868), Lyman Trumbull at 4008 Lake Park, and was at his son's wedding at Vincennes and 45th. Later he visited the Farwell home, 120 E. Pearson. **Garfield and Arthur** were at the Grand Pacific Hotel at Jackson, Clark, and LaSalle. **Hayes** visited friends in town on several occasions. **Cleveland** was in town several times, visiting the Potter Palmer home in 1887 and the Joy Morton home, 638 Groveland, in 1893 when he opened the Columbian Exhibition where Soldier Field now is; the ceremony was attended by **TR** and other presidents. **Wilson** stayed then at 321 Huron. **B. Harrison** and **McKinley** visited the Peck House, 1826 S. Michigan. **Coolidge** stayed at the Drake Hotel, 140 E. Walton, in 1924.

After **Theodore Roosevelt's** first wife died, he stayed in the Grand Pacific and helped in a political fight to keep James G. Blaine from being nominated for president. **Roosevelt** made a name for himself with his organizational skills and met many people important in his later political career. Biographer David McCullough writes that this time was of critical importance in **Roosevelt's** career and his first appearance on the national stage. He proved himself to be a force to be reckoned with. In 1904 he visited 1430 Astor. After the assassination attempt in 1912 in Milwaukee, he was brought to the Mercy Hospital at Stevenson Expressway and King Drive.

When the 1920 Republican Convention deadlocked over a presidential candidate, a group of senators met political manipulator Harry Daugherty, who told reporters, "After the other candidates have failed ... the leaders, worn out and wishing to do the very best thing, will get together in some smoke-filled room about 2:11 in the morning.... I will be with them and present the name of Senator **Harding**. When that time comes, **Harding** will be selected." The "smoke-filled room" was suite 404–6 at the Blackstone Hotel, although it took ten ballots. **Harding** then had a personal suite at the LaSalle Hotel, 720 N. LaSalle, and arranged for his mistress Nan Britton and her child to stay at 6103 61st Street.

FDR was nominated in 1932, 1940, and 1944 at the Chicago Stadium, 1800 W. Madison, then the largest indoor arena in the world, built in 1929. It was demolished in 1995. He dramatically flew to town and was at the Congress Hotel, 520 S. Michigan, in July 1932 to accept the nomination. He was back for the 1932 World Series and threw out the first pitch at Wrigley Field in the game where Babe Ruth "called the shot." (**TR** was at the Congress in 1912.) **FDR** might have lost the nomination in 1932 as he could not muster the two-thirds requirement and a compromise candidate was about to be proposed. Then Joe Kennedy called newspaperman William Randolph Hearst to talk John Nance Garner into giving up his votes. At that time he sat next to Mayor Cermack, who was shot and killed a few weeks later while riding with the president-elect in Miami.

The Blackstone Hotel, at 636 S. Michigan, claims all presidents from **Theodore Roosevelt** through **Clinton**. Near the end of World War I, former close friends turned bitter enemies, **TR** and **Taft**, accidentally met one another in the dining room here, embraced, and ended their estrangement, to the cheers of the packed room. Their young children had been playmates and best friends when **Roosevelt** was in the White House. Charlie Taft was serving in France when Quinton Roosevelt was killed in combat there, prompting **Taft** to send a heartfelt letter of condolence. The meeting here took place shortly thereafter.

FDR was here in 1944, after **Truman** got his arm twisted to be the vice-presidential nominee via a phone call to Chairman Hannegin's suite (rooms 708–9) from the president, then in San Diego. **Truman** had spent part of his 1919 honeymoon at the hotel. In 1944 **Truman** was staying across Balbo Street at the Stevens, and there prepared his speech to nominate James Byrnes for the vice presidency. Most, including Byrnes, felt that he, Byrnes, had the nomination in the bag with **Roosevelt's** endorsement. But **Truman's** name began to surface. **Truman** still rejected the honor until **Roosevelt** changed **Truman's** mind by allowing the reluctant, balking senator to hear him shout over the telephone, "Well, you tell the senator that if he wants to break up the Democratic Party in the middle of the war, that's his responsibility." Opposed by a bitter floor fight with Henry Wallace diehards, the little-known senator from Missouri began a road to the White House. Most of the politicians in 1944 knew that the presidency was at stake, or should have known that **Roosevelt** was very sick and had a limited life expectancy. The president should have known the implications of his health, but did little or nothing to prepare the new president for his responsibilities that came less than three months after the next inauguration. In fact **Roosevelt** only met twice with the new vice president after the election to discuss minor matters. In 1952 **Truman** stayed in the same room (708–9) at the Democratic convention.

Several hotels in the "Convention City" claim multiple presidential visits. The Conrad Hilton (also known as the Stevens), 729 S. Michigan, claims **Truman** through **Carter**, and the Palmer House, 17 E. Monroe, claims **Cleveland** through **George W. Bush.**

Kennedy trained at Northwestern University's Chicago Campus in the Midshipmen's School in 1942. He lived in Abbot Hall at 710 N. Lake Shore Drive.

Three-year-old **Reagan** moved to 832–4 E. Seventh Street in 1914. Later presidents include **Ford** at the Congress Hotel (1960), **Nixon** at the Nickerbocker, 163 Walton, **George H.W. Bush** at the Hyatt Regency, 151 E. Wacker, and various others at sites too numerous to mention individually around the city, except for Hillary Rodman's home, 236 Wisner in Park Ridge, where **Clinton** visited while escorting his new girlfriend to a summer job in California. **George W. Bush** addressed the nation from the Science and Industry Museum* in July 2006.

CLINTON • On May 22 and 23, 1840, **Lincoln** and Stephen A. Douglas worked together on the first murder case in the county. The courthouse was a frequent stop and on the NW corner of the square, now a park with no building. He first met future general and his 1864 Democratic opponent, George B. McClellan, in 1855 as a witness opposing Douglas, his 1860 opponent. The general wrote that he often traveled "with him [**Lincoln**] in out-of-the-way county seats where some important case was being tried, and, in the lack of sleeping accommodations, have spent the night in front of a stove listening to the unceasing flow of anecdotes from his lips."

DANVILLE • **Lincoln** tried at least 209 cases here from 1841 until 1859, second in number only to Springfield. The **Lincoln**-Lamon Law Office and his only permanent office on the circuit is marked on the NW corner of Public Square, Main and Vermilion. The 50-square-foot 1832 courthouse was on the current site. The railroad tracks are still where **Lincoln** made his final address in Illinois bound for Washington, except for a short statement at Tolono to the east.

A boulder on the lawn marks an 1858 impromptu speech, delivered barefooted out Dr. William Fithian's* southeast second story window, 116 Gilbert St. The home is now the county museum with **Lincoln's** memorabilia and bed. He was followed from the depot by a demanding crowd and went upstairs to take off his boots. Fithian realized that the crowd wanted a speech and told **Lincoln** that he should go out even when he could not get his boots back on his swollen feet.

Lincoln ate often at the Reason Hooton House, 207 Buchanan, and told tales at Dr. Woodbury's store, 14 W. Main, where he bought a humor book quoted from during the debates. When Lincoln Hall was built on the site, claimed to be the first so named, he wished it success. He stayed at the McCormick House at 103 W. Main and frequented the homes of Rev. Enoch Kingsbury, NW corner of Walnut and Water, and Oscar F. Harmon, at 522 E. Main. He ate "many times" at Amos Williams Home on South Clark Street, on the bluff overlooking the river, and traded at the Hubbard Trading Post, SE corner of Public Square.

DECATUR • **Lincoln's** first Illinois home, now Lincoln Homestead State Park,* is six miles west, three miles south on the Sangamon River. A direction marker is on I-72 at Niantic, and signs will direct five miles south.

A bronze tablet at the southwest corner of the square marks the campsite where **Lincoln's** migrating family first arrived in 1830, now Lincoln Square where North and South Main crosses East and West Main. In the summer of 1830, he was working at the farm nearby, came to investigate a commotion, and heard a political speech. The young farmhand hopped up on the stump to speak in defense of a Whig. A statue on the northeast corner commemorates "**Lincoln's** First Political Speech," showing him barefoot with one foot on the stump, where splinters hurt his bare feet. The crowd cheered wildly as he learned that he could speak.

Lincoln became friends with Uncle Jimmy Renshaw, who lived on the NE corner of Broadway and Condit, and used his store, now the Lincoln Theater site, just south of Prairie Street about a half a block north on the west side of North Main or Lincoln Square. He practiced in the first courthouse on the SW corner of the square, known as the Log Cabin Courthouse, now at 5580 North Fork Road, and the second courthouse, built in 1838 on the SE corner. He stayed with relatives including John Hanks, and at the Revere House, on the SE corner of Franklin and Prairie, also called the Macon House. **Lincoln** was here when a wagon bearing a piano arrived with no one to get it inside. **Lincoln** insisted that he and his friend Leonard Swett could; they did, and then heard "Old Dan Tucker," "Rocked in the Cradle of the Deep," and other favorites.

The Cassell House, later the St. Nicholas Hotel, was on the west side of South Main midway between Wood and West Main, back from the SW corner of the square. In February 1856 **Lincoln** met with a political committee drafting Anti-Nebraska resolutions and organizing disorganized factions to suggest a governor. This led to organizing the Illinois Republican Party in Bloomington. He also spoke at the closing dinner.

In 1858, he gave his last speech before the senatorial election at Powers Hall, 135 E. Main, now a parking lot. In May 1860 the Illinois Republicans endorsed **Lincoln** as their candidate for president and gave him the sobriquet of "Rail Splitter" at the temporary Wigwam, marked on South Park Street, at the SW corner of State Street just north of East Main between Water and Franklin, a block and a half east of Lincoln Square. The state convention to nominate state officials spent most of its time discussing possible presidential candidates, with **Lincoln's** supporters hoping for a unanimous Illinois endorsement in the divided party. The platform was at about the middle of the block on State between Park and East Main. **Lincoln** spoke there and stayed at the Junction

House at the depot, about two blocks NE of the NE corner of Martin Luther King and Eldorado, about where extensions of Cerro Gordo and Hinton would cross. Supporters felt that he needed a label like Jackson's "Old Hickory" and Harrison's "Tippecanoe." Fence rails were brought in with the sign: *ABRAHAM LINCOLN The Rail Candidate for President in 1860.* With little ceremony the convention passed the following resolution: *That Abraham Lincoln is the choice of the Republican party of Illinois for the presidency.*

DIXON • **Lincoln** camped several times along both sides of the river for about eighteen days in May and June 1832 during the Black Hawk War at what is now the Lincoln Monument State Memorial on the west bank of Rock River. He was part of a volunteer military group of about 1200 called to force Chief Black Hawk out of Illinois. **Davis** and **Taylor** were here also. "Lincoln the Solder" is the only statue depicting him in military uniform. Stories persist that he and **Davis** saw one another, but **Davis** did not arrive until after **Lincoln** left.

He was here to speak on the north lawn of the Courthouse on July 17, 1856, where a stone marks the rally. One journalist wrote that he and **Lincoln's** future friend and secretary, Noah Brooks, sat together and "made fun of **Lincoln's** excessively homely appearance." He probably stayed then in the Nachusa Hotel after being entertained in the Joseph Crawford home on a bend in the river east of town, and was also at James Charter's home at Brinton and Everett. The Nachusa, at 215 S. Galena, claims to be the oldest hotel in Illinois, and that **Lincoln, Grant, Teddy Roosevelt, Taft,** and **Reagan** stayed.

Reagan lived in several houses in Dixon, including one at 816 South Hennepin,* the only one mentioned in his autobiography. By the time he moved here at age nine, he had lived in five towns in five years (Tampico, Chicago, Galesburg, Monmouth, and Dixon), making him introverted with a reluctance to get close to people. His alcoholic father managed a shoe store. Still standing are his nearby school at Fifth and Peoria, library at 221 S. Hennepin, and Christian church—called the center of his life—where he taught Sunday school, at 123 S. Hennepin. A school at Morgan and North Ottawa has been destroyed. While he was in high school, 415 S. Hennepin, the **Reagans** lived at 338 Everett. He learned to swim at the YMCA located a block east of his South Side School, one block north of the library where he checked out several hundred books. As a result of learning to swim he got a job as lifeguard beginning at age fifteen for seven summers in Lowell Park, where he saved seventy-seven from the swift Rock River current. He knew the number exactly because he made notches in a log. This was also a center point that he continued to talk about when his mind faded at the end of his life. After going to Eureka College about eighty miles south, he returned to his parent's homes at 26 Lincolnway from 1928 to 1931, 207 N. Galena Avenue in 1931, and 107 Monroe from 1932 until 1937. He only made mediocre grades in school, and wondered on comedian Jay Leno's television show how far he might have gone if he had only applied himself more. The former South Side School on Hennepin is now an historical center* and one place where the Ronald Reagan Trail Tour Map is available.

ELKHART • **Lincoln** stopped at the Latham Tavern, also known as the Kentucky House, on the Edwards Trace when he rode the Eighth Circuit. The site is now on private land on the east side of Elkhart Hill, east of the business center.

FREEPORT • The site of the second **Lincoln**-Douglas Debate, N. State Ave. and East Douglas St., is marked by a boulder dedicated by **TR** in 1903 with a life-size statute. About 15,000 swelled the town of 7,500 to hear Douglas's "Freeport Doctrine," said to have cost him the presidential election, or at least the presidential nomination of the full Democratic Party, in 1860. Both parties stayed in the Brewster House and appeared together on the balcony, two blocks from the debate site at the NW corner of Stephenson and Mechanic, on August 27, 1858.

GALENA • **Lincoln** passed through on June 10, 1832, with his military company camping at Apple River Fort,* just southeast, restored as a state park just east of Elizabeth. Later he stayed at the DeSoto House at Main and Green Street* and spoke from the balcony on July 23, 1856.

Grant's home was at 121 S. High from April 1860, until he left to rejoin the army at the beginning of the Civil War. The **Grant** leather goods store site where he worked for his family is marked at 120 Main. "High" Street is aptly named, as he had to climb 200 steps each way. His pew is marked in the Methodist church at 125 S. Bench. His wife had to leave her slaves back in Missouri since Illinois was free. **Grant** volunteered for duty at a mass meeting at the courthouse in the spring of 1861. At that time he was the soul of mediocrity, at best, after having failed at almost everything. Four years later he was one of the most powerful men on earth, supreme commander of the greatest army ever assembled, and heir apparent to the presidency. His family remained for part of the war, although they did spend time with the general at various locations. Afterwards the town presented him with a new home at 500 Bouthillier St.* on August 19, 1865, at a DeSoto House reception. This was one of four houses that wealthy friends would provide him in Galena, Philadelphia, Washington, and New York City. He had told a reporter that he wanted to go back here and see that a decent sidewalk was built. A banner upon his arrival read, "General Here is Your Sidewalk."

Grant so hated **Johnson** that he did not want to be in Washington while the latter was president, and possibly accepted the home so he would have somewhere to go besides the capital, including during the 1868 election. This is open with period furnishings, trophies, souvenirs, and family heirlooms including china and silver used by the family in the White House. He and his family stayed at times before and after his presidency from 1879 to 1881. He was at his and **Lincoln's** close friend Elihu Washburne's home at 908 Third* when he learned he had been elected as the then youngest president ever, and left from the depot at the foot of Bouthillier near the current visitor center. **McKinley** spoke at the **Grant** sites 1899. **TR** visited in 1900 and spoke at Turner Hall, 115 S. Bench.

GALESBURG • **Taylor** left his family here to command at Fort Armstrong. **Lincoln** spoke on August 24, 1858, at the Bancroft House, located south of Bernen Street between Prairie and Kellogg Streets, just north of the depot and railroad tracks, still used. The depot site is marked at the end of Depot Street east of Knox College.

The fifth **Lincoln**-Douglas debate was on a temporary platform at the east side of Old Main on the Knox College* on South Street, the only building associated with the debates still standing. A large procession accompanied **Lincoln** on October 7, 1858, to the home of Mayor Henry Sanderson at the SE corner of Simmons and Broad, now the library* site. He probably ate here and with Mrs. Abram S. Bergen on Main four doors west of the NW corner with Cedar Street. **McKinley** visited the debate site and 560 N. Prairie in 1899.

Five-year-old **Reagan** lived first in an apartment at 1260 North Kellogg (1915), then across the street in a house at 1219 (1915–8). He went to the still-standing Silas Willard School at 495 E. Fremont and the Disciples church on Northwest Street.

JACKSONVILLE • **Lincoln** made his first strong anti-slavery speech in the Square; the courthouse was then at the northwest corner. **Lincoln** and Douglas were involved in many legal cases and speeches over the years at this site, now known as "Central Park," a block east of the present 1868 courthouse. On March 16, 1840, he spoke here and at the Market House, arguing corruption in the Van Buren administration. Evidently no markers in town relate to **Lincoln. Grant** and his forces camped on the way to Missouri, as marked on the square and fair grounds. **Lincoln** and **Van Buren** were entertained at Duncan Park, 4 Duncan Place at State and Webster, west of the square.

John Hardin's home is marked at the NE corner of E. State and Hardin, just east of Our Savior Church Rectory at 462 E. State and Brown Streets. He succeeded **Lincoln's** law partner Stuart in Congress and became **Lincoln's** rival in the 1846 congressional election. **Lincoln** came to confer in the fall of 1845 about running for Congress and told him that he expected him to abide by an informal agreement to serve only one term. It appeared that Hardin would run again, but he withdrew, joined the army and was killed in Mexico. **Lincoln** attended the funeral here.

On March 21, 1854, **Lincoln** was at the Mansion House on North Main across from the courthouse. From August 25 to 27, 1854, he stayed with future Governor Richard Yates on East State, where "he was always welcome," just west of where Yates Street would dead-end if it ran as far as State. A flat monument on the north side of State in front of McMurray College marks the spot. On February 11, 1859, he made one of several presentations of his unsuccessful "Lectures on Discoveries and Inventions" at the Congregational church, then known as Union Hall, on the east side of the square about midway between State and Morgan, set back from the street. Afterward he was a guest of honor at a tea party a block north at "C" Alley and Court.

LINCOLN • This was the only town named for him with his knowledge and consent. The first courthouse was in Postville Park, where **Lincoln** engaged in horseshoe pitching and other games. It is now the Postville Courthouse Shrine and Museum,* 915 Fifth St. off U.S. 66N. Once when

Lincoln christened the new town of Lincoln, Illinois, the only town named for him while alive, with watermelon juice at this site, reenacted later by Ford.

Lincoln was absent when due in court, the sheriff found him here playing townball. The present 1953 structure is a replica of the original now in Greenfield Village, Dearborn, Michigan.

The county seat from 1847 until 1853 was Mt. Pulaski, ten miles southeast on Route 121, but a more central location was needed after the railroad came. So three partners acquired land and granted the railroad a right of way through a potential town site with **Lincoln** preparing the legal documents. The promoter bestowed the name of **Lincoln**, and **Lincoln** christened the site with watermelon juice poured from a tin cup on August 29, 1853, apparently with son Robert. This spot is marked at the modern Amtrak station, Sangamon and Broadway. **Lincoln's** funeral train stopped on May 3, 1865, under an evergreen arch with the words, "With Malice toward none, with charity for all." **Ford** rededicated the town with watermelon juice and a tin cup at the same spot on October 16, 1976.

The 1905 Logan County Courthouse at Pulaski and McLean Streets stands on the site of two buildings where **Lincoln** practiced law and acted as judge for the absent Judge David Davis. The first structure marked on the NE corner was used from 1854 until it burned in 1857, destroying most of the records of **Lincoln's** practice at all three county locations. Lawyers then used the Christian church on Pekin between Kickapoo and McLean as a courtroom, now a parking lot. He spoke twice at the later courthouse for presidential candidate John C. Frémont. **Reagan** spoke from the sidewalk plaza on the north side in 1980, commenting that polite society looked down on **Lincoln** because he told too many jokes, but he shook the world by concentrating himself and his nation to liberty.

Lincoln often visited the Old Primm Store and post office on the NE corner of Fifth and Washington, a home at the corner of Delavan and 400 Kickapoo, and Deskins Tavern, corner of Fifth and Madison, all marked. Leonard Volk met **Lincoln** in front of the Lincoln House, 501 Broadway on July 16, 1858, and arranged to make **Lincoln's** life mask. A plaque marks the lot at 523 Pulaski, of the few pieces of real estate **Lincoln** owned. James Primm found **Lincoln** in New York City in 1857 and got him to guarantee a loan that he was unable to pay. The lot was in settlement of the debt when **Lincoln** paid the creditor. Once when **Lincoln** came to examine his property he found an unauthorized shed and asked the police magistrate who was responsible. The official told **Lincoln** that some fellow whom **Lincoln** knew needed room for his horses. **Lincoln** then explained that he felt the fellow ought to pay the taxes since he was benefiting and **Lincoln** was not. The magistrate then confessed that he was the one.

MARSHALL • **Lincoln** made speeches in the square, practiced law, and stayed at the Archer House,* as did **Cleveland**.

MATTOON • **Lincoln** stayed at the Pennsylvania House on September 17, 1858, and spent the day in town. **Lincoln** probably spoke at the Essex House several times and stopped on his way to see his stepmother in 1861. It was the depot at the SW junction of the tracks, now the NW corner of the tracks and bridge across the street from the Pennsylvania House to the south. The tracks running northeast have been lowered below street level as they pass through town now, and the east-west tracks have been removed. Two **Grant** markers at the depot and about a hundred feet east note that he, without uniform or commission, mustered in the Seventh District Regiment on May 15, 1861, and took command of his first Civil War troops on June 15.

MONMOUTH • **Reagan** lived from 1917 until 1919 at three houses including 218 S. Seventh, 1918–9. He went to Central, now Lincoln Elementary while his father worked at 208 S. Main.

MOUNT PULASKI • The Greek Revival Courthouse* was built in 1847 at the cost of $3000 when Postville was succeeded as county seat. **Lincoln** helped persuade voters to move back to a more central location, the town of Lincoln. *The History of Logan County* comments: "Abraham **Lincoln** was present oftener in this building than in any other in the county and during the existence of the county seat in Mount Pulaski, he was on one side or the other of every important case on the docket. Every plank in the structure is therefore sacred with historical significance." The small two-story structure is only 30 by 40 feet. One of **Lincoln's** cases involved an alleged patent for a "horological cradle," which, **Lincoln** explained to Judge Davis, would not "like some of the glib talkers you and I know ... stop until it runs down."

During court days **Lincoln** stayed often in private homes, including the middle of the 100 block of North Marian, west side, and on the west side of the square. He was also at the Mt. Pulaski House Inn (NW corner of the square), where his friend Samuel C. Parks lived. In 1860 Parks sent his copy of Howell's campaign biography, now displayed in the Lincoln Museum in Springfield, for **Lincoln** to read and correct. **Lincoln's** pencil comments are clearly seen.

NEW SALEM • **Lincoln** floated through in the spring of 1831 accompanied by his half brother and cousin on the way to New Orleans with a load of goods for Denton Offutt. The raft got stuck and was freed with town help and **Lincoln's** ingenuity. He liked the town and Offutt decided to open a store with **Lincoln** employed. **Lincoln** arrived back in July 1831, before Offutt, and boarded in the cabin of John Camron (also spelled "Cameron"), located where the museum* is now. He cast his first ballot here on August 1, 1831, at the polls in Camron's home.

The New Salem State Park is just south of Petersburg with most of the cabins of **Lincoln's** friends reconstructed near their original locations. **Lincoln** spent time at many places around the community including homes of Mentor Graham, Bowling Greene, and Jack Armstrong outside the village, and with the Camrons, the Offutt Store, Rutledges, Burners, and others. He worked at Offutt's and the Hill and McNeil store, the center of activity and "headquarters for all political discussions." Offutt's was located on the bluff above the mill about fifty feet from Bill Clary's store or tavern, which served local toughs from nearby Clary's Grove. Showoff Offutt bragged about the strength of his clerk, producing an inevitable wrestling match between the stores, with **Lincoln** either winning or holding his own, gaining mutual respect and friendship, and establishing himself as a popular member of the community.

Lincoln worked at odd jobs at the sawmill, splitting rails, and clerking in several stores after Offutt's failed. The schoolteacher Mentor Graham helped him develop speaking skills, and he ran for the legislature, winning most of the local votes. But the Black Hawk War broke out in April

1832 during the election, and **Lincoln** joined up at the Scott farm on Richland Creek, nine miles southwest. He stated later that his election as militia captain gave him as much satisfaction as anything that ever happened. Scott's was about two miles east of Pleasant Plains, and north of Route 125, just northeast of Claysville, west of County Road 11W with County Road 6AN running through it with the NE curve in the road forming part of the eastern boundary.

When he returned he went into business with a preacher's drunkard son and was awarded the local postmaster's job, allowing him to read newspapers and get free mail. Once **Lincoln** walked six miles to the Hornbuckle house, just SW of the intersection of Clemens and Harris Roads, about 1.5 miles west of Athens, to return the overage when he accidentally overcharged several cents. He loafed and studied on a knoll nearby as the town and store dwindled. His partner Berry died, and **Lincoln** took years to pay off the debts. He stayed with Graham for about six months, learning trigonometry, geometry, and logarithms to become a surveyor. As deputy surveyor he surveyed many area farms and towns including the future county seat, Petersburg. Graham's home was due west of the village park, about ½ mile south of Lake Petersburg at a private drive on the east side of South Shore Road and south of Ill. 550, about 100 feet east of a lone tree.

A "literary society" or debating club met in the Rutledge Tavern, where **Lincoln** entertained with stories, original verses, and debates on local issues and had some sort of relationship with nineteen-year-old Ann. She was to be married to another in the fall of 1832, but her intended left town "to bring his parents there" and did not write for months. She expressed her anxiety to the young clerk at the post office. Naturally two young people in a small town grew closer. Rutledge went bankrupt and moved to a farm at Sand Ridge, about seven miles north of New Salem. Many believe that **Lincoln** fell deeply in love, courted, and then proposed to Ann before going to the legislature in late 1834. She became ill, probably from typhoid, and lingered until she died August 25, 1835, with **Lincoln** alone at her bedside.

He then went into a deep depression, supposedly threatening to kill himself, and is quoted saying, "I can never be reconciled to have the snow and rains and storms beat upon her grave." He walked many times to her grave. (See Petersburg for these sites.) Bowling Greene, a sort of father figure, took him into his home, where his melancholia remained and deepened throughout his life. Their home was due north of the village across the road north of the east end of the camping ground at New Salem, now a depression or gully on the north side of Ill. 550 (South Shore Drive), at the top of the hill west of Ill. 97 and just northwest of a private park road into a maintenance area on the south side of the road.

PEORIA • **Lincoln** came here often even though Peoria was not on the Eighth Circuit where he generally practiced law. He spoke in the courtroom and on the grounds, Main and Adams, for Harrison, Clay, and Taylor during their presidential campaigns. He crossed the ferry at the foot of Franklin and ate at Fulton House, Fulton and Adams. During the middle of October 1844, he participated in heated debate at the Main Street Presbyterian, about a block and a half north of the courthouse on the east side of Main, just north of the alley between Jefferson and Madison. He stayed at the Peoria House, east side of Adams at Hamilton. On October 5, 1858, he stayed at the Clinton House at Fulton and Adams. He is claimed to have stayed "many nights" at Liberty and Jefferson, and told stories at the Market House on Washington between Main and Hamilton.

He began his race for the presidency at the Courthouse Square on October 16, 1854, where a tablet and statue at the SE corner of Jefferson and Main commemorate the site of his first great speech, and his longest, at over 17,000 words. Here he reportedly denounced slavery publicly for the first time. The crowd came to see Douglas, who did not have to let **Lincoln** reply. But he did not object when **Lincoln** told the crowd to go home and eat, then return for his remarks that turned out to be about three hours long.

PETERSBURG • **Lincoln** was hired to complete the town survey as noted by a plaque set in the pavement at the SE corner of Jackson and Seventh, on the SW corner of the square where he began. He spent most of March 1836 finishing the survey and planning the town, including Bennett's Addition, running along Cherry Street between Fourth and Seventh. **Lincoln** shopped at his friend John Bennett's store and stayed with him frequently, about four blocks northwest of the courthouse at 313 N. Ninth, where he made a speech on the foundation as the house was being built. Petersburg became the county seat and was on **Lincoln's** Eighth Judicial Circuit from 1839 until 1847. The courthouse was then on the northeast corner on the square at Jackson and Sixth, Routes 97 and 123, where **Lincoln** practiced law and made speeches. He often stopped at the Menard House, NE corner of Sixth and Jackson.

One of the mysteries of **Lincoln's** life is his relationship with Ann Rutledge. After his death, law partner William Herndon dedicated his life to collecting information and documenting **Lincoln's** life. He then gave lectures and wrote, insisting that Ann was **Lincoln's** lost and only love. (See New Salem.) The grave of Ann was relocated to the Oakwood Cemetery south of Washington and Oakland Streets in May 1890 from an almost inaccessible original location, maybe partly to help sales in a new cemetery and partly to provide for perpetual care of her memory. **Lincoln** visited her grave in the Old Concord Cemetery about four miles away, then along the mail road. A marker there notes, "Abraham **Lincoln** made many pilgrimages alone to this sacred spot. He often said, 'My heart is buried there with Ann Rutledge.'" Other markers note, "Where **Lincoln** wept," and quote **Lincoln**: "I can not bear to think of her out there alone." The spot is north on Rte. 97 three miles from the courthouse to a narrow "Lincoln Trail Road," just north of the Worthington Road, running east and west, the only road crossing the highway between here and Atterbury. Go north on Lincoln Trail about a half-mile to a narrow private road west with an unmarked "path" a few yards north leading east along an easy "path" about a half-mile between cornfields to the high flagpole and fenced cemetery. Ann was buried with her family in a plot neglected for many years, but now well marked and maintained when visited in 1999 and 2006. Other friends of **Lincoln** are also here, including Jack Armstrong.

Ann's home was northwest on the "Lincoln Trail Road" about a mile past Atterbury Road and just north of Concord Creek along several sharp turns to a sign in a yard about a half-mile south of White Crossing Road on Lincoln Trail Road. The sign reads: "On this very spot stood the log

Lincoln visited his sweetheart, Ann Rutledge, at her grave in Old Concord Cemetery, now in the middle of corn fields.

cabin in which Ann Rutledge died, Aug. 25, 1835. On the hillside to the west stood a large oak tree under which Abraham **Lincoln** wept bitterly after leaving the sick room of Ann Rutledge, where their last communication was held."

PITTSFIELD • This town claims more original homes with documented **Lincoln** visits than any other. Many sites are marked and illuminated by available radio presentations.

Lincoln tried at least thirteen cases at the courthouse, Washington (Route 106), Madison, Monroe and Adams Streets. A marker on the southwest side commemorates many appearances of **Lincoln**, and a boulder shows the site of "decidedly the largest gathering of people that ever occurred here," **Lincoln's** speech of October 1, 1858. After the two-hour speech a friend asked for a picture, and **Lincoln** posed for the itinerant ambrotyper, Calvin Jackson.

Lincoln often visited at 626 W. Washington Street, another home west of the library at about 219 West Adams, and many times at the home of John Shastid, 326 E. Jefferson. Shastid made his son break out laughing when he told **Lincoln** that he was nothing but a hog. He introduced **Lincoln** to John Nicolay, later his presidential secretary, at the newspaper office on the east side of the square. Nicolay introduced him to John Hay, another secretary and biographer.

Lincoln stopped September 30, 1858, at the pretentious home of Colonel William Ross, a mile east of the courthouse on the south side of Washington at Washington Court. He was a dinner guest on at least one occasion in Reuben Scanland's home at the NW corner of West and Washington. A procession traveled from here taking **Lincoln** to the courthouse with 100 girls dressed in white. **Lincoln** possibly stayed and surely visited with his friend Milton Hay at the NE corner of West and Washington where Hay's nephew, John, moved at age twelve to attend Thomson Academy. Other homes and sites are marked around the town.

PONTIAC • **Lincoln** first came to Pontiac in 1840, drenched to the skin, to the county's first circuit court term. Court was held in a cabin on the banks of the river on the east side of town, and he stayed in a cabin, now a parking lot by the Mill Street Bridge. Most of the court records from **Lincoln's** law practice have been lost.

In 1855 **Lincoln** was marooned here when his train was mired in a snow bank at nearby Cayuga. Newspapers relate that the passengers "were in imminent danger of freezing to death or dying of starvation" until rescuers hurried to the site to carry passengers to town in snow sleds. **Lincoln** then stayed with John McGregor at the NE corner of Oak and Madison, where he came when he rode the circuit. His hostess refused payment, but the two young daughters did not when he gave them a gold dollar each. He ate in a home at 633 W. North Street.

In 1860, he stayed with Jason W. Strevell in a house still at 401 W. Livingston. Strevell asked **Lincoln** to stand in his stocking feet next to a door casting where his height was marked, six feet four inches. When his son moved to Utah many years later, he took this as a **Lincoln** memento. During this visit he addressed the Young Men's Literary Association at the Presbyterian church at the NW corner of Mills and Livingston.

ROCHESTER • **Lincoln** traveled the road from Springfield to Decatur many times, south of the Sangamon River, through Bolivia and Mt. Auburn, stopped at many taverns and surveyed farms along what is now Routes 556, 2, and 28. He came here on June 17, 1842, as part of a committee to welcome former President **Van Buren** in the Doty Home, located about two blocks east of the current City Hall, just before a dip in the road, near the funeral parlor at 200 E. Main. **Van Buren** said his sides were sore from laughter from **Lincoln's** well-known humor. **Lincoln** spoke later at the top of the hill opposite this home and probably at other times.

Lincoln gave a temperance lecture in 1846 at the South Fork School, now the site of a church marked about three and a half miles south and just east of town, south of Ill. 29, on county roads 7S and 7.5, just west of the 8E intersection.

SPRINGFIELD • The **Lincoln** Home,* Eighth and Jackson, was built in 1839 for Rev. Charles Dresser, who married the **Lincolns** in 1842. The family moved during the first week in May 1842 to what was the edge of town and lived here until 1861 except while he was in Congress. The home, displayed as of 1860, was changed beginning in 1846, with the north porch being removed and a

Opposite: **Lincoln lived in this Springfield home, where three of his sons were born and one died. Many presidents have visited and spoken on the site.**

back bedroom added that is thought to have been the **Lincolns'** bedroom where the rear of the double parlor is now. Eddie, Willie, and Tad were probably born there, and Eddie died there. The front formal parlor, separated by a wall and door from 1846 until 1856, was only for guests and clients. There was always room for bedrooms upstairs in front on the north and south sides, although the ceiling was somewhat lower.

The home was enlarged to include two full stories in 1856. Now all of the bedrooms were upstairs and a dining room was created. The marital bedrooms were separated, with **Lincoln's** in the northwest front, also his home office. His writing desk and shaving mirror are still here with the mirror hung so that he could look straight into it at his 6' 4" height. He used it every morning to shave and straighten his unruly hair. Mary's bedroom adjoined, maybe half of a master suite.

A ten-member committee came to the home on May 19, 1860, to officially inform him of his nomination. Before leaving they sold furniture and burned many personal letters and items that would be treasured today. On their last day in their home, the **Lincolns** held a grand public levee for maybe "thousands" as reported, who greeted **Lincoln** in the center of the parlor. Many presidents have visited. **Taft** was shown outside, then **Eisenhower** and **Hoover** went inside; **FDR** came by the front. **Ford** was the first president to give a talk here.

The two blocks on Eighth between Edwards and Capitol Streets have been preserved with many original structures frequented by the **Lincolns**, restored to their 1860 appearances. These include Julia Sprigg's home at 507 Eighth. She was a widow with seven children and close friend of Mrs. Lincoln. Tad was a frequent visitor and would hide under the furniture when his father came looking for him, then squeal with delight when found.

The **Lincolns** often visited Mary's sister's family, the C.M. Smiths, at 603 S. Fifth,* on the corner of Edwards, across from the governor's mansion. The president-elect may have begun his first inaugural speech here to avoid the crowds and continued composition at Smith's store. Poet Vachel Lindsay later lived here, and it is open honoring him. **Lincoln** also frequently visited Smith's brother's home at the NE corner of Jackson and Seventh where the Visitor Center now is.

The Illinois Governor's Mansion is located between Jackson, Edwards, Fourth, and Fifth Streets. The 1855 section of the new mansion is at the north end and was the center of Springfield social life where **Lincoln** attended many parties. Governor William H. Bissell's daughter wrote that **Lincoln** came often for quiet talks with her father, sometimes bringing Willie and Tad, who apparently always made themselves at home wherever they were. Once they climbed through a window and hung out through a bay window roof enjoying the fright of those trying to get them down. **Lincoln** was unofficially a behind-the-scenes strategist and chief legal advisor for the governor. **TR** ate here in 1903 while visiting the **Lincoln** monuments and was there before 1900, in 1900, and 1901. Other visitors to the Capitol, Mansion, and **Lincoln** sites, including the tomb, were **Grant, Hayes** (1879), **B. Harrison, Wilson, Hoover, Taft, Eisenhower** (1954), and **FDR. TR** spoke in front of the prominent Lincoln statue on the Capitol grounds.

The **Lincolns** were married on November 4, 1842, in Ninian Edwards' house, originally standing on an entire block located at the south end of the new Capitol Building begun in 1868. Old maps show the exact location to be where Jackson and First would have intersected if they were extended. It had a Second Street address. As seen in old photographs, the site was in the present parking lot between the Howlett and Capitol Buildings. Mary stayed here when she came to Springfield. Of course the **Lincolns** were here many times where Mary lived late in life and died as the new Capitol was being built next door.

Lincoln used the Chicago and Alton Station many times on the east side of Third between Jefferson and Washington, marked on the current depot. He introduced former President **Fillmore** to a large crowd on June 14, 1854. **Lincoln** had been introduced to **Fillmore** in 1848 in Albany. **Lincoln** was too busy to stop by to see the Prince of Wales, the future Edward VII, when he also made a stop in the fall of 1860, or felt like he should not initiate a meeting. **Lincoln's** body was received here on his last journey home. President **Johnson**, General **Grant**, and many other dignitaries arrived here in 1866 to pay homage. **FDR** also arrived here.

Just north was First Presbyterian at 302 E. Washington. Mary had been raised a Presbyterian, but joined her sister and family at St. Paul's Episcopal until after her marriage. When Eddie died, the minister of First Presbyterian conducted the funeral after previously talking with the **Lincolns** and making a lasting impression. The **Lincolns** became regulars at the Sunday service. **Lincoln** bought, not rented, a pew after Mary joined the church on April 13, 1852, the first church she had ever joined. The boys attended Sunday school. Tad was baptized here on his second birthday and eulogized after his death in 1871. Governor Chase of Ohio, later secretary of the treasury and chief justice, sat with **Lincoln** on January 6, 1861. The pew now is at the present church, NW corner of Capitol and Seventh, where the congregation moved in 1872.

The **Lincolns** moved on their wedding night to the Globe Tavern (or hotel) at 315 East Adams, the nicest place **Lincoln** had yet lived, but Mary's worst. **Lincoln** was vice president of a celebration here on October 5, 1836. Robert was born here August 1, 1843. A few months later they moved to 214 S. Fourth until May 1844. They stayed here before leaving for Washington in 1847 and after returning, since they rented their home. When **Lincoln** left for Congress in late November 1848, the family continued at the hotel until reunited on May 31, 1849.

The St. Nicholas Hotel still occupies 400 E. Jefferson at Fourth in a newer building, now an apartment house. **Lincoln** attended many social events here, used it as an office while preparing to leave for the presidency, and sat for a sculpture now in the Old State Capitol. **Johnson** and a number of generals and cabinet members, including Generals **Grant**, McClernard, and Custer, Secretaries Seward and Welles, and Admiral Farragut, stayed here when they came to pay homage to **Lincoln** at his temporary tomb on September 7, 1866. **Johnson** was booed when he tried to speak from the balcony. Presidents **Kennedy** and **Truman** were here in the 20th century.

Lincoln waited for election returns at the Chenery House on the NE corner of Fourth and Washington. **Grant** moved in when it looked like a civil war was coming. He tried to find a place for himself, almost gave up and moved back to Galena when Governor Yates came by to ask him to become an aide. The **Lincoln** family moved here on February 6, 1861, and lived until Feb. 11. The NW corner of the street is the site of the Johnson Building that served as **Lincoln's** office from the end of December 1860 until February 11, 1861. **Lincoln** used the governor's office in the Capitol when not needed before the legislature convened.

When the capital was moved to Springfield, the House first met in the Methodist church at the SE corner of Fifth and Monroe. **Lincoln** was here in 1840 when he abruptly jumped out the window to avoid a quorum call when he realized his party was not well-represented for a vote.

The Melvin Drug Store, NW corner of Fifth and Washington, was frequented by **Lincoln**, who liked to play checkers with the owner, a neighbor. **Lincoln** transferred his business here while president. **Lincoln's** first law office (marked) in 1837 was at 109 N. Fifth, where he began practice with Major John T. Stuart, whom he had met in the Black Hawk War. Stuart became friends with Captain **Lincoln**, and encouraged him to consider law as a profession, giving him free access to his legal library. **Lincoln's** friend, Dr. Anson G. Henry, had an office next door. **Lincoln's** brother-in-law Dr. William Wallace was on the first floor with his medical office and drug business with partner J.R. Diller. The drug stores here and later were favorite loafing places for **Lincoln**. The County Circuit Court was located on the first floor while **Lincoln's** second-floor office faced the front and served as a jury room. The ceiling contained a trap door opening below, similar to the Tinsley Building, discussed later.

Lincoln had seven law offices at six locations. The second office was across the street from the first described above, at 106 N. Fifth (marked), with Stephen T. Logan, for a firm formed in May 1841. The firm moved around January 1844 to the Tinsley Building, where **Lincoln** had two offices including one with William Herndon. Two other sites are not generally known. About 1850, the **Lincoln** and Herndon law firm moved to the south side of Adams Street midway between Fourth and Fifth. Herndon had been elected city clerk, and the firm then took over that office for their work also. About two years later, they occupied 110 North Fifth, remaining until 1856, when they moved to their last office over what had been Speed's Store (marked) at the SW corner of Fifth and Washington facing the square.

When **Lincoln** moved to town on April 15, 1837, he wandered in to buy supplies and asked Joshua Speed if he knew where he could stay. He admitted, though, that he had no money to pay rent, and if his legal experiment were not a success, he would never be able to pay. Speed offered to share his room and bed. **Lincoln** continued to trade at the combination store and bank there. Herndon lived here shortly and called the store "**Lincoln's** headquarters" in the late 1830s, a sort of informal literary and debating society where men told stories, read each other's poems and writings, and debated politics and religion.

In 1856, the firm moved to the same building in

Lincoln had two law offices in the Tinsley Building in Springfield.

a back room law office on the second floor that they occupied until **Lincoln** left for Washington. The twenty-by-twenty-two-feet space was about 30 feet from the corner of Washington, called "the dingiest and most untidy law-office in the United States, without exception." Herndon wrote that **Lincoln** frequently brought the "little devils" (Willie and Tad). "They would take down the books, empty ash buckets, coal ashes, inkstands, papers, gold pens, letters etc. etc. in a pile and then dance on the pile. **Lincoln** would say nothing, so abstracted was he, and so blinded to his children's faults."

During his single years, **Lincoln** boarded with William Butler at the SW corner of Madison and Third, and evidently paid nothing during these five years, either for food or clothes that Butler bought. He moved here after Speed left Springfield, and lived from January 1841 until November 1842. When Butler's son asked where he was going before his wedding, **Lincoln** responded, "To hell, I suppose."

Lincoln came to a jewelry store in the Chatterton Building on the west side of the square, one-third of the block north of Adams, on his wedding day to buy the ring that Mary always wore and was buried with. The building was rebuilt after a fire in 1855 and is one of the town's few original buildings with **Lincoln** associations. He frequented the building and came to James Conkling's office on May 18, 1860, stretched out on a short settee, and received his first-hand impressions of the convention meeting in Chicago. Conkling was optimistic, unlike **Lincoln**, who stated that had better go back to his office and practice law. An upper floor was occupied by Christopher Smith German, who there on January 13 and February 9, 1861, took the last known photographs of **Lincoln** in Springfield.

Lincoln and sons frequented Watson's Saloon site, 514 Adams, an ice cream and snack parlor where he may have been when he received word that he had carried New York, assuring election. David H. Donald traces his activity waiting for election reports from the Capitol, to here, and then back to the local source, the telegraph office. Here he was first called "Mr. President" by an enthusiastic crowd. **Lincoln** traded in C.S. Smith's Store next door, where he used the third-floor office to write much of his inaugural address. The store had been part of the Tinsley Building, and was remodeled, or extensively reconstructed.

The Tinsley Building, now known as the **Lincoln** and Herndon Law Office,* is at the SW corner of Sixth and Adams, the only remaining original law office building. It appears much as it did when built in 1840. **Lincoln** moved in 1844 with Logan. Until around 2006, it was thought that his office was "probably" in the front of the third floor, next to the jury room, with windows facing north to the Old State Capitol and also to the east. **Lincoln** continued to occupy the office after his partnership with Herndon began. Among others, **Taft** visited the office, home, tomb, and other **Lincoln** sites. Exactly what space was used and when is still debated, but it is now thought that the law offices were in the rear one-third and extended next door to Smith's store. The store was probably also in what is now called "**Lincoln's** office." The other half of the building, identical but now missing, was on the west side. Here, in his brother-in-law's store, **Lincoln** completed his First Inaugural Address, probably at the desk now in the restored law office. **Nixon** used the desk when it was in the Old Capitol.

The door from the street leading to **Lincoln's** office was just north of the restored post office on Sixth Street where he got his mail. The stairway up was much narrower then, but at the same location. The original wooden floors are still here, as is a trap door that opened into the federal court below, allowing **Lincoln** to listen to the proceedings. This second-floor courtroom was the only federal court in the state until 1848. After **Lincoln** left for Congress in 1847, Herndon moved to a smaller room.

In the center of the square is the reconstructed Old State Capitol.* The original was begun in 1837 after the 1831 courthouse here was torn down. It served as Capitol for about 40 years, and was **Lincoln's** focal point for activities in Springfield. His last session in the legislature was in the building in 1840 and 1841. The House was the scene of many important speeches, including **Lincoln's** political rebirth in October 1854. Here he answered the powerful "Little Giant" Stephen Douglas's defense of the Kansas-Nebraska Bill, reopening the question of slavery extension, and later Douglas's position on the Dred Scott Supreme Court decision declaring that Negroes could not be citizens and that the Missouri Compromise was unconstitutional.

Lincoln was the front-runner for the U.S. Senate election in 1855 but lost as the legislature elected Lyman Trumbull, the husband of Mary's best friend (soon to be former best friend), as they both watched from the gallery. On June 16, 1858, **Lincoln** delivered his most famous pre-presidency speech, discussing a "House Divided," arguing that the country could not continue forever half slave and half free. This was the last speech at the Republican State Convention that nominated **Lincoln** for the Senate, and the first speech of the campaign that gained him national reputation. The president's body was placed here on May 3 and 4, 1865, and viewed by an estimated 75,000. (Senators were elected by the legislature, so the campaign was for Republican candidates for that body.)

During the 1860 campaign and after his election, the governor allowed him to use his offices and reception room for the never-ending throng. The portraits of Lafayette in the Senate Chamber and Washington in the House were hung in the building in 1841. Various state offices were frequented by **Lincoln**. The State Supreme Court, located on the first floor, was where **Lincoln** had his greatest impact as a lawyer, and maybe his greatest success. He tried more than 200 cases and spent countless hours in this only full law library on the circuit. **McKinley**, **Wilson**, **Ike**, and **LBJ** spoke at the Old Capitol, the latter two on the south side grounds. **Nixon** used **Lincoln's** desk, where it is claimed **Lincoln** wrote his First Inaugural Address, to sign a bill here designating the four-block area around the Lincoln Home as a National Historic Site.

The Supreme Court Law Library is across the central hall from the State Library. The first person to borrow a book from the latter was **Lincoln**, who made liberal use of both libraries to study, brief cases, play chess, and tell stories for hours in an informal "men's club." His famous Cooper Union Address and others were researched and prepared here. A fellow lawyer remembered that he never knew a night when **Lincoln** did not put in an appearance with an endless supply of new stories and seemed never to tell the same one twice.

About two months after **Lincoln** left for Washington in 1861, **Grant** arrived and worked in the building for a while before moving his troops off to glory. It would not be until March 1864 that the two Illinoisans would meet in the White House. The building was later remodeled, enlarged, and sold to the county when the new Capitol Building opened. It was almost destroyed in 1899 but preserved due to historical importance. In the mid–1960s it was torn down and reconstructed to its original size, using original outside façade and a new interior to match the original. All offices and areas mentioned are open as a museum and memorial.

LINCOLN-HERNDON LAW OFFICES
ADVERTISING

LINCOLN-HERNDON LAW OFFICES

The American House was directly across from the Tinsley Building at the SE corner of Adams and Sixth. The 1838 hotel, the largest and finest in the town, was where the **Lincolns** attended many social functions. He was one of the managers of a "Cotillion Party" held here in late 1839 and possibly here when he first met Mary. She told the story that he had blurted out, "Miss Todd, I want to dance with you in the worst way." And she said, "He certainly did!" Exact dates and locations of that event vary and include the Edwards' home. **Lincoln** was probably here at a reception to honor former President **Van Buren** on June 17, 1842, since he was on the welcoming committee and assigned to escort him.

Lincoln would occasionally attend services at the First Baptist, then at the SW corner of Seventh and Adams, where he made a speech on January 27, 1838. His barber was Billy (Florville) the Barber, between Sixth and Seventh on the north side of Adams, sometimes called a "clubhouse" and "second home" for **Lincoln**. He spoke several times at Cook's Hall, 122 S. Sixth, including a repetition of his lecture on Discoveries, April 26, 1860. Corneau and Diller's Drug Store was in the middle of Sixth on the east side north of Cook's, just south of an alley then between Adams and Washington. **Lincoln's** bank from 1853 until his death was located at 104–108 S. Sixth, with Greek pillars dating to **Lincoln's** era. He made deposits as president. This is now Bank One and displays **Lincoln's** ledger. Beginning in 1846 the courthouse was located at 100 S. Sixth at the corner of Washington; here **Lincoln** handled numerous cases. The 1860 presidential election voting was on the second floor. From his temporary office in the Governor's Chamber, **Lincoln** watched voters going and coming all day on November 6, and went to vote himself when he noticed a lull in the crowds. He refused to vote for himself.

Lincoln tried more than ninety cases in the federal court on the NE corner of Sixth and Washington after it moved here in 1855. He played handball on the north side at a vacant lot on the day that he was nominated. North of the center alley, on the east side of Sixth between Washington and Jefferson, was the office of the *Illinois State Journal*. **Lincoln** sometimes wrote editorials and articles. Accounts differ as to where **Lincoln** was when he received word of his nomination to the presidency. Some believe here, as stated in Howells' biography that **Lincoln** read and approved. **Lincoln** expert Dr. Wayne Temple strongly believes that he was then in a telegraph office in the middle of the block north of the courthouse, where Professor David Donald and others locate him when the final word of his election was received in November. On May 18, 1860, **Lincoln** had stopped here after making numerous trips to the telegraph office to check on the status of the nominating convention. While he was on the second floor, a messenger boy burst in with a telegram that **Lincoln** had won. After receiving many congratulations, he hurried home, saying, "There's a little woman down the street who would like to know something of this." But she already knew and had started the party to celebrate.

The home of Simeon Frances was at the SE corner of Sixth and Jefferson where the Abraham Lincoln Library* is now. After **Lincoln** and Mary broke up in early January 1841, they did not see one another for many months. Sometime in 1842, Simeon invited **Lincoln**, while Mrs. Frances invited Mary, to their home, where they were reunited. Mary and Abraham continued to meet here, probably so Mary's family would not find out.

Lincoln attended political meetings at the Christian church on the NE corner of Sixth and Jefferson, now the site of the Abraham Lincoln Museum,* dedicated by **George W. Bush** on April 19, 2005. The Concert Hall or Myers Hall on the top floor of the Henry C. Myers Building on the north side of the square, midway between Fifth and Sixth, was the site of **Lincoln's** lodging when he came to campaign for the legislature or visit before he moved from New Salem. On February 21, 1859, **Lincoln** gave his unsuccessful lecture there on "Discoveries." Next door just east of the middle on the north side is the site of the Buck

Opposite, top: **Lincoln's law offices were in the Tinsley Building, shown on the right. The building at the left was the site of a ball hosted by Lincoln and others for Van Buren. Here he supposedly met future wife Mary and told her that he would like to dance with her "in the worst way." Mary agreed, "He surely did."** ***Opposite, bottom:*** **The Tinsley building and Old Capitol in Springfield are where Lincoln made some of his most famous speeches. McKinley, Ike, Wilson, Nixon, and LBJ have spoken here.**

Hat Shop, an original building (marked) used by **Lincoln**. He treated his boys and their friends to nuts and candy at the Webster Grocery on the south side of Monroe between Ninth and Tenth. The Great Western (Lincoln) Depot is still located at Tenth and Monroe, on tracks where **Lincoln** loved to walk with Willie and Tad, deep in thought as the "dear little codgers" skipped from tie to tie. He left and returned to Springfield often at this building, where he made his famous "Farewell Address."

Lincoln's partner and friend Stephan Logan lived between North First and Rutledge, north of Miller, across from the hospital. The house was north of where Klein intersects Miller. **Lincoln** visited often and played marbles and games with Logan's eight children. He visited his banker, Robert Irwin, in what is now known as the Iles House,* the oldest home in Springfield. It was as the SE corner of Sixth and Cook, and now is at the NE corner of Seventh and Cook.

The **Lincoln** Tomb* is located in the center of Oak Ridge Cemetery, several blocks north of the Old Capitol, where the family, minus Robert, is buried. Many presidents including **Hayes, Benjamin Harrison, McKinley, TR,** and **Taft** visited the tomb before the reconstructed tomb was rededicated in 1931 by **Hoover. FDR** and **LBJ** visited afterwards, among others.

Grant lived at a home now at 119 S. Walnut for a short time while his headquarters were in Springfield. The original site was at Camp Yates. He stood at the well on the north side of the home at 107 S. Douglas as his troops lined up for their first expedition in the Civil War. His campsite is marked on the Old Jacksonville Road west of town. **Grant's** eleven-year-old son stayed with him for much of the war and was here also.

The State Armory on the site of the Arsenal, at the NW corner of Second and Monroe, has been the site of speeches by **TR, Hoover**, and **Truman**.

Lincoln served in the Illinois Legislature in the Old Capitol in Vandalia, Illinois, where he was sworn into the Illinois Bar.

A number of presidents have spoken at the Fair Grounds north of town, including **TR** (1903 and 1918), **Ike**, **Reagan**, and **Nixon**.

TAMPICO • **Reagan** was born in 1911 at 111 S. Main Street* above a bank, in a house long gone. His mother's labor was so long and difficult that his father, fearing for her life, set out in a blizzard to find a midwife. Finally a doctor showed up and delivered a plump baby who bellowed incessant as his father muttered, "For such a little bit of a Dutchman he makes a hell of a lot of noise." **Reagan** later said he did not think his father changed his mind any time later. As a boy he requested that he be called "Dutch" as he thought this was more masculine. After a few months the family moved to Glassburn Street, across from a park and the depot. They moved away in 1914 and back in 1919 for about a year to another apartment on Main Street.

VANDALIA • Vandalia was the second capital of Illinois. The first Capitol burned in 1823. The second was on the west side of Fourth Street just north of Gallatin. This was in the state of collapse when **Lincoln** arrived to begin his political career in late November 1834. It was replaced by the building seen today at Third and Gallatin. This Old State House* housed all three branches of government and **Lincoln's** service in three sessions from December 3, 1836, until 1839.

Lincoln and his "Long Nine" friends were largely instrumental in removing the capital to Springfield in 1839. They celebrated in Ebenezer Capp's Tavern, Fourth and Main. **Lincoln** rented rooms at 615 W. Johnson, 419 Gallatin, and in hotels on the NW and SW corners of Fourth and Gallatin. Only the Statehouse survives, which includes the Supreme Court Chamber where **Lincoln** was sworn as a member of the bar, and returned to speak September 23, 1856.

INDIANA

CORYDON • **William Henry Harrison** founded this town in 1800; it became the first state capital. He built the Branham House Tavern,* now a gift shop a block north of the square on the west side in the mid–400 block of North Capitol, and owned all the land for the first several years. The Capitol Building* is still on the east side of Capitol Avenue between Chestnut and Walnut, the town square by the courthouse. **Monroe** and **Jackson** visited together in June 1819.

FORT WAYNE • **William Henry Harrison** negotiated treaties with the Indians at counsel houses located in what is now the 300 block of Main. He also was at and worked on several forts in the downtown area, including 211 S. Barr. **Lincoln** stopped briefly at the train station on the way to his Cooper Union Address in New York in 1860.

INDIANAPOLIS • **Lincoln** first spoke here on September 19, 1859, after being entertained at the America House at 18 Louisiana Street where Union Terminal is now. He spoke in the evening at the Masonic Hall, then on the SE corner of Washington and Capital, the present site of the Hyatt Hotel. He next came on February 11, 1861, on the way to assume the presidency, at the railroad siding at Missouri and Washington. A marker on the north side of Washington between West and Senate Streets shows where he began the parade route, heading east along Washington, north along Pennsylvania, west along Ohio, and south on Illinois to the Bates House at the NW corner of Illinois and Washington, now Claypool Court. He appeared three times on the south hotel balcony and met with the legislature and public. The next morning he walked to the Governor's Mansion at the NW corner of Illinois and Market, the current location of the Adam's Mark, and then addressed the legislature. **Hayes** met **Lincoln** here to escort him to Cincinnati. The Capitol was then on the southern half of the current location, Washington and Capitol. **W. Harrison** had been there in 1832 and 1833, when the building was under construction, to meet with the legislature at the courthouse. The old building was replaced in the 1870s with a much larger one two blocks long. The funeral train carrying **Lincoln's** remains passed through the city on April 30, 1865, where 100,000 viewed them at the State House from 9:00 A.M. until 11:00 P.M.

It was probably here that Robert lost the only copy of his father's Inaugural Address, although this may have occurred elsewhere. He was told to be careful with the package, not what it was, and left it with a desk clerk. After it was found his father handed it back and just told him, "Now you keep it." Biographer David H. Donald believes that **Lincoln** did then show anger at one of his children for the only time in his life. A close friend said he never saw **Lincoln** angrier.

Benjamin Harrison moved here in 1854 and lived in several homes no longer standing, including the 600 block of North Pennsylvania (1854), corner of New Jersey and Vermont (1854–61), and the SE corner of North and Alabama (1865–75). In 1874 he built the 16-room Italianate home at 1230 N. Delaware,* where he lived until his death there in 1901. The home, one-half mile north of Washington, U.S. 40, has relics of both **Harrison** presidents. His law offices were on Washington between Meridian and Illinois (1854–5), 30½ W. Washington (1857–60), and in the Supreme Court in the Statehouse (1860–62 and 1865–81). He then had an office at 120 E. Market from 1887 until 1889. He believed that he had a reputation of "almost getting there." He was defeated twice for governor and once for the Senate after serving one term. His 1888 winning presidential campaign was run from the home, where he gave nightly speeches from the front porch. When his wife died during the losing 1892 reelection campaign he ceased electioneering, but the results were already certain. He returned home and remarried against the wishes of his children, whom he partially disinherited. His new wife was 25 years younger, and he had a child in 1897 when he was 63. His funeral, after he had lain in the rotunda of the Capitol, was at First Presbyterian, SE corner of Pennsylvania and Vermont, where he had been an elder for 40 years. His grave in Crown Hill Cemetery,* 700 West 38th, is easily found by following signs. Other **Harrison** sites include the Columbian Club, 121 Monument Circle, Union Station,* 39 Jackson Place south of George St., and James Whitcomb Riley's House,* 528 Lockerbie.

Johnson stayed at the Bates House in 1863 and spoke at the Capitol, as have **Cleveland, Reagan, Theodore Roosevelt,** and **Taft. Grant** and **Johnson** came to the Bates House in 1866. **Harding** supposedly met his mistress, Nan Britton, at the Bates, registering as "Mr. Harding and niece." He is also claimed to have been at the Claypool. **Ike** spoke at Butler University, 46th and Clarendon, in 1954.

LAFAYETTE • General **William Henry Harrison** gained his nickname and much of his political fame when he defeated Indians led by the Prophet, the brother of Tecumseh, in 1811 at Tippecanoe Battlefield,* seven miles north near State 43, just over a mile south of I-65. Tecumseh had traveled extensively to organize an Indian confederation to band together against the white man. His plan was working well until his less talented brother committed hostile acts, surprised the Americans, and provoked **Harrison's** attack when Tecumseh was absent. **Harrison** lost 179 men and was severely criticized at his handling of the campaign until it was later realized that the Indians' defeat broke the mystique and promise of a united front. His bravery was profound, as was his luck, as he had hastily mounted a black horse rather than his own, thwarting a hundred warriors who had sworn to kill the white chief on the gray mare. His aide, who did ride his horse, was killed, and is honored by a monument on the field. The Indians attacked at **Harrison**'s campground, the battlefield at the visitor center and museum.*

Grant visited a West Point classmate at 622 Main. **Taylor** marched here in 1815.

LINCOLN CITY AND GENTRYVILLE • Lincoln City, now on Route 162, was established in 1872 on the site of the **Lincoln** farm, part of which is open as the Lincoln Boyhood National Memorial.* The home site and the grave of **Lincoln's** mother are about a mile and a half east of Gentryville, a town platted in 1854. Seven-year-old Abe settled here in 1816 and lived on various unknown sites until 1830. The reproduction cabin was built from several period structures near where it was believed by old-timers that **Lincoln's** last home was, and is marked by a low rectangular wall containing the fireplace, now replaced with replica stones. This may have been a new site and fireplace that his father was working on when the family left for Illinois or was possibly where the cabin was located before moving. As in many respects, when **Lincoln** was young, no one knew he would be famous and documentation is sparse.

Lincoln's mother Nancy is buried on a hill opposite the visitor center beside her aunt and uncle who raised her. All of these died of a mysterious illness, later known to be caused by drinking milk from cows that had eaten a poisonous plant. Nancy's nephew Dennis Hanks, ten years older than Abe, moved in with the **Lincolns**, married his stepsister, and remained a friend for life and an endless source of stories, some probably true. The grave remained unmarked during Abraham's lifetime so that only an approximate spot is marked. **Lincoln** visited the site many times as a boy and probably in October 1844 when he returned to speak in the area. Probably **Lincoln** never recovered from the death of his mother. Much of his sadness and near-suicidal depressions relate to the early loss by this lonely little boy. About a year after his wife died, his father went back to Elizabethtown, Kentucky, and brought back a new wife with her three children.

Lincoln State Park* on the south side of Route 162 contains many sites of his boyhood years. The present Little Pigeon Primitive Baptist Church* incorporates the original cornerstone and stands about 90 feet to the northwest of where the original church stood when attended by the **Lincolns**. Guide maps to the area erroneously state that this is the historical site at a spot now in the middle of the graveyard, but it was then a little south of the present, larger structure. At age 12 he helped his father and others build the small church and make the pews. At 14 he was the church sexton in charge of keeping the facilities in order and supplying firewood and candles. **Lincoln's** sister's grave was one of the first. **Lincoln** worked to remember sermons to quote to his stepmother when she could not attend and would stand on a stump and recite them from start to finish to his friends and family, mimicking the gestures and voices of the preachers.

Lincoln attended three schools nearby, including several months with Andrew Crawford, 200 yards east of the church, the first time he had been to school in about four years. In 1822, he irregularly attended the James Sweeny or "Swaney" school, just southeast of the current lake in the park. Swaney was 21 and could barely read and write himself. For about six months in 1823, he attended Azel Dorsey's school near or in the church before Dorsey's building was completed. In 1830 the family moved to Illinois with the families of the two married daughters of Mrs. Lincoln. Abraham at 21 was no longer legally bound to his father, but he joined the move.

His last visit to the area was in 1844 when he revisited to campaign for Henry Clay for president. He spoke in Carlin Township to an audience of old friends at the community center about two miles west of the last home, and spent a day in Gentryville with his old employer, William Jones, and visited the area around the church and cemeteries. Jones' store site, frequented by **Lincoln**, is marked on a side road west of U.S. 231. He called at James Gentry's home, site* marked on Route 162, to the north, but little detail is known. Maps of other **Lincoln** sites are at park headquarters.

TERRE HAUTE • Fort Harrison was built here on a bluff overlooking the Wabash in 1811 by General **William Henry Harrison** and defended by Captain **Taylor** in 1812 when he repulsed an Indian attack. **Taylor** had only 16 healthy men, 34 sick ones, and a few women to fight off about 450 warriors, but held the fort with the loss of only two dead. The survivors then had to withhold a siege with little food until a relief force could reach them. The fort is marked three miles north on Fort Harrison Road and Route 41 at the Elk's Lodge near the actual site at the north end of Fifth Street.

VINCENNES • The **Lincoln** family traveled this way in 1830 while migrating to Illinois and stayed a day to see the largest town in Indiana. They probably followed the Troy-Vincennes trail passing through Polk Patch (now Selvin), Petersburg, and Monroe City, probably up present Highway 61. They saw the site of George Rogers Clark's important Revolutionary War victory over the English that captured Fort Sackville, of decisive importance to the Colonial cause and the winning of the West. Afterward Virginia claimed all the lands northwest of the Ohio and the County of Illinois was organized. The fort was just south of the current Lincoln Memorial Bridge that marks the family's Wabash River crossing point. **Franklin Roosevelt** dedicated the Clark Memorial Building* now on the site.

Lincoln enjoyed the *Western Sun* and visited the editor at Elihu Stout's Printing Office,* then on First between Perry and Buntin, where he saw his first printing press. **William Henry Harrison** brought Stout to publish the legislative laws when this was the territorial capital. A replica of the office is open near the still prominent 1804 **Harrison** Mansion, "Grouseland"* at Park and Scott, surely the grandest home **Lincoln** had yet seen. This "Red House" had served as the Territorial Capitol. A small building now at First and Harrison, moved from the original site at 217 Main, is considered the first Capitol, where **Harrison** served.

Harrison made this first brick home in Indiana

his base while territorial governor. The mansion, patterned after his Virginia birthplace, was the site where he met with an Indian delegation in the front yard. When negotiating with the great chief Tecumseh, **Harrison** ordered that a chair be brought. The servant told Tecumseh, "Warrior, your father, General **Harrison**, offers you a seat." But the leader exclaimed, as he sat on the ground, "The sun is my father, and the earth is my mother; and on her bosom will I recline." He then warned **Harrison** that he would not sit still if his lands were threatened. Eight of **Harrison**'s ten children lived here with him and four were born in the home. A hole in the window shutter in the dining room shows where a bullet entered, barely missing the future president and his young son, John, later the father of **Benjamin Harrison**. In 1812 **Harrison** was named commander in chief of the Army in the Northwest, and moved his family to North Bend, Ohio.

Fort Knox II was built in 1788 on a bluff on the Wabash, now a mile northwest of the Route 67/41 intersection on Fort Knox Road, three miles from the center of town and near the railroad tracks. **Harrison** assembled troops here, leading them to the Battle of Tippecanoe, and **Taylor** was stationed there beginning in 1811. The site is outlined with posts and well marked. His home site is marked at the NE corner of First and Hart, a few blocks west of Grouseland, where **Taylor's** daughter, Sarah Knox, was born in 1813. She later married Jefferson Davis.

Lincoln returned later to stay at 505 Main* and 111 N. Second.

IOWA

COUNCIL BLUFFS • **Lincoln** stayed at the Pacific House, located on the north side of Broadway between Main and Pearl, August 12–15, 1859. The Lincoln Monument is at Point Lookout at the head of Oakland Drive and Lafayette, near Fairview Cemetery and Sixth and "G," where **Lincoln** looked over the river. He spoke at Concert Hall, NE corner of Broadway and Sixth, and attended a reception at the Pusey home, SE corner of Willow and Sixth, First Presbyterian services held in Concert Hall, and dined in a home at 533 Willow. While here he showed an old land warrant issued for land near Schleswig on U.S. 59, given for his services as a captain in the Black Hawk War, but never filed. President Buchanan issued a second warrant in 1860.

DAVENPORT • From 1932 until 1933, **Reagan** faked play-by-play descriptions of football games on broadcasts for the radio station WOC, 800 Brady. He lived near where he took his meals at 202 E. Fourth, and went to First Christian, 510 15th.

DES MOINES • **Grant** and **McKinley** visited General William Sherman's brother at his home in the 1870s, at Woodward Avenue and 15th. **Grant** stayed at the Slavery Hotel, Fourth and Locust. **Reagan** lived at 330 Center in 1933–4 and later at 400 Center, 1934–7, when he became a Midwest celebrity by making up sports commentary from wire service statistics for the radio station WHO in 1933–4. He attended the Capitol Hill Christian, 3322 E. 25th from 1933 until 1937.

TR stayed at the Wellington, 415 Fifth, in 1901. In 1903 he spoke in Iowa at Keokuk and Waterloo. Many presidents have stayed in the Hotel Fort Des Moines, Tenth and Walnut, including **Wilson** (1919), **Harding** (1920), **Coolidge** (1922), **Hoover** (1932), **Truman** (1948), **Kennedy** (1960), **LBJ** (1960), **Nixon** (1971), **Ford** (1974, 1975), **Reagan** (1974), and the first **Bush** (1976). He visited the State Historical Museum on Sixth and Locust on October 16, 1990. All were in the Capitol, as were **FDR** (1936) and **Taft** (1909). **Wilson** attended Central Presbyterian, 3829 Grand, and **Ford** visited the State Fair, 13th and Grand.

DUBUQUE • **Grant** was a guest in the Ryan House,* 1375 Locust Street, now a restaurant.

WEST BRANCH • The **Hoover** National Historic Site contains the Presidential Library Museum, birthplace, and burial site of the first president born west of the Mississippi. **Truman** helped dedicate the library. The burial site is on a hill where **Hoover** slid down in winter. The two-room cabin birthplace at Downey and Penn* measures 14 × 20 feet, and his Quaker Meetinghouse* has been restored on Downey north of Main. The family lived in the little birthplace house for about five years after Herbert (Bertie) was born, and then moved a block south on Downey to a home now destroyed, and then to Downey and Cedar. When his father died in 1880 when he was about six, the three children moved in with relatives scattered across the country. "Bertie" moved to Pawhuska, Oklahoma, then "Indian Territory," to live about nine months with his government agent uncle and attended school with half-tamed young braves. He roamed streams and forests to acquire a lifelong love of the outdoors and returned to his mother at Downey and Cedar. When she died in 1883, he moved about a mile north of the depot on Route 2 to be with an aunt and uncle, and then was sent to live with another aunt and uncle in Oregon. The poor boy was maybe the most financially successful president, who devoted his later life to public service and helped feed 1.2 billion people after the World Wars, according to the Director of the Hoover Library.

KANSAS

ABILENE • **David Dwight Eisenhower** was born in Denison, Texas, in 1890, and moved to Kansas in 1891 to live at 112 SE Second Street, still standing. His names were later reversed to avoid confusion with his father, also "David," who had been one of the founders of nearby Hope, Kansas, before moving to Texas. In 1898 the family moved to 201 SE Fourth Street,* adjacent to the later Presidential Library and burial site. It had been the home of his uncle, a veterinarian, for whom Ike had his first job, for a penny a day, to run into town to fetch a paper. Uncle Abraham Lincoln Eisenhower left to spread the gospel, and his father bought his house, occupied by the family until 1946. They were members of a strict, fundamentalist religious group, the River Brethren, later known as Jehovah's Witnesses. Later in life Dwight rarely attended church and joined none, but supporters found him praying before the presidential nomination in Suite 600 at the Sunflower Hotel, still the town's "skyscraper" at 407 NW Third.

Dwight shared a bedroom with his five brothers in the 818-square-foot home where daily prayer and Bible study were a habit. His mother commented, "Boys are the best investment in the world. They pay the biggest dividends. The boys were our bank. We invested in them every spare penny we could save." (Another brother died in infancy at the Second Street home.) Ike loved baseball, fishing, and swimming in Mud Creek, and worked in a lumber company at 306–320 W. North Second, and at Belle Springs Creamery, marked at the SE corner of Court and Cotton, just east of the courthouse. He knew about the famous incident when Wild Bill Hickock killed a cowboy and then turned to shoot his deputy dead when he heard footsteps behind him. **Ike's** imagination no doubt envisioned the incident when he came by the site about two blocks west of the creamery at the NE corner of Cedar and Texas. As president, he urged the country to return to Hickock's code of honor as town marshal.

When **Ike** was twelve, a rare flood almost buried the town. **Ike** and his brother, Edgar, floated down the main north-south street, Buckeye, on a board as it rushed through the town in a raging torrent toward the main river. They didn't realize the danger until a stranger on a horse forced them to get off before being completely swept away. **Theodore Roosevelt** was photographed speaking in the central business district in front of the Central Hotel in May 1903, surely witnessed by 12-year-old **Ike**. **TR** also spoke then in Hays, Junction City, and Manhattan.

Eisenhower's first school was across Fourth Street at Lincoln Elementary, 308 S. Buckeye, now the visitor center site. He once developed blood poisoning from a scratch on his leg, and the doctors wanted to amputate. But he and his brothers refused to allow it, to the consternation of the doctors, causing him to miss much of a semester that he had to repeat, but he saved his future career.

It took all the money his father made just to feed the family, leaving nothing for sports equipment and other pleasures, so Mr. Eisenhower gave each boy a plot to raise vegetables to sell going door-to-door for spending money. Ike even learned a profitable skill that his mother had picked up in Texas, making tamales, and the boys had no trouble disposing of the leftovers.

After his first school he went to the Garfield School on the other side of town, 215 N. Seventh, and then went to high school in the old city hall on the SE corner of Fifth and Broadway, now the site of the new city hall. Then he went to Abilene High, where he was on the football and baseball teams with his brother, Edgar, who was two years older, but had lost time in school due to illness. Edgar was "Big Ike," and Dwight was "Little Ike," as the nickname applied to most boys named **Eisenhower**. The site of the second high school is now the Frontier Estates on the SE corner of Buckeye and Seventh, across the street from his church on the NE corner. Both historical structures are gone.

He seemed destined for greater things, but his parents could not send both boys to college. They had graduated together, and a fellow classmate predicted that Edgar would be president. (**Ike** used to tell the story of a friend who wanted to be president while he himself wanted to play professional baseball. He lamented that neither got his wish.) So Dwight spent two more years at various jobs to help Edgar, who intended then to help Dwight. His work included the creamery, where, after several promotions, he was able to work up to $90 a month for his 84-hour weeks. In his short spare time, a friend talked him into studying for admission into the U.S. Naval Academy. He worked hard for the appointment, but discovered that he would be too old (21) by the time he would have entered Annapolis, and wound up applying for West Point Military Academy, where age restrictions were more lenient. By then it was too late to get into cram school to study for entrance exams, so at age twenty, he re-entered Abilene High for several months. He came out behind another appointee, who then failed the physical exam. His pacifist mother gave her OK, but when he left it was the first time he had heard her cry.

All of the Eisenhower sons were successful. When Mrs. Eisenhower was asked here after World War II if she was proud of her famous son, she responded, "Which one?" **Ike** is buried in a $95 soldier's casket, as per his request, with his wife and infant son at the Eisenhower Library and Museum, for which he broke ground on October 13, 1959. **LBJ** and **Nixon** attended his funeral. **Reagan** and **Ford** are pictured on his porch here among the presidents to have visited.

ATCHISON • **Lincoln** spoke on December 2, 1859, at the Methodist church (destroyed), now the courthouse site, marked by a plaque at Fifth and Parallel Streets, north of the business district. A band drummed up interest and escorted **Lincoln** from the Massasoit House, 210 Main Street, to the church, where there was a full house. The Massasoit was on the NW corner of Second and Main Streets and is noted by a stone marker at Third and Main.

FORT SCOTT • the fort* was established by Taylor in 1842.

LEAVENWORTH • A number of presidents have visited Fort Leavenworth, including **Taft, Grant, McKinley, Wilson, Eisenhower** (who was assigned here in 1917 and 1925), and **Theodore Roosevelt. Truman** trained here in 1923.

Lincoln was met at the Fort Leavenworth Military Academy on December 3, 1859, and escorted to the Mansion House, SW corner of Shawnee and Fifth. The carriage is now in the Fort Leavenworth Museum. He spoke at the Stockton Hall, marked on the SW corner of Fourth and Delaware. Back at the Mansion House, he swapped stories with local men and guests who were mostly supporting William Seward for the Republican nomination. As the wood fire died in the stove on the cold night, they threw some government patent office reports into the fire and asked, "Mr. **Lincoln**, when you become president will you sanction the burning of government reports by cold men in Kansas?" **Lincoln** joked, "Not only will I not sanction it, but I will cause legal action to be brought against the offenders." This was the only reference to the presidency during the trip, which included Elwood, Troy, and Doniphan.

People heard of the speech and prevailed upon him to make the address again on December 5. In the meantime he visited and maybe stayed with Mark Delahay and his wife at Third and Kiowa. There was no hall large enough, so they gathered in front of the Planters Hotel, and he gave an "unplanned" but by now well-rehearsed address called "The largest mass meeting ever assembled on Kansas soil and the greatest address ever heard there," still considered the largest crowd ever gathered in Kansas Territory. He possibly stayed at the Planters, a city landmark for many years, where **Arthur** stayed in 1856, now a parking lot at the foot of Shawnee Street in the same block as the Riverfront Community Center.

LAWRENCE • **TR** made a whistle-stop speech in 1903 and came by on August 31 and September 1, 1910, to dedicate the John Brown Monument in Osawatomie. He also dedicated the marble drinking fountain at Ninth (Warren) and New Hampshire, and spent the night.

OSAWATOMIE • The *Kansas Historical Quarterly* calls **Theodore Roosevelt's** speech on a kitchen table here the most important ever given in Kansas. One historian called it the most radical speech ever given by an ex-president. The speech to 30,000 at John Brown Park* at Main and Tenth on August 31, 1910, was expected to be controversial. In fact he dedicated the monument to the controversial Brown without mentioning his name. The spot was near the pre–Civil War battle between proslavery forces and the abolitionist Brown. Republicans were divided over President **Taft's** policies. **TR** wanted everyone to expect a condemnation of the incumbent, and then intended to try to unite the party with a unifying policy statement for the future. It did become the policy statement of the Progressive Party. He favorably received party rebels before coming, heightening the anticipation. But this was unsuccessful as he was perceived a communist in some areas and highly anti–Taft and anti-government in others. The speech, written by others, was perceived to be anti-capitalistic, and he could not later change the minds of many that he claimed had misunderstood him. This might have cost the presidency in 1912.

TOPEKA • According to a local yarn, a huge cottonwood tree grew from a stake driven into the ground near the south and east wings of the Capitol, under which **B. Harrison, McKinley** and **Taft** spoke. But more probably, the tree was here before the stakes. It fell in the 1980s. **TR** was at the Capitol and Governor's Mansion, then at Eighth and Buchanan. **FDR** is pictured here also with his vice president campaigning in September 1932. **Taft** laid the cornerstone at the State Historical Society. **Ford** visited the Capitol in 1975 and stayed at the Ramada, I-70 and E. Sixth. Every succeeding president through **Reagan** since Governor Alf Landon lost to **FDR** in 1936 was entertained by Landon at his home, 521 Westchester Rd. **Eisenhower** waved to the crowd from the train station on June 20, 1945, having just returned from Europe. On May 17, 2004, **George W. Bush** dedicated Moore Elementary a National Historic Site. This is where the noted school desegregation case *Brown vs. Topeka* originated.

WICHITA • **Theodore Roosevelt** was at City Hall, 204 S. Main. **Franklin D. Roosevelt** was the first sitting president to visit. **Taft** spoke here on May 29, 1919, and stayed as Supreme Court justice at the home of Sen. Henry Allen, still at 255 N. Roosevelt. The common story that he got stuck in the bathtub is not believed accurate since a man this smart would have learned from all of the other times this supposedly happened, including in the White House. **Harding** made a speech at the Forum, west on Douglas where the Conference Center* now is, between the library and river. **TR** spoke there in 1912, as did TR Jr. a few years later.

Truman stayed at what is now the Broadview Radisson* at 400 W. Douglas and River. **FDR** rode from Union Station* to Lawrence Stadium* in 1936 for a major speech. The stadium is still west of the river and was said to have hosted the largest political gathering in its history when it heard **JFK** on October 22, 1960. **Wilson** was to stop at the station in 1919, but passed through without stopping. Large crowds had gathered without knowing that he had suffered a debilitating stroke. On June 15, 2007, **George W. Bush** joined in during a "heated game of [table] football" at the 21st Street Boy's and Girl's Club, 2408 E. 21st. **Clinton** toured nearby in November 1998 at 21st and Grove, a workforce training

KENTUCKY

ADAIRSVILLE • Two miles west of U.S. 431, southwest of Bowling Green on the Red River near Harrison's Mill, is the site of the 1806 **Jackson**-Dickinson duel. A dispute had arisen over Charles Dickinson's repeated slurs of **Jackson's** beloved Rachel. **Jackson** prepared to get hit first since his opponent was a better shot and put on oversized clothes to disguise his thin body frame. Dickinson, an expert with .70 caliber dueling pistols, misjudged where his heart was by a fraction of an inch. **Jackson** was so severely hit that he suffered for the rest of his life. The same was true for Dickinson, but **Jackson** lived another 39 years and Dickinson, only a few hours.

BARDSTOWN • The Talbot Tavern* at 31 E. Court Square claims that the **Lincoln** family stayed there during a trial over title to their farm. It also claims that **Jackson**, **William Henry Harrison**, and **Taylor** were guests. **Monroe** passed through with **Jackson** in 1819.

COVINGTON • **Grant**'s parents lived at 520 Greenup while his father had a leather goods store on Madison. The dejected future general visited here before going to Cincinnati to try to get a position on General George McClellan's staff. McClellan ignored him. In 1862 **Grant** sent his wife and children to stay here. He attended his father's funeral at Union Methodist Episcopal at Fifth and Greenup in 1873 and burial at Spring Grove Cemetery.*

ELIZABETHTOWN, HARDIN COUNTY • A few blocks southeast of the courthouse on the Dixie Highway is a marker at the bridge showing the site of a mill raceway built in 1796 and noting that **Lincoln** crossed here with his family when they migrated to Indiana in 1816. While the Lincolns lived nearby, **Buchanan** came in 1812, involved in legal actions at the courthouse concerning his family's land interests, and stayed at the Eagle House or Smith Hotel on the square.

FAIRVIEW • The monument* at **Davis'** birthplace is the fourth tallest in the country. He was born at a site now occupied by a Baptist church that **Davis** came back in 1885 to dedicate.

FRANKFORT • One of the most beautiful homes, Liberty Hall,* 218 Wilkinson, claims to have welcomed eight presidents, but only three can be documented in spite of claims in several sources, including a souvenir booklet available there. The current curator believes that the historical marker is correct in showing only that **Monroe** was entertained in 1819 with heroes of the late War of 1812, **Jackson** and **Taylor**. They stayed at the Mansion House on the NW corner of Main and St. Claire and breakfasted at the (Old) Governor's Mansion at 420 High, visited later by **William Henry Harrison**, **TR**, and **Taft**. **Taylor** was back on the way to his inauguration in 1849 to the John J. Crittenden home (private) at the NE corner of Main and Washington to consult about his cabinet. He was again at the Old Governor's Mansion, now the official residence of the lieutenant governor. The uncompleted First Presbyterian Church,* 416 W. Main, midway between Wilkinson and Washington, opened for him then.

In March 1854, **Fillmore** stayed at the Capitol Hotel on the NE corner of Main and Ann. He later was in town and attended Thanksgiving services at the Ascension Episcopal Church, 311 Washington. Surely all of these would have visited the 1830 Old Capitol* at Broadway and Lewis, on site of an 1817 structure. **Lincoln** surely saw the Capitol and other sites mentioned when he came through in 1841, 1847, 1849, and 1850. **Taft** dedicated the Lincoln statue in the Capitol. Some sources claim **Madison** was at the Todd House, west of the SW corner of Washington and Wapping, Liberty Hall, Locust Grove in Louisville, and Spring Hill Mansion on Colby Road, six and a half miles west of Winchester. But I can find no documentation or convincing argument that he was ever in Kentucky.

HODGENVILLE • The Abraham **Lincoln** Birthplace National Historic Park* is about three miles south on the Cumberland Road. He was the first president born outside the original thirteen colonies. The small town contained a store and mill used by the **Lincolns**. **TR** laid the cornerstone and **Taft** dedicated the temple under which a "symbolic birthplace cabin" sits. **Wilson** came

Lincoln's birthplace was visited by both Roosevelts, Taft, Wilson, and others.

later for another ceremony, and **Franklin Roosevelt** was here during his 1936 campaign. The cabin was on the property at the end of the Civil War, dismantled and hauled around, then dismantled again with **Jefferson Davis**' claimed birthplace cabin. Apparently the logs of both may have been mixed, according to park rangers' stories told on site and national TV. So the scaled-down structure here now may be all or part **Lincoln**, **Davis**, or neither.

About six miles northeast on U.S. 31E, then the main route from Louisville to Nashville, is the rebuilt Knob Creek cabin, **Lincoln's** Boyhood Home* from 1811 until 1816, on the **Lincolns'** 228-acre farm. This is probably the same site, but it may have been closer to or in the present road. The cabin was rebuilt in 1931 with logs from the cabin of **Lincoln's** boyhood friend, Austin Gollaher. **Lincoln's** earliest recollections are of this farm and his younger brother born here and buried a short distance across the road at the top of a knob hill seen to the right across the road. The site was not generally known until WPA workers in 1933, clearing the old pioneer burying ground, found a small stone believed to be the gravestone. The dates of his birth and death are not known, and there is also a question of the boy's age and name, presumed "Thomas." Abe and his mother visited the grave just before they left to go to Indiana. A grown-over Boy Scout trail across the road from the home leads to the cemetery on private land. It can also be reached by turning north on the Joe Brown Road just east of the Pleasant Grove Baptist Church, where Austin is buried, and going to the end. Permission from the owner should be obtained to cross over private land.

Austin was a close friend of Abraham, source of many adventures and stories of his youth, and tells of stopping with Abe many times at the old stone house, visible to the west of 31E, just south of the cabin, and of Abe's many visits with his hero, John Hodgen, and his mother at Hodgen's Mill. A newer dam is still behind the Hodgen home site, northeast of the square a block east of Lincoln Blvd. on Water Street in Hodgenville, a

Lincoln's boyhood home: Lincoln lived here from age two until seven.

block north of 31E, marked with a plaque on the city office complex. Abe is said to have spent many days and nights here on a trundle bed. Mrs. Hodgen told many stories of Washington, Columbus, and Robinson Crusoe and helped Abe with his ABC's and the Ten Commandments. Austin's detailed stories and conversations are questionable, although the most famous is generally accepted, about Abe falling into the creek when neither could swim. Austin says he fished him out with a pole and waited until their clothes dried before going home since they were too scared to tell their mothers. It is believed that the incident took place about 100 yards from the replica cabin in front of the bluff, although **Lincoln** expert Louis Warren believed it was about .8 mile north.

LEXINGTON • Transylvania University hosted **Monroe** on his 1819 tour with **Jackson. Monroe** had also been in town in 1785. On the way they stayed at Chaumiere du Prairie, nine miles southeast in Jessamine County on Catnip Hill Pike. The university buildings were then in the center of Gratz Park,* south of Old Morrison Hall* that replaced the buildings that burned in 1829. **Eisenhower** visited here on the 175th anniversary of the school, the first west of the Allegheny Mountains, in 1954. **Davis** used the old buildings when he attended, one of which still occupies the east side of the park.

Monroe and probably **Jackson** were also guests at the Pope Home, 326 Grosvenor, and stayed at the Postlethwait Tavern on the SE corner of Main and Limestone. This later became the Phoenix Hotel, where **Lincoln** ate during his 1849 visit. A park and the Central Library are now there. **William Henry Harrison** stayed there in the 1830s. **Jackson** returned in 1832 and worshipped at First Presbyterian, SW corner of Broadway and Second.

Lincoln came to Lexington four times, first in 1841 to see Joshua Speed's fiancée, while Speed's guest at Louisville. The next three visits were with his wife and family, and included visits to Mary's Main Street home and other Todd homes where the family still lived. On the way to Washington in November 1847, the family spent almost a month with the Todds. Then it was necessary for **Lincoln** to return in 1849 after his father-in-law died and in 1850 after the death of Mary's grandmother to handle estate legal problems and family lawsuits.

Lincoln spent time admiring the city's large homes and lawns, including all the Todds,' Mary's birthplace at 501 Short Street, later Levi Todd's (torn down in the 1880s), her grandmother's home at 511 Short Street,* and the Todd House, 578 W. Main,* Mary's home from 1832 until 1839, where they stayed. **Lincoln** encountered apparently contented slaves and spent many hours with Grandma Parker at her home. Here he could look over into a structure that housed and sold runaway slaves nearby on Mechanics Alley and Broadway. **Lincoln** could see slavery first-hand at the public meeting places still around the courthouse called "Cheapside," where slaves were sold, and had time to swap stories with lawyers there and on the east side in Jordan's Row. He heard Dr. Robert J. Breckenridge, the famous preacher-orator, at Mary's Second Presbyterian (destroyed) at 184 Market Street and visited a famous confectionery of Monsieur Giron who also served **Monroe** in a building partly remaining at 125 Mill.

Lincoln spent several days at the Todd summer home, Buena Vista, on Leestown Pike, 18 miles toward Frankfort, destroyed in the late 1940s. This is two miles east of the current intersection of U.S. 421 and U.S. 60 with Rte. 676. A historical marker on the south side of Rte. 421 shows that the home was about a half-mile south, but north of the main road when Mary lived here. A modern black barn is near the site now between the fifth tee and eighth green on the golf course, Links at Ducker Lake. The original springhouse is nearby at a small pond.

The family returned in 1849 and 1859 as Lincoln worked on the estates and surely visited the family graves at the Lexington Cemetery,* a few blocks west of Mary's home, north of the center of Section F, north of the Henry Clay gravesite. **Fillmore** visited Clay's grave in 1854.

Davis went to school at Transylvania at age 14 and lived from 1823 to 1824 in the building (marked) still at the SW corner of Limestone and High. His classmates included his old playmate at the Hermitage in Nashville, Andrew Jackson Donelson. He visited his friend Henry Clay Jr.'s father at Ashland,* the Clay mansion on the Richmond Highway, where **Lincoln** visited his hero, as did **Fillmore** in 1854, **Van Buren** in 1842, and **Pierce** in 1856. The restored home is still one of the landmark homes of America, located about a mile and a half east of the courthouse. **Houston** attended Clay's funeral in the home.

LOUISVILLE • **Monroe, Jackson,** and **Taylor** were guests in June 23, 1819, of Locust Grove* at 561 Blankenberger Lane and were served in the state dining room. This was the last home of George Rogers Clark, the famous frontiersman and Revolutionary War general, who lived with his sister and her husband. **Jackson** came through on January 22, 1829, and no doubt many other times. **Taylor** grew up nearby, probably was friends with the owner's son, and visited as a boy. **Monroe** was also entertained then at Washington Hall, Union Hall, and the Presbyterian Meeting House, probably with **Jackson**, who traveled with **Monroe** on his tour through Kentucky, including Bowling Green and Danville.

Taylor moved in 1785 as an infant to "Springfield," seven miles from downtown, now at 5608 Apache Road, in a residential area where his much-restored private home blends in with the neighbors' modern ones. In his early years, his father kept several loaded rifles in strategic spots around the house in case of Indian attack. He spent most of his first 23 years here, first in a log home later moved and used for slave quarters, and then in the current house built between 1785 and 1790. He was here when he received a commission as first lieutenant in 1808, and was married in 1810 in the home of his sister-in-law, two miles from Harrod's Creek Station on Wolf Pen Road at the Mercer County line. As a wedding present he got 324 acres at the mouth of Muddy (Sinking) Fork of Beargrass Creek near downtown, now near Interstate 71, where he lived on occasion. Five of his six children were probably born at his Apache Road home. **Taylor**'s brother acquired the home at the death of the father. He lived at several other sites around town, including on the east side of First Street near Jefferson, during an extended furlough in 1830. Zachary was buried in the family burial grounds and is now buried in the nearby Zachary **Taylor** National Cemetery,* 4701 Brownsboro Road. Rumors existed for years that he was poisoned, and his body was exhumed for an autopsy in 1991. No trace of arsenic was found, but some still argue that he was murdered by other means.

Taylor opposed the marriage of his daughter

to **Davis**, because he was a soldier, but they married at **Taylor**'s sister's house, Beechland, three miles from downtown, marked at Number 2 Rebel Road, a short street that intersects Hillcrest Ave., an extension of Zorn Ave. at the northwest corner with Brownsboro Pike. **Taylor** approached **Davis** twelve years after her death to tell him that his daughter had been a better judge of character than he, and the two men became friends and served together during the Mexican War.

Lincoln was a guest for several weeks in August 1841 at Farmington,* the home of his closest friend, Joshua Speed. The home, at 3033 Bardstown Road, exit 16 off I-264, contains the original floors, stone barn and springhouse and much original furniture. **Lincoln** was assigned a servant, one of the 70 slaves on the 554-acre hemp plantation, and spent his time tramping the fields, woods, and roads around here and in Louisville. His room was probably in the basement in the corner to the left facing the entrance. In Louisville he spent long, delightful hours with his later attorney general, Joshua's brother James, then on the west side of Centre, now Amory Place, midway between Jefferson and Green, now Liberty Street.

Andrew Johnson and **Grant** were at the Louisville Hotel, west of the southwest corner at Main and Sixth, in 1866. They took the steamer from Third Street and the river. At the beginning of the war, **Grant** stayed at the Galt House, where a marker notes the site, then at W. Second and Main, the east side of the Highway 31 bridge. He was in town February 1, 1864, and also later paid tribute to Robert E. Lee in 1879 at the hotel, now at First and Main, where **Hayes** and **TR** stayed. **TR** campaigned in the Square in 1900 and was in town April 4, 1905. **Davis** stayed at the Galt in 1873. The hotel later moved to where it is now, 140 Fourth,* where many presidents have stayed, including all from **Carter** through **Clinton**.

The Seelbach Hotel,* 500 Fourth, has hosted **Taft, Wilson, FDR, Truman** (room 940), **Kennedy, Johnson, Carter, Clinton,** and **George W. Bush** (room 920). The grand lobby is relatively unchanged from the 1905 opening. **Reagan** was at the Hyatt, 328 W. Jefferson, in 1984.

MAYSVILLE • **Grant** went to school at age 14 for about a year at Maysville Academy, 1616 W. Fourth Street, that survived until 1997. He visited Cedar Hill four miles south on U.S. 68 overlooking Washington. **W. Harrison and Jackson** stayed at the stagecoach stop on the Maysville-Lexington Road at Carlisle Pike. **Taylor** headquartered in the area at an unknown site.

PADUCAH • **Grant** took the town in the fall of 1861, "to protect it from Confederate invasion." A marker shows his landing site at Grant Landing, First and Broadway. He built Fort Anderson on Trimble between Fourth and Fifth and visited headquarters on the NW corner of Sixth and Clark and the supply base at N. Eighth and Julia. While here he attended Broadway Methodist, NW corner of Broadway and Fourth. **Jackson** and **Lincoln** in addition to **Taylor** and **Polk** are claimed on the marker to have been at the Gower House in nearby Smithland, abandoned on Water Street.

SMITHLAND • The Gower House at U.S. 60 and Water hosted **Polk** and **Taylor**.

SPRINGFIELD AND WASHINGTON COUNTY • **Davis** went to Saint Rose Priory,* a Catholic school, from age eight until ten, then known as St. Thomas Aquinas. The 1806 church still prominently stands one-half mile south of U.S. 150 on Route 152, less than a mile from the 150/152 junction down Route 152. He started in 1816 when seven-year-old **Lincoln** was growing up about twenty miles west at Knob Creek, attending a school also taught by a Catholic. Jeff and Abe both had Baptist fathers.

Early on, Jeff decided that he wanted to be a Catholic and was shocked when the priest suggested that he wait a while to decide. He did not join any church until he was president of the Confederacy. **Davis** was the smallest boy there and was a special favorite of one of the priests. When he was involved in a school prank where the lights were shut off and the priest pelted by food thrown in the dark, the priest tied down the only one caught, Jefferson, and pleaded with him to tell all he knew and thus not be punished. The priest kept his word when Jefferson said he knew only one thing, who put out the lights. He had.

The **Lincoln** Homestead Park, seven miles north, has the replica home on the original site where the president's grandmother moved after Indians killed her husband near Louisville. The life of **Lincoln's** mother is somewhat clouded. It is probable that the president's grandmother, Lucy Hanks, and her only child had moved nearby to live with Lucy's sister and her husband. Lucy married and moved out, leaving Nancy to live with the Berrys, according to tradition. Nancy thus lived in nearby Beechland, up Beechland Road from the **Lincoln** cabin, with Richard Berry and his wife. The exact site is at the tiny community of Poortown, on Route 438, two miles northeast on a knoll overlooking Little Beech Creek. When Berry's wife died, Nancy probably moved in with Frances Berry, where she lived while Tom was courting. This cabin has been moved across the lawn from the **Lincoln** cabin at the park. They were married June 12, 1806, in Richard Berry Jr.'s cabin, now in Harrodsburg. The Berry Mill Road now surrounds the community; the eastern end runs north of Route 438 at the bridge over Beech Fork, loops and narrows to the west, hitting Route 438 again. Richard Berry Jr.'s cabin was just northwest of the present bridge. Frances's cabin was about a hundred yards due north. Richard Sr.'s cabin and Nancy's girlhood home was a little west, southwest of the Routes 438 and 528 junction.

Louisiana

Baton Rouge • **Taylor** "retired" after the Mexican War to his prior home at 727 Lafayette, a vacant site now marked on the Capitol grounds, from which he was elected president. A British officer had built the structure much earlier when Britain controlled the area, and Spanish commanders used it. Mrs. Taylor preferred this to the Pentagon Barracks when he was the commandant. He was the first regular army officer elected, no politician, and the only president who never voted, not even for himself, and truly never wanted the office. He stated, "Such an idea never entered my head, nor is it likely to enter the head of a sane person. I did not vote for General **Taylor**; and my family, especially the old lady, is strongly opposed to his election." He refused notification of his nomination when it arrived with postage due. He owned plantations near the Mississippi River nearby and east of here in West Feliciana Parish, attended the Episcopal church at 208 N. Fourth, and visited the Cottage Plantation* on La. 327, ten miles south, 18666 Perkins Road.

On the east side of the Capitol is the Old Arsenal Powder Magazine,* built in 1838 under **Taylor's** command. The Pentagon Barracks* are now just southwest of the new Capitol near the river bluff. These military buildings, completed in 1824, replaced a 1779 star-shaped earthen fort, and housed **Taylor**, **Davis**, **Grant**, and many future Civil War generals.

The Louisiana Bicentennial Commission believes that **Lincoln** was in town in one of his trips down river. He and companion Allen Gentry beat off attackers near the riverbank about six miles south on their 1828 flatboat trip to New Orleans.

Fort Jesup and Natchitoches • **Taylor** built Fort Selden, twelve miles north of Natchitoches and two miles north of Grand Ecore, on a high bluff overlooking Bayou Pierre and the Red River where he wintered in 1821. This was not a healthy location, so he scouted for a better one and established Fort Jesup* between the Sabine and Red Rivers, on the El Camino Real, now State Highway 6, in 1822 to serve in the event of a boundary dispute with Spain over the western limits of the Louisiana Purchase. A treaty had been signed in 1819, but the land west of there was a sort of neutral zone for outlaws. United States troops were sent here at the time of the Texas Revolution supposedly to enforce neutrality laws and then to aid Texas in case they voted for annexation. **Taylor** was back in 1844 and notified a year later to expect trouble when it became evident that Texas would be voted into the Union. He left from here for the opening campaign of the Mexican War from riverboats at the Natchitoches landing.

Grant was at Fort Jesup and nearby Ft. Salubrity, north of Natchitoches at Grand Ecore, that he helped set up at the town with the same name. He described it as living in a small tent that rain ran through like a sieve surrounded by a swamp full of alligators and woods full of red bugs and ticks. He visited plantation homes in the area to relieve months of boredom and stayed in Natchitoches at an inn then at the SW corner of Touline and Front. **Houston** passed through Fort Jessup and Natchitoches several times, once to deliver a letter to **Jackson** about his initial meetings with Texas leaders, and got a gift of an officer's sword.

New Orleans • The War of 1812 Chalmette National Battlefield* is on SR 46, six miles down river from the French Quarter. Here, for the first time, Americans learned that they could defend their freedom. General **Jackson** arrived in New Orleans on December 2, 1814, to command the military district and established headquarters at 106 Royal. (He also had offices at 6400 St. Claude.) He met here a few days later with the notorious pirate Jean Laffite, who boldly walked through the streets even though a wanted outlaw, and who offered his services to the United States rather than accept a British offer. The British under the Duke of Wellington's brother-in-law shocked the city when they made a surprise landing nearby, attempting to capture the key city controlling the Mississippi. **Jackson** immediately surprised them by attacking their camp 22 miles east, now marked on State 39. The British then attacked three times, December 28, January 1, and January 8, all at the American lines, and all failed. On January 8, 1815, **Jackson**'s makeshift command of 4000 militiamen defeated British regulars attacking his lines at Chalmette, securing his country's claim on the Mississippi River and the Louisiana Territory. Neither side knew that the treaty ending the war had already been signed in Europe, but England may not have honored the treaty if they had won here, or may not have given up the area wanted as a buffer.

The war commenced with the young country trying to end the bully treatment by the mother country, prove its right to independence, and show that it could maintain permanent government. The war gained little if anything toward these ends, but the victory here gave the new republic new prestige and self-confidence lacking from the Revolution and earlier setbacks and fostered western expansion. It also made **Jackson** a national hero. President **Madison** and others considered the victory more important to maintaining peace than the treaty. Indeed, he has been called the luckiest of presidents, and the battle may have saved his presidency. Secretary of War and State, **Monroe**, told **Madison** that had **Jackson** lost this battle, Britain would have insisted that the entire Gulf Coast belonged to Spain, Mobile was illegally seized, and Louisiana was illegally purchased. (France had contracted not to sell it when they acquired it from Spain.) The victory legitimized the Purchase and led to the United States' acquisition of the Gulf Coast. If Spain or Britain had maintained a foothold on the coast, an Indian buffer state might have blocked southwest expansion and protected Spanish Florida. If the British had controlled New Orleans they would have controlled the Mississippi and joined their Canadian army. The British general was charged with carving off a part of the continent here. **Jackson** felt January 8 should be remembered like July 4. Maybe he was right.

Jackson's battlefield headquarters site is now in the river, southwest of the battlefield visitor center. His command post was first at the Pakenham Oaks, marked along the St. Bernard Highway, running along the northern battlefield border. The spot where the British commander fell mortally wounded is also marked. Several spots are marked in New Orleans claiming to be where **Jackson** and Lafitte planned the battle, including 440 Chartres, Absinthe House at 400 Bourbon, and the Old Absinthe House at 238 Bourbon. **T. Roosevelt, Davis,** and **Taft** as well as many others are claimed on the tablet at the Old Absinthe House. After the battle **Jackson** stayed at 619 St. Peter (private) in what is now called the Jackson House. **Davis** camped on the battlefield with his First Mississippi Volunteers before shipping out to the Mexican War in 1846.

After the battle, rumors of peace circulated, but **Jackson** declared martial law and considered the country still at war unless some official message was received. A judge in court at 919 Royal fined him for contempt for failing to honor a court order to release dissidents held under martial law. **Jackson** then jailed the judge, and a crowd gathered at the Coffee Exchange or Maspero's Slave Exchange at 440 Chartres, marked at the SE corner of Louis Street. **Jackson** spoke from the top of a marble table taken out into the street. Money was raised for him to pay his fine, but he refused to take it, asking it to be given to the widows and children of the battle dead. (Congress remitted the fine later.) **Jackson** revisited in 1824 and 1838 to be hosted in giant celebrations at 417 Royal, now Brennan's Restaurant, where he had lived for five months in 1815 at the home of Colonel Livingston. In 1840 he made an arduous trip back to revisit the battlefield in another anniversary celebration to dedicate his still prominent equestrian statute. The cathedral* is listed as dating from 1794, but was mostly rebuilt between 1849 and 1850. **Jackson** was given a place of honor near the altar during the battle celebrations in January 1815 and later and honored in

Many presidents have spoken near Jackson's statue at the Old Cathedral in New Orleans, including Jackson himself.

Jackson Square. **George W. Bush** spoke on the south side of the square after the destruction caused by Hurricane Katrina in 2005, pledging to rebuild the city.

Lincoln came in 1828 and 1831 delivering goods and apparently rented a room on St. Ann in 1828. Little is known about either trip except that he saw slaves being sold at the St. Louis Hotel near the Cabildo* and is quoted saying that he would hit the "thing hard if he could." He is also thought to have gone to the American Theater on the lakeside of Camp near Gravois and Poydras.

Army headquarters were in City Hall, 545 St. Charles, when **Taylor** commanded in the area, and he lived at 621 Royal. A crowd of 40,000 honored him in December 1847, in the square and church. **Fillmore** (1854), **Davis, Harding** (1920), **Hoover, TR,** and **McKinley** (1901) were received at City Hall. **Houston** came here for medical treatment after being wounded at San Jacinto, almost died, and stayed at the Col. William Christy mansion on Girod Street. **Polk** came through on the way back home after leaving office, stayed at the St. Louis Hotel, 730 Bienville, made a speech, got sick, and died two months later in Tennessee.

Davis spent his month-long honeymoon at the St. Charles Hotel, 211 St. Charles, in 1844 and stayed many times before and after the Civil War. **Fillmore, Cleveland, McKinley, Hoover,** and **TR** also stayed there. Expert horseman **Grant** was thrown from a horse nearby. In 1875, **Davis** worked at 33 Camp. In 1876, he stayed at 327 Bourbon, two blocks from Canal. At this time he met Mrs. Sarah Dorsey and agreed to live at her house in Mississippi, where he could write his book. The Lee Monument at Lee Circle was dedicated in **Davis**' presence.

Davis died in 1889 at 1134 First Street at the SW corner with Camp, where he was often a guest. He was preparing to go home to Biloxi after getting sick while visiting his old plantation in Mississippi but lingered here, as he was too sick to travel. He was first buried at Metairie Cemetery and later moved to Richmond. The spot in Metairie is marked and is on the west side enclosed by Avenues A and D, and west of the end of Avenue I.

McKinley, TR, Taft, and **Eisenhower** were at the Cabildo adjacent to the St. Louis Cathedral that surely all visited. **G.H.W. Bush, Carter, Coolidge, Ford,** and **Truman** all stayed at the Fairmont Hotel, formerly the Roosevelt, 100 University. **Hayes** got deathly sick in the Planter's Hotel in 1848 on the way to Texas and reminded himself to "never get caught in a cheap tavern in a strange city."

ST. FRANCISVILLE • **Davis** often rode his horse to Locust Grove as a boy to see his sister and brought his bride of three months in 1835 to escape from an unhealthy location at his plantation near Vicksburg. He had married Sarah Knox Taylor, the daughter of **Zachary Taylor**, against Taylor's strong objections to her marrying a soldier. **Taylor** had land near the **Davises** and had lost two daughters and almost Sarah and his wife to malaria at nearby Bayou Sara on the Mississippi. He did not want his daughter brought back to this unhealthy place where, in fact, both newlyweds did come down with malaria while visiting. **Davis**, who had resigned from the army, knew of the unsafe conditions in the area during the summer months, but probably convinced her to leave Kentucky earlier than expected to come to his home in Mississippi. This decision haunted him for years. Sarah died just past her twenty-first birthday on September 15, 1835, about three weeks after Lincoln's sweetheart died in Illinois. **Davis** almost died also, first physically and then emotionally. After years of seclusion he married again in Natchez.

Sarah is buried at Locust Grove Cemetery* four miles east of U.S. 61, on La. 965, off La. 10, near the home site. The death changed the normally friendly, personable, happy **Davis** into a sour, cantankerous, bitter recluse. He returned the day after his second marriage with his second wife to visit the grave. Her thoughts are not known. On the way here then he had met his former father-in-law, **Zachary Taylor**, for the first time since the prior wedding and was reconciled.

The Cottage Plantation,* on U.S. 61 nine miles north of the U.S. 66 interchange, hosted **Jackson** in 1815 after the Battle of New Orleans. South is Fairview Plantation, once **Grant**'s headquarters.

WINTER QUARTERS* • The 1805 plantation where **Grant** is claimed to have stayed during part of the Vicksburg campaign is three miles southeast on SR 698, off U.S. 65 north of Lake Bruin, although there is a dispute that he was ever here. The owners were pro–Union and approached **Grant** to spare their home in exchange for food and hospitality. None of the other fifteen plantation homes in the area were spared destruction. He crossed the Mississippi nearby at Hard Time Landing to begin his famous Civil War campaign.

MAINE

AUGUSTA • **Buchanan** (1847), **Grant** (1873), **B. Harrison** (1889), **Polk** (1847), and **TR** were honored at the James G. Blaine mansion, 162 State, now the Executive Mansion. **Polk and Buchanan** visited the Capitol in 1847 and stayed in the Augusta House at Green, Grove, Water and Gage Streets, where **Grant** stayed in 1865.

BRUNSWICK • **Pierce** went to Bowdoin College here, 1821–1825, on Main, Bath, and College, and stayed at various locations including Massachusetts Hall on the north side of the quadrangle; the oldest college building in Maine, Maine Hall; and boarding houses on Cleaveland Street and Park Row. He visited the Stowe House, 63 Federal, where *Uncle Tom's Cabin* was written. While here he developed a close, lifelong friendship with author Nathaniel Hawthorne. He attended the First Parish Church, 9 Cleaveland, near his boarding house.

Grant came in 1865 to get an honorary degree and visited General Joshua Chamberlain in 1868 and 1873 at 226 Maine* and was at the Tontine Hotel, site at School and Maine.

BUCKSPORT • **Van Buren, W. Harrison,** and **Tyler** were guests at Prouty's Tavern, 52 Main.

DRESDEN • **Adams** tried a case in the state's only remaining colonial Courthouse, Route 128.

KENNEBUNKPORT • **Monroe** stayed at the Jefford Hotel in 1817. **George H.W. Bush's** summer home is at the easternmost point of Ocean Avenue at a small peninsula called Walker's Point, easily identifiable on abundant local tourist maps, although not linked to his name. It was his maternal grandfather's property. Both **Bushes** came here for summers all during their lifetimes and through their presidencies. Neil Bush's wedding was at St. Anne's on Ocean Avenue, and his brother **George W.** and father attended. Senator Prescott Bush, George H.W.'s father, was married here in 1921. The two presidents saw Florida Gov. Jeb Bush's son married at St. Anne's in August 2004. The elder **Bush** hosted **Clinton** in mid–2005, and both Presidents **Bush** hosted Premier Putin of Russia on July 1, 2007.

One of **George W.'s** "two life-changing events" occurred on the beach here with Baptist Evangelist Rev. Billy Graham, who had taken an interest in him. He reminded the preacher of his own son, who had led a life of hell-raising and hard drinking before he had committed his life to Christianity. Graham asked the young Bush if he was "right with God." Bush answered that he attended church and taught Sunday school. Then Graham said that his question wasn't answered. "Do you have the peace and understanding with God that can only come through our Lord Jesus Christ?" Then he explained, "To be without God in this life is terribly lonely," and asked him to take back to Texas the knowledge that God loved him and could make him a new man. Shortly thereafter he quit drinking and changed his ways. (See Colorado Springs, Colorado.)

LUBEC • **Franklin D. Roosevelt**'s home* on Campobello Island, New Brunswick, Canada, is just across a short bridge here from Maine. He spent most of his summers from age one in 1883 until 1921 at his father's cottage adjacent to the north of the home. Franklin's mother Sara was not happy with his choice of a bride, his distant cousin Eleanor, but she was allowed to come to get to know his mother better in 1904. A neighbor had known **Franklin** for years, took a liking to his intended, and gave her large cottage to Sara for a token $5000 with instructions to transfer it to **Franklin** and his bride. A year after their marriage Sara presented them the large, Dutch colonial cottage next to hers, although they did not own it for many years. They spent many summers with the later family of five children. Franklin Jr. was born here. Eleanor considered this the only home that was her own until Val-Kill was built.

The family was here when **Franklin** was struck with polio in 1921. He had taken the kids swimming in the chilly waters and got overheated putting out a wildfire. Exhausted when he returned home, he went to bed and never walked again. The illness kept him out of political office for seven years, but made him more sympathetic to others and gave him insights into human nature that he did not previously have. Eleanor too found herself by going into the public to speak, and for the first time she had to confront her domineering mother-in-law, who wanted to keep Franklin a helpless invalid. It is possible that isolation during childhood left him more vulnerable to sicknesses and disease from lack of exposure to mild cases, including, in addition to polio, the lifelong attacks of sinusitis, lumbago, colds, etc. The strain of the Lucy Mercer affair might also have left him physically weak and more vulnerable. He was the only person chosen to lead the country who could not walk. Only two of his 35,000 pictures show him in a wheelchair, and the public was largely deceived as to his infirmity that he never mentioned. After leaving then, he returned for only three short stays during his presidency, although the family continued to summer here. The Queen Mother dedicated the site as an International Park in 1967.

YORK • When **Adams** served on the Provincial Court in 1770, he stayed in the Woodbridge or Ritchie's Tavern and attended the 1774 Meeting House. **Monroe** visited Judge David Sewall in 1817, the courthouse in Portland, and the Old Meeting House in Saco, Maine.

MARYLAND

ANNAPOLIS • **Washington's** diary records 18 visits before the Revolution to this colonial vacation spot. In his earliest visits he stayed with Daniel Wolstenholme at the end of Maryland Street, now Naval Academy Gate 3, in a house long gone. In September 1771, he went to the theater on West Street four times and danced at three balls in the city hall.* He played cards and gambled at the races held at what is now West and Cathedral Streets. October 1772 produced comparable activity, and he stayed with "Mr. Boucher at the parsonage of St. Annes," much changed at 215–7 Hanover. His stepson, Jacky, went to school taught by Boucher, first in Caroline Co., Va., and then here. **Washington** frequently came, and enjoyed lively discussions with the rector until his Tory views became too pronounced. He finally went back to England, but still wrote the commander in chief of his problems.

Jacky's son, **Washington's** step-grandson, George Washington Parke Custis, attended St. Johns College, as did two nephews. (**Washington** raised and treated Jacky and Parke as sons.) Ogle Hall* or the Alumni House, marked at the SW corner of King George and College Avenues, entertained **Washington** on September 1, 1773. During his last visit to town in 1791, **Washington** strolled through the campus and complimented the school on its progress. He would have known McDowell Hall,* still prominent on College Street, that **Jefferson** said in 1766 was the only building in town worth noting. **Coolidge** visited it in 1928, and **Ike** dedicated the Key Memorial Auditorium in 1959.

Washington also made purchases at Jonas Green's,* 124 Charles Street, now a bed and breakfast, and visited Governor John Howard at the head of Calvert, south of Chase Street. He and Martha frequently visited at the Ridout House,* marked at 120 Duke of Gloucester Street, as noted in his diary. Martha once left her nightcap behind as a symbol that she wished to return. She never did, and it is still there, as political differences ended friendship with the loyalist.

Later **Washington** generally stayed at Port of City Hotel, or Mann's, extending from Main and listed at 162 Conduit. This is where he stayed when he came to the then federal capital to resign his military commission. Congress honored **Washington** at a public dinner at Mann's on the day before he resigned. The original part where the presidents stayed is gone, as seen by the marker on the present Masonic Hall. It was toward Main, north and adjacent to the Hall. **Washington** stayed there, also in Mann's home, but on the then fourth floor of the altered current building. The Annapolis Convention met at Mann's in 1786 as **Madison** and **Monroe** came from Congress, meeting in New York City. No Maryland delegates attended, and only 12 from five colonies appeared. So the convention decided to meet again next year in Philadelphia, a meeting that resulted in the new Federal Constitution. **Jefferson** and **Madison** also stayed here in 1790.

Washington's diary notes visits to the Jockey Club at the Maryland Coffee House, 199 Main, prior to 1770. Later he also attended the Club when it met at the Middleton Tavern,* at the head of City Dock directly across from the Market House on the northeast side of Market Space, Randall and Dock. All mentioned used the ferry at the City Dock. **Washington** left from here to see his friends at White Hall or Rock Hall on White Hall Creek and U.S. 50, across the Severn River on the Eastern Shore. **Monroe** was entertained at Middleton's as president in 1818. **Washington** had his hair cut at Number 6 Cornwall, and **Jefferson** kept his horses at Number 37–9. **Washington** was a frequent guest of the governor who lived on a peninsula in the river.

Washington, **Jefferson**, **Madison**, and **Monroe** frequented the Reynolds Tavern,* Church Circle and Franklin, and the Carroll home at 107 Duke of Gloucester, now behind the church. **Jefferson** lodged in Middleton's on June 17, 1775, and climbed to the top of the 1771 State House* dome before taking the ferry to Rock Hall, twelve miles from Chestertown, which the other presidents listed also frequented. **Jefferson** and **Madison** once waited a whole day in Rock Hall for a boat. The present State House dome was completed in the 1780s. **Jefferson** made the climb again, with **Madison**, in September 1790.

Congress with **Jefferson**, **Madison** (for a few

days), and **Monroe** met in the State House* from November 1783 until the next August 13. While here Congress negotiated treaties and voted to send **Jefferson** to France and **Adams** to England as ambassadors. At noon on December 23, 1783, **Washington** entered the Hall of Congress and surrendered his command of the army before **Jefferson**, **Monroe**, the rest of Congress, and many generals, ending fearful talk that he would become a Caesar. A picture shows **Madison** here, but he was then back in Virginia as his three-year term limit had expired. He came with **Jefferson** and left several weeks before **Washington** arrived. A bronze plaque in the floor marks the spot where Washington stood to give his commission to the president of Congress and receive an overwhelming ovation from members and spectators. Most wept when he read his formal reply that **Madison** felt **Jefferson** had written at least part. He told Governor Clinton of New York, "I felt myself eased of a load of public care," and he intended to spend the remainder of his days in the "practice of domestic virtues." Afterward there was a large banquet and celebration for him at City Hall,* marked at 150 Duke of Gloucester. During this visit he visited Governor Ogle at 247 King.

Jefferson stayed at the Ghiselin House,* 26–28 West Street, in January 1784 with **Monroe**. The back part is now the visitor center. They also shared quarters at Mann's, then called Dulany's. When **Jefferson** went to Paris in the spring of 1784, **Monroe** purchased many of his law books and inherited his French cook. **Jefferson** and **Madison** earlier rented a residence where Gate 3 now is at the Academy and walked down Maryland Avenue by the Hammond-Harwood* and Chase-Lloyd* Houses, at the Maryland-King George Street intersection. **Jefferson**, the amateur architect, admired the prominent homes, which offer tours today, and made a sketch of the Hammond-Harwood while sitting on the steps of the Chase-Lloyd, where Frances Scott Key later married. (A copy of the original sketch in Boston is shown in the Hammond House.) **Washington** dined with Mr. Lloyd at an unknown location while this house was being built and would have also passed both of these mansions between the St. Anne's Rectory and State House. He also dined at Strawberry Hill, then across Dorsey Creek where the cemetery is on Academy grounds.

Madison stayed at 10 Francis and the Maryland Inn,* Church Circle at Main in the triangle with Duke of Gloucester. The Brice House* on the NE corner of East and Martin entertained **Washington**, **Adams**, and **Madison**. The equally imposing and similar Paca House* is the next lot north and must have hosted these and certainly impressed all. Both mansions were built in the 1760s. It is claimed that all prominent mansions in the city hosted **Washington** at some time. William Paca was in Congress from 1774 until 1779, signed the Declaration of Independence, and was governor during the Revolution and when **Washington** resigned. Many other colonial buildings impress those who visit the beautiful little town called an open-air museum.

The Naval Academy has hosted many presidents including **Carter**, who attended and stayed in the world's largest dormitory, Bancroft Hall,* dominating the campus. **Washington** visited a friend whose house was on the site. Other presidents on campus include **Ford** in 1942, **Truman** in 1948, **Kennedy** in 1961, **Eisenhower** in 1953, 1958 and 1959, **Nixon** in 1974, **Reagan** in 1985, and **George W. Bush** in 2005. **TR** laid to rest national naval hero John Paul Jones beneath the chapel on April 24, 1906, amid pomp and fanfare never seen here before.

North is Crownsville, where the Rising Sun Tavern (private) still stands on the west side of SR 178 just north of the town, 1090 Generals Highway, just north of Layfield Road. It is marked, not with that name, but as French General Rochambeau's campsite. This was the busiest highway in Maryland before the Revolution. **Washington** and other leaders stayed there.

ANTIETAM BATTLEFIELD (SHARPSBURG) • **Lincoln** stayed two nights shortly after the battle on the field next to General McClellan's headquarters when he visited October 1–4, 1862. The battle witnessed more casualties than any other day in American history and gave **Lincoln** enough of a victory to issue the Emancipation Proclamation, without which the Union may not have survived. Historian William C. Davis deems this **Lincoln's** most important visit as it showed McClellan had to go. He probably would not lose the war, but he also would not win it.

Lincoln traveled by train through Elliot City, Sykesville, Mt. Airy, Monrovia, Monocacy Junction, Berlin, and Harper's Ferry, where he spent the night. On the next day he visited troops nearby and arrived at the general's camp late in the afternoon, probably via Weverton, Brownsville, Gapland, Rohersville by Route 67, Mount Briar, and the infamous Burnside Bridge,* a center point during the battle, where he was met by Burnside himself.

Lincoln was photographed in and outside McClellan's tent with various other generals. The location is questionable as McClellan had left his headquarters at the Pry House north of Sharpsburg and moved to a new site from September 27 until October 8. The site was until recently thought to be slightly less than two miles south of Sharpsburg on the east side of Harper's Ferry Road. But Chief Historian Ted Alexander and present consensus place the site on Mill Drive .6 mile west of Burnside Bridge Road. This is east of the 1763 Antietam Furnace at Harper's Ferry Road and Mill Road, south across the Antietam Creek Bridge and east of Burnside Church at the white stone Showman Farm House (private) on the south side. He also reviewed the Ninth Corps near the Furnace.

Another **Lincoln** photograph was taken in front of the prominent Grove House (marked and private), also known as Mt. Airy, visible several hundred yards south of the Shepherdstown Road just west of Sharpsburg. These are the only battlefield photos of **Lincoln**. The president reviewed soldiers just across the road northwest, visited wounded in the house where he apologized to the owners for the damage caused, and walked down the big hallway talking to wounded from both sides. With not a dry eye among Union or Confederates, he explained that solemn obligations owed to our country and posterity compelled the prosecution of the war, and it followed that many were our enemies through uncontrollable circumstances. He bore no malice, and could take them by the hand with sympathy and good feeling.

Lincoln reviewed troops at Bakerfield, three miles away on Bakersfield Road, west of Route 65, and the Bakersfield Church, now Salem Church, and at South Mountain via the Middle Bridge, Bloody Lane, and Pry House. The landmarks are marked, but no markers or National Park guidebooks refer to his visit. Wounded General Israel B. Richardson was dying at the Pry House,* where the president climbed the stairs to comfort him. The National Park Service owns the home west of Route 34. He visited the Miller Cornfield and Dunker Church* being used as a hospital, near the visitor center, and campsites along the Chesapeake and Ohio Canal from Antietam Aqueduct to Shepherdstown Ford. On one trip across the Middle Bridge* (Route 34), he got a drink from the creek. The modern bridge is at the same site where **Washington** also passed to visit the Orndorff house (site), marked south of the bridge. Most sites mentioned above are part of the park tour. **Lincoln** is mentioned only at the Grove House. McClellan accompanied him to the summit of South Mountain.

Colonel **Rutherford B. Hayes** was wounded at Fox's Gap during the Battle of South Mountain that preceded Antietam. The spot is near the original stone wall south of an unmarked paved road one-half mile west of Reno Monument (Old Sharpsburg) Road, less than a mile from the gap. **Hayes** thought his wound was mortal and requested a wounded Confederate lying nearby to relay his dying message to his wife. (He was reported dead in newspapers.) When a scared Union sergeant ran by him, fleeing to the rear, Hayes arose, pointed with his bloody arm to the battle and told him to return to his place, then fainted. He recovered at the Jacob Rudy home (private), still on Alt. 40, 504 W. Main Street, at the north end of nearby Middleton, where his wife came to nurse him back to health. When he returned to Ohio to recover he recommended that 19-year-old Commissary Sergeant **McKinley** be promoted to lieutenant. A long-term effort to get a Congressional Metal of Honor for **McKinley** failed. He had repeatedly carried provisions to weary troops during the Battle of Antietam, and returned many years later to the site of his monument, up the hill from Burnside Bridge toward the parking lot, where he was during the fighting. He also dedicated the Maryland Monument in 1900 with former Confederate General James Longstreet after an informal reception by the Dunker Church.

Johnson dedicated the National Cemetery on September 17, 1867, with **Grant**. The high point was where Robert E. Lee had watched the battle. With the governor of New Jersey, who had been 16 years old here during the battle, **TR** dedicated the New Jersey Monument on September 17, 1903, and toured the battlefield, including Dunker Church. He stated, "You men of the Grand Army

Opposite, top: **Antietam Dunker Church, a battlefield landmark, was visited by various presidents including Lincoln, McKinley, and both Roosevelts after the Battle of Antietam.** ***Opposite, bottom:*** **Grove House at Sharpsburg, Maryland, where Lincoln is pictured in 1862 visiting soldiers on the Antietam Battlefield.**

by your victory not only rendered all humanity your debtors. If the Union had been dissolved, if the great edifice built with blood and sweat and tears by mighty **Washington** and his compeers had gone down in wreck and ruin, the result would have been an incalculable calamity, not only for our people ... but for all mankind." **FDR** came on September 17, 1937, by way of the old National Road, Alt. 40 and Mountain House at South Mountain, to speak to up to 40,000 on the battlefield, and **Eisenhower** toured while Chairman of the Joint Chiefs. **JFK** arrived secretly by helicopter near Burnside Bridge and toured on April 7, 1963. **Carter** came from Camp David on July 6, 1978, after touring the Seton Shrine in Emmitsburg, Gettysburg, and Mercersburg. Like others he visited Dunker Church and Burnside Bridge.

BALTIMORE • **Washington** visited at least 36 times and stopped a few miles south in Waterloo, at least 25 times on his way to and from Philadelphia between 1789 and 1798, according to a Maryland marker at Spurrier's Tavern, 125 feet east of U.S. 1 and .2 miles north of Route 175. **Jefferson** stayed here when it was owned by Mrs. Ball. Among others, **Washington** visited Dr. McHenry at Baltimore and Fremont, shopped at the Lexington Market, 400 W. Lexington, and was at Mount Clare,* the home of Charles Carroll, "the Barrister," in Carroll Park. **Adams** noted the home in his walks around the town he called "the dirtiest Place in the World."

Congress met in Congress Hall, at the SE corner of Liberty and Baltimore Streets between Sharpe and Liberty, from December 20, 1776, until February 27, 1777. Congressman Benjamin Harrison (father of William Henry) called it "the Damndest Hole in the World," but Samuel Adams believed that the adverse conditions here improved the work of Congress. It was here that Congress voted **Washington** full military powers. **John Adams** arrived on February 1 and left on March 2. He stayed at Mrs. Ross's boarding house at East Redwood or Nine Market Street, a few doors below Grant's or Fountain Inn, at the NE corner of Redwood and Light, said to have been **Washington's** favorite stop in the city as he stayed there at least in 1775, 1789 (on the way to his inauguration), 1792, 1797, and with Rochambeau in 1781 on the way to Yorktown. **Jefferson** also stayed here when Brydon owned it. Frances Scott Key finished "The Star Spangled Banner" in the inn. **Jackson** also stayed, as did **Monroe**.

Jefferson stayed in town for a month, February 1783, among many other times, and spent time at the Indian Queen, on the SE corner of Hanover and Baltimore, where Congress was in 1776 when members fled Philadelphia as the British approached. **Jackson** met Indian leader Black Hawk here in June 1833 and warned him to "bury the tomahawk" or his people would be wiped out. This was also the occasion of the first presidential train ride when **Jackson** rode in from about twelve miles away. He was entertained at the Front Street Theater at the NW corner of Front and Low, where **Lincoln** was renominated in 1864 with **Arthur** present. **Jackson** was so weak on this trip that he felt it would be his last, and the journey had to be cut short and plans altered in New Hampshire for a quick return back to the capital. This was only the fourth long trip by a president before the Civil War. (**Washington, Monroe**, and **Tyler** made the others. **Jackson** followed **Monroe**'s route.) **Monroe** began his foreign service by sailing from Baltimore harbor on Boston Street at the foot of LeHarve.

In suburban Towson, **Washington** is thought to have stayed at Hampton,* the home of Captain Charles Ridgely, a confidant. It is located at 535 Hampton Lane northeast of exit 27 off I-695. **Madison** accidentally met Lafayette here in 1784, and the two went to Fort Stanwix (also Schuyler) in New York and toured New England together.

John Quincy Adams, Van Buren, Andrew Johnson, Buchanan, Fillmore, Monroe, Taylor, Davis, Wilson, and **T. Roosevelt** stayed at Barnam's Hotel at the SW corner of Fayette and Calvert. The claim that **Washington** also stayed is doubted. **Pierce** stayed several times, including two days before his inauguration, appealing to his distraught wife, who had just found out that he had actually wanted and sought the nomination. He had told her otherwise, and she blamed the election for the death of their small son, who was killed in a train accident on a trip taken to say goodbye to relatives. **Houston** also stayed when it was his headquarters as supporters sought to get him nominated for the National Union Party in 1860. Mrs. **Lincoln** and her family stayed several times, and **Lincoln** spoke there during his 1864 trip. All of those mentioned in this paragraph would have seen the pretentious War of 1812 Battle Monument* erected between 1815 and 1825 in the middle of the intersection at Barnam's, being constructed when **Monroe** visited in 1817. They also saw the Washington Monument,* completed in 1829 at the top of the highest hill in downtown,

Barnam's Hotel site in Baltimore, where many presidents stayed, including Quincy Adams, Andrew Johnson, Monroe, Pierce, Wilson, Taylor, Buchanan, Theodore Roosevelt, Houston, and Davis. Lincoln spoke there. In the foreground is the 1812 Battle Monument erected in 1815.

and most saw nearby Fort McHenry.* **Harding** dedicated the Key Monument in 1922 at the fort near where "The Star Spangled Banner" was written. **Ford** spoke there July 4, 1975.

W. Harrison was at the Eutaw House (destroyed) in 1836, NW corner of Eutaw and West Baltimore. **Grant, Andrew Johnson,** and **Pierce** stayed several times later at a newer structure. **Jackson** and **Van Buren** were both at the Athenaeum at the SW corner of Lexington and St. Paul for the Democratic National Convention in May 1832. **Polk** was nominated in 1844 at Odd Fellows Hall,* 320 S. Highland, and **Pierce** at the Maryland Institute, SW corner of Baltimore and Market Place, in 1852. **Buchanan** was at the Universalist Church, Calvert and Pleasant, in 1848 for the Democratic National Convention. Little-known **Pierce** wound up with the nomination when the convention was unable to select from better-known candidates.

On February 23, 1861, **Lincoln** arrived at 3:30 A.M. incognito at the President Street Station, President, Canton, and Aliceanna, in a sleeping car to thwart a suspected plot to kidnap or kill him. It is now the Civil War Museum.* (After **Lincoln's** assassination, **Grant** was met here with a large armed guard on the way back to Washington.) The railroad car was pulled by horse down Pratt Street to the Camden Station, Camden and Howard, now adjacent to the Camden Yards Ballpark, and attached to the last train to Washington. (Later the Sixth Massachusetts Infantry had to make the same transfer and were attacked on Pratt in what is known as the Baltimore Riot, April 19, 1861.) **Lincoln** was supposed to arrive from Harrisburg at the Centre Street Station, also known as the Calvert Station, the terminus of the Northern Central Railroad to Harrisburg. This was in a block bounded by Calvert, Orleans, and opposite the Franklin intersection with Calvert. Here a Baltimore barber and conspirators planned to assassinate **Lincoln**. Three **George Bushes** were at Camden Yards on April 6, 1992, when George P., in the next generation, threw out the ball perfectly at 39 miles per hour. **Carter, Reagan** and **Bush Sr.** attended several games as president here.

Lincoln went to Gettysburg in November 1863 by way of the B&O Camden and Calvert Stations via the Northern Central. On April 18, 1864, he stayed at 702 Cathedral on Mt. Vernon Place, facing the Washington Monument,* when he came to speak at the Maryland Institute and spoke at the American Institute at Mt. Royal and Lanville. Large crowds greeted him at the station and throughout a long parade, a warm reception much different from the 1861 trip. He lay in state at the Merchant's Exchange on South Lombard at Gay and South, where **John Quincy Adams** had likewise been honored in death. **Andrew Johnson** was there after leaving office for a large reception where **Pierce** visited and **Fillmore** was nominated.

Johnson attended the laying of the cornerstone for the Masonic Hall at 225 N. Charles in 1866. In March 1863, he gave a speech for the Union at the Maryland Institute. **Grant** visited his friend George Small several times at Mt. Vernon Place at the Washington Monument.

Wilson attended graduate school at Johns Hopkins University in 1883 and lived at 906 (then 146) North Charles (current site of the Walters Art Gallery) and later at 909 N. McCulloch. He lectured in Hopkins Hall. His church was Scotch Presbyterian at 53 W. 14th. He met his first wife at this time. He also attended the Franklin Street (Bread of Life) Presbyterian Church at the NE corner of Franklin and Cathedral. Several have been to Memorial Stadium, 39th and Ellerslie, including **Carter** in 1979, **George H.W. Bush** in 1989, and **Clinton** in 1993.

Two future five-star generals, **Eisenhower** and his friend George Patton, were both almost killed twice while serving at Camp Meade, SW of the Baltimore–Washington Airport on Chamberlain Avenue. The first time was when a cable towing a heavy tank up a grade snapped and whipped within, by **Eisenhower**'s estimation, "five or six inches" of their heads. Saplings and brush around them were shaved as if by a razor. Later as they practiced with a machine gun and went in front of it to inspect the target, the overheated gun began to spontaneously fire haphazardly in their direction. Although the near tragedies were averted, **Eisenhower** suffered here what he termed "the greatest disappointment and disaster" of his life. For the first time, he and his wife had saved enough money to hire a neighborhood girl to help with chores. They did not know that she had recently had scarlet fever. Although she showed no signs, she evidently brought the disease, causing the death of his three-year-old son. The only building that **Eisenhower** would have known is the bachelor quarters on Taylor Avenue off of Mapes Road.

BETHESDA • **All presidents since FDR** dedicated it in 1936 have gone to the Naval Hospital, 8901 Wisconsin Ave. **JFK's** body was brought here after his assassination. Most presidents starting with **Harding** played golf at the Burning Tree Country Club, Burdette and River. **Nixon** visited his daughter and her husband David Eisenhower at their home, 7000 Armat Dr.

BLADENSBURG • **Washington, Jefferson,** and **Madison** stayed in an inn run by a black lady who had a reputation of keeping the best hotel in town. **Washington** also stayed at Indian Queen, later known as the George Washington House* at Baltimore and Upshur, now restored. This is just north of the Bladensburg Road (Alt. U.S. 1) junction with Annapolis Road (Route 202, 450). **Jefferson** was at the Rhodes Tavern six miles north on Route 1 near Beltsville on June 29, 1798. He also stayed at Van Horn's Tavern on the east side of U.S. 1, 1000 feet north of the Route 212 crossing at Beltsville. U.S. 1 follows the route used by **Washington** and the other Virginia presidents to and from the north, passing by many places and sites where they stopped.

BROOKVILLE • In 1814 **Madison** fled the British to the Caleb Bentley House (private), 205 Market two blocks east of the "S" curve on Maryland 97 at the center of town, where **Monroe** met him. There they heard the British had gone, so they proceeded back to see what was left.

Opposite, top: **Bladensburg Inn, where Washington, Madison, and Jefferson stayed.** ***Opposite, bottom:*** **Ft. Lincoln Cemetery near Bladensburg. Madison and Monroe watched the Battle of Bladensburg from the top of the hill by the mausoleum in the distance. Lincoln met officers at the Old Spring House, Maryland's oldest structure, in the foreground and drank from the adjacent spring at the "Bladensburg Oak," where the tree's remains are seen.**

BUSH • The old Bush Tavern on SR 7 near the SR's 136 crossing of I-95 near exit 80 claims **Washington**, **Jefferson**, **Madison**, and **Monroe**. This vanished town was the county seat at one time, but is not listed on any state map now.

CHESTERTOWN • **Washington** served for five years on the Board of Visitors and Governors of Washington College, Route 213. No building from the period survives on the campus. He visited at least eight times, as shown on the marker at the courthouse, saw the colonial homes still standing mostly on High Street at the river, and was present when the design of the school and buildings were planned. On March 23, 1791 (and apparently other times), he stayed at Worrell's Tavern, site marked on the SW corner of Queen and Cannon. **FDR** delivered an address in October 1933 and received a degree, as did **Truman** in 1946 and **Eisenhower** in 1954. **FDR** came by yacht and was entertained at the river estate (Godlington) of the chairman of the visitors. **Jefferson** spent two nights in town in 1797. He made at least 33 trips between Virginia and the north, traveling different routes. At least six were through Rock Hall and Chestertown's waterfront, some with **Madison**. **Garfield** spoke at the courthouse in 1863. **Kennedy** visited the campus before his presidency, promised to return as president, but never made it back.

CUMBERLAND • Known as Wills Creek in its infancy. **Washington's** military career began and ended at the important border to the wilderness. British King George II heard that the French were encroaching on his territory and wanted to send a messenger to discover the situation and deliver a warning. The 21-year-old **Washington** rode to Williamsburg to present himself, offered to go, was sent, and came four times in the mid–1750s. The first was in late 1753 to meet frontiersman Christopher Gist on the way to Fort Le Beouf. In 1754 he came leading Virginia forces, again to warn the French, but he wound up starting the French and Indian War. (See Fort Necessity, Pa.)

Then in 1755 **Washington** came as a military aide to General Braddock on the way to Fort Pitt, following a route west paralleling U.S. 40. He got sick at Tomlinson's Tavern in Little Meadows, today's Grantsville, recuperated some at Fort Cumberland, and then joined Braddock in time for a disastrous defeat near Pittsburgh. He was back in 1756 to the settlement now known as Fort Cumberland, as commander of Virginia forces sent to capture the French fort at the forks of the Ohio, later known as Pittsburgh. But he was only deemed second in overall command here since the fort was in Maryland, and a Marylander was a captain in the British regular army. There was a question as to proper military ranking, and **Washington** went to Boston to plead his case before the overall British commander.

In 1794 he returned to speak to troops before the Whiskey Rebellion, and is said to have appeared in military uniform for the last time, thus closing his military career where it started. He met a nephew at the fort and told him to set an example for the army.

The only remaining structure from Fort Cumberland is a small one-room cabin* used by **Washington**, moved to Riverside Park at the eastern end of Greene Street, south of the Baltimore Street Bridge over Wills Creek and opposite the train station and visitor center on the opposite side of the creek at its junction with the Potomac. It was originally on a hill within the fort about where the Episcopal church is now, next to the courthouse on Washington. The site is prominent just to the north along I-70. During the French and Indian War he built a series of forts along the Allegheny border, including Fort Ashby,* about ten miles south of here in West Virginia at the intersection of V.W. Routes 28 and 46. He came back several times following the same route as U.S. 40, through Hagerstown, Williamsport, Fort Frederick, Grantsville, etc.

Truman stayed in the large Fort Cumberland Hotel at Baltimore and Liberty in 1928, now a retirement home.

DONCASTER • Two **Washington** sites are near this small town south of Waldorf near the Potomac River. He met with his friend William Smallwood at his home, now in Smallwood State Park,* southwest of Marbury off Route 224. With Smallwood he visited Christ (Durham) Church* in June 1771, still active on Route 425 south of Ironsides on Route 6, west of La Plata.

ELKTOWN • Known during colonial times as "Head of Elk," this is where the Elk River flows into Chesapeake Bay. The landing, used by all the early Virginia presidents, is marked at the end of Landing Street, where colonial taverns still stand. British General Howe landed there in August 1777 on the way to Philadelphia, the capital. **Washington** watched the arrival from the top of Gray's Hill, north of town near Highway 40 and Graymount Mansion, and then moved his troops to White Clay Creek at Newark, Delaware. The day before he had slept in the Hollingsworth Tavern,* 205 West Main, west of the bridge on Bridge Street, on August 27, 1777, as shown by a small plaque on the building's south side. Howe slept there the next night. Washington would have seen Hollingsworth's nearby mansion, Partridge Hill,* on the north side of Main between Bow and Bridge Streets. In 1781, **Washington** came through toward Yorktown. He also stayed at the tavern at other times, including his trip home in 1797 with Martha and Lafayette's son, who was staying with him. **Jefferson's** Memo Book also shows that he stayed here.

ELLIOTT CITY • When **Jackson** boarded the B&O train at the now restored station, 2711 Maryland Avenue at Main,* in 1833, he became the first president to travel by train.

FREDERICK • **Washington** occupied an office in April 1755 on the south bank of Carroll Creek, generally in the second block west of All Saints Street, a block south of the John Hanson House at 108 Patrick. Hanson was president of the United States under the Articles of Confederation, really just the head of Congress. **Washington** met with General Braddock and Benjamin Franklin at this location, and was probably here other times. **Washington** and Franklin correctly supposed that Braddock underestimated the Indian threat and style of warfare. **Washington** later stayed in Brothers Tavern, Patrick and Church Streets, while coming back from his 1791 Southern tour. The bells of the still present churches rang in salute.

In August 1785 **Washington** visited his friend Thomas Johnson at his home, Richland, four miles northwest, north of Tuscarora Creek and west of Monocracy on the Frederick and Emmetsburg Turnpike. (**Harding** visited a friend here much later.) Johnson's nearby Catoctin Furnace* made cannon balls for the Revolution, was visited by **Washington**, and is now a state park. Johnson was a Washington Supreme Court appointee and turned down the president's request that he replace **Jefferson** as secretary of state. **Washington** also was honored a year later at Mrs. Kimball's, just east of the city, and at Rose Hill Manor,* north of town just west of North Market, now the Children's Museum. In the 1790s, **Washington** stopped at Cookerly's Tavern* at nearby New Midway, marked on Maryland Route 194 by the railroad track. He got refreshment, probably did not spend the night as claimed by the marker, but slept in Taneytown.

Jefferson's diary showed that he stayed at Crush's here on his way to and from Philadelphia when he wrote the Declaration of Independence, but the site is unknown, as is that of Peter Hanson's home, where **Washington** stayed in 1755. Frederick was on the National Road, now Alt. 40, and saw many prominent figures traveling from the west to the capital including **Monroe**, **Polk**, and **Houston**.

On February 5, 1841, **W. Harrison** stayed at Dorsey's City Hotel on the north side of Patrick between Market and Court. He is said to have caught a cold here speaking from the doorway, and carried it into his inauguration, maybe leading to his death a month later. (Actually he probably caught his final illness later in March.) The captured Mexican president, Santa Anna, also stayed here in captivity after the Texas Revolution, on the way to Washington. **Wilson** is pictured here in the twentieth century. **Jackson** frequently stayed at the Old Stone Tavern at Patrick and Jefferson, and Talbert's, NE corner of Patrick and Court.

In October 1862, after his visit to Antietam Battlefield, **Lincoln** visited General George L. Harsuff, recuperating from a battle wound at the Ramsey House, 119 Record Street, still facing the courthouse and city hall on the square. He traveled in a procession down Patrick Street to Court Street, then spoke briefly to a large crowd on the front steps and later at the B and O Station* still at the SE corner of All Saints and S. Market. He may also have visited wounded at the Presbyterian church,* 115 W. Second. In 1912, **TR** spoke at the courthouse* and at **Lincoln's** train station. In 1899 he spoke at the Opera House, 100 N. Market.

FDR and Churchill visited the Barbara Fritchie House* at 154 W. Patrick on May 17, 1943, on the way to Shangri La (Camp David). She supposedly challenged Confederate soldiers to shoot her "old gray head, but spare" their country's flag. **Roosevelt** was surprised and embarrassed that Churchill knew more about the questionable story than he did, so they made a point to see the structure, although it is a reconstruction.

FDR, **Nixon**, and **Truman** were entertained at Prospect Hill,* just northwest of the U.S. 15 and I-70 junction, west of town on Route 340 at 889 Butterfly Lane. It is assumed that **Washington** also visited as he knew the owner and received a horse "from here." General George Meade took over command of Union forces there before the Battle of Gettysburg.

Camp David, the presidential retreat for all

Lincoln visited a wounded general in the white home in the center here in Frederick, Maryland.

presidents beginning with **FDR**, is northwest in the Catoctin Mountains near Thurmont. **Eisenhower** named it after his grandson, who became Nixon's son-in-law. **Roosevelt** first came here in the summer of 1942 and quickly discovered that this was a more practical retreat than Hyde Park. **George H.W. Bush's** daughter was married here. It had been a CCC camp built for tourists. A visitor center is located in nearby Catoctin Mountain Park on Foxville Road, Route 77, two miles west of U.S. 15, although the exact location of the retreat is a secret and it is inaccessible to the public. A marker on a boulder on Catoctin Mountain notes that **Washington** and General Braddock passed on the National Trail here. **Hoover** fished at Trout Run, its stone buildings still at 12929 Catoctin Hollow Road nearby.

The village of Braddock Heights a few miles west on Alt. 40 still contains the resort Vindobona at the SW corner of Jefferson Blvd. and Clifton Road. **FDR** visited his former secretary Grace Tully here several times. **Ike** worshipped with Prime Minister McMillam on March 22, 1959, in Thurmont at Trinity Church of Christ, 101 E. Main.

HAGERSTOWN • **Washington** stayed at Beltzhoover's Tavern (also called Globe Tavern, Bell's, Washington House, and Baldwin House) on the north side of Washington Street, just west of Potomac, on October 12, 1790. It is thought that he was then traveling to nearby Williamsport to check out the site for the location of the nation's capital. **Jackson** stayed there in 1829. Since it is on the National Road, now U.S. 40, several presidents passed through. The list includes **Monroe** at Edward's Hotel on Washington Street and **William Henry Harrison** at McIlhenny's Tavern on the NW corner of Washington and North Potomac Street, now an antique shop. Many then came from Virginia and Pennsylvania to shout themselves hoarse and share in the 112-pound cake in his honor. **Jackson's** reception was somewhat more subdued, and he attended the Presbyterian church, then at the east side of the bend in Potomac Street, now just south of the library where a Baptist church is now. **Madison** and **Monroe** visited the Gen. Samuel Ringgold house, on College Road near the junction with MD 68, in 1801. **Harding** passed through the area in 1921 on a camping trip with Henry Ford, Thomas Edison, and Harvey Firestone.

HANCOCK • **Washington** stayed at Cohill's Manor, 5102 Western Pike, now a B&B.

LAURE • **Washington** often stayed with his friend Thomas Snowden at Montpelier,* now on Muirkirk Road .025 miles NE of the exit off SR 295 at Route 197. Since Abigail **Adams** also stayed here and described it in her diary, we might assume that her husband also was here. Ike stayed at 327 Montgomery while assigned to Camp Meade.

LA PLATA • **Washington** visited La Grange (private), the home of his friend and doctor, James Craik, on numerous occasions. It is located on Route 6, west of U.S. 301.

OAKLAND • **Garfield, Grant, Cleveland,** and **B. Harrison** vacationed at nearby Deer Park Hotel and attended St. Matthew's Episcopal, Second and Liberty. The hotel became **Cleveland's** honeymoon cottage and the most famous house in America for five days in June 1889. The 49-year-old president brought his 21-year-old wife, Frank, here hoping to find privacy, but was besieged by reporters who had followed, lurked in the woods, and climbed trees to spy on the famous couple. **Cleveland** wrote that he loved the cottage and felt quite at home. (Frank later had her named changed to Frances.)

OLDTOWN • One block south of SR 51 is the Cresap House, visited by **Washington** as a surveyor in 1748, probably on his other trips from Winchester to Cumberland, and later in 1770, as shown in his diary.

PERRYVILLE • Washington, Jefferson, and Madison frequented the Rodgers Tavern* on their trips to Philadelphia. It still stands on the south side of the Post Road, now Route 7, at the Susquehanna River, south of the U.S. 40 bridge. In fact Washington's incomplete diary recorded 30 trips through this area.

PINEY POINT • The "Lighthouse of the Presidents," off Maryland 249 east the U.S. 301 Bridge on the Potomac, served as summer White House for **Monroe, Pierce,** and **TR.**

TANEYTOWN • **Washington** stayed in the Adam Good Tavern on July 1, 1791, then at Route 140 and 194.

UPPER MARLBORO • **Washington** traveled the route of present U.S. 50 on many occasions and stayed at various sites along the route. One frequent stop was the Widow Ramsey's Tavern about halfway to Baltimore from here. He used room number seven on the second floor at the Marlboro House on Main Street across from the courthouse. He was a frequent visitor to Mount Airy,* just south in Rosaryville, and attended the wedding of his stepson there at the bride's parent's home, even though he considered the couple too young for marriage. The home is located about five and a half miles south on 301 and about a mile west on Rosaryville Road, marked in a state park. The union produced a daughter and son raised by **Washington.**

WARWICK • On May 14, 1773, **Washington's** diary shows that he dined and lodged at Worsell Manor while taking his stepson to King's College in New York. He also dined and lodged at his factor's house as shown by a plaque on Main Street.

WILLIAMSPORT • The Potomac River town was once considered as a possible site of the capital of the United States. **Washington** came to examine the area and discussed this proposal in the Springhouse* at the end of Springfield Lane, south of Potomac Street off U.S. 11. It was decided that since this was too far beyond the navigable section of the river, the capital would be further downstream. He lodged here in 1794 during the Whiskey Rebellion.

MASSACHUSETTS

AMHERST • **Coolidge** graduated cum laude from Amherst College, where he attended from 1891 to 1895. He went to the Johnson Chapel on campus and lived in several places including the Avery House on Prospect. **Kennedy** made one of his last public appearances before 10,000 at the field house where he got an honorary degree as Doctor of Laws and attended the groundbreaking for the Robert Frost Library on October 26, 1963.

ANDOVER • In November 1790, **Washington** ate at Abbot's Tavern (private), still at 70 Elm Street, and visited Judge Samuel Phillips at the Mansion House on the Academy campus, west side of Main facing Salem Street. **Washington's** grandnephews attended and stayed in the home.

After visiting his sister-in-law at 48 Central (private), President-elect **Pierce**, his wife Jane, and their surviving son, eleven-year-old Bennie, traveled back to New Hampshire on January 6, 1853, when their train derailed a mile north of the depot. The spot is near Shawsheen Village along the tracks at the still present steep embankment about 100 yards northwest of Penguin Park on Burnham Road and 150 yards from where the track crosses over the road between Rock O' Dundee Road and Arundel. The parents were uninjured, but Bennie was mangled before their eyes. This severely affected **Pierce** for his entire presidency and indeed, the rest of his life.

Jane became a recluse hidden away upstairs in the White House, writing letters to her dead son, when she normally would be the unofficial hostess of the nation's social center. She had concluded that God had taken her boy to leave the president undistracted. But it left him a broken man in "hopeless sorrow" and destroyed his prospects for an effective presidency, affecting the history of the country. Bennie's body was taken to the Andover Arms House, an imposing red brick tavern still 100 yards south across the field between Argyle and Arundel, and then to 48 Central, where a wake was held several days later. Jane died in 1863 at 48 Central, a frequent summer destination for the president while in office.

Both **Bushes** went to Phillips Academy at Phillips and Main. **TR** enrolled his son Archie here after being expelled from Groton. **George W.** stayed in the American House on Main Street, where "My Country 'Tis of Thee" was written. The elder **Bush** was celebrated for at least 23 distinctions including "Best All-around Fellow," president of the senior class, and captain of the baseball team, and was "an omnipresent checkpoint" of what was wanted and expected. The younger **George** said his mission was to instill frivolity.

BOSTON • The 22-year-old commander in chief of Virginia military forces, **George Washington**, came to see British military commander Governor Shirley at his Roxbury home, then off of Dudley, now at 33 Shirley St.,* in February, 1756. Or so it's claimed; actually there is no proof where he met with Shirley, there or at his town house, the Province House. (During the Revolution, the Continental Army stayed here, and **Washington** was at least nearby.) But surmise and tradition says that he was at the home and improved Mt. Vernon the next year based on ideas he got from the mansion. He lost playing cards at the Province House, on Washington Street at the head of Milk Street, across the street from the Old South Church, and stayed about two weeks nearby at the Cromwell Head Inn, 15–17 School Street. **John and John Quincy Adams** also came here when it was called Brackett's Tavern. Steps of the old Province House can be seen, marked on Province Street just east of Bromfield.

Washington was on the only unwounded officer in Braddock's 1755 defeat. It was well known that the British commander had failed to heed **Washington's** advice that might have saved his forces. Shirley's son was killed fighting at **Washington's** side. Now the young militia commander was receiving no respect from junior officers among the British regulars whom he was supposed to command, and he wanted to know where he stood. He lost his appeal. (See Cumberland, Maryland.) Later the Province House was British Commander Gage's and then Howe's headquarters. From here Gage sent out troops on April 18, 1775, to start the Revolutionary War at nearby Lexington and Concord, and later Howe decided to evacuate Boston.

Washington returned in summer 1775 to Cambridge across the Charles River to command the Continental Army. The British evacuated on March 17, 1776, after **Washington** moved cannon to the domineering Dorchester Heights* south of downtown, where a monument was placed in his honor. This is clearly visible from the Southeast Freeway, Exit 16, and reached by taking Telegraph Street due east from Dorchester Street at Eighth in South Boston. It humiliated the greatest military power on earth to be forced to retreat by an army of amateurs.

After the British left, **Washington** inspected their fortifications on and around the Boston Common* across from the present State House* on Beacon Hill. He stayed about six days at Court and Tremont, Scollay Square, inspected Faneuil Hall, and went to the Concert Hall just up Court at Hanover. On his last Sunday in Boston, **Washington** went to Trinity Church on the corner of Haley and Summer, facing west on Copley Square, near his headquarters two blocks south of Old South Church, where he attended often and had come in 1756.

Washington came to survey from the gallery the British destruction of Old South Church,* 310 Washington at Milk Street, a meeting place for patriots before the Revolution. The current Washington Street was the street entered by all coming into the city down what was the narrow "Boston Neck" to the mainland. Benjamin Franklin was born up the street (marked on the Freedom Trail) and brought that day to be baptized in a prior church on site. The church overflowed after the Boston Massacre while Samuel Adams went back and forth to the State House,* then the Town House, Washington and State Streets, with demands for troop withdrawal. Citizens also met here on December 16, 1773, to march to the Boston Tea Party, a protest of English taxes, held at Griffin's Wharf, marked inland on the south side of Congress St. between Purchase and Atlantic near Pearl. The oceanfront is now several blocks away. **John Adams** was often at the church. British General Burgoyne turned it into a British riding school in revenge for the tax protest here. He was later held prisoner in the Apthrop House on the Harvard campus, near the northeast corner of Mount Auburn (Lampoon) and Plympton.

In 1789 **Washington** returned, parading down Washington Street as the first president of a new country, and was honored at many sites still on Boston's well-marked Freedom Trail. While in the state he toured Springfield, Leicester, Worcester, Middlesex, Marlborough, Weston, Shrewsbury, Sudbury, Newburyport, Marblehead, Salem, Amesbury, Lynn, Malden, and Salisbury. **John Adams** escorted him to the Old State House and Faneuil Hall. **Washington** spent six days at the Ingersol Inn on the south corner of Tremont and Court, directly across from the Sears Block, now the State Street Bank, and ate there with **Adams. Jefferson** stayed with a Col. Ingersol in 1784 on the way to Europe, and the location is thought to be the same.

Washington was a guest twice at the Bowdoin Mansion, 10½ Beacon, where the Bellevue Hotel now is, and was honored at a large feast at Faneuil Hall. **Washington** also visited Brattle Square Church on the square and the First Meeting House at the site of the Boston County Building. He heard an oratorio on October 27, 1789, at Kings Chapel,* School and Tremont, where he had also attended in 1776, sitting in the governor's pew (marked) both times. **Adams** was here several times where in 1803 he heard **John Quincy** deliver an address.

John Hancock inherited his uncle's mansion, site marked on Beacon Street on the top of Beacon Hill, in 1777, now occupied by the west wing of the new 1798 State House.* As governor he invited **Washington** to stay with him during the first presidential visit, but **Washington** declined in favor of a public inn. Then Hancock pleaded sickness, real or pretended, and could not call first on **Washington**. This created a public stir, as there was still a question of the relative importance of a president of the federal government and state governor. **Washington** held his ground and sent word that he would not see Hancock unless it was at his own lodgings. Hancock gave in, "even at the hazard of [his] health," a step that helped to establish federal supremacy. It was hoped that the mansion would be preserved when the new State House was occupied in 1798, and new additions were later added, but it was destroyed in 1863 after a long preservation campaign. **John and John Quincy Adams** stayed there after they returned from Europe in 1788.

Washington reviewed a parade on the steps (marked) of the (New) State House while he passed a handkerchief in front of his eyes as an ode was sung to him. Many presidents have been to the State House including the **Adamses, Mon-**

roe, Fillmore, Jackson, Van Buren, Taft, and probably **Lincoln,** but he did not speak there as claimed. **TR** always admired the Shaw Statue in front of the Capitol. **Coolidge** served here as governor as well as president of the senate.

The **Adamses** were familiar with all sites on the current Freedom Trail. In 1758 **John** lived in the nearby town of Arlington at Pleasant and Massachusetts as shown by a marker on the Green. As a lawyer and leader, he kept diaries that show many details of the town's political gatherings at the Old State House,* Faneuil Hall,* and Old South Church,* leading to the Revolution, for which he presented legal and political arguments. **John** was honored several times at each location, including at Faneuil in 1789 with **Washington** and in 1797. Guides insist that all presidents have spoken here, but the official brochure lists only **Jefferson Davis** and documentation in the Park Service library shows only those listed here. **Davis'** speech was in October 1858 when he argued that slavery was not denounced in the Bible or the Constitution and had helped blacks more than anything else, to Christianize and civilize them. **Adams** was brought here two weeks after his beloved Abigail died to see the huge John Trumbull painting of the signing of the Declaration of Independence that now hangs in the Capitol Rotunda in Washington. He pointed to the back door on the right side of the painting and commented, "When I nominated **George Washington** of Virginia for Commander-in-Chief of the Continental Army, he took his hat and rushed out that door." **Adams** had lectured the artist on accuracy. His son was nominated for president in 1817 in the hall where he later lay in state. Official documentation by the National Park Service also lists **Truman** in 1948 as the last president who spoke there, although **Carter** visited in 1976 as well as both **Bushes. Clinton** spoke outside on the south side, and **Kennedy** gave his last campaign speech inside. **Grant** was given a reception in August 1865.

In the late 1760s **Adams** lived at the White House, NE corner of old Brattle and Court, across from the Brattle Square Church. Brattle ran north from Court, east of Cambridge toward the west end of the city hall, less than two blocks from Faneuil Hall. **John Quincy's** homes were with his father until 1782. In 1770 **John** moved to Cold Lane by the Mill Pond, where his son Charles was born. This street ran northward from Hanover to the Mill Pond and was indiscriminately called Cold or Cole Lane. At the time, Hanover ran from where it now ends to Cambridge, parallel to and about 50 yards south of the Federal Building. They then moved back to his own home in Braintree (now Quincy) in mid–1771 for a short time before moving back to Boston, where they lived from 1771 to 1775 on Court opposite the courthouse, where it was convenient for him to practice law out of the home. This was South Queen at the time, about a block west of the Old State House. **John Quincy** lived in and practiced law in the Court Street house in 1790. When the war started in April 1775, **John** first stayed here and moved his family back to Quincy.

Adams attended the Unitarian church, Marlborough and Berkeley, after 1768. His office was on King (State) Street, and he frequented the Green Dragon, called "the headquarters of the Revolution" and marked 81 Union Street at Hanover, and also the American Coffee House at 66 State. (The present Green Dragon is several blocks away.) **Adams** landed at the Long Wharf at the end of State Street upon his return from Europe, the site of the present aquarium.

Jefferson had to wait in 1784 for a ship to carry him to France, and spent time touring Ipswich, Salem, Marblehead, Exeter, Portsmouth, and other nearby towns. **Monroe** visited the city in 1817 and stayed at the NW corner of State and Congress. He visited Faneuil Hall and the Old North Church* at 193 Salem at the foot of Hull Street. The lanterns hung by Paul Revere's friend before his famous ride were in the bell tower. **TR** occupied pew 25 in 1912, and **Franklin Roosevelt** spoke in 1920. **Ford** used the pulpit to initiate the nation's Bicentennial. A reception was held for **Monroe** at 45 Beacon Street,* the home of Harrison Gray Otis.

Across the river near Old North, as the Freedom Trail continues, is the Bunker Hill Monument, dedicated by **Tyler** in 1843, where **Pierce, Jackson** (with **Van Buren**), and many others have spoken and visited. (The monument is on the site of the famous battle, Breed's Hill. Before the fight it was thought that the higher Bunker Hill should be fortified, but it was determined that Breed's had more military value. Also the British got the names reversed on their maps, resulting in the misnamed battle.) **JFK's** mother brought him to Bunker Hill at age five and expected him to remember the details of her historical lecture to him. Down the hill west of the monument is the Warren Tavern* at Two Pleasant Street at the NE corner of Main between Main and Warren Streets, where **Washington** stopped in 1789.

John Quincy Adams's home from 1801 to 1803 was at 39 Hanover Square, Tremont and Boylston, where his son Charles Frances was born. He served the country well as ambassador to Great Britain during the Civil War. This is the site of Hotel Touraine, where **Coolidge** lived from 1907 to 1921. **Adams** used 57 Mt. Vernon Street as a winter home beginning in 1842. Charles was living here later when, at age seventy-nine, **John Quincy** insisted on taking a walk and had a stroke in front of the home. He was unable to resume his service in Congress for a while, but returned to have a fatal stoke the next year.

Lincoln arrived on September 15, 1848, and made speeches in the area until September 22. He would have had time to see the sights including State Houses and Faneuil Hall. On the 15th, he spoke before the Boston Whig Club for Taylor's election at Washingtonian Hall at 23 Bromfield Street. This was a preliminary speech to his main event at Worcester. (Several sources, including *Following Abraham Lincoln,* inaccurately show a speech at the State House. He may have brought his family as sometimes related.)

Lincoln stayed in the Tremont House on the Freedom Trail, located just north of the Granary Burial Ground, where he may have stood at the graves of those whom he would have read about: Paul Revere, Samuel Adams, John Hancock, and others of the Revolution. On September 22, he spoke at the Tremont Temple,* 275 Tremont, marked across from the hotel. It burned in 1852, but later buildings with the same name have occupied the site. He visited the telegraph office daily on Court Square, one block northeast of the Tremont. The hotel also hosted **Jackson, Pierce, Tyler, Houston,** and **Van Buren. Jackson** was sick here, bled over two days and almost died before the doctors stopped the flow. Extra carpet was put in the halls to keep noise down. **Davis** stayed with a desperately sick son in 1858. **Pierce**'s presidential campaign headquarters were here, and he came many times before and after his election. **Houston** is said to have won the crowd when he gave the Southern viewpoint on slavery at the Temple in 1855. He argued that all states had slavery during the Revolution when slave owners won freedom. But the institution became unprofitable in the North as immigrants provided cheap labor. Now it was under control, would soon die, and it was not worth the trouble to hasten the inevitable end. He argued that there would be no conflict except for the Northern unrest.

Lincoln's 1848 program at Tremont Temple included his later secretary of state, William A. Seward, probably their first meeting. (But see Worcester.) Seward spoke first and his speech appeared in full in the Boston papers. **Lincoln** had no manuscript, and thus no words were recorded. He commented to Seward, "I have been thinking about what you said in your speech. I reckon you are right. We have got to deal with this slavery question and got to give much more attention to it hereafter than we have been doing." A plaque at the present 1896 Temple boasts of having a number of famous speakers and performers: Jenny Lind, Daniel Webster, Charles Dickens, John Gilbert, etc. **Lincoln** is not mentioned, but it is claimed elsewhere that all presidents from **Lincoln** until **Hoover** spoke there. Lincoln passed through again in 1860 on his way to and from New Hampshire, using the Boston and Providence Depot just west of the present intersection of Eliot and Broadway. This is several blocks south of the Charles/Boylston intersection, south of the public gardens. He then and in 1848 had time to see various landmarks.

Pierce came to 20 Bromfield to take his college roommate, author Nathaniel Hawthorne, back to New Hampshire when he was sick. **Johnson** dedicated the Masonic Temple at Tremont and Boylston in 1867. **Grant** stayed in St. James Hotel at 11 W. Newton Street in 1869. The Hotel Vendome, Commonwealth Ave. at Dartmouth, saw **Cleveland, Grant, B. Harrison,** and **McKinley. Wilson** was at the Central Congregational Church in April 1896. The Revere House hosted **Fillmore, Pierce, Andrew Johnson,** and **Grant.** It was located in the middle of the present Saltenstall State Building on the east side of Bowdoin, south of Cambridge St. **Kennedy's** voting residence was 122 Bowdoin on Beacon Hill facing the State House.

Several presidents have been to the theaters at 539 Washington, as well as many other famous royal guests and performers. As part of a club initiation, **Theodore Roosevelt** sat in the balcony and applauded during the most intense emotional moments of a play until he was thrown out. The night before his wedding, **TR** stayed in the Brunswick Hotel, Berkeley Street. He married in 1880 in the Unitarian church at 382 Walnut Street in Brookline and invited his old childhood friend Edith Carow, who would later become the second Mrs. Roosevelt.

Coolidge served in the State House in four capacities: both houses, lieutenant governor, and governor. He commuted from the Adams Hotel,

553 Washington Street, for business and rented two rooms when he became lieutenant governor. During his stay he made the famous remark, "There is no right to strike against public safety by anyone, anywhere, anytime," leading to his nomination as vice president. **FDR** is pictured at many locations in Boston.

The birthplace of **Kennedy** is at 83 Beals Street, Brookline.* He was baptized at the baptismal font still at St. Aidan's Catholic Church, 158 Pleasant. In 1923–4 he attended the Edward Devotion School, 347 Harvard, a couple of blocks from the birthplace near the corner of Stedman Street. The family moved to a larger house nearby at the NE corner of 131 Naples and Abbottsford, where Robert and two sisters were born and the future president lived from age four until ten. He and his older brother were altar boys at St. Aidan's, and both attended the Dexter School, then at 169 Freeman Street, and Edward Devotion School, 345 Harvard. (These sites are between Beacon and Commonwealth.) His father, millionaire Joe Kennedy, was not too happy when he considered himself snubbed at the country club because of his religion, so he packed up and moved to Bronxville, New York. When **John** later ran for president, his headquarters were at the Bellevue Hotel, 10½ Beacon near the State House, and he stayed at the Ritz Carlton at 15 Arlington in Boston. Joe Kennedy once confronted vice presidential candidate **Truman** at the hotel during the 1944 campaign to complain about **Truman**'s support for Roosevelt, "that crippled SOB that killed my son Joe." **Truman** threatened to throw him out the window, and said in 1960 that he was not afraid of the pope, but the pop. The birthplace was repurchased in 1966, when restoration was started by his mother, whose recorded voice guides visitors today. Several presidents have visited the **Kennedy** Museum at Columbia Point south of downtown including **Clinton** on May 28, 2003. **Carter** spoke at Logan Airport on August 21, 1980.

Boston suburbs include:

Beverly: While president, **Taft** vacationed at 55 Ober Street at Burgess Point and 70 Corning. He worked at 244 Cabot, and went to church at 225 Cabot in the First Parish Church. His July 5, 1912, parade through town drew 10,000.

Cambridge: **Washington** took command of the Continental Army on the Common between Garden, Waterhouse, and Massachusetts Streets on July 3, 1775. Three cannon mark the site on the west side not far from the church. They were abandoned by the British at Fort Independence (Castle William), when they left on March 17, 1776. Three buildings fronting the common survive: Christ Church, the Waterhouse House, and the gray house on the northern end. **Washington's** headquarters were at the Wadsworth House* from July 2–9, 1775, on the north side of Massachusetts, just east of Harvard Square at Boylston Street, now used by Harvard. From July until the next spring, **Washington**, with Martha part of the time, used a house later owned by the poet Henry Wadsworth Longfellow, known as the Vassall or Craigie House,* 105 Brattle Street, just west of the Common. (**Pierce** was here just after his nomination in 1852.) It is now the Longfellow National Historic Site. Martha did not come until a British warship landed near Mt. Vernon, and George sent a courier for her to join him, which is what she wanted all along.

John Adams was here as a member of Congress on January 16, 1776, when **Washington's** officers rejected a plan to attack Boston by sending troops across the frozen bay. The commander approved a suggestion by 25-year-old Henry Knox to bring captured British cannon 300 miles from Ft. Ticonderoga to Boston and named Knox to lead the endeavor. **Washington** and General Putnam used the Hicks House as an army office at the NW corner of Eliot and Boylston, south of the Common.

Several buildings on the Harvard campus predate the Revolutionary Period, including Massachusetts Hall, where **John Adams** lived as a student in number 3 and later number 19 in the lower northwest chamber. **Adams** studied in the lab of his favorite professor in the Philosophy Room and dined on "wretched" fare in the ground floor dining hall of Harvard Hall, north and parallel to Massachusetts Hall, just inside the campus at Massachusetts Ave. In 1779 he attended a diplomatic dinner honoring the French minister in the Philosophy Hall. **John Quincy** entered as a junior and stayed with his brother in adjoining Hollis Hall, also dating to the same era. All period buildings were used by colonial troops. Tradition says that **Washington** broke up a violent snowball fight among his troops on the yard here. Both **Adamses** attended the First Church of Cambridge, then at the SW of present Lehman Hall. **John** took notes, criticized the sermons in his diary, and got a divinity degree at age fifteen. In August 1779, the state constitutional convention was held in the church with **Adams** in attendance, back from his European assignment. He was chosen to write the Massachusetts Constitution and drafted it at his Braintree home, now the oldest functioning constitution in the world. The standing desk that he used is now in the library adjacent to his final home.

Christ Church on Garden Street still faces the Common. After the loyalist Anglican congregation departed with the British, it was used as barracks. But when Martha Washington arrived she requested that it be returned to a state so that church services could be held. **Washington's** pew, number 93, is marked at the far left front. During this time a funeral was held for a British officer, and a mob wrecked the church again. A prominent bullet hole near the entrance, easy to spot just inside over the door, still remains from this incident.

Various other presidents have gone to Harvard including the **Roosevelts**, **Hayes**, **Kennedy**, and **George W. Bush. Hayes** was the first president with a law degree and **Bush** the first with an MBA. Energetic **TR** ran from class to class and talked so much that a professor finally shouted, "See here, **Roosevelt**, let me talk. I'm running this course." His sister had picked out Number 16 Winthrop Street as his apartment, had the rooms painted, and got the furniture. Like **FDR** later, **TR** had lived a rather sheltered life as of his first schooling. His adolescent activity consisted of too much book reading and dead bird stuffing, so it took him most of two years here to figure out where he fit in and how he measured up. Since he was relatively frail as a boy, it was thought that New England winters might be too much for him. He sometimes had to stand for Philips Brook's sermons at the overcrowded Trinity Church on Copley Square and taught Sunday school at Christ Church. When a boy came to class with a black eye and confessed that he got into a fight with a bigger boy who had been pinching his sister, **Roosevelt** told him he had done right to fight and gave him a dollar. This did not fit the "turn the other cheek" principles. Then, after teaching for three and a half years, he was found to be Presbyterian, not Episcopalian. The rector told him he must join or quit; so he then left to teach elsewhere. **Monroe** got an honorary degree at Harvard in 1817. When **Jackson** visited in 1833, the university felt they had to do the same for him. **John Quincy Adams** was invited but refused to sit next to "a barbarian who could barely write his name or a sentence." When the ceremony was completed after the Harvard president's Latin address, a student supposedly cried out for the new doctor to address them in Latin. Instantly Jackson (supposedly) replied, "E pluribus unum, my friend, sine qua non!"

When **Pierce's** wife heard that he had been nominated, she promptly became distraught and fainted. So he brought her to the Brattle House, 105 Brattle, as he tried in vain to calm her, since she constantly tried to stop his political career. **Lincoln** came by the Fitchburg Railroad Depot on Causeway between Haverhill and Beverly and spoke on September 20, 1848, at City Hall, then at the NE corner of Harvard and Norfolk. The *Boston Atlas* reported, "Mr. **Lincoln** ... is a capital specimen of a 'Sucker' Whig, six feet at least in his stockings, and every way worthy to represent that Spartan band of the only Whig district in poor benighted Illinois."

Hayes lived where Mathews Hall stands today. When **Cleveland** made a speech at Memorial Hall, a row of newspapermen whom he hated was near the platform. He made everyone very uncomfortable by snarling very audibly, "Oh, those ghouls of the press."

FDR lived in Adams Hall in 1899, between Harvard Square and the Charles River, where the facilities, including the always running toilet, are the same as then. It is called the most historic house at Harvard. **Kennedy** met his senior thesis advisor in the Coolidge Room here. **Roosevelt** then lived in some of the most expensive rooms at the university at Westmorly Court from 1900 until 1904. **Kennedy** lived in the Freshmen Dormitory, Weld 32, and Winthrop House, NW corner of Boylston and Mount Auburn, while attending Harvard. **John Adams** stayed there in the early 1750's. **Kennedy** also roomed at 32 Weld Hall in the Yard's south boundary. Although frail and undersized he tried to play "third rate" football, but hurt his back, giving him a lifetime of misery. He spent most of his free time at his club at 76 Mount Auburn. His first two years were heavily involved with the opposite sex, but he became a scholar during the last two, involving himself in world affairs. He ran for Congress from here in 1946. From then until his death, his legal address was 122 Bowdoin Street, Apartment 36.

***Chelsea*: Lincoln** spoke on September 19, 1848, at Gerrish Hall, northeast of the square at 165 Winnisimmet, near the NE corner with Park, between the Pearl Street Bridge and Mystic River Bridge. The *Boston Atlas* described the speech, "which for aptness of illustration, solidity of argument, and genuine eloquence, is hard to beat."

Concord: **Washington** visited the historic sites in 1789 and ate in the Concord Tavern* on the west side of Monument Square, still open for business. A marker that in prior years was on a house across from the Wright Tavern claimed that he noticed the house across Lexington Road, and patterned the outside of Mt. Vernon on the style existing then and now.

Dedham: **Lincoln** spoke September 20, 1848, at Temperance Hall near the train station on Pleasant Street. The hall site is on the east side of Court Street about midway between High and Church Streets, around the corner from the present courthouse, where Sacco and Vanzetti were tried in 1921. **Lincoln's** escort described him as withdrawn, awkward, and ill at ease on the train ride and at the reception at the Haven House, now the community center* at the NW corner of Court and High. Newspapermen with him felt that his invitation was a great mistake, but when introduced, **Lincoln** instantly transformed his demeanor and expression to "bubble out humor and charm." After thirty minutes when the train bell signaled that his train was leaving, **Lincoln** announced that he had to go. The crowd yelled "No, no!" and urged that he continue. But he ran, saying that he was committed to speak in Cambridge. He might have stopped at the inn at 19 Court. **JFK's** father sent him and his older brother as probably the only Catholics in Noble and Greenough School to test their mettle.

Lexington: **Washington** was a guest at the early 18th-century Monroe Tavern,* 1332 Massachusetts Avenue, in 1789 as he came to visit the site of the opening battles of the Revolution. His table and chair used during his upstairs meal are still displayed. As the war began up the street on April 19, 1775, the British commander used it for a while after his troops ransacked it and killed the man in charge. The Battlefield Green a short distance west still has several structures **Washington** observed where the first shots were fired, including the Buckman Inn,* Monroe, and Harrington Houses, all marked. **Grant** attended the celebrations on the one-hundredth anniversary of the battles here and at Concord, as did **Ford** on the 200th.

Lynn: **Taft** attended First Unitarian at Main and Summer, and **Coolidge** used the seventh floor of the Security Trust Co. on Central Square.

Marblehead: The Jeremiah Lee Mansion,* on Washington Street opposite Mason Street, received **Washington** in 1789 and later **Monroe** and **Jackson**. It was the home of a leading merchant who led in preparing Massachusetts for the war, but died just as it started. **John Adams** was at the Azor Orne House, 18 Orne Street, and Old Town Hall on Washington.

Medford: General John Stark made the Isaac Royal House* at 15 George Street his headquarters during the Revolution, and was frequently visited by **Washington**.

Milton: **George H.W. Bush** was born at 173 Adams Street, about two miles up the same street as the Adams' Old House in Quincy. These two men, who lived on the same street, shared other characteristics besides being the only presidential fathers of presidential sons and were the only sitting two-term vice presidents elected directly to the presidency. They had served as vice president with a political rival and were then were defeated for reelection by a Southerner (**Jackson** and **Clinton**), born after his father died, accused of sexual impropriety, who was reelected. Their Harvard graduate sons, each with their same first name, but a different middle initial, were elected by the Electoral College after losing the popular vote to a Tennessean.

Quincy: The **Adams** National Historical Park Visitor Center at 1250 Hancock Street (the town's main street) has a trolley to the historic **Adams** homes. (It's quicker and easier to drive yourself unless you want a guaranteed interior tour since bus tour members get first choice to enter.) Here are the oldest presidential birthplaces and the only two adjacent.

John Adams was born in 1735 in the 1681 house at 133 Franklin,* then known as the Penn's Hill Farm, where he spent his formative years before going to Harvard. He studied at home with his mother, then at Dame Belcher's across Coast Road from 1741 to 1743, and then with an indifferent teacher he hated at Free Latin School near the Meeting House, about one mile from home, 1743–50. In 1750–1 he was at Marsh School on Franklin Street, two doors from his home. He wanted to leave school when he was fifteen to be a farmer against the strong wishes of his parents, who wanted him to study for the ministry at Harvard. In an attempt to bring him back to his senses, his father put him to work shoveling manure and doing other equally appalling work. When asked if he was satisfied, he replied that the liked it very much. The family ignored him, but he soon decided that Harvard was not so bad after all. He got his bachelor's and master's degrees, but still wound up a lawyer by studying law in Worcester. He then came back to live with his parents, who still called him "Johnny" or "Jack," and opened an office in the home.

Like many houses then, it had hidden stairs around the chimney in case of an Indian attack, but that danger had passed by **John**'s birth. The old house was stifling hot in summer, while in winter, overcoats were worn inside all day as water left in glasses turned to ice. **Adams**' father bought the adjacent, similar house at 141 Franklin in 1744. **John** inherited it in 1761 when he was almost 29. The inheritance made him a property owner, allowing him to take part in town meetings, be a fuller member of the community, and marry Abigail. This was always an isolated farm, but the street was the coastal road from Maine to Cape Cod. He spent many hours before the fireplace listening to his father and prominent men discuss current issues and various subjects like predestination. But **John** preferred action rather than theological discussions.

His father-in-law had not considered a lawyer and son of a farmer to be decent husband material for the daughter of a clergyman descended from a long line of clergymen. This 1663 structure at 141 Franklin was where he brought Abigail, his new wife, in 1764, and where his son **John Quincy** was born in 1767. Author David McCullough believes that Quincy probably had the highest IQ of any president. His parents realized while he was young that he was a prodigy. **John** used this as a home and law office for much of the time until moving back and forth to and from Boston several times. **John** purchased his adjacent birthplace house from his brother in 1774, and in 1803 gave or sold both houses to **John Quincy**, who lived in his own birthplace until 1807. When the houses were restored, much of the original material was saved. For about twenty years **John** was gone about half the time while Abigail took care of family business.

Nearby Penn's Hill was a favorite spot for **John** to wander and survey the countryside during his lifelong daily walks. He came here for a private place of meditation and rode over the hill on the way to see Abigail in Weymouth. The hill is now in a residential neighborhood about a third of a mile down Franklin Street. At 3:00 A.M. on June 17, 1775, Abigail roused seven-year-old **John Quincy** when she heard cannon fire, and the two went to the top of the hill to witness the Battle of Bunker Hill. This now seems to be an impossible view, but evidently it could be seen then without the modern buildings. She emphasized that some day schoolboys would memorize the momentous date. Eight months later they watched from here as what they called "the largest fleet ever seen in America" sailed out of Boston. In 1843 the former president commented: "Do you wonder that a boy of seven who witnesses this scene would be a patriot?" A water tower and plaque on a cairn mark the spot in a small park at 353 Franklin.

The nicest house in town belonged to Josiah Quincy. Abigail was a descendant and gave the name to her first son. This was also where John Hancock was born. That fact is marked in front of the present structure, the Adams Historical Society,* at the NW corner of Hancock and Whitney. **John Adams** once worked up enough nerve here to propose marriage to Quincy's daughter Hannah, when cousins entered the room and broke the spell. A second chance never came, which is probably good, since Abigail provided him with an ideal partner for life. When historians later rated first ladies, she was ranked number two after Eleanor Roosevelt.

A later (1770) "Josiah Quincy House"* at 20 Muirhead is open to the public, but unrelated to the events related in the above paragraph. Both **John** and **John Quincy** were familiar with this house and also the Quincy Homestead* at 1010 Hancock. When **John Quincy** walked by the latter with the daughter of the Quincy who had been president of Harvard, he told her, "Sixty years ago, I used to visit the family ... who resided here ... and more beautiful women I have never seen in Europe or America."

In 1787 the family purchased "Peacefield,"* or "The Old House," at 135 Adams Street, and moved in after **Adams** had been in Europe on various diplomatic duties for ten years, with less than three months spent at home. That short home period was productive, though, as he wrote in his home the Massachusetts Constitution. He named the home, at least partly, because of his pride in negotiating the favorable peace treaty ending the Revolutionary War. Both **Adamses** came here during their presidential terms, including much of **John's** time in 1798 and 1799, as yellow fever then had driven most of the population away from the capital. Retirement was the happiest time in **Adams's** life as he was in relatively good health for many of these years and surrounded by grandchildren who lived here for years at a time. He was affectionate and indulgent as he had never been with his own children. **Monroe** ate with him here in July 1817.

From here he carried on his prolific and remarkable correspondence with his once close friend, later enemy, then friend again, **Jefferson**. On the fiftieth anniversary of the Declaration of Independence, July 4, 1826, **John** had a stroke in a chair still shown and died in a bed placed in the room. His last words were, "**Thomas Jefferson** still survives." But he was wrong; **Jefferson** had died a few hours before. **John Quincy** then lived here, as did later generations of **Adamses**.

Both **Adams** tombs are in the crypt at the Adams Temple, United First Parish Church* at 1306 Hancock, where both men were baptized and attended. **John** had been a deacon. This is the only location where two presidents and their wives are buried side by side, although **Tyler** and **Monroe** are almost as close in Richmond. **John** had been buried at 1266 Hancock in the churchyard next to the city hall. (The church is open, but open hours are limited.)

Salem: **Washington** stayed in the northeast chamber at the Joshua Ward House, 148 Washington,* October 29, 1789. A chair **Washington** used was later owned by a resident of San Francisco who let **Grant** and **McKinley** sit in it during visits there. Citizens flocked to the house for weeks afterward and many were seen kissing the door latches. He also visited the Lee House on Washington and the courthouse on Federal. **Adams** was at the Old Courthouse* on the Town House Square in 1769. In 1817 **Monroe** visited the Silsbee House at 94 Washington Square East, now the Knights of Columbus Hall, as well as the Almshouse on the Neck from lower Essex Street and the Town Hall.* **John Quincy** dedicated the East India Marine Hall* at 173 Essex in 1825. In 1833, **Jackson** visited 21–23 Chestnut (private), marked. **Pierce** was at 328 Essex, several times. **Taft** unveiled the tablet at the Essex Institute,* visited in 1882 by **Arthur**.

Waltham: **John Adams** and **Monroe** both visited the Gore Mansion,* 52 Gore Street. **Truman** spoke at Brandeis University during his term, and **Carter** agreed to speak in April 2007.

Watertown: **Washington** stayed in the Marshall Fowle House, 28 Marshall, in 1791.

Weymouth: **John Adams** courted his future wife, Abigail, at her birthplace for five years, then at North and East Streets. Her father had been pastor for 49 years at First Church or Weymouth Meeting House, 17 Church Street, where **John** married in 1764. He attended while courting and afterward. **John Quincy** attended later and stayed at his grandparents' home at times, partly to get away from his aggressive mother. A large section was torn down with part of the lumber used to construct 8 East Street. The ell of the home is now at Norton and North.*

BOURNE • **Cleveland** bought "Gray Gables" in 1891, located on President's Road at Monument Point in Buzzards Bay, where he spent several summers and recuperated from his operation in 1893. In fact the public knew nothing about the surgery on his cancerous jaw until many years later. **Cleveland** used the home until 1904. It burned down in 1973.

DORCHESTER • With his head almost touching the ceiling, **Lincoln** gave a speech at Richmond Hall, Washington and Sanford Streets, on September 18, 1848, and spent the night at the home of Nathaniel Safford, a local Whig leader, at Washington and Morton, Churchill Place, just to the north on the north side of Norton, north of the Richmond intersection with Washington. Papers referred to "Abram" **Lincoln** here and in other towns. Only Washington Street remains.

GLOUCESTER • The Sleeper-McCann House at 75 Eastern Point Boulevard hosted **Taft**.

GROTON • **FDR**, like **Eisenhower**, wanted to go to Annapolis, but he went to school here in the Spartan existence of the Academy under Rev. Endicott Peabody. His mother did not want to part with her "especial treasure" so young, so he started at age fourteen rather than twelve. Peabody had won the respect of Wyatt Earp and the rest of Tombstone, Arizona, and now greatly influenced young **Roosevelt**. He later officiated at Franklin's wedding, his children's weddings, and led his inaugural services. The young, rich boy had not gone to school before or played much with other boys and did not fit in too well. He tried too hard and struggled to find his place in society. After graduation, **Franklin** proposed marriage to Eleanor in a maze, now the lawn behind the Pleasure Dome, while both visited Eleanor's brother. Both buildings mentioned survive. The chapel was being completed as **Franklin** graduated. Many alumni were not happy when as president he was asked to come back and speak for the fiftieth anniversary in 1934.

Distant cousin **Theodore Roosevelt** spoke at **Franklin's** graduation, probably in Peabody's office in Hundred House. All of **Franklin**'s and **Theodore**'s sons went to school here. **TR** visited his sons several times including 1901 as vice president and as president to be with Ted, who almost died of double pneumonia. He spent Thanksgiving here in 1911 with Quinton. None evidently liked the school or the strict Peabody; Archie was expelled.

In 1869, **Grant** visited the Gov. Boutwell House, now the historical society, directly across the street from the town hall at Station and Main.

HAVERHILL • **Washington** deemed this "the pleasantest village he had past through" after his stay at Harrod's Tavern on Main Street on Nov. 4, 1789. After he left, the town changed the name of the main meeting square to "Washington Square." In 1791 he stayed at the Mason Arms on what is now the site of the town hall. As was his custom, he walked through the town seeing structures still here. **John Quincy Adams** stayed with his uncle at the parsonage while preparing for Harvard on the site of the present public library, and attended the adjacent First Parish Church on Main Street.

HYANNIS PORT • **Kennedy** frequented his father's home as a youth most summers and lived here as an adult in one of three family homes known as the Kennedy Compound, Irving and Marchant, where his presidential campaign was largely conducted and his summer White House and retreat were. These are not open but can be seen from a distance.

LOWELL • On September 16, 1848, the *Boston Atlas* reported, "The Whigs of Lowell had one of the tallest meetings on Saturday night that they have yet had ... addressed by Hon. Abraham **Lincoln**." The site was the city hall, Merrimack and Shattuck, now a bank at the SE corner next to a small park where the passenger railroad station was then located and a tourist passenger car now operates. (**John Quincy Adams** also spoke here.) Tradition says that he was the guest of a reputed cousin of his mother, the wife of Reverend Stedman Hanks, or at the Child-Bartlett House at Kirk and French. **Jackson** and **Van Buren** toured New England together in 1833 and stayed at the Merrimack House at 310 Merrimack Street, where **Polk** and **Tyler** later stayed.

NEWBURYPORT • **Washington** rode his carriage to the edge of town and then switched to a horse. His diary shows that he was "received with much respect and parade." **John Quincy Adams** studied at the law office of Theophilus Parsons, 98 High Street. He lodged and boarded at the Leathers House on the SE side of Market Square at the NW corner of Green on Washington. Young **Adams** rode in **Washington's** welcoming procession on High to State and also wrote the welcoming address for the town celebration where **Washington** stayed at the Tracy House,* 94 State near Tremont. This has been the town library for many years.

NORTHAMPTON • **Coolidge** lived at 40 Round Hill from 1895 to 1898, and later at 162 King Street until 1905. After his honeymoon, he and his wife stayed three weeks at the Norwood Hotel, Bridge and Market, and then moved to 5 Crescent at Prospect until 1906. They then made their permanent home in a rented duplex at 21 Massasoit through all of his political offices until 1930. He spent several days here during his presidency. He studied law in an office in the First National Bank Building at Main and King, worked in the courthouse and city hall, and had an office at 25 Main. While in the legislature and as governor, he lived in the Adams Hotel, 553 Washington in Boston, and commuted back home on weekends. The **Coolidges** were active in Edwards Congregational Church on Main and South. When his wife missed a sermon, **Calvin** told her it was on sin. When asked what the preacher said, **Calvin** said he was against it. His funeral was here, with **Hoover** in attendance.

His wife was always worried about the lack of money and her tight husband's reaction to any spending. She once bought an $8 book, *Our Family Physician*, but dared not tell Calvin. She just put it out where he would see it. He said nothing, but in a few days she found a note saying, "Don't see any receipt here for curing $8 suckers! C. **Coolidge**." She played baseball with the two boys in the back yard, and **Calvin** was noted for reading to them. He held several public offices here in the city hall and courthouse. His rent was raised to $40 from $28 per month when he became governor. After returning here, the former president liked to sit on the porch until the inevitable parade of curiosity-seekers drove him inside. In 1930, the **Coolidges**, craving privacy and space, moved to "The Beeches," overlooking the Connecticut River, at the end on Munroe Street, where he died in 1933 at sixty. He went most days to his "law office," really just a getaway in the Masonic Building on Main. When told that the reticent "Silent Cal" had died, some asked, "How could you tell?" This and the other house are privately owned.

Jefferson and **Madison** traveled through in 1791 on a 920-mile trip taking them through New England and upper New York, including Lanesborough and Pittsfield, Mass.

PALMER • **Washington** and both **Adamses** stayed at Scott's Tavern, marked, at an ancient tree on the lawn of the Kmart parking lot just beyond the western town limits on U.S. Route 20.

SPRINGFIELD • **Washington** stayed in the Zenas Parsons Tavern in 1789, marked near the corner of Court Square, Main and Elm. The front entrance was on Elm St. in 1775, when he also stopped on the way to Boston and met with an escort to Brookfield, where another party escorted him to Worcester. He toured the magazine and armory* east of downtown on Federal Street where **Jefferson** and **Madison** came in 1791. **John Adams** had stayed here in the 1770s, as did **Monroe** in 1817. **John Quincy Adams**' body was honored in the church on the square dating to the 1600s, although the present building dates to 1819. In 1880, **TR** honeymooned his first night near the railroad in the Massoit House, Main and Gridiron or Lyman, where the Paramount Theater later was built. **Lincoln** ate at the Massoit, where **Davis** stayed.

TAUNTON • **Lincoln** spoke on September 21, 1848, at Union Hall, west of the river close to the center on Winthrop between Mill River and today's Winthrop Street Baptist. He arrived at the Boston and Providence Station near Park Square and first spoke in Mechanics Hall at the SE corner of Hopewell and Danforth.

UXBRIDGE • **Washington** was at the Taft Tavern on Sutton and Sylvan in 1791.

WORCESTER • **John Adams** taught school and lived here from 1755 to 1758. His 1755 school is marked on the courthouse and was on the NW side of Main near Mechanic overlooking the square. The 19-year-old Harvard graduate first stayed with Major Nathaniel Greene at 306 Main, midway between Walnut and Sudbury. He later moved to Dr. Nahum Willard's, on Franklin between Portland and Main, and in 1756 moved to the home of James Putnam on Franklin, around the corner of Main facing the Common. During this time he wrote that he had no books, no time, and no funds, and that he must therefore be contented to live and die ignorant and obscure. But living with a lawyer rekindled an interest leading to a legal and political career. He studied law in the evening with Dr. Nahum Willard at Main across from Franklin, a site now occupied by the Boston Store, and stayed with James Putnam across the Green, where the Park Building now stands. Willard and Putnam were Tories in the Revolutionary War. Willard made peace with the town by apologizing, but Putnam fled to England. **Adams** attended the Congregational Meeting House on the Green known as Old South Church at the site of the present city hall.

On October 23, 1789, **Washington** came to the U.S. Arms Inn on Main for breakfast and noted the meetinghouse. **Lincoln** attended the state Whig convention and made speeches in the Old South Church and town hall, SE corner of Front and Main, on September 12 and 13, 1848. The church was at the south side of the common, and the hall was on the west side at the site of the present town hall. He arrived at the Foster Street Station that was east of the present plaque on the SW corner of Norwich and Foster. He was entertained at the home of Levi Lincoln, Jr., on the north side of Elm Street, between Lindon and Ashland. The house has been moved to nearby Old Sturbridge Village and is the Country Curtains Store.*

The former governor and future president were descended from Samuel Lincoln. **Lincoln** observed, "...we both belong, as the Scotch say, to the same clan; but I know one thing, and that is, that we are both good Whigs." During the Civil War, Levi visited the president, who told him that he remembered his meal in Worcester as the best dinner of his life and could remember every guest and where they sat at the great table. He remembered that he "went with hayseed in my hair to learn deportment in the most cultivated state in the Union." **Quincy Adams**, **Taft**, and **Coolidge** also visited the home. **Lincoln** may have stayed at the home overnight as reported in various modern local newspaper accounts or at the Lincoln (Worcester) House back of the west side of Main with wings extending back to Elm and Maple, the pre–1835 home of Levi. It was also about a block west of the depot mentioned. William Seward wrote that he and **Lincoln** spent the night together after the speech, but numerous Boston newspaper stories through the years mention their later Boston addresses as their first meeting, and that appears correct.

Grant (1869) and **Hayes** (1877) stayed at the Bay Street Hotel on Bay. **TR** (1905) was at the Rockwood Hoar House, 16 Hammond. **LBJ** visited Holy Cross College on June 10, 1964.

MICHIGAN

ANN ARBOR • **Ford** attended the University of Michigan from 1931 until 1933; he was an outstanding athlete, playing center for the national football champions of 1932 and 1933. His presidential library is here, where **Carter** has attended several meetings including 1983 and 1984. **Bush** attended the football stadium in 1991, and **LBJ** gave the commencement address on May 22, 1964.

BATTLE CREEK • **Harding** made five visits here to a sanitarium run by Dr. J.P. Kellogg, at North Washington and Champion Streets. He had invented corn flakes and various other modern products. **Harding** had suffered a nervous breakdown at age 24, and came out of the facility more outgoing and a general "good ol' boy."

DETROIT • **William Henry Harrison** captured Fort Shelby, at about the site of the Penobscot Building between Shelby and Griswold, north of Congress, in 1813. He then worked at the Hull House, SW corner of Jefferson and Randolph, now the oldest brick house in Detroit. **Taylor** reported here in 1816 on the way to Fort Howard at Green Bay, Wisconsin. **Monroe** came in August 1817 and landed at Government Wharf at the foot of Randolph, where the tunnel to Canada now is. He visited the Steamboat House at the NW corner of Woodbridge and Randolph, now the Renaissance Center, and visited Fort Shelby with Governor Cass on Larned between First and Second. He also visited the Indian Council House, SE corner of Jefferson and Randolph.

In 1842 **Van Buren** stayed at the American House on the south side of Jefferson just east of Randolph and went to several churches on the same day, the Methodist at Woodward and Congress, the Catholic at the NE corner of Russell and Jefferson, and the Episcopal at Larned and Woodward. September was a popular month to visit, as **Fillmore** visited the town on September 20, 1849, **Grant and Andrew Johnson** on September 4, 1866, **Hayes** on September 18, 1879, **TR** on September 20, 1902, and **Taft** on September 18, 1911.

Grant later attended the same churches mentioned above when he was stationed here. **Taylor** was at Ft. Wayne,* foot of Livernois Avenue, in 1845, as was **Grant** later. **Pierce** lodged at the Russell House, NE corner of Woodward and Cadillac Square, in 1861, near where **Truman** gave a "Give 'em Hell" campaign speech in 1948. **Hayes** attended a reception at 110 W. Fort in 1879. **FDR** spoke in front of Old City Hall on the square in 1936.

Grant was transferred to Detroit Barracks with his new wife in November 1848, soon transferred to Sackets Harbor, New York, but then came back the next March. He and Julia first lived in the National Hotel (Russell House) in 1848–9. After a few weeks they moved to 253 Fort, between Russell and Rivard, not far from the Barracks bounded by the two latter named streets, Catherine and Graviot. The house was later moved to the Michigan State Fair Grounds off Woodward at Ralston. During this time he loved to race his horse down Jefferson and Grand River Avenues and attend weekly balls at the Exchange Hotel on the SW corner of Jefferson and Shelby. He did not dance, and just stood around looking bored. Two of his favorite hangouts were The Shades, on Shelby between Larned and Jefferson, and a sutler's store on Jefferson two doors south of Woodward, where he played cards and drank freely from the always-available barrel of whiskey. When Julia left for St. Louis to have their first child, **Grant** stayed with friends on the NE corner of Jefferson and Russell. Mayor Zachariah Chandler, lived in a mansion on Jefferson. The city required homeowners to keep their walkway free of ice. **Grant** sued the mayor when he slipped in front and collected a judgment of six cents plus costs. Chandler was a powerful senator during the Civil War and appointed by **Grant** to his cabinet. **Grant** visited him after the war at 144 Fort.

Lincoln came through Detroit in early October 1848 on the way back from New England by way of the steamer *Globe* from Buffalo, and then proceeded to Chicago. He was the only president to receive a patent even though it is referred to as a perfect failure since no practical use was ever made of it. He got his inspiration probably on the Detroit River when he saw a steamer piled up on an island, or maybe when his boat got stuck on a sand bar in Lake Erie, according to another story.

Lincoln got the idea for "expandsible [sic] buoyant chambers placed at the sides" that would enable a boat to ease itself off a bar. This was made later into a model for a patent granted in May 1849 and can be seen today at the Patent Office in Washington.

The Henry Ford Museum in Dearborn has the chair that Lincoln was sitting in when he was assassinated on April 14, 1865. This was confiscated by the government from Washington theater owner John Ford. The blood on the chair was probably from Lincoln's guest, who was stabbed. **Lincoln's** shawl carried that night and part of actress Laura Keene's bloodstained dress are also here. Also the museum contains the car that **Kennedy** rode in Dallas at his assassination as well as presidential limousines since **FDR**. Adjacent Greenfield Village has Lincoln, Illinois,' original relocated Logan County Courthouse, where **Lincoln** practiced law. TR rode the steamer *Tashmoo* to the dock here in 1901.

In 1866 **Andrew Johnson** and **Grant** arrived at the railroad station at Michigan and Griswold and stayed at the Biddle House (same as the American House), where a grand reception was held. **Grant** revisited the Episcopal and Methodist churches he had attended earlier, but the Methodist was now located at Woodward and State. **Garfield** visited several times from 1863 until 1866 and went to the church at the SW corner of Jefferson and Beaubien.

Kennedy addressed an estimated 100,000 on the Campus Martius in 1960. The 1980 Republican Convention was in Cobo Hall, where **Reagan** and **Bush** were nominated. (**Ike** had been there in 1960, and **Clinton** spoke to the NAACP on April 29, 2007.) They visited the Detroit Plaza Hotel, and **George H.W. Bush** was at the Pontchartrain, 2 Washington Blvd., when he learned of his nomination. It was here that **Ford** revealed to TV news reporter Walter Cronkite that he and **Reagan** were discussing an arrangement where he would be nominated as vice president. He made it clear that he wanted a serious impact on policies and cabinet members, almost a co-presidency. (This was not the first time such an arrangement was considered, as ex–President **Monroe** almost was teamed as **John Quincy Adams's** vice president.)

GRAND RAPIDS • **Gerald Ford**'s mother brought him to his grandparents' at 457 Lafayette in 1914–16 and later to 1960 Prospect, S.E. (later renamed "Terrace"), before she married a paint salesman in 1916. The boy was born Leslie King, Jr., in Omaha, Nebraska, but the parents were divorced after his mother moved to Oak Park, Illinois, when he was six weeks old. The new husband adopted him and renamed him **Gerald Ford**, Jr. They lived at 716 Madison (1916–1921), 630 Rosewood (1922–1923), 649 Union (1923–1929), 2163 Lake (1929–1933), and 1011 Santa Cruz (1933–1948), where **Nixon** was a guest. He worked in law firms at 40–50 Pearl in the Michigan Trust Building, N.W. All other addresses are S.E. He was not told of his adoption until after his birth father appeared when he was 16 and confronted the shocked boy on his schoolyard in 1927. From his clothing and fancy car, Jerry thought he was rich, although he was too polite or intimidated to ask why he did not send any money for support. Three years later when he needed money for his college tuition, he wrote his father, who never wrote back.

While president, **Ford** had an undeserved reputation for clumsiness. But he did write that when his jalopy once died at the house he put blankets over the fiery red motor, went inside and forgot it until the fire trucks showed up. He then borrowed his stepfather's car to get to a track meet and backed out into a tree. The impact snapped the clamp that held the spare tire, but he felt, "No problem; I'll simply tie the tire on the back." The heat from the exhaust then burnt a hole in the tire. He married at the Grace Episcopal, 1815 Hall, where he went from 1922 until 1951. His funeral was later here. After that he moved to his wife's apartment at 330 Washington, S.E. In 1950 they moved to 1624 Sherman, in East Grand Rapids. Workplaces include Ford Paint and Varnish, 601 Crosby, N.W. (1930–33) and his law firm at 620 Michigan Trust Building, 40–50 Pearl, N.W. (1941–8). His museum* is at 303 Pearl. **Reagan** and **Bush** visited in 1981, and **Bush** made a campaign speech in front in 1992. **George W. Bush** laid flowers at the gravesite here on April 20, 2007. **Clinton** spoke at DeVos Place on June 18, 2007, 187 Monroe, N.W.

JACKSON • **Taft** dedicated a plaque at Second and W. Franklin, the birthplace of the Republican Party, where men met in 1854 to oppose the Kansas-Nebraska Act and name the national party.

LANSING • **Taft** visited the Capitol in 1919. **Bush** and **Clinton** debated at the Performing Arts Center at Michigan State on October 19, 1992. **Theodore Roosevelt** spoke to the legislature and boys at an industrial school in late May 1903.

MACKINAW CITY • Taylor was at Fort Mackinac* in 1819. Lincoln would have seen it while passing through the straits connecting Lake Huron and Lake Michigan as he was returning from Congress in 1849. TR's favorite watering hole was said to be the Lighthouse Restaurant* at 618 S. Huron.

MINNESOTA

MINNEAPOLIS/ST. PAUL • Fort Snelling* is now a state park on Post Road off SR 5 at the Mississippi and Minnesota Rivers' junction. **Taylor** was the founder and commander and the grandfather of the first white child born in the state. His oldest daughter married an army surgeon here. **Taylor** dressed like a slob, and it is thought that **Grant**, also here, modeled his famous disheveled appearance after him.

That **Lincoln** was, as shown in more than one source, at Nicollet House, then on Washington Ave. between Hennepin and Nicollete Ave., now occupied by the Nicollet Hotel, or anywhere else in the state cannot be confirmed, but **TR** was here as well as numerous places in town before and during his presidency. He and **Arthur** took the train at the Fourth and Sibley Station. **Cleveland** was at the West Hotel, Hennepin and Fifth, in 1887. **Taft** was at Westminster Presbyterian Church, Nicolete Mall at Twelfth, in 1909. **Carter** attended former Vice President Hubert Humphrey's funeral in 1978 at the Hope Presbyterian Church, 797 Summit Avenue. The State Capitol has seen **Harding, McKinley, TR, Wilson,** and **Cleveland**, and probably most of the rest during the last few decades. **McKinley** visited J.J. Hill's home, 240 Summit.

Probably the most important event in the history of the Minnesota State Fair was the address by **TR**, who told listeners on September 2, 1901, four days before McKinley was assassinated, to "Speak softly and carry a big stick." The fair is held in Falcon Heights adjacent to the University of Minnesota, St. Paul campus. On October 9, 1936, **FDR** told his St. Paul audience about how much he enjoyed his two hours driving around the area that day. **Truman** campaigned at the railroad station in St. Paul on October 13, 1948. **Carter** spoke in the Plaza Room at the Minneapolis Auditorium on October 28, 1978, to raise funds for the governor. It was at the corner of Main and Nicollet. **Ford** addressed the National Press Club newsmakers on June 5, 2000, at 480 Cedar in St. Paul. **George W. Bush** gave a political speech on November 2, 2002, at the Xcel Energy Center at 175 Kellogg W. He was back for a speech on October 30, 2004, at the Target Center, 600 First St. N. **Clinton** wound up a campaign bus trip in St. Paul in August 1992, later spoke in the emergency room at the St. Joseph's Hospital on May 13, 1998, and campaigned in town on September 17, 2006. **FDR** told crippled children at the Dowling School for Crippled Children, Dowling and 38th, on October 2, 1936, that even though he saw many wheelchairs and crutches, he saw also many cheerful faces.

ROCHESTER • The Mayo Clinic on Second Avenue S.W. has treated **JFK, LBJ, Reagan,** and then **Ford** in August 2006. **FDR** honored the Mayo brothers here in 1934. **Kennedy** came at age seventeen to try to find out what was wrong with him. He had little luck in getting a diagnosis, but, if we believe his letters to friends, better luck getting nurses.

MISSISSIPPI

CORINTH • **Grant's** Civil War headquarters were 615 Jackson, across from the Curlee House, 711 Jackson, headquarters for Union General Halleck and Confederates Bragg and Hood. All businesses closed when **T. Roosevelt** came through in 1901 and spoke at the depot.

GULFPORT-BILOXI AREA • **Davis** visited the Gulf Coast in December 1876, and saw Beauvoir,* now open as the **Jefferson Davis** Home on U.S. 90, the Gulf Coast Highway. Mrs. Sarah Dorsey, the owner, had heard that he was looking for a quiet place to write his memoirs, and offered him the use of the east cottage. She was an author, aged 48, whose husband had died in 1875. He then began the writing task and lived there. His wife became jealous of the hospitality and aid. She was already in bad mental and physical health, and continued to live in Europe and then in Memphis, pouting about the rumors of a physical relationship with the young widow, but none is provable or probable. Varina **Davis** finally came to live there as she realized they had no other good option, and the two women became friends. In 1879 Sarah sold the property to **Davis** for an installment note, and then died a few months later, forgiving the note in her will and giving him clear title. **Davis** thus acquired the home, with liabilities, where he lived and greeted many prominent guests until his death in New Orleans. The two women acted as secretaries as he took four years to write the dry, argumentative *Rise and Fall of the Confederate Government*. **Davis** worshipped at the Church of the Redeemer, Bellman and E. Beach, in what is now the parish house in back of the present church. Mrs. Davis later refused $90,000 from a promoter who wanted to turn the home into a hotel, but took $10,000 from the Sons of Confederate Veterans, who turned it into a memorial and veterans home. Beauvoir is now restored after severe damage by Hurricane Katrina in 2005. Most of the presidents listed below at least noted the home as they passed by on their trips down U.S. 90, including **Wilson** and **FDR**, who were noted to pause in front.

Twelve presidents visited the coast. **Jackson** traveled through on the way to New Orleans in 1814, and **Taylor** built a road on the coast from the Pearl River to Bay St. Louis in 1820. While he was speaking in Bay St. Louis, a hastily constructed platform collapsed. The not-so-mild-mannered candidate let loose a tirade of profanities, but this went unreported by the national press. **Monroe** is claimed here but unverified. An exhausted **Wilson** spent three weeks in 1913–4 at 767 E. Beach, U.S. 90 in Pass Christian, and regained his "glow of health." He was once stopped on U.S. 90 in Gulfport by a young woman who gave him a package that he was told not to open until he got to his vacation home, Beauliau, called the "Christmas" or "Dixie" White House. When he did, he found a live white dove that he released at the end of 1913. The symbolism, reported worldwide, was not lost in later wartime. St. Paul's Catholic, when he attended, flew the American flag for the first time. He also went to First Presbyterian in Gulfport. On another occasion **Wilson** was returning from his favorite golf course at Gulfport's Country Club, when he noticed flames shooting out of Judge James Neville's home on U.S. 90. He stopped, ran to the house, and was greeted by Neville's surprised wife, who did not know that her house was on fire or that the president was coming to call. **Wilson** drew water from the well as the Secret Service battled the flames until the fire department arrived. Beauliau, marked at the last corner of Lang, was badly damaged in Hurricane Camille in 1969 and torn down.

Taylor owned a house in Pascagoula. **Grant** also at least passed through. Both **Roosevelts** fished here, and **TR** last came for a visit in 1915, with **FDR** coming in 1917 as assistant secretary of the Navy to examine port sites. He later came to fish in 1937. Silent Cal **Coolidge** proved that his nickname was accurate by once appearing on the railroad platform and not speaking. **Truman** also vacationed on the coast several times, first in 1933 for six weeks at a cottage at Biloxi and once as his daughter Margaret recuperated from a heart attack. He liked the area pralines at Margaret's candy shop in Biloxi, where a surprised tourist once took his picture. He spoke at the Markarm Hotel in Gulfport in 1944 and at Keesler Airforce Base in 1956. **Nixon** spoke at the Gulfport Airport in 1969 after flying over hurricane damage, as did **Carter** (1979), **Reagan,** and both **Bushes** later. The earlier visit endeared **Nixon** to Gulf Coast residents, who cheered when he came out of retirement in 1978 for a Veteran's Day address and "rousing reception" at the Mississippi Coast Coliseum. **Ford** drove down U.S. 90 with his head and arms out of the top of the limousine.

HOLLY SPRINGS • **Grant** lived at 331 W. Chulahoma in 1862 with his family, visited 330 Salem, and kept his mules in the basement of the Methodist church at 175 E. Van Dorn and Spring Street. He first removed the stained glass for safekeeping.

JACKSON • One of the largest acquisitions of land in U.S. history took place due to General **Jackson's** 1820 Treaty of Doak's Stand with the Choctaws. The treaty site was north on the Natchez Trace and is marked a few miles south on the Parkway at mile marker 128.4. This was the culmination of seven years of treaties negotiated by **Jackson** where the country acquired much of the several Southern states. Other **Jackson** campsites near the Natchez Trace include the business district of Kosciusko and the north entrance to Tishomingo.

Jackson was given a hero's welcome in 1828 at the Old Capitol,* State and Capitol, now a museum. He returned in 1840 to speak before the legislature. **Davis** served in various capacities and spoke at various times, including 1884. He was hailed here with his Mississippi Volunteers after returning from the Mexican War. **Grant** used the 1842 Governor's Mansion* as his headquarters after he captured the capital in 1863. Later **Theodore Roosevelt, Taft, Kennedy**, and Eleanor Roosevelt were entertained and **Nixon** used it during his stay in 1962. **Grant** spent the night in the same room that the Confederate commander Joseph Johnston had used the night before at the Bowman House, Amite and State, across (north) from the old Capitol.

The first Grant to enter the town and the Capitol was his twelve-year-old son who, with his mother's blessing, was with his father but mostly on his own during the famous Civil War campaign. Fred Grant had been shot at and grazed, and wandered in alone in advance of Federal forces as Confederate troops were leaving, while his father and most of the Union troops were elsewhere. He could have been killed or captured, but later he joked about how he had single-handedly captured Jackson.

Taft paraded up Capitol Street in 1909 and is pictured at the Poindexter Auditorium. **Ford** spoke at the airport in 1974, and **Carter** spoke there in 1978 on the way to Yazoo City for a town hall meeting. A nine-year-old girl who asked a question then became a short-time national celebrity. In 1977 he spoke at the high school on MLK Jr. Drive. **George H.W. Bush** became the first president to speak at the new Capitol in 1992 and spoke at the Ramada Plaza in 1994.

NATCHEZ • **Davis** went to Jefferson College in nearby Washington, now off U.S. 61 near U.S. 84E. **Jackson** camped here going to and coming from New Orleans in 1814 and 1815, and Lafayette watched cadets drill in 1825. In 1813 **Jackson** and his troops camped for several weeks around the town before they were ordered back to Tennessee before seeing any action. **Jackson** rightly considered this 500-mile trip without pay or supplies an insult to him and his men.

Davis was married in 1845 at a very private and small ceremony at the Briars Plantation,* one of the many old mansions open to the public. He was double the age of his 18-year-old bride, and still grieving the death of his first wife. It is now by the parking lot of the Ramada Inn at the west end of Irvine Ave., south of the bridge and on the river. **Grant** made his headquarters in Rosalie Mansion,* at the foot of Broadway. The family later joined him there.

North of town on Miss. 553 near Fayette, one mile from the Natchez Trace, is Springfield Plantation,* where **Jackson** first married his beloved Rachel, probably during the first few months of 1791. (No marriage record has been found.) He had been trading here for about two years. The story goes that he had escorted her either down the Natchez Trace or on a flatboat to help her escape the wrath of her abusive husband after she left him at his home in Kentucky. Then permission to file a rare divorce petition was granted to her husband in the legislature that then, for residents of Kentucky, was in Richmond, Virginia. While the divorce was pending, the family sent her to some friends here under the care of family friend and lawyer, **Jackson**. He evidently went back, heard that the divorce was completed, and then returned to marry her at the mansion. But although her husband had been granted permission to file, he had not and did not obtain the divorce until September 1793. By then the **Jacksons** considered themselves married for two years. When they found out the truth she insisted upon a remarriage in Tennessee the next January. Political enemies accused them of bigamy and took political advantage of the indiscretion from then on.

Slander resulted in at least one fatal duel with **Jackson**, and probably contributed to Rachel's death from grief in 1828, after her husband had been elected president. Actually it is somewhat unclear exactly when and how Rachel got to Natchez, or if **Jackson** came with her, or when their love heated up. And probably the marriage was illegal anyway, as this area then was Spanish territory that required a Catholic priest. She had been married maybe by her host, a former judge, but his authority had ended anyway years before in Georgia. She must have arrived at about the time the house was ready in 1791 or stayed in Natchez before it was completed. **Jackson** then took her fifteen miles up river to Bruinsburg, where he had a trading post, where they stayed for six weeks. (This is marked near the ruins of Windsor Mansion.*) **Grant** crossed the river at nearby Bruinsburg during the Vicksburg Campaign in 1863, and ten historical markers follow his route to Port Gibson.

Jackson spoke in town in 1828, visited the Mercer House, NW corner of Wall and State, in January 1840, and Elms Court,* south on U.S. 61. He also stayed in the Moss House (ruins) on Raymond Road in Clinton in 1818, the Ford House off SR 24 in Foxworth in 1814, and on the banks of Pottoxchitto Creek near Hickory in 1815.

Taylor had 81 slaves on his 2100-acre Cypress Gross Plantation northwest of Springfield Plantation on the Mississippi, ten miles south of Rodney. The absentee landowner visited each year and owned it at the time of his election. More than half of **Taylor**'s $116,770 estate was in the value of the slaves. **Fillmore** spoke in the New Institute Hall in 1854.

PORT GIBSON • **Grant** reportedly stood on the porch of the Williams home at the NE corner of Church and Walnut and commented, "Port Gibson is too beautiful to burn." The battle on Highway 61 secured his position on the east side of the Mississippi River that he had just crossed in order to capture Vicksburg. Ten historical markers show his route to here from his Bruinsburg landing. **Jackson** supposedly found the Hermitage on U.S. 61 nearby so beautiful that he used it for a model for his home in Tennessee.

VICKSBURG • Nearby at Davis Bend, now Davis Island after the river washed away the narrow land connection, is the site of Hurricane, the home of **Davis**' brother Joe. **Davis** came here in 1835 after his wedding as his brother had given him land to start to build his nearby plantation, Brierfield. His new wife died while visiting nearby in Louisiana, and he remained mostly in seclusion for seven years. Millionaire Joseph Davis was 23 years older and still treated his brother like a son.

In December 1843 he fell in love with 17-year-old Varina Howell at Hurricane as she visited for several weeks, probably as Joseph engaged in matchmaking. Almost immediately Jefferson wanted to marry, did, and they lived at Brierfield until the Civil War. **Davis** was cutting roses in the garden in 1861 when a messenger summoned him to hurry to Montgomery to accept the presidency of the Confederacy that he did not want. Hurricane, with the large library, was burned by Federal troops during the Civil War, but Brierfield remained, although ransacked and pillaged. The property was sold to its former slaves after the war, but they defaulted, and **Davis** finally got the title. But it took long litigation in 1881 with Joseph's heirs as the elder **Davis** never deeded the property rights to his younger brother, either because of Joseph's paternal feeling or lack of confidence. Even though the retention of title in his brother's name caused family grief, it shielded Jefferson's name from ownership after the Civil War was lost by the South.

He visited annually, including his last journey. These two plantation home sites were cut off from easy access in 1867, being completely surrounded by the river between Vicksburg and Grand Gulf. The ruins of Brierfield (burned in 1931) are directly east of Somerset and directly south of New Carthage, Louisiana. Hurricane is five miles northwest in the direction of Ione.

Joseph's residence in Vicksburg was Anchuca* at 1010 First Street, where you can still see the balcony used by **Jefferson Davis** for a public address in 1867 after his release from prison. He also danced in the ballroom at Cedar Grove,* 2200 Oak Street, and slept in the master bedroom. The old courthouse,* now an excellent museum, was used by both **Davis** brothers.

This important town was the object of **Grant's** brilliant military campaign in 1863, and surrendered to him on July 4, the day after the Battle of Gettysburg ended. **Grant** wanted to cross the river from Louisiana at Hard Times Landing on the west side opposite Grand Gulf. The site now is on La. 608 near the northeast end of a loop on a cut-off lake called Yucatan Lake on the Mississippi, now near a cooling tower of the nuclear station. This belonged to Mr. and Mrs. Sarah Dorsey, who later owned Beauvoir in Biloxi, which they sold to **Davis**. Not able to cross there, he had to go five miles downstream to Disharoon Plantation, now inaccessible, at a point midway between Winter Quarters and Grand Gulf. After crossing the Mississippi he fought his way east and north to Raymond and Jackson, and then west to Vicksburg by way of several battle sites around today's U.S. 80 and I-20 marked at Champion Hill* and the Big Black River. Interstate 20 passes over the center of action of the latter battle. (When **Jackson** addressed the people of Raymond at the Old Oak Tree Inn, people took bed sheets to make him a carpet to walk on.)

Grant's battlefield headquarters and the site where he negotiated surrender terms are marked on the Vicksburg National Battlefield. The surrender site is not listed on the tour map, but is marked on Pemberton Road, south of the Great Redoubt and Louisiana Monument toward the battlefield route, Union Avenue. A small obelisk with a ball on top marks the spot where **Grant** met the Confederate commander, a former Pennsylvania Yankee. The Confederates were starving, and **Grant** was planning another assault. Terms were discussed, but the two commanders reached an impasse, and **Grant** suggested that several subordinates try. They then talked and an agreement was reached the next day, July 4. **Grant** met Pemberton again at the Rock House on the Jackson Road west of the Great Redoubt. **Grant** then rode in on the Jackson Road, now Openwood Road and Martin Luther Ling Jr., and then reviewed troops from the courthouse.* The courthouse was the pride of the city when the Union was claimed to have used the clock on top for target practice. According to a questionable local story, the Confederate commander then moved Union prisoners to the top floor and notified **Grant** of their presence.

After the surrender **Grant** used the 26-room Lum House, site marked at the car dealership on the east side of Washington between Belmont and Bowman, for headquarters. A later Union commander had it destroyed to improve fortifications. **Grant** was also at the Balfour House at 1002 Crawford, next to the Confederate headquarters* of General Pemberton, and many of the old homes now open for tours. He also came to the landing at the foot of Grove Street and Levee Street to greet Admiral Porter. The site was later used by **McKinley** (1901), **T. Roosevelt** (1901 and 1907), and **Taft** (1909 and 1911). **Grant** returned in 1880, had no desire to visit the battlefield, but did visit the cemetery and spoke between the columns on the north side of the old courthouse at the present entrance. **McKinley** is pictured at the national cemetery and Grant-Pemberton Monument. **Ike** visited in 1947 and made a speech generally said (erroneously) to be the first time July 4 was celebrated here since the surrender on that date in 1863.

As shown in one of the several historical markers on the courthouse lawn, **Taylor** was honored at the site and spoke here in 1849. Several presidents visited the area. **Jackson** is said to have always stopped to visit friends three blocks down the hill on Grove Street at the Gwine House. **TR** once spoke on Monroe Street on the south side of the courthouse later on the west side, then the main entrance, or Walnut Street. **McKinley** spoke from a platform on the north side near Cherry Street. **Fillmore** visited as a former president and stayed in a hotel then on the NW corner of Washington and China. Four presidents came via the steamboat landing according to several local newspaper sources: **TR, Davis, Fillmore,** and **Taylor**. When **Taylor** left for the White House, rival steamboats vied for the honor of taking him. The "wrong one," the *Saladin*, showed up early at his home at Spithead Point, sounded the whistle, and "kidnapped" him when he sleepily and innocently got on board. He later admitted that this "got him into a whole mess of trouble" since he was supposed to ride on the *Tennessee*. **Polk** owned a plantation near Coffeeville, but may or may not have visited.

Teddy Roosevelt's most famous bear hunt was 15 miles east of Smedes, due north of Vicksburg 25 miles, near U.S. 61, and marked two miles north. He refused to shoot a bear in a cage, prompting many cartoons and leading to the production of the "teddy bear," popular with young children ever since. He hunted in the state several times, once guided by former Confederate General Stephen D. Lee.

WOODVILLE • **Jefferson Davis**' boyhood home from age two, Rosemont,* is one mile east of U.S. 61 on the north side of State 24. **Davis**' Baptist father thought his youngest child was being spoiled, and sent him away to a Catholic school at age seven. When he returned two years later, he had changed so much that he tried to pretend to his mother that he was a lost boy looking for directions. She was not fooled, and he was smothered with parental affection from both parents, the only time his father showed such emotion. About this time he decided he did not want to go to school. His father put him in the cotton fields, and he changed his mind about physical labor versus mental challenges. He went to Wilkerson Academy in Woodville. His mother died here in 1845 after being visited by her son on his wedding trip, and is buried with numerous family members in the family cemetery. Some of her rose bushes still bloom.

Missouri

Excelsior Springs • As crowds swarmed around **Truman's** residence and election headquarters on the night of the 1948 election, **Truman** escaped to the Elms Hotel,* 401 Regent, escorted by Secret Servicemen. **FDR**, John D. Rockefeller, Jack Dempsey, and Al Capone had also escaped public view at the hotel. During the night **Truman** woke up and heard popular broadcaster H.V. Kaltenborn predict his defeat. **Truman** later mimicked Kaltenborn's forecast before the cameras.

Grandview • **Truman** moved to 12301 Blue Ridge* in 1887 and lived until 1890 in the farmhouse owned by his paternal grandparents. It burned in 1894 and was immediately replaced by the home open now just west of U.S. 71. It took them a month to get here by horse and buggy from Lamar, and they could not take much because his mother insisted that they bring her piano. In 1906 his father asked him to return to help on the farm that he now owned. Harry then lived as a dirt farmer until 1917 (ages 22–33), when the United States entered World War I. At one time there were 14 people living in the house. He didn't like farming much, but the property later gave him his first financial independence after the end of his presidency when it was sold for development.

He joined the Grandview Baptist Church, SW corner of Grandview Boulevard and Main, in 1887, again in 1916, and stayed a member until his death, although he was a member of or attended Baptist churches in Independence, Kansas City, and Clinton, Missouri, and courted Bess at the Presbyterian church in Independence, 16 miles away. The president dedicated the modern church at the NW corner of Main at 15th on December 24, 1950. After Harry joined the National Guard and proudly wore his new blue uniform to his grandmother's home, she made it clear that this was the first time a blue uniform had been in her house since the Civil War, and it had better be the last! It was. As president and throughout his life he returned many times to see his brother, mother, and sister, including every day for two weeks when he worked in Kansas City as his mother lay dying in 1947 and a hurried trip after he heard of the North Korean invasion before rushing back to Washington. He also visited 604 High Grove Road where his mother and sister moved 1940 and after 1955 at his sister's, 13106 13th.

Hannibal • **Lincoln** traveled this way to and from Iowa in August 1859 and again to and from his Kansas speaking trip in late 1859. He may have visited at Judge John B. Helm's home at the NW corner of Sixth and North. A marker shows that he stayed at the Planter's Hotel, then located on the west side of Main between Bird and Hill. He told the judge and crowd at his office, located where the drive-through of the Hannibal National Bank is now, on Main just north of Broadway, that he had known the judge as a boy in Kentucky and his mother brought him to Helm's store in Elizabethtown. "This man was the first man I ever knew who wore store clothes all week. My ambition when I was a boy, was to reach his position in society." His route here was through Palmyra, Ely, Monroe, Bevier, Callao, Utica, Osborn, Easton, etc.

Wilson was a great admirer of Mark Twain, and ordered his campaign train stopped to visit the sites recreated in several of his books. **Wilson** supposedly asked a man on the street where Tom Sawyer was supposed to live. The local said he never heard of him. The president then asked about Huck Finn, but the man had never heard of him, either. "How about Pudd'nhead Wilson?" The man answered, "I heard of him all right. In fact, I even voted for the durn fool." **Carter** and **Hoover** also visited the Twain sites. **TR** was photographed in the central business district, and **FDR** dedicated the Mark Twain Bridge in 1936.

INDEPENDENCE • **Truman** moved to 619 S. Crysler in 1890 so that he could get town schooling, and then to 909 West Waldo and River Boulevard (1896–1902), which become a meeting place for many neighborhood friends. His chores included driving the family cows to pasture and retrieving them in the evening. Not being able to play outside like the other kids because of poor eyesight, he enjoyed reading history and taking piano lessons. His parents loved books also, so he was never bored, always having books around. He was probably the most musically accomplished president. His eyes were always weak, and he had to have expensive glasses, rare for the area, preventing his participation in rough-and-tumble sports. They also prevented him from achieving his goal of attending West Point or Annapolis Military Academies. As a result he spent many hours at the library next to the high school where he and Charlie Ross claimed to have read all 2000 books.

He went some to First Baptist, 500 W. Truman Road, in 1896–1902. His schools included Noland, 1892–4, at 533 S. Liberty, and then the Columbian School, 300 block S. River Blvd. near Walnut, where he was now in the same class with Bess. (This is now a parking lot for the Latter Day Saints Auditorium.) He then attended the Ott School, SW corner of Liberty and College, from the middle of the fifth grade through the first year in high school. The rest of his high schooling was at Independence High at the NW corner of Maple and Pleasant. His best friend Charlie Ross was valedictorian and got an on-stage kiss at graduation from the English teacher. When asked why she kissed him, she said jokingly that she hoped to kiss a president of the United States. Harry was standing nearby and asked if he got one too. She said he had to do something to deserve it. Later Charlie became his press secretary. As the two reminisced, the new president called his old teacher to see if he could now get his kiss.

When he was ten he suffered a severe case of diphtheria, paralyzing him for a time so that he had to be carried around. After several months he miraculously recovered and was rarely sick again. (**Eisenhower's** brother died of the same disease at this time, not too many miles west in Abilene.) At about age 14 he worked as a soda jerk at the Clinton Drug Store* at the NE corner of the square at 101 West Maple, still operating as such. This was his first paying job and required him to arrive at 6:30 A.M. to sweep, mop, and clean the medicine bottles. Whiskey was kept behind the prescription case for those prominent citizens who opposed saloons, but wanted a ten-cent shot in the morning. This led Harry to learn about hypocrisy among the socially elite and "amen-corner-prayers." During his teen years, Harry was invited to a few parties attended by Bess and her social group and became somewhat of a loner although friends did frequently meet at his home. His best friends during school were actually his two female cousins. He was able to meet twice a week at their house, 216 Delaware, where one helped a group including Harry and Bess with their Latin. Cousin Ethel was one of the few who knew of his infatuation with Bess.

He met Elizabeth ("Bess") Wallace in Sunday school at the nearest Protestant church, First Presbyterian, between Maple, Spring, Lexington, and Pleasant. His mother felt that the minister of that church was especially welcoming to the family, so she sent Harry there rather than the Baptist church. He secretly admired the popular belle, who generally sat behind him at the Columbian School, all through high school. He didn't dare speak to the pretty little girl for five years after he first saw her, even though he confided his feelings to his cousins. Bess never showed any particular attention to him, and the relationship was interrupted when he moved to Kansas City after high school graduation. When his father lost a huge amount of money from speculation, removing the chance for Harry to go to college in 1901, the family moved to 902 N. Liberty for several months and then to Kansas City. Until after high school Bess lived at 608 N. Delaware. While Harry was in Kansas City, her father killed himself in the home, and she moved with her family to the nicest house in town, that of her Gates grandparents, 219 N. Delaware and Truman Road,* her permanent home for the rest of her life.

After Harry began work on the family farm in Grandview, 16 miles away, he visited frequently with his cousins, who lived across the street from the Gates House. They remembered his fondness for the girl now living across the street, and he volunteered to take a cake plate back, "with something approaching the speed of light." More visits followed, and in 1913 Harry wrote Bess, "It seems a hollow week if I don't arrive at 219 Delaware at least one day of it." Harry had a standing invitation for several years to eat Sunday dinners with Bess, although Mrs. Wallace felt Bess could do better. He returned after World War I, soon married Bess in 1919 at the church she had attended since about 1902, Trinity Episcopal, 409 N. Liberty, and moved into her home, as he had agreed to live with her possessive mother, brother, and grandmother. Bess's mother was so possessive that she probably drove away potential suitors long after high school, leaving her available to Harry. Even as she lived in the White House with her famous son-in-law, she let it be known that she did not feel that he was good enough for Bess. His daughter Margaret was born in the home in 1924 and married at Trinity in 1956.

The **Trumans** lived in the home until 1935, when he went to Washington as a senator. This was also his permanent home for the rest of his life and a summer White House. The home was inherited in 1924 by Bess's mother, and later by Bess and her brothers, who were bought out by the **Trumans**. His two brothers-in-law lived in houses still standing just to the east on Truman Road, built in the rear of the Wallace home. The home is near his Presidential Library,* retirement office, and burial site at U.S. 24 and Delaware Street. Bess couldn't bear to live elsewhere and spent much time here during the presidency. Most of subsequent presidents have been to the home, donated to the nation. Here **Truman** addressed the nation on the eve of his 1948 election and received word of the North Korean invasion in 1950, which resulted in 33,629 U.S. battle deaths with no congressional authority for the resulting war. The fence was put up in 1949 to keep the public from carting off the house bit-by-bit. Bess lived in the home until she died at age 97, the oldest of the first ladies. The second floor cannot be shown to the public as the family still has the right to stay there.

After retiring he continued for years to take his daily walks around familiar neighborhoods, the town square, and his courthouse. **Truman** had worked in the old courthouse as county judge and supervised the construction of the new courthouse* on Independence Square in 1934. He then made sure that the square had a statue of his hero, Andrew Jackson, from whom the county got its name. Young Margaret pulled the string that unveiled it. In 1924 he was the president of a savings and loan at 204 N. Liberty that, in his words, "went to pot." He also oversaw the construction of the Memorial Building, still at 416 W. Maple, and frequented the Harpie Club at 101 N. Main to play cards, some thought badly. He got his hair cut at 214 N. Main before 1965, and later at 417 W. Maple when the barber moved.

The **Truman** Presidential Library was dedicated in July 1957 with **Herbert Hoover** in attendance. When **Truman** was back in town he worked behind his White House desk here for six and a half days a week for nine years, longer than his two White House terms, and then for the rest of his life on a more limited schedule. His office recreation contains a globe that was presented to him by **Eisenhower** and many duplications of White House pictures and furnishings. He began to write his memoirs here that relieved somewhat his financial position. **Truman** retired from the presidency without a pension or allowance for expenses, a large estate such as many ex-presidents enjoyed, or willingness to accept gifts or corporate positions. (A pension with expenses was voted for former presidents beginning in 1958.) And he paid a top 67% income tax on his book profits rather than the 25% that **Eisenhower** had managed to pay as capital gains tax on his *Crusade in Europe*. The IRS had ruled that **Ike**, being a nonprofessional writer, could do this.

Eisenhower finally came to the library in 1961 to get ideas for his library in Abilene. During his campaign **JFK** came to see **Truman** at the library and home, and the former president was happy to tell a friend, "The boy is learning—I hope." **LBJ** came twice in 1966 and signed the Medicare bill here, for which **Truman** had fought. **Nixon** personally delivered **Truman's** White House piano and played the "Missouri Waltz" for **Truman**, who liked neither **Nixon** nor the song. He turned to his daughter when **Nixon** was playing and blurted out, "What's that?" **Nixon** was back with **Johnson**, who had just three weeks to live, for **Truman's** 1972 funeral. **Carter** (1980), **Ford** (1976), and **Reagan** (1985) have also visited the Truman sites.

The area around the home is preserved as a historic area relatively unchanged since Harry's courting days. A National Park map, "**Truman** Places," available in the area, notes many of the area **Truman** sites and the Missouri Pacific Depot, 600 W. Grand, where he was welcomed at the end of his historic 1948 campaign and by 10,000 upon retirement in 1953.

IRONTON • **Grant** received his commission as brigadier general in present day Emerson Park* at the monument, erected in 1886.

KANSAS CITY • **Truman** came as a twelve-year-old piano student with his teacher to see renowned pianist Ignace Paderewski. As vice president he reminded the later prime minister of Poland that he had to play his piece three times before the artist was satisfied. He later came as a 16-year-old page to William Jennings Bryan's nominating convention in 1900 and then moved here with his parents in 1903 to 2108 Park Avenue. His Kansas City activity included:

1900–17, Convention Hall, NW corner of 13th and Central: 1900 Democratic convention; attended various functions later, including being taken by cousins to a season of opera (from which he said it took him years to recover); and drilled his men during World War I.

1901, 814–818 Delaware, near NW corner Ninth and Baltimore: Went to Spalding Commercial College, but abandoned it as too costly after taking typing and shorthand.

1901, 4515 Kansas Ave.: Worked at Santa Fe RR for Smith Construction Co., from which he moved around to several construction camps.

1902–3, 1729 Grand: Mailroom clerk two weeks for the *Kansas City Star*. He wrote a letter, never mailed, that if the *Star* were to be known in history, it would be because a future president had worked there.

1903–5, 2108 Park: Resided with family and attended Benton Boulevard Baptist, 25th Street and Benton Boulevard, now Macedonia Baptist.

1903–5, National Bank of Commerce, Tenth and Walnut: Worked in basement where his boss wrote that he was very careful and caught many errors others would miss.

1903, Grand Theater, 704 Walnut: Usher.

1904, 506 Bodine, Clinton, Mo.: Lived at the end of 1904 with his parents.

1905, 2650 East 29th Street: Lived with his aunt after his parents moved to the farm, but this was too far from downtown, so he moved to 1314 Troost.

1905–6, 214 E. 35th Street: Roomed with Arthur Eisenhower, also a messenger for the same bank, whose brother Dwight was in high school in Abilene. Arthur later recalled that they only had about a dollar a week left over from room and board, but Harry managed to catch every vaudeville show at the Orpheum and Grand.

1905–6, Northeast of Ninth at Baltimore: He was doing well making $75 a month at the Union National Bank as bookkeeper, but the family farm was failing. By 1906 the entire family had moved there to work it, including 22-year-old Harry. This physically built up the large farm and the owlish-looking bank clerk.

1914–53, Union Station, 2400 Main: Began and ended many trips here.

1919, 703 Ridge Arcade: Worked at Morgan and Co. Oil Investments.

1919–1922 and later, 104 W. 12th, the Muelebach Hotel: Went into partnership at a haberdashery, north of the Muelebach Hotel,* still at 12th and Baltimore, where 13 presidents have been guests. **Truman's** interest in the clothing store came after selling off livestock and machinery from the Grandview farm. As his store was failing, the father of an army buddy came by the store and asked him to run for county judge, equivalent to county commissioner. The father was also the brother of the county political boss, Tom Pendergast. (Before the war he had attended Mike Pendergast's Tenth Ward Democratic Club at 2535 Prospect.) His political career was now started, although he was tainted with the bad reputation of his political mentors. **Truman** himself was never shown to have compromised his office. He did have to hide at the Pickwick Hotel, Tenth and McGee, at times to escape pressures of those hounding him to do their will.

Truman spoke for his law school class at the Muelebach in 1925 and stayed many times, including the night of his vice presidential election in 1944. This was his election headquarters in 1948. The presidential suite on the eleventh floor was his political headquarters from 1945 until leaving office in 1953. He signed the Truman Doctrine here in 1947 and celebrated his 1948 win amid "a madhouse" of joy. He arrived here at 6:00 A.M. to a surprised crowd and later learned he had been reelected. He was here when he heard **Kennedy** had been shot in 1963.

Eisenhower celebrated his first-place finish in Staff School here. When he was staying in 1953, **Truman** called to pay his respects, but an aide told him the president's schedule was full. They did have lunch together here in 1966. **Johnson's** speech was canceled in 1961 as the hotel was evacuated because of a fire.

1920, 3404 Karnes: The only house **Truman** ever owned until he bought the Wallace House was deeded to him as part of an investment. He never lived there and used the proceeds from the 1921 sale to purchase an apartment at 3932–34 Bell and then traded for a farm near the intersection of K 7 and K 10 in Lenexa, Kansas.

1920s, Engineers Armory, 3620 Main: **Truman** met for several years here with the Reserve Officers' Club that he helped found.

1922–1924, Courthouse in block bounded by Fifth, Oak, Missouri, and Locust: Served as county judge. The firetrap was replaced by a new structure in 1934 at 12th, 13th, Oak and Locust. (He lost his reelection bid in 1924.)

1923–5, 1013–5 Grand Avenue: Went to law school for two years of a four-year course while he was county judge, but had to leave due to pressing county business.

1924–6, Tenth and Central: Worked for Kansas City Automobile Club.

1926–34, Courthouse, second floor: As presiding county judge of Jackson County, **Truman** made it clear that he would not award contracts based on favoritism, but only on low bids that Pendergast honored. (Jackson County includes Independence, Kansas City and Grandview.) He later had an office as senator.

1928, Jackson Democratic Club, 1908 Main: Tom Pendergast's office was the scene of meetings with the refuted political boss of the area.

1930s, 822 Club, NW corner 13th and Baltimore: Played poker on the eighth floor and made a life member. 110 E. Tenth: Plaques mark the spot where an army buddy cut his hair for years and his favorite booth (number four) at the Savoy Grill, SE Ninth and Central.

1944, President Hotel: Accepted James Byrnes' request that **Truman** nominate him for vice president at the upcoming Democratic convention, and then turned down Alben Barkley's identical request.

1939–45, U.S. Courthouse, 811 Grand, Room 649: Offices as senator and vice president.

1953–7, Federal Reserve Bank Building at Tenth and Grand, room 1107: Offices after leaving office until the Truman Library was completed.

1945, Visitation Catholic Church, 5141 Independence: Created a sensation as vice president when he attended the funeral of his friend, "Boss" Tom Pendergast.

1972, **Truman** Medical Center, Little Blue and Lee's Summit Roads: Died at age 88.

Other presidential visits include **Cleveland** at the Coates House in 1887, 1003 Broadway; **Coolidge** dedicating the Liberty Memorial in 1926; **Ike** at the Baltimore Hotel, Baltimore Ave. from 11th to 12th, in 1915 and 1939; and **Reagan** in 1976 at the (now) Ritz Carlton, Warnall and Ward Parkway. **Ford** beat **Reagan** for the 1976 nomination at the Kemper Arena, 1800 Genessee, and stayed at the Crown Center, 2345 McGee. **George W. Bush** told the VFW at Bartle Hall, 301 13th, on August 22, 2007, that as long as he was in charge he would fight to win.

Lamar • **Harry S. Truman**, named after his Uncle Harrison, was born in 1884 in a 20x28-foot house in a 6x6-foot-10 inch bedroom, still at 1009 Truman Avenue.* The tree his father planted on the day he was born is still growing here. His grandparents were named Solomon and Shippe, and he was given the middle initial "S" after both, even though a middle name sometimes appears in print. It is sometimes stated that the "S" should have no period, but "S." is used in his daughter's biography as well as David McCullough's. When the Chief Justice swore in **Truman** in 1945, and stated, "Harry Shippe Truman." **Truman** restated it correctly. His name was put on the cradle roll at First Baptist, 108 Gulf. In 1885 they moved to an unknown site near Harrisonville and to a farm southwest of Belton. The family lived there from 1885 until they moved in 1887 to Grandview, southeast of Belton.

Mexico • **Grant** visited the Ross House,* 501 S. Muldrow.

St. Louis • **William Henry Harrison** visited Augustine Chouteau's home in 1804, a house fronting Main and occupying the whole square between Market, Main, Walnut, and Second. He was here to organize the District of Upper Louisiana, attached to his Indiana duties. The **Lincolns** stayed at the National Hotel, also called Scott's, SW corner of Third and Market, on the way to Washington in 1847. It was across the street from the famous Old Cathedral* in the widened street across from KMOX-CBS. He may have visited a block away at the old courthouse,* where the slave, Dred Scott, began a legal action to gain his freedom. **Grant** freed his only slave there in 1859. **Lincoln** also passed through at other times, including 1841, returning to Washington in 1849, and probably in his trips to Lexington. **Taylor** had his headquarters in the National in 1814 and 1820 and commanded at Jefferson Barracks* in 1836, then the largest military post in the country.

Grant began his army career at the Barracks, still covering a large area south of downtown. **Davis** was also stationed here and brought the captured Indian chief Black Hawk at the end of "his" war. The Barracks are open on Alternate 67 and Bypass 50, SE of Kirkland. **Eisenhower** came there in 1911 to take exams for West Point and got lost in the big city. He and a friend got back after curfew, and had to sneak into the barracks in order to be at the proper place on time to take the qualifying exam. None of the buildings from the Civil War era, where 200 future Civil War generals served, are still present except three buildings from the 1850s near the river, marked and serving as a museum near the visitor center. The area in operation while **Taylor** and **Grant** were here is located in the present National Guard area along Hancock. **Ike** would have been in these red brick buildings and was treated at the old hospital now belonging to the school at the NW corner of Sherman and Worth, west of the Guard area. **Ike** was in the Statler Hotel, 822 Washington, on September 20, 1952.

Grant visited the family of his best friend, Frederick Dent, outside St. Louis at White Haven,* clearly marked on Grant Road, north of Gravois Road. He enjoyed the family atmosphere that he missed and spending time with two of Dent's younger sisters. But when the oldest sister Julia returned from school, it was love at first sight. When **Grant** was ordered to Louisiana, he rode out to tell her he was leaving and almost drowned getting across a normally shallow stream. He made it to the house, changed clothes with one of her brothers, and left with an understanding about the future. He did not see Julia again for four years, but returned to marry her in the Dent town home at the NE corner of Fourth and Cerre Streets, about four blocks south of the National Hotel site, now a vacant lot adjacent to the exit ramp of I-55 and I-44. Future Confederate General James Longstreet was his great friend and best man. He and two ushers surrendered to General **Grant** at Appomattox in 1865. The **Grants** failed to come for the wedding owing to the disagreement with the Dents over slavery, a favorite arguing point when **Grant** lived in the White House as president. (Actually **Grant**'s mother, about whom very little is known, failed to travel almost anywhere, including the White House, and **Grant**'s relationship with her was almost unknown, similar to Washington's and Jefferson's cases.)

Julia remained at White Haven as **Grant** was stationed on the West Coast, but he resigned in 1854 to join his family, now consisting of two sons. Two of their four children, the oldest and youngest sons, were born in the house. White Haven is now a part of the **Grant** National Historical Site,* and is painted green as it was in the 1870s, rather than cream as it was when **Grant** was here; Dent painted it gray during the Civil War, showing his feelings. He is said to have tried to get his son-in-law to go south, stressing that he would get to general quicker.

The **Grants** moved back after he resigned from the army and realized that he could not work for his own family. He lived for a while in the big home with Julia's three slaves. Everyone thought it was peculiar for a farmer who did his own farm work to have three house servants. They then moved to a nearby home of his brother-in-law Lewis, known as Wish-ton-wish, where his daughter was born. This was located about 150 feet in from the east corner of Eddie Park Road and Pardee, in Grant Farm Park. Probably because of Grant's arguments with Julia's father over slavery, he built his own log house known as Hardscrabble,* now located at 10501 Gravois Road. The original site is marked* a mile or so north on the grounds of the present St. Paul's Cemetery on Rock Hill Road. It was begun in the fall of 1855, and the family moved in in September 1856. It is said to be the only thing **Grant** ever built. To access Wish-ton-wish and the original site of Hardscrabble, go west from the current location of Hardscrabble along Gravois to the next intersection, which is Eddie Park. Turn north, and Pardee is the next intersection. Pardee winds around to Grant Road, north of White Haven, and continues on generally north to Rock Hill. St. Paul's Cemetery is to the east. Much of the **Grants**' furniture was in Wish-ton-wish when it burned while **Grant** was president.

After the **Grants** had lived just a few months at the crude, primitive home, his mother-in-law died, and the family moved back to White Haven in January so that Julia could help raise the younger sisters. Old Man Dent moved into St. Louis, and **Grant** rented the big house, where his youngest son was born in 1858. The farm had to be abandoned in 1858 because of illness, weather, and an agricultural depression. Mr. Dent persuaded him to go into a real estate partnership, so he took a room at 209 S. 15th, and walked 12 miles to and from White Haven on weekends. He acquired a slave of Dent's, but later freed him rather than sell him for the $1000 or so he desperately needed.

After four months of this, he moved his family to Ninth and 1008 Barton, for which he had traded his farm and Hardscrabble. But the new owners defaulted, and **Grant** got it back. The original but heavily modified Barton Street home is in an older section about a mile and a half south of downtown. His office was at Pine and Memorial Drive, and he also lived at 209 S. Pine and 632 Lynch at Seventh Street, now a park across from the Busch Brewery. He also served as clerk in the U.S. Customs House, SE Third Street and Olive, in 1859, but the collector died within a short time, and the new one let him go. Everything failed, so he tried selling firewood on street corners, where friends were appalled by his appearance. He ran into his old friend Longstreet in front of the Planters Hotel, at 410 Fourth Street between Pine and Chestnut. **Grant** was in shabby clothes but insisted on paying him back a $5 gold piece he had owed for many years, although Longstreet tried to refuse. He had been surprised the day before when **Grant** had been brought in obvious poverty to a game of brag (poker) at the hotel. The next time they met was in 1865 at Appomattox. **Grant** then stopped alongside Longstreet and said, as if nothing had happened in between, "Pete, let's have another game of brag, to recall the old days which were so pleasant for us all."

In 1860, **Grant** appealed to his father and was sent again as a failure to Galena, Illinois, to help in a family business there and to work under his younger brothers. During the Civil War the family spent much of the time here with Julia's family, and **Grant** began to purchase White Haven in 1863 from his father-in-law. He had hopes of returning here after the war, and did return shortly for rest and relaxation, but the world was bigger then and demands and opportunities called beyond this peaceful place.

In 1886 **Johnson** and **Grant** stayed at the Lindell Hotel, Washington Broadway, between 6th and 7th and attended a banquet at the Southern Hotel between Broadway, 4th and Walnut. **Grant** spoke from the balcony of the Campbell House,* now a museum, at 15th and Locust. **TR** was at the Planters in 1906 and 1916, 4421 Maryland in 1903 and 1904, and attended Second Presbyterian in November 1904 at 2608 Washington. **Cleveland** visited the Presbyterian church, on the SW corner of Washington and Compton, in 1887. **TR** visited the St. Louis Exposition World's Fair in 1903 at Forest Park, now the home of most of the city's museums and zoo. **Cleveland** visited the fair the same year, and **Harding** did the next, and was also at the Coliseum, at 2608 Washington and Union Station on the south side of Market at Eighteenth Street, in 1920. **TR** also visited the Planter's Hotel (1903, 1904) and Second Presbyterian, 2608 Washington at Jefferson (1904). **FDR** dedicated the Soldier's Monument opposite City Hall in 1936. **LBJ** helped celebrate the city's bicentennial on February 14, 1964, at the St. Louis University, 221 N. Grand, and at a dinner at the Chase-Park Place Hotel, 212 Kingshighway. **Clinton** debated the elder **Bush** at the Washington U. Gymnasium, 1635 Washington, on October 11, 1992. **Bush** then visited the Catholic church at 2653 Ohio. **George W. Bush** debated Vice President Al Gore at Washington University, 900 Walnut, on October 8, 2000.

Montana

Billings • **Wilson** spoke at the Fair Grounds Auditorium in 1919, a year after **Theodore Roosevelt** had spoken there. **George W. Bush** spoke at the Billings Arena in March 2001. **FDR** came here as a vice presidential candidate in August 1920. He was honored in a tent at Division and Clark before playing golf at the country club.

Butte • **TR** spoke at a local ball park in 1900 and pleased miners, who had expected the worst, with his remarks on the rights of labor. **Taft** visited the Leonard Copper mine off U.S. 91 at Noble Street in 1909 and also the courthouse. **Harding** came in 1923 via the Great Northern Station and visited a mine. **Truman** returned in 1950 and in 1956 to the Finlen Hotel, where he said his campaign really got started on June 8, 1948. (**TR** had also been to the hotel.) Someone at Naranche Stadium yelled for **Truman** to "give 'em hell," and he did. **Harding** also had addressed a large crowd there. **Truman** also had been to Butte in 1944, when he donned a hardhat, went into the Leonard Mine, and formed what he referred to as the "Hard Rock Club," which reporters referred to in subsequent visits. He also then got a war bonnet and was inducted into the Blackfeet Tribe at the Harve station, where he spoke five times. Even earlier **Truman** came to Glasgow to register a homestead. **FDR** spoke at nearby Glasgow and Harve from the train.

GLACIER NATIONAL PARK • **FDR** spent the night at Two Medicine Chalet* in 1934 after a day-long park tour. This is now the store at Two Medicine Lake. From the chalet he addressed the nation in a radio fireside chat that described and praised the beauty of the area. Blackfeet Indians greeted him in the park and pronounced him "Chief Lone Wolf." **Truman** threw the switch of the Tiber Dam* near Chester from the nearby Kalispell gym. He also visited Grand Coulee Dam* and Hungry Horse Dam* at Columbia Falls. **Nixon** flew into Glacier Park International Airport* near Kalispell, greeted large crowds, and, with Senator Mike Mansfield, pulled a rope at Libby Dam* to place the 3.5 millionth yard of concrete.

GREAT FALLS • **Truman** was the first president to visit when he came in 1950 at the Great Northern Station. **JFK**, **Nixon**, both **Bushes** and others have since visited. The first **Bush** delighted in telling his audience of the hairdresser's delight in December 2000, when, in fixing his wife's hair there, she learned her client was the mother of "the governor of Texas." He greeted about 400 at the Heritage Inn* at 1700 Fox Farm Road. On September 26, 1963, **Kennedy** also spoke at the Memorial Stadium,* where he broke through the ranks of Secret Servicemen to greet thousands, and stopped at Mike Mansfield's parent's home on Sixth Ave. at Sixth Street. **George W. Bush** spoke at the Four Seasons Arena, Northwest Bypass and Third Street, on February 1, 2005. Thousands stood in line for hours for tickets.

HELENA • **TR** visited the Capitol on Sixth between Montana and S. Roberts on May 28, 1903, as did **Taft** in 1909 and **Wilson** in 1919. **Roosevelt** spoke for 30 minutes on the grand stairway at the main entrance and then toured the interior. **George H.W. Bush** spoke on the lawn and visited inside in 1989. He planted the centennial tree and addressed the House. Other visits to the capital city include **Taft** (1909), **Wilson** (1919), **Harding** (1923), and **Truman** (1950).

TR spoke on April 12, 1911, at the high school at Lawrence and Warren, torn down in 1975. **Harding** spoke at the civic center after going to Yellowstone. Crowds standing on the train track delayed the train for 20 minutes. Almost 20,000 heard **Wilson** at the now destroyed Marlow Theater. **Taft** was at the state fair. **JFK** and **Nixon** came before taking office.

Kennedy came to the Rebir home on June 27, 1960, at 801 Floweree Street where he was pictured by the pool, made a speech, refused, as was his habit, to eat at the banquet, and then left out the back door. When he could not find his limo, he yelled, "Where the hell is my car?" A businessman whom he knew offered to rush him to the airport in his gaudy red, white, and blue station wagon. The candidate professed that he "would not ride in that damned thing." The owner then said, "So walk." **Kennedy** smiled and did ride, licked all the way by the driver's dogs.

MISSOULA • **FDR** announced at the train station here in 1932 that he had been up and down seven states and had found no one who would vote Republican, but many Republicans who would vote for him. **Truman** later spoke from the rear train platform at the station. In April 1950 he visited the power station at Hungry Horse Dam.* **Carter** spoke in the Mansfield lecture series in 1986 at the University of Montana on University Ave.

WIBAUX • **TR** drove cattle to the town's large holding pens from nearby North Dakota.

YELLOWSTONE NATIONAL PARK • Many presidents have visited, including **TR**, who dedicated the Roosevelt Arch* at the Mammoth entrance on U.S. 89. **Arthur** came in August 1883. **Harrison** visited in 1881, when he stayed in Marshall's Hotel on the confluence of the Firehole River and Nez Perce Creek. **Harding** came through during his last trip in 1923 and stayed at the Mammoth Hot Springs Hotel. (Also see Wyoming.)

NEBRASKA

GRAND ISLAND • **George W. Bush** explained how liberty can transform former enemies into allies and a region of hate into a region of hope. He predicted that someday a U.S. president will be talking with elected leaders of the Middle East about peace, and America will be better off. He spoke November 5, 2006, at the Heartland Events Center, 700 E. Stolley Park Road.

KEARNEY • **Clinton** told 6000 at the University of Nebraska that he was glad he "finally" made it on Dec. 8, 2000, the last of the 50 states he visited. He called on his successor to help unite Europe to help the United States in international peacekeeping. Students at Park Elementary, 29th and University, were surprised when a limousine stopped and the president got out and greeted several. He stopped at 39th and N and mingled in with 1000 as spectators screamed. He stopped at Horizon Middle School and the Great Platte River Road Archway over I-80.

LINCOLN • Campaigning in 40 Nebraska towns in four days in 1900, **TR** spoke to 300,000, including 30,000 between Falls City and McCook and "a monster rally in Lincoln." He spoke in front of the Capitol* in 1903, as did **FDR** in 1936 and **Taft** in 1911. **Wilson** visited three-time presidential loser William Jennings Bryan's home, Fairview,* in 1919, now a museum on 49th Street on the north side of Sumner. **Ike** honored veterans at the state fair on September 1, 1946, telling them that the barriers to neighborliness are fear and ignorance spawned by ignorance, but these had been largely destroyed and the road to world peace was seen clearly. He spoke at the McCook Airport on September 4, 1954. **Ford** told listeners on October 16, 1974, at the Lincoln airport at 3:18 P.M. that he had breakfast in Kansas City, a meeting in South Dakota, was going to dinner in Indianapolis, and would be back in Washington that evening.

OMAHA • **Grant** and his wife were served a buffet at General Crook's home,* now a museum, at Fort Omaha, 30th and Fort, one of the last surviving Italianate arch-style homes in the area. Crook's furniture had not arrived for the important reception, so all furnishings were borrowed from Omaha citizens. **Hayes** and his wife were honored here the next year.

McKinley saw his official chief executive's flag floating over the Omaha Club, NW corner of 20th and Douglas, on his 1898 visit. **TR** ate here twice, and when he later learned that the U.S. marshal had turned over two wealthy ranchers to their lawyer so that they could eat here during their six-hour sentence, fired the marshal. On October 10, 1936, **FDR** told a crowd at Ak-Sar-Ben Coliseum, 302 S. 36th, that he enjoyed returning after a few weeks' absence. He had spoken at Sidney on August 31st. In 1920, **Harding** stayed at the Fontanelle Hotel on Howard between 14th and 15th. **Truman** spoke at Ak-Sar-Ben ("Nebraska" spelled backwards), where he dedicated the War Memorial and visited Boys Town, 132nd and W. Dodge in June 1948.

Ford was born under the name of Leslie King, Jr. on June 14, 1913, at 3202 Woolworth. The home burned in 1971, killing an inhabitant, and was torn down in 1975. The lot was purchased to build a memorial, but the city could not come up with the money. **Ford** visited the site on May 7, 1976. On December 8, 2000, **Clinton** spoke at Offutt Air Force Base, telling the crowd that his critics said it would be a cold day when he came to Nebraska, but he enjoyed the warm welcome. **Carter** spoke there on October 22, 1977, telling them that he was there studying the readiness of forces under his command. He toured SAC headquarters and met many soldiers.

NEVADA

CARSON CITY • **Grant** (1879), **Hayes** (1880), **TR** (1903), **Eisenhower** (1919), and **Kennedy** (1960) have visited the Capitol,* on the east side of North Carson Street at Musser. **Ike** was on his cross-country survey of roads for the proposed Lincoln Highway, later Highway 50. Later his observation of German Autobahn led to the creation of the Interstate Highway System. **Carter** appeared at the Legislative Building south of the old Capitol on February 6, 2006, to support his son's announcement that he was running for U.S. Senate. Gov. **Reagan** may have visited his friend the governor at the governor's mansion at the NW corner of Mountain and Robinson.

Grant was the first president to visit the state when he was returning from a trip around the world after he left office. He arrived at the north side of Lake Tahoe on October 26, 1879. The party then steamed across the lake and rode the narrow gauge at the top of Spooner Summit where U.S. 50 and Nev. 28 now cross. From there **Grant** took a stage to Carson City, where he spent the night with Governor John Kinkead and spoke in the Capitol. Kinkead lived in a rented house, still at 502 N. Division, now a law office, where Mark Twain stayed with his brother Orion Clements, who was Territorial Secretary and acting governor. **Grant** then took the Virginia and Truckee Railroad to Virginia City from the depot at 729 N. Carson, also used by **TR** and **Hayes. Hayes** traveled to the west while president a year later and was taken from Carson City to the lake by stage driver Hank Monk, made famous by Mark Twain.

Kennedy visited nearby Lake Tahoe in November 1960. **Clinton** came to Incline Village in late July 1997 to host the Presidential Forum at Sierra College, 999 Tahoe, and signed an executive order on the beach declaring national concern for the area. He stayed at the Hyatt Regency Lakeside Lodge, 111 Country Club Drive.

Hoover Dam: **Hoover** inspected the dam named in his honor on November 12, 1932. **FDR** dedicated it on September 30, 1935.

LAS VEGAS • **JFK** met Frank Sinatra in February 1960, and frequently during his presidential campaign, at the Sands Hotel,* where he met various entertainment stars and a girlfriend, Judith Campbell, that he shared with mobster Sam Giancana. Many gamblers and show business personalities believed Sinatra "won the election for **Kennedy**." And "all the guys knew it." The hotel was at 3355 Las Vegas S. and hosted many well-known entertainers, including the rest of Sinatra's "clan," and maybe, as the hotel claimed, all presidents from the time they opened in 1952, including **Truman. Kennedy** was in town twice as president and watched "the clan" perform here. The Venetian Resort Hotel occupies the spot now. **LBJ** was here October 11, 1964. **Kennedy**'s visits included December 8, 1962, when he traveled to the atomic test site at Indian Springs with noted scientist Glen Seaborg. He visited Las Vegas Country Club, September 28, 1963, as did **Nixon,** October 31, 1970, and **Ford** on May 24, 1976. **Kennedy** (1963), **LBJ** (1964), and **Nixon** came to the Convention Center, 3150 Paradise, torn down in 1990. The current Center is at the same location.

Reagan was in town many times as an entertainer, governor, president, and former president. He played two weeks as a song and dance man at the Last Frontier in 1954, and joked as president in 1986 at the Hilton* (3000 Paradise Rd.), "Some predicted that I'd never play Las Vegas again, but here I am, playing a full house." He spoke to county Republicans at the Circus Circus,* 2880 Las Vegas S., on February 18, 1975, and denied here later that year that he would run on a third-party ticket with George Wallace. He came to a fund raiser at Wayne Newton's home in 1982 and took up 250 rooms at the Sands later that year. In 1990 he told a convention at the Mirage* (3400 Las Vegas Blvd. S.) that he was proud that a spiritual revival had occurred when he was president.

RENO • **Grant** and **Hayes** (September 1880) passed through, as did **McKinley** on a train, May 26, 1901, that did not stop until it got to Carlin to add engines to make the high grades further east. **McKinley** did not get off there, but spoke to the crowd from the train platform. He also stopped at Wells. **TR** made speeches at the University of Nevada on North Virginia on May 19, 1903, and the steps of the current courthouse in 1911 and 1912. In 1903 a vast crowd watched as he was paraded down Virginia Street to the park across from the courthouse. On April 3, 1911, he urged Nevada to keep out those who wanted to get quickie divorces by moving here, and congratulated the state for recently outlawing gambling.

Wilson spoke at Reno on September 22, 1919. **Harding's** body passed through the state by train, stopping at several places, including ten minutes at Sparks. **Hoover** made one of his final campaign speeches from the train at Elko and Carlin on November 7, 1932, before passing through here on the way to his Palo Alto home. An attempt was foiled to blow up the track as he passed over a bridge at Palisade west of Elko. **FDR** made a similar trip east in 1938, stopping also at Carlin to speak as locomotives were changed. He commented that the population of the state was too small for what it should be. He also stopped briefly in Reno and Sparks. **Truman** spoke in front of the State Building on September 22, 1948, in what is now Powning Park. The building has been replaced with the Pioneer Center on Virginia opposite the courthouse. The *Evening Gazette* officially estimated 2500–4000 heard him, although supporters argued that there were 25,000 present. On October 12, 1964, **LBJ** flew in on Air Force One, the first time the plane was used, and spoke for a Democrat candidate to about 20,000 in front of the State Building. The speech was worth a visit as his candidate won by 84 votes.

Ford was at the International Airport and convention center on May 24, 1976, to disagree with opposing candidate **Reagan** that America was now number two in the world. In 1997 he got an honorary degree from Sierra Nevada College at 999 Tahoe, Incline Village. **Carter** was also at the airport and the Incline Village in 1997. **Reagan** made three trips as president (Oct. 2, 1982, October 30, 1986, and Nov. 1, 1988) and became the second president to speak at the University in 1982. He spoke at Morrill Hall on the Quad, east of N. Virginia, north of Ninth Street, at where Lake Street would run if it went north of Ninth. In 1986 he spoke at the Lawlor Center. **George W.** spoke at the convention center at 4001 S. Virginia on June 18, 2004; at Ranch San Rafael nearby on October 14, 2004; and on October 2, 2006, at the Reno and Elko Airports. The elder **Bush** spoke in August 5, 1992, to 5000 disabled at the Hilton, 2500 E. Second.

Virginia City • **Grant** visited in October 1879, upon returning from his long world tour. The papers reported that 2000 flag-waving school children marched to greet him along with fire companies, veterans of both sides, Indians, and many miners. He stayed at the International Hotel on the NW corner of C and Union, now a parking lot, and went twice to the Piper Opera House* on the northeast side of Union at B Street, just east of the courthouse,* where he was also honored, as was **Theodore Roosevelt** later, or at least so some claim. Although **Roosevelt** is "pictured" in Virginia City, there is some dispute that he was ever in town. Local expert Guy Rocha at the State Library can find no verification. Edwin Booth and Buffalo Bill Cody, among many others, performed here.

Grant was served dinner at the Savage Mansion, still west of the center at 146 "D" and visible just south of the main ("C") street. He also visited the Mackay Mansion on W. "D" Street with John Mackay, the richest mine owner. The party, including his wife and Ulysses Jr., visited the Comstock Mine with Mackay and proclaimed that it was the most wonderful site he had seen in two years of travel. The visit lasted two days here while he attended many functions at the Piper, Pioneers' Hall, Savage Mine Office, and other locations. He went the entire length of the railroad tunnel through Silver City to Dayton's Odeon Hotel,* where he made a speech from the balcony, and the Sutro Mansion in Sutro east of Dayton, where another speech was delivered. The party then returned via the tunnel to Virginia City, the Savage Mine, and Reno, where they caught the Central Pacific on route to his Galena, Illinois, home.

Hayes came September 7–8, 1880, with General William T. Sherman and stayed at the same hotel and saw the Comstock. He also visited Glenbrook at Lake Tahoe. Again the town went wild with festivities, parades, hundreds of Chinese lanterns at the hotel, and lavish decorations. In a speech from the International, **Hayes** related that he would rather rule the nation from here than Washington.

NEW HAMPSHIRE

AMHERST • In 1827 **Pierce** attended the Methodist Chapel on Middle Street and the Congregational Church, on Church Street near the Boston Post Road, when he studied law at the home of Edmund Parker at 12 Main. He met his future wife and was married in her grandparents' home, the Means (Appleton) Mansion at 1 **Pierce** Lane.

CONCORD • **Jackson** and **Van Buren** visited the State House in 1833 and spoke at First Congregational at 177 N. Main, as had **Monroe** in 1817. **Jackson** also spoke at the Unitarian church at 274 Pleasant and the Baptist church on State. He stayed at the Eagle Hotel, still on Eagle Square across from the State House and up the hill from the train station site where **Lincoln** and the others arrived. **Monroe, Hayes**, both **Harrisons, Grant, Davis,** and **Nixon** also were guests, and **Eisenhower** had his picture taken in front. It was a major strategy meeting site for local politician **Pierce. Monroe** was also at Barker's Tavern on Main. Later presidents, including those listed plus **Arthur, George H.W. Bush, Eisenhower, Ford, Polk, Reagan**, and **Taft**, also visited the State House. **Jackson**, an old man at age 66, grew physically worse due to the strain of endless parades and receptions as his trip progressed from Baltimore to here, finally collapsed while in town, and had to be taken back to Washington by ship in mortal danger. Even at this late date in medical history, he was bled, making his condition worse.

While in the legislature in 1829, **Pierce** lodged with his father, the governor, in John George's home near the North Church and moved the next year to the Eagle Hotel until 1833. From 1833 until 1842 he served in both houses of Congress, then resigned from the Senate and moved back to what is now called the Pierce Manse at 18 Montgomery to live until after the Mexican War in 1848. This was his first real home away from a domineering father and senior party members at boarding houses in Washington. One of his sons died there near the present location at 14 Penacook,* at the end of Main. It was reconstructed at a new location since he owned it, although he lived longer at the destroyed rental home on Main. By 1848 the **Pierces** had lost two sons, and they did not want to return to the former home. He then lived at 52 S. Main until leaving for the presidency. The indulgent parents doted on the surviving son, who would scamper downtown to wait outside his father's law office and share a walk home. The eleven-year-old was killed after his father's election. (See Andover, Ms.) He and his wife returned and lived here from the time he retired from office in 1857 until his death in 1869. It is now a vacant lot with a few remaining steps just south of the Water Funeral Home and a block south of the Capitol Center for the Arts, between Thorndike and Concord.

Pierce attended South Congregational at 27 Pleasant from 1842 until 1863 and was baptized at St. Paul's Episcopal, 18 Park, where he attended from 1863 until he died. His funeral was there. This preacher was not political like the one at South Congregational. **Pierce** worked at several places on Main including his Merrimack Bank Law Office, County Courthouse, and Ayer's Block over Franklin Book Shop near the State House.

When he left for Washington to be inaugurated, the youngest elected president up to then, he was probably the most loved man in New Hampshire. When he returned, the town refused him an official welcome because he had signed the Kansas-Nebraska Act, called the worst legislation in American history, renewing the rift between the states. He stayed even though the town seemed to turn against him as he battled alcoholism. One of the bedrooms was set aside for his old friend, author Nathaniel Hawthorne, who often visited.

After **Lincoln** was assassinated, an angry mob gathered to demand that **Pierce** show his loyalty, as he had not flown his American flag. In fact he was stricken with grief and prostrate on his library sofa when the sound of approaching mayhem gathered. **Pierce** went out carrying a small flag, expressed horror at the deed, and exclaimed that it was not necessary "to show my devotion for the Stars and Stripes by any special exhibition upon the demand of any man or body of men." The "first alcoholic president" probably drank himself to death at his home in 1869. After reposing in the State House, he was buried with his wife and sons at the Old North Cemetery, North State between Walker and Franklin, in an enclosure on the north side of Kearnes Lane.

On March 1, 1860, **Lincoln** was first introduced as "The Next President" in Phenix Hall, 40 N. Main, and was so surprised that he made no comment. He later asked the speaker if he really meant it. He stayed in the Phenix Hotel connected by a second story bridge from the hall.

CRAWFORD NOTCH • **Pierce, Grant, Hayes,** and **Harding** stayed at the Crawford House near the top of the Notch, on the west side of Route 302 just north of Saco Lake, the Willey House marker, and gift shop near the intersection with Mount Clinton Road. **Davis** spent the night on top of Mount Washington while secretary of war. **Eisenhower** saw the Old Man of the Mountains on June 24, 1955, the state symbol until it fell into the valley on May 3, 2003. A little north in Jefferson, **Garfield** visited the Cheshire House, at the SE corner of Central Square between Roxbury and Church Streets, and dedicated the Soldier's Monument. **Monroe** is claimed to have stayed at the Kent House on Pleasant Street during his 1817 tour.

DOVER • **Washington** stayed at the Folsom Tavern, 21 Spring, now a vacant lot, on November 4, 1789. **Monroe** visited the Episcopal church in 1806 and the William Hale House at 5 Hale Street, now 192 Central, where Lafayette stayed in 1825. **Lincoln** spoke at the city hall, then on Central Square, Central and Washington, on March 2, 1860, and slept in the northeast bedroom at the George Matheson home at 113 Locust, now called the Lincoln House. He visited the New Hampshire Hotel on Third, and got a shave at a barbershop on the corner of Central and Orchard.

TR was given a large reception on Franklin Square at Main and Central in 1902, as was **Taft** in 1912. The American Hotel was on the site of the present Days Inn and claimed to have hosted "many presidents." The Mobil station, where Central, Court, and Church meet, marks the site of Tuttle Square, where the courthouse was and where the legislature met when Dover was state capital for one year. **John Quincy Adams** and **Monroe** stayed in the adjacent Wyatt's Inn.

EXETER • Revolutionary War officers formed the Society of Cincinnati at the Folsom Tavern, NW corner of Spring and Governors. **Washington** was served a meal at the original site, Front and Water, in 1789. He did not know when he came that the legislature alternated between here and Portsmouth, or he would have planned more time for a public dinner that he missed.

Lincoln visited his oldest son at the boarding house of Mrs. J.B. Clark, located at High and 7 Pleasant. Robert failed his Harvard entrance exams and came to study at the academy here to get the foundation to reapply. With Tad and Willie not around, they were probably close for one of their few times and attended the Second Church of the New Parish. **Lincoln** probably stayed with Robert at least one night, February 29, 1860, maybe also March 3, and spent at least one night at 89 Front, the home of his Congressional colleague, Amos Tuck, one of the founders of the Republican Party. **Lincoln** spoke at the Town Hall at 7 Front on March 3, 1860. Ulysses Grant, Jr. and Richard and Francis Cleveland also attended the academy.

HILLSBORO (HILLSBOROUGH) • **Pierce** was born in 1804 in the family homestead three miles west on State 31. This old home site is now under a lake, and no one is quite sure where it was. But the boyhood home where he was brought from the age of three weeks, the Pierce Homestead,* is nearby at the junction of State 9 and 31. He went to school in the Hancock Academy, just down the road in Hancock, the first building east of his church on Main, NH 123, and he lodged in the boarding house across the street from the bandstand. A turning point in his life came when he ran away at age twelve to go back home. His father said nothing, invited him to dinner, and then rode him back to school. In 1820 he went to the Francestown Academy, stayed next door and attended the Meeting House on routes 47 and 136. He built his law office directly across the road from the family home, where he continued to stay until his marriage in 1834, although he had purchased another home about a quarter of a mile away on NH 31 and Old Turnpike. But he was frequently in Washington, and his wife visited her relatives so much that they did not feel they had a real home. After their first son died, the **Pierces** moved to Concord, but he always thought of this home as his own after it had been owned by siblings whom he visited. He worshipped at the South Congregational in the Town Center and studied law on Main. **Pierce**'s biographer states that **Jackson** visited **Pierce**'s father here "many times," but I can find no specific verifications.

MANCHESTER • **Lincoln** and Robert stayed at the City Hotel, NE corner of Elm and Lowell, on March 1, 1860, after **Lincoln** spoke at Smyth Hall. After the "immense gathering" in the Smyth Block on Elm between Water and Spring Streets, they then went to the Amoskeag Mills on the east side of the Merrimack River at Canal Street. **Hayes** was at the Maplewood House in May 1877. **Bush** and **Clinton** engaged in a TV debate at the WMUR station in 1992.

PORTSMOUTH • **Washington** visited several friends and state officials in late October and early November 1789. He arrived traveling roughly what is now U.S. 1. A marker at NH 84 and U.S. 1 in Hampton Falls Village notes that he halted there to greet and shake hands with many soldiers. These included the "president" (governor) of New Hampshire, General John Sullivan. Thirteen gentlemen in a red, white, and blue barge rowed him around the harbor as hundreds cheered from the shore. He got a good view of Fort Constitution. The president tried his hand at the fishing grounds near the bridge, but only caught a half-pounder. On Sunday he went to two churches, both since rebuilt. A marker on the current 1854 Old North Church at the square, replacing the 1713 meetinghouse, notes that **Washington** worshipped there. St. John's on Bow Street still displays **Washington**'s chair from the earlier Queen's Chapel on the site. **Monroe** worshiped there in 1817. **Washington** visited his private secretary Tobias Lear's mother at her house, 51 Hunking, south of Strawberry Bank. The Old State House was on Market in the center of the present square between the Athenaeum and present Old North Church. **Washington** addressed the people from a balcony facing Pleasant. Part of the Old State House was moved to 429 Court, but the remnants are in storage in Concord.

As the first president attended a ball in the Assembly Rooms he referred to the building as "one of the finest halls he had been to in the United States." As was his custom, his diary mentions the number of handsome ladies. There is nothing remaining today, not even a marker, but it was on a small shopping street, Vaughn, north of Congress, that was once Raitt's Court, in the middle of the short block. He was entertained at the Pitt Tavern on the corner of Court and Atkinson. This is now on the north side of the Strawberry Bank Restoration Area. It was originally a meeting place for the Tories, but when the Patriots attacked it in 1777, the penitent host changed the name to honor William Pitt, the colonies' great friend.

Washington dined several times at the home of Governor John Langdon,* 143 Pleasant at Junkins, and is said to have enjoyed the hospitality and praised the home of Portsmouth's leading citizen. Langdon signed the Constitution and was president of the Senate at the first session. **Washington** also visited Governor Goodwin's Mansion on Hancock and Wentworth's house at 346 Pleasant. **Monroe** stayed at the latter in 1817. **Washington** came back in 1791 and visited Langdon again and the Chase House on Court. He also stopped at Stoodley's Tavern, on Hancock across the street from the Goodwin Mansion. His diary shows walks around the town and general comments on the architecture from the era that still exists. He found some "good houses," but a number "indifferent."

John Adams' appearance in 1777 at the courthouse was his last representing a client anywhere. This occurred while the congressman was on recess and just before he sailed with ten-year-old John Quincy for the beginning of their foreign diplomatic careers. **Monroe** was in Portsmouth in 1817 to visit the Cutter House, at the corner of Congress and Middle, and toured several forts in the area. All visiting presidents must have been impressed with the pretentious Moffatt-Ladd House* at 51 Market, just north of the square. One of the residents, William Whipple, knew **Washington** and **Adams** and signed the Declaration of Independence.

TR chose the Naval Yard on Seavey's Island (Kittery, Maine) for his conferences that ended the Russo-Japanese War with the Treaty of Portsmouth in 1905. **Clinton** and **George H.W. Bush** spoke at the 2007 commencement at the University of New Hampshire in Durham.

Pierce (1865–1869), **Garfield**, **Arthur** (both in the 1880s), and **Taft** vacationed at Little Boar's Head a few miles south. **Taft** (1884, 1909) stayed in the second house north of Atlantic on Ocean Blvd. and the beach. **Pierce** and **Garfield** stayed at the Bachelor hotel on the beach north.

NEW JERSEY

BURLINGTON • **Grant's** family lived for much of the time from 1862 until 1865 at 309 Wood, where he was going when **Lincoln** was shot. He visited his daughter Nellie as she attended nearby St. Mary's Hall, near the Delaware River Bridge, Route 413. The house and school are still standing. Elias Boudinot built the home at 207 W. Broad in 1798. As president of the Continental Congress when the Revolution ended, he has been referred to as the first president of the United States. But the president then only chaired meetings and had no real powers.

CALDWELL • **Cleveland's** 1837 Presbyterian manse birthplace is at 207 Bloomfield.* He was baptized in the Presbyterian church at 814 Madison. A more recent church is still on site. His father was a kind, diligent man with too few talents and too many children. The home was rather extravagant, but his salary was not. A year later he moved to Fayetteville, New York, where the manse was less stylish and the salary larger.

CAPE MAY • **Buchanan** sometimes vacationed at his brother's cottage at 205 Howard, and **Benjamin Harrison** used the Congress Hotel, 251 Beach Drive, as a summer White House.

ELIZABETH AREA • **Washington** attended a wedding in 1778 at the Belcher-Ogden Mansion, 1046 E. Jersey, in 1778 with Lafayette and Alexander Hamilton. On April 23, 1789, traveling to his inauguration, **Washington** stopped at Boxwood Hall,* 1073 E. Jersey Street, another home of Elias Boudinot. **Monroe** visited Liberty Hall,* the home of Gov. Livingston, on the west side of 1003 Morris Ave., east of Garden State Parkway exit 140A in Union. His friend **Washington** is believed also to have visited and also stayed three times at Merchants and Drovers Tavern, Westfield and Grand Avenue in nearby Rahway. He spent his last night before his first inauguration in Woodbridge at Amboy and Main, where the Knights of Columbus Hall now is. The old tavern where he stayed was later moved a short distance and is now at 142 James.

ENGLISHTOWN, FREEHOLD AND MONMOUTH BATTLEFIELD • While **Washington** shivered in the winter of 1777–8 at Valley Forge, the British enjoyed Philadelphia and then decided to march back to New York in the early summer. They could not return by sea due to lack of supplies and fear of the French fleet. When their march north was detected, **Washington** learned which route they were taking and decided to slug it out when he caught up with them on June 28. This resulted in the longest battle of the war, the last major battle of the north, and the last for second-in-command, General Charles Lee.

On June 26, as the army camped around Cranbury, **Washington** made his headquarters in the Stites House (private), marked at 53 S. Main, Route 535. He and his officers dined a few miles away on June 27, 1778, at the Village Inn* in the center of Englishtown at the NW corner at the intersection of N.J. 52 and 527, Water and Main, the oldest continually operated inn in New Jersey. Various sources claim he drew plans for the battle here, but this is questioned. The commander was also believed to have been here after the battle and offered Lee a hearing for his questionable actions. A few doors away is the Moses Laird Home. He was **Washington's** guide before the battle and his host afterward. A plaque on the door of the Hulse Memorial Home on Main marks a site of **Washington's** army before the battle, where it is claimed that he ordered General Lee to lead the attack.

Lee had doubts about attacking and waived his command position to Lafayette. But as the battle loomed, Lee reversed himself, ineptly led the troops, then panicked and fled directly into the path of **Washington**. When the enraged commander in chief encountered Lee, he had one of the most celebrated tirades in history, screaming abuse toward Lee, then assumed command and saved the day. The spot of the encounter is marked northwest of Freehold on Route 522, although the marker is about 500 yards away from the exact site believed to be the top of the hill SW of the intersection of Ilene and County Route 522, and SE of the 522/Wemrock Road intersection. It is south of the railroad tracks in Battleview Orchards north of the Rhea House. Lafayette, who witnessed the scene, said it was the only time he ever heard **Washington** swear and that his fury was terrible to behold. Near the spot is the 1751 Old Tennent Church* or Freehold Meeting House, a battle landmark that **Washington** referred to as "the new church." The military draw was a political triumph for **Washington**, who had met the British in the open field and forced them to retreat. This was also the last battle for **Monroe**.

GLASSBORO • The Holy Bush Mansion on the north side of Whitney at Victoria, now the administration building for Rowan University, was used in a three-day summit by **LBJ** and Soviet Premier Kosygin in 1967. **Reagan** delivered a high school graduation address there in 1986.

HACKENSACK AREA • **Washington's** headquarters from November 18 to 24, 1780, were at Peter Zabriskie's,* where he stayed when he had fled with the army from Fort Lee in 1776. A plaque at Washington Mansion House at the NE corner of Washington Place and Main, the courthouse Square, notes the site. Here the commander was shocked to learn that the British had crossed the Hudson, requiring an immediate retreat. The present 1791 First Reformed Church, at 42 Court between Main and the river, incorporates some of the 1728 church used by **Washington** when he attended the funeral of Gen. Enoch Poor.

Just north of Ho-Ho-Kus is the Hermitage* at 335 North Franklin Turnpike, where **Washington** and his staff frequently visited, open as "**Washington's** headquarters.*" This was the home of Theodosia Prevost, who later married Vice President Aaron Burr here. She was a patriot in spite of her British officer husband and entertained patriot leaders. Supposedly while visiting, **Monroe** fell in love with a local girl, who was already pledged. **Madison** later visited.

Washington frequently visited his mapmaker at the predecessor of Ringwood Manor* off Route 511 and 1304 Sloatsburg Road, four miles west of Ringwood State Park, just south of the New York State border, west of the I-87 and I-287 junction.

In nearby Oakland, **Washington** used the Van Allen House* on Franklin, just east of Route 202, north of exit 58 on I-287, in August 1777, when he heard that British General Burgoyne had captured Fort Ticonderoga. In nearby Paramus, **Washington** established headquarters in the Hopper House in September 1778, and supposedly drank from the spring in Van Saun Park on Forest Avenue, the center of the camp. He was at the Paramus School House, 650 E. Glen, in 1778 in Ridgewood. After the war a grateful nation presented a home in River Edge to Baron Von Steuben, the Prussian officer who taught military discipline and European training methods to colonial troops. It is now known as the Steuben House,* New Bridge Road just NE of the Main-Hackensack intersection, near 1209 Main. **Washington** used the 1713 house as headquarters on September 4, 1780, as had Cornwallis.

JERSEY CITY • **Washington** is claimed to have come through the area known in 1775–6 as Bergen and was presented a lace handkerchief at Stuyvesant Tavern at the foot of Glenwood Avenue. He and Lafayette visited the Van Wagenen House* or Apple Tree House at 298 Academy and dined under an adjacent apple tree in 1779. They were trying to get Bergen farmers to supply the colonial troops. When the tree fell in 1821, many came to make souvenirs of the remains, some of which were given to Lafayette when he visited in 1824. The old house is off Bergen Square. He may have also visited the Van Vorst House, now the oldest house in New Jersey, as his officers were staying there. This is located on Palisade between South and Bowers.

Lincoln passed through the railroad station, then at the site of Pennsylvania Station, several times going to and from New York City, including his inaugural trip and in his journey to West Point in 1862, when he made a brief speech.

LAMBERTVILLE • **Washington** and **Monroe** used Coryell's Ferry from New Hope, Pennsylvania, several times and then set up headquarters at the Holcombe-Jimison Farmstead* on Route 29 between Routes 179 and 202 from July 18 until August 1, 1776, July 18 through July 31, 1777, and again on June 21 and 22, 1778. The ferry site is marked just north of the bridge. The Lambertville House,* just south in the business district, still operates as a hotel at 32 Bridge Street and once hosted **Andrew Johnson** and **Grant**.

LONG BRANCH • Seven presidents, **Grant**, **Hayes, Garfield, Arthur**, **Benjamin Harrison**, **McKinley**, and **Wilson**, came here for summer getaways and attended St. James Chapel,* the "Church of the Presidents," at 1260 Ocean Boulevard and Lincoln, near Takanasses Bridge. All went to Oceanfront Park, Ocean and Joline Ave., NJ 35. Nearby areas were destinations of these presidents, plus **Taft**, who honeymooned at the long-gone Albemarle in Sea Bright.

The **Grant** family spent summers in an extravagant red brick "cottage" given to him at 991

Ocean Avenue, demolished in 1963. The site is now covered by the south side of the Stella Morris Retreat Center. The president loved the place, and his vacations got longer and longer. He also visited "an architectural wonder," Bricksburg or Laurel House, in 1869. A little south in Lakewood, on Main east of the present post office, it was later **Cleveland's** home in 1889. **Cleveland** also stayed in the Grover Cleveland Cottage, on Lexington north of Carey, and Lakewood Hotel, on Seventh between Clifton and Lexington, called the Winter Headquarters of Tammany Hall (New York's Democratic Party). The hotel once stayed opened after their normal season so that the dying **Cleveland** could rest in peace.

After being shot in Washington, **Garfield** was brought to his summer home in 1881, a cottage near the beach at the grounds of the Elberon Hotel, Ocean Avenue opposite Lincoln Avenue, not far to the south of Grant's cottage. It was hoped that cool ocean breezes would aid healing. The bullet, lodged near his spine, was probed for with dirty fingers and instruments, probably causing the infection that killed him on September 19. **Arthur, Hayes,** and **B. Harrison** also stayed at the hotel. **Taft** came by on his honeymoon to see where **Garfield** had died. The site is now a residential area east of the Elberton Train Station on Lincoln Avenue. A marker shows the site of **Garfield**'s death at 12 Garfield Terrace, a circular street opposite the end of Lincoln Ave.

Wilson came a number of times while president to stay at Shadow Lawn at Cedar and Norwood in West Long Branch. A new building, Woodrow Wilson Hall of Monmouth College, was built on the site after it burned. He made many speeches from the porch and was notified of his nomination in 1916.

MADISON • **Washington** visited the Sayre Mansion, 31 Ridgedale, in 1777. Young **TR** stayed at a summer place, Loataka, between 1863 and 1866. This is on the west side of Kichell Road between Madison and Woodlawn. **Washington** spent the night of August 27, 1781, in nearby Chatham on the way to Yorktown, in the Morrell House,* now a restaurant. He also is said to have frequented the Day's Tavern just east of the center.

MORRISTOWN • While **Washington** was camped in New Jersey in the winter of 1777 the Revolutionary cause experienced its darkest hours. **Washington** somewhat redeemed himself as commander in chief by holding the army together here. He was nearly "the Revolution," bringing his weary but elated troops here after the great victories at Trenton and Princeton that revived the failing cause. The Watchung Mountains presented a perfect defensive position against the superior British force in New York City, 30 miles away. **Washington** rested and rebuilt his undisciplined army that raided peaceful nearby farms. Cold and sickness dominated the harsh months. The Presbyterian and Baptist churches dominated the town and became hospitals for the sick and dying during a smallpox epidemic. He worshiped at the Baptist church on the NW corner of the Green and the Presbyterian church, where he took communion, on the north side of the Green at Speedwell and Morris, now occupied by a later church. Much business was conducted in Jacob Arnold's tavern, then on the western side of the Green in the middle of Park Place. **Washington** used this as headquarters and issued a proclamation in 1777 that all people in America swear allegiance to the United States. **Washington** ordered barrels of sand rolled in and out of the storehouse on the Green (now the SE corner of South and Marker) to deceive British spies into believing there was an abundance of provisions.

One defensive position was later called Fort Nonsense* when a legend arose that **Washington** had it built only to keep the soldiers occupied. But **Washington** wanted to guard supplies when the army moved to the field in 1777. The area is open by the National Park Service down Western Avenue, southwest of town. As warm weather returned, the British moved in strength. **Washington** countered by moving to Middlebrook, where he could better oppose the advancement. Then the British returned to New York and sailed south.

He returned two years later to encamp again during the terrible winter of 1779–80, the harshest in a century, known as the "starving time." Again **Washington's** leadership and ability held the Revolution together in another severe time of starvation and mutiny. As many as 28 snowstorms blocked supply roads and further weakened the health and resolve of troops. During this period he and Martha lived in the Ford Mansion,* 230 Morris, from December 1, 1779, until June 10, 1780, as his troops camped nearby at Jockey Hollow,* also on Western Avenue. When Martha arrived, some observers thought she looked so "simple, easy," and plain that she was taken as a servant and were shocked when **Washington** rushed up to embrace her. Troops only had used the home the winter before. The quartermaster could not clothe the army since Congress was stymied with inflation and lack of resources. **Washington's** call on the governors of the surrounding colonies was answered by New Jersey in an effort which **Washington** said "saved the army from dissolution or starving." Daily conferences at the mansion dealt with problems, strategy, and coordination with the new French ally. Mrs. Ford and her four children were here during the time and frequently huddled with **Washington** and Martha in front of the kitchen fire to keep warm through the night. In May Lafayette arrived with momentous news that the French fleet of six warships and 6,000 soldiers were headed for Rhode Island to aid the Americans.

Washington knew many sites open as Morristown National Historical Park. He is thought to have visited the Wick House,* General St. Clair's headquarters, still north of Tempe Wick Road near Jockey Hollow Road and encampment. The owner's daughter hid her horse in her bedroom to keep it from being stolen by the British. Among other presidential visits, **Grant** came to 50 MacCulloch Avenue.

NEW BRUNSWICK • **Washington** came here at least five times and used Cochrane's Tavern, on the SE corner of Albany and Neilson (now Hyatt Hotel site), from November 29 until December 1, 1776, in the retreat across New Jersey when he wrote frantic letters to Congress. He and his staff stayed at the White Hart Tavern on the NE corner after the battle at Monmouth. (Markers are at the SW corner.) General Charles Lee was held for insubordination in Cochrane's. In 1783 **Washington** is believed to have visited the 1739 Buccleuch Mansion,* overlooking the Raritan River in Buccleuch Park off Easton Avenue.

On the way to the conference with British commanders in September 1776, **John Adams** and Benjamin Franklin shared a bed in the crowded Indian Queen Tavern (destroyed in 1974), in the vicinity of Albany Street and Route 18 (once Water Street). **Adams** feared the night air and wanted to leave the window closed, but Franklin was convinced that outside air was better than the stuffy air produced by no ventilation. **Adams** was not persuaded, but Franklin's long scientific explanation put **Adams** to sleep. During other visits, **John Adams** was a guest at the Henry S. Guest House at Livingston and Morris and also stayed at the White Hart. **Jefferson** and **Madison** stayed there several times and in Crane's in September 1790.

NEWTON • **Washington** was at the Cockran House near the Courthouse Square, on July 26, 1782, and ate at the White House Inn in nearby Fredon during the same month.

NEWARK AREA • **Washington** passed through on June 25, 1775, and later led his men down Broad on November 22, 1776. On February 21, 1861, two-thirds of Newark's 70,000 lined the streets when **Lincoln** passed through en route to his inauguration. His train from New York brought him to the "lower depot," and he rode in an open carriage for one and a half miles to the "upper" depot. He made speeches at both. The route was along Chestnut, past the Ninth Ward School to the Chestnut Street Station. **TR** dedicated Lincoln's statue at the courthouse in 1911.

Just northwest is South Orange, where **Washington** stayed at the Timothy Ball House, 425 Ridgewood. The walnut tree where he tied his horse is still here. The Washington Rock in the nearby South Mountain Reservation is where he observed his troops intercepting efforts of the British to reach Morristown. **Washington** came to lodge at the Davis House, at 409 Franklin in Bloomfield, but soon left, according to two stories. One is that Gen. Benedict Arnold had already established himself there, and the other is that he found sick solders all over the home. **Washington's** headquarters on October 26, 1780, are marked at Valley Road and Claremont in Montclair. He might also have been here the following night on this trip to visit Lafayette's camp in the vicinity of 551 Valley Road, now in the business district of Upper Marlboro.

Nixon lived in nearby Saddle River from 1981 until 1990 and then in Bears Nest, a Park Ridge condominium in Woodcliff Lake, 239 Spring Valley Road, about a mile from the first mentioned home. It was here that he had a stroke in 1994 preceding his death.

PAULSBORO • **Washington** and Lafayette visited Fort Billings, on Beacon Avenue between Fifth and Sixth, across the river from Philadelphia, on August 1, 1777.

PRINCETON • British General Cornwallis told **Washington** at Yorktown: "Fame will gather your brightest laurels rather from the banks of the Delaware than from those of the Chesapeake." Historian Sir George Otto Trevelyan wrote, "It may be doubted whether so small a number of men ever employed so short a space of time with greater and more lasting effect upon the history of the world." **Washington's** battle here on January 3, 1777, ended the miracle of "The Nine Day's Wonder" when he breathed new life into the failing Revolution with three small but major victories. But for these surprise victories reversing what seemed to be a lost cause, the middle colonies would probably have fallen almost immediately. America may well have been on the way to becoming a replica of Canada. But now British scattered garrisons were called into the main base at New Brunswick, and the enemy abandoned most of New Jersey.

Washington's army followed up their surprise victory a few days before at Trenton by leaving Cornwallis there and moving to Princeton, winning, and marching north. Twelve stone monuments along Routes 206 and 533 mark the route from Trenton. Now **Washington's** army reached its physical limits and was ready to be rebuilt. He moved north through Kingston, Somerset Courthouse, Bound Brook, and Morristown for the winter.

The battlefield is a part of the town, a little southwest of the university campus down Mercer Street, and few sites are marked. Three are the Mercer Oak (which recently died), where General Mercer was wounded; the Clarke House,* in the park at 500 Mercer, where he died nine days later; and Nassau Hall,* where many British defenders were forced to surrender after an artillery bombardment. **Washington** must have visited Mercer, his friend and fellow townsman from Fredericksburg, who had received seven bayonet wounds, stayed under the oak to encourage troops, and refused to leave the battlefield. **Washington's** rallying the troops while on horseback in full view of the enemy was one of the most dramatic events of the war.

Morven,* 55 Stockton Street, Route 206, was owned by a signer of the Declaration of Independence, Richard Stockton. He was captured and incurred injuries until he signed an amnesty proclamation, discrediting him with fellow Americans. He died a broken man in 1781. British officers, including maybe Cornwallis, used the house and looted it. **Washington** stayed there when he visited in 1783 when Congress was meeting in Princeton to get away from mutinous soldiers in Philadelphia. He enjoyed listening to Mrs. Stockton's recitations of her verse. **Jefferson** may have visited Morven on November 4, 1783; **Madison** maybe on July 4, 1783; and **John Adams** described it in his diary from his 1774 visit. Many presidents have visited, including **Cleveland, Harding** (1922), **JFK** (1960), and **Truman**.

The town sites mentioned are within walking distance of Nassau Hall, at the head of Witherspoon Street on Nassau, at the heart of the campus. It was the only building of the College of New Jersey, the predecessor of Princeton University, when **Madison** went here and stayed in a 20-foot-square room with three others for three years. Congress (including **Madison** and **Monroe**) met in the hall from June until November of 1783 and thanked **Washington**, in person, for his conduct. Here they received the treaty ending the conflict. **Jefferson** was in Congress for only about a day, November 4, when they adjourned to Annapolis. **Washington** had been to the hall in 1773 visiting his nephews in school. Many members of Congress stayed at Bergen's or Hubibras Inn opposite Nassau Hall. Congress wanted **Washington** handy for final conferences on military matters as the Revolution was drawing to a close. He visited the Olden House at 344 Stockton, U.S. 206, in 1776 and also in 1791. Here he observed troop movements from the porch before the Battle of Princeton, and later returned to instruct that British prisoners here be treated humanely.

The college commencement in 1783 was at First Presbyterian Church, 61 Nassau with **Washington** and Congress. Nassau Hall claims also that nearly every president of the United States has entered the building, and has the distinction of being the site of the only known "joke" told by **Washington**. At a dinner when someone commented that the superintendent of finance had his hands full, **Washington** said he wished that he had his pockets full.

A few miles northwest on Route 518 is the town of Hopewell, where **Washington** arrived on June 23, 1778. He set up headquarters near the Baptist Meeting House on West Broad (Route 518) and began to get detailed reports about the evacuation of Philadelphia by the British. On the next day a council of war was held in John Hunt's home, with its commanding view midway between Hopewell and Blawenburg off Route 518, on County Line Road 603 just west of the county line. Here the officers debated about what to do. Most agreed not to molest the British on the way back to New York City, which Alexander Hamilton, Washington's aide, said "would have done honor to the most honorable body of midwifes and to them only." Generals Wayne and Lafayette argued strongly that they must be attacked. (See Freehold.)

While the Continental Congress was meeting in Princeton, they made Rockingham, also called Rocky Hill or the Berrien House,* available to the commander and Martha from August 23 until November 10, 1783. **Washington** entertained lavishly, met with **Jefferson** and other members of Congress, and wrote to Fraunces Tavern in New York for a cook. Martha was sick during much of this time, and slept in the small bedroom beyond the entrance hall. It was on the second-story porch that he read his "Farewell Orders to the Armies of the United States." The house has been moved several times and is now on County Road 603, Kingston/Rocky Hill Road just north of Kingston, five miles north of Princeton and west of the junction with N.J. 27 and east of Rocky Hill where it was for years. It was originally a quarter mile away toward the river.

On his inaugural trip in 1789, **Washington** stayed at the Merchants and Drovers Inn, at the junction of Westfield and Grand, where he also stayed in 1791. **Madison** came for schooling in Princeton rather than his state's William and Mary College for several reasons. His tutor was from here, and he felt the climate for his perceived precarious health was better. Also he perceived a lack of proper student discipline at the Virginia school. He went to Trinity Church on Stockton Street and lived in Nassau Hall with future vice president Aaron Burr, future general Henry Lee (Robert E.'s father), and Henry's brother Charles Lee, later U.S. attorney general and Washington's personal attorney. Madison brought his 12-year-old brother in 1774. The College of New Jersey was then little more than a junior high/high school. **Madison** ruined his health by completing the four-year curriculum in two years, stayed an extra six months to study with the college president, and then went back home and took five years to restore his health. (Actually he was a hypochondriac, like his mother, although they lived to ages 85 and 98.) He stayed then in the President's House,* adjacent to Nassau Hall on the south, built at the same time as the Hall and

It is claimed that all presidents have visited Nassau Hall at Princeton University, where Congress (with Jefferson, Monroe, and Madison) once met. Madison lived here while in school.

used as the president's house from 1756 until 1879. **Adams** visited it in 1774. It is also known as the Dean's House and currently the Maclean House.

Cleveland lived at Westland, 15 Hodge Road, from 1897 until his death in 1908. Today privately owned, it is the second house from the west of the NW corner on Hodge at Bayard, set back off the street. In 1891, when **Cleveland** was 54, his first child was born, with four more later; so his old age was lively and anything but quiet. The aging father liked to lounge on the portico watching his toddlers frolic and conversing with passing students. He attended the Presbyterian church at 61 Nassau, where a plaque is now on his pew, and worked in 1899 at 185 Nassau Street. He was a trustee of Princeton and sometimes clashed with **Wilson**. He died at his home in 1908 (**TR** attended the funeral in his library), and is buried at Princeton Cemetery,* Witherspoon and Wiggins. The grave is east of Witherspoon between Green and Quarry Streets. Maps are available at the entrance at Greenview and Humbert. (Former Vice President Aaron Burr is buried a few feet away off Wiggins.)

Wilson came to the College of New Jersey, later Princeton, in 1875 to study for the ministry, but changed his mind and decided to become a statesman. He later lived at the SE corner of Washington and Nassau and then at Witherspoon Hall off University Place, graduating in 1879. As a university professor he lived at 72 Library Place (1890–96) and then 82 Library Place (1896–1902). These locations are just north of Stockton across from Morven. In 1907 the trustees, including **Cleveland**, chose **Wilson** to be the president of the university, and he lived in the president's house on campus from 1902 until 1911. Now the Prospect House, it is part of the Faculty Club one-fourth of a mile from the library and chapel. His office was Room 1 in Nassau Hall from 1902 until 1910. While university president, he ruffled the conservative feathers of the establishment for condemning the privileges of the few and gained a reputation of a fighter for democracy. This led to his election as governor in 1910 and as such, lived at the Princeton Inn opposite Trinity Church, on Stockton next to the current police station, since the state then did not provide a home. In 1913 he became the first Democratic president since **Cleveland**, and moved to temporary quarters behind **Cleveland's** house at 25 Cleveland Lane. In addition to Trinity, he also attended First Presbyterian, 61 Nassau, from his student days, 1875–1897. His pew 57 is marked. From 1897 until he was elected U.S. president, he attended Second Presbyterian, now Nassau Christian Center at 26 Nassau.

Harding dedicated the War Memorial across from Morven, which he visited, in 1922. **Kennedy** attended the university for a short time in 1935, when he stayed in S. Reunion Hall (torn down) next to Nassau Hall and attended St. Paul's Catholic, 214 Nassau. One of the reasons he came was to get away from his big brother, but he had to leave because of illness.

SOMERSET COUNTY • **Washington** visited General Knox's headquarters in 1778–9 at the Vanderweer House* on the west side of U.S. 206 north of River Road and exit 22 off Interstate 287, about a mile south of the U.S. Route 202 junction. Just south on 202/206 is the Pluckemin Community that has two house sites associated with **Washington**. He had several conferences in the Fenner House, 264 Highway 202/206, east side of the main street, just south of the historical church on the west side, and stayed there two nights. The commander in chief had also been in the "Mathew Lane" or "1750 House," torn down several years ago for a parking lot on the south side of the church. **Washington** also visited two homes on the NW and SW corners of Lamington Road (Route 523) and Larger Cross Road, about five miles west of Bedminster in Lamington. (The Bedminster and Somerville libraries have various sources of documentation for the area included in this entry.) Only the Vanderweer House is marked.

The Middlebrook encampment area is on the north edge of Bound Brook on Mountain Avenue. **Washington** used the area as a main base camp in May and June 1777 and from November 1778 to June 1779. The location allowed the army to cover Philadelphia and check operations in New Jersey, contributing to Howe's 1777 decision to withdraw from New Jersey. **Washington** is believed to have used Chimney Rock in Watchung Mountain County Park* (marked), on a road with the same name, north of exit 14 on I-287 and south of Route 620, to observe British troop movements.

Washington stayed at the Drake House,* 602 Front on Route 28 in Plainfield, during the Battle of Short Hills or Watchungs, June 25–27, 1777. The home is now the Plainfield Historical Society.* The British captured Philadelphia in 1777 in a campaign starting here. **Washington** feared an offensive on his position at Morristown and advanced the army in May to around Middlebrook, where he was protected by hills and could observe from protected positions. The British maneuvered and tried to trap him, but **Washington** flanked skillfully, preventing an overland advance by the British, who then went to Philadelphia by sea. **Washington** was back in November 1778, and he and Martha lived at the Wallace House,* on U.S. 22 and 527 at 38 Washington Place in Somerville, from December 1778 until June 1779 while the Continental Army was at Camp Middlebrook. They also frequented the Old Dutch Parsonage* at 65 Washington Place, the home of Jacob Hardenbergh, who became a warm friend.

Several acres of sites of the Revolutionary activities are preserved near Bound Brook, on Route 527, Mountain Avenue. **Washington** also frequented Tunison's Tavern, Main and Grove, where he exchanged toasts with the innkeeper to "the American victory." Twenty-one-year-old **Monroe** came to **Washington** at the Wallace home to get his written recommendation for a military command and also used it later politically. Many markers show **Washington's** route.

Nearby just off the road south of Finderne in Bridgewater (east of Somerville and not on most maps), and north of Manville at the end of Van Veghten Road just north the Raritan River Bridge, is the Van Veghten House* (marked), General Greene's headquarters. Here on March 19, 1779, **Washington** danced for two hours with "the charming Mrs. Greene." This is west of Main Street, Route 533 in an industrial area, 9 Van Veghten Dr., reached by following National Starch Chemical Drive winding in from the north. **Washington** was also at the Van Horne House,* marked at 941 Main, east of the Target Store and across (north) from Somerset Stadium. His headquarters before the victory in the Watchung Mountains were also in the Van Dorn House on West River Road, Route 533, one mile south of Amwell Road, Rte. 514 in Millstone.

After **Washington** left the Wallace House, Greene moved to Lord Stirling Manor* (marked), at 96 Lord Stirling Road at South Maple in Basking Ridge, now a park. William Alexander laid claim to a Scottish title, Earl of Stirling, rejected by Parliament, but he used it anyway. **Monroe** was on Stirling's staff and spent time here after the Battle of Monmouth. **Washington** stayed here as the mansion was nearing completion on June 25, 1773, and later attended Stirling's daughter's wedding here in July 1779. Two brick slave quarters remain. **Washington** is believed to have eaten under a 600-year-old oak at Basking Ridge Presbyterian Church, 1 East Oak. The town also is where the second-ranking general in the colonial army, Charles Lee, was captured by the British after fleeing New York. He either defied **Washington** or at least moved slowly in his retreat to allow this to happen at White's Tavern (site), S. Findley and Colonial Drive, while his commander huddled south of the Delaware River near Trenton. The capture was probably a blessing in disguise, as it temporarily eliminated a major problem for the commander in chief. The White Horse Tavern, at U.S. 206 and I-95, in the town of the same name, lasted until 1972, and was named after **Washington's** horse when he visited.

On the west side of the Route 22 and 28 traffic interchange is the Frelinghuysen Mansion, where **Harding** signed the Knox-Porter resolution on July 2, 1921, formally ending the state of war between the U.S. and Germany and Austria-Hungary. He had been called in from playing golf, sat down, and signed the document without ceremony. The Baltusrol Golf Club at 201 Shurpike in Springfield was the first golf club to host a president (**Taft**) in 1912.

TRENTON • **Washington** retreated through town on December 3, 1776, after repeated defeats further north. He stayed near Trenton Falls across the river, and then moved north on the Pennsylvania side. British general Howe faced the Continentals across the river, but decided further military operations were ended for the winter and went back to the comforts of New York, leaving a holding force of Hessian (German) allies. He felt the war was about over, and indeed it seemed so to all. Then, on Christmas evening, **Washington** moved his forces, with **Monroe** in his boat, and crossed the Delaware River northwest of Trenton at Johnson Ferry House,* opposite Pennsylvania's McKonkey Ferry, on Route 29, River Road, in Titusville, and attacked the celebrating 1,200 unsuspecting Hessians in the town center. The present ferry house may be an ancient reconstruction. Washington Crossing State Park* is on the east end of the Route 532 bridge down Route 29.

Washington and his officers conferred briefly at the Bear Tavern at the NE corner of 546 and 579. The Continental Lane route some used is now Route 29. **Washington's** forces attempted the crossing in several sections with about 2,400 troops, but only those with the commander made it to the battle since the others felt that the extreme weather conditions made movement impossible. Swift action by the British and their Hessian troops now would put the Colonials in grave peril. Even a drawn battle would place **Washington** in a position where he could be easily surrounded by nearby enemy forces at a time when his troops were demoralized and leaving, and Congress seemingly could do nothing. The British might have ended the war if they had responded accurately and timely to the correct location of the advance and then stood up against **Washington's** main strength. A disastrous Hessian attack directly against **Washington's** main strength was an enemy mistake of historical consequence, allowing the war to proceed, ultimately to independence. **Washington** prevailed, but retreated as the many Hessians escaped.

Washington placed his artillery on high ground with a commanding view, now at the Battle Monument, Broad and Warren. Almost a thousand Hessians were captured with only four Americans wounded, including 18-year-old Lt. **Monroe**. He and Capt. William Washington, the commander's cousin, led a detachment on today's Broad Street and captured British cannon. **Monroe** would have died but for the swift services of a doctor who volunteered during the march. The New Jersey capital had been held by the competent Hessian Colonel Johann Rall, who loved the bottle and was so contemptuous of the Americans that he did not make proper preparations for a surprise. And when warned with a note that something was up and an enemy may be approaching, he did not want to interrupt his card game and put the note in his pocket. It was still there when he died a few hours later in his headquarters, marked at the west side of Warren between Hanover and Bank. The rectory of St. Mary's is on site. **Washington** received the surrender on East State near Broad, and then visited the dying Hessian commander.

After the battle **Washington** retreated back to Pennsylvania for a few days, then camped on the south bank and recrossed to south of Trenton behind the twisting bed of Assunpink Creek and the bridge. He wanted to strengthen his position with another victory and prevent the British from easily crossing the river if it froze, as they might take Philadelphia. The capital was now open, and **Washington** made his headquarters south of Assunpink Creek in the John Barnes House on Queen (Broad), knowing that Trenton was not easily defended. British General Cornwallis attacked Trenton on January 2 and drove the Colonials through town. **Washington** heroically poised on his horse at the Broad Street Bridge as his men crossed and then held off repeated attacks of Hessians trying and failing to get across.

After this critical Second Battle of Trenton, Cornwallis backed up, pondered whether or not to finish off the trapped **Washington** then or the next day, and decided to get him a little later. **Washington** met with his officers in the Douglass House* near the bridge. There they decided to go to Princeton, where a third important battle was fought, leaving Cornwallis wondering what happened back in Trenton. The home has been moved several times and is now about where it originally was, at Montgomery and Front.* His headquarters were adjacent in the True American Inn (destroyed).

In 1794 **Washington** and Congress met at the State House* to escape the yellow fever epidemic in Philadelphia. (The present building incorporates the original 1792 structure.) They crossed the ferry at the head of Ferry Street, east of the U.S. 1 Bridge where the railroad tracks now cross. **John Adams's** diary shows that he stayed in the ferry house here several times. They would have been familiar with the Old Barracks* on South Willow opposite West Front, still on the east side of the State House Grounds. Built during the French and Indian War, it quartered the Hessians at the time of the battle.

Washington is claimed to have visited the Masonic Lodge* at Willow (Barrack) and Lafayette, now a museum and visitor center. The building was moved from Front and Barrack in 1915. The claim that he presided over a meeting is questioned. A brother of John Dickinson lived in the Hermitage, now a derelict apartment building in a slum area on the east side of Colonial Avenue between Riverside and State, about a mile west of the State House. Hessians used it as their main outpost on the River Road. **Washington** knew it and passed nearby to get into town. Martha brought her grandchildren here when **Washington** was president. The first three presidents were claimed to have been entertained there and several sources claim **Lincoln** visited, although this does not seem probable.

In April 1789 the town celebrated the nation's first citizen on the way to his inauguration with a huge parade. The depiction of him crossing under 13 arches with 13 maidens and matrons singing and throwing flowers on the Broad Street Bridge* over Assunpink Creek was probably his most popular image of the 19th century. (A modern, wider bridge is here now, marked as the site of the battle.) Biographer Douglas S. Freeman described it as "...something altogether unique, something far beyond the usual measure of public acclaim. Here was something from a page in Roman history, something very like the triumphal return of a Caesar...." **Washington** wrote a letter of thanks at the City Tavern, marked on 1 West State, SW corner State and Warren, to the ladies who had planned such an enormous reception. The oldest and "most historic" house in the city is the Trent House Museum* at Market and William Trent Place. **Washington** was an acquaintance of the owner, and there are questionable stories of his presence in the home, although Martha was undoubtedly here.

Jefferson and **Madison** came through many times, crossed the ferry at Ferry Street, and stayed in town, probably at the hotels shown here. **Monroe** met with Congress in October 1784 at the French Arms, as the City Tavern was then called. When the government moved here temporarily because of a yellow fever scare in 1798, President **Adams** stayed in the Phoenix Hotel at Hanover and Warren, next to the Rising Sun Hotel at the SW corner of Hanover and Warren, where he had earlier stopped. He is also listed at the Barnes's home on King Street near St. Michael's Church. **Monroe** later stayed at the Rising Sun in 1794 and 1817. **Jackson** ate there June 11, 1833. **W. Harrison** stayed September 9, 1836, as did **Polk** on July 4, 1847, after his speech at the State House. By that later date the hotel was called the American House. In 1817 **Monroe** attended First Presbyterian at 120 E. State, just east of Warren. The present building dates to 1840.

On February 21, 1861, **Lincoln** arrived at the station, State and Canal (U.S. 1), and spoke to the both legislative houses.* Both halls were later destroyed by fire and rebuilt, although the rotunda is original. He ate lunch and stayed at the Trenton House on the SE corner of Warren and Hanover. (This is across from the Rising Sun site and a block north of the old French Arms.) His room on the second floor faced Warren and he spoke from the balcony there to a large crowd. The 1824 hotel had hosted Lafayette and later **Taft**.

Governor **Wilson**'s office was on the first floor of the State House, first office right from the main entrance. **Pierce** and his cabinet, including **Davis**, were at the State House July 13, 1853. **Truman** and **Kennedy** spoke at the War Memorial across from the visitor center. Note that most of the sites mentioned in this entry are within a short walk east of the State House.

WAYNE • **Washington's** headquarters were in the c. 1740 Dey Mansion,* 199 Totowa Road at Preakness Valley Park, from June 11 until July 29, 1780, and later the same year from October 8 until November 27. This was a strategic location close to British-occupied New York City where the colonial army could get food and forage. While here **Washington** heard that the French allies had landed in Newport, Rhode Island, and he left to go there. Soon afterward it was discovered that traitor Benedict Arnold was campaigning against his former comrades. His accomplice, Major André, had been captured and hanged, leading the British commander to vow to capture **Washington**. So the general came to this relatively safe place again where he was visited by Alexander Hamilton and Generals Wayne, Greene, Sterling, and Lafayette. It is believed that 364 letters and orders were written from here by or on behalf of **Washington**.

WEST ORANGE • **Hoover** spent the night with Thomas Edison in his home at Main and Lakeside.

NEW MEXICO

ALBUQUERQUE • The Alvarado Hotel, Gold and First, entertained **TR** in 1903 as the territory appealed for statehood, and **Taft** in 1909 before the hotel was destroyed. **TR** was back for speeches in 1905 and on October 16, 1916. **Truman** spoke from his train platform at the station on June 15, 1948, and also at Gallup, Las Vegas, and Raton. He mentioned his first trip to the state in 1909 and another where he set up a monument here to pioneer mothers. **George W. Bush** came to the Intel Corporation in nearby Rio Rancho on February 3, 2006, to promote a greater emphasis on math and science education. In March 2005, at the Bear Canyon Senior Center, 4645 Pitt N.E., he told residents that Roosevelt had done the right thing with Social Security.

LAS VEGAS • **TR** came here in 1899 for a reunion of the Rough Riders.

ROSWELL • **George W. Bush** addressed a large audience on the War on Terror, January 22, 2004, at the Convention and Civic Center. He joked that the unfamiliar aircraft reported that morning was just him.

SANTA FE • **TR** and **Taft** visited the Capitol on Galisteo and Montezuma at the dates shown above. The building has been considerably modified over the years and now serves at the Bataan Memorial Building. In 1880 **Hayes** visited the Capitol, still at the Governor's Palace, on the historic downtown square, the oldest government building in the United States, dating to 1610. **Clinton** visited the nearby Los Alamos lab.

New York

ALBANY AND VICINITY • **Washington** visited in 1782 and first went to Denniston's Tavern, NW corner of Beaver and Green, where he was granted the freedom of the city. He then was a guest of General Schuyler at his 1761 mansion* at the NW corner of Clinton and 32 Catherine, the unofficial patriot military and political headquarters of the area. British General Burgoyne was a prisoner-guest in the home after he lost the Battle of Saratoga, even though he had burned Schuyler's home in that vicinity. Alexander Hamilton married Schuyler's daughter here in 1780. A tomahawk cut can still be seen in the stairs, left by an Indian who was after Schuyler. **Jefferson** and **Madison** were guests in 1791.

Washington also visited the Pruyn House,* 19 Elk, Whitehall Mansion (burned in 1883) at 73 Whitehall Road, an extension of Second, and the First Reformed Dutch Church, then in the center of the intersection at Broadway and State. After touring the town he traveled to nearby Schenectady and visited the John Glen House, still at 58 Washington, and then went to Cherry Valley, Ft. Plain, Solomon's Lodge in Poughkeepsie, Fort Frederick, and visited Saratoga Battlefield. In Cherry Valley he was a guest of Col. Campbell, who had been burned out by the Indians during the war and had his wife and children carried off. This home, Auchinbreck, is still located at the SE corner of Montgomery and Old Fort Plain Road at the northeast edge of town.

Monroe visited Albany in 1784, as did **Madison**, who had also visited in 1774. In 1832, **W. Harrison** visited the Van Rensselar Mansion, still on Cherry Hill,* at 5231/2 Pearl, between McCarty and First, as did the governors of New York who became president. **Fillmore** served in the legislature and as state comptroller at the Old Capitol, then located at the head of State at Eagle on Capitol Hill at a spot now in the front lawn facing the southeast corner of the new building built after the Civil War. He lived in the Delavan House that was on the north side of Broadway between Columbia and Steuben where **Johnson** and **Grant** stayed in 1866, now the site of a park. **TR** stayed there and attending many state hearings and conferences. He had a habit of reading a stack of newspapers every morning and then throwing them on the floor, unfolded.

Van Buren attended the Dutch Reformed Church at Pearl and Clinton Square and lived from 1815 until 1827 in a house on State big enough to also contain his law practice. In 1828 he moved to 92 State and lived in the Congress Hall Hotel between the Capitol and Washington. His first wife died in 1819, leaving him with four sons aged from two to twelve. She was buried at the Second Presbyterian Church. His second marriage took place in the Schuyler Mansion* in 1858, in the same room as Hamilton's. **Van Buren** was governor for 64 days when he resigned to become secretary of state under **Jackson**. His office was behind the Old State Capitol in a square made by Washington Avenue, Park Place, Congress and Hawk. **Arthur** lived with his family at 626 First in Troy from 1846 until 1849 as his preacher father served the First Baptist Church* at 82 Third. He also went to First Baptist in West Troy at Canal and Ohio, 1853–1855.

Lincoln met on September 26, 1848, with **Fillmore**, probably at the home of influential Whig editor Thurlow Weed on Green Street near the Capitol. On February 18, 1861, no one recognized the new president-elect with his new beard when he arrived in a railway car previously used by the Prince of Wales. The station was at the Broadway railroad crossing with Lumber (now Livingston) Street. Finally the crowd realized who the little-known westerner was and flooded the area, with children climbing all over the engine. He and the family stayed at the Delavan House where **Lincoln** received many before dining at the governor's mansion, 144 State. He rode to the (old) Capitol to address the legislature and then through the crowds down Broadway and up State. He was honored at Congress Hall at the SW corner of Washington and Park. **Davis** was inaugurated President of the Confederacy on the same day in Montgomery, Alabama. On April 26, 1865, 55,000 viewed **Lincoln's** body in the Assembly Chamber of the Capitol. Many were turned away at the doors after the time came to close the viewing. The funeral procession passed State, Dove, Washington, and Broadway to the depot on Broadway.

In 1865, a crowd trying to get near **Grant** at the Capitol overloaded and collapsed a grandstand. **Johnson** and **Grant** were together at the Capitol in 1866. Both **Roosevelts** served in the legislature and held the office of governor. The 1871 Capitol was declared complete by Governor **Theodore Roosevelt** in 1899.

Arthur lived in North and South College Buildings, still at Union College in Schenectady, across the yard west of the Nott Memorial. (**Carter** and **Grant** both visited the college.) He is buried in the western end of Rural Cemetery* on Cemetery Avenue off Broadway in Menands, just west of I-787, north of downtown Albany. His prominent gravesite is marked by a flag and angel at the NE corner of South Ridge and Linden Ave., west of the superintendent's office.

The **Franklin Roosevelts** lived at 248 State Street from 1910 until 1912. Eleanor wrote, "The house seems palatial after New York, and it is a comfort to have only three stories instead of six." In 1913 they lived on the site of the Hilton Hotel at the NE corner of State and Pearl. **Franklin's** path to the White House, like **Theodore's**, ran through Albany. It did not hurt that all through his career, personal and political, some thought he was **Theodore's** son.

The Governor's Mansion, SW corner of Eagle and Elm, was first occupied in 1874 by Samuel J. Tilden, who almost became president. He got the most popular votes in 1876, but didn't make it, although three other occupants of the mansion did: the **Roosevelts** and **Cleveland**. (Three other occupants were "also-rans": Charles Evans Hughes, Alfred E. Smith, and Thomas E. Dewey.) During the 1898 gubernatorial nominating convention, it was discovered that war hero **TR** had signed an affidavit that he was a resident of low-tax Washington, D.C., rather than high-tax New York, making him ineligible for the governorship. The convention ignored it. His daughter Alice described the house as "big, ugly, rather shabby," but his four little boys must have brought some life to it by bringing a menagerie of pets, a gym with frequent boxing matches refereed by the governor, and frequent antics that continued in the White House. One official party ended when the doors to the reception room were opened to reveal the smell of a barnyard from the basement menagerie. A visitor was once astonished to see **Roosevelt** lowering his children by a rope out of a second floor window. But it was explained that Indians were attacking, making a quick emergency escape necessary. Winston Churchill visited while **Theodore** was governor and discussed the Boer War. **TR's** pew in the Dutch Reformed Church at the SW corner of Pearl and Orange is marked. **FDR** created more of a museum by soliciting furnishings and objects used by former governors, and built a swimming pool in a greenhouse. **Truman** planted a tree in 1958.

AUBURN • The home* of Lincoln's secretary of state, William H. Seward, is still maintained at 33 South Street, where **John Quincy Adams**, **Van Buren**, **A. Johnson** (1866) and **Grant** (1866) visited at various times.

BEACON • **Washington** was entertained at Madam Brett's Homestead* on the SW corner of Fishkill and Van Nydeck Streets.

BUFFALO • **Monroe** came to Forts Erie* and Niagara* in 1784 and stayed more than a week at the latter. He was back in 1817 and stayed at Landen's Tavern before going again to Fort Niagara.

In 1826 **Fillmore** built a home in East Aurora, 20 miles southeast, where he lived for four years. This is the only remaining presidential home built partly with a president's own hands. He had studied in Buffalo, but came to this small town for experience and self-confidence. His home, a few doors from his law office at 686 Main, has been moved a mile to 24 Shearer Avenue.* He later moved to 180 Franklin in Buffalo before being elected to Congress, and returned after the presidency, when he was married to his second wife in 1858. It now contains furniture from the destroyed Buffalo home.

His law office in Buffalo, where **Cleveland** was a clerk, was on Main between Eagle and Court. **Fillmore's** first wife caught a cold at **Pierce's** slush-soaked inaugural, and died within three weeks in Washington. He moved his new wife to a more suitable location for a former president, the largest mansion in Buffalo, at 52 Niagara Square, NE corner of Delaware, between Delaware and Genesee. Here he hosted **Lincoln** in 1861, **Johnson** and **Grant** in 1866, and died there in 1874. The site is now just west of the convention center, now at the Statler Towers, formerly the Statler Hotel, once the largest hotel in the country. It hosted **FDR**, **Truman**, and **Ike**. **Fillmore** occasionally went to the Baptist church at 965 Delaware after being rebuffed by the Episcopals. He is buried at Forest Lawn, 1411 Delaware at Delavan, where maps are readily available. His red obelisk memorial is near the western edge, north of Scajaquada Creek, in Section F, and can be visited or seen at a distance through the fence on the east side of Delaware.

Lincoln boarded the steamer *Globe* here for Chicago in late September 1848. On February 16, 1861, **Fillmore** and 10,000 greeted the president-elect at the Exchange Street Depot as soldiers and police were unable to prevent almost complete disorder. **Lincoln** stayed at the American House Hotel, on the west side of Main between Eagle and Court, where he had a public reception. He spoke from the balcony asking that the people maintain their composure, but stated that he could not speak more until waiting for further developments.

Fillmore took **Lincoln** to a service the next morning at the First Unitarian Church,* NW corner of Eagle and Franklin, now marked as the oldest building in downtown. Afterwards they returned for Mrs. Lincoln and dined at **Fillmore**'s home. (Generally she went to church while he stayed home.) Then they went into seclusion while Willie and Tad had the run of the hotel with the proprietor's son, who was forever known as the boy who played leapfrog with **Lincoln.** He survived until 1951. That evening **Lincoln** attended a service unannounced at St. James Hall, on the south side of Eagle, east of Main, led by a preacher to the Indians. **Fillmore** did not support the Republicans and voted Democratic in 1864. When **Lincoln** was assassinated, the crowd remembered **Fillmore's** southern leanings and demanded that he drape the house in mourning cloth, considered appropriate symbols of mourning. Some irate neighbors smeared the beautiful mansion with black paint. On April 27, 1865, **Lincoln's** body was viewed in St. James Hall.

Fillmore introduced **Johnson** for a speech in Niagara Square in 1866, with **Grant** along as "window dressing." **Cleveland** stopped in town on the way west to make his fortune. He was headed for Cleveland, Ohio, as he liked the name, but his uncle had a farm on Grand Island in the Niagara River, and he agreed to work there. Before long, the uncle got him a job as clerk in a law office, leading to a legal career. He lived in various places, including the Southern Hotel at Seneca and Michigan, and then a decade in the Weed Block at 284 Main and Swan, where he also worked. His church was First Presbyterian at Mason and Breckinridge. He was mayor (office at Church and Franklin), assistant district attorney, sheriff at the old courthouse* (now library) on Lafayette Square, and then governor by 1882. As sheriff he personally hanged criminals on the site of the central library. Rather than spend evenings courting like most bachelors, he found grown women left him cold, and fawned over the infant daughter of a close friend. He changed her diapers, rocked her to sleep, waited for her to grow up, and married her in the White House. He was then 49; she was 21. One woman found him not so cold and named him as the father of her son. He supported her and the boy, although the boy could have been another's, sued for removal of custody when her alcoholism worsened, and arranged for the boy's adoption. This came back to haunt him later, but he admitted all and suffered no political setbacks.

McKinley delivered one of his most important speeches to 50,000 highly enthusiastic supporters during the Pan-American Exposition on September 5, 1901, a site now near Lincoln Parkway. He was at the height of his career. The next day he shook hands with many of the several thousand who had waited for him for hours at the Temple of Music. When his secretary told him that he was exposing himself needlessly to danger, he said, "No one would wish to hurt me." Then a Polish anarchist with a gun concealed in a bandage in his right hand took the president's hand with his left, and shot him twice. The Secret Service had been watching the black man next to the assassin, maybe too closely. The assassin had nothing against **McKinley**; he just thought all governments were evil and wanted to stamp them all out, staring here. Horrified onlookers wrestled the assassin to the ground and almost killed him as **McKinley** cried, "Don't let them hurt him," and then pleaded that his secretary be careful how his wife was told. He was doomed from the time the shot was fired, as gangrene started forming and could not be prevented in those days before penicillin. The assassin was tried, convicted in an eight-hour trial, and executed October 29, 45 days after the president's death and 53 days after the shooting. The exhibition area and site became a residential neighborhood. A bronze tablet set in a rock in the median at 30 Fordham Avenue, between Elmwood and Lincoln Parkway, marks the spot and is easy to find. The site needs to be entered from Elmwood, north of the homes mentioned below on Delaware Avenue.

The president lingered for several days at the Milburn home, 1168 Delaware, where he and his invalid wife had been staying. Vice President **Roosevelt** hurried to town, stayed with his friend Ansley Wilcox, 641 Delaware,* and was assured by September 10 that **McKinley** would recover. The vice president then returned to join his family on an Adirondack Mountain outing and climbed Mt. Marcy, where he was informed that the president had taken a turn for the worse. Shortly after returning to his cabin he was summoned to Buffalo again as **McKinley** was dying. His wife pleaded that she wanted to go too, and he embraced her, saying, "We are all going." **McKinley** used the same words to his wife when she said she wanted to go with him. As **TR** boarded the train at North Creek Station,* North Creek, New York, near the Hudson River, he was handed a note saying that he was president. The station is now a museum and serves a tourist train. The death site is marked on the grounds of a high school built later. **Roosevelt** came here and then took the oath of office as president on the same day in the library at the Wilcox Mansion, open by the National Park Service. He had left in a rush and had no formal clothes, so he borrowed everything from shoes to coat from his host and the members of the cabinet assembled there in order to be sworn in properly. More than 50 people witnessed the ceremony, and the cabinet members stayed for their first meeting.

FDR dedicated the U.S. Courthouse on the SW corner of Franklin and Court.

CANAJOHARIE • **Washington** stayed at the Van Alstype House* on Moyer Street, south of Highway 5 S, in 1783, an important meeting place during the Revolution.

CARMEL • **Washington** stayed in the Fowler House on the way to an engagement at Pawling.

CLINTON • **Cleveland** lived with his family at 22 Utica from 1850 until 1853. He then moved to Holland Patent at 9573 Main in 1853 while his father was a pastor at First Presbyterian for about a month before he died. **Cleveland**'s mother and sister remained there after he went off to college and returned to visit.

FAYETTEVILLE • **Cleveland** lived at 109 Academy Road from about age four. His preacher father moved the family here when Grover was one year old in 1838 to become the pastor of the Presbyterian church on Genessee Street. Grover went to the Fayetteville Academy at 402 Elm. Once during the middle of the night, the young boy woke up the whole town by climbing into the bell tower and vigorously ringing. The family moved again in 1850, to Clinton, but Grover was soon sent back here to the academy and to fend for himself as a store clerk where he lived, over McVicar's Store. This still exists near McVicar's home, now the library at 111 Genesee.*

FISHKILL • **Washington's** headquarters was at the John Brinkerhoff House, October 1–8, 1777, 1.3 miles east on SR 82. Mrs. Brinkerhoff is said to have tucked him in every night. On one night John tried to coax some military information. **Washington** asked if he could keep a secret. The host said, "Yes," and **Washington** responded, "So can I." Three miles east of Fishkill at SR 52 and 82 is the Derick Brinkerhoff House, where Lafayette was sheltered in the upper southeast bedroom while sick. **Washington** is also shown to have stayed here. Brinkerhoff's Mill was burned during 1777 and ordered rebuilt by **Washington** to provide grain for the army. He evidently stayed on other occasions.

Washington was at Wharton's on September 24, 1780, also known as R. Van Wyck's. This is all that remains of the large supply depot known as the Van Wyck Homestead Museum* at the junction of Route 9 and I-84, west of the village. There were various military trials or courts-martial here including that of Enoch Crosby, counterspy for American forces. That was a mock trial, and he was allowed to escape to continue supplying **Washington** with information. He became the model for the famous James Fenimore Cooper novel, *The Spy*. **Washington** also visited Griffin's Tavern at 231 Route 82 and the Kip House (private) on Old Glenham Road, von Steuben's headquarters, one of the area's best surviving Dutch stone farmhouses. Storm's House at Sylvan Lake Road and Route 9 hosted **Washington** and **Adams,** just east of the Parkway.

Fort Edward • A copy of **Washington's** handwritten bill is displayed in the Old Fort House Museum* showing that the general dined here, at least twice, in 1783 at the Old Fort House,* on Route 4 at 29 Broadway. **Jefferson** and **Madison** also visited on their New England tour.

Greenwich • Arthur moved to New York with his family when he was five and lived in Perry, York, and Greenwich at 22 Woodlawn (private). He went to school in Schenectady, taught school in Schaghticoke and Cohoes, and studied law in Ballston Spa and Lansingburgh.

Hyde Park • **Franklin Roosevelt** was born at a house known as Springwood,* now a National Historic Site two miles south on U.S. 9. After a 24-hour, difficult birth, he was born limp and did not breathe until the doctor desperately breathed into his mouth. He was named Warren D. after his grandfather. But a cousin with the same name died a few days later, and it was decided to change the name rather than keep the unhappy reminder. His godfather, Elliot Roosevelt, Theodore's brother, was present, and **TR's** mother frequently visited. The two **Roosevelt** fathers were close friends. **Franklin** grew up here and returned 200 times as president via a railroad landing on the river at the foot of the property. He hosted the King and Queen of England just before World War II and Prime Minister Churchill in 1942 as they signed an historic agreement in his first-floor office resulting in atomic bomb development. When the president's mother entered the library during George VI's visit and saw that **Franklin** had opened the bar, she pronounced that the king would prefer tea. When she left he apologized, but the king related that his mother did not approve either. From the same room in 1944 he broadcasted his last campaign speech. He is buried between the home and presidential library on the grounds. **Truman** was present at the burial. **Ike, JFK,** and **LBJ** also have visited.

His half-brother, 28 years older, James Roosevelt Jr., or "Rosey," lived next door at the "Red House" to the south, where young **Franklin** frequented. He was the same age as Franklin's mother, Sara. Rosey's son, about two years older than **Franklin**, was a boyhood friend. When Rosey's first wife died, **TR's** sister, Anna, made a play for him, but she did not know about his long-time mistress. She chased him to London, met another, and finally married a naval commander there. The National Park Service headquarters is in the Rodgers House on the grounds to the east frequently visited by **FDR**, as he was a friend of the children of the owner.

He was baptized as a baby downtown in St. James Chapel, and went to church all his life at St. James Church* on the north side of town, U.S. 9. His parents and three of his six children (both FDR Jr.'s and Anna) are buried there directly east of the parking lot with graves behind a high hedge near the middle of the cemetery. **Franklin** long remembered the impassioned address his father gave here about the sufferings of poor children in London. Later in life, the president was a long-time senior warden and worshipped in 1939 with George VI and Queen Elizabeth.

He spent an isolated childhood roaming the woods, a constant companion of his father. **Franklin's** future wife, Eleanor, had been brought here as a child by her father Elliot. The four-year-old boy let the younger girl ride him as a horse and piggyback around the playroom. He built crow's nests in trees and learned to swim in the ice pond where he taught his sons to swim later. He roamed the hills, generally alone, and shot birds that he stuffed. His parents overprotected him, knowing that they could not have other children. His mother doted on her child all his life and saved everything, all toys, drawings, books, and the curls that were not cut until he was six. Some are on display at the adjacent museum. He had worn dresses at age five and did not take his first private bath or wear pants until the age of eight. He was raised apart from other children, tutored in the home until fourteen, as was the custom of the large estate holders. Being "the boy" here made it hard to become "one of the boys" later on.

This remained his home all his life, where he raised his children, pored over his world-class stamp collection (sold by his children) and other collections, battled polio, and received world leaders. He returned in 1921 after being stricken with polio and drove himself back to health here by the force of his will. He felt that he would walk again and pushed himself down the tree-lined drive striving to "get all the way down the driveway." He never made it on his own strength, but went far beyond that doing what he could do. His four boys, in turn as each became the oldest still living at home, were ceremoniously installed into his old bedroom opening on to the main staircase. It was a Christmas tradition here for the man of the house to read Dickens's *A Christmas Carol* in the library. Although he saw no future in the newfangled TV invention, he had one of the first.

His wife, Eleanor, never considered herself more than a visitor in the home and resented the lack of privacy with the looming presence of **Franklin's** mother, Sara, in their homes at various locations. Sara seemed to feel that if she could control Eleanor, she would not lose **Franklin**. Eleanor felt out of place especially when Sara seasonally closed the big house, and Eleanor had her own friends invited from New York for long periods; so **Franklin** suggested that they build a large cottage near the main house. Thus Val-Kill,* off SR 9G, one-half mile north of St. Andrews Rd., became Eleanor's getaway, finally a home of her own, where she cooked the only dish that she could make, scrambled eggs. Here she found emotional closeness with her friends that **Franklin** could not provide. Churchill was entertained during the war and swam in the pool. He borrowed a bathing suit, kept his cigar in his mouth and his big brimmed hat on all the time except in the pool. **Kennedy** came in 1960 seeking Eleanor's blessing. **Franklin** came often as president, swam, and after his death, this became her home until her death in 1962.

Nearby on the highest hill east of SR 9G, just south of East Park, is **Roosevelt's** "Dream Cottage,*" open now as "Top Cottage." Servants left bread and marmalade for his frequent visits, although he promised his mother he would not spend the night. This was built in 1938 and hosted the king and queen for a frankfurter roast in 1939. Their visit was punctuated by a series of accidents that **Roosevelt** enjoyed telling about as the "Hyde Park Cataclysm." During dinner a rickety table suddenly collapsed with a weight of dishes. The noise drowned out all conversation. **Roosevelt** relieved the silence by exclaiming, "Oh, this is just an old family tradition." Later, when they went to the library for drinks, the butler missed his footing, hurled the tray into space, and bounced along with it. **Roosevelt** roared with laughter and explained, "That's number two! What's next? These things usually happen in threes." The next day the party went to Val-Kill for a swim. When the president finished and was sitting by the pool, he decided to move to the lawn. Instead of waiting for the Secret Servicemen to carry him, he tried to move himself by putting his palms downward and then raising his weight toward where he wanted to go. After several false starts he tipped over into the serving tray, with all sorts of delicacies, iced tea, and glasses flying everywhere. When he recovered, he grinned and told the king, "Didn't I tell you there would be a third? Well, now I can relax; the spell is broken."

Many presidents have been here. **Clinton** enjoyed fall colors with Russian Premier Boris Yeltsin in 1995. **FDR**'s adjacent library and museum is the only presidential library used by a president still in office. He laid the cornerstone in 1938.

Young **FDR** often visited his neighbors, the Vanderbilts, at their mansion* two miles to the north on Route 9. The president helped it to be named a National Historic Site and enjoyed contrasting this spectacular home with the "comparatively simple style of living" of his own.

Naturalist John Burroughs's home, Riverby, and retreat, Slabsides, were across the river off Route 9W at West Park. **Theodore Roosevelt** visited his long-time friend here on a hot day, and Burroughs reported, "We walked from the river up to Slabsides, and **Roosevelt** sweat his white linen coat right through at the back."

JOHNSTOWN • **Washington** came by the imposing home* of "baronet" William Johnson and inspected Fort Johnstown (marked) in 1783, now the site of the county jail in the center of town.

KINDERHOOK • The first president not born a British citizen, **Van Buren**, was born in a farmhouse/tavern holding eight children, six slaves, and varying numbers of guests. (This was 1782, after the Declaration of Independence, but before the formal recognition of peace was signed.) It was on the post road between Albany and New York City, site marked on the west side at 48 Hudson just south of Jarvis, between U.S. 9 and State 9H, 24 miles south of Albany. This was near the then town center, east of the present center, the enclave of Dutch customs made famous by Washington Irving's *Legend of Sleepy Hollow* and *Rip*

Van Winkle. Young **Martin** delivered vegetables from his father's garden to town and sometimes acted as barkeeper. He was educated by listening to debates at the bar and attended local schools including the Kinderhook Academy, on the west side of Albany Avenue, State 14, north of State 9 and south of Water Street.

At 14 he began his legal career in a different kind of bar, with an apprenticeship beginning in 1808 to Francis Sylvester in his home still at 5 Sylvester, in the town center across from St. Paul's Episcopal, founded later by **Van Buren's** son and brother. Later he lived in his law office at 309 Warren, not marked, still in nearby Hudson, and moved to Albany in 1815. As president he wrote "OK" on notes to his staff ("Off to Kinderhook") and became known as "Old Kinderhook," or "OK," one theory of the origin of the popular expression. ("OK" is now the most recognized word or phrase in the world. "Coke" is second.) He visited the Vanderpoel House,* home of his daughter-in-law, south of the County Museum on the SW corner of Route 9 and Albany.

Van Buren retired to his estate of Lindenwald,* three miles south on Highway 9H, just north of the Route 25 junction, where he died in 1862. This had been the inheritance of a lifelong friend who had lost it to creditors and had let it run down. Shortly after **Van Buren** purchased it, his youngest son and family moved here to keep him company on condition that he could transform the Georgian mansion into a fairy-tale castle, which he did to **Van Buren's** chagrin. His funeral was where he had been baptized at Kinderhook Reformed,* SW Church and Broad Street, U.S. 9, where he attended all his life and sang so loudly that he drowned out those nearby. It burned in 1867 and another was built on the site. His is the tallest monument towering over graves in the east section of Kinderhook Cemetery on the east side of Albany Avenue, Route 21, the same street as Hudson. He was the last sitting vice president to be elected president before **George H.W. Bush** in 1988, although eight succeeded due to death. After his death his home was owned by Winston Churchill's maternal grandfather.

Lakes George and Champlain Area • In 1783 **Washington** visited several areas, battlefields, and forts around the area. Reconstructed Fort William Henry* is open at the southern edge of the lake, and the site of Fort George* is marked just south. He also inspected the historic fort at Crown Point,* now restored, about 25 miles north on Route 9N. Ruins here date to French occupation in 1734. The fort played a major part in the French and Indian War, as did Fort Ticonderoga* five miles to its south, also inspected by **Washington**. Patriots at the beginning of the Revolution, Benedict Arnold and Ethan Allen captured British guns at these two forts and hauled them to Boston to force the British to give up the town.

Jefferson and **Madison** inspected Ft. Ticonderoga and Crown Point during their 1791 travels, as well as the ruins of Fort William Henry and Fort George. **Jefferson** thought Lake George was the most beautiful body of water he had ever seen and fished there. They stayed at an inn down the hill between Fort "Ti" and the lake. On this trip they visited Poughkeepsie (Market Street Tavern), Albany, Troy, Glen Falls (where they saw the falls and Baker's Falls), and Saratoga and Bennington Battlefields. **Monroe** (1817) and **Van Buren** (1847) visited the area.

Moravia • **Fillmore** was born in 1800 about one mile south in Fillmore Glen State Park, Route 38, where a replica cabin* now stands as a tribute. This is southwest of town on Skinner Hill Road. His father had been lured here with rapturous tales of rich black loam. But the farm was poor, and his father was completely swindled and lost the farm due to a faulty title. This was a blessing in disguise for the future. After a short time, the family moved to Sempronius, but after living in isolation on a farm until 1815, **Fillmore's** father felt his son should not spend his life as a farmer and sent him to apprentice as a clothmaker in Sparta. He could only go to school in the three winter months when he was not needed for labor. While serving as a bound boy, similar to **Andrew Johnson**, **Fillmore** attended a one-room school and fell in love with his teacher and future wife, who coached him until he was able to teach school himself. He also lived in Sparta as an apprentice and studied law with a judge in Montville. He left at age 18 to study law with a judge in Montville and then practiced three years in East Aurora.

Mount Vernon • **Washington** paid off his troops on October 28, 1776, at the Guion Tavern after the Battle of White Plains, now the corner of Kingsbridge Road and Columbus.

Newburgh • **Washington's** extraordinary strength and character in holding the army together, not abusing his powers, and then willingly and happily relinquishing them, is seen once again here in this long encampment. **Washington's** headquarters were first at William Ellison's home (destroyed) on SR 32 at the junction with SR 45, just southwest at the south side of the town of New Windsor, on the river two miles south of the Hasbrouck House, from mid–June until July 20, 1779, March 20 until May 18, 1781, and May 25 until June 24, 1781.

After the British surrender at Yorktown, peace negotiations opened in Paris early in 1782. Many considered the Revolution practically over although the British still occupied New York City. Congress and **Washington** agreed that vigilance could not be relaxed until the treaty was signed. In October 1782, he ordered the troops into camp at nearby New Windsor* encampment, one mile south on Temple Hill Road, SR 30. A military village of 700 buildings housed about 6500 soldiers during this time. The one building left is the only known wooden building to have housed Revolutionary soldiers. **Washington's** headquarters and home with Martha were in the Hasbrouck House,* Liberty and Washington Streets, from the end of March 1782 until August 1783. His bedroom was on the east or river side, in the middle room with seven doors and one window because of a prior addition. Here he created the Badge of Military Merit from which the Order of the Purple Heart takes its design. The first one is displayed in the adjacent museum. **Washington** found his headquarters dreary and confining and sometimes visited Knox's headquarters,* marked near New Windsor, and William Denning's house on Orrs Mill Road (private) in Salisbury Mills.

While here he met a major challenge to the authority of the Continental Congress and future of the new nation. As historian James Flexner states, "Almost every revolution in the history of the world, however idealistically begun, had ended in tyranny. The American Revolution had now reached its moment of major political crisis." In the spring of 1782, there was a push led by Colonel Lewis Nicola to make **Washington** king. No man held more awesome power than **Washington** did at this time. His leadership had held the army together and won the war. Some thought that the royalty form of government was good, with only George III at fault, and that **Washington** was the obvious successor. Democracy was unknown and untried, and voting by the common man was not universally accepted. Republics were thought by many to be the weakest form of government. But the strength of character in **Washington's** refusal to be so considered preserved the great hope and promise that the Revolution had presented to the future. **Washington** wrote that he received the proposal with "surprise and astonishment," and viewed it with "abhorrence" and "reprimanded with severity." Author Michael Lee Landing's book *The Military 100*, that rates the top 100 military leaders in history, rates **Washington** number one, over Julius Caesar, Alexander the Great, Napoleon, and others. This was not because he was the greatest battle captain or brilliant military strategist, but because he was the most successful and influential in terms of final results. He argues that there would have been no lasting Continental army without **Washington**, and thus no United States. But while he was here, only a military victory appeared successful, not a new form of government. Hamilton and **Madison** feared that this could end the advantages of the successful Revolution and the future of a republic or democracy.

Washington knew that the men were weary from long periods of deprivation, sacrifice, and suffering from the Revolutionary cause that now seemed won. Promised benefits were not forthcoming. The slender bond holding the solders together in times of uncertainty now was strained by feelings of frustration, contempt for congressional leadership, and futility. The "Newburgh Letters" were circulated, urging officers to rebel and force payment of back wages and pensions. Many had given up careers and positions for many years and spent their own money to clothe and feed themselves and their men. **Washington** had sent representatives to Congress with appeals for aid that appeared fruitless. The army was restless and became more ill contented. **Washington** knew there was a drive to overthrow the government.

A meeting was called in the Temple,* reconstructed as the Temple of Virtue at the New Windsor camp, held on March 15, 1783. Biographer James Flexner called it probably the most important single gathering ever held in the United States. Here **Washington** stood between the new nation and the folly of military rule as seen in the history of our sister nations to the south. His words pledged personal involvement and argued reason and forbearance to preserve the ideals so long fought for. He urged them to look with "utmost horror and detestation" on any man who "wishes, under any specific pretenses, to overturn the liberties of our country." But faces remained hard. Resistance was tense. Then a miracle happened. Feeling that a congressman's statement of their difficulties might carry extra conviction to the men, he introduced a letter. But as he tried to read the words, he fumbled and pulled out a pair of heretofore unknown glasses, saying, "Gentlemen, you must pardon me. I have grown gray in your service and now find myself growing blind." A wave of emotion swept over the officers. This act effectively demolished almost every man in the hall. From that point on, the words were insignificant, and men began to weep openly. The officers passed a vote of confidence and the tide was turned. This prevented, in **Jefferson**'s words, "this revolution from being closed as others have been by a subversion of that liberty it was intended to establish." The speech had preserved the republic. The Temple Hill Monument marks the spot, known as "The Birthplace of the Republic."

In the book *What If?,* historian Thomas Fleming traces many ways the Revolution could have been and almost was lost, including the last noted event. Years later **Washington** decided against writing a memoir. As Fleming has written: "It was decided that it would be too disillusioning if the American people discovered how often the Glorious Cause came close to disaster." He believed that the real secret to America's final victory in the eight-year struggle could be summed up in two words: "Divine Providence."

Also here **Washington** drafted a circular to the governors of the states setting out his views on the future development of the country, a basis of its future development. On April 19, 1783, he announced the signing of a preliminary peace treaty and the troops began to go home.

FDR's parents married several miles south at Algonac, a family home now rebuilt and in a housing addition in Balmville on Susan Drive. It stands out as oversized with large trees. His mother grew up here, and he frequently visited as a child. A highlight of his young life occurred here when at age eight, his mother allowed him to take his first bath alone.

New York City • In 1756, **Washington** traveled to Boston and stopped off in New York for two weeks. Some believe that he proposed to Mary Philipse, who turned him down and later married Robert Morris. Family members, whose money built the Morris-Jumel Mansion,* were staunch loyalists that would have made an interesting family situation in 1776 if **Washington** were included in it. He would have used Bowery Lane and the old Boston Post Road, running northwest from today's Washington statue in Madison Square, to continue to Boston. In 1773 **Washington** brought his stepson to Kings College and stayed at Hull's Tavern on Broadway.

The new commander in chief landed between Hubert and Laight on June 25, 1775, and stayed at about 200 Hudson. He was on the way to Massachusetts to assume command of armies in the Revolution, and delayed his journey to make an important speech at the site of Federal Hall. Some citizens feared that **Washington** had secret ambitions to make himself a military dictator. In fact, **Washington** is one of the few, if not the only major leader in history, even into the twenty-first century, not to do so in such a position. He spoke to the people to assure them that he "would not lay aside the citizen" and would happily return to "our private stations in the bosom of a free, peaceful, and happy country." He bypassed his favorite restaurant, Fraunces Tavern, and ate at Col. Leonard Lispenard's, where Canal Street crosses Desbrosses and Hudson Streets, and camped where City Hall is now. He is also reported at Cox's Tavern, Broadway and 230th Street, and Hyatt's Tavern at Broadway and 223rd Street.

He returned with most of his army after the British evacuated Boston and made his headquarters at the Kennedy Mansion, 1 Broadway, April 13–16, 1776, anticipating the next British attack. The mansion was described as the height of elegance, and Howe's headquarters were later there. **Washington** here refused his letter, addressed to "Mr. **Washington**." When Martha arrived, **Washington** then moved to Abraham Mortier's, Carleton and Varick, from April 17 to May 22. Number 1 Broadway remained his base of operations until he moved to City Hall, later known as Federal Hall, and Henry Knox and his wife moved to the Broadway mansion. After a brief trip to Philadelphia, where Congressional delegates were debating independence, he was back from June 6 to August 27, and maybe here in early September. **Monroe** joined **Washington** in August and fought in the Battles of Harlem Heights and White Plains. Mortier's was later used by the British commanders and then in 1789 by **John Adams** as vice president. The house was moved (and later destroyed), and the hill was leveled in 1811.

Washington read the Declaration of Independence to the troops on July 9, 1776, just south of where the present city hall later was built in the commons. Then the British began to assemble on Staten Island for an attempt to take the city with the most powerful navy in the world and the largest expeditionary force of the 18th century.

Not knowing where the attack would come, **Washington** had to split his meager forces between Brooklyn and Manhattan.

The military battles for New York City began when the British made their long-awaited landing on August 22, 1776, on Long Island at the site of later Fort Hamilton and chased the Americans to Prospect Park. This is called the first battle of the new country, as it was the first after the Declaration. Then more troops landed at Dyker Beach and Bensonhurst Park, a spot buried today under the Shore Freeway and apartments. The British then chased the Americans through Brooklyn at today's Greenwood Cemetery, with heavy fighting at 39th and Third Avenue and Jamaica Pass at Jamaica Avenue and Euclid.

Washington was in Brooklyn at the Cortelyou House, called the Old Stone House at Gowanus, where Fifth Avenue and Third now intersect. He and American General William Alexander (Lord Stirling) tried to save the army as the center of the fighting raged nearby at the present site of Byrne Memorial Playground. The house was rebuilt in 1935 as the First Battle Revival Center, 87 feet from the F subway line stop at Smith and Ninth above the Gowanus Canal. The British came over Jamaica Pass near the old Howard Tavern site, Atlantic and Alabama. The heaviest fighting was in the vicinity of Flatbush and Fulton. **Washington** watched the retreat of his shattered forces at a site marked on a building at Court and Atlantic. This had been the first great battle of the Revolution, the largest battle ever fought in North America, and a fiasco for **Washington**. Howe did not follow up his success enabling **Washington** to save most of the army by a daring rescue, "The Dunkirk of America."

Washington met at the Joralemon House (400 feet south of Joralemon on the east side of Hicks) for a council of war and executed a secret withdrawal on August 29 and 30 to save the army. This was the home of Philip Livingston, where **Washington** was again in 1781, when he met to determine what course to take, attack in New York or go to Yorktown. (A marker at Montague and Pierrepont incorrectly marks the site.) The commander went back to Manhattan and got every boat he could to Brooklyn's old ferry site, now the foot of Fulton westward to the Fly Market Slip on Manhattan, at Fireboat Station 77, end of Fulton, near the foot of Maiden Lane. He dangerously stayed behind until the last man was safe and left on the last boat, saving the army and the chance for independence. At least 9,000 troops, baggage, provisions, horses, and other goods were rescued to fight another day that came soon. The orderly withdrawal in the face of a superior enemy is considered very difficult even for the best-trained soldiers. Secrecy and silence were essential. **Washington's** luck again was present. Weather conditions were perfect. If the wind had not persisted from the northwest the British could have isolated and captured the army, probably ending the Revolution. This same wind almost made the evacuation impossible because of rough water, but then died just in time as the retreat began. And daylight would have revealed the Americans escaping, but for a fortunate fog appearing at the escape point in Brooklyn, but not Manhattan. This was just south of the present Brooklyn Bridge. He is also listed just before the retreat at a house where Montague meets the Brooklyn Esplanade, or the southern end of the boardwalk. A British officer called the operation "particularly glorious," and a modern scholar has written, "A more skillful operation of this kind was never conducted." The ferry operated here when **Jefferson**, **Madison**, **Monroe**, and **Lincoln** later used it.

American General John Sullivan was captured in Brooklyn. The Howe brothers, the British commanding general and the admiral, paroled him to go to Congress, saying that they could negotiate liberal terms to the Colonies. On September 11, 1776, in an attempt to end the war, **Adams**, Benjamin Franklin, and Edward Rutledge came to Staten Island at 7455 Hylan to the Conference or Billopp House,* to meet with Admiral Howe. This is just south of the Outerbridge near Exit Two, on the southern end opposite Perth-Amboy. (The admiral's brother was too busy planning the invasion of Manhattan to attend.) Franklin assured him that Americans would not go back to British rule after the Declaration had been signed. Howe expressed affection for America and said, "If America should fail, I should feel and lament it like the loss of a brother." Franklin replied that they would do their utmost to save him such "mortification."

New York City itself was south of where the city hall is now. After the Battle of Long Island in August, about a third of lower Manhattan burned on September 20, 1776, possibly due to a fire set by a patriot to destroy the area's usefulness to the British. The fire destroyed Trinity Church, not rebuilt until after the war ended. At that time those loyal to England were forced to leave the town and most of their possessions. No city suffered more in the Revolution, although there was little fighting here. During much of the war it was the largest military base in the world. The fighting was in central and northern Manhattan.

Washington then spent September 14 to October 18, 1776, planning the next moves at the Morris-Jumel Mansion* in Harlem Heights at 160th and Edgecombe. The large drawing room was the council chamber where plans were made and courts-martial were held. **Washington's** private quarters were immediately above. (It was later Vice President Aaron Burr's home, after he left office; he was married in the front parlor.) **Washington** came back as president for dinner on July 10, 1790, with the **Adamses** and **Jefferson**. (Queen Elizabeth II visited in July 1976.) French General Rochambeau's headquarters were here from July 6 until August 18, 1781, and at the Odell House at 425 Ridge Road in Hartsdale. Here he offered half of his military fund to **Washington** when the Continental Army was nearly bankrupt. The Jumel House was occupied in November by Sir Henry Clinton, the new British commander, for much of the time later that the British controlled New York City. Seventeen-year-old Prince William Henry, later King William IV of England, was here in the autumn of 1781 as a young naval cadet and stayed at the Beekman House near Hanover Square, at the NE corner of Sloat Lane, now about Beaver and William. He worshiped at St. Paul's and saw the pedestal that a statue of his father George III had stood on. A plot to kidnap him failed to materialize.

The British also had headquarters at 91st and Columbus, 51st and First Avenue (now PS 135), and the Mortier House, mentioned earlier at Carleton and Varick. **Washington** is thought to have earlier visited 51st and First, the Beekman Mansion that was the headquarters of Howe in September 1776, as Howe supervised the battles in upper Manhattan and received the captured spy Nathan Hale. (Hale was thought to have been discovered by British officer Robert Rogers, of earlier fame in the French and Indian War.) Hale was renowned as having said, "I regret that I only have one life to give for my country." His execution site is listed at various places around the city, including 66th and 3rd Avenue, 46th and First Avenue, 45th west of Park (plaque), and at the SW corner First Street and 46th Street (plaque).

While at the Jumel House, **Washington** directed the building of various defenses, including at the south end of Jerome Reservoir in the Bronx. He had to decide to retreat against the much larger force or stay and fight against unfavorable odds. Staying may not have been a wise military decision, but he felt that a retreat would be demoralizing, with men drifting away.

On September 15, 1776, the British landed at Kip's Bay and moved toward Murray Hill to capture Manhattan. When **Washington** learned of the invasion, he raced from the Jumel Mansion to a site now at 34th and Lexington. It is believed that Mary Murray delayed the British two hours by entertaining Howe, Clinton, and Cornwallis at her home, Murray Hill, by coaxing them with a lavish meal. The site would now be on Park Avenue between 36th and 37th. Kip's Bay was where 34th Street meets the East River, although the inlet has been filled in. The Americans were pushed first to the site of the present Empire State Building and then to the site of the current Main Public Library at 42nd and Fifth Avenue. **Washington** met his retreating troops at about the site of Grand Central Terminal and chased the British to about the library site. (Most presidents from **Grant** forward have used the station.) He grew choleric with rage, pleaded, then lost his temper and slashed at the men with his riding crop to force then back into the fight. An aide took his bridle and led the horse away before the commander was shot or captured.

The Battle of Harlem Heights is marked on Broadway at 147th, 153rd, and 159th. The center of the fighting was where Columbia University is now, around Amsterdam and Broadway between 116th and 120th. This was somewhat successful, but the British escaped a trap planned because some officers gave a premature order to open fire. The Americans were then chased north up Fifth Avenue past McGown's (or McGowan's) Pass at 107th. The British camped there, at the NE corner of present Central Park, from September 15, 1776, until November 21, 1783, long before the park and streets were there. **Washington** retreated to White Plains across King's Bridge, as the British dallied and let him go again, but controlled Manhattan with headquarters at First Avenue and 51st. King's Bridge, destroyed as **Washington** retreated, was at King's Bridge and W. 230th at the place where the Boston Post Road crossed Spuyten Duyvil Creek.

The next action was the Battle of White Plains on October 28, 1776. **Washington's** headquarters were at the Elijah Miller House* on Virginia Road in North White Plains. He was also at Miller's on November 10, 1776, and from July 20 until September 16, 1777. The British landed at Pell's Point, now in Pelham Bay Park in the Bronx off I-95. Near the time of the opening of the battle, **Washington** is thought to have been at a site marked by a cannon in the lawn of the modern home at Whitney and Wayne. He also used the Purdy House at 60 Park Avenue from October 23 to 28 during the battle and again for two months during the summer of 1778. Another landmark is Chatterton Hill, just south of I-287 in the vicinity of Bronx River Parkway and Battle Avenue. This was a key to the battlefield where **Washington** erected defenses attacked by Howe. The Patriots were clearly defeated, but again British General Howe did not follow through and force a showdown that might have ended the Revolution. **Monroe** fought in the battles around the city, including White Plains.

Fort Washington, constructed under **Washington's** direction, occupied the highest point on Manhattan and is now marked in Gordon Bennett Park at Fort Washington Avenue and 183rd and 185th, north of the present George Washington Bridge. (**Washington** also visited here as president with **Jefferson** and the **Adamses**.) He also supervised improvements and installations at Horn's Hook at 89th and East River. The commander was at Fort Lee across the Hudson in New Jersey by mid–November when he urged Greene to abandon the fort and cross the river.

On November 15 **Washington** rowed from Fort Lee across the Hudson to meet Greene and Putnam, but met them rowing back midway and came back. On the next day they recrossed from Fort Lee to inspect Fort Washington, heard the sound of guns, got to near the Morris home, started to the fort, but then decided to go back to New Jersey, barely escaping capture. The fort was just north of the George Washington Bridge leading to Fort Lee, where **Washington** watched his troops evacuate the island. Fort Lee was then abandoned when it was learned that the British were about to take it. The loss of the fort and almost 3000 men at Fort Washington was the worst loss for General **Washington** during the war and the lowest point of his career.

The British under Cornwallis also crossed here and marched south down what is now Route 9W in New Jersey to the fort at about 141 Old Palisades Road in the present town of Fort Lee, where 2000 American troops were captured in November 1776. The boundaries of the fort were about Federspiel, English, Cedar, and Parker. **Washington** then retreated along a route that approximates the New Jersey Turnpike. He now knew he could not successfully face British regulars with militia, and planned to fight only small actions and not major battles in the future. On July 23, 1781, **Washington** was at Van Courtlandt Mansion,* Broadway and 242nd, on the way to Yorktown, Virginia, and again in 1783 as the British were evacuating. He had headquarters in various locations, including Philipse Manor Hall,* SW of the corner of Riverdale and Ashburton in Yonkers, on the Hudson River. As the British were leaving in November 1783, he waited in a tavern then near Frederick Douglass Boulevard (Day's Tavern at St. Nicholas and 126th) until the British gave word of their final departure. He stayed at the Bull's Head Tavern on the Bowery, November 25. The British commander then surrendered the city to **Washington** at the old Fort Amsterdam, built in 1625 by Gov. Peter Stuyvesant at what is now Broadway, Battery Place, and Whitehall, where the 1907 Custom House* was later built. The old fort was not demolished until 1790, when it was torn down to construct the President's House in an attempt to keep the capital in the city.

After the 1783 evacuation, the city celebrated the government's return as **Washington** proceeded down Bowery to Pearl, then west along Wall to Capp's (Cape's) Tavern, 18 Broadway. A grand banquet was then held at Fraunces Tavern,* largely reconstructed or heavily restored at 54 Pearl Street at Broad, also the scene of **Washington's** emotional farewell to his officers on December 4, 1783. Henry Knox and Governor Clinton were known to be here then, and it is supposed that Alexander Hamilton and Generals Greene, Lincoln, Schuyler, and Kosciuszko were in attendance. **Washington** then proceeded south from the foot of Whitehall Street. (This was the location of White Hall, the 1653 mansion of Peter Stuyvesant.)

After 1783 the government operated loosely under the Articles of Confederation, and met beginning in January 1785 in city hall. **Monroe** was in Congress, an association of sovereign states with each state having one vote. After the 1787 Constitution was approved, the first U.S. Capitol was created at the expanded city hall, Wall and Nassau, at the head of Broad Street, where Federal Hall National Memorial* now stands. The first president was elected in January 1789 by ten of the eleven states that had ratified the Constitution. New York could not get organized to cast votes by the prescribed time. North Carolina did not ratify until the next November, and Rhode

Island finally ratified on May 29, 1790. Only three states chose electors by popular vote. The Constitution did not say how the electors who actually chose the president would themselves be selected. Even by the second presidential election, when there were fifteen states, most electors were not chosen by a vote of the people. **Washington** did not learn that he was elected until April 14, but was in New York by the 23rd. Now it was his play to mold the sketchy office of the presidency.

The new president landed at Murray's Wharf, 120 Wall Street at the East River, and was inaugurated on April 30, 1789, at Federal Hall by the Chancellor and presiding judge of New York, Robert Livingston, since the Supreme Court had not been set up. (Livingston later negotiated and signed the Louisiana Purchase as French ambassador.) The vice presidential oath had not been drafted by Congress, so **Adams** could not be sworn in until June, although he had assumed the office. **Washington** set many traditions, including using a Bible and uttering "So help me God," followed by all except **Quincy Adams**, who did not use the Bible, and a few like **FDR**, who once omitted the phrase. The Masonic Bible that **Washington** used is displayed here, also used by **Eisenhower**, **Carter**, and **George H.W. Bush** at their inaugurals. **Washington** stood on a second floor balcony where his statue is now located, diagonally across the street now from the New York Stock Exchange, and then went inside to nervously and clumsily deliver his inaugural address. (A hundred years later, **Benjamin Harrison** traced his footsteps, using **Washington's** Bible and chair.) **Washington**, **Adams**, and other dignitaries then walked to St. Paul's* since the crowds were so large they could not use their coaches. (This old church near the World Trade

Federal Hall, the old City Hall of New York, was at this site and served as the first Capitol of the United States under the Constitution. Washington was sworn in where his statue stands in front. Adams, Jefferson, Madison, and Monroe served inside the original building and many later presidents have visited and reenacted the first ceremonies. Many presidents lived and worked nearby within a block or two of this site, across the street from the New York Stock Exchange.

Center barely missed being destroyed on September 11, 2001.) The inaugural ball was held north of Wall on the east side of Broadway. The current building at the inaugural site was completed in 1842 as the U.S. Customs House. A newer Customs House* was at the SE corner of Wall and William, where **Arthur** worked until President **Hayes** removed him for alleged corruption. Actually **Arthur**'s profession was as a "spoilsman" to find federal jobs for others for money. The Custom House position was his only government office before election. Ironically he signed the Pendleton Act revising civil service to help end the spoils system.

Congress and federal officials (including men who served as the first five presidents) met in the Federal Hall until August 1790. **Washington's** office was on the second floor toward the East River from his present statue in front. Great precedents were started. **Adams** and **Washington** exhibited little intention of working together, and the vice-presidential office that could have been as powerful as a prime minister, has been insignificant ever since. Many questions had to be answered such as how to address the president, how to act when he came to Congress, and whether they should stand or sit when he talked. When **Washington** came to get "advice and consent" on a treaty, **Adams** read the provisions, but Congress told the president that more information was needed. **Washington** "wore an aspect of stern displeasure," then "started up in a violent fret." He came again and still received no answer. At that he said "he would be damned if he ever went there again," and presidents never did for "advice and consent."

The Bill of Rights, or first ten Constitutional amendments, were drafted and adopted at this location largely through the guidance of **Madison**. Alexander Hamilton lived at 57 Wall, met with **Madison** there as they worked on *The Federalist Papers* to promote the Constitution, and opened the Bank of New York at 56 Wall and the First Bank of the United States at 52 Wall. The leading architect of the American capitalist system and path to economic success, resigned as treasury secretary at age 40, and was shot dead in a duel near Fort Lee at age 49 by the vice president, Aaron Burr. Hamilton had been secretary of the treasury at age (about) 34 in our youngest cabinet, with **Jefferson** at 46, Edmond Randolph at 36 and Henry Knox at 38. (Hamilton's birth date has been speculated in William Sterne Randall's 2003 biography to be about January 1755, earlier than normally shown.)

President **Washington's** first modest residence from April 1789 until February 1790 was Dover, Franklin, and Number 3 Cherry Street, now covered by a pier of the Brooklyn Bridge. (Dover is the first street south of the bridge and Cherry is an extension of Pearl.) **Madison**, who came to escort him to his inaugural, wrote **Washington's** inaugural address, the House's reply, and **Washington's** reply to the reply. So he was sort of talking to himself. **Washington** later moved with his family to a larger house at 39–41 Broadway just below Trinity Churchyard, now marked with a plaque, where he stayed for five months until the government moved to Philadelphia. **John** and **John Quincy Adams**, **Jefferson**, and **Madison** are shown from **Washington's** diary to have come to formal dinners and levies that started exactly on time. Late arrivers were told, "My cook never asks whether the company had arrived, but whether the hour has." He, Martha, and the grandchildren took many rides around the town, including fourteen-mile carriage rides around Manhattan up Bloomingdale Road (about where Bowery Street continues north today), to Harlem Heights, across Kingsbridge, back along the Boston Post Road on the east side. He was hosted at Governor George Clinton's, at 10 Queen near the end of Cedar, and Chancellor Robert Livingston's home a short distance away at 3 Broadway, where he saw a fireworks display on inauguration day. Clinton was vice president under **Jefferson** and **Madison**.

St. Paul's,* Broadway and Fulton, still has **Washington's** pew, used with **John Adams** and **Madison** on inauguration day and for about two years after that. **Washington's** diary mentions attending St. Paul's and Trinity numerous times and walking around the Battery area. He and **Madison** watched fireworks from Battery Park. **Adams** went to both churches as vice president and when he passed through in 1774. Then he stayed at the Stoutenburgh house on Nassau Street near the city hall. **Jefferson** attended with **Washington** later after he had been appointed secretary of state in 1790 and arrived in the spring. He had gone to Trinity during his first visit in 1766. St. Paul's was built on a field outside the town in 1766 and is the oldest public building in continuous use still standing in Manhattan. **Monroe's** funeral was there. British officers used this as their church during the occupation, including Lords Howe, Clinton, and Cornwallis. On the centennial of the first inauguration, **Cleveland** and **Benjamin Harrison** worshipped at the church. The pulpit contains the only surviving emblem of British nobility in New York. **John Quincy Adams** once commented on an old gentleman reading from a text here "...so slow that the first part of a phrase was lost before he finished the last."

The president worshipped at Trinity Church, on Broadway at the end of Wall Street, before the war, and he went to the consecration of a rebuilt church in 1790. **Washington** had attended Trinity while headquartered here in the summer of 1776, but the church burned in the September 1776 fire and had not been repaired at the time of his inauguration. **Madison** attended also. The church burned again in the Great Fire of 1835 and was reconstructed at the same site. Hamilton and Albert Gallatin, the first two secretaries of the treasury, inventor Robert Fulton, and seaman James Lawrence are buried in the churchyard. The present 1846 steeple was the tallest structure in New York City for many years. **Monroe** lived at 15 Wall, married at Trinity in 1786 where he attended when he later lived in town, and then lived at his father-in-law's house, 90 Broadway, until Congress adjourned. In 1813, **Van Buren** lived across from Trinity at 1 Wall Street. **Madison** lived at 19 Maiden Lane from 1787 to 1793. (**FDR** worked at 54 Wall in 1908 and 52 Wall in 1915. **TR** worked at 44 Wall from 1909 to 1919.)

Adams arrived in New York on April 20, 1789, stayed with John Jay at 133 Broadway, and then lived at the Mortier House mentioned earlier, then known as Richmond Hill. When a yellow fever epidemic broke out in Philadelphia in 1797, he moved back to 3701 Provost Avenue at 233rd Street (altered) in the Bronx for two months.

Two great questions confronted the young country in 1790, and little business could be conducted until they were settled: the site of a permanent capital, and how the debts of the Revolution would be paid. Secretary of State **Jefferson** first got to the capital on March 21, 1790, where he lived at City Tavern, 115 Broadway, and then 57 Maiden Lane (marked), where he had extensive alterations inside and out even though New York was to be the capital only temporarily. On one occasion, Hamilton and **Jefferson** met outside of **Washington's** home at 39 Broadway, walked up and down in front of it, and agreed to meet later at **Jefferson's**, on Maiden Lane, with **Madison**. This meeting resulted in the Great Compromise whereby, among other things, it was decided that the federal government would pay the war debts of the states, benefiting mostly the North, and then move the capital south to the Potomac River after ten years in Philadelphia, because it was not felt that the Pennsylvania delegation would agree to a move further south without some concession. Secretary of the Treasury Hamilton was convinced that the government could not survive without Southern consent for the payment of the war debts incurred by the Northern states. Congress then moved in August 1790. The Great Fire of 1835 destroyed most of the buildings mentioned above.

Monroe moved after his presidency to the home his daughter, 65 Prince Street on the NE corner of Lafayette (then Marion), in a structure still standing, although damaged by a fire in 1905. He died there on July 4, 1831, the third of the first five presidents to die on Independence Day. His coffin rested on a platform in front of the new city hall, built in 1803 at the present location, Broadway, Park Row, and Chambers, which still serves as the oldest local government house in the nation. After the funeral in St. Paul's, he was buried in Marble Cemetery on Second Street near Fifth Avenue. It was the largest funeral in the city's history up to that time. The body was moved in July 1858 back to city hall and then permanently to Richmond.

Little is known about **Lincoln's** first two visits. In 1848 he passed through to Boston by train at the New Haven Depot, on the south side of 27th between Lexington and Fourth (now Park Ave.), the site of Old Madison Square Garden. He came again in 1857 with his family to collect a court-ordered fee and evidently stayed in the Astor Hotel and toured Central and Battery Parks.

In late 1859 **Lincoln** was invited to lecture or speak at famous preacher Henry Ward Beecher's Plymouth Church* in Brooklyn. Beecher was one of the most famous antislavery speakers in the country and his church was well known to feature abolitionists. Fortunately **Lincoln** delayed his trip unintentionally and, unknown to him, when he arrived the lecture series in the church no longer existed. The place was switched to the available Cooper Union, where the largely unknown westerner spoke in February 1860, leaving a few days later nationally known. (The popular term "Cooper Institute" is not correct, as this referred to a private group that sometimes used the facility.) He got off the Paulus Street-Courtland Street Ferry from the end of the train line from Exchange Place in Jersey City. In New York he walked alone over ground later occupied by World Trade Center Two to the Astor House on February 25, and stayed until the 27th and

The Cooper Union has heard several presidents speak, including Lincoln, who gave the address without which he probably would have not have become president.

probably March 10–11. The hotel was across from city hall at 217–225 Broadway, west side between Vesey and Barclay Streets. Much earlier the site was the home of John Jacob Astor and then Vice President Aaron Burr, listed as "Official Residence of the Vice President," although the capital was then in Washington. The site is just south of the Woolworth Building,* 237 Broadway, once the tallest building in the world. (**Truman** went to the top in 1917 on his way to fight in World War I.) **Grant** had come to the hotel in 1854 on the way back from California; broke, he had to borrow money from Simon Buckner for his hotel bill. **Grant** returned the favor after his friend surrendered his Confederate army to him at Fort Donelson, Tennessee. He also stayed at the Astor in June 1865 just after the Civil War ended. Other presidents at the now demolished hotel include **Fillmore, Pierce, Buchanan,** and **Wilson.**

After arrival **Lincoln** went to see Henry Bowen, the publisher of the *New York Independent,* at 4 Beekman Street, where he learned that the speech was rescheduled for the Cooper Union,* still at Cooper Square, where Third and Fourth Avenues and Seventh Street meet, considered the most elegant auditorium in the world. He paid two cents to take the Fulton Street Ferry to Brooklyn to hear Beecher on Sunday, February 26. The ferry ran from Fulton Street in Manhattan to Atlantic and Fulton Streets in Brooklyn, the same route used by **Washington** in his retreat after the Battle of Long Island. **Lincoln** sat in pew number 89, left side of the center section, four rows from the front. This 1829 church* is still located at 69 Orange Street between Henry and Hicks Streets. **Cleveland** and **Wilson** attended later.

Afterward he went to the Bowen House, at Clark and Willow in Brooklyn, but refused to eat lunch as claimed, stating that he needed to work on his speech. The next morning he toured Broadway, and bought a hat at the Knox Great Hat and Cap Establishment, 212 Broadway and Fulton. He must have visited or surely seen St. Paul's, across the street from his hotel, and at least saw Trinity Church, then the tallest building in town.

The famous photographer Mathew Brady from 1844 had a studio across the street on the corner south of St. Paul's, at 205 Broadway at Fulton, photographing some of the most famous men in the world. From 1853 until 1859, Brady was located at 359 Broadway, still standing but unmarked. Then in 1860 he moved temporarily to 643 Broadway, on the NW corner of Bleecker, and then to 785 Broadway at Tenth. Various sources list each of the above Brady addresses as the location of **Lincoln's** famous 1860 photograph, but the correct location is 643 Broadway. The famous photograph was later published as "an official campaign picture." **Lincoln** said that the Cooper Union speech and photograph made him president.

His February 27 speech contributed more than any single event to his nomination. He was not well known outside of Illinois before, but appeared before the "pick and flower of New York." An excellent crowd of 1500 paid 25 cents to hear the great Stephen Douglas's rival. At first his impression and words failed. His new $100, ill-fitting and wrinkled suit and appearance were awkward and uncultivated. When they heard "Mr. Cheerman," in his high falsetto and country dialect, many shook their heads in disappointment and laughter. But a witness wrote, "As he spoke he was transformed; his eyes kindled, his voice rang, and his face shone and seemed to light up the whole assembly ... as he held the audience in the hollow of his hand."

He now became a major political figure. Influential newspaperman Horace Greeley was impressed and promoted **Lincoln** over then front-runner, New York's William Seward. Other notable speakers have used **Lincoln's** lectern, still in the hall, including **Grant**, **Andrew Johnson**, **Hayes**, **Cleveland**, **Theodore Roosevelt**, **Wilson**, **Taft**, and Mark Twain. The only incumbent president to speak was **Clinton**, who gave a major address on May 12, 1993.

After the speech **Lincoln** ate at the Athenaeum Club, 108 Fifth Ave., SW corner of Sixteenth and Fifth Avenue, and went to the *Tribune* office, at Nassau and Spruce across from City Hall Park, to have the speech published, and maybe left the blue foolscap manuscript after proofreading the copy. He then went to New Hampshire to see his son in school, and also to let himself be seen and heard by potential voters on a two-week trip through New England without which he probably would not have been nominated. Going and coming he used the New Haven Depot he'd used in 1848, then returned to New York and attended Plymouth Church again, sitting in the balcony to hear Beecher on March 11. That afternoon he toured Five Points, Division and Bowery, and the House of Industry, 155 Worth, before going to the Church of Divine Unity on Broadway between Prince and Spring.

President-elect **Lincoln** and family arrived on the Hudson River Railroad on February 19, 1861, going from the 30th Street Station on the south side of the street between Ninth and Tenth Avenues. An estimated 250,000 people watched as he rode in an open carriage 60 blocks to the Astor House. (In 1916, presidential candidate Charles Evans Hughes was at the Astor on election night when several newspapers declared him the winner over **Wilson**. Times Square flashed the news to 100,000 gathered there to cheer him. After Hughes went to bed here a reporter, who heard subsequent results that **Wilson** had won, asked to see him. His aide announced, "The president can not be disturbed." The reporter then said, "Tell him when he wakes up that he is no longer president.")

Lincoln dined with the family at the hotel, received numerous delegations, and ate the next morning at the home of former congressman Moses H. Grinnell, at Fifth Avenue and 14th. Later he met with the mayor and council in the Governor's Room at city hall,* across from his hotel, still used by New York governors. **Lincoln** shook hands for two hours beside **Washington's** writing desk and then spoke from the balcony. (**Andrew Johnson** spoke here as president.) He refused P.T. Barnum's invitation to his American Museum (destroyed), at the corner of Ann Street and Broadway, across from and prominently visible from their hotel.

Vice President-elect Hannibal Hamlin and his wife met the **Lincolns** at the Astor and dined in the **Lincoln** suite. The men attended the Academy of Music at 4 Irving Place (an extension of Lexington Avenue), on the NE corner with Fourteenth, and left the next morning via the Cortlandt Street Ferry to Powles Hook in Jersey City at Exchange Place.

Lincoln passed through on the way to and from West Point on June 24 and 25, 1862. His body lay in state April 24–25, 1865, outside the Governor's Room on the staircase landing across the rotunda, where more than 120,000 paid their respects for almost 24 hours. The room is on the second floor, just inside the balcony. **Grant** was also so honored as his body lay under the rotunda. Afterward, **Lincoln's** body was moved up Broadway to the Hudson River Depot.

As the funeral cortege passed the south side of Union Square, Broadway and 14th, a photograph was taken showing two small boys in the window of their grandfather's house, then at the present 853 Broadway, on the SW corner. These were future President **Theodore Roosevelt** and his brother Elliot, the father of Eleanor Roosevelt, wife of **FDR. TR** frequently visited here and met as a child his future wife, who lived nearby. The boys might have been searching for their father marching in the parade. The camera is facing north on Broadway, just south of 14th. **Lincoln** passed this way in 1861 as the Academy of Music was just east, and would have passed the Washington statue, now on the southern edge of the park, but then at Park or Fourth Street, facing the **Roosevelt** home less than a block away.

After leaving office **Andrew Johnson** stayed at the Metropolitan Hotel, 578 Broadway, where he was serenaded. **Grant** passed through town several times prior to living here after leaving office and returning from a two-year trip around the world. He was stationed in Officer's Row, Governor's Island, before being sent by the army to California. He visited in 1866 with **Johnson**, and beat the president in a carriage race through Central Park. In the early 1880s **Grant** lived at Three East 66th (marked), purchased by rich friends, with a view of Central Park. He went to work every day at Two Wall, first as president of the Mexican Southern Railroad until it became bankrupt, and then with his son at an investment firm, **Grant** and Ward, until it also failed, owing $16 million with $57,000 in assets. Ward was thought to be a financial genius, but was not investing **Grant's** and his clients' money, just paying dividends out of investments. The day before the failure became known, **Grant** had received $150,000 from his friend William H. Vanderbilt at his home, 640 Fifth Ave., for "a day until the banks opened." Grant gave it to Ward, who absconded. **Grant** thought he was worth $2.5 million, but had only $180 when the bubble burst, realizing that he, his friends, and clients had been swindled. He sold everything, including his military memorabilia, although much was purchased by friends who gave it back.

Grant is buried at the General Grant National Memorial,* at Riverside Drive and 122nd Street, in one of the largest mausoleums in the world. He wanted to be buried at West Point and probably would have been, but his wife could not have been buried there without Congressional consent, and he did not make his wants known in time to Congress. **Benjamin Harrison** laid the cornerstone. **Hayes, Arthur,** and **Cleveland** were at the funeral. **Grant's** wife visited the site in 1897 with **McKinley** and **Theodore Roosevelt,** when **McKinley** formally dedicated the tomb. **Truman** came in 1917 and asked, "Is he really dead?" Some of the heaviest fighting of the Revolutionary War battles for New York was here on September 16, 1776. **Washington** was at the site during part of the Battle of Harlem Heights and heard a British bugler blow a foxhunting tune, meaning the fox had gone to ground. The Virginia gentleman bridled at the insult.

The Gracie Mansion, home of the New York mayor, sits on a high spot in Carl Schurz Park along Gracie Square at East 84th Street and the East River. Guests have included **John Quincy Adams, Carter, Reagan,** and **Truman. Washington** was on the site also. **Hayes** was at the Metropolitan Museum on Fifth Avenue for opening ceremonies in 1880.

Arthur was staying at the Bancroft House, a family hotel at 904 Broadway, when he met his future wife, who was visiting relatives there. After his marriage they lived with their children at 34 W. 21st Street, his wife's old home. During the Civil War, they moved to a hotel near 22nd and Broadway, and then to 123 Lexington, his official residence for the rest of his life. He entertained frequently and stylishly in several large parlors. His office was in the basement, and he carefully stocked a large library mostly for show. He worked at 289 Broadway before the war, 51 Walker Street during the war, and later had a law office at 155 Broadway. He preferred the company of cronies to that of his wife, who died shortly before his nomination as vice president. His election was his first to any office. He was sworn in as president in the house after Garfield died. Reporters soon came for an interview, but the doorman informed them there would be none. **Arthur** was "sitting alone in his room sobbing like a child." After his term ended he returned to his home, where he died less than two years after leaving office. Little is known about his private life today as he destroyed all of his papers the day before he died, since he believed that his "personal life is nobody's damned business." The run-down building is still standing.

Cleveland lived in the city between his two

presidential terms. His residences were 816 Madison Avenue, 1889–1892, and 12 W. 51st, 1892–3. During his presidency he often stayed at the Hotel Victoria, 4 West 22nd, and held cabinet meetings there. He often ate at The Players, 16 Gramercy Park, owned by Edwin Booth, famous brother of Lincoln's assassin. **Cleveland** became secretly engaged, and the public did not know officially, although rumors abounded. When his fiancee returned from a trip to Europe, she stayed at the Gilsey House at Fifth Avenue, two blocks south of Madison Square. The public then besieged this address when the announcement was made. **Cleveland** met her there and then came to watch a parade at the Square. She leaned out the window to wave a handkerchief as he waved back, and the band played the wedding march. While at the first listed residence, he had his first child at age 54. Four more followed. He stayed also at the Murray Hill Hotel, Park Avenue between 40th and 41st, as did **McKinley**.

Benjamin Harrison's second wedding, avoided by his children, was at St. Thomas Episcopal,* Fifth Avenue at 53rd, in 1896. He then had a daughter, born in 1897 when he was 63. His children never forgave him, and refused to sit with the widow at his funeral.

The two **Roosevelts** lived similar lives, and had numerous ties with the city. Only **FDR's** houses survive as **TR's** have been destroyed. **TR's** birthplace was at 28 East 20th,* where a replica building now stands. This home and the identical one next door had been wedding presents from their father to Theodore Sr. and his brother. (Fifteen presidents, **Madison**, **Quincy Adams**, **Jackson**, **Tyler**, **Buchanan**, **Hayes**, **McKinley**, **TR**, **Coolidge**, **Hoover**, **Eisenhower**, **Ford**, **Carter**, **Clinton**, and **George W. Bush**, had the same first name as their fathers, although not all were considered "juniors." **Adams** and **Bush** each had a different middle name and **Eisenhower** had his first and second names reversed. **Ford** and **Clinton** took the names of their stepfathers, although they were Jrs. at birth with their real father's names.)

TR was the first president born and raised in a large city. The entire family suffered medical problems, and **TR's** parents died in their forties. (He was the first president known by initials.) As a child "Thee" was the frailest and weakest. He suffered many ailments, and his father installed a gymnasium for him on the second-floor back porch where he exercised to build up his puny body. The father lovingly forced his son to drink strong coffee and inhale cigar smoke, thinking it would clear his frail lungs and end his asthmatic coughing. Whether this worked or not — he did get better as he grew older — he at least learned to strive to overcome limitations and problems and to improve situations as he found them. Here "Teedie," another nickname, had all the books and presents he wanted from his prosperous father, who also forced him to take midnight carriage rides to aid his poor health. He was mostly home schooled and had few playmates. One was his younger sister's friend, Edith Carow, who became his second wife. Also he collected many specimens of insects and animals, studied taxidermy, and set up what he called "The Roosevelt Museum of Natural History." Some of his specimens were donated to the new Museum of Natural History,* whose charter was signed in this house. When the museum opened on the west side of Central Park, he escorted President **Hayes** through the building. The much-altered home was destroyed in 1910. The replica birthplace house is now a shrine with many personal items. The property was purchased by his sisters just after his death and reconstructed by measuring the identical house next door, before it was destroyed, and through the memories of **TR's** sisters and wife. Forty percent of the furnishings are from the original house and another 20 percent are from family members.

As a child **Theodore Roosevelt** was scared to death to go to the Madison Avenue Presbyterian Church, SE corner of 24th and Madison Avenue. The family could not understand the extreme fear. It was finally discovered that he was terrified of the "zeals" that he feared were crouched in the dark corners. He knew they were there; the preacher had read it from the Bible. It was finally determined, using a concordance, that the source of the terror, as "Teedie" screamed for his mother to stop reading, was John 2:17: "And his disciples remembered that it was written, 'The zeal of thine house hath eaten me up.' "

At age 14 he set out on a year-long tour of Europe with his family and returned to Six West 57th Street, near Fifth Avenue and Central Park. (He had also traveled in Europe for a year in 1869.) Theodore Sr. felt that the proximity to the park would improve the boy's health. **Franklin Roosevelt's** mother, Sara Delano, was a frequent visitor with her close friend, **TR's** sister Anna, nicknamed Bamie. When TR Sr.'s cousin James's wife died, he called on the family here. Bamie fell in love with James, or the other way around depending on which story you read. The 22-year-old's relationship was thwarted by her mother, or Bamie gently rebuffed his proposal. He then rebounded into Sara's arms. Sara was escorted by Bamie and TR's mother to James's Hyde Park home, where love blossomed, resulting in marriage and the birth of **Franklin**. Sara later told **FDR** that she would have been an old maid if **TR's** family had not provided her a place to meet and then court James. (Franklin's half-brother Rosey's daughter married Theodore's sister Corinne's son. So James, **Franklin's** father, had descendants in **TR's** family as **Franklin** married **TR's** niece, and **FDR**'s half-niece married **TR's** nephew.)

After marriage, **TR** moved to 55 West 45th, then back to live at the family home on 57th, so his mother could take care of his pregnant wife Alice when he was in the legislature. He walked from here to Columbia Law School at 8 Great Jones Street. The close-nit family continued to dote on **Theodore**, and biographer Kathleen Dalton relates that Alice compliantly called upstairs to the rest of the family when he returned each day from law school, "Teddy is here; come and share him." In a remarkable coincidence, his wife and mother both died there on the same day, Valentine's Day 1884. (Both were buried in Greenwood Cemetery.) When his wife died less than 48 hours after the birth of their daughter, he wrote in his diary, "The light has gone out of my life." In later years, he wrote the same words and added "forever." He never spoke of her again, not even to their daughter, and did not mention her in his autobiography.

The funeral for his mother and wife was at Fifth Ave. Presbyterian,* where he also gave his sister Corinne away at her marriage. The **Roosevelts** had attended the church since it opened in 1875, and it is still in use at the NW corner of 55th and Fifth Avenue. He attended his son's wedding there in 1910. He left the baby, Alice, with Bamie for three years at 422 Madison and spent time on a ranch in North Dakota. He had already purchased 155 acres on Long Island, sold 60 to relatives, and signed a contract on March 1, 1884, for the construction of a 22-room house there. When this was completed the next year, he sold the two New York City homes, and Bamie and little Alice moved to the new estate, Sagamore Hill, near Oyster Bay. The next year he lost a bid for mayor of New York, but married his childhood friend, Edith Kermit Carow, in London. Edith had lived next to Roosevelt's grandfather on Union Square and over the years had remained close to Corinne, who got them back together. They renewed their relationship at Bamie's house, 422 Madison Avenue. Edith was his first love, but they had a falling out as teenagers. She had always remained in love with him, then grew impatient waiting after their reunion and went to England, where he followed her to marry.

TR's brother Elliot was married at Calvary Episcopal Church,* Park Avenue and 21st, with **TR** as the best man. During the mid–1890s **Roosevelt** was president of the Police Commission, with offices at 300 Mulberry, and governor in 1898. He then met with party boss Senator Tom Pratt at Bamie's to avoid being seen at Pratt's Hotel, in order to intimidate the profane senator in a woman's house, and provide himself a witness, if needed. He accidentally (maybe) bumped into Edith here after not seeing her for several years. He and the family stayed here at times in years when their Oyster Bay home was too expensive to heat and then worked in town.

FDR stayed with his mother Sara at 200 Madison when he went to Columbia Law School in 1904. He worked briefly at 120 Broadway, and then from 1907 to 1911 at 54 Wall. In 1915 he was at 52 Wall and in 1924 back at 120 Broadway. He tried to return to work in the 1920s after getting polio, but getting out of the car and into the building was a disaster and terrible ordeal, so he gave up on that. He never discussed his polio affliction, and many could not or did not accept that he could not walk. He did not use crutches in public and instead learned to shuffle or move his body while holding on to others. Of the thousands of photographs of him, only two show him in a wheelchair, and there are only four seconds of known film of him "walking."

From 1905 to 1907 **FDR** and his mother had a house at 125 E. 36th. He and Eleanor were married in 1905 on the southeast side of Fifth Avenue at 76th, in the same block as the Whitney Art Museum. **Franklin** courted Eleanor there while she had been living at her aunt's half of a double house joined by sliding doors that could be opened to make a large room. Uncle **Teddy**, president at the time, gave away the bride and stole the attention of all the guests, telling **Franklin**, "...there's nothing like keeping the name in the family." **Franklin's** choice of a seemingly passive and unemotional mate seemed strange as evidently they had not even kissed before the wedding, but maybe he wanted something different from his mother, who had always dominated him. Even so, after the wedding they were dependent on Sara for financial support and lived in the Webster Hotel at 40 West 45th while he finished his first year in law school. When Eleanor got pregnant, they were given the small townhouse at 125 E. 36th. Eleanor was "jubilant," or at least she said so, but never mind about adding electricity, since "they would not be there long." Her brother, Hall, lived with them at the hotel and here. Eleanor was, however, not too jubilant that **Franklin's** mother was constantly afoot to direct the management of the house.

After a short time Sara gave them 49 E. 65th, a five-story double house and basement, with her on the other side at Number 47. Both still exist, but only the latter is marked as a memorial to Sara. Each floor had a sliding door from one house to the other so that she could intrude at any moment, and there was never any privacy. **Franklin** returned home here sick and bedridden from a trip to Europe in 1918 as assistant secretary of the Navy. According to the accepted, vague story, **Franklin** was in Granny's bedroom when Eleanor discovered a packet of love letters from her secretary, Lucy Mercer, to **Franklin** revealing his affair with her. She was devastated. The marriage was almost broken up when he had to choose Lucy or give up his family, his mother's money, and his political career. Sara and Eleanor stuck together for maybe the first time. Among other things, Sara said she would cut him off financially and disinherit him if he divorced his wife. The three **Roosevelts** never discussed this, so what we suspect comes from the children and others. The couple stayed together, but the relationship was permanently changed. From that point on there was no intimacy, and the two began to lead mostly separate lives. They were bound by affection, respect, and a common interest in politics and children. She had never felt love growing up and needed intimacy. The shy, quiet woman with the inferiority complex knew now she would have to make a life on her own. Later he sought to recover here from polio after leaving Presbyterian Hospital. While **Franklin** suffered through his illness, quiet Eleanor was forced to emerge from her private shell to campaign for the party and keep her husband's name before the public until he could return to politics. The personal transformation led later to her being ranked as the best first lady and to be called "First Lady of the World."

After striving to overcome the effects of polio, the former vice-presidential candidate made his political comeback in 1924 by nominating Al Smith at the National Democratic Convention. The heroic physical effort of mounting the platform showed great courage and marked **Roosevelt** as a shining light in the party. Smith won the governor's office over Theodore Roosevelt Jr., with the help of Eleanor and **FDR's** tough campaigning and tactics, preserving **FDR's** future political future through the governor's office. During his presidency he stayed at 29 Washington Square at the corner of Waverly Place.

Kennedy maintained an apartment suite on the 35th floor of the Hotel Carlyle, on Madison Avenue at 35 E. 76th, while senator. It is rumored and written that he had liaisons with actress Marilyn Monroe here. After she sang happy birthday to him in 1962 at Madison Square Garden, they reportedly came here for several hours for the last time. **Truman** stayed at the Carlyle while visiting his daughter.

Summary of New York City—The Battery to City Hall

Castle Clinton* on the battery at the tip of Manhattan, built in the early 19th century, was converted into a place of entertainment known as Castle Gardens in time to honor the return of General Lafayette in 1824. **Washington** received the British surrender near here. Most presidents from **Washington** to **Pierce**, and probably most since then, visited. **Pierce** and Secretary of War **Davis** spoke there in July 1853. **Jackson**, **Tyler**, and **Polk** were honored inside. **Jackson** landed in 1833 and rode a horse across the bridge from the then island castle. It fell, carrying "cabinet members, governors, mayors, and other celebrities" into the water. **Grant** left from here for West Point in 1865. **JFK** dedicated the East Coast Memorial in 1963.

3 Cherry (Frankfort and Dover): As president, **Washington** first lived at the site, now covered by the piers of the Brooklyn Bridge, a few doors east of Franklin Square. The bridge was dedicated by **Arthur** with Governor **Cleveland** leading a procession over it in 1883.

SE corner of Pearl and Broad, Fraunces Tavern:* **Washington** frequently ate here in 1776 and later, and met in 1783 with his officers for the last time as commanding general. It is presumed **Adams**, **Jefferson**, and probably **Madison** and **Monroe** also were served.

15 Broad: **Cleveland** worked in a law firm, 1889–1893. (East side north of Exchange Place.)

20 Broad: **Nixon** worked in a law firm, 1963–1969, now the entrance to Stock Exchange. (Near NW corner with Exchange Place.)

30 Broad: **Van Buren's** law office was here in 1801. (Just south of Exchange Place)

1 Broadway: **Washington's** headquarters in 1776 were at Broadway and Bowling Green. (West side at Battery Place.) **Jackson** and most others paraded up the famous street.

3–11 Broadway: **Washington** and others visited the home of New York Chancellor Robert Livingston, who swore in the first president.

15 Broadway: **Van Buren** lived here. (South of Morris Street, west side.)

18 Broadway: **Washington** and **Adams** were entertained at Capes Tavern in the 1780s, as were **Jefferson, Madison**, and **Monroe** later.

39–41 Broadway: **Washington** lived here as president, with 21 servants including seven slaves. (Marked with plaque, west side.)

Broadway and Wall: The first five presidents attended the old Trinity Church.* The new church attracted Queen Elizabeth II in 1976 and many presidents; **Monroe** was married here.

90 Broadway: **Monroe** lived here in 1786. (Opposite Trinity Church, north of Wall.)

115 Broadway, City Tavern: **Washington, Adams, Jefferson, Madison, Monroe**, and **Van Buren** frequented. **Van Buren** lived here from 1829 to 1833; torn down in 1850. (West side between Thames and Cedar Streets, north of Trinity. The tavern was the second of four small lots north of Thames, now a passageway under a building.)

120 Broadway: **FDR** worked for a law firm 1924. (South of the SE corner with Cedar.)

133 Broadway: **Adams** visited John Jay in 1789.

155 Broadway: **Arthur** worked at a law firm 1878–1881. (West side, north of Cedar.)

176 Broadway: **Houston** stayed in the old Howard or Barnam's Hotel, his headquarters for busi-

Washington and the other leaders worshipped at Trinity Church in the distance, where Monroe was married. Lincoln and the others here must have noticed the tallest building in New York during their time here.

ness trips in the late 1850s. (East side, north of Maiden Lane.)

St. Paul's Chapel,* Broadway between Fulton and Vesey: Many presidents have visited, including all of the first six. **Monroe's** funeral was then the city's largest. **George W. Bush** stood at the site of the World Trade Center just west to tell the terrorists that they would be hearing from us soon.

212 Broadway and Fulton: **Lincoln** bought a hat in 1860. (NE corner, across from St. Paul's.)

225 Broadway between Vesey and Barclay: Astor House site, where **Jackson**, **Fillmore**, **Pierce**, **Buchanan**, **Lincoln**, **Grant**, **Houston**, and **Wilson** stayed.

237 Broadway (Woolworth Building): **Van Buren** lived on site (SW corner) in 1822. Doughboy **Truman** stopped off on the way to World War I to climb to the top of the world's tallest building. At that time he also walked across the Brooklyn Bridge.

289 Broadway: **Arthur** worked in a law firm, 1852–56.

Broadway and Chambers: As president, **Van Buren** often stayed at the Washington Hotel.

1 Wall Street: **Van Buren** lived and studied law here in 1813. (SE corner with Broadway.)

2 Wall: **Grant** worked in 1881 as president of a railroad and later at the firm of Grant and Ward. (NE corner with Broadway.)

4 Wall: **Van Buren** lived here, 1802–3.

28 Wall and Nassau, NE corner: **Washington** was inaugurated in 1789 at the old city hall, now Federal Hall.* **Adams**, **Jefferson**, **Madison**, and **Monroe** worked at the site. Many presidents, including **George W. Bush**, have spoken here.

44 Wall: **TR** worked for a law firm, 1909–1919. (West of William Street, south side of Wall.)

Washington, Adams, Jefferson, Monroe, and many other presidents have worshiped in St. Paul's Church in New York, where the leaders came after the first inauguration. Monroe's funeral was here, and George W. Bush stood just behind at the site of the World Trade Center to inspire the nation. The Astor House site, where Lincoln, Grant, Wilson, and others stayed, is across the street on the right.

52 Wall: **FDR** worked for a law firm, 1915. (North side, east of William Street.)

54 Wall: **FDR** worked for a law firm in 1905, then 1907–11.

55 Wall: **Arthur** worked in the Customs House, 1872–8.

57 Wall: Home of Alexander Hamilton, where he met with **Madison** as they wrote *The Federalist Papers* and conferred to pass the proposed Federal Constitution.

120 Wall and South Streets: **Washington** landed on the way to his inauguration.

Wall Street, National City Bank Building: **Arthur** worked here, 1871–8.

135 Fulton (east of Broadway): The American House was where **Jackson** and **Van Buren** stayed in 1833 and **William Henry Harrison** stayed in 1841.

End of Fulton Street and East River: **Washington** retreated in 1776 during the Battle of Brooklyn to where Fireboat Station 77 is now located. **Lincoln** used the ferry here to go to Brooklyn in 1860. Both went from Fulton Street in Brooklyn to Fulton Street in Manhattan. **Jefferson** and **Monroe** among others also used the ferry. President-elect **George H.W. Bush** and **Reagan** are pictured with Russian Premier Gorbachev with the skyline in the background from about here in 1989.

4 Beekman: **Lincoln** ate here with a friend. (East side of City Hall Park, NE corner with Park.)

Nassau and Spruce: **Lincoln** visited the *Tribune* office, where his Cooper Union address was transcribed. (North of above, NE corner, now Pace University.)

Nassau and Frankfort: The Democratic Party headquarters, Tammany Hall, was here between 1812 and 1868 and hosted Democratic presidents.

82 Nassau Street: **Arthur** worked in a law firm in 1871, as well as at 117 Nassau Street, 1856–61 and 1863–71.

Nassau Street near City Hall: **Adams** stayed in Stoutenburgh house in 1774.

19 Maiden Lane (Atlantic Bank): **Madison** lived here, 1787–89. (North side of street between Broadway and Liberty.)

57 Maiden Lane: **Jefferson** lived here while secretary of state, 1790–93. (Plaque, north side east of Nassau.) The Great Compromise making **Washington D.C.** the capital was initiated here with Hamilton and **Madison**.

155 Worth (Five Points House of Industry): **Lincoln** visited. (North side between Center and Baxter.)

160 Duane running south to Hudson, north of Chambers and West Broadway: **Lincoln** used Hudson Street Depot in 1861.

26 Federal Plaza: **Nixon** had an office in the 1980s.

City hall,* Broadway and Park Row: **Monroe**, **Lincoln**, and **Grant** lay in state. **A. Johnson** and many others visited. **Lincoln**, **Hayes**, and **Grant** were received in the Governor's Room.

City Hall to the Empire State Building

NW corner of Broadway and 23rd: The Fifth Avenue Hotel was a Republican headquarters hosting **Grant** through **Hayes**. **TR** met Republican boss Tom Platt.

Broadway and Reade: **Arthur** worked for law firm, 1852–1856, NW corner.

346 Broadway: **Van Buren** lodged here in 1802.

349 Broadway:* Celebrated photographer Charles D. Fredericks had a studio where he took **Houston's** picture.

Broadway and Chambers: **Van Buren** lodged here, 1837–1841.

240 Centre: **TR** worked as police commissioner from 1895 to 1897 at the police headquarters, also listed as 300 Mulberry. (Between Broom and Grand.)

Hubert and Laight: **Washington** landed south of today's Holland Tunnel.

Charlton and Varick, SE corner, Mortier House or Richmond Hill site: **Washington's** headquarters in 1776. **Monroe** joined him. One of **Washington's** bodyguards tried to give him poison peas and was hanged. **Adams** lived here as vice president, visited by **Jefferson**.

Broadway between Prince and Spring: **Lincoln** attended the Church of Divine Unity.

63–65 Prince and Lafayette: **Monroe** lived at the home of his daughter on the NE corner in 1830 and died there on July 4, 1831. Parts of the original house survive. He was first buried in the Marble Cemetery* on Second Street between First and Second Avenues before being moved to Richmond, Virginia.

East side of Lafayette, between Catherine and Leonard, originally 346 Elm: **Arthur** worked here.

51 Walker: **Arthur** had an office in 1862 and was promoted to quartermaster general.

8 Great Jones Street at the NW corner of Lafayette Place: Columbia Law School was here when **TR** attended in 1880.

Many presidents visited New York's city hall, including Lincoln, Grant, Hayes, and Andrew Johnson. Monroe, Lincoln, and Grant's bodies lay in state inside.

521 Broadway: **Van Buren** (1840s) and **Fillmore** (1854) both stayed in the St. Nicholas Hotel. (West side south of Spring.)

578 Broadway: **Andrew Johnson** stayed in July 1869 at the Metropolitan Hotel, where he was honored and serenaded.

643 Broadway at NW corner of Bleecker: Photographer Mathew Brady took **Lincoln's** picture here in 1860. **Lincoln** credited it and his speech at the Cooper Union with making him president. Brady also had studios at 205, 359, and 785 Broadway, where the picture is sometimes incorrectly said to have been made.

Broadway and Worth, 28 Federal Plaza on Foley Square: **Nixon** worked in a law firm, 1988–94.

36–38 Fifth Ave. and NW corner with 10th Street: **Tyler** married at the Church of the Ascension.* The original building is marked. Just west and south of the back side of the church is 12 W. Tenth, where author Emily Post tells of having **Wilson** to Thanksgiving dinner in her 1846 townhouse, where he proposed to his second wife.

48 Fifth Ave.: **Buchanan** attended Fifth Avenue Presbyterian in 1856, between 11th and 12th.

428–434 Lafayette, Colonnade Row just south of Astor Place: Remains of the original home of **Tyler's** second wife, where he courted her; marked, but **Tyler** is not mentioned. Franklin Delano, **FDR**'s grandfather, also lived here.

Fifth Avenue and 14th: **Lincoln** visited Moses Grinnell.

4 Irving Pl. on NE corner at 14th: **Lincoln** and his wife attended the Academy of Music in 1861. Tammany Hall was moved next door from Nassau Street to the east side of the Academy of Music in 1868 and was visited by **Andrew Johnson** and other presidents.

853 (then 849) Broadway, SW corner of 14th, south of Union Square: **TR's** grandfather lived in a mansion on site, frequented by young **Teddy**, who was photographed looking out the window at **Lincoln's** funeral parade in 1865.

The camera was facing north along Broadway. **Washington** met grateful New York citizens where his statue is now across the street when he arrived in November 1783 to receive the British surrender of the city.

14th near Union Square: **Arthur** lived at the Continental Hotel, 1853–5.

904 Broadway: **Arthur** lodged here, 1856–7.

14 E. 16th: **Hoover** lived from 1909 to 1911. (South side, east of Fifth Avenue.)

28 E. 20th: **TR** was born in a house* reconstructed by the National Park Service.

34 W. 21st: **Arthur** lived here, 1859–61. (South side, east of Fifth Avenue.)

21st and Fourth Ave.: **Arthur** was married at Calvary Episcopal and attended for more than twenty years.

Gramercy Park and 2 Lexington Avenue: **Kennedy** lived in the Gramercy Park Hotel* as a boy in the 1920s and played in the park. (West side of street between 21st and 22nd.) The hotel is still on the north side of the park. Samuel Tilden's home is marked on the south side at 15 Gramercy Park South. He had the most popular votes and apparently the most electoral votes in the 1876 election. Four states were disputed, and he lost all by one vote in a decision by a commission, voting down party lines. (**Jefferson** almost lost his first presidential election by one vote to Aaron Burr.) Several months of strategy and legal maneuvering during this time were planned here. Fearing hostile mobs, he put up an iron grill defensive barrier behind his windows, and then, in case this failed, built a tunnel to escape to 19th Street. The home later became the National Arts Club, where **TR** frequented.

Greene St. and Waverly Place near Washington Arch: **Van Buren** stayed in the Benjamin Butler home upon leaving the presidency.

338 Fifth Ave. (NW corner of 33rd): John Jacob Astor House, visited by **Hayes** and **TR** in 1877.

Madison Square Garden: Attended by all virtually presidents since **Hoover**. It was at Eighth Avenue and 50th until it moved to the site of old Penn Station, 31st, 33rd, and Eighth Avenue. **Carter** was nominated in 1976, **Clinton** in 1992, and **George W. Bush** was renominated here in 2004. It was originally at the NE corner of Madison and 26th, also the depot of the Harlem Railroad.

Fourth and 21st, Calvary Episcopal:* **Arthur** attended this original building from 1859 to 1880, and was married in 1859. **TR** was best man for his brother in December 1883.

Broadway and 22nd: **Arthur** lived here, 1861–65.

4 W. Broadway and 22nd: **Cleveland**'s residence.

Fourth Ave. and 22nd: **TR** had an office here upon returning from Europe after his term, under a contract to write magazine articles.

Fifth Avenue, Broadway, and 23rd-24th Street: Headquarters of the Republican Party, on the east side of the street, visited by **Grant**, **Hayes**, **Garfield**, **Arthur**, and **B. Harrison**.

24th and Madison, SE corner, east side of Madison Square: Site of Madison Avenue Presbyterian, where **TR** attended. (Verified from maps of the era of **Roosevelt's** childhood.)

Park (Fourth) Ave. and 27th: **Lincoln** used the depot that was on the south side of 27th between Park and Lexington.

4 W. 27th: **Cleveland** lived here, 1889–92.

123 Lexington:* **Arthur** was sworn in as president in his front parlor by a judge of the New York Supreme Court and later died in the home, now an altered commercial building. It is on the east side of the street, north of 28th. He knew he had a terminal illness as president, but kept it from the public, who had just experienced Garfield's assassination.

South side of 30th between 9th and 10th Avenues: **Lincoln** used the depot here to go to the Hudson Street Depot, on Duane between Hudson and West Broadway.

Eighth and Ninth Avenues, 33rd Street and 34th Street: **Cleveland** and his brother were in charge of the boys' dormitory at the Institute for the Blind, 1853–54.

Third, Fourth Avenue, 7th Street and Astor: The Cooper Union* hosted presidential addresses.

32nd and Broadway: **Harding** supposedly visited his mistress at the Imperial Hotel, built 1897; now the Holiday Inn.*

34th and East River, Kip's Bay: British landed in September 1776 in pursuit of **Washington**.

125 E. 36th (between Park and Lexington): **FDR** lived here, 1905–07.

Fifth Avenue and 29th: **Nixon** attended daughter Julie's wedding to David Eisenhower at Norman Vincent Peale's Marble Collegiate Church,* where **Nixon** attended frequently.

200 Madison: **FDR** lived here while attending law school.

411 Fifth: **Hayes** visited the Morgan House in 1877.

North of the Empire State Building

Fifth Avenue and 42nd, SW corner: In October 1842 **Tyler** dedicated the waterworks where the

New York Library is now with former presidents **John Quincy Adams** and **Van Buren.** **Taft** dedicated the library when it opened in 1911. It is the largest library in the country after the Library of Congress.

Sixth Ave. and 42nd, Bryant Park:* **Pierce** opened the first world's fair in America here in 1853, just west of library.

42nd Street and Park Avenue, Grand Central Terminal:* Used by many presidents. Earlier during the Battle for New York, **Washington** furiously raged at his retreating troops between here and 43rd Street and Fifth Avenue.

125 E. 42nd, NW corner with Lexington: **Eisenhower** stayed at the Commodore Hotel in 1952 and 1953, and **Nixon** met Whittaker Chambers here in 1948. Near Grand Central Terminal, it is now the Grand Hyatt.*

43–44th Street and Madison: **FDR**'s campaign headquarters for governor in 1928.

40 W. 45th: **FDR** lived here for a short time after he married.

44th and Broadway: **Washington** met Israel Putnam in retreat.

55 W. 45th: **TR** rented in 1882 and first lived alone with his first wife after living in the family home. (North side of street just west of Fifth Avenue.)

277 Park between 47th and 48th: **JFK** had an apartment.

301 Park Ave, NE corner of 49th Street, Waldorf Astoria Hotel: **JFK** lived in the early 1940s.

551 Fifth Avenue near NE corner of 45th Street: **Arthur** went to the Church of Heavenly Rest in the 1880s; his and his wife's funerals were held here. **Wilson** also attended in 1884.

Fifth Avenue and 48th: **TR** was a member of the Collegiate Church of St. Nicholas.

422 Madison: **TR** stayed with sister Bamie from 1895 to 1897, and left his baby daughter with her for several years after his wife died. He met his future second wife here after not seeing her for several years. While governor he met a party boss here.

109 E. 50th, Park Avenue and 50th to 51st and Madison: **Hoover**'s funeral was at St. Bartholemew's Episcopal* in 1964, attended by **LBJ**; still one of the more beautiful churches in the city.

50th and 5th Avenue, St. Patrick's Cathedral: **Johnson** and **Nixon** attended Robert Kennedy's 1968 funeral in the country's largest Neo-Gothic church building.

315 Park and 100 E. 50th: **Hoover** (Suite 31-A, 1933–64) and **Nixon** (35th floor) both lived at the Waldorf Towers Hotel.* **Hoover** was visited by **Kennedy** and **LBJ** and died there at the age of 90. For most of the time he was alone after his wife died there in 1944. **Kennedy** spent the first night of his honeymoon here, and **George W. Bush** visited his **father** in Suite 42-A, the official residence for U.S. Ambassadors to the UN. General MacArthur lived here, and the Duke of Windsor, later King Edward VIII, stayed.

12 W. 51st Street: **Cleveland** lived here in 1892.

Fifth and 53rd Street, NW corner: **Benjamin Harrison** was married at St. Thomas Episcopal to his second wife. (The present building replaced the one burned in 1907.)

705 Fifth Avenue at the NW corner of 55th, NW corner: **TR** attended Fifth Avenue Presbyterian* for the funeral of his mother and first wife in 1884 and his sister's and son's weddings. **Wilson** and **Carter** also attended the original church, dating to 1875.

2 W. 55th: **Hoover** lived in the Gotham Hotel from 1914 to 1917, now the Peninsula Hotel.*

6 W. 57th Street: **TR** lived here with his wife and mother, who both died here on Valentine's Day 1884. (South side of street just west of Fifth Avenue.) He walked from here 50 blocks to Columbia Law School in lower Manhattan.

Seventh Avenue and 57th: **TR** spoke at Carnegie Hall* in 1917.

North side of W. 57th, between Sixth and Seventh Ave.: **Clinton** attended Calvary Baptist* in 1993.

Fifth Avenue between 59th and 60th, now Sheray Netherland Building: **Hoover** lived here, 1903–4. It is on the west side of Fifth Avenue, across from the Plaza Hotel 59th Street, where **Kennedy** stayed and met with Judith Campbell.

421 E. 61st Street: Contrary to various sources, **John Adams** was never here at the site of land owned by his daughter.

689 Madison: **TR** rented in 1886 from his sister. A plaque on the SE corner with 62nd Street shows that he also lived here from 1895 to 1898.

810 Fifth Avenue: **Nixon** lived here, 1963–69, in a 12-room cooperative apartment at the NE corner of 62nd and Fifth Avenue, when Governor Rockefeller arranged for him to be accepted.

1335 Avenue of the Americas: **Carter, Ford, LBJ, Kennedy**, and **Reagan** stayed at the Hilton.*

49 E. 65th: **FDR** lived here from 1908 for several years and stayed periodically until 1943 in a

double house, with his mother at number 47, where he convalesced from polio on the fourth floor. (North side of street, east of Madison.)

142 E. 65th: **Nixon** lived here, 1980–81, in an apartment bought for $750,000 and sold for $2.9 million in 1981.

3 E. 66th: **Grant** lived from 1881 to 1885 in a house bought with donations of $350,000. It is marked. He fell on ice in front and was on crutches for months and a cane for the rest of his life. As noted in the plaque near the NE corner, he worked feverishly to finish his memoirs here before going to Mt. McGregor, where he died.

525 E. 68th: **Nixon** died at the Cornell Medical Center* in April 1994 after being taken from his home in Park Ridge, New Jersey.

801 Seventh Ave., Americana Hotel:* All presidents from **Kennedy** to **Carter** stayed here.

816 Madison: **Cleveland** lived here, 1889–1892.

Park Avenue: **Hoover** lived at three addresses, 876, 950, and 993, in 1920, all north of 70th.

United Nations Building:* Every president since **Truman** laid the cornerstone has addressed the UN. **George H.W. Bush** worked as ambassador from 1971 to 1973 on the eleventh floor of the U.S. Mission across First Avenue from UN Headquarters.

Madison and 35 E. 76th, NE corner: **Kennedy** stayed at the Carlyle Hotel. **Truman** usually stayed from 1953 to 1972 and had the same suite.

Fifth Ave. and 8 E. 76th Street: **FDR** married, with **TR** giving away the bride, his niece. (South side of street, just east of Fifth.)

Central Park West at 79th Street, Natural History Museum:* **Grant** laid the cornerstone, **Hayes** formally opened, and both **Roosevelts** contributed specimens.

82nd and 18th Avenue: **Washington's** headquarters in 1776.

West side Park Ave. between 83rd and 84th: **JFK** worshipped at St. Ignatius, his wife's childhood church, where her funeral was later held.

86th and 137 Riverside Drive: **Pierce** was at the Clarendon Hotel several weeks, 1859–1860.

89th and East River: **Washington** supervised the military installations.

Eighth Avenue and East End Avenue: Various presidents, including **John Quincy Adams** and most recent ones, have visited the Gracie Mansion* c. 1799–1804, at the river. **Washington** was on site during the Revolution.

60 Morningside Drive at 106th Street: In May 1948 **Eisenhower** served as president of Columbia University and lived at the university president's 21-room mansion until 1951. He spent most of his time upstairs, as the house was too palatial for his tastes. He was living here when elected to the presidency.

435 W. 116th: Columbia Law School was here when **FDR** attended, 1904–7.

Bronx, Yankee Stadium:* **George W. Bush** threw out the first pitch on October 10, 2001, as the first president to see a World Series game here. **Harding** saw Babe Ruth hit a home run on April 24, 1923, in the first shutout in the new stadium.

160–162nd and Edgecombe Ave.: **Washington's** headquarters in 1776 were at the Morris-Jumel Mansion,* where he lived on the second floor. Afterwards the British used it until evacuation in 1783. **Washington**, the **Adamses**, and **Jefferson** visited in 1790.

622 W. 168th: **FDR** was treated at Presbyterian Hospital for polio in 1921 and 1938.

183–185th Streets and Fort Washington Blvd.: **Washington** was at Fort Washington during and after the Revolutionary War, NE of the present George Washington Bridge.

233rd and 3701 Provost Avenue: **John Adams** stayed for two months, escaping the yellow fever epidemic while he was president.

242nd Street and North Riverside: **Washington** occupied the Van Cortlandt House* "a number of times during the Revolution" and for a short time afterward. Evidently he was here in 1776, and then near the end in 1781 to meet with French General Rochambeau to plan final strategy, and then again in 1783 to form a triumphant march into the city as the British evacuated. He was also at the Van Cortlandt Manor House on SR 9 at Harmon, two miles north of Ossining.

675 West 252nd Street:* **Theodore Roosevelt** was at the Wave Hill House.

SE corner 252nd and 5040 Independence: **Kennedy** lived from 1928 until 1929. He went to the Riverdale County Day School on Fieldstone Rd. from 1926 to 1928, and claimed that when he grew up he would be president.

294 Pondfield Road in Bronxville: **Kennedy** lived from 1929 to 1942 in the nicest house in town. It no longer survives. He attended St. Joseph's, 15 Cedar.

NIAGARA FALLS • **Lincoln** supposedly visited the falls in September 1848, probably with the family (Mary, Robert, and Eddie), on the way back from a New England speaking tour, although there is some question if the family was with him then or if he was at the falls then. But they all were clearly here on July 24, 1857, when he signed, "A. **Lincoln** and Family, Springfield, Illinois." They stayed on the American side at the Cataract House, located generally between the present Comfort Inn and Goat Island, west of Main between the two bridges to Goat Island. The register from the hotel, showing **Lincoln's** signature, is in the city library. **Franklin Roosevelt**, Churchill, and the future Edward VII of Great Britain also stayed there. Mary Lincoln came back in 1861 to stay in the International Hotel, across the street north of the Cataract and south of Falls Avenue, where **Johnson** and **Grant** stayed in 1866. **McKinley** was there on the day he was assassinated in 1901. His assassin came too, could not get close enough, and carried out the deed later. **Taylor** visited the same sites in 1850, as have many other presidents over the years.

The Niagara Falls Museum has a register to show that **Lincoln** came when the museum was near the river bluff on the Canadian side, down from the Horseshoe Falls; no doubt he arrived via the 1855 railroad suspension bridge. He may have gone across the Maid of the Mist Ferry in 1848. **Lincoln** jokingly said that he wondered where all the water came from. A register shows that they went to Goat Island and surely to Terrapin Point, where a prominent tower then gave a spectacular view. That point of the island no longer exists. The museum's register also shows that **Grant** visited. **McKinley** also went to Goat Island just before he was killed; he went only halfway across the suspension bridge, as it was against protocol to set foot in a foreign country.

OYSTER BAY • **Washington** visited the area in 1790 and slept in Sagtikos Manor, Appleneck, Bay Shore and Roslyn. In the latter he had breakfast at Henry Onderdock's on Main Street and made several sheets of paper, now displayed in the local library, at the Roslyn Paper Mill. In Oyster Bay he stayed at Mr. Young's on Cove Beach Road.

Theodore Roosevelt's home is preserved here as Sagamore Hill National Historical Site,* three miles east via Main Street and Cove Neck Road. The area had been a favorite haunt in his late boyhood, when he roamed spotting and shooting various small game. As he grew older he romped here with his sweetheart, told her that this was his favorite place in the world, and promised to build a home for her here. After marriage the home was planned; she died, but the home was started anyway two weeks later. He then went west, letting his sister Anna (Bamie) settle here with his infant daughter. After marrying again in London he brought his new wife home in 1887. Theodore Jr., Kermit, and Ethel were later born here. (His last two children were born in **Washington**.) This was the summer home when he lived elsewhere, and here he received official notifications of his nominations for the governorship of New York in 1898, vice presidency in 1900, and presidency in 1904. He hosted a conference of college men, including **Wilson**, here in 1901 as vice president to determine how to get students into politics.

Although other presidents went home for extended periods, the telephone made this a more fully working summer White House, at least until Teddy, suffering from nearsightedness, mistakenly chopped down the telephone pole. Here the six children and innumerable cousins, including **Franklin Roosevelt** and his future wife Eleanor, played tennis and other games, rode, boxed, wrestled, swam, went on arduous hikes, shot a .22 rifle, and courted, 13-year-old Alice with 15-year-old **FDR**. When his youngest son got his first rifle, too late in the day to try it outside, **TR** took the boy upstairs and let him take the first shot into the ceiling, warning him not tell his mother. He once went in swimming with the kids and got chilled, and upon their returning home, Mrs. Roosevelt made all the children go to bed after taking a dose of ginger syrup. His wife believed her most troublesome "child" was **Theodore**. When the kids complained to their father, he told them, "I'm afraid there's nothing I can do. I'm lucky that she did not give me a dose of ginger too."

The home was the scene of many domestic and foreign policy conferences taking place in the library or piazza constructed in 1905. **TR** became the first man to be elected after succeeding to the office, and made a pledge he came to regret, that he would not run again, called the worst mistake of his life and one of the greatest presidential blunders in history. The statement weakened his second term, forced him to give up the office, and provoked a statement that he would have cut off his right hand to take it back. Maybe he could not imagine life after the age at which his father died. He was only fifty at the end of his second term. He did not run in 1908, when he probably would have been elected then to a third term, but spent the rest of his life seeking the power that he gave up. Bolting the Republican Party that nominated **Taft**, **Roosevelt** ran in 1912 on an independent ticket, got more votes than the Republican incumbent, but angered the party enough not to be considered in 1916, when he might have won. Ironically his loss in 1912 paved the way for the victor, **Wilson**, to promote **Franklin Roosevelt's** career by naming him assistant secretary of the Navy, allowing him to follow Teddy's path to the presidency. **TR** was again a leading candidate for the 1920 nomination, when he would have been only 61, but the apparently vigorous physical fitness advocate died here in 1919 at the age of 60. His grave* is a short distance away on Main Street at Young Memorial Cemetery.

Harding and **Taft** attended his funeral at Christ Episcopal,* 61 East Main, **Roosevelt's** church. **Taft** had been **Roosevelt's** best friend, but the two had become bitter enemies. **Taft** openly wept over the grave. **Theodore's** widow lived here until her death in 1948. **Eisenhower** and **Hoover** dedicated the public opening of the home in 1953.

PAWLING • **Washington** made his headquarters in the fall of 1778 in the John Kane House,* 126 East Main, south of the Couiter Avenue intersection, west of Route 22. Kane was a Tory and was forced to leave his home. Only the kitchen is believed to be a part of the original house.

PERRY • As a boy, **Arthur** lived from 1835 until 1837 at 7 Elm Street as well as several other parsonages as his father served the Baptist Church of Perry at 77 N. Main.

PLATTSBURG • **Harding** (1917) and **Coolidge** (1924) both stayed at the Witherill Hotel, 25 Margaret. **McKinley** attended three churches here in 1897: the Methodist Episcopal at 19 Oak, First Presbyterian at 34 Brinkerhoff, and Bluff Point Trinity Episcopal on Trinity Square.

POESTENKILL • A marker is in front of the church where **Garfield** preached and conducted a school to earn tuition to Williams College.

RHINEBECK • **Washington** watched troops in the square and stayed in the Beekman Arms at 4 Mill Street, one of the oldest and most historic hotels in America. **Van Buren** and **FDR** also stayed.

ROME • **Madison** came here with Lafayette in October 1784 for eight days to negotiate a treaty with the Indians at Fort Stanwix,* prominently restored in the center of town. They traveled through the Oriskany Battlefield ravine nearby, where the battle began.

RYE • The stage stop known as the Square House* or Haviland Inn, west of the Green at One Purchase Street, was turned into city hall. **Washington** called it "A very neat and decent Inn" when he stayed in 1789. **John Adams** and Lafayette also stayed and danced in the second-floor ballroom. **George H.W. Bush** married here in Barbara's hometown at First Presbyterian at 882 Boston Post Road. She lived at 25 Onondaga, where he courted her.

SACKETT'S HARBOR • **Monroe** saw a fireworks display in 1817, when he also inspected Madison Barracks and Fort Pike. He also then toured other New York towns including Altona, Malone, Plattsburg, and Ogdenburg. **Grant** served in the army here twice, once in 1848 when he was ordered here by mistake, and later when he chose this post after Detroit Barracks was reduced in 1851. His family came also, including his oldest son. They attended the Presbyterian church, and **Grant** even pledged to give up drinking, joining the Sons of Temperance. He took his Masonic Degrees in the Temple, and also stayed the Union Hotel, now a visitor center at the NW corner of Ray and West Main. They lived in Madison Barracks* on Pike Street around an oval-shaped parade ground, the quarters to the left of the sally port, at the east village line. When part of the post burned in 1877, **Grant** was able to have it rebuilt, and it remains open today. This was the **Grants'** happiest place. He left from here for California. Julia, who was eight months pregnant, wanted to travel with him, but agreed to go to her home by way of **Grant's** family home in Ohio, where their second child was born. This was a blessing, as all children with **Grant**'s party died crossing Panama to get to the Pacific. **Grant** came back in 1854 to collect payment from an absconding California business partner, but he left town when he heard **Grant** was coming, not the last time **Grant** was swindled.

SAGTIKOS MANOR, WEST BAY SHORE, LONG ISLAND • At 15 First Avenue is Sagtikos Manor,* dating to about 1692, where **Washington** stayed in 1790. General Sir Henry Clinton was an unwanted guest during the Revolution. The British used the Union Depot in the village author Robert Lewis Stevenson called the "Switzerland of the Adirondacks."

SARANAC LAKE • Several presidents vacationed at this mountain retreat, including **Arthur** and **Cleveland** in 1881 and 1884 at Camp Alpha,

Coolidge in White Pines in 1926, and **McKinley** two miles south in Hotel Champlain.

SARATOGA SPRINGS • It is claimed that 18 presidents visited here. **Washington** visited the High Rock Spring, High Rock Avenue opposite Rock Street, in 1783 with the possibility of exploitation in mind. **Washington** had visited the nearby Saratoga Battlefield, as did **Jefferson** and **Madison** on their 1791 New England trip.

Van Buren stayed at the United States Hotel in Saratoga at Broadway and Division and the Congress Hotel at Broadway and Spring, as did **Wilson** much later. **Fillmore** was here at the New Congress in 1869 after the old hotel burned in 1866. **Taft** stayed there between 1909 and 1913. **Arthur** proposed to his future wife on the porch at the United States Hotel. Both **Roosevelts** have also visited the town.

Grant was at the Grand Union Hotel, on Broadway between Washington and Congress, in July 1865 and several times while president. **B. Harrison** stayed in 1891. **Grant** accepted a warm and shrewd invitation to stay here in a mountain cabin* at Mount McGregor, ten miles north of Saratoga Springs, near Wilton, for six weeks prior to his death on July 23, 1885. Here he struggled to complete his memoirs. His illness was common knowledge, and his presence attracted many to an area being developed. This is clearly marked off Highway 9 at Ballard Road to Corinth Mountain Road, and remains much as it was when **Grant** died here, with his chairs, bed, tables, clock, etc., as they were when he died. However, it is on the grounds of a correctional facility, and the grounds are closed when the house is not officially open.

Grant had suffered financial reverses and was almost penniless, but had sold to Mark Twain the rights to his unwritten memoirs that he knew must be completed to provide security to his family. He felt that the summer heat of New York City would make it difficult to concentrate, and so moved here on June 16, 1885. In July, Twain arrived to assure him that he would earn at least $300,000, and they did earn $450,000. He wrote mostly on the porch or on a grassy area about 200 feet away from the house and marked today. He didn't seem to mind as tourists strolled by in a steady stream as he waved or tipped his hat. Confederate General Buckner, from whom **Grant** had demanded "unconditional surrender" at Fort Donelson, also came. The manuscript was finished on July 11 and revised until the 19th. Because of his illness he had to sleep sitting up in two leather armchairs, his feet in one. Almost near death, in a coma and without his consent, Grant was sprinkled in baptism by a minister, something that his pious Methodist mother was never able to accomplish. The chairs are still here, as is the clock, stopped by his son when he died. *The Personal Memoirs of U.S.* ***Grant*** is ranked among the finest military memoirs ever written.

SCHUYLERVILLE • British General Burgoyne burned General Philip Schuyler's home* here before the nearby Battle of Saratoga. Burgoyne had used it for headquarters and did not want the Americans to use it during the campaign that he lost, changing the course of the war. Schuyler immediately had it rebuilt, and **Washington** was hosted in June 1782 on a visit to review troops, and again in July 1783 to visit Forts Edward, Crown Point, and Ticonderoga before continuing to Saratoga Springs. This is now a part of the Saratoga National Historical Park.* **Jefferson** and **Madison** made a similar trip through the area in May and June 1791, visiting the forts mentioned and crossing the Hudson near Fort Edward at the present Northumberland Bridge. Their friend **Monroe** was too poor to come with them and had to practice law and farm to build up his cash.

SLOATSBURG • The Smith Tavern is at the southern edge on SR 17, at exit 15A off I-87, and was where **Washington** stopped in June 1775 to send instructions to General Wayne, copies of which hung on the wall for years.

TAPPAN • **Washington** used the De Wint House,* 20 Livingston and Oak Tree Road, as his headquarters four times during the Revolutionary War, including September 28 until October 26, 1780. During this time, the British officer considered a spy, John André, was tried and hanged. Here **Washington** gave command of West Point to a favorite, Benedict Arnold, who immediately wrote to the British commander at New York City, offering to turn over the garrison. The British sent Major John André to arrange details, but he foolishly changed into civilian clothes, meaning if he were captured, it would be as a spy, not a military prisoner. Arnold and André met at the site of the State Rehabilitation Hospital, just north of West Haverstraw, two miles south of Stony Point on Route 9W, at the home now known as the Treason House. Upon returning to British lines, André was stopped at Tarrytown at what is now the André Monument at northern end of village on Route 9. Soldiers searched everything, including his boots, and found incriminating documents revealing the deception.

TARRYTOWN • **Pierce** visited Washington Irving's home, Sunnyside* at Tarrytown. **Ford, Reagan** and **Nixon** visited Governor Rockefeller at 555 Bedford in North Tarrytown.

At the moment **Washington** was arriving at the Robinson House, Arnold's headquarters, on the east side of the Hudson at Glenclyffe as he intended to visit West Point, Arnold received word at West Point and fled. (See West Point.)

André was kept in the nearby Seventy-Six House, also known as the Yoast Mabie Tavern, on the SW corner of Washington and Main, and tried across the street in a church then on the site of the present (1835) Reformed Dutch Church on the NE corner. **Washington** and his officers were hosted there. British General Clinton met General Greene at Dobbs Ferry to try to save the popular André. (These are near Sleepy Hollow Church, bridge, and burying ground, made famous by Washington Irving's *Legend of Sleepy Hollow*.) He was executed on André Hill, André Hill Road out West Tappan Road, a continuation of Washington Street, .4 of a mile from the historic area. All sites are marked. He requested a soldier's death by firing squad, but was hanged, considered a humiliating death, in retaliation for the unceremonious hanging of patriot Nathan Hale in New York City. In 1821 British authorities requested that André's body be given in return for that of General Richard Montgomery, killed at Quebec in 1775. The owner of the land where it was buried agreed, even though he had turned down offers from speculators who wanted to purchase the land. André's body is now in Westminster Abbey. Montgomery is buried in the front of St. Paul's in New York City.

In 1783 **Washington** again used the De Wint House. British commander Sir Guy Carleton came ashore to meet with **Washington** at nearby Piermont and continued to the De Wint House to discuss peace terms and withdrawal of British forces. Upon **Washington's** return to Carleton's flagship, the British for the first time saluted the flag of the United States.

WESTFIELD • **Lincoln** stopped at the depot to meet eleven-year-old Grace Bedell to see how she liked the whiskers that she suggested he grow. He told the crowd he had a friend in town and surprised everyone by asking Grace to come forward to shake hands and kiss the president-elect.

WEST POINT VICINITY • This is America's oldest military post, where the country's flag has flown continuously. **Washington** called it "the key to America." His headquarters were at the Moore House on Route 9D about 5.5 miles north of Bear Mountain Bridge from July 21 until November 27, 1779. He came back in late September 1780 to inspect fortifications where his favorite warrior was in charge. As he neared, Benedict Arnold, the greatest combat commander on either side, was fleeing southward after having been warned that his co-conspirator, British Major John André, had been captured. Arnold felt slighted by Congress, was plagued by financial difficulties, and was urged by his young wife to enter into an agreement with the British to allow the capture of West Point. When **Washington** arrived at his headquarters on the east or opposite side of the river, the Robinson House, then known as Beverly, with Lafayette and Alexander Hamilton, he was told that Arnold had to make a trip across the river. **Washington** followed him across to West Point and then returned later that day to the house, where he learned of Arnold's betrayal from captured material. Arnold's wife Peggy, very much involved in the plot, pleaded such shock and fits of hysteria that she was not charged or held. **Washington**, at first mentally immobilized, regained his abilities and stayed for several days as the plot was uncovered, the fort made stronger, and André brought here and then taken to Tappan. The Beverly site was once marked opposite and just south of West Point, south of Garrison on the east side of Route 9D about a half a mile south of the Garrison Road (Route 403) intersection, but no marker is there as of the end of 2004. There is a marker for Arnold's escape route on the west side of 9D. Beverly was then on the east side just south of that marker. Both sites are south of the Glencliffe facility and Beverly Road. **Washington** was also at West Point from November 14 to 18, 1783.

Just south, two miles north of Peekskill on U.S. 9, is the Van Cortlandt Manor House, where **Washington** often stayed. **Washington** visited the Mandeville House, marked, and still at the NW corner of SR 9D and CR 403, on July 26, 1779, as shown by his expense record. This is west opposite the library. East of the library on the nearest hill, a bald spot is visible, marking the spot of **Washington's** visit to South Redoubt—

sometimes called "Middle Redoubt"—where mounds and gun emplacements are still visible. A trail leads to the top. His visit here caused him to miss breakfast and Arnold.

Almost every president beginning with **Monroe** has visited West Point. **Houston** was on the Congressional Board of Visitors and came annually to inspect. **Jackson** reviewed **Davis's** class. **Grant** came in 1839 to take the admissions test. It is sometimes said, although disputed, that he did not want or expect to pass, as he had no interest in being a soldier. His name was "Hiram Ulysses," but there was no such name on the register. The congressman who had obtained the appointment evidently did not know the correct name and had assumed that it was "Ulysses S." (The "S" is sometimes said to mean "Simpson," his mother's maiden name, but he said it meant nothing. While at Camp Salubrity in Louisiana, he wrote to his future wife, "Find some name beginning with "S" for me ... I have an "S" in my name and don't know what it means." So he shared with **Truman** a meaningless "S" for a middle initial.) Now the young man, who to his surprise and disappointment passed the test, could not be admitted unless he changed his name, which he did, since it was easier than changing a bureaucratic foul-up. It was just as well; he did not like his initials on his luggage, HUG. And his new initials, U.S., sounded so patriotic that they gave him a new nickname, "Uncle Sam," or Sam, that he carried for the rest of his life. (Actually, earlier in Ohio, during the Civil War, and even for years afterward with some die-hard Confederates, his nickname was "Useless." Contrary to most biographies that show **Grant**'s reluctance and unwillingness to go, he wrote in his *Memoirs* that "he had no objection" to going here and always liked to travel.

Cadet **Davis** came back drunk from a popular tavern late at night and almost fell off a steep cliff. **Lincoln** made a "mysterious" last-minute trip to see General Winfield Scott on June 24, 1862, to seek advice at his retirement summer home. His train passed to and from New York City and from Dock Street Ferry at Garrison across from West Point. While here, he stayed at the Cozzens (or Couzzens) Hotel, where Scott was living, on the hill behind the new West Point Museum near the main street in Highland Falls. (**Grant** visited Scott there in 1865.) A historical marker at the Abrams Gate from the town to West Point states "This is the site..." of the hotel, but the site is now a parking lot for the Five Star Hotel, up the hill from the marker, near the bluff overlooking the Hudson River, recently occupied by the Ladycliff Academy.

Eisenhower came here to get a free education only because he could not get into the Naval Academy, since he was too old.

Several old buildings remain at West Point that **Lincoln** must have seen, including the 1837 chapel, the 1841 library at Jefferson and Cullum, and the 1820 superintendent's quarters on Jefferson Road, where Robert E. Lee had lived when in that position.

NORTH CAROLINA

ASHEVILLE • The Grove Park Inn at 290 Macon has seen **Taft, Coolidge, Hoover,** and **FDR. McKinley** stayed at the Glen Rock Hotel in 1897, 400 Depot. **Wilson** stayed at the Eagle at the corner of Eagle and Biltmore, two blocks from the square, and at the Swannanoa, 49 Biltmore.

CHAPEL HILL • **Polk** went to the university and was at Old Chapel in Old East Hall at various times from 1816 and lodged on the third floor of New College. He was also at Hilliard's Hotel, later the Eagle, and then Chapel Hill Hotel fronting Franklin Street. He came back for a reception at Gerald Hall in 1847. **Buchanan** (1860), **Johnson** (1867), and **Kennedy** (1961) spoke here.

CHARLOTTE • The town center still is Trade and Tryon Streets. The first courthouse was there in the center of Independence Square, where in May 1775, the Mecklenburg Convention issued a Declaration of Independence and the Mecklenburg Resolves. The finest house in town, the

Thomas Polk Home, was on the NE corner, but marked on the SW corner where the tallest building in town is now. He was a kinsman to the future president. British General Cornwallis used it for headquarters, and **Washington** later stayed on his 1791 tour. A short distance west of Trade Street is a tablet marking the site of Cook's Inn, where **Washington** was entertained.

Jackson was at Queen's College at 301 Tryon on the SE corner of Third and Tryon from 1783 to 1784. Later the school's name was changed to Liberty Hall.

Davis fled to the Bates home at Tryon and Fourth in his flight from the victorious Union army. He spent a week, from April 19 to 26, 1865, in the home of a Massachusetts Yankee, where he got a telegram that Lincoln had been assassinated. He expressed the view that, if true, he feared it would be disastrous for his people, not because he shed tears for Lincoln, but because he feared the new president. He also heard from Lee as his old commander set out details of the surrender terms and explained that he had to surrender since supplies had not reached him. **Davis** and the cabinet also worshipped in an earlier St. Peter's Church on North Tryon. The Confederate president was unnerved when the preacher glared in his direction in denouncing the Lincoln assassination. Cabinet meetings were held at **Davis's** office at 122 S. Tryon, the Bank of Carolina Building (marked). On April 26 they adjourned to William Phifer Home at 722 N. Tryon, to consult with the Secretary of the Treasury Trenholm, who was ill and a guest there. **Davis** was livid with rage at his longtime problem general Joseph Johnston, who had just surrendered against **Davis's** wishes to General William T. Sherman. **Davis** had wanted his army to escape to the west and keep fighting. This is sometimes called the last full cabinet meeting.

George H.W. Bush, Carter, and **Clinton** helped dedicate the Billy Graham Museum in May 2007. Graham said he that he felt like he was attending his own funeral. It is located off the Billy Graham Parkway, west of I-77 at 4330 Westmont.

CONCORD • Nearby is the site of the Pheifer home, where **Washington** had been a guest, marked one and a half mile west of the U.S. 29/601 bypass and SR 1394, Popular Tent Road. He also had lunch with Major Robert Smith at Smithfield, five miles west of Concord on the Old Charlotte Road. He was upset to learn that he had left his powder puff in Charlotte. **Davis** spent the night of April 18, 1865, in a house marked on Union Street, U.S. 29A, as he fled the Yankees.

DAVIDSON • **Wilson** stayed in room 13, Old Chambers Hall, in the center of the campus when he attended Davidson College in 1873. He came here at age 16 to study for the ministry, but soon had to withdraw because of ill health. Many old buildings dating to the mid–1800s remain. He made his first speech at the Eumenean Literary Society Building and stayed at a boarding house next to the 1848 Carolina Inn, Depot and Main, at the site of the present computer center.

DURHAM • **Nixon** went to Duke Law School from 1934 until 1937 and lived at 814 Clarendon. He worked in the library and went to Friends Meeting House, 404 Alexander. While a student in Georgetown, **Clinton** brought his stepfather to the Duke Chapel and visited him on weekends during the older man's cancer treatments at Duke Medical Center.

EDENTON • **Monroe** was welcomed at the courthouse on East King in 1819 with a 21-gun salute. He also visited Washington and Roanoke Island.

GREENSBORO • **Washington** toured nearby Guilford Courthouse Battlefield,* well marked off Battlefield Avenue and U.S. 220 north of Greensboro. Here patriots lost an important battle, but helped win the war by depleting the British strength. **George H.W. Bush** gave a commemoration speech on the battlefield in 1976. **Jackson** spent a short time in town practicing law and stayed at the McNairy House,* 1130 Summit Avenue. **Davis** and his cabinet met at 300 Elm and McGee (marked), April 12–13, 1865. He was not well received here as antiwar feeling was growing. **Davis** was for continuing the war even when Lee's dispatch explaining his April 9 surrender to **Grant** reached the cabinet. Generals Johnston and Beauregard, **Davis's** top field commanders, meeting with the president, believed, "It would be the greatest of human crimes for us to attempt to continue the war." All but one of the cabinet agreed. **Davis**, who wanted to fight a guerrilla war in the hills, broke down and wept bitterly as his aides left him alone. Official word of Lee's surrender arrived on the 13th. **Davis** then decided to go to Charlotte. Union cavalry had cut the railroad so the fleeing Confederates had to ride in the rain, camping out as people feared reprisals if they used their homes. Johnston went back to meet with

General Sherman and ultimately surrendered against **Davis's** orders. **Davis** then escalated their bitter lifelong feud.

GREENVILLE • **Washington** is believed to have eaten in a tavern then at 200 E. Fourth at Cotanche Street in April 1791, as he traveled from Tarboro to New Bern on his Southern tour. His route is marked north at Halifax on the 16th and 17th, and in Tarboro, where he stayed April 18 at the Exum Lewis home near the junction of State Routes 1409 and 1428. He was not much impressed and referred to the stop as "a trifling place called Greenville," but he used "very trifling" for Charlotte. Family journals recorded that he stated it "was a dirty little mudhole on the Tar." But it was the momentous occasion of the century for the little town, from which all other events were measured, even though there are no surviving records of any particulars about the visit. He must have made quite a scene since he traveled in a style unimaginable to the backwoods areas. His coach, or chariot as some referred to it, was trimmed in gilt and enameled with his coat of arms and pastoral scenes. He had a coachman, footman, and outriders with smartly tailored uniforms of scarlet and white. Meticulous about his appearance, he powdered his wig and polished his boots several times a day, and stopped before arriving in each town to change into a fresh set of attire.

He probably spent the night in Shadrach Allen's Crown Point Inn seven miles east of Ayden. On April 20, he ate at Col. John Allen's plantation home, marked on NC 55 at Fort Barnwell. He thought it was a public house, ordered breakfast from the startled hostess, and then found out, to his embarrassment, that it was a private home that he said he would not impose on during the tour. He refused the feast offered and just took a boiled egg and coffee with rum.

LEXINGTON • As **Davis** and several cabinet members fled at the end of the Civil War, they spent the night in a pine grove marked by a historical marker on U.S. 29 and 70, four miles east.

NEW BERN • Tyron Palace,* 613 Pollock, called the most beautiful building in Colonial America, was used by royal governors, the last of whom made a precipitous flight in 1775. **Washington** visited for two days in 1791 and observed that it was "now hastening to Ruins." His diary noted 70 ladies at a ball that evening, most of whom danced with him. After drinking many toasts in his honor, he retired at 1:00 A.M. as the ball continued. The president danced the first dance with the daughter of Colonel Joseph Leech and then visited his home at the SW corner of Front and Change for a small party. The Palace ceased to be used by the government a few years later and burned in 1798, but has been carefully and beautifully restored to be a showplace today.

Washington spent April 20 and 21 at the Stanly home,* now in front of the Palace, at 307 George Street. Then it was in the street near the SW corner of New and Middle, where it was noted and visited by Union soldiers during the Civil War. Lafayette visited it in 1825. General Burnside used it as his headquarters, and Confederate General Lewis Armistead was born in it. It was later moved back to where the federal building is now and then moved to its present location. It contains much of the same woodwork and floors.

Washington and later **Monroe** attended Christ Church* at 320 Pollock Street. The present church was built in 1858, but the old structure's foundations are marked adjacent. Young boys had shouted, "Off with his head," outside the church during the Revolution when the rector offered a prayer for King George. On April 23, Washington stayed further south at Sage's Inn, 200 yards east on U.S. 17, in Onslow County at Pender County line, and at Shine's Inn, seven miles southwest of NC 12/41 intersection, Jones County, both marked.

Monroe was entertained at the Coor-Bishop House, 501 East Front, and at a dinner at the Masonic Hall, 516 Hancock. **Truman** attended services at First Baptist,* 239 Middle, just after his 1948 election, to the disgust of many, who were inconvenienced by his motorcade.

PINEVILLE • **Polk**'s reconstructed birthplace cabin* is about a half-mile south on U.S. 521, just south of Charlotte at exit 64, Interstate 285. **Polk** lived here for eleven years, with nine siblings and five slaves, before moving to Tennessee. The replica cabin, made from material dating from about 1835, was reconstructed in the mid-twentieth century and dedicated by **Lyndon Johnson** in 1968, as he stood on the steps. The exact location of the original birthplace cabin is unknown, and has not been discovered by metal detectors or satellite pictures. It was probably closer to the highway where the creek flowed. An original well is on the west side of the cabin. Several original pieces of **Polk** furniture are displayed, including his college desk from Chapel Hill. **Polk's** old church, Providence Presbyterian, built by slaves, is on NC 16 south of Charlotte toward Waxhaw. His mother brought him there to be baptized when he was very young, but the preacher would not unless his parents made professions of faith. The father refused and quarreled with the preacher, and **Polk** remained unbaptized until his deathbed.

RALEIGH • **Andrew Johnson's** 1808 birthplace site is on Union Square, east across from the State House, at 123 Fayetteville at the corner with Morgan Street, where his father was a janitor. The small cabin was then in the yard of Casso's Inn. **Johnson** returned in 1845 to investigate his paternity and 1867 when he visited the old cabin. It was later moved to Carrabus Street, where much of it was dismantled for souvenirs. A replica cabin,* sometimes claimed to have some original material, is located on the North Carolina State University Campus, 1 Mimosa Street.

Church services at the time of his birth were being held in the State House across the street, and **Johnson** may have been baptized there. The building burned in 1810. He was probably born into the lowest level of poverty of any president. When **Andrew** was three, his father died from overexertion in helping to rescue two friends from drowning. Congressman **Johnson** came to Raleigh in the 1840s to visit his father's grave in the city cemetery, at South East and East Hargett Streets, just inside the gate at a stone marked "JJ." He returned as president to dedicate a monument over the grave.

Andrew was apprenticed out at age fourteen to a cruel taskmaster and fled the slave-like conditions at sixteen when he threw rocks at a neighbor's window and got caught. (He and **Fillmore** were indentured and are called the two slave presidents.) He returned to ask forgiveness, but was refused, meaning that he could not be hired elsewhere, and had to move to Tennessee.

Grant met General Sherman at the Haywood House, NW corner of Blount at 127 Edenton, to discuss the surrender terms that Sherman had offered General Joseph Johnston, considered too generous by the secretary of war. **FDR** called the governor's mansion at 200 N. Blount the most beautiful in America. **TR, Buchanan,** and **Van Buren** have visited the Capitol, and **Truman** dedicated the statute of the three presidents on the grounds.

SALISBURY • **Washington** was here in 1791 and spoke at the courthouse on the square, Main and Innes. It has long since disappeared, as have all other structures mentioned. His journey was tiring on the bumpy, primitive roads, and he stopped to get something to eat at the Brandon House, site marked on the west side of Route 29, Main Street, five and a half miles south of town. No one was home but Betsy, who was about twelve years old. She said that all the family had gone to town to see President **Washington**, and she was not sure whether if she could fix him anything. He told her if she fixed breakfast, that she would be the first to see the president. She did, and when he left he told her to tell "your people when they get home that you not only saw George **Washington** before they did, but that he kissed you."

He also spoke and probably stayed at 201 S. Main (SE corner with Fisher Street), where **Jackson** had lived in 1785. The 59-year-old president told the people, "My friends, you see nothing before you but a gray-headed old man." **Washington** was also entertained at the Yarborough House, 118 N. Main, where there was a ball. Several sources indicate that he stayed at this location rather than the one mentioned above.

Seventeen-year-old **Jackson** moved here at the end of 1784 and studied law under Spruce Macay for two years, one block west of the marker on U.S. 29, at 200 W. Fisher Street. (This is the only **Washington** or **Jackson** marker in town.) The 1760 town well remains on the property. British General Cornwallis's headquarters were half a block south on the SW corner of Church and Bank. Actually **Jackson**, who was admitted to the bar here, was said to have spent more time in the stable and raising hell than with law books and was known to be the leader of all the rowdies and misfits in the community. He paid his room and board from card playing, winning mostly from the owner of his lodging. He attended dancing school so much that he was asked to manage the Christmas ball, and invited, as a joke, the two "fanciest" prostitutes in town, who actually appeared, to the dismay of the respectable society. He went to Third Presbyterian between Iredell and Thyatira Streets, although his rival for the hand of his sweetheart also went here, and **Jackson** lost the contest.

SALEM • **Washington** stayed two nights at the Salem Tavern,* 800 S. Main, between West and Walnut, from May 31 until June 2, 1791, probably in the northeast corner bedroom, and attended the Salem Church. He came up the route of today's Highway 150. The Moravian brass band played as he ate in the inn. The Moravians gave him a tour of the town including workshops,* choir houses,* the Single Brother's House* at 600 S. Main, and Boy's School, now the Wachovia Museum* at the NE corner of Main and Academy. The latter building dates to 1794, but the other buildings are original. The tavern and Stanly house in New Bern are the only structures in the state still standing where he stayed.

A nervous 13-year-girl played the piano. **Washington** thought that he was being helpful when he told her how to get rid of a wart, but she "fled in humiliation." The piano is now in the c. 1769 Vierling House,* 463 Church, although the story is questioned by those who feel that **Washington** would not have been so insensitive. The president had only planned to stay one day, and preparations and food supplies for the party were planned accordingly. But he learned that the governor was hurrying here to meet him, so he stayed another day, causing the staff of the hotel to scurry for more provisions. The Old Salem historical area, including the structures mentioned, is restored and open for tours.

Jackson is also claimed to have been admitted to the bar in Richmond, North Carolina, several miles northwest at Highway 67 and the Yadkin River. It also serves the distinction of being the only town in the state to be completely destroyed by a cyclone, and nothing remains.

George H.W. Bush stayed in the Robert E. Lee Hotel, W. 5th and Cherry, when winning the Eastern championship with the Yale baseball team in 1948. The hotel was torn down in 1972, with the Embassy Suites now on site. **Bush** and Dukakis debated on national TV at Wait Chapel, Wake Forest University, in 1988.

WAXHAW • George McKemey's (also "McAmey" or "McCamie") cabin, one of **Jackson**'s "two birthplaces," is a few miles south of a marker at the west end of town down Rehobeth Road at the border. North Carolina claims him and gives evidence that he was born here. (See Lancaster, South Carolina.) His mother was traveling to see both her sisters at the time he was born, and there remains a question as to which home was the site. Jackson's father had died shortly before his birth. Both aunt's cabins were then in South Carolina, but the boundaries were fixed in 1813 with McKemey then in North Carolina. Mrs. **Jackson** and her sons lived with the Crawfords in South Carolina, and **Jackson** himself said he was born there, as pointed out on the South Carolina markers. Some biographers and "oral tradition" put the birth here. The McKemey site is noted with a monument on a dead-end dirt road, Old Church Road, just east of Mt. Zion Baptist Church. The monument is made with hearthstones and chimney stones from the cabin. This can be reached from signs near the South Carolina State Park also. Young **Jackson** visited often and lived at McKemey's for a while after his mother died.

WILMINGTON • **Washington** came in 1791 and was to stay at Dorsey's Tavern, on the east side of Front Street between Princes and Market. He possibly ate there, but when he arrived his room was not ready. As he waited he asked the owner about the water, and Dorsey replied that he could not speak on the subject because he never drank it. So a widow with a large family then gave up her house, noted by a marker on the SE corner of Front and Dock. **Washington** walked around town and was surely shown Cornwallis's imposing headquarters at 224 Market,* the SE corner of Third. The basement was a prison for rebels. He attended a grand ball at the Assembly Hall on the east side of Front between Orange and Ann.

A marker across the street on the SW corner of Front and Dock notes that Senator John C. Calhoun was entertained there in 1819. This was on his trip with **Monroe**, who surely must have seen or visited also, although not mentioned on any marker found in town or in historical data in the library. He also saw Fort Johnson,* on Bay Street in Southport, a few miles south. **Taft** is pictured reviewing school children on the corner of Front and Dock.

Thomas Woodrow **Wilson** lived on Third from 1874 to 1882 with his family, as his father was pastor from 1874 to 1885 at First Presbyterian, reconstructed at Third and Orange, noted with a marker on Third. The marker also notes his home at the Manse on the corner of Fourth and Orange, now the church playground. He was also a guest of the Robinsons on the NE corner of Front and Nun. **Taft** was a guest at the SE corner, both original and marked. While at Davidson, "Tommy" suffered a digestive disorder. His father purchased a high-wheel bicycle for him, thinking it would correct the problem. He once came down the steep incline on Orange so fast that he plunged into the river. He also liked to swim in the river at the foot of Dock Street.

NORTH DAKOTA

BISMARCK • **Theodore Roosevelt** spoke in front of the Old Capitol in 1903, as well as in Fargo and Jamestown. He also visited the Governor's Mansion, 320 Ave. B. **Wilson** visited the Old Capitol in 1919, as did **FDR** in 1920. That building was replaced in 1934 and visited by **George H.W. Bush** in 1989 when he dedicated an American Elm near the steps to commemorate the 100th birthday of statehood.

MEDORA • **TR** came here in 1883 at age 25, mainly for the hunting, stayed at the hotel at the depot, met Joe Ferris, who acted as his guide, and continued to the Maltese Cross Ranch to hunt buffalo and big game. He wound up buying the ranch and 400 cattle, and then settled down here after his first wife died in February 1884 to become a part-time rancher after the Republican Convention in June. The ranch site is ten miles south, accessible on dirt roads.

He was successful at first and bought more cattle for another ranch 35 miles north, the Elkhorn. He spent most of his time there in a ranch house called the finest in the Badlands. Real cowboys were never impressed with his skills, but they had respect for his tenacity and courage in pursuing ranching despite difficulties including disastrous weather and tough guys. They laughed at such expressions as, "Hasten forward quickly there." But when he told a foul-mouthed bully at the saloon here, "I can't tell you why I like you for you are the nastiest talking man in the world," everyone expected gunplay. The loudmouth dropped his hand to his pistol, then admitted he had been a little too free with his mouth and added himself to the list of **Roosevelt's** friends.

He lost much of his investment in the ranch due to bad weather and bad luck but stated that he would not have been president but for these experiences. Future ranchers learned to use better breeds and store hay for feed during the harsh winters. The Elkhorn was abandoned around 1891, with activities concentrated at the Maltese Cross. He came back various times, including 1887–8, 1890 (with his wife), 1892–3, 1896, 1903, and 1911. Loss estimates vary; maybe $20,000 out of $82,500 invested, plus the interest he missed of another $30,000.

The National Park Service has a good map to the three ranch units, now Theodore Roosevelt National Park. No original building is on its original site now, but the Maltese Cross cabin* is at the visitor center with various **Roosevelt** items, including the rocking chair that he rocked all around the room while discussing politics. The outside walls still contain graffiti from the cabin's exhibition sites in Bismarck, St. Louis, and elsewhere. He wrote several magazine articles here and finished much of his Thomas Hart Benton biography at the Elkhorn. The other ranch units are near Watford City and along the Little Missouri west of and about midway between the other two and near Elkhorn. He was the chief orator at the July 4th picnic in 1886 in nearby Dickenson.

He stayed at the Rough Riders Hotel* (Metropolitan), at the NE corner of 3rd Avenue and Main, in 1883–9, 1900, and 1903 and patronized his friend Joe Ferris's Store,* on the east side of Main between 3rd and 4th Avenues, where he slept in the upstairs southeast bedroom. He also attended St. Mary's Church,* still at the northeast corner of 4th Street and 3rd Avenue. Several other period structures are restored and marked in town. The DeMores Chateau* is open west of the river south of Route 10. **Teddy** visited here, but is not believed to have spent the night, as he had some personal problems with this leading citizen. The depot serving **Roosevelt** on his visits was then at the entrance road to the chateau at the still present Northern Pacific tracks.

Ohio

Bethel • **Grant's** parents moved here to the SE corner of West Plane and N. Charity in 1840 to take over a tannery after Ulysses went to West Point. He visited numerous times, and his second child was born in the home. Slaves in Grant's wife's home gave the boy the name "Buck," for the Buckeye State, which he carried for the rest of his life. By this time, **Grant's** father was worth well over $100,000, maybe $2 million today. When Ulysses sent his family here from Sackets Harbor for the birth, he did not know that he would not see the family for two years since he was soon transferred to the West Coast. When he returned here completely broke, he did so in disgrace after having resigned. The elder Grants moved from Bethel to Covington, Kentucky, in 1854.

Blooming Grove • **Harding's** 1865 birthplace is marked at the spot of the long-gone cottage east of the town on Route 97, one mile west of Route 288. A couple of years after his birth, the family moved to a location six-tenths of a mile west on Route 97. His mother repeatedly told the story that she took him to the Methodist church on the south side of town, down County Road 20, when he was ten days old to have him baptized, since she predicted that he might be president. The current church is dated 1870. He attended the school in the town center and Methodist Sunday school. The community is still so small that it is not noted on nearby highway signs. He visited family graves in the cemetery north of town. The **Hardings** are near the highest spot on the hill.

Caledonia • **Harding** moved here in 1872, as shown on the marker, at age eight and lived on the NW corner of South and 139 Main, south of the public square. Caledonia Methodist in the 200 block of Main was his church, across the street on the southwest corner, where he attended all meetings, suppers, and entertainment. The sites are three-tenths of a mile north of the Route 309/Main Street junction. At age ten he helped his father at the *Argus* newspaper and set type as a printer's devil. After going to grammar schools in nearby Corsica and Caledonia, he left to go to Ohio Central College in Iberia. At age 14 he attended a college about halfway to Blooming Grove. In 1880, his family lost the house in town and moved to a farmhouse that still stands, marked two miles east of town, behind another house off the road. He earned extra money by painting another church that he attended, Iberia Methodist, at 3607 County Road 30.

Canton • **McKinley** moved here to practice law in 1867 at the SW corner of Market and Tuscarawas. He lived with a sister at the corner of Shorb and W. Tuscarawas, nine blocks west of his parent's house at 131 Tuscarawas. The young lawyer walked to church and probably met his wife as she walked to her church, First Presbyterian, SW corner of McKinley and W. Tuscarawas, where they were married by ministers of both churches. Her absent-minded pastor almost forgot to show up. Afterward they lived in the St. Cloud Hotel and then were given a house at the SW corner of Eighth and North Market, now the site of the main city library, by Mrs. McKinley's father. They lived here for a few years, but when her mother died they moved to the home of his wife's parents, the Saxton Home,* 331 Market at Fourth Avenue, where they had their wedding reception. They sold their home before moving to Washington after his election to Congress, as the expensive home proved to be a liability. **McKinley** worked at the courthouse, same site as now, and was on the board of directors at the bank at Seven East Tuscarawas. Soon after the marriage they went to **McKinley's** First Methodist* at the SE corner of W. Tuscarawas and Cleveland. His pew, fifth back of the left center aisle, is marked. He was very active, being superintendent of Sunday school and serving in many capacities including the board of trustees. His funeral was here, and the flag from his casket is displayed in the small museum. When Congress was not in session the **McKinleys** stayed in the Saxton House. **McKinley** established a law office there, where it remained for 20 years as the retreat from public life and political headquarters.

After they had passed several blissfully happy years, their second child died in infancy, leaving his wife Ida with a deep depression and symptoms of epilepsy, and completely dependent on him. In 1896 they leased their old home on North Market when he ran for president and used it during the campaign for his "front porch speeches" to 750,000. Ida by now was an invalid, and he refused to leave her side. So he gave carefully rehearsed speeches from his porch, where he also liked to sit with her by his side, knitting. After he became president, he repurchased the home in 1899 with the thought of retiring there, and he set up a miniature executive office in the library. **Theodore Roosevelt** visited during the 1896 campaign and was later given the post of assistant secretary of the Navy, launching his broader career.

Pandemonium broke out at the house when he won. A friend fled in panic, shouting, "You have my sympathy!" The fence was torn down, and the bushes, flowers, and grass were torn up as great crowds descended, demanding a speech. He also spent much of his 1900 campaign here and returned shortly after the election to where his sickly wife could recover from an illness. She continued to live in the Saxton home until she died in 1907. **TR** attended her funeral. The house was ready for the wrecking ball, but the home (now Saxton-Barber) still exists as the National First Ladies Museum,* owned by the National Park Service. This is the only private house still existing where the president lived. The **McKinleys** are buried in an imposing tomb and monument in Westland Cemetery on Seventh Street N.W., off exit 106, Interstate 77. School children from across the country contributed pennies to build the monument for the martyred president.

CHESTERFIELD • **Garfield** lodged with a local family at 12570 Chillicothe* when he went to Geauga Academy from 1848 until 1850. The old Chester High School is now on the site. He is associated with several churches, including a Presbyterian (site) at the SW corner of Sherman and Chillicothe, a Baptist (site) on the east side of Chillicothe just south of Sherman, and Disciples Church, 250 feet north of Mayfield Road facing Chillicothe.

CINCINNATI • The town began as Fort Washington, the principal military outpost of the Northwest Territory, where **William Henry Harrison** began his army career in 1791. **Harrison** was first aide-de-camp to General Anthony Wayne and then commander by 1795. (During his career he served at various Ohio forts, including Forts Amanda, Fayette, Greenville, Hamilton, Jefferson, Meigs, Recovery, and St. Claire.) He met his wife here, where he built a cabin, then a house. (Maybe this was where the mansion-born general got his "log cabin" roots touted in his 1840 election.) She was the daughter of the man who owned the land between the two Miami Rivers and lived on his river farm near North Bend on the north side of the Ohio River, 17 miles west of Cincinnati, now on U.S. 50. They were married in 1795 in the house owned by the father-in-law, at 116 Nebo in North Bend, and honeymooned at the fort in Cincinnati. A monument at the corner of Third and east of Broadway, near the intersection with Ludlow, marks the side of the fort, bounded by River, Broadway, Ludlow and Fourth. He attended the church meetings held in the Drake House, 429 E. Third, from 1791 until 1798. From 1817 until his death, when in town, he attended Christ Episcopal at 318 E. Fourth, north side between Sycamore and Broadway. From 1812 until 1814 he lived at 30 N. Front and rented a home on Broadway just south of Fourth.

His wife's family still lived in North Bend, and he moved there to build the 22-room Big House at the SW corner of Symmes and Washington Avenues. Here his grandson **Benjamin**, the only president other than **John Quincy Adams** born in the home of another, was born in 1833, as the baby's father was building a home five miles west. **William Henry** liked to open a closet door and show visitors a section of the original logs. He was the first candidate to make campaign speeches and did so to "acres of men" in front of the home. It burned in 1858.

He was very active in his North Bend church and sometimes invited the entire church congregation home to eat lunch. His funeral was at the Wesley Chapel Methodist, 322 E. Fifth, in Cincinnati, and he is buried on Mt. Nebo in North Bend, overlooking the Ohio River, just off U.S. 50 and OH 128. This is clearly marked and visible on Loop Avenue south of Harrison Avenue in **William Henry Harrison** State Park. The tomb remained unostentatious after years of neglect until 1924, when the memorial obelisk and tomb were dedicated. The body is buried inside five caskets to discourage grave robbers in view of what happened to his son John. His body was stolen and found hanging by the neck in a medical school, prompting stringent laws against grave robbers. Various family members are buried here, including **Benjamin**'s father John, the only man who was the son of a president and the father of another.

Shortly after **Benjamin's** birth his family

moved to The Point, on Brower Road, razed in 1959. This was so named because it was where the Ohio and Big Miami Rivers meet. He attended the North Bend Presbyterian, 25 E. State Road, from 1833 until 1854 and was often at the homes of both grandparents. His family lived well, although his father was always complaining about being almost bankrupt. **Benjamin** was educated here until age 14, when he was sent to Farmers College in College Hill, and later Miami University. In Cincinnati he attended First Presbyterian between Fourth, Fifth, Walnut and Main. After graduating, he lived with a married sister at 323 W. Third while practicing law on E. Fourth in Hart's Building. He then married and moved back to The Point. His father had gone to Congress, so he and his wife volunteered to stay with his younger siblings, before moving to Indiana.

Monroe visited Cincinnati in 1819 and was fascinated by the Pearl Street Market on Pearl between Broadway and Sycamore. Seventy-six-year-old **John Quincy Adams** came in 1843 to dedicate the naming of Mount Adams in his honor and laid a cornerstone at the first professional observatory in America, Avery Lane at Observatory Place. He also spoke at the Wesley Chapel mentioned above. **Jackson** stayed at Yeatman's Tavern in 1829, at the NE corner of Front and Sycamore. **Taylor** and **Polk** both stayed at the Southgate House at 24 Third, across the river in Newport, Kentucky. The first national political convention outside the original 13 states was here in 1856, at Smith and Nixon's Hall, when Democrats nominated **Buchanan**.

Lincoln appeared in court in Ohio, as shown in a letter written from Cincinnati on December 24, 1849, implying that he might go to Columbus. In September 1855 he and his future secretary of war, Edwin M. Stanton, appeared for a case at first scheduled in Illinois' Federal Court. **Lincoln** was probably hired to be local counsel, and no one told him the trial was moved or in fact tried to communicate with him for any reason. He found out from the newspaper and just showed up. He stayed with the William Dicksons at 321 Longworth, now just west of the Convention Center downtown, under Interstate 75. (Longworth Street was between Fifth and Sixth.) When he came to the Burnet House at the NW corner of Third and Vine to meet his notable eastern co-counsels, they were so unimpressed that Stanton reportedly exclaimed, "If that giraffe appears in the case, I will throw up my brief and leave." Thus, **Lincoln** was ignored or dismissed.

But he toured various points, including the county and city courts, and spent about a week here meeting a number of lawyers, including **Taft's** father. He visited the estate of Nicholas Longworth at 316 Pike and Fourth, just east of the Ft. Washington site, to see the grounds, now between I-71 and I-471. The gardens are still open, and the home is now the Taft Art Museum,* after Charles Taft, the half-brother of the president, who later owned it. **Taft** dedicated the Lincoln statue there now and was formally notified of his nomination in 1908 on the portico.

Lincoln came to the Burnet House on September 17, 1859, and then by open carriage to the Fifth Street Market Place at Vine, where he spoke from the balcony at the Kinsey Jewelry Store on the north side of the square, marked on the Federal Courthouse, NE corner of Walnut and Fifth. A plaque across the street marks the site of a **Kennedy** speech. **Hayes** was one of the members of the committee to receive **Lincoln**. The family, consisting of Mary and Tad, also spent part of the 18th with Mrs. Dickson, mentioned above.

The president-elect received an immense reception at the train station on February 12, 1861, his 52nd birthday. He then rode in a two-hour procession to the Burnet House, where he addressed a huge crowd inside from the balcony and in the dining room. After a large reception, **Lincoln** returned to the room to find his youngest son waiting to be carried to bed as was their custom, continued in the White House. He left the next morning from the Little Miami Railroad Depot, then east of today's L and N Bridge, near the river and under Interstate 471.

When **Andrew Johnson** left his home at the beginning of the war, the only Southern senator to remain loyal to the Union, he stayed at the Burnet House and made several speeches outside and in, as he did later during and after the war. In 1866, he and **Grant** stayed here and were given a lavish reception at the Spencer House on the NW corner of Front and Broadway.

Grant's headquarters were at 739 W. Eighth when he came in March 1864, to confer with General Sherman. The tables were too small to spread out the maps, so they had to adjourn to the Burnet House to consider the grand plan to end the war. He also worked at the Union Army headquarters at the SW corner of Arch and Broadway. In 1879, after his world tour, he was honored at an extravagant reception at the Grand Hotel at the SW corner of Fourth and Central. **Taft** was on the committee to organize the event.

Hayes' first office was at 127 E. Third while he was boarding at Fourth and Vine from 1849 until 1852. He used his 12-foot-square office also as his lodgings. Later his office was at 17 W. Third, between Main and Walnut. After several years of courtship he moved in with his wife and mother-in-law after he married at their home, 141 W. Sixth. The long engagement might have ended when his domineering, rich bachelor uncle questioned within his hearing why "the young fool" had not married, and stated, "I don't believe she will have him"; and, "If he didn't marry soon he [the uncle] would get mad and marry some old maid himself." The couple then lived there for about a year and embarked in what he called "the boy business." After his first son they moved to 383 W. Sixth until 1872 and had a total of seven boys, plus a girl, and twin girls who died there. Nothing remains of any of these homes. He had an office at Old City Hall, Eighth and Plum, as city solicitor. Although he never joined a church, he went to several: the Presbyterian, on the north side of East Fourth near Main; the Episcopal, on the SE corner of Seventh and Plum, 1849–52; and later St. Paul's Methodist, Seventh and Smith. He considered his activity at the Literary Club at the Presbyterian Church to be the most educational adventure of his life. After the war and two terms as governor, he returned, sold his home, lived temporarily at the Carlyle House, NW corner of Sixth and Mound, and then moved to Fremont.

Garfield had a law office at the beginning of the Civil War on what is now Garfield Place between Vine and Elm. **Taft's** 1857 birthplace home, where he lived into his adulthood, is open at 2038 Auburn.* His prominent father moved to the hill away from the coal dust and noise in 1851. His school from 1862 to 1870, now the William H. Taft School at Southern and Young, is marked by a plaque. He sledded down the hill in winter and walked it each day into and out of the city to school. His high school was Woodward High, 13th, Woodward, Sycamore, and Broadway. After his 1886 marriage at his wife's home, 69 Pike Street, he and his wife moved to The Quarry at 1763 East McMillan. The family home was at 118 E. Third from 1892 to 1898, and then at Madison Road east of Annwood Avenue in Walnut Hills until 1900 in a house still standing. He moved to Washington, D.C., in 1890, but came back here a short time later to live in the Burnet House and then at Third and Lawrence. His church was First Congregational at the SE corner of Fourth and Race from 1857 to 1900, although after his marriage he sometimes went to Christ Episcopal, 318 East Fourth, and St. John's Unitarian, NE corner of West 12th and Elm. He attended Cincinnati Law School, 414 Walnut, later was a dean and professor, and worked in the city hall, courthouse, and federal buildings on Government Square.

CLEVELAND • **John Quincy Adams** visited in 1843 and spoke at the Congregational (now Presbyterian) Church,* on the north side of the public square at Ontario St. and 91 Public Square, now known as the Old Stone Church, where comedians George Burns and Gracie Allen married.

On February 15, 1861, **Lincoln** traveled in a snowstorm two miles from the center of the city from the depot, Euclid and 79th, to the Weddell House Hotel (marked) on the NW corner of W. Sixth (Bank) and Superior. He spoke from the balcony, stating, "If all do not join to save the good ship of the Union in this voyage, nobody will have a chance to pilot her on another." His suites covered the block along Superior. On April 28, 1865, his body was viewed by 100,000 (including **Garfield**) in a building hastily erected for that purpose in City Park, Public Square, Superior and Ontario, in what is now the street north of the Soldiers Monument.

Grant and **Johnson** stayed at the Stadium Hotel in 1866 at the SE corner of Sixth and St. Clair. The president made a speech on the balcony for leniency toward the South, with **Grant** at his side, and was hissed by the antagonistic crowd. **Grant** shouted, "Gentlemen: Remember this is your President." The text of the speech was used against **Johnson** at his impeachment trial.

The last "log cabin president," **Garfield**, was born in 1831, just southeast in what now is 4350 S.O.M. Center Road in Moreland Hills, on the crest of a hill above the Chagrin River, northeast of the I-271 and U.S. 422 interchange. He was baptized in the river, maybe at Miles Road, and went to church at the junction of two branches of the river a mile west of Chagrin Falls. His father died 18 months later, and the widow refused to do the common thing and split the family. So she labored in the fields beside her children to manage a rough living out of the 30 fertile acres. The old rough log cabin had chinks filled with mud to keep out winter winds and windows of greased paper. He wrote later, "I lament sorely that I was born to poverty." His poverty was the worst of the several presidents who grew up poor. But he felt that this "chaos" prepared him for "fight and storm ... in the little great things of life." His impoverished home life was happy with a cheerful mother, but he felt ridiculed by boys with fathers and finer things in life. His mother remarried, but deserted her husband a year later, inviting divorce, scandal, and ridicule anew for James. His one-room River Road School, which he attended from 1841 until 1847, can be found by taking S.O.M. Center Road between Solon and Moreland Hills to the corner of River Road. He wandered off at 16 to find work as a canal driver in Cleveland. At 19 he found religion and in 1849 went to Chester Seminary, where he met his wife. He went to the Disciples Church at several locations, but it was at 24 Walnut, which he helped build, where he became the minister, gaining experience as an orator and contributing to his political career. He then lived at 23 Walnut.

In 1876 **Garfield** bought Lawnview,* now 8095 Mentor Avenue* in Mentor, a northeast suburb off I-90. The home was almost rebuilt as of his election, and he produced a lovely country estate out of a run-down, reeking pigsty. He went to the Disciples Church on Main and conducted his 1880 campaign from the home. **Grant**, who had almost been nominated for a third term, visited there to help unite the bickering party. The family returned to the home after his assassination. His wife added a memorial library wing to the house, with a vault to store presidential papers, setting a precedent for later presidents up to the present day.

He lay in state in the Pavilion at Cleveland's Public Square, where his funeral was held with **Grant** and **Hayes** in attendance, and is buried at the prominent hilltop Garfield Monument in Lakeview Cemetery, 12316 Euclid Avenue at 123rd Street. **Benjamin Harrison** dedicated it in 1890 and stayed at the Stillman Hotel, north side of Euclid just east of Erie (Ninth Street).

Hayes had a heart attack in the railway station at the foot of Water and Bank, now between W. Sixth and W. Ninth, and was brought home to die. He had been visiting his son at 3625 Prospect, the former home of his cousin. **Chester Arthur** and **TR** stayed at the Grand Hotel on the SW corner of Fourth and Central. **TR** came for a wedding at St. Paul's, 14th and Euclid. **Harding** and **McKinley** were at the Hollenden Hotel, Sixth and Superior, long since closed. **Coolidge** was at the Municipal Auditorium, NW Sixth and St. Clair, and **Carter** and **Reagan** debated at 3100 Tower City Center, near Superior and Euclid, in 1980. **G.H.W. Bush** and **Clinton** were honored by the National Underground Railroad Association at the Duke Energy Center, 525 Elm, on June 2, 2007.

COLUMBUS • **Monroe** stayed at Broderick Tavern and saw the State House in 1817. This 1814 building at High and State served as Capitol until the present one was built at the same site. It was started in 1839 and was ready for the legislature in 1857 and the governor in 1861. **Monroe**'s Ohio trip included Sandusky Bay, Worthington, Circleville, Chillicothe (Watson's Hotel and Prospect Hill), Lancaster, Zanesville (courthouse and Few's Tavern), and the new village of Monroe. **William Henry Harrison** worked from 1819 to 1821 at the former courthouse, 55 S. Hague, just south of Broadway. During the War of 1812, he served in a building located at 570 W. Broad. **Fillmore** visited the Capitol* or State House in 1854, where **Johnson** spoke in 1861 and 1866, as did **TR** in 1912, **Hoover** in 1931, and **Ford** in 1976, and no doubt others. The first governor in the new 1861 State House was Salmon P. Chase, who became **Lincoln**'s secretary of the treasury. **Grant** accompanied **Johnson** here during his later tour. **Hayes** (governor), **Garfield** (state senate), and **Harding** (senate, lieutenant governor) worked in the Capitol and lived nearby at various locations. **Garfield** lived at 193 S. Third, and **Harding** lived at 310 S. High.

On September 16, 1859, **Lincoln** spoke from a platform at the east terrace of the Capitol, High and Broad, and made an address that evening at city hall, located on the second floor of the Central Market House, 165 S. Fourth. He also attended the Franklin County Fair with Mary and Tad, staying at the Neil House mentioned later.

Lincoln was a guest of Governor William Dennison on February 13, 1861, and addressed the Legislature in the House Chamber.* He got an enthusiastic welcome from a crowd of 60,000 as he moved up High Street. At the Capitol he remarked on the beautiful building and told them, "We entertain different views upon political questions, but nobody is suffering anything." A plaque on a pillar in the north first floor reception hall notes **Lincoln's** presence.

The governor's office still has its 1861 appearance and the desk **Lincoln** used. No order existed in the rotunda, where he was almost crushed. Finally the exhausted president-elect mounted the staircase and waved to the crowd before addressing them outside from the western steps. Later there was an informal reception in the courthouse

The Capitol in Columbus, Ohio, has seen many presidents, including all of the Ohio presidents who served there and Lincoln. The building is directly across from the Neil House site (behind the camera), where about 19 presidents stayed, including Lincoln.

rotunda at 352 S. High, SE corner of Mound Street, just before he received a telegram informing him that he had been duly elected by the Electoral College. There was another public reception at the Capitol after supper and a levee in full evening dress at Deshler Hall on the SE corner of Town and High. The **Lincolns** spent the night at the residence of Governor Dennison, 211 N. High. **Lincoln's** body lay in the rotunda of the Capitol on April 29, 1865, after moving down High and Broad from the depot where the Convention Center now is, east of High, south of Spruce.

The Neil House, 41 S. High, across (west) from the Capitol, hosted **Jackson, Van Buren, William Henry Harrison**, and all presidents from **Lincoln** to **Wilson. McKinley** lived here from 1893 to 1896 as governor. He moved in when his first lodging, the Chittenden Hotel at the NW corner of High and Spring, burned in November 1893. Every morning when he walked to the Capitol, he turned and waved to his invalid wife, watching him from the window. Then promptly at 3:00 every afternoon, he opened the window of his office to wave with his handkerchief and waited for her to return the wave.

After graduating from Kenton College in Gambier, **Hayes** complied with his sister's wishes that he live with her and her family at their home on High near Spring while he practiced law. But even though there was an intense, lifelong love between the siblings, he felt dominated when near her. He probably felt that she was emotionally disturbed and avoided her as she was institutionalized shortly. Also he felt that a legal education of just reading law limited him, so he decided to go to Harvard Law School. After the Civil War he was governor three times and lived in several houses, including 51 E. State, 96 S. Grant, and 60 E. Broad. He was at the last address, across from the Capitol, as governor when he went to bed on election evening thinking that he had lost the presidential election, and was here while monitoring the long process of determining who actually won that did not end until he was declared the winner the day before being sworn in. He was in his Capitol office when notified of his nomination and was at home after the election when a bullet was fired through his window, just missing him. It was never determined if it was an assassination attempt or just a stray, but passions ran rampant during the disputed election.

The Great Southern Hotel* opened in 1897 at 310 S. High and still operates as the Westin. It hosted **McKinley**, **TR**, **Taft**, and **Wilson. Ford** dedicated the Plaza at the Ohio Theater* on October 21, 1978.

DAYTON • On September 17, 1859, Lincoln arrived at Union Station, freshened up at the Phillips House on the SW corner of Third and Main, spoke at the courthouse at the NW corner of Third and Main, and shook hands for about two hours. He inscribed a Bible for a young admirer, "Live by the words within these covers and you will [be] forever happy." He told the photographer taking his picture at Cridland's Photographic Gallery a few doors east of the hotel at 264 Third, "Keep on. You may make a good one, but never a pretty one."

DEFIANCE • The site of Fort Winchester, built by **William Henry Harrison** in 1812, is marked, as are many other forts, including Forts Amanda, Fayette, Greenville, Hamilton, Jefferson, Recovery, St. Clair, and Meigs, at Fallen Timbers Battlefield.

DELAWARE • **Hayes'** 1822 birthplace site is marked on 17 East William, north side of the street near Sandusky, the town's main streets. His father had died of typhoid fever three months before he was born and is buried in the nearby Old Burying Ground, on the east side of Henry Street, a favorite playground for the young boy and his extremely close, domineering sister. When he was born the still grieving mother was told that the puny baby could not live, and it would be a mercy if she allowed him to die rather than waste strength to try to save him. But the strong-willed matriarch saved her frail son, who was sheltered and spoiled until at age nine he at last could play with other boys. His uncle, Sardis Birchard, a wealthy, lifelong bachelor, provided a comfortable living and education. When "Rud" was about a year old he moved a short distance west to the NE corner of William and Franklin, where he lived until he went to school in 1836 at Norwalk, near his uncle. He continued to visit his mother for ten years. A marker is in front of the church on the home site now. He was baptized in Presbyterian services held in the courthouse, where **Monroe** once attended, located where the present courthouse is, at Central and Sandusky. When **Monroe** came, the preacher became flustered upon seeing the president, recovered, and is said to have given the devil his just due. A hat was passed and the guest's lodging bill was paid. **Hayes** later attended church at the SE corner of Washington and Winter. Part of this original 1844 building still stands.

Hayes' school also stands on the west side of 15 N. Franklin between Winter and William, and he also attended at the SW corner of Winter and Franklin. He returned in 1844 to a temperance convention and met his then 15-year-old future wife at the Sulphur Spring* on the Ohio Wesleyan College campus, behind and east of the Admissions Office. **Hayes** was almost nine years older. She was going to the college with her brothers, although no female was allowed to actually enroll. It is claimed that he later proposed in the Mansion House, now Elliott Hall,* by the spring. This was a student center at the time, and he supposedly courted her there, although he was involved with a woman more nearly his age in Cincinnati, where he then lived. The campus is south of William Street on Sandusky.

FREMONT • **Hayes** lived at Spiegel Grove,* 1337 Hayes Avenue at Buckland Avenue, beginning in 1873. He moved to town in 1845 and had lodged with his uncle at 1829 Buckland, and also at the Thompson House at 323 State, SE corner with Arch. He worked at a law practice, NW corner of Front and Croghan, from 1845 to 1849, but this was a waste of time as the town offered few opportunities. His all-knowing, affectionate, benevolent uncle also was an impediment to full maturity. After five years of sedentary life leading to depression and physical ailments, he moved to Cincinnati. He moved back in 1873 to Spiegel Grove, where he had wanted to move much earlier, but his wife had not been ready to leave big city life, and the Civil War and politics had interfered. He conducted his 1876 campaign from here until he was persuaded to rent a modest place in Columbus for political reasons so as not to seem too ostentatious. As president he was the first to have a telephone and typewriter in the White House. His wife and a son predeceased him, and he frequently visited her grave, even by sleigh when the weather dictated. He stated that he longed to be quietly resting by her side. He died in Spiegel Grove in 1893, saying that he was going to where she was. **Cleveland** attended the funeral, held in the house due to the five-below-zero weather. **McKinley** visited the grave in 1899.

The State Memorial Library (now Hayes Presidential Center), built in 1916, the first presidential library and museum, and his tomb are now on the site with the home. **Harrison's** walk* south of the mansion follows a trail cut by **William H. Harrison** across the land during the War of 1812. The trail to the tomb follows an Indian trail from Lake Erie to the Ohio River. Captives were brought up the trail toward Detroit. One of **Hayes'** favorite stories was of Peggy Fleming, a pioneer girl who was tied to a tree on the grounds near the later gravesite. Delaware Indians were going to burn her there the next morning, but she was freed during the night and fled, disguised, to freedom. The stump remains off the grounds.

The 1873 Dillon Home, across the street from the Presidential Center, was often visited by **Hayes**, a close friend of the owner. Other **Hayes** sites include the Old City Hall, dedicated by **Hayes** in 1877, at the SE corner of Croghan and Arch, just east of the library on the site of Fort Stephenson. **Hayes** and his uncle earlier opened the library at the SW corner of State and Front, but wanted it located at the site of the fort to honor the heroics of George Croghan during the War of 1812 battle here. **Harrison** (who must have been to the site) was nine miles away at Lower Sandusky and told the 21-year-old Croghan to burn the supply post and retreat. Croghan was determined to face the 1200–1300 enemy (or 2400, according to the marker on site) with his 160 men and cannon, "Old Betsy." He held off the British, who were attacking from the future location of the 1840 courthouse, at Croghan and Clover. (That site is marked as an Indian town site where Daniel Boone and others were held captive.) **Harrison** first sought to punish Croghan for disobeying orders. Finding that he could not punish a hero, he dropped the charges, saying, unconvincingly, that he did not come to his aid as he felt that he could hold out. **Hayes** had become friends with Croghan, and was honored to have the town enshrine a monument to the battle and preserve "Old Betsy." The current library, fort site, monument, and "Old Betsy" are surrounded by Croghan, Arch, High and Garrison Streets.

Hayes' church is at the NW corner of Birchard and 216 S. Park. He helped to build it in 1883 and to restore it after a fire a few years later. **McKinley** reviewed a parade here and was the keynote speaker at the reunion of the 23rd Ohio in 1899 at the Old City Hall.

GEORGETOWN • Hiram Ulysses **Grant** moved to what is now 219 E. Grant Avenue* (formerly Main Cross) at Water Street, at about six months of age and lived here until 17. This home and the others mentioned still exist. His five siblings were born in the house. He worked at his father's hated tannery across Grant Street, now at 300 E. Grant. Tanning was the most ostracized profession of the time because of the odors clinging to the building and its workers.

One school is still nearby on 508 S. Water,* south of State. He was shy and seldom got into trouble, but was once switched here when he refused to obey his teacher by handing over a knife that was his and demanded by other boys. He went to the Methodist church, east across the street from his home, now a vacant lot. Another school was on the SW corner of Apple and 208 E. Grant, where the boy went beginning at age four. **Grant's** teacher lived on the south side of Grant at Vine, high on a hill, and was known to liberally apply beechwood switches. The old teacher had little control over the children, and **Grant** was shocked at the amount of whipping since he was never switched by his parents. A boyhood friend lived at 115 S. Apple. **Grant**, while president, kidded him for saving him from drowning in the local swimming hole on White Oak Creek, just west and north of Route 125, and causing him so much misery.

Two early predictions are claimed to have been made in the town. When Grant was age two, someone decided to see what he would do if a pistol were placed in his hands and fired. It went off with a loud report, but the boy did not flinch or show fear, and begged for it to be "ficked" again. A bystander said, "That boy will make a general, for he neither winced nor dodged." When Grant was ten, a traveling phrenologist examined his head before a large crowd and announced, "You need not be surprised if you see this boy fill the Presidential chair!" Joke or part of the act or whatever, this confirmed Jesse's insistence that his son would be great, and he arranged for him to be schooled rather than spend his life in the tannery.

At age five, he began riding horses to bring water to workers. By age eight he won $5 in a traveling show from the showman, who bet no one could ride his "trick pony," trained to throw riders, around the ring, just east of the square. The showman even trained a monkey to jump on riders to throw them off, but "Lyss" rode like a trained performer. By nine or ten he was breaking all fiery, pitching, rearing, and kicking mavericks in the square. He drove a wagon for his father's livery business, starting at age ten, delivering passengers to Cincinnati, Maysville, and Chillicothe. Some complained that it was not safe to send one so small into the forest, but Jesse felt Lyss could take care of himself. At age 13 he carried two lawyers to Toledo. A large stone that he transported to town is just inside the main gate at Confidence Cemetery on Mount Orab Pike.

In 1824 Jesse contracted to build a jail at the NW corner of Cherry and Pleasant. Lyss, 12 years old but very small, hauled logs and stone after convincing his father he could handle the job. Jesse hired a man to help, who finally told the father after a short time that there was no use in his following little Lyss, around since the boy was amply capable of driving and taking care of the team by himself. One day he came home to tell his father that he did not need to go back that day as none of the cutters were at work to help him load. When the father asked how he had loaded the wagon with logs that seemed to require about 20 men, the boy explained an ingenious way that he had moved the logs over a stump and worked the horse and wagon forward and back to perform the seemingly impossible task.

My favorite version of a varying story follows a version reported in the local library about a time when Lyss wanted a horse very badly. His father gave him $60 to go to the owner and see if he would sell for $50, or if not, $55, or if not, to offer the $60. The owner asked the youngster what his instructions were, and Lyss, who had been taught not to lie, related the entire plan. The owner then announced he would not take less than $60. The story generally ends here, but other sources in Georgetown continue, stating that Lyss then said he had been told to make up his own mind, and upon examination felt that the horse was not worth more than $50 and he would pay no more. The owner, noting the determination, made the sale for $50. **Grant** refers to this in his *Memoirs* as a story told by another of a time when he was about eight, blurted out to the owner that he was to pay $25 if a lesser amount was not accepted, and paid the higher figure. He states this was nearly true, and that it caused him embarrassment, then refers to it later, presenting a question whether the former version is accurate or relates to another incident.

Grant attended nearby Ripley College at Third and Mulberry in Ripley, just southeast of Georgetown, and boarded there at 206 Front Street. Close friend Bart Bailey lived at 112 N. Water, near his home. Bart's father Dr. Bailey liked to read family letters to a crowd of family and friends. On a Christmas vacation from Ripley, according to local stories, **Grant** was present when they gathered here to read Bart's letter from West Point, and learned that he had failed and was leaving. **Grant** immediately thought that the military academy was a way out of his humdrum existence. He immediately ran to Rep. Thomas L. Hamer's home, covering the block on the east side of North Street between Apple and Main, and requested that he be considered for appointment. A sort of political feud was going on between the congressman and **Grant's** father, but Hamer agreed to consider it. This account of how he wound up in West Point differs from most biographies and even **Grant's** *Memoirs*, as he states there that his father applied without his knowing, and he just went based on his father's wishes. **Grant** expert John Simon accepts this version. When he left in 1839, he was five-foot, one inch and weighed 117 pounds.

HIRAM • **Garfield** and his wife were married at her parents' home, on the north side of OH 305 east of Hiram Center, in 1858 and lived there before moving to a boarding house at 11221 OH 700. He then bought a home, still across the street from the Institute at 6825 Hinsdale, while he was in the army. He preached in various churches around Hiram, mainly Hiram Christian at 6868 Wakefield at Garfield Road, and maintained the home after the Civil War, even after he bought another in Washington. He started at Hiram Eclectic Institute as a janitor and graduated two years later, then served as president and remained actively involved as trustee after the war. **Arthur** was also here. When the war started, **Garfield** got 60 students to join up with himself as colonel. After selling his home in 1872, he traveled back as a tourist to the area of his youth, remembered his love for the farm and felt that he needed to get somewhere where his boys could learn to work and touch the earth. He then bought his farm in Mentor, near Cleveland.

LEBANON • Among the guests at the Golden Lamb Inn, at 27 S. Broadway north of Main, were **William Henry Harrison, Hayes,** and **McKinley.**

MARION • **Harding** was born in 1865 about 25 miles east and moved here with his family in 1882 to N. East Street. This is now Prospect Street, opposite the interurban station, second door from the jail, behind the Fite Building, where the *Marion Daily Star* was published. His father's doctor's office was 193½ Center, where he frequently visited. The future president had just graduated from college and rode home on a mule. Later the family moved to 498 E. Center, where **Warren** began teaching school at the SE corner of Main and Williamsport. This was the home he returned to as president and where his body was brought after death.

He taught one term at a school, now the site of the radio station at 1330 N. Main. Warren's mother joined the Seventh-Day Adventist church at the SW corner of Center and Mill. He attended, but became a Baptist and went to Trinity Baptist at 1330 North Main before 1901 and 220 South Main afterward. At 19 he and some friends bought the *Star*, and he soon emerged as the sole owner. After several moves the paper wound up at 131–134, then 195 E. Center, 1885–1890. From then until 1915 he was located on the south side of 229 E. Center, next to the Methodist church. Six-time losing Socialist Party presidential candidate Norman Thomas worked for **Harding** at the newspaper.

Florence Kling gave piano lessons to Warren's sister at the family home at 498 Center, where she met Warren. She was the daughter of the richest man in town who shared, with her father, the headstrong trait of getting what she wanted. Earlier she had wanted the boy next door, got pregnant, forced him into marriage—although no marriage certificate has ever been found—and then was powerless to prevent him from abandoning her and the baby. Her father offered to take her back if she would change her name back, but she refused, gave him the baby, and then taught piano lessons. She went after "Wurr'n," who could have had almost anyone, but felt the dour older lady might bring wealth and prestige. In 1891, he built the large home at 380 Mount Vernon Avenue* where they were married. He was 25, five years younger than his wife. Her father did not approve of Warren any more than he had her first husband, and refused to give up custody of her son. The boy visited and was said to be close to **Harding**.

It is claimed that there was no love between the **Hardings**. Florence (Flossie) had no feminine charms, but she made **Harding** and the paper. He remained the sole owner until 1923 when he sold it. She nagged and carped about everything, including the fact that he should work harder. This led to nervous indigestion and a breakdown, causing him to seek help at Dr. Kellogg's sanitarium at Battle Creek, Michigan. While he was there, Florence came to the newspaper to straighten it out and stayed for 14 years so she could watch the paper and Warren. There is a question as to which needed it more.

His ambition did not go beyond being just one of the boys at the Saturday night poker games, the brass rail, and an occasional stag party. Marriage was little hindrance to his infatuations with other women, his mistresses, and rendezvous. When their best friend, Jim Phillips, got sick, Warren helped with his business, and then helped himself to his wife, Carrie, at their home, 417 S. Main. Florence's biographer Carl Sferrazza Anthony calls Carrie the love of **Harding's** life. (A large number of **Harding** "love letters" to her was found in the 1950s and locked up by the courts, to be released in 2014.) He backed off when she pushed for marriage, then allegedly became involved with 18-year-old Nan Britton at 733 E. Center. Most historians agree that he made love to her in his senate and later White House offices, and sent Carrie and Nan money to take long trips when he was nominated. During the 1920 campaign, Carrie came by the house as Warren sat on the porch. Flossie knew all by this time and ran out of the house throwing a feather duster, then a wastebasket, and then a piano stool. Carrie threw back a kiss. **Harding's** daughter by Nan lived into the twenty-first century. (At least one historian and author, Robert Ferrell, disputes the truth of any involvement with her, generally accepted by others. He also disagrees that **Harding** should be rated the worst president, also generally accepted.)

When Warren ran for office he started making speeches from the front porch, starting with his campaign for lieutenant governor in 1903. At one time the porch collapsed and a new one was built running the full length of the house, with a speaker's platform. Here he conducted his "Front Porch Campaign" during his 1920 election race. The party bosses had no thought of letting Warren go out into the country to actually make speeches and embarrass himself in the first election in which women could vote. **Taft** and **Coolidge** visited during the race. He never returned after leaving to go to the White House and left the home to the Harding Memorial Association. After death, **Harding** lay in state at his father's home at 498 Center while **Coolidge, Taft,** and thousands paid tribute. The clock is still here which allegedly stopped at the moment of his death. He is buried at the Harding Memorial,* Delaware Avenue at Vernon Heights Boulevard. **Hoover and Coolidge** were here a few years later for the dedication of the Greek Temple memorial and tomb. There are no markers in town to these many sites except for the home and memorial.

OXFORD • **Benjamin Harrison** attended what is now Miami University and lived on West High, now a women's dormitory. He held debates at Old Main, now Harrison Hall. Several buildings from the period remain. His 1853 marriage took place at the home of the bride, whose father was a minister at 121 High on the corner of College. Prior to that he had lived at Main and High.

POINT PLEASANT • North on U.S. 52 and State 232, 27 miles east of Cincinnati, is the one-room, 16-by-19-foot birthplace* of Grant. Actually he was named Hiram Ulysses, after a family vote, and changed his name after a clerical foul-up when he went to West Point. The birthplace cabin traveled around for some time and was under glass in Columbus for many years, but is now back on site and open. Or at least what's left of it is back, probably little more than its structural framing. One Ohio Historical Society director called it the most traveled, butchered, and maligned building in Ohio. The Grant Memorial Church occupies the site of his church near the home. Harding visited this area, including all Grant sites in nearby towns, in 1922.

YOUNGSTON, POLAND, NILES • **McKinley** was born in Niles in 1843 at 40 South Main, Highway 422, where he lived until he was nine. A reconstructed replica home and research center is now on the spot. The **McKinley** National Birthplace Memorial, also a museum and library, is down the street a block north at 40 North Main on the site of his school, the center of town. The home was moved, divided into two parts, rejoined years later, and then was destroyed by fire in 1937. In fact, **McKinley** is the only president who now has no surviving home other than the White House. (His wife's home, where he stayed, is still open in Canton.) He attended the Niles Methodist Episcopal Church, still a block west at the SW corner of Park and Arlington. His boyhood is described much like **Lincoln's** as "he always had a book in his hands." He swam in the creek about a block east of Main and was an expert with the bow and arrow, marbles, and kites, but there were limited educational opportunities here.

He moved to Poland and lived at 111 S. Main (now the fire department) from 1853 to 1855, since his father felt the schooling opportunities were better. He lived at 212 S. Main from 1855 to 1867 (Rte. 170) and when he returned from the Civil War, where he had served in the same regiment as **Hayes.** He shopped at the old general store at 101 S. Main* and worked at the post office, 221 S. Main,* now a gift shop. His sister's home is still at 301 S. Main. He would have known the Old Dormitory at 307 S. Main and many marked old homes from the period in the blocks north and south on Main, Water, and Pittsburgh Rd. He went to school on the Green by the Presbyterian church on the west side of Rte. 170, south of Riverside Street on Main, swam at the town swimming hole in Yellow Creek marked by a large black oak at the end of Main, played ball on the site of the town hall, and enlisted at the 1804 Sparrow, also known as Old Fowler or Stone Tavern,* 121 Main. His schools included the Methodist Seminary at 47 College off Main, marked by a plaque on the school still at 24 College, near his home. He was active in the Methodist church that he joined in 1858, then at the site of Bank One, Rte. 224, now across from Walgreens.

After returning from the war, he studied law at an office in Youngstown near Boardman and Youngstown Streets and lived there at 210 Main, south on Ohio 616, and at 36 Joy while working in a law office. In 1887, he made an address at the Soldier's Monument in Poland's Riverside Cemetery, Water and Riverside. He announced for the presidency at the still prominent home at 4 Riverside, on a hill just south of the Main Street locations listed in Poland.

OKLAHOMA

DURANT • **Taylor** established and inspected Fort Washita* in 1842, northwest on State 199, in the newly opened Indian Territory as a stopping place along the Southern Overland Trail.

FORTS GIBSON AND TOWSON • **Houston** came to Fort Gibson in 1829 via Memphis, Little Rock, and Ft. Smith, after his young wife left him. He had just resigned the governor's office in Tennessee, leaving a promising career as Jackson's protégé. He moved in with his old Indian mentor from earlier days in Tennessee, old chief Oo-loo-te-ka, on a knoll separating the Arkansas and Illinois Rivers. He acquired a common-law Indian wife, Tiana Rogers (Will's aunt, three generations removed), and then lived on the Neosho River, 30 miles from Oo-loo-te-ka. She died of pneumonia in 1838. He acquired the nickname "Big Drunk" and more or less lived in a stupor for two years until the problems of his Indian friends aroused his indignation, causing him to go to Washington to appeal to his friend President **Jackson**. He came back in 1832 after moving away as ambassador for **Jackson**, probably to convey an understanding with the Indians about western migration, and then went by way of Ft. Towson to Texas. At this fort, **Houston** met with Pawnees and Comanches to promote or negotiate peace between them and the eastern tribes migrating into the territory. Rumors had it that **Houston** was off to Texas to conquer it for the United States. A friend from Arkansas parted with him at Towson and gave him a razor. **Houston** responded that it would someday shave the chin of the president of a republic. Restored Fort Gibson* is north of the town with the same name on Route 80.

He tried to get the Choctaws and other tribes to sign with the Comanches to agree to let whites move west. No evidence about the purpose of his mission from **Jackson** exists. He settled his affairs in the area, and, in effect, divorced Tiana, who understood that she would not go with him when he went back to white civilization.

Davis was stationed here, with his slave, after arriving in a snowstorm with pneumonia in late 1833. He helped build nearby Camp Jackson and received his promotion to first lieutenant. When he and **Houston** were later U.S. Senators, he liked to tell a story of finding **Houston** here telling stories in return for drinks. **Houston** was in Texas by 1832 and generally recovered from his earlier troubled days, but was back here shortly in mid–1833. So the story could be true, but is questioned. **Davis** spent a troubled 1834 in ill health and conflict with his commander and was tried by court-martial for conduct subversive to good order. He was acquitted, but his inability to compromise or back down was clearly displayed in this early stage of a lifelong career exhibiting these traits. After acquittal, **Davis** resigned from the only career he knew. He said later he resigned to get married, but there was no hint before the court-martial that he would do so, even though his father-in-law (**Taylor**) strongly objected to his daughter marrying a soldier.

The remains of Towson* are east of Hugo, north of U.S. 70. Towson was established by **Taylor**, who was in command in 1841. He inspected Fort Washita,* on Route 199 between Durant and Madill, just west of Brown. He held two grand councils with representatives of civilized and uncivilized tribes to keep them out of Texas, and to negotiate peace and the release of white captives. The first, with 17 tribes, was at the junction of the Deep Fork and Canadian Rivers near Eufaula, now under Lake Eufaula, and the second, with 18 tribes, was at the capital city of Tahlequah.

OKLAHOMA CITY • On April 19, 1995, a bomb in a truck in front of a federal building on Fifth Street between Harvey and Robinson killed 168 people, injured hundreds more, damaged 312 buildings, and destroyed 14. **Clinton** attended a memorial service on April 23, at the State Fair Arena* five miles west of downtown, and returned to the site April 5, 1996, and April 19, 2000. **George W. Bush** dedicated the Memorial Museum* on February 19, 2001, saying, "America will come here and be better people for having walked through the Memorial Museum." **Carter** and **George H.W. Bush** also visited the site.

Prior presidential visits include **Reagan** at the

Skirvin Plaza Hotel* on June 5, 1985, for a fundraiser, and later at the Capitol rotunda for a speech. The hotel is still at the NE corner of Broadway and Park. **Ford** had earlier been to the Skirvin and Myriad Convention Center. **FDR** and **LBJ** visited the Fair Grounds* in 1938 and 1964. **George H.W. Bush** ate at the Cattleman's Restaurant,* 1309 S. Agnew, and stayed at the Marriott,* southeast of Pennsylvania and 63rd Street at 6300 Waterford. **JFK** spoke at the Redding Shopping Center, 3903 S. Western Ave., and at the Municipal Auditorium on November 3, 1960.

Theodore Roosevelt made at least three trips here before the town was Oklahoma's capital. In a July 1900 speech in front of the Lee Hotel, where he stayed on Broadway just north of Main, he stated that he hoped Oklahoma would be a state on his next visit. He signed the bill in 1907 that made it so. (The prestigious hotel burned down in 1908.) He paraded with his Rough Riders around town, including all the way out Grand Avenue where their camp had been set up, and also spoke from his train, now on Santa Fe Plaza,* just east of the Skirvin. He drove around town unofficially in 1910 on the way to a wolf hunt in the Tillman County community of Cross Roads, and returned to speak at the Fair Grounds in 1912. The 1910 trip took him through Durant and various Texas towns: Denison, Sherman, Plano, and Dallas.

OREGON

NEWBERG • Orphaned **Herbert Hoover** came to 115 South River and East Second Streets* in 1885 at age ten to live with his affectionate aunt and uncle, who had recently lost a young son. He was fully accepted into the family of several girls and did heavy man's labor that was needed in the home since his relatives were very active elsewhere in churches and the school. Here he learned independence and self-reliance, feeling rich working for 50 cents a day pulling weeds in an onion field. He attended George Fox College (then known as Friends' Pacific Academy) at Fourth and College from age 11 until 15 when his uncle was principal of the Quaker academy and went to the Meeting House at 414 N. Meridian. He moved in 1889 to Salem. His aunt and uncle shared responsibilities in the then male-dominated society, and she always owned the property when they moved about. The example of a mobile lifestyle and shared marital responsibilities is felt to have influenced his later marriage with a strong, educated wife who also shared in family decisions and accomplishments.

The former president came back on his 81st birthday to dedicate the home in 1955. Earlier in 1947, his boyhood friends weren't sure, but thought that the much altered house then for sale was his old home and requested that he come to make sure. He looked at it from the outside and sadly stated that he hated to disappoint his friends, but this was not the home that he remembered. But when he went inside, he turned down the upstairs hall to his small bedroom and remembered it. Friends then purchased the home. His bedroom furniture is among the few original pieces of furniture there now since furniture was sold upon frequent moves. Two rockers have been recovered and are displayed. He recalled that he loved the pear tree in the yard that bore such wonderful fruit that he had never heard of when he moved there. His aunt told him that he could eat all he wanted if he would stir without stopping the pear butter she was making. He stirred, ate, got sick, and had to be put to bed so that he could not look at another pear for some time afterwards. The tree is still in the yard north of the home. The pretentious, more modern home to the south was the site of the family barn. The site is just west of the Routes 99W/219 junction, a block south of First, the main street.

PORTLAND • **Grant** supposedly climbed Mount Hood east of town while he was stationed at Fort Vancouver, Washington. **Hayes** dedicated the North Pacific Industrial Exposition Building downtown in 1880. He stayed at Esmond Hotel, Front and Morrison, and with General William Sherman, and visited Jacksonville, Roseburg,

Eugene, Junction City, Harrisburg, Albany, and Salem. **Benjamin Harrison** is pictured in a parade near First and Taylor on May 5, 1891, and visited the Exposition Building. He also visited Ashland, Eugene, Albany, Salem, and Oregon City.

TR visited several times and dedicated the Lewis and Clark Centennial Exposition on May 21, 1903, laid the cornerstone at the Multnomah Athletic Club in 1911, and had dinner at the Portland Hotel, SW Sixth Street between Yamhill and Morrison, as did **Taft** and **Wilson. Taft** attended Grace Lutheran on NE Broadway in October 23, 1909. He also attended First Unitarian and laid the cornerstone of First Universalist Church in East Portland. **Wilson** came here on September 15, 1919, to try to convince the public to support the League of Nations. There was such a demand for tickets to see him at the auditorium that a statewide lottery was held. He spoke in the public auditorium then and in 1911. **Coolidge** visited in 1922. **Harding** appeared at the Oregonian Press Building with **Hoover** on July 4, 1923, declaring Meacham the capital of the United States for a day after dedicating the Old Oregon Trail Monument. They stayed in the Multnomah Hotel, 319 SW Pine.

Truman was here in April 1945 and in June 1948 to view flood damage. **Clinton** also viewed damage from the 1996 flood on February 14, and came to two conferences on April 2, 1993, and in June 1995. He was here campaigning on September 20, 1996. **FDR** visited in 1934 and dedicated the Timberline Lodge on Mt. Hood in 1937. As shown in the Washington chapter, he dedicated Bonneville Dam on the Columbia River and was there also in 1934. **Carter, Ford,** and **Nixon** stayed in the Benson Hotel, 309 SW Broadway. **George W. Bush** viewed fire damage in Medford in August 2002, and spoke at the Tower Hotel, 921 S.W. Sixth.

SALEM • **Hoover** lived here in 1889, first in a barn and then at Hazel and Highland. He served as clerk for his uncle and office boy for the Oregon Land Company, 325 Commercial, where he learned accounting and typing. He went to Highland Ave. Friends Church on south Highland. His chance meeting with an engineer instilled the desire to be a mining engineer, and he took night classes to prepare to go to Stanford University. The local historical society believes the "HH" still on an exposed brick at Boone's Treasury, 9–12 Liberty, was carved by him. He returned several times after leaving for Stanford. In 1955 he landed at McNary Field and stayed in the Senator Hotel located where Courthouse Square now is.

TR visited the Capitol in 1903, as did **Taft** in 1911, and **Nixon** was here for the 100th anniversary of the Capitol on the same location in 1959, although the building was rebuilt in 1938. **Truman** landed at McNary Field in 1948 to examine what he characterized to the mayor as the "son of a bitch flood." He stopped his convertible downtown to be able to stand up and wave to the crowds.

PENNSYLVANIA

BEDFORD • **Washington** used the Espy House* at 123 Pitt as headquarters in 1794 while leading troops during with the Whiskey Rebellion. This was the only time a president has led troops in the field, although **Madison** and **Lincoln** were involved in some field action. His presence quelled the opposition to the whiskey tax, the first major test of the new republic. His hostess planned an elegant dinner, leaving her turkey cooling in the window. The temptation was too great for the soldiers camped all around as it was soon impaled on a bayonet and disappeared. A marker at 106 Pitt, east of Juliana, notes the site of the fort then covering the downtown area.

The original King's Tavern is still at 109 Pitt, almost across from the Espy, where British officers were quartered during colonial days. **Washington** came in 1758 and may have stayed then in the "pre–1761" tavern, or at least nearby. **William Henry Harrison** stayed in a log cabin near the site. **Benjamin Harrison, Polk, Taylor,** and **Tyler** also are claimed to have stayed at the Espy House (questionable), but they were at the hotel mentioned next.

As **Washington** traveled east, he was entertained at Mount Dallas, where he stayed with the William Hartleys and played backgammon with Mrs. Hartley. This is still one mile east of the Lutzville-Peenknoll Road, north side of U.S. 30 just east of Rte. 1005 on the outskirts of Everett.

Buchanan liked to stay at the immense Bedford Springs Hotel* beginning in 1816, about two miles south on Bus. 220, and enjoyed walks up Constitution and Federal Hills. He used it as his summer White House, and received the first trans-Atlantic cable here, from Queen Victoria, saying, "Come let us talk together." In 1859 a slave or "body servant" of a member of **Buchanan's** party was kidnapped here by abolitionists, distressing the president so much that he returned early to Washington. Among others here were **William Henry Harrison**, **Polk**, **Taylor**, **Tyler**, **Garfield**, **Eisenhower**, and **Reagan**.

BETHLEHEM • The Sun Inn* is still at 556 Main, where many famous Americans stayed including Franklin, **Washington**, **John Adams**, and **Buchanan**. **Adams** called it "the best inn I ever saw." **Washington** and **Adams** attended the Old Chapel* on Church and Heckewelder Place in what is now the Moravian restoration area, with many old structures they would have seen.

BRISTOL • **Jefferson** was entertained at the Crossed Keys Tavern,* still at Radcliff and Market, on November 6, 1783. The WPA Guide claims that "many presidents from **Washington** to **Buchanan**" stayed here.

CARLISLE • **Washington** assembled his army at the time of the Whiskey Rebellion in 1794 at the Carlisle Barracks, established in 1757, one mile north on U.S. 11. Hessian prisoners that **Washington** had captured at Trenton in 1776 built the guardhouse still here. The Mill Apartments there date to 1761. The Whiskey Insurrection was the first challenge to the new government, and **Washington** marched here, literally assuming his commander in chief responsibilities as president. He heard a political sermon at the First Presbyterian Church* at the NW corner of Carlisle Square, Hanover and High, Routes 11 and 34, as the pastor praised the order, good government, and excellence of the United States. A historical marker at the home site of General Ephraim Blaine, a block south on South Hanover at Liberty, notes that **Washington** stayed October 4 through 11, 1794. He also was honored in a formal ceremony at the courthouse on the square and presented the proper replies. The Green Tree Inn, marked across west from his headquarters, is where his officers stayed, including Knox and Hamilton. The spot where he reviewed troops is also marked a block west of the square, at West and High at Denny Hall. An estimated 10,000 to 15,000 troops encamped on the common. **Washington** then left for Shippensburg, where he dined.

Buchanan graduated from Dickinson College, West High Street, in 1809, in spite of the fact that he was kicked out for disorderly conduct in 1808 and had to beg to be readmitted. Old West Hall, dating to 1803, still stands from his time west of the North West and Dickerson intersection. **Eisenhower** was honored with a downtown parade on May 21, 1947.

CHAMBERSBURG • **Washington** lodged at the Morrow Tavern at 35 S. Main (site marked), just south of the square on October 12, 1794, while traveling to review troops at Bedford.

CHESTER • **Washington** retreated here after defeat at Brandywine and stayed in Mary Withy's Inn or Washington House, marked on the east side of Avenue of the States (formerly Market Street) between Fourth and Fifth. He, **Jefferson**, probably **Madison**, **Monroe**, and other colonial leaders also spent many nights here across from the colonial courthouse.* **Washington** encamped again on September 5, 1781, on the way to Yorktown. The campsite is on U.S. 13 on the east side at Morton and McDowell. **Jefferson** was also at Withy's, called the best-kept tavern in America, in June 1775.

EPHRATA • **Washington** and **Jefferson** are shown in some sources to have visited in Johann Peter Miller's House, site marked in the Ephrata Cloisters Historic Park,* on Rte. 322 at the western boundary. However, historians there and the local historical society believe that while **Washington** may have visited the hospital he established during the revolution, no record is shown of either's visit to Miller. **Buchanan** is claimed to have been here in the 1860s. The WPA Guide claims that the Mountain Springs Hotel,* Camp Silver Bell, at the NW corner of Main and Spring Garden, now the Hampton Inn just east of downtown, hosted **Buchanan** and **Lincoln**. The historical society verifies **Buchanan**, who carried a first mortgage on the hotel, but doubts **Lincoln** would have been anywhere near here.

Fort Necessity National Battlefield: Here in 1754 the French and Indian War began, leading to the British conquest of much of the continent. It was begun by a young militiaman who here started a war and began a road to immortality. The British claimed this territory under various treaties, and the French claimed it based on discoveries by the explorer La Salle. The Virginia governor sent an expedition to French Fort Duquesne (Pittsburgh), where the French had expelled a detachment of Virginia soldiers building a fort. The commander of the expedition was fatally injured at Cumberland, Maryland, and his aide, Major **Washington**, took over. When he got to the Great Meadows here, he threw up poorly planned, located, and constructed breastworks along what later was the National Road, the main east-west highway (later U.S. 40) crossing a region long fought over by the French and British.

Washington then led a scouting tour when he encountered of Frenchmen under Coulon de Jumonville. The colonials attacked, and Jumonville was killed. The site, Jumonville Glen, is marked north of U.S. 40, about five miles from the fort, on County 2021. Half Moon's Rock marks the spot where the Delaware chief met **Washington** in what is now a Methodist camp. The parties were not at war, no French attack had been made, and the Virginia governor had just ordered **Washington** to warn the French to leave before engaging in hostilities. The Virginians retreated here to convert the breastworks into a makeshift fort that the Indians called "that little thing in the meadow." The main French force then approached after about six weeks, led by Jumonville's half brother, and **Washington** stood his ground against a superior force. The French and Indians probably could have annihilated their enemy, but offered to parley. **Washington** signed surrender papers that he understood said the French officer had been "killed," although the actual wording in French meant "assassinated." **Washington** was discredited, and King George stated that this showed colonial officers were inferior to British. The Indians perceived a loser in the British, and allied with the French. **Washington** resigned, and the French and Indian War had begun, with the North American continent as the prize.

General Braddock later led the British in 1755 to capture Ft. Duquesne and passed by. **Washington** accompanied as a volunteer aide, got sick on the way, maybe with malaria, recuperated some as the army moved ahead, and then followed past the old fort to catch up. (A number of historical markers can be found along highway 40 east of Pittsburgh tracing Braddock and **Washington's** march and campsites.) After Braddock's defeat and wounding near Pittsburgh, the army again trudged back to Fort Necessity, where Braddock died nearby. He was buried under the road so that wagons could obliterate and hide the gravesite, rediscovered in 1820, and now marked by the road a little over a mile from Fort Necessity, and about a hundred yards from where it was found. The fort's 53-foot diameter would have not held more than 200. The Old Orchard Camp* is on the site of **Washington's** ninth encampment, about a mile north of the fort.

Washington must have liked the area because he bought nearly 2000 acres thirty miles north toward Pittsburgh in 1770 near Perryopolis. A marker on Route 51 directs you .9 mile east down Independence to the old mill at the creek on Lawton Road at Strawn Roads, where his gristmill* is reconstructed on Washington Creek. The site was lost in later times until discovered by archaeologists in 1932 and rebuilt the next year to its original size. He came back to the site for several days in September 1784 down the old Braddock Trail.

FRANKLIN: To the Indians and pioneers of the Upper Ohio Valley, this was an important site in the network of waterways where French Creek enters the Allegheny River. In 1753 the French began a road and a string of bases from Lake Erie to the Forks of the Ohio (Pittsburgh), passing here, where they took over an English trader's post. The Virginia Royal Governor sent a mission to warn the French to leave, wanting to arouse the compliant Virginia legislature to the presence and intentions of the French expanding into territory desired by the British and the Colonies. Twenty-one-year old Major **Washington** was selected. His four years spent surveying the wilderness had toughened him to bear the brunt of the brutal winter climate and travel. **Washington** was to deliver an ultimatum, determine French intentions, decide where to build a fort to claim the territory, and observe French activity. With several companions, including frontiersman Christopher Gist, he stopped first at Logstown, eighteen miles northwest of present-day Pittsburgh, to powwow with Indians and find a guide. The powerful chief Half King expressed hatred for the French and affection for the British, and offered to lead.

Here at Fort Machault, marked at 616 Elk at Sixth, **Washington** found a strong French presence over which flew a French flag. He encountered a polite French captain who, when "doused plentifully with wine," informed the messenger that the French would take the Ohio Valley. Wine flowed freely, the Indians became befuddled, and it was hard to determine where they stood or if the Frenchmen knew the young militiaman's mission was half diplomacy and half spying. But he was able to pry Half King away from the jug and continue. Since the commander here lacked official authority to answer, **Washington** continued on to Fort Le Boeuf. (See Waterford.) Monuments and markers are located near Eighth and Elk in a residential area where Fort Venango was built in 1760.

GETTYSBURG • **Washington** traveled to the Russell Tavern (private) in 1794, west of Route 34 (Biggerville Road), about four miles north of town and one mile west on the road to Mummasburg, then the main road from Philadelphia to Pittsburgh. The tavern looks the same as he saw it, although it was severely damaged by fire in 1917. He evidently watered his horses, ate, and then moved on rather than spend the night as claimed. **Madison** traveled here in the mid–1780s, passing through York and Lancaster also.

On November 19, 1863, "the best known speech in the history of the planet" (as per author and historian Gabor Boritt) took place just south of town at the dedication of the National Cemetery. **Lincoln** almost didn't come. His son Tad was sick, and Mary urged him not to leave. He probably wasn't feeling well as he returned with a slight case of smallpox and was quarantined, saying that at last now he had something to give everybody. (**Lincoln's** valet, who came along, died from catching the sickness allegedly from the president.) **Lincoln** arrived shortly before dusk on the day before the speech at the depot* still on Carlisle Street, where orator and main speaker Edward Everett, and local attorney David Wills met him. They walked the two blocks to the Wills House,* the largest structure on the circle (Diamond), now "Lincoln Square." **Lincoln's** bedroom is open to the public, and the first-floor parlor where **Lincoln** and twenty-one other guests were served is a visitor center. He appeared before the crowds but declined to make an impromptu speech at a door then on the north side, as shown in the photograph on the marker. In response to demands, he also spoke from a window of the house.

Lincoln greeted arriving Pennsylvania Governor Curtin at 11:00 that evening, and walked through heavy crowds next door to the Harper House, probably to show his speech to Secretary of State Seward, getting no useful suggestions. This house site is now the Masonic Hall. Many historians believe that he took a battlefield tour with Seward that **Lincoln** had wanted the next morning for about an hour to view the first day's fighting area, toward the Seminary, as Seward later claimed. He is said to have seen the spot where General John Reynolds was killed, marked on the battlefield tour route. This would have taken him past Lee's headquarters site and the stone house* across the road where Lee ate, now at the Quality Inn on U.S. 30. At about 10:00 he mounted a horse too small for him in front of the home and waited about an hour for the procession to get organized for the parade down Baltimore Street. Many houses of the period and the tall sycamore trees on the east side of Baltimore Street at Levering Street remain along the parade route toward today's Holiday Inn. The route turned again shortly at the Taneytown Road, near where future President **Nixon's** grandfather had been killed in the battle, about where McDonald's Restaurant is now.

Lincoln's startlingly brief "dedicatory remarks" set the war goals into ideological terms rather than military, constitutional, or property arguments. Stories that he was dissatisfied with his performance are thought to be a myth. There were some unfair and shortsighted newspaper accounts. Some dignitaries are quoted as being "disappointed" although these may not be accurate. Curtin commented that the speech was highly "impressive." Time was needed to reflect upon the words intended for beyond that day and place. (Chairs from the speaker's platform are displayed in the Gettysburg National Park Museum.*) After the ceremonies, **Lincoln** returned to the Wills House for lunch and to meet with local hero John Burns. Burns had fought in Canada during the War of 1812 and had volunteered to fight rebels at age 73 when they invaded his hometown. He had been wounded and left for dead. **Lincoln** requested to meet him. The two then walked arm-in-arm to the Presbyterian church, NE corner of Baltimore and High, sat side-by-side on the second row, and listened while Ohio's lieutenant governor condemned traitors. His and **Eisenhower's** pews are marked. The church is more recent but the rafters and floorboards are original. **Nixon** attended on Easter Sunday in 1972. Many houses and buildings are marked as witnessing the battle and served as hospitals afterward.

The most often asked question in Gettysburg is: "Where did **Lincoln** give his address?" No site can be supported with certainty, but it was probably near the prominent Brown Family vault in Evergreen Cemetery, toward the fence between the vault and Soldiers Monument. **Cleveland** was criticized as appearing reticent and apparently indifferent, but it was learned later that he was overcome with grief thinking about his $300 (some say $150) substitute killed here. (One reporter wondered if his grief was over the $300.) On the way back to Washington **Lincoln** was stunned by three shots fired in the nearby town of Fairfield, but it turned out to be an overenthusiastic supporter.

Other presidential visits include several on various Memorial Days: **Hayes** (1878), **Theodore Roosevelt** as president (1904) and as former president (1909, 1912), **Coolidge** (1928), **Hoover** (1930), and **Franklin Roosevelt** (1934). **Hayes** used the depot that **Lincoln** had used and was honored at the McPherson House, still at the SW corner of Carlyle and Stephens, adjacent to the college campus. **TR** toured the battlefield with Generals O.O. Howard and Daniel Sickles and discussed the battle with other participants, including Alabama Major William Rollins. He commented, "This country is all right so long as we can have this kind of talk on Little Round Top." His speech from a platform in the cemetery before 10,000 during a deluge of rain noted, "...he is but a poor American who, looking at this field, does not feel within himself a deeper reverence for the nation's past and a higher purpose to make the nation's future rise level with her past...."

Taft dedicated the U.S. Regulars' Monument and attended a reception at the Eagle Hotel that stood for a hundred years at the NE corner of Chambersburg and Washington before it burned in the 1960s. His parade traced **Lincoln's** to the site of the speaker's platform erected near the memorial. **Wilson's** visit was the shortest, only an hour, when he spoke in a giant, hot tent near the Codori House to 50,000 veterans. He told them, "We have harder things to do than were done in the heroic days of the war, because [they are] harder to see clearly, requiring more vision, more calm balance of judgment, a more candid searching of the very springs of right." **Harding** watched a reenactment of Pickett's Charge from Ziegler's Grove observation tower. **Coolidge** was here at the same time as 2,000 KKK members and discussed the cost of almost $7 billion in pensions to date. **Hoover's** speech was the shortest since **Lincoln's**, 1,200 words. **Carter** came twice in 1978, once with Egyptian President Anwar El Sadat and Israeli Prime Minister Menachim Begin. **Carter** wanted a break from the negotiations for peace in the Middle East then going on at nearby Camp David. Sadat and the other military men from Egypt knew all about the battle here, but Begin knew very little. But when they got to the spot where **Lincoln** gave his address, all were dumbfounded when Begin quoted it verbatim.

The Hotel Gettysburg on the NE corner of the square (diamond) has hosted **William Henry Harrison** in 1836, **Grant** in 1868, **Ike** in 1915, 1946, and various times from 1952 to 1961, and later **Nixon**. The Holiday Inn, south on Baltimore Street, has hosted **Ford** and **Clinton**. **George H.W. Bush** was photographed jogging near the impressive Pennsylvania Memorial. **Kennedy** was familiar with the battle details and came with his wife and daughter in March 1963 before the 100th anniversary. No one knew they were there except the guide who escorted them around the battlefield. He was unable to keep his promise to return for the next anniversary celebration of the Address because of a trip to Dallas later that year. He drove his own car, as did **Truman**, who held a press conference by Lee's statue at the Virginia Monument in 1946 and recalled being here when **FDR** dedicated the Eternal Light Peace Memorial in 1938. **Ike** got an honorary degree from the college, where **George W. Bush** later spoke.

Eisenhower lived at 157 Washington Street from May until November 1918 with his wife and infant son, just south of Water Street on the east side. The marker notes that this was their first family home. The family also lived at an apartment at 237 Spring. The young soldier got his wife interested in the Civil War by taking her around the battlefield and explaining the action. He came through the next year as part of a slow, two-month, 3200-mile (at six miles per hour) truck convoy on the new Lincoln Highway (U.S. 30) from Zero Milestone, south of the White house in Washington, D.C., to San Francisco. (After seeing the German Autobahn, he was instrumental as president in the 1950s in starting the Interstate Highway program.) In the late 1940s he later purchased a farm,* at the southwest edge of the Military Park. It took much convincing and $40,000 to get the owner to part with the place. This was the only home they ever owned. Once remodeling of the home began after purchase, it was found to have been built around a 200-year-old log cabin, and this was somewhat retained in the

present structure, mostly a reconstruction. While living here, **Ike** occupied an office on the Gettysburg College Campus marked by his statue in front at the NW corner of 300 Carlyle and Stevens Streets. **Nixon**, **Reagan** (1966), **LBJ** (1963), and **Ford** (1965) met with **Ike** at his home, visible from Seminary Ridge. Many distinguished visitors came, including Nehru of India, Charles de Gaulle, and Winston Churchill, who once corrected a guide's incorrect information. But German General Rommel never was on the battlefield or anywhere in the country, as is popularly supposed.

HANOVER • **Washington** came through at least in 1791 and breakfasted in town. At Carlisle and Park Streets, a marker notes: "One-half block east of here, on November 18, 1863, **Lincoln** spoke briefly to townspeople from his special train. The president was traveling to Gettysburg for the dedication of the National Cemetery." This spot is two blocks north of the town square on Routes 94, 116, and 194, between Park and Railroad Streets. An old railroad track is still on the side of the street just west of an old depot, but does not extend east.

HARRISBURG • **Buchanan** stayed at the Golden Eagle on Market Square while in the Assembly, 1814–16. The Capitol then was at the head of the square, about three blocks from the river. **William Henry Harrison** was nominated for president at the Zion Lutheran Church* (marked on South Fourth Street) in December 1839. **Tyler** came as a delegate and was put on the ticket as **Harrison's** running mate. He laughed at and disavowed the still popular story that he cried so much when Henry Clay failed to be nominated that he was given the vice presidential nomination to soothe his feelings. **TR** was at the church in 1903 and dedicated the new Capitol in 1906 at the spot marked on the floor just inside. **FDR** visited the building later.

On February 22, 1861, President-elect **Lincoln** arrived at the depot northeast of Fifth and Market and spoke from the portico at the Jones House, marked on the east side of South Market Square, the SE corner of Market and Second. **Washington** had stayed at the site (marked) in October 1794 and went to the Presbyterian church at the NE corner of the square. **Lincoln** told the crowd, "It shall be my endeavor to preserve the peace of this country."

Members of the legislature and military then escorted him to the State House, where he spoke to the General Assembly. (That building burned in 1897.) After a return to the Jones House, where he was supposed to stay, he learned of new plans for his trip to Washington. An assassination plot had been uncovered, canceling plans to visit Governor Curtin's home. He secretly left the hotel and drove to the outskirts of the city to board a special train to Philadelphia in time to catch the special 11:00 P.M. train to Washington, D.C. **Lincoln** hated to sneak into Washington "like a thief," but was convinced that the plot were real, as is so thought today.

The president's body arrived on April 21, 1865, after passing through Shrewsbury and York to lie in the State House from 8:30 P.M. until midmorning on April 22. Thousands lined the streets to and from the train station.

Johnson with **Grant** visited the Bolton (Eagle) House (marked), at the NE corner of Second and Strawberry in 1866. He had spoken at large Union rally at the courthouse in 1863 during the war. A marker in front of the Cameron Mansion, on the SE corner of State and Front, shows that **Grant** visited and could easily be seen smoking his cigar on the south side veranda. **Hayes** spent nights in the Ramsey House on Exchange Street in 1878 and 1886.

JOHNSTOWN • Before the devasting 1889 flood, **Andrew Johnson** and **Grant** came through on September 14, 1866, and stopped at the station on Iron Street, now Walnut, 100 yards east from where it is today. A crowded former canal bridge over the main line, with thousands waiting to see mainly **Grant**, collapsed, killing about 28 and injuring 350. The presidents stayed on the train, waved, and then left for Pittsburgh.

KUTZTOWN • **Washington** and **John Adams** were at the Old Kept House in 1777, now called Whispering Springs, U.S. 222.

LANCASTER • Although Douglas Southall Freeman states that **Washington** did not come here until 1791, several sources, including **Washington's** own diary, show that he was here in 1773, 1777, and later in 1794 (from York, Chambers-

Opposite: **"The most famous speech in history" was probably made near the Brown Family Vault in the cemetery adjoining the National Cemetery in Gettysburg.**

burg, Bedford, and the Whiskey Rebellion) and 1796. In 1777 he stayed at the Salisbury White Horse, Cross Keys and West King Streets, one block from the Center Square. He stayed at the White Swan Tavern on July 4, 1791, at the SE corner of Penn Square, dined at the courthouse, and took a long walk through town. **Jefferson** passed through on the way to Congress in May 1776 and other times. He stayed at Ryckhart's or the Bear Tavern, at 32–34 North Queen (marked as "Reigart's" Grape Inn), and ate at the Bull Tavern, SE corner of East King and Christian Streets, just east of Queen toward Duke Street. His route was from Frederick, Taneytown, and York.

Congress, including **Adams**, had been forced to meet at the courthouse, then in the center of Penn Square, on September 27, 1777, when the British captured Philadelphia. They brought the Liberty Bell with them. That courthouse burned in 1784 to be replaced with another visited by **Washington** in 1791 and used as the Capitol of Pennsylvania from 1799 until 1812. **Adams** came through town on the way to the new capital of Washington in 1800, stayed in the White Swan, and was entertained with a fireworks show at Prince and King. **Houston** and **Wilson** also were guests later at the hotel, as were **William Henry Harrison** and **Taylor**, as shown on the marker that claims **Lincoln** was there in 1861. The courthouse was razed in 1853 and the present one is a block east. **Kennedy** spoke on the north side of the square in 1960.

Buchanan moved to town in 1809 to become county prosecutor. He stayed at various times at Widow Dutchman's Inn on East King, a block and a half from the old courthouse and across the street from his law teacher James Hopkins at King and Duke. **Buchanan** purchased a tavern in 1813, at 42 East King Street about halfway between Penn Square and Duke, where he lived until 1821.

Lancaster, Pennsylvania, was the capital of the United States when Congress fled the British. The courthouse that was in the square was the Capitol where Adams worked, Washington and Jefferson visited, and many stayed in a hotel on the corner. Buchanan practiced law here. Kennedy and Lincoln spoke nearby.

He had an office at various times until 1853 at mid-block, north side of King, and one-half block east of the square. He was there infrequently after he became active in politics. He took his meals at the White Swan, where he probably met his fiancée, the beautiful daughter of a millionaire. They quarreled and broke up, maybe because she thought he was after her money (although **Buchanan** was worth $300,000 through earnings from his law practice), maybe because of false reports of his philandering, or maybe because her father objected. Then she went to Philadelphia and suddenly died mysteriously. Her friends said it was suicide; the doctor called it "hysteria." Possibly the drug laudanum was involved, as it was widely used then without knowledge of its dangerous side effects. His letter to her father, expressing grief and pleading to come to her funeral, was returned unopened, and is now in the museum at Wheatland. She is buried with her family in the churchyard at St. James, NE corner of Orange and Duke. He could not be prevented from frequently visiting her grave at the rear of the church nearest Orange Street at the point where the brick and iron fence meet. A marker here is inscribed, "...beloved of James **Buchanan**."

In 1833 he bought her house, 52 East King, where he lived until 1848. Only a few rooms were used until he decided to have the house fully furnished in 1848 and got furniture for all seven bedrooms. He joined the lodge at Heritage Center and went to church at First Presbyterian, on the south side of 140 East Orange between Lime and Duke, from 1812 to 1868.

In 1848 **Buchanan** purchased Wheatland,* one and a half miles west on State 23, 1120 Marietta. He never married, but adopted his seven-year-old nephew and nine-year-old niece, who lived there. The niece traveled with him to England when he was ambassador, and was his hostess at the White House. She married in the parlor of Wheatland. He returned here after his presidency to live under a cloud as many blamed him for the war, and militiamen had to guard his house for months while he was a virtual prisoner. **Lincoln** inquired about it on his way through in 1861, and the home was pointed out to him from the train. The former president later watched **Lincoln's** funeral train from his buggy. **Buchanan** died in 1868 and is buried at the center of Woodlawn Hill Cemetery* near the brick chapel. A wide path leads east from the 500 block of South Queen Street to the prominent grave under the flagpole.

The Fulton Opera House,* at 12–14 N. Prince, is called the oldest building in the United States in continuous use as a theater, highlighting such talent as Mark Twain, Buffalo Bill, Victor Herbert, and John Wilkes Booth, whose performance was witnessed by **Buchanan**. On February 22, 1861, **Lincoln** spoke from the balcony of the Cadwell House (destroyed), on the SE corner of Chestnut and Queen, across from the depot where he arrived. He only said, "I think the more a man speaks in these days, the less he is understood. As Solomon says, there is a time for all things, and I think the present is a time for silence."

LIGONIER • **Washington** joined General John Forbes's army at Fort Ligonier* to proceed to capture the French fort at today's Pittsburgh. Forbes took over after the fallen Braddock had failed to drive the French away. **Washington** had argued that his route, roughly today's U.S. 40, from Fort Cumberland, Maryland, past Fort Necessity (used by Braddock), was the best way to approach Fort Duquesne at the forks of the Ohio. This would presumably make Alexandria a great metropolis at the end of a great road. But Forbes had to be supplied out of Philadelphia, and chose another route leading roughly down today's U.S. 30. After about a month the force moved toward Fort Duquesne, which was found abandoned. The fort site is marked on U.S. 30 east of the square, and the reconstructed fort is nearby, just north of U.S. 30.

MCCONNELLSBURG • **John Adams** occupied the front room to the right of the stairs on the second floor at the Fulton House,* marked at 110–12 Lincoln Way East, where **Buchanan, W.H. Harrison, Taylor,** and probably other presidents also stayed along the National Road. This is now the police station on the north side of Route 16, just east of Route 522.

MEADVILLE • **Washington** may have stopped at the Bicentennial Oak near the NE corner of Main and Randolph. **McKinley** came here in 1860 to attend Allegheny College for one term until financial problems and illness forced him to leave. He attended Bentley Hall between Park and North Main, still the main building on campus. Legend says **McKinley** led a cow up three stories to the bell tower, and learned that cows can go up easily, but not down. He stayed at 400 N. Main, which became the Odd Fellows Orphan's Home, destroyed in the 1920s.

MERCERSBURG • **Buchanan** was born in 1791 at what is now Buchanan State Historical Park, marked by a pyramid of stone* four miles northwest of State 16, up a narrow road in the forest. The log cabin birth home is now SE of Seminary and Fayette Streets on the campus of Mercersburg Academy, next to the Nolde Gym at the southern end of the athletic field. From 1794 until 1796 the family lived at Dunwoodie Farm along West Conococheague Creek, and in 1796 moved to 17 Main Street in Mercersburg, now the James Buchanan Hotel,* where they lived until 1809. His niece, who was the mistress in his bachelor White House, was born across the street at 14 N. Main. Both original structures are marked. He attended the Presbyterian church at Seminary and Park Streets and the Old Stone Academy (now gone) at 43 W. California, the northeast corner with Park. His parents and various siblings are buried in the Spring Grove Cemetery* east of town, where he frequently visited. The plot is a chained rectangle next to a narrow road. The Mansion House on the SE corner of the square was a local gathering point where he made a speech from the balcony in 1852 and another in 1856. Political opponents then persuaded a bunch of rowdies to harass the presidential candidate, but he refused to take action, calling their disturbance "a trifle." **Coolidge**'s sons went to the academy here when he was vice president and later president. **Carter** visited the sites in 1978. A well-done town walking-tour guide is available at several locations, pointing out numerous historical structures.

NEWTOWN • **Washington** was at 2 S. Sycamore before and after the Battle of Trenton. From here he wrote two famous letters to Congress reporting on the battle.

PHILADELPHIA AND AREA • **Washington** and **Jefferson** (and probably **Madison**) frequently stayed at the Blue Bell Inn, ten miles south of central Philadelphia at the NW corner of Island and Woodland Streets, about three miles north of the airport. It was on the road from Philadelphia to the Southern colonies. Once when all was quiet, **Washington** overheard three young girls talking in another room when one remarked that she would like to see if a kiss could change **Washington's** somber expression. **Washington** surprised all by springing to his feet and confronting the girls to demand to know who had made the remark. None confessed so he announced that he would have to kiss them all.

The City Tavern,* reconstructed on the west side of Second, midway between Walnut and Spruce, was a major gathering place for colonial discussions and political meetings. Here a proposal first went out that the thirteen Colonies meet together. **Washington** and many members of Congress then met regularly at the tavern before and after the Revolution. **Adams** took his meals here throughout his term and called it the "most genteel place of its kind in all the colonies." He first met **Washington** inside. In 1790, **Washington** and his family stayed here while traveling from New York to Mt. Vernon, and he was honored with banquets. When **Adams** first came to Philadelphia, he lived at Mrs. Yard's Stone (or "Slate") House, at the SE corner of Norris Alley, Sansome, and Second, marked opposite the City Tavern, and then nearby at a boarding house on Arch, halfway between Front and Second. **Washington** had stayed at the Slate House (marked) in 1773 while taking his stepson to King's College in New York. Across the street from the City Tavern is the Thomas Bond home,* now a bed and breakfast, where **Washington** visited. It was the home of several prominent residents and **Washington's** business agent. (Note that the river was then about where Interstate 95 is now.)

The First Continental Congress met for six weeks beginning September 5, 1774, at Carpenter's Hall,* in the middle of a block bounded by Third, Fourth, Chestnut, and Walnut. **Washington** and **Adams** were delegates to the convention, which was concerned about the closing of the port of Boston and other British policies. They chose to meet in a private building rather than a public facility like the nearby Pennsylvania State House. Virginia's Patrick Henry made a revolutionary declaration: "The distinctions between Virginians, Pennsylvanians, New Yorkers, and New Englanders are no more. I am not a Virginian, but an American." They adopted a Declaration of Rights and Grievances and pledged not to use British goods until their rights were recognized. **Washington** then was at the Harp and Crown on North Third just south of Arch. Pennsylvania Hospital,* the first hospital in the country, is still in the same location between Eighth, Ninth, Pine, and Spruce, as it was when **Washington** visited in 1774 and probably other times. Then as was his custom, he and the others attended most if not all of the churches in town, mostly still here.

The Revolutionary War Period

The Second Continental Congress met May 10, 1775, at the Pennsylvania State House, known now as Independence Hall,* south side of Chestnut, between Fifth and Sixth. Delegates used the entire building, including the courtroom and second-floor hall shown on public tours. Historian James Flexner called it an illegal junta representing thirteen mutually jealous and independent sovereignties. The shooting had already begun on April 19, in Massachusetts, and **Washington** attended in his old army uniform to show his feelings about the hostilities. The five-foot-four president of the Congress, John Hancock, had an army commander in mind who he thought was the best man for the job: himself. But his fellow delegate from Massachusetts, **John Adams**, arose on June 15 and proposed, to Hancock's dismay, an experienced man from Virginia, who promptly left the room while his qualifications were discussed. **Washington** accepted and was off to eight years of military leadership, without which the new country could probably not have survived. In effect he became the chief executive of the nation, as there was no other. On the night he was nominated he went to Burns Tavern at Tenth and Vine. After he accepted he went to Peg Mullin's Beefsteak, at Passyunk on the Schuylkill River, where he said that his fall and ruin would date from this time. Earlier he ate at Peg's when it was located at Water and Tun Alley.

Jefferson arrived on June 21, 1775. At various times he lived on Chestnut between Third and Fourth, at the Indian Queen Hotel, also known as the Francis Hotel, 15 S. Fourth, in 1774; in 1790, at the SE corner of Market and Fourth; and at the Spread Eagle Inn at 715 Market. He also generally ate at the City Tavern. **Madison** later thought that the Indian Queen had the best food in town. Ben Franklin hosted all of the future presidents in his house on the eastern side of the Indian Queen, now outlined with a skeleton structure* in a square in the middle of the block surrounded by structures on four sides. **Jefferson** also frequently dined at the Indian King Tavern, on the south side of Market between Second and Third.

Slowly the concepts of independence evolved as war raged. In 1776, **Jefferson** was an alternate delegate for Edmond Pendleton, who had to leave. **Jefferson** really wanted to go to the Virginia Convention then meeting, that he felt was more important. On May 15, 1776, **John Adams** called for the Colonies to organize as states. On May 24, **Washington** returned to report on the army and tell war stories at the City Tavern. Richard Henry Lee moved on June 7 that the Colonies declare their independence. When Congress appointed a small group to draft the Declaration of Independence, the other members asked **Jefferson**, who arrived May 14, to draft a proposal. He first stayed at the Benjamin Randolph House, on Chestnut between Third and Fourth, where he had stayed in 1766 and 1775. **Washington** had also lodged there. On May 23, he moved to the Graff (or Declaration) House,* at the SW corner of Seventh and Market, where the document was drafted. When this house was torn down the bricks were numbered and stored so that the historic building could be preserved, but they could not be found when it was rebuilt. The reconstruction house has a glass wall to recreate **Jefferson's** room where he wrote the Declaration. Actually **Adams** and Franklin changed some of the document, to his dismay, but most agree that the final version was better. For instance, his often-quoted words, "We hold these truths to be *self-evident* [emphasis added], that all men are created equal..." were changed from "clear and undeniable." (The Library of Congress sometimes displays **Jefferson's** handwritten draft.) Note that one-fifth of the 2.5 million inhabitants of the colonies were slaves and one-third of the delegates (including all of the Virginians) were slave owners.

Independence was approved on July 2. The Declaration was adopted on July 4, and signed by John Hancock, the president of Congress, and the secretary. Most of the other delegates signed without ceremony on August 2, when an engrossed copy was available. Some signed as late as January 1777. The names of those who signed were kept secret as each committed treason, and the British were near. Few outside Congress knew who wrote it until much later, and it did not appear in the newspaper until 1784. The now faint and almost unreadable Declaration is displayed in the National Archives Building in **Washington**. For many years it was displayed in bright light and used for a wet copy process that faded the document. (**Lincoln's** Gettysburg Address asserted that the country was "brought forth" then, fourscore and seven or eighty-seven years before 1863, not at the later date of the Constitution.) Biographer David McCullough said of **John Adams**, "Few Americans ever achieved so much of such value and consequence in so little time.... **Adams** made the Declaration of Independence happen when it did." **Jefferson** called him the "colossus in Congress." **Jefferson** was the pen; **Adams** the voice. If the Declaration had been delayed much longer it may not have happened, as

Above and opposite: **Probably our country's most important building outside of Washington is Independence Hall, where all presidents have visited. Lincoln spoke in front, and his picture taken there was the first of a president-elect. Kennedy's speech site is also marked. Lincoln's body was viewed inside with visitors entering through the windows up steps. The interior shot shows where the Declaration of Independence (with Adams and Jefferson) and Constitution (with Washington and Madison) were debated and signed and where Lincoln's body lay.**

the British were about to land in New York, not a good sign of hope for the future.

Congress remained in the State House off and on throughout the war and moved several times depending on where the British were. **Jefferson** left in September 1776 to go to the Virginia convention and was out of Congress until 1783. **Adams** was on a naval commission meeting at the Tun Tavern on the waterfront between Walnut and Chestnut. This was a recruiting place for marines in 1775 and is called the "Birthplace of the U.S. Marines." From March 14 until September 12, 1777, **Adams** lived at Mr. Duncan's, on the south side of Walnut between Second and Third, and then for the next three days he was at Rev. Sprouts on Third, a few doors from the Arch Street Meeting House. He then fled the British through Trenton on the way to Lancaster.

Most historians doubt that **Washington** ever came to Betsy Ross House* at 239 Arch with the design of the first American flag, and question if she ever even lived there. The general design of the flag was adopted on June 14, 1777, in Congress. She did make flags for the government, but the story of her designing the first flag with **Washington's** instructions did not arise until many years after everyone who could have known first-hand was dead. The world first heard this from her grandson in 1870, who claimed to have been heard it from her when he was eleven in 1836. But **Washington** knew her and was in town in June 1777, when he was supposedly said to have come to her house to get her to make the flag and gave her a general design. She supposedly changed the six-point star to a five-point. Regardless of how questionable it is, the story has credence and the house is the city's third most popular tourist destination today. She is highly honored in Philadelphia and at the State Museum in Harrisburg.

Near the end of December 1776, it seemed that the Revolution was lost. The Continental Army had been chased out of New York, through New Jersey to Pennsylvania. The army was deserting as Congress was fleeing to Baltimore. Enlistments of many soldiers were up in a few days, and the British and their allies were bearing down. Once the Delaware River froze the British could move men and artillery over the ice to Philadelphia. Having no boats, they stopped north of the river. **Washington** got to the river first and ensured that all area boats were destroyed or hidden. (His December 1 order to do so is in the New Jersey museum at the crossing.) His troops then escaped to the south side of the river, but some bold move was needed, now! **Washington** then surprised the British and their Hessian allies with two courageous moves and battles at Trenton and Princeton, New Jersey, to extend the Revolution.

Washington's headquarters were at the Falls of the Delaware for much of December 1776, in nearby Summerseat* or William Keith's home in Morrisville, Pennsylvania, on Legion Avenue near Clymer Avenue and Alt. U.S. 1, just northwest of the U.S. 1 bridge to Trenton. He was also at Thomas Barclay's near Trenton Falls. On December 24, **Washington** moved to the Thompson-Neely House,* near the embarkation and the present Memorial Building.* This is called the House of Decision as it is where he finalized his plans with his commanders, probably in the basement kitchen, about crossing the river to attack. Eighteen-year-old **Monroe** was a lieutenant with General Lord Stirling (William Alexander) as they made their headquarters for most of December at the house. The central section dates to 1702. A cedar tree that was twenty-seven years old then is marked in the rear of the structure.

Detachments went to Coryell's Ferry, between modern New Hope and Bristol. The crossing was centered around the McKonkey Ferry House* to the east, but took place for maybe a mile along the Delaware. The present structure dates to 1780, rebuilt on 1740 foundations. **Washington** ate Christmas dinner at McKonkey's, also called the Old Ferry Inn. The famous picture of **Washington** crossing here is accurate insofar as he did have to stand because of ice in the bottom of the boat, although **Monroe** is shown in the picture carrying the flag that in reality had not yet been adopted. The river had more water then as towns draw from it now. **Monroe** was severely wounded during a heroic capture of a cannon, and recuperated in the Thompson-Neely House.

Washington's Crossing State Park,* northwest at the bridge over the Delaware, Route 532 along Route 32 for several miles, preserves sites of the famous event that probably preserved the Revolution and independence. Troops assembled near Bowman's Hill,* four miles north across from the Thompson-Neely. **Washington** used the top of the hill as an observation post where a tower* now stands. The hill was named for a surgeon with the infamous pirate Captain Kidd, who built a house here saying the high spot was as near to heaven as he would get.

British commanders did not properly guard for surprise. Snowstorms made conditions miserable for the Continentals. Shoes and socks for some were nonexistent in many ranks, and the soldiers left bloody footprints. All were supposed to be across by 12:00 A.M., but did not make it; only **Washington's** direct command arrived at 3:00. Two other groups felt that the weather was too bad, and gave up. Then **Washington** and his officers met in the Bear Tavern northeast of the present Routes 546 and 579. They had to march miles to attack by dawn. Greene used Pennington Road, and Sullivan used River Road (not Route 29) and Route 31, not 579. (See the entries on Trenton and Princeton in the New Jersey chapter.)

After the Trenton and Princeton victories and spending the winter of 1776–7 in Morristown, New Jersey, **Washington** found out that the British again would try to take the capital in Philadelphia, leaving New York City and heading south by sea. **Washington** used the Moland House,* just north of Bridge Creek, north of Hartsfield (north of I-295 and Philadelphia), as his headquarters from August 10 to 23, 1777, waiting for intelligence as to where they were headed. This is marked on the Old York Road, Old Highway 263 north of Bristol Road. It can be seen but not accessed just west of the present 263, south of Mercer Way leading to Doylestown and about twelve miles west of Washington Crossing State Park. During this time **Washington** returned to Philadelphia to confer with Congress and met a young dandy at the City Tavern. The red-haired, white-wigged nineteen-year-old did have money and had left his pregnant sixteen-year-old-bride to spend his own money to aid the Colonies. He presented his credentials to Congress before joining the army at the Moland House, where he received his commission as major general even though he had no military experience. Strangely the seemingly immature Marquis de Lafayette seemed more interested in service than military rank and quickly became a major leader and national hero to America and France. **Washington** was tired of French dandies who wanted glory, but the childless **Washington** and the orphaned Frenchman quickly formed an almost father-son bond lasting for their lifetimes.

The British arrived in late August 1777 with 15,000 men at the northern end of Chesapeake Bay, where they moved north to occupy the rebel capital. It is supposed that British General Howe wanted to divert **Washington's** forces so that British forces under Generals Burgoyne and St. Leger could move more easily down from Canada. Or Howe might have intended to capture key areas west of Philadelphia in addition to occupying it. So **Washington** moved the army south of town to head off the British advance. In order to boost the city's sagging morale, **Washington** marched the army down Elfreth's Alley* in Philadelphia on the way to meet the British. This became a failed effort to prevent the advance along the Baltimore–Philadelphia Road over today's U.S. 1. **Washington's** army of 14,000 met them at Chadd's Ford on September 11, resulting in the Battle of Brandywine,* the largest one-day battle of the Revolution. A local farmer barged past guards at **Washington's** headquarters to insist that the British were about to encircle the colonials, unbeknownst to the army. The commander himself investigated, finding that Howe and his subordinate Cornwallis had almost flanked and captured the smaller rebel force. Howe, who had bet that **Washington** would consider himself secure in a defensive position by the river, hit his flank and rolled up the American line. The colonials quickly retreated, suffered a defeat, but escaped a disaster.

Washington's reconstructed headquarters* are just north of the bridge over Brandywine Creek on U.S. 1. **Monroe** was near Lafayette when the latter was wounded at Birmingham Meeting House.* Lafayette's headquarters,* just north of **Washington's**, and these sites are clearly marked. The Frenchman revisited the house in 1825 where he had been treated and where **Washington** told doctors, "Take care of him as if he were my son, for I love him the same."

After the battle, before retreating to the west, **Washington** ate "a hearty breakfast of boiled river fish and mountains of meat chops swimming in thick brown gravy with corn and greens" at Wayside Inn, now General Wayne Inn.* This is at 625 Montgomery in Merion, just south of the city, near Highway 1 off Old Lancaster Road, just west of the I-76 and U.S. 1 split, northwest of downtown, said to be the oldest continually operating restaurant in North America.

On September 16, the armies met again northeast of West Chester and southwest of Malvern, south of present U.S. 30 along Route 352. A record-breaking rain ruined most of the colonial musket cartridges due to faulty boxes although the British lost none, and **Washington** had to call the engagement off. **Washington's** headquarters were at Malin Hall* on September 16, 1777, on a side road off Swedesford Road, Route 401 on the north side of Malvern, west of Morehill Road. The battle was between two still existing taverns, the Admiral Warren* and White Horse,* landmarks of the action sometimes called the Battle of the Clouds. The British had no trouble capturing Philadelphia, where they spent a comfortable winter while **Washington's** army ultimately froze at Valley Forge.

Congress fled west to Lancaster and then York. **Washington** retreated to Chester and camped at what is now U.S. 13 east of the present city line at Morton and McDowell Streets. **Washington** later camped at the same spot on the way to Yorktown, Virginia, in 1781. His September 17 headquarters after the Battle of Brandywine are marked on SR 113 at Chester Springs. He is also known to have inspected the works at Fort Mifflin* (east of the airport) and Fort Mercer. (**Jefferson** toured Fort Mifflin on October 17, 1775.) From September 19 to 22, **Washington** was at the Castleberry House on Level Road (private) in Evansburg.

Then he moved, from September 22 until 26, to the nearby Antes House* on Colonial Road south of Route 73 east and a little north of Pottstown, and visited several churches serving as hospitals, also open in town. He probably visited Pottsgrove Mansion* on High Street, east of 100 West King Street, marked on the west side of Route 100 north U.S. 422 in Pottstown. The Pottsgrove Camp for about 10,000 soldiers was between the center of Pottstown and **Washington's** headquarters at the Antes House. **Washington** had to determine whether to possess Philadelphia or protect the interior of Pennsylvania and his supply base at Reading. His diary shows that he stayed in Pottsgrove also on October 1, 1791. Many sources put him at the manor house, and some later sources describe the "earnest consultations with his staff inside," although there is no documented record that he came into the mansion.

Howe refused to follow the Americans "into the woods of the country." Then **Washington** stayed September 26 to 30, 1777, at Pennypacker Mills and Mansion* just east of Route 29 on the corner of Route 73 and Haldeman Road in Schwensville, east of Pottstown. The house has been expanded, and the original is on the south side. He returned October 4 to 7, after the Battle of Germantown. All sites are still surrounded by many period homes and churches that served as hospitals and shelters.

On October 4, **Washington** tried to recapture the capital by attacking nearby Germantown, then a separate small town about seven miles north of Philadelphia. Before and after the Battle of Germantown, he stayed in the Wentz Farmhouse,* marked off Route 73 and Shearer Road, just a mile SE of the intersection of SR 73 and SR 373 in Worcester. As his troops headed down Skippack Road and Germantown Avenue, he got to the Michael Billmeyer House, 6505–7 Germantown Road, north of Cliveden* (Chew House), 6401 Germantown, where British soldiers had barricaded themselves inside. It should have been left contained and bypassed, but **Washington** ordered it shelled and stormed, thus delaying further advance and maybe costing him success in the battle. **Washington** went inside the Billmeyer home to view the situation and is said to have directed the action from its steps. Cliveden is now shown by the National Trust for Historic Preservation basically as it was when **Washington** shelled it in 1777. The walls proved too thick. Deadly assaults were repulsed and an officer was shot trying to present a white flag of parley to the British. The house was finally contained and bypassed, but the Continental Army was beaten back in another defeat. **Washington's** generalship has been questioned, but the French, considering an alliance, were very impressed at the rebels' quick recovery and willingness to persist. The troops' morale remained high to try again somewhere else. **Washington** returned to dine at the Chew House on May 23, 1787. **Monroe** also fought in the battle and visited, while president, the houses listed here on Germantown Avenue.

Washington then moved his forces to Whitemarsh, open today as Fort Washington State Park, twelve miles north and now just west of the I-276/Route 309 junction. **Washington's** headquarters were at Dawesfield (private), at 525 Lewis Lane in Whitpain north off Rte. 73, south of the 73/202 intersection, from October 21 until November 2, 1777. While here he and his officers heard unofficially about the great American victory at Saratoga, New York, a major turning point of the Revolution. The victorious General Gates reported only to Congress, bypassing the commander. **Washington** wrote to congratulate him and sent his aide Alexander Hamilton to try to get him to comply with his orders to return loaned soldiers. Not only had a large, important British force and commander been beaten, but the French now decided the cause had hope and joined the fight to aid the Colonies. The commander allowed his exposed men to cut the owner's trees for firewood. Lafayette slept in the entrance hall because his Brandywine wound would not allow him to climb the stairs to a bedroom. **Washington's** bed is still here. General Anthony Wayne received a court-martial here at his request to be cleared of charges that he was to blame for the disaster at Paoli, where British troops caught the Americans asleep and massacred many. This site is in the town of Malvern, west of Paoli, at the northeast intersection of Monument Avenue and Sugartown Road, south of the midpoint between exits 23 and 24 on the Pennsylvania Turnpike. He was acquitted and honored for bravery. Howe moved against the position and then retreated back to Philadelphia.

Washington visited his surgeon general's headquarters, Hope Lodge,* 553 S. Bethlehem Pike, in Fort Washington south of Exit 26 on I-276 of the Turnpike, and moved to George Emlen's home for headquarters from November 2 until December 11, 1777. This is on Pennsylvania Avenue in Fort Washington but not open. **Washington** now felt that this base was too near the British and moved to Valley Forge, where he spent the next several months.

Valley Forge National Historic Park,* eighteen miles west, contains reconstructed soldiers' huts and fortifications where **Washington's** army of 12,000 encamped during the winter of 1777–8. The commander, with his wife, lived most of the time in the Isaac Potts House* from December 19, 1777, until June 18, 1778, the center of activities, planning, and courts-martial. It is estimated to be 90 percent original with original flooring (except in the entrance hall) and paneling. Martha was at all eight winter encampments and spent February until June here.

Here, as depicted in popular prints, Potts supposedly found **Washington** on his knees in prayer, and stated, "Till now I have thought that a Christian and a soldier were characters incompatible: but if George **Washington** be not a man of God, I am mistaken, and still more shall I be disappointed if God does not through him perform some great thing for this country." Potts described the questionable scene he claimed to have witnessed, since depicted in paintings, of **Washington** on the ground praying that so moved him, he told his wife that surely God would, "through him, work out a great salvation for America."

Washington is said to have stayed in the King of Prussia Inn* on U.S. 202 and Gulph Road in King of Prussia, now isolated on a traffic island in the middle of the road. He and Martha visited troops hospitalized at Historic Yellow Springs* several times. This is just east of the Yellow Springs Road at 1685 Art School Road in Chester Springs, near exit 23 off I-76, west of Valley Forge.

Out of fear, **Washington's** personal cook locked himself in the kitchen with the commander's food to thwart the possibility of poisoning. In this area the army could control roads leading to supply depots near Reading. On December 23, **Washington** wrote, "To see men without clothes to cover their nakedness, without blankets to lie upon, without shoes ... without a house or hut to cover them until those could be built, and submitting without a murmur, is a proof of patience and obedience which, in my opinion, can scarcely be paralleled." No battle was fought here except that against disease, hunger, and the elements. **Washington** reported that almost 3000 of his men had no shoes, and sentries had to stand on their hats to keep their feet from freezing to the ground. Typhus, typhoid, dysentery, and pneumonia killed about 2,000 as Congress tried to get help from the states. Skilled Prussian drillmaster "Baron" Von Steuben, recently arrived, drilled and taught military discipline.

Uwchlan Meeting House* in nearby Lionville was used for sick and wounded. **Washington** stayed across the street at the Red Lion Inn.* He inspected the forges and foundries at East Nantmeal supplying the army. Of these the Redding Furnace* survives. When the army broke camp in June 1778, **Washington** advanced toward Philadelphia and camped in the yard of the Fell House in Doyletown and ate inside. This is in the 400 block of East State Street, private and not marked, across (north) from Chapman Pond Park, a half mile east of the courthouse.

The British left Philadelphia in June 1778, pursued by **Washington**, resulting in the Battle of Monmouth, New Jersey. **Washington** was at Henry Laurens' from December 23, 1778, until February 3, 1779, in Philadelphia. During 1780 to 1783, **Jefferson** and **Madison** generally stayed at the home of Mrs. Mary House, although **Jefferson** was not in Congress and only infrequently here. He did pass several months in vain here and Baltimore waiting for a ship to Europe to help negotiate peace. Congress eventually moved to Princeton and was there with **Jefferson**, **Madison**, and **Monroe** when the Revolution ended in 1783. **Washington** was nearby. Even King George III had said he would be the greatest man in the world if he actually resigned his military commission and reassumed civilian life. Certainly this voluntary surrender of power at the time of triumph is unique in world history, and left **Washington** "first in the hearts of his countrymen."

The Constitutional Convention

The Articles of Confederation were adopted in 1781 as the war ended and proved weak and ineffectual in uniting and organizing the former colonies and their commerce. In effect the former colonies were independent states in a "firm league of friendship," without a leader or real executive, and a congress that could only suggest and request. In 1787, after years of struggle under this weak government, a Grand Convention met again here to revise the Articles, but wound up drafting a new government and Constitution, seeking and accomplishing what no other group had ever done in the history of the world, inventing a government based on "liberty and justice for all." From that standpoint, the convention, not called the Constitutional Convention until later, was illegal as they were not authorized to do away with the government as it existed. They knew this and met behind closed doors and windows in the heat of the summer, in heavy woolen suits at the point of near heat exhaustion, to hide what they were doing. They were wary of a strong leadership position, but knew **Washington** would be it, and created the office of president that **Washington** framed, destined to become the most powerful and important office in the world. Rhode Island, called "Rogue Island" by some of the other angry delegates, never showed up. **Washington** presided over the nearly four months of continuous sessions meeting again in the Pennsylvania State House (Independence Hall*). His prestige united the independent twelve squabbling separate states. Without his presence there possibly would not have been a Constitution or united country, as we know it, as there would not have been an army that would have lasted the eight years of the Revolution without this indispensable man. He deserves his title, "The Father of his Country." **Jefferson** wrote that he was "the only man in the United States who possessed the confidence of the whole."

Madison is known as the Father of the Constitution because of his preparation, leadership, and voluminous, informative convention notes. (He refused to release his notes to the public until the death of the last signer of the Constitution, who turned out to be him.) During the convention, he and the Virginia delegation stayed at Mrs. House's, on the SW corner of Fifth and Market, where **Jefferson** stayed several times before. In fact **Jefferson** and **Madison** stayed here from 1783 until 1793, before and after Mrs. House died. **Madison** became engaged to a 16-year-old in 1783, but she lost interest and married someone else. **Madison** met frequently with the Virginia delegation here, setting up the meeting and trying to persuade the members to illegally throw out the Articles of Confederation for a new government. George Mason objected to this mood, and stayed elsewhere. Many informal meetings were held in Benjamin Franklin's garden* next to the Indian Queen. **Madison** came early and spent many hours alone in the meeting room at Independence Hall planning where he and others would sit and how ideas would be conveyed. He met with the South Carolina delegation at the Indian Queen and agreed that the convention would not attack slavery or the Carolinas. Mason challenged this, which was admirable, but unpractical at the time. This would have produced an unwinnable debate, as there was not the slightest chance that South Carolina, and maybe other Southern states, would concede slavery.

When the Constitution was adopted by the convention, subject to ratification by the States, Franklin remarked that the sun carved on **Washington's** chair must be rising rather than setting. The chair is sometimes displayed in the room, as is other original furniture, and the inkstand is next door on display where the chair is sometimes shown. (Note that over the years the chair, furniture, and inkstand are moved around, in and out of storage, or displayed elsewhere.) On June 1, 1787, John Penn, the grandson of Pennsylvania's founder, entertained **Washington** in his home, at the NE corner of Chestnut and Sixth across from Independence Hall, and at Solitude, now used as an office in the Philadelphia Zoo.

The Capital of the United States

The capital of the United States, with President **Washington**, Vice President **Adams**, and Secretary of State **Jefferson**, moved here from New York City in 1790. **Madison** and **Monroe** were in the House and Senate respectively after **Madison** defeated **Monroe** for the House and then **Monroe** was appointed to the Senate. Philadelphia put forward their best in high hopes that the government would stay rather than move to the Potomac River as then planned. In 1791, **William Henry Harrison** was in town as a young medical student at the College of Pennsylvania, 19 S. 22nd. He served in Philadelphia in the House as a delegate from the Northwest Territory in 1799. The new city hall became Congress Hall,* next to Independence Hall, and was the site of the inauguration of **Washington** and **Adams** in 1793, that of the president in the senate chamber on the second floor. **Washington** gave his second inaugural, the shortest in our history. By this time, all of **Washington's** teeth had long since gone and his uncomfortable hippopotamus ivories made his lips stick out. He still visited his favorite chef at Fraunces Tavern on the south side of Chancellor at Dock, a short block south of the City Tavern. Other historic houses visited by **Washington** and others are marked in the historic areas south of Independence Hall.

On March 4, 1797, President **Adams** was inaugurated in Congress Hall, after **Washington** gave his farewell address there. At the time six of the first seven presidents were in the hall; only **John Quincy Adams** was missing. **Jefferson** was sworn in as vice president in the Senate Chamber on the second floor, where **Adams** and then **Jefferson** presided over the Senate as vice presidents. **Madison** left Congress then after seeing the inaugurations. **Washington**, **Adams**, and **Jefferson** were together then for the last time in "the most affecting and overpowering scene **Jefferson** ever acted in," according to **Adams**. **Jackson** served as the only member of the House from the new state of Tennessee, in 1796–7, and then in the Senate in 1797–8. He heard **Washington's** farewell speech, but would not vote to honor him because of his opposition to Jay's Treaty, and because he felt **Washington's** Indian treaties gave too much away. **Jackson** hated the Senate, was outclassed as an inexperienced thirty-year-old, accomplished virtually nothing, and resigned after one session. He did meet with President **Adams** in the Morris home, known as the "President's House," to convince him to negotiate a new Indian treaty. Most if not all of our presidents have been to Independence and Congress Halls.

When **Jefferson** arrived to greet **Adams** in 1797, they had not seen one another for three years after **Jefferson** had resigned as secretary of state. A great crowd followed **Washington** here as he paid his respects to the new president before he left Philadelphia. When **Adams** was sworn in as the second president, he sat next to **Jefferson** and **Washington** on the dais in Congress Hall. **Washington** insisted that **Jefferson** leave the building first at the place of honor as after the ceremony, **Jefferson** held office, and he did not. **Washington** now did something no other revolutionary leader in history ever did: he stepped down from power. When Napoleon lost everything, he commented that the people had wanted him to be another **Washington**.

Washington lived one lot east of the SE corner of Sixth and 526–30 Market in the Robert Morris House (marked) for most of this presidency, as did **Adams** as president. (This had been Howe's headquarters. It is sometimes listed at 190 High, an obsolete number and street name. Traitor Benedict Arnold also stayed there.) **Washington** had come here before in the early 1770s and 1781, and Morris insisted that the president make it his home rather than at the other end of the street where he had planned. Morris did get an exorbitant $225 rent per month. **Adams** described the furniture as in a "deplorable condition," and bed and bedding in a "woeful pickle." The Liberty Bell Pavilion* was moved to just east of the site in the late 20th century. Morris was one of the wealthiest men in the Colonies and had used much of his personal fortune to finance the Revolutionary effort. Later he became bankrupt, hid out in his country estate, but was arrested and put into debtors' prison. **Washington** had dined with him there at the Walnut Street Prison, in the debtors' section, south of the SE corner of Sixth and Walnut midway in the block toward Spruce Street. **Jefferson** (and probably the others mentioned herein) watched America's first manned balloon ascent from the grounds on January 9, 1793. **Washington's** coach was kept and repaired at a coach maker's shop around the corner on Sixth Street just north of the middle of the block. **Quincy Adams** ate with **Washington** at the Morris House in 1791 and 1794, and heard debates in Congress.

Washington's pew, near Betsy Ross's, can be seen at Christ Church* on Second between Market and Arch. **Adams** and **Jefferson** took delight in climbing the stairs to the tower, the tallest building in the Colonies. It also had the largest window in the Colonies, with a huge tree still outside. **Washington** was a member for seven years, but went to the other churches. **Adams** was technically a member, but he preferred the Presbyterian at the NW corner of Third and Arch. Seven signers of the Declaration and five of the Constitution are buried at Christ Church and in the church's other graveyard up the street. On one occasion **Adams** attended St. Mary's Catholic Church on the west side of Fourth, about one-third of the block north from Spruce (224–250 S. Fourth), with others, including **Washington**, and remarked about how the "unfettered daylight through clear window glass allowed no dark or shadowed corners, or suggestions of mystery." The expanded church still retains the same sanctuary used four times by the Continental Congress.

Washington frequently worshipped at St. Peter's* at Third and Pine, using the Powell family pew (number 41), when he lived on Third Street near the church below Willings Alley. He had worshipped here on his first Sunday in Philadelphia, September 25, 1774. **Madison** favored this church, especially after his marriage. **Jefferson** and **Adams** also came. Actually **Adams** tried all the town's churches, including the Baptist Meeting House at Lagrange Place just north of Christ Church; St. George's Methodist, 235 N. Fourth, now the oldest continually operating Methodist church in the world; Pine Street Presbyterian at 412 Pine; and St. Paul's, on the east side of Third, midway between Spruce and Walnut.

During the summer of 1793, yellow fever struck the capital in one of the most murderous epidemics in American history, forcing the president and others to move out of the city to safer locations while the government formally met. **Washington** stayed a few days in September, went back to Mount Vernon for about two months, and then returned to Germantown. His temporary home with Martha and his two step-grandchildren was the Deshler-Morris House* at 5442 Germantown Avenue, which could be called the earliest "White House" since earlier presidential homes no longer exist. It faces Market Square with a Presbyterian church on the former site of the German Reformed Church, attended by the family, dominating on the east side. Howe used the home as headquarters after the Battle of Germantown.

Christ Church, Philadelphia, was attended by Washington through Monroe at least. Washington's pew can be seen. Adams and Jefferson delighted in climbing the tower, the tallest in the Colonies.

Washington had planned unsuccessfully for his forces to converge at this square, then to drive the British back. During the last two weeks of November 1793, this was the seat of government as he held four cabinet meetings in the house before returning to the city on November 30. **Jefferson** moved to the King of Prussia Tavern, 5516 Germantown, and then to 5275 Germantown, next to Grumblethorpe,* c. 1744, during this time. This architectural gem and others still along the avenue must have attracted his architect's eye.

Washington visited Gilbert Stuart's studio at 5140 Germantown in 1796, and sat for at least two portraits at his studio, at the SE corner of Fifth and Chestnut. **Washington**, **Jefferson**, and the others were frequent visitors to the John Bartram Home,* 54th Street and Eastwick, at Lindbergh, now a memorial to the pioneer botanist, where **Washington** purchased seedlings for Mount Vernon. He and **Jefferson** often visited a friend at Belmont,* in Fairmount Park, 2000 Belmont Drive, and once dug a hole in the ground with his walking stick and planted a Spanish chestnut that still survives. **Washington** and **Jefferson** and probably **Adams** and **Madison** also were guests at the country estate, renamed Lemon Hill,* now in Fairmount Park on Kelly Drive, and Strawberry Mansion* (near the Dauphin Street entrance). **Washington** also was entertained at Woodford House,* 33rd and Dauphin in Fairmount. On May 23, 1787, he noted in his diary that he and **Madison** visited Woodlands,* north of Bartram's Garden on Lindberg, now in Woodlands Cemetery on Woodland. In the southern part of Germantown is Stenton,* Courtland and 18th, used by **Washington** on the way to Brandywine. Howe used it during the Battle of Germantown. **Jefferson** visited his friend Dr. George Logan here.

Benedict Arnold bought Mount Pleasant,* now in Fairmount Park, for his wife, but never occupied it as the government confiscated the mansion after his betrayal. Baron von Steuben leased it briefly, and **Adams** called it the "the most elegant country seat in Pennsylvania." **Washington** and **Jefferson** would have seen it on their visits to the other houses in the area. **Adams** ate at John Dickinson's country seat, Fairhill, and his town house, cater-cornered to the State House on Chestnut. **Washington** liked to attend the theater across from the State House on the NW corner of Sixth and Chestnut. The London Coffee House at the SW corner of Front and Market was a noted meeting place for the patriots.

Washington continued to visit the city after leaving office. He attended Congress with **Adams** on December 7, 1798, after being named commanding general of the army as war with France loomed, with Alexander Hamilton second in command. **Adams** made a speech in their presence in Congress Hall that they would prepare for war, but still try to negotiate with France to settle differences. **Washington's** diary notes that during this November 9–December 14, 1798, visit, he stayed with Mrs. White at 9 North Eighth and ate at the following locations: 187 S. Third; Thomas Willing, 100 S. Third; Bishop William White, 89 Walnut; 113 S. Third Street; Eleventh and Chestnut; Sixth and Arch; 85 Walnut; 217 Arch; Trench Francis on Market between 11th and 12th; plus several addresses on Market.

John Adams lived as vice president in Bush Hill, a structure about two miles outside the city, off Vine Street at the NE corner of 18th and Buttonwood, with a view of the Schuylkill River. When it became too expensive, he moved to Fourth and Arch. When Abigail went back to Boston, he lived with the secretary of the Senate, Samuel Otis, and his wife. He then went to Vice President **Jefferson** at the Francis Hotel, where **Jefferson** then liked to stop, as well as the Spread Eagle or Dunwoody's Tavern at 715 Market. **Washington** came to the Francis for social and business reasons with **Adams** before going back to Virginia. As president his official residence was the Morris House, but **Adams** preferred another, on Market between Fifth and Sixth, probably because of the high rent Morris was charging. **Adams** also spent long periods, March 11, 1798, to October 10, 1799, and July through October 1800, at his home in Massachusetts. The representative of San Domingo once dined at the Morris House, the first man of African descent to be a guest of an American president.

Madison and **Jefferson** stayed together, after traveling through Philadelphia to New York and other places, a block from Independence Hall at the SW corner of Fifth and Market at the House-Trist home, where **Washington** planned to live while president. **Madison** was here at various periods until he married, as was **Monroe**, who stayed near his close friends. Secretary of State **Jefferson** stayed a short time at Mrs. House's in November 1790, and shortly moved to 806 Market, the Leiper House, south side of Market, fourth house west of Eighth. His office across the street was at the NW corner of Market and Eighth. He was here until March 1793, when he resigned. Later the office was on Arch Street, two doors east of Sixth.

Oeller's Hotel, on Chestnut between Sixth and Seventh, was probably the most popular and finest hotel in the capital, and hosted many gatherings, concerts, and meetings involving the presidents during this time. **Jefferson** hosted **Monroe** upon his return from Europe in 1797. Later after the hotel burned, **Jefferson** contributed to the replacement. From April 1793 until January 2, 1794, **Jefferson** lived near Gray's Ferry on the east side of the Schuylkill River between 36th, 37th, Reed, and Dickinson Streets. **Washington** visited, trying to talk **Jefferson** out of resigning as secretary of state. While there, **Jefferson** enjoyed wading in and walking or riding along the river with **Monroe** and **Madison**. Then, from 1797 to 1800, **Jefferson** was back at the Francis, which became headquarters of his party's inner circle.

Vice President **Jefferson** and President **Adams** walked to the American Philosophical Society,* 104 S. Fifth on Independence Square, one of the few things they did together in four years in office. The former close friends, now heading different political parties, further shaped the office of vice president by an almost complete lack of cooperation or communication. A museum was once in the building where **Washington**, a Society member, bowed to a painting with two lifelike figures standing at the head of painted stairs. The painting is now at the Philadelphia Museum of Art. **Jefferson** was president of the Society from January 1797 until 1814, and liked to spend time in various rooms inside. The Society sometimes met at Shippen House, SE corner of Fourth and Locust, where they all visited.

The Powell House,* 244 Third between Walnut and Spruce, famous for its hospitality, was where all the notables dined and drank tea. **Adams** described in great detail lavish dinners in his diary, as well as Benjamin Chew's Town House, where **Washington** stayed from November 26, 1781, until March 23, 1782, among other times. This home was on the west side of Third Street midway between Walnut and Spruce. When the children of his friends, the Powells and Chews, were married in 1787, **Washington** attended. Franklin's daughter wrote to her father in London that she had danced with the president in the great drawing room. The **Washingtons** and Powells were great friends who visited Mt. Vernon.

Dolley Todd lived in the Todd House* at the NE corner of Walnut and Fourth when her husband died in 1793. A year later she married **Madison**, who courted her here. Afterwards they lived at 429 Spruce from 1795 to 1797, **Monroe**'s former home, where **Madison** visited in 1794. **Monroe** had been appointed minister to France.

Washington lodged with Mrs. Rosannah White for a month in 1798, 9 N. Eighth, and visited the Half Moon Tavern, directly across Chestnut from Independence Hall, in the 1790s. Like **Washington's** diary, **Jefferson**'s memo book shows him at many locations in Philadelphia, too numerous to mention other than those shown before, plus his shoe shop at 268 Market, daughter Maria's music teacher at 163 N. Third, and her boarding school at 113 Arch, where **Jefferson** visited every Sunday. Southwest of Independence Hall is Washington Park, where a marker notes that **Adams** once spent an hour in April 1777, silently honoring soldier-prisoners buried there.

After Washington's Death

The memorial service for **Washington** was on December 26, 1799, at the Lutheran church, marked at the SE corner of Fourth and Cherry, north of Arch, which had the town's largest seating capacity. Here Congressman Henry Lee, Robert E.'s father, gave **Washington** the honor, "First in war, first in peace, first in the hearts of his countrymen." **Adams** and Congress were here; **Jefferson** was conspicuously absent, as he purposely delayed his trip from Virginia.

Prior to 1824 there was little interest or regard in the Old State House, and it was almost torn down. Lafayette's 1824 visit changed public feeling and an eternal reverence began preserving the structures. **Jackson** came here in 1833, stayed in the City Hotel, went to First Presbyterian, and sought medical help from a specialist because of bleeding lungs caused by the bullet he received in a duel. The doctor could not alleviate the problem or pain, and just told him to "keep up the good fight." He used Dr. Philip Physick, who lived at 321 S. Fourth,* and whom **Adams, Jefferson,** and **Monroe** also visited. Physick introduced carbonated water for gastric disorders and thus is called the father of the soft drink industry. The crowds were so heavy and unruly in Independence Hall to greet "their president" that six-foot windows were pushed out onto passersby. He lived at Third and Arch when **Madison** brought Dolley.

Houston visited in 1834. On the way to his inauguration, **Franklin Pierce** stayed at the Merchant's Hotel, 40–48 North Fourth, south of

Arch. **Buren** also stayed there in 1839. **Pierce** and **Davis** spoke at Independence Hall in July 1853. **Lincoln** and **Fillmore** attended just as spectators the Whig National Convention, held at the Chinese Museum on the NE corner of Ninth and Sansom, June 7–10, 1848. Surely they must have visited Independence Hall* (although **Lincoln** said that he was not permitted inside) and other historical sites. After the nominations of **Taylor** and **Fillmore**, speeches were made in Independence Square, including one by **Lincoln**. He visited the Musical Fund Hall, 810 Locust and Darien, where the first Republican Convention was held. **Johnson**, military governor of Tennessee, spoke in the hall on March 11, 1863.

Lincoln changed trains here on February 25, 1860, on the way to New York and attempted to meet Simon Cameron and David Wilmot at the Girard House at the NW corner of Ninth and Chestnut. He traveled here on the way to **Washington** on February 21, 1861, and came from the Kensington Depot to the new Continental Hotel, at the SE corner of Ninth and Chestnut, through a crowd of 100,000. The Ben Franklin Hotel now occupies the site, and there is a plaque along the Chestnut Street side, the same block as the Whig convention of 1848. **Lincoln** used the Ninth Street door and spoke from the balcony, although probably no one heard a word. The Kensington Depot was used to and from trips to the north and was several miles north of Independence Hall, on Front between Berks and Montgomery Streets, where the Kensington Recreation Center now is. **Lincoln** used this station also in 1848, 1860, and in 1862 on the way to West Point. The various depots were not connected by rail to the others so that it was necessary to travel over city streets from one to the others.

The next morning **Lincoln** attended a flag raising ceremony at Independence Hall and made a short speech in the room where Congress met and the Liberty Bell then stood. He then spoke in front on a platform where the first photographic image of a president-elect was made. A marker in front of the Hall on Chestnut Street marks the spot, a few feet away from another marker where **Kennedy** stood in 1962.

Afterward, **Lincoln** left from the hotel by way of Pennsylvania Depot, at the NW corner of 32nd and Market, for Harrisburg, refusing to change plans until his obligations were completed. He did skip the ball in Harrisburg, returning to the Pennsylvania Depot for Washington on the Philadelphia, Wilmington, and Baltimore Station at Broad and Washington Streets, at 11:00 P.M.

On June 16, 1864, the **Lincolns** attended the Philadelphia Sanitary Fair or Great Central Fair, held at Logan Square where the main hall was, in the center of Benjamin Franklin Parkway between 18th and 19th Streets. They had little time for exhibits as crowds pressed him everywhere. He again stayed at the Continental Hotel. **Grant**, **Hayes**, and **Andrew Johnson** later came and spoke there and at the Union League Club, then at 1118 Chestnut.

On April 22, 1865, his remains arrived at the Broad Street Railroad Depot at Broad and Prime (Washington) Streets and proceeded over the following jammed route: north to Walnut, west to 21st, north and east on Arch to Third, south to Walnut, and west to the south-center entrance of Independence Hall. His body lay near the Liberty Bell, and was carried past the bell to the middle of the room where Congress met. **Quincy Adams**'s body had earlier lain in state here. The public was allowed to pass by in two unbroken streams for twenty hours and numbered 85,000 to over 300,000. Public viewers entered through the windows directly into the room by specially constructed stairs on Chestnut, passed both sides of the president, and then out the windows via stairs onto the square. After leaving Harrisburg, the funeral train had passed through great crowds at Middletown, Elizabethtown, Lancaster, Parkesburg, Coatesville, Downingtown, West Chester, and Paoli. (None of the Philadelphia railroad stations listed is in existence today.)

After the Civil War, **Grant** lived at 2009 Chestnut in a home given to him by the Union League. He intended to commute on weekends to his duties in Washington, but found this too difficult. So this house was rented, and he accepted another gift house in the capital. He attended the first world's fair held in America, the Centennial Exposition of 1876 in Fairmount Park along the Schuylkill River, as did **Hayes** and just about everyone else of any importance in the country.

The Academy of Music, SW corner of Broad and Locust, has hosted "presidents from **Buchanan** to **Hoover**." **Theodore Roosevelt** stayed at the Hotel Walton at Locust and Broad for the 1900 Republican Convention at the Exposition Hall. **McKinley** was there the year before.

Wilson's first job was teaching young women at Bryn Mawr outside of Philadelphia. He and his wife lived between the home of the dean, the "Deanery," and a house called the "Greenery."

They called their home "Betweenery." Normally a Presbyterian, he went to the Baptist church at 905 Gulph Rd. Every president from **TR** to **Reagan** is claimed to have visited the Bellevue Stratford Hotel* at 200 Broad and Walnut. Thirty-four convention attendees died here in July 1976 from "Legionnaire's Disease." The Convention Hall at 34th and Vine has seen all the presidents from **Franklin Roosevelt** to **LBJ**. **FDR** made his famous "Rendezvous With Destiny" Speech in 1936 there, and **Truman** began his surprising campaign in 1948. **George W. Bush** was nominated in 2000 at the Wachovia Center (then First Union Center), 3601 S. Broad. He and all recent presidents have been here many times. **Ford** and **Carter** debated on September 23, 1976, at the Walnut Street Theater at 823 Walnut. **Clinton** and **H.W. Bush** were presented the 2006 Liberty Medal at the National Constitution Center, 525 Arch, on October 5, 2006.

PITTSBURGH • After the French began invading the Allegheny region in the 1750s, young **Washington** and several guides scouted the area for the British in December 1753. (See Franklin.) After several days scouting the area he determined that the point where the Allegheny and Monongahela form the Ohio River, now Point Park,* was "well situated for a Fort." This was the beginning of the later great city. He scouted further north, near today's Waterford, and raced to get back to Williamsburg to deliver intelligence and the French answer to the British ultimatum to the king's representative. When he arrived at the river crossing here, the solid ice that he expected had not formed. So he attempted to cross in freezing water with ice floes, about where the Washington Crossing Bridge now is at 40th Street. He almost drowned on his first attempt when he fell in the freezing water, since he could not swim, and spent a freezing night rubbing snow on his feet. He then crossed here the next morning when the river did freeze. Virginians later came and began building a fort until they were driven off by the French, who completed it and named it Fort Duquesne. The young militiaman then was sent back with a force of several hundred, but ran into the French near Fort Necessity, starting the French and Indian War.

The British then sent a force under General Braddock to recapture the fort, remnants of which are still preserved at the Point. The British would not change their European tactics despite the urging of **Washington**, frontiersman Daniel Boone, and others among them. Other Revolutionary War figures—Charles Lee, Horatio Gates, Daniel Morgan, Hugh Mercer, and Christopher Gist—were also in the company. Nor would the British respect the French-Indian allies. Rather than take packhorses and scout the woods, Braddock lumbered slowly on at a snail's pace without proper scouting. After all, what did the colonials know, especially the volunteer militia officer, who was under no obligation to stay and could have left any time? But even after getting sick and being left behind, **Washington** rejoined just before the July 9, 1755, attack that historian James Flexner called "the most catastrophic [day] in all Anglo-American history." All officers were then killed or wounded, except **Washington**.

When Braddock was attacked in the present suburbs of the future city he was appalled at the cowardliness exhibited by the Virginians coolly firing from cover and the more simple-minded British following them. He ordered formations in the open to make frontal attacks, exposing and devastating his own ranks. **Washington's** luck would hold up all his military life, as he was never wounded even after frequent exposures to fire. (Some believe that a major factor in Benedict Arnold's defection was his feeling that the later Revolution rested on **Washington's** shoulders, and the commander could not survive his frequent exposures to fire.) Officers on horses were perfect targets. At least four bullets tore **Washington's** uniform, his hat was shot off, and two horses were killed beneath him. The attack came as the British were attempting the double-crossing of the Monongahela River where Turtle Creek joins it in the area of Braddock and North Braddock, eight miles east of Fort Pitt, near Highway 30 in the vicinity of Braddock and Center Avenues and Sixth Street. The 800 to 900 French and Indians inflicted 977 casualties on the British force of about 1459. The British could not fight as individuals, out of formation. The Indians could have done more damage if they had not taken time to loot and scalp as the survivors fled. Prisoners were burned alive about where Three Rivers and Heinz Stadiums were later built on the north side of the Ohio River just beyond the river junction. Braddock, gravely wounded, was carried back toward Virginia, but died near Ft. Necessity. **Washington** was regarded as a hero as the only unwounded officer, who had tried to correct British tactics and had ridden for reinforcements while sick.

Now the twenty-three-year-old hero commanded the Virginia militia for two years after Braddock's defeat. Promoted to colonel, **Washington** was ordered to build Forbes Road to the east of Fort Pitt. His base camp, set up in November 1758, is marked on U.S. 22, east of Murrysville. (Forbes Road is generally along U.S. 30.) On November 24, 1758, **Washington** and Forbes camped on the site of Braddock's defeat, intending to attack the next day. During the night they heard a large explosion and found out that the French had blown up the fort. The old French Fort at the Point was rebuilt as Fort Pitt, which grew into Pittsburgh. **Washington** later returned to Ft. Pitt on a surveying mission and drifted for 250 miles "through a pristine empire so vast and empty that imagination was staggered." In 1770 **Washington** was at Samuel Semple's Tavern, northeast corner of Ferry Street and the Monongahela River, one block south of First Street. The address is not current, but was near the fort.

William Henry Harrison was at Ft. Pitt in 1791, and Watson's Tavern at the northeast corner of First and Market, and traveled through in 1841 on the way to his inauguration. **Monroe** came here on the way to attend a conference with the Shawnees to the west, but low water prevented his going much further. During his 1817 tour he visited the courthouse, then at First and Market on the Diamond, and the Presbyterian and Episcopal churches. These two old churches were at 320 Sixth (Presbyterian) and the triangle with Wood and Liberty (Episcopal). The Episcopal has moved a short distance east on Sixth and is now next to the Presbyterian.

On his inaugural trip, **Lincoln** made short stops in nearby Rochester and Allegheny City and arrived on February 14, 1861, north of the river and on South Commons. He then traveled through huge crowds in the rain down Federal Street, over a suspension bridge to St. Clair (about the present Sixth Street Bridge), to Market, Fifth, and Smithfield to the Monongahela House at the NW corner of Fort Pitt and Smithfield. He spoke standing on a chair in the lobby and made his longest address of the journey from the balcony before a multitude of five thousand. He returned to the train via Fourth, Grant, Fifth, Wood, Liberty, Hand, Penn, and St. Clair Streets. **Jackson, John Quincy Adams, Benjamin Harrison, Garfield, Hayes, Cleveland, McKinley, TR,** and **Taft** were also at the Monongahela House. **TR** made a speech on the water side.

Johnson and **Grant** were also at the hotel in 1866 and attended a banquet at the St. Charles Hotel at Wood and Third. **Benjamin Harrison** dedicated the Carnegie Library at 4400 Forbes in 1890, and **McKinley** attended Christ Methodist Episcopal at Penn and Eighth in 1899. Freshmen congressmen **Kennedy** and **Nixon** first debated each other on opposite sides of the Taft-Hartley Bill in April 1947, in suburban McKeesport, sharing the same sleeping car on the train.

READING • **Washington's** October 1794 headquarters during the Whiskey Rebellion was at the Federal Inn, marked on Penn Square between Fourth and Fifth Streets. **FDR**, as assistant secretary of the Navy, dedicated the statue on Penn Commons, Penn and Eleventh Streets.

SOMERFIELD • The Great Crossing Bridge was dedicated on July 4, 1818, by **Monroe** at what became the National Road Crossing of the Youghiogheny River. Various presidents traveled the road proposed by Jefferson, now U.S. 40 east of route 281. **Washington** crossed here to forts north, and then with Braddock. **McKinley** vacationed at the Endley House. The town was covered by a lake in the 1940s.

WASHINGTON • **Washington** was presented two lots at the SE corner of Wheeling and College when he visited. Several presidents stayed about two blocks west at the Sign of General Jackson Inn at Main and Strawberry (northeast of the U.S. 40/19 intersection), including **W. Harrison, Monroe, Jackson, Polk,** and **Taylor. Grant** laid the cornerstone for the town hall in 1868. Lafayette, **Jackson**, and maybe others stayed at the still operating Century Inn* in Scenery Hill, just east on U.S. 40, the old National Road.

WATERFORD • **Washington** stepped on to the world stage here in his first public mission in December 1753 to the French Fort Le Boeuf, now marked on U.S. 19 two blocks south of the central green. A museum adjoins. When the Virginia governor got word that the French were trespassing on British soil, blocking a move by wealthy Virginia investors to settle homesteaders on British grants in the upper Ohio Valley, he looked around for someone to deliver a warning to the French to peacefully withdraw. The eager volunteer was a twenty-one-year old adjutant with the Virginia militia, selected largely because of his frontier surveying experience. The 1000-mile, ten-week adventure began in Williamsburg on October 31, continuing through the winter with constant bad rains and severe cold causing numerous water crossings in freezing water and ice.

Washington and a few rough companions met the French here. The twenty-one-year-old hoped his manner and grave face would make him seem older and stronger than his years would have indicated as he could have been executed as a spy. He quickly determined the strength and plans of the French, presented his king's ultimatum, and received a negative response. Legend says he climbed a tree, now behind a supermarket a half-mile from the Eagle Hotel down U.S. 19, to reconnoiter the French Fort.

The information was desperately needed back at the Virginia capital. He skillfully and firmly maneuvered the Indian allies out of the French camp before liquor completely changed their allegiances, and started back toward his superiors in Williamsburg. The Indian allies were left behind until he and Christopher Gist were alone with one Indian, who fired directly at **Washington** from fifteen paces and missed. (The event is marked on Pa. 68, 1.8 miles northeast of Evans City.) This was the first of many bullets and potential disasters that would have changed the course of world history, but that the "indispensable man" survived. When the traitor was subdued, **Washington** would not let Gist kill him, so they had to send him away while they traveling night and day in the freezing weather to leave the area. This included a dangerous crossing of the Allegheny River described in the Pittsburgh entry. Governor Dinwiddie printed Washington's journal/report, bringing great fame and admiration among the colonists, leading to future opportunities.

Taylor lodged at the Eagle Hotel* on U.S. 19, High and First Streets, in 1848.

YORK • From September 30, 1777, until June 27, 1778, Congress met in the courthouse in the center of the square, with the main entrance on George Street, after fleeing the capital in Philadelphia. The building has long since vanished and the current courthouse is a little east, with a replica of the building used as a visitor's center at Market and Pershing. **Adams** and many others stayed at the Globe Inn marked at the SW corner of the square. He presided over the Board of War at a law office at George and Mason Alley. He was also frequently at the Golden Plough Tavern* on West Market. While Congress was here General Horatio Gates is believed to have either led a conspiracy to place himself at the head of the army, and given tacit approval of such thinking, or at least was a part of a major malcontent uprising. This ended, according to an unproved legend, at the Gates House, Market and Pershing, next to the Golden Plough. Here Lafayette supposedly observed after a series of toasts, "Gentlemen, there is one you have forgotten. I propose a toast to our Commander-in-Chief: George **Washington**. May he remain at the head of the army until independence is won." This display of his important individual opinion, as well as that of a spokesman for France, ended the "Conway Cable."

Washington passed through Frederick, York, and Lancaster in 1791 on the way to Philadelphia by a route he had not traveled before, although he probably passed through York in the 1750s. He was honored at the courthouse on April 2, 1791, when every window was lit with candles, and either stayed or dined at the Thomas Harley House on Market, marked, then east of and next to the Zion Reformed Church one block west of the square. He went to Zion on April 3, 1791, since there was no Episcopal church here. The service was in German, and he wrote in his diary that there was no chance of the preacher "making a proselyte" of him since he could understand not a word. He was also seen in front of the George Irwin home at Market and Beaver talking with friends. He visited the Baltzer Spangler Tavern, later called the Washington House, on E. Market and Centre Square near Duke. (He might have stayed here rather than the Harley House shown above as sources vary.) He also was at the First Presbyterian at the NE corner of Market and Queen, where **W.H. Harrison** attended in 1836 and 1840. **Washington** generally noted in his diary, as he did in 1791 here, that he walked through the town noting houses, some still here.

Jackson was brought into town in February 1819 by a sled after his large sleigh broke down just south. He stayed at a hotel on the SE corner of Centre Square and George. **Van Buren** stayed at the White Hall Hotel, NE corner of Beaver and Market, in 1839, and the Washington House in 1840, as did **W. Harrison**. In 1840 **Buchanan** gave campaign speeches at the Golden Horse Inn from the balcony at the corner of Market and Water. He also made speeches from the courthouse in 1848 to returning Mexican War veterans. **Taylor** was at the Washington House in August 1849. Funeral processions for both **Harrison** and **Taylor** went through York. **Johnson** came to town in 1866 with **Grant** accompanying and stayed at the Washington House. **Grant** met a boyhood friend at the station. **Garfield** came several times and stopped at the train station after his inauguration. His body was honored by 10,000 on the way back to Ohio. **Theodore Roosevelt** passed through the Centre Square in 1906 to address the town at the Agricultural Society grounds on Market Street. All were welcomed with processions, speeches, and responses.

RHODE ISLAND

BRISTOL • In March 1781, **Washington** visited Governor William Bradford at his home at 250 Metacom Avenue, Route 136, now an inn,* north of the center of town. The site is known as Mount Hope Farm and was the home of the Indian leader King Philip, who led a war in 1675. **Washington** returned in 1793 to spend another week at Bradford's home, then at the NE corner of Hope and State,* now also a B&B. For years the students at one school had to learn and recite:

> In fourteen hundred ninety-two
> Columbus sailed the ocean blue.
> In seventeen hundred eighty-one
> I saw General Washington.

Next door to the above is Linden Place* at 500 Hope St., Route 114, at the town center visited by **Arthur**, **Jackson**, **Grant**, and **Monroe**.

KINGSTON • When the British occupied the Rhode Island capital, the Assembly met in a building now the library* at SR 138 and Upper College Road. Following the war, **Washington** met with Ben Franklin and the Assembly there.

NEWPORT • **Washington** was first here in 1756 on the way to Boston, and then to meet French General Rochambeau on March 6, 1781, at the 1739 Old Colony House* (Old State House) on Washington Square, Touro and Broadway. They met with French Admiral d'Estaing to plan a campaign, which ended in victory at Yorktown. A banquet was held in his honor on the first-floor hall where the legislature met from 1790 until 1900. The building is claimed to be the second oldest Capitol and to be America's real Independence Hall, since Rhode Island declared its independence here on May 4, 1776, thus making it the first independent republic in the Americas. **Quincy Adams**, **Jackson** (1833), **Van Buren**, **Fillmore**, **Buchanan**, **Grant**, **Arthur**, **Hayes**, **Taft**, **FDR** (1936), **Eisenhower**, and probably all of the presidents ever in town were here.

Meetings then were at Rochambeau's headquarters, where **Washington** stayed seven nights, the Vernon House (private), 46 Clarke Street at the NE corner of Mary. When **Washington** entered, a small boy in his father's arms called out, "Why father, General **Washington** is a man," to which **Washington** replied, "Yes my son, only a man." The Europeans were said to be much impressed with his demeanor and presence when they met him at a ball in the home. The town was illuminated, and he walked all over as he did when he visited other places all of his life. Balls were also held at Mrs. Cowley's Tavern nearby, at the SE corner of Church and Thames, and "French Hall" erected just north of the Vernon House.

Rhode Island did not approve the Federal Constitution until May 29, 1790, by a vote of 34 to 32, and finally became a part of the new country, more than a year after **Washington's** inauguration. To honor the new member of the Union, he and Secretary of State **Jefferson** landed at the Long Wharf,* east of the visitor center and south of Washington Square, in August 1790. The party stayed at Mrs. Almy's on Spring near Thames Street, south of Mary Street, where they were escorted by a procession from the dock. They attended the Touro Synagogue,* to which **Washington** later sent a letter of recognition, read there every August. Although there is no documentary evidence for any year, he traditionally worshipped at pew 81 at Trinity Church,* Queen Anne Square, although the church may have then been out of repair due to the occupation by the British. (Queen Elizabeth II attended Trinity in 1976.) They walked extensively around town, went to the Benton House behind the Thames Street shops, walked Bellevue Street, saw many houses and buildings still in town, and attended a banquet at the State House.

Monroe paid a visit in 1817 while president and visited Forts Adams* and Wolcott, Trinity Church, and the Baptist church* on Spring Street. The present church dates to 1846, the fourth since 1638. He visited William Ellery, one of the two Declaration signers still alive other than **Jefferson** and **Adams. John Quincy Adams** came several times, inspected Fort Adams on Harrison Avenue (named for his father), and the Redwood Library* at the north end of Bellevue Ave., the oldest library in America. **Polk** arrived at the Newport wharf in July 1847, long enough for the steamer to unload. A large crowd did hear a brief speech. **Pierce** left from the fort to go to the Mexican War in 1847, and came back after his nomination in 1852 to the City Hotel and the Bellevue House. **Grant** and **T. Roosevelt** made extended trips here as president, the latter as secretary of the Navy also, and spoke at a naval conference at the Naval War College, as did **George W. Bush** on August 28, 2007, his first appearance as president in the state.

One of the most elegant balls ever in Newport was at the Stone Villa on Bellevue for **Arthur** in 1884. **B. Harrison** toured the naval facilities in 1889, and **Cleveland** fished in the area in 1893, anchoring his yacht off Jamestown, and stayed at Chateau Nooga at Bellevue and Narragansett in 1889 and 1893. **TR** visited Cliff Lawn, at the Cliff Walk and Bush Rd., in 1902 and Beaulieu on Bellevue Ave. between the Marble House and Clarendon Court. **FDR** witnessed the defense of America's Cup against the British challenger in 1934 and inspected military and naval installations in 1940. **Truman** visited the Naval Training Station in 1946 and later dedicated the servicemen's club.

Kennedy married at St. Mary's Church,* 70 Church, on September 12, 1953, and his wedding reception was at Hammersmith Farm,* on Ocean Drive, the bride's mother's home. He was hosted here often and used it as the summer White House from 1961 to 1963. He met the Pakistani president at the Breakers,* the most elaborate of estates along Bellevue, in 1962.

Ike spent three-month vacations in town, golfed most days at Newport Country Club,* went to several churches, and dedicated the park named for him in Washington Square* in 1957. He was here in 1958 and 1960, staying at the commanding officer's quarters at Fort Adams, now administrative offices for the state park. While here he conferred with **Nixon**, who had been assigned to Quonset Naval Air Station during World War II.

Providence • **Washington**'s headquarters were at Stephen Hopkins's House,* where his bed is still kept, from April 5 to 7, 1776, and again in 1781. This was on the NE corner of Hopkins and Main where the Court Building now is, later moved across the street, then north toward Benefit Street, and now it sits on the SW corner of 15 Hopkins and Benefit, southeast of the courthouse. When it was announced that **Washington** would be here, various neighbors rushed to allow his host to use their fancy linen, china, and silver, but Hopkins' stepdaughter, who kept house, told them that what was good enough for her father was good enough for the president.

The Old State House,* capitol from 1762 until 1900, still stands on North Main between North and South Court. Providence makes the same claim as Newport for the Old State House, where the Declaration of Independence was read from the balcony, and the Constitution was ratified. (The legislature met here and in Newport.) A plaque inside notes the 1790 visit of **Washington** and **Jefferson** when they came to honor the state for having finally joined the Union. **John Adams**, **Jackson**, and **Hayes**, among others, were honored here.

The Golden Ball Inn at 159 Benefit, opposite the Old State House just to the east, was the social center of the town, known by various names over the years. Among those entertained were all of the **first seven presidents**. University Hall, east of College and Prospect, was used as a barracks during the Revolutionary War. **Washington** received an honorary doctorate of law there in 1790, and **Monroe** stayed in 1817. **FDR** spoke from the steps of the new Capitol in 1936, and **LBJ** spoke at Brown University in 1964.

In 1789 **John Quincy Adams** described the John Brown House,* 52 Power Street, as "the most magnificent and elegant private mansion I have ever seen on this continent." But it is believed this statement was based on his view of the outside, as there is no proof that he was inside. But **Washington**, **John Adams**, and **Jefferson** were. **Washington** was entertained at the Jabez Bowen House (site) at 20 Market Square on March 13 and 14, 1781. **Hayes** was at Governor's Mansion, 83 John Street, in 1877 and stayed at the Hopkins Mansion.

Lincoln gave his "recycled Cooper Union

Speech" on February 28, 1860, at overflowing Railroad Hall, located on the second floor at the northern end of a station that burned in 1870. The spot is marked at the Federal Building at the east end of Exchange Place, Exchange Terrace and Exchange. He stayed with John Eddy at 265 Washington Street. He is also claimed to have been to Howard Hall at the NE corner of Westminster and Dorrance Streets, as was **Houston.**

Just south in East Greenwich is the Varnum Museum,* a house used by General **Washington** during the Revolution, 57 Pierce Street, southwest of Main (U.S. 1) and Division.

WOONSOCKET • On March 8, 1860, **Lincoln** spoke on the third floor of Harris Hall, now the town hall,* at 157 Main, and stayed with Edward Harris at the corner of Harris and Blackstone in the North End. A Yale professor was so impressed by the speech **Lincoln** had given in New Haven that he rode the train here to hear it again and lecture on it to his class.

SOUTH CAROLINA

Washington made a tour of all Southern states in the spring of 1791. He came with a riding horse, baggage wagon, private secretary, and his pet greyhound, Cornwallis. He hoped to promote the new federal union, conduct a fact-finding mission, and restore his health. His route through the area was roughly down U.S. 17, the King's Highway through the Carolinas. The best source of the exact route is in *South Carolina in 1791*, an out-of-print publication by the South Carolina Department of Archives and History, summarized in this chapter. But no one source is complete, and various other sources are also used here.

ABBEVILLE • The town is often referred to as the cradle and the grave of the Confederacy. It is claimed that a meeting held on Secession Hill began the movement, and what is called the last cabinet meeting of the Confederacy was held on May 2, 1865, at the Burt Mansion* at the corner of Main and Greenville. But that was when the cabinet was scattered and with **Davis** and several generals, including Braxton Bragg and John C. Breckinridge, secretary of war, but now acting as a general, fleeing the Yankees. The civil government was by now just symbolic with no real function. Though thoroughly beaten, the still defiant **Davis** was only willing to discuss the future course of the war. He proclaimed that the cause was not lost, and the 3000 brave men now there could be a nucleus to form a rallying point. The amazed, dumbfounded generals could not believe their leader and sat silent as he seemed to age and sank in his chair. Finally they told him that there was no war to continue, there should be no guerrilla actions, the cause was hopeless, and the only recourse was to aid his escape. He fled federal patrols at 11:00 that night.

AIKEN • **Taft** visited the Beech Island Agricultural Club in 1908 on CR 125 before the clubhouse burned. **Ike** was at Uncle John's Cabin, 467 Newberry; **Kennedy** was at CaneBrake, 531 Coker Springs; and **George W. Bush** visited the area of his grandparents as a baby. They lived on Magnolia Street, at the present site of Whitehall, and attended St. Thaddeus, 125 Pendleton.

BRANCHVILLE • At least three presidents, **McKinley, TR,** and **Taft**, have eaten at the depot on Main, claimed to be the oldest railroad junction in the world, dating to 1832.

CAMDEN • Fourteen Revolutionary battles were fought in the area with one witnessed through chinks in the stockade jail by barely fourteen-year-old **Jackson** and his brother, sixteen-year-old Robert. This was the April 25, 1781, Battle of Hobkirk Hill as the American army attacked the British just north. The boys were confined to jail, in the 600 Block of S. Broad at the SE corner of King, for having been present at a Patriot gathering near their home. There were huddled with about 250 others with no beds, no medicine, and little food with constant threats of being hanged. Although his British jailers boarded the windows so that the prisoners could not see the progress of the battle, Andy was able to cut out a peephole to describe the battle for his fellow prisoners. Both boys caught smallpox and almost died from maltreatment before being surrendered to their mother in an exchange. She got them home, Andrew walking the forty rain-soaked miles, but Robert died of an infection caught here. When Andy appeared to be recovering, his mother set out for Charleston to nurse other prisoners including his Crawford cousins, living in horrible conditions. She succumbed to a camp disease, leaving her remaining son an orphan. This was the genesis of **Jackson's** hatred for the British, culminating the in the Battle of New Orleans.

Washington came from Columbia in 1791 through what he called "the most miserable pine barrens he had ever seen." The town greeted him at the ferry where modern I-20 crosses the Wateree River, two miles south. He was honored at King and Fair, the Chestnut House, now moved to the NW corner of 1413 Mill and Laurens. He was also greeted and made an address at the NE corner of Bull and Broad, the center square of the old town. He visited the Fowler Mansion at the SE corner of Fair and York, and probably stayed there or at the Brisbane House (burned) on the east side of Fair near the Chestnut House. Going and coming he traveled roughly U.S. 1 and 521. After leaving he spent the night just northeast of Kenshaw on U.S. 521. As he moved north he toured the battlefields, with scattered bones of soldiers still present, and sites in the area including Hobkirk Hill, on the north edge of town, and the battlefields of Camden and Gum Swamp, a little further north, all marked. The former commander questioned his guides about battle positions and how Greene could have been surprised by British General Rawdon at Hobkirk's Hill. He paid his respects to the tomb of DeKalb, wounded at the Battle of Camden, then in the yard of the house where he died at the NW corner of Meeting and Broad. The tomb is now in the Old Presbyterian Cemetery* at Market and DeKalb. The foreign-born general had helped save the army from further disaster at the Battle of Camden, one of the greatest losses ever suffered by an American army. But at least it ended any talk of General Horatio Gates replacing **Washington**. The site where DeKalb fell is marked on the field. **Washington** would have seen Lord Cornwallis's headquarters, near the SE corner of Broad and Meeting, that General Sherman's forces burned during the Civil War. Lafayette later stayed in the 1100 Block of Broad in 1825, later the site of the courthouse and next to the birthplace of financier Bernard Baruch.

CHARLESTON • **Washington** spent May 2 to 9, 1791, in the former state capital. He spent the night before in a long-destroyed house known as Joseph Manigault's Salt Pond Plantation, on the ocean directly south of Awendaw. In the morning he had breakfast at Governor Charles Pinckney's Snee Farm,* now a National Historic Site at 1254 Long Point Road, west of U.S. 17 a few miles north of Charleston, east of Interstate 526 and SR 517. (This archeological site is open near the more famous Boone Hall Plantation,* called "the most photographed plantation in America," on the north side of the road a little further west.) He then proceeded toward Charleston, saw Christ Church, marked on the east side of Highway 17 near the turn to Snee Farm, and landed amid a great crowd at the foot of Queen Street. A parade of followers then moved up Queen to East Bay and then down Broad to the Old Exchange* at 122 E. Bay, the end of Broad, still an elegant building, where the Declaration of Independence and Constitution had been proclaimed. Here he stood on the steps to witness a parade in his honor, later attended several dinners and receptions, danced at a ball, and went to a concert. He refused to walk on red carpet rolled out for him and reproached the citizens that such adulation should be for the Creator alone.

The parade proceeded several blocks south on E. Bay, back up to Broad, to Church Street and down to the Heyward-Washington House* at 87 Church, where he stayed. Tradition says he spoke from the balcony of Sixty-nine Church across the street. Other large homes had been offered and considered, including his cousin's and Edward Rutledge's, mentioned later. His host, Thomas Heyward Jr., had been a signer of the Declaration and sent to prison at St. Augustine by the British when they captured Charleston. His wife kept her sister and her children here until Loyalists so harassed them that the sister died, and Mrs. Heyward moved to Philadelphia. **Washington** dined with Governor Pinckney on Meeting Street on one day and attended a ball there on another. The destroyed Pinckney home was between **Washington's** cousin's on the south and **Washington's** host Heyward's 1803 home at 18 Meeting on the north, both still standing.

On his Sunday in town **Washington** worshipped in a morning service at St. Philip's* on the east side of Church Street, north of Queen.

(This church burned later and was rebuilt.) That afternoon he sat in the large Royal Governor's pew, number 43, at St. Michael's* at the SE corner of Broad and Meeting. The day before, he had ascended the 186-foot steeple, then the tallest structure in town, for a bird's-eye view. The pew box, baptismal font, and organ case are original to that time. Lafayette, **Theodore Roosevelt**, Robert E. Lee, and other prominent men used the same pew. (John Rutledge and Charles Pinckney are buried in the graveyard.) This is the "corner of the four laws," as here were located three levels of government, the State House, city hall, Federal Post Office, and the moral law represented by the church. The State House on the NW corner was being rebuilt when **Washington** visited, since it was then hoped that the capital would be lured back. The site was used by the royal governor and partially destroyed in 1788. The design might have influenced the White House. After church he dined at General William Moultrie's.

The city hall was then where the Federal Building is now, the SW corner. **Washington** was there several times where he dined and attended a concert. His diary comments about the 256 ladies at the dinner. (*South Carolina in 1791* says that this event was at the Exchange and the city hall chambers were the grand ballroom.) **Davis** spoke there in 1863 during the Civil War.

On May 4 the president was given a tour of the battlefield and area fortifications and honored at a dinner and ball with members of the Society of the Cincinnati in the Long Room at McCrady's Tavern,* 63 East Bay, 2 Unity Alley at Queen, now restored as a restaurant. The next day he saw Fort Moultrie,* then in ruins. This is restored across the U.S. 17 Bus. Bridge on Sullivan's Island and administered by the National Park System. He also visited Ft. Johnson on James Island, now in ruins, down S.C. 171 on Fort Johnson Road at the grounds of the Marine Laboratory of the College of Charleston. One morning he visited the orphans' home then on Market Street about two blocks north of St. Philip's.

The 1760 home of John Rutledge, president of the Independent Republic of South Carolina during the Revolutionary War, governor, and second chief justice of the United States, was 116 Broad.* **Washington** breakfasted there with his wife as Rutledge was out on the judicial circuit. (**Taft** visited in 1909 with the then owner and mayor. He stayed at the Charleston Hotel on Meeting St. and attended the Unitarian church at 4 Archdale.) Rutledge's brother Edward signed the Declaration of Independence. His prominent house is still across the street, marked, and must have attracted **Washington's** notice. On May 6, the president toured the streets and the city's elegant homes, many still here. Surely he must have seen the Miles Brewton House* at 27 King, British headquarters of Clinton and Cornwallis and later the Union headquarters during the Civil War. Some believe this is the most complete, elegant, and best-preserved Georgian mansion in the country. The owner hid her daughters in the attic while Cornwallis was here and thought their existence remained a secret. As the British general was leaving he rolled his eyes to the ceiling and expressed his regret at not having met the rest of the family.

On the way south **Washington** visited his kinsman, William Washington, at his home, Sandy Hill, toward Savannah, north of U.S. 17 about five miles northwest of Ravenel. His townhouse is still at 8 South Battery at the NW corner with Church Street. Further on the way to Savannah he ate at Thomas Bee's, a site a few hundred yards east of the Edisto River, on the north side of U.S. 17. Northwest of Jacksonboro are the marked ruins of Bethel Presbyterian Church that he passed to get to the bridge over the Salkehachie now marked on U.S. 17A.

St. Andrew's Hall was next door to John Rutledge's at 118 Broad where **Monroe** and Lafayette were guests. (The Ordinance of Secession was passed in St. Andrew's on December 20, 1860, and signed later at Institute Hall, 134 Meeting Street.)

Monroe stayed where the Maritime Museum now is for a week in 1818, visited many of the same sites as **Washington** including area forts, orphans' house, museum, city hall, etc., before going to Beaufort. The only marker of the visit is at 62 Broad. **Jackson** visited the Dock Street Theater, at 135 Church at the SW corner with Queen, and McCrady's Tavern mentioned above. **Van Buren** visited the Poinsett House, 110 Broad, in 1827. **Davis** attended the funeral and burial of prominent senator John C. Calhoun at St. Philip's Church.* **TR** was entertained in 1905 at the Mills House Hotel, 1905 Meeting and Queen Streets. He also saw Fort Dorchester at nearby Summerville and stayed in the Pine Forest Inn there in April 1902. **Grant** stayed two nights in town in late 1865. **FDR** spoke at the Citadel in 1935.

Kennedy supposedly met his girlfriend, Ingrid Arvad, in room 132 of the Fort Sumter Hotel* at the Battery. She had been a former Danish beauty queen cited by Hitler as a perfect example of Nordic beauty. According to several biographies of **Kennedy**, she was married and was sleeping with JFK in 1941 and 1942, as shown by FBI wire taps. The FBI also believed that she had been intimate with Hitler and was the mistress of a pro-Nazi journalist. So the story goes, the FBI bugged them here and in Washington, where she told **JFK** that she was pregnant, and heard **Kennedy** reveal sensitive information. His commander wanted him out, but the director of the Office of Naval Intelligence got him assigned to Charleston, where the affair continued. **Kennedy** wanted to marry her, but his father ended that by interceding with the undersecretary of the Navy and getting him transferred to sea duty. **Kennedy** lived at 48 Murray Road in January 1942 and attended the Catholic Cathedral on Broad.

COLUMBIA • **Washington** traveled from Augusta in late May 1791, over roads following the modern-day routes of U.S. 23, 25, and 1, through Leesville, Lexington, and long-vanished Granby, crossing the Congaree River to the new town of Columbia. A marker south of Trenton marks the site of Piney Woods Tavern, where he ate on May 21, amidst a crowd of locals. At the junction of Highways 21/23 and 19/28 between Edgefield and Ward is a marker noting the Lott Tavern, where he was entertained. Another marker about seven miles into Saluda County on Highway 23 near Ridge Springs notes the site of Jacob Odom's house, where he spent the night. He gave Odom's youngest stepchild a gold coin when he found out the father had been killed in the Revolution.

The colonial State House, visited by **Washington**, **Van Buren** (1827), and **Polk**, was burned during the last days of the Civil War. The site is marked just west of the present Capitol, under construction during the Civil War, that still shows damage from cannon balls. **LBJ, Nixon,** and **FDR**, among others, visited the current Capitol. **Washington's** diary mentions the sixty ladies whom he received there. He dined at the home of Alexander Gillion and maybe lodged directly across the street at Rive's Tavern, although this is questioned. All records were lost in Columbia during the fires at the end of the Civil War, and no one knows where he stayed. A formal dinner was given in the Senate with a reception in the House Chamber. He spent two days and left by the Old Camden Road, through today's Forest Acres, Fort Jackson, Forest Drive, and Dixie Road.

Davis visited Chestnut, the home of the famous diarist Mrs. James Chesnut, at 1718 Hampton (private). As he sat on the front porch, some boys stopped and pointed to tell their friends, "Come look! There's a man on the front porch who looks just like President **Davis** on the postage stamp." Years later he was in town and seen by fourteen-year-old **Wilson**, who had moved here in 1870. **Wilson** lived first at Pickens and Blanding, then 1531 Blanding, and later 1705 Hampton* until 1875, open with some original furnishings. This was the only home his parents ever owned. He also lived a brief time with his aunt in 1870 at 1301 Washington. His father was a teacher of theology at the Presbyterian Seminary. They attended First Presbyterian, NE corner of 1324 Marion and Lady. The first week of his honeymoon he was at back at 1531 Blanding, where his sister was now living.

GEORGETOWN AND AREA • **Washington** entered the state on April 27, and stopped at several places, but exact sites are not fixed. These included Little River and the James Cockran House south of Lake Arrowhead, both on U.S. 17. Just south of the latter is Singleton Swatch, where he was piloted across a low area at low tide. He then stopped at George Pawley's house in Garden City Beach, and continued through an area described as "gloomy and lonesome woods" until he got to Brookgreen Plantation. The house where he spent the night on April 28 burned in 1901. This is now Brookgreen Gardens,* just west of U.S. 17 three miles south of Murrell's Inlet. He left early the next morning and got to Clifton Plantation by mid-morning, where he spent the day and night. Here he was met by his cousin, William Washington, a hero of the Battle of Cowpens, and others from the Charleston welcoming committee. The site is nearby, about two miles east of the U.S. 17 crossing of the Waccamaw River, and marked on the highway.

In Georgetown he was saluted by guns at the foot of Broad Street near Market Square. Then a reception followed at 1019 Front Street, where he spent the night, between Wood and King, back of the southeast corner, facing the river. The house is next to the Kaminski House Museum,* but not open. That afternoon he spoke at the Masonic Temple, still on the NE Prince and Screven Streets, and visited the Winyah Indigo Society Hall at the corner of 632 Prince and Cannon. Future generals Lafayette and DeKalb had first arrived from Europe on the North Island across the bay on June 13, 1777, to join the Patriot cause.

As his southern journey continued, **Washington** ate breakfast in the long room at Hampton

Plantation,* c. 1750, the home of the governor's sister, Mrs. Daniel Horry, fifteen miles south, about four miles west of U.S. 17 on Rutledge Road, preserved in a state park. Her mother was there and so charmed **Washington** that he asked to be a pallbearer when she died in 1793 in Philadelphia. While here she commented that she was going to cut down an oak in front as it spoiled her view. He urged her to let it stand, and it still does, noted with a marker.

Between U.S. 17 and Hampton is an unpaved section of the original Georgetown-Charleston road that **Washington** traveled by the St. James Church,* two miles south. Hampton had been the headquarters of the "Swamp Fox," Frances Marion, during the Revolution, and he was almost captured here by Lt. Col. Banastre Tarleton. The two were roughly portrayed as the main characters of the Mel Gibson movie *The Patriot*. Tarleton (claimed in *Partisans and Redcoats* to be more cruel than depicted in the movie) then made the plantation his headquarters.

In 1821 **Monroe** was welcomed at Arcadia (then known as Prospect Hill) with a real red carpet rolled out to the Waccmaw River. Joel Poinsett lived at the White House Plantation on the Black River and Georgetown Rd. and welcomed **Van Buren**, and **Cleveland** was a guest of the Annandale Gun Club for duck hunting in 1894 and 1896.

Among financier Bernard Baruch's guests at his home known as Hobcaw Barony* were **Franklin Roosevelt** and Winston Churchill. Baruch was an advisor to presidents from **Wilson** to **Kennedy**. The home is one mile north on U.S. 17. **Roosevelt** came for a month in April 1944, after he had been shown to have congestive heart failure with a limited life expectancy unless he rested. His headaches were severe and his wandering mind forced him to shorten his workweek to twenty hours. He had his daughter arrange for him to meet here his old flame Lucy Mercer (Rutherford), now a widow, and the two renewed their friendship. The president needed a close personal friend to provide an emotional understanding that Eleanor could not give, and their probably platonic relationship continued until his death in Georgia with Lucy by his side.

LANCASTER • In 1791 **Washington** visited Barr's Tavern on the east side of U.S. 521 at the northern city limits, a mile and a half north of the Courthouse. He gave a large tip to the innkeeper's daughter by taking out a Spanish silver dollar and cutting it, giving half to the young girl. The souvenir is kept today in the Wofford College controller's office in Spartanburg. He followed present route of U.S. 1 and 521 from Columbia and Camden and stayed at the Ingram House, destroyed but marked on Highway 58 south of Heath Springs, across the road from a fortified British post and the great Hanging Rock, from which the battle took its name.

Waxhaw Church* is located southwest of the **Jackson** birthplace down County 35, Old Hickory Road, heading south off State 5, just west of the marker at the approximate site of Major Robert Crawford's house just west of the US521/5 interchange, on the south side of the road. Robert was another of **Jackson's** Crawford uncles who hosted **Washington** in 1791. The marker also tells how the house was used for two weeks as Cornwallis's headquarters and how **Washington** met a delegation of chiefs from the Catawba Nation who set forth fears of attempts to deprive them of their land. The village of their once powerful tribe was then four miles west. **Washington** took no action then or later, and an Indian delegation met again with him at Mt. Vernon in 1796. No one knows if **Washington** slept in the same bedroom as the British general.

There has always been some controversy as to where **Jackson** was born in 1767, but he believed that it was near here in South Carolina. Both Carolinas claim him. It was probably at the Andrew Jackson State Historical Park,* eight miles north on U.S. 52, the approximate site of James Crawford's home. The area known as the Waxhaw was the site of his mother's sister's home that stood maybe 100 yards north of the park museum near the monument. The birthplace could have been at another aunt's home, Mrs. George McCamie (also "McKemey"), now just across the North Carolina border. Also there is confusion as to where the border was in 1767. After Andrew's father's burial, his pregnant mother traveled from one sister's home to the other, and it is unclear where she was when Andrew was born. But he stated many times that it was at the Crawford home, and he probably knew. In any event, he was the first president born in a log cabin and spent his first thirteen years in the area, most of the time at the Crawford plantation with his two older brothers and eight cousins. His childhood ended at age thirteen when he served as messenger and orderly in the militia during the Revolutionary War, with his next older brother, and was at the Battle of Hanging Rock. (The speculation that he was born in Ireland or on a ship coming here does not appear credible.) Andrew Jackson Sr. died a few days before his son's birth and is buried at the Waxhaw Church at the back border away from the highway. A granite block marks his grave. Andy was baptized here, went to church, and suffered through long sermons. Later his family tended soldiers here, wounded in Buford's Battlefield in the spring of 1780 after a "massacre" by British Lieutenant-Colonel Banastre Tarleton. He and his brother Robert then went on several expeditions with the army and in some accounts carried muskets.

After one engagement the boys fled to the home of Thomas Crawford, where they were surrounded after being informed on by a Tory neighbor. After the boys were captured, an officer ordered fourteen-year-old Andrew to clean his boots. When he refused, the officer slashed at him with his sword. He swung up his arm in a reflex movement and was cut. He carried the scar and resentment for the British all his life. The officer also sent Robert sprawling across the room after he too refused. They were then taken away as prisoners to Camden. There is a statue honoring **Jackson's** mother near the southern edge of the cemetery between the church and most of the graves. A row of markers in front of the statue honors various Revolutionary soldiers, including **Jackson's** brothers, who are buried in unmarked and unknown graves. His seventeen-year-old brother Hugh died from exhaustion and wounds received at the Battle of Stono Ferry. Andrew then was bounced around between the Crawfords (Robert, James, and Thomas) and McKemeys in North Carolina. He got into an argument with a fellow boarder probably at Thomas Crawford's and left. After carousing in Charleston, where he claimed and then lost his grandfather's inheritance, he returned at age seventeen to teach school in the Waxhaw area by preparing the night before every session. He then left for Morgantown to study law, but could not find a room and wound up in Salisbury, North Carolina.

Note that the exact home sites discussed above are not known. Historians have traced old deeds and historical remembrances to approximate locations of the Robert and James Crawford sites. The Thomas Crawford site is probably near the church, but not located with enough accuracy to enter any hypothesis here.

LAURENS • In 1825 **Johnson** came here by way of Carthage, N.C., and set up a tailor shop reconstructed on the north side of the courthouse. He attended the Methodist church and visited Sarah Wood's house on Harper Street. He had been an apprentice in Raleigh, committed a prank by throwing rocks at a house and fled the law. He wound up here for about a year and then returned to apologize. His shop in Carthage is also marked on the square there.

YORK • On his flight from Richmond, **Davis** stayed at Eight Congress Street on April 27, 1865.

SOUTH DAKOTA

MITCHELL • Four presidents, **TR**, **Taft**, **FDR**, and **Hoover**, are claimed to have spoken at the Corn Palace at 601 N. Main in the center of town, although I can verify only **Taft**.

MOUNT RUSHMORE AND RAPID CITY • **Coolidge** spent the summer of 1925 here and dedicated the Doane Mountain sculptor's studio* for the monumental carving of four presidents, the largest work of sculpture on earth, in August 1927. He called it "a cornerstone that was laid by the hand of the Almighty." He then spent two months at the Black Hills State Game Lodge,* in Custer State Park, near the current visitor center on Route 16A, just west of the Wildlife Loop Road. His office was at the Rapid City High School, now DeSoto Middle School, at 601 Columbus, where he issued his famous statement, "I do not choose to run." He drove back and forth each day from the Lodge. He also dedicated the Boy Scout camp. He was deemed "Chief Leading Eagle" at the Deadwood "Days of 76 Celebration." This was a turning point in the history of the area and its memorial as funds now became available due to publicity and his backing. **Ike** spent three days here and Mt. Rushmore in 1953 and fished in

French Creek. **Ike** was inducted into the "Singing Tribe of Wahoo" during Indian ceremonies at the Coolidge Inn, where **Coolidge** had been.

FDR visited in August 1936 to dedicate the just-finished Jefferson figure and stated that he "had no conception until ten minutes ago ... not only of its magnitude, but of its ... permanent importance." The president arrived at 2:30 P.M., two hours late for the optimum viewing in the sun, according to the boiling mad sculptor, Gutzon Borglum, who almost lowered the flag covering the face before the shadows covered it. **Roosevelt** wanted to know, "Where are you going to put Teddy?" Earlier he had attended the Emmanuel Episcopal Church,* 717 Quincy, in Rapid City, suggesting that if no church were available there, they could hold an outdoor service at the memorial site. He sat in the fifth pew from the rear on the right hand side.

Ike spoke at the memorial and dedicated Ellsworth Air Force Base in June 1953. **George H.W. Bush** is pictured in the visitor center, and all presidents are believed to have visited since **Coolidge** except **Hoover** and **Nixon**, although **Nixon** campaigned in Rapid City.

SIOUX FALLS • **McKinley** was the first incumbent president to visit the state, stopping at 13 places in one day. He pulled into the Milwaukee Depot amid "deafening noise of screaming whistle blasts, clanging bells, and prolonged cheers by the high-spirited crowd." He was paraded in a horse-drawn carriage to a reviewing stand at Ninth and Main. **TR** attended what is now East Side Presbyterian at Fairfax and 6th and the German Lutheran at 214 S. Walts in April 1903. He stayed in the Cataract Hotel at Ninth and Phillips and is pictured in a Fenwick Flyer automobile in 1910 on Philips Ave. as he was honored in a large parade. **Wilson** jammed the coliseum in 1919 at 5th and Main to promote the League of Nations. **Nixon** spoke here on Sept. 26, 1960.

WOUNDED KNEE • This site of an Indian engagement where 200 mostly friendly Sioux and a few soldiers were killed in 1890 was called a "battlefield" for many years, but is now referred to as a "massacre." It is claimed that most of the soldiers died from "friendly fire." **TR** visited, as did **Clinton**, who came down in a limo from Mt. Rushmore. He is pictured under the arch at the cemetery on the hill, just south of the massacre site that crosses Route 27.

TENNESSEE

BOLIVAR • **Jackson, Houston, Polk,** and **Davis** have been guests at the Pillars* on Washington Street. **Grant's** 1862 headquarters were at Magnolia Manor, 418 N. Main.

CHATTANOOGA • In 1861, **Davis** had a violent quarrel with the Crutchfield House owner's Unionist brother at the hotel marked on West Ninth between Broad and Chestnut. **Davis** had just resigned from the Senate, made a speech in the dining room suggesting that Tennessee should also secede, and was denounced as a traitor. The mostly Unionist crowd became agitated only at Crutchfield's inflammatory response. Pistols were drawn, but cooler heads prevented seemingly inevitable bloodshed. The hotel hosted **Jackson** and **Andrew Johnson** before burning down in 1869. The Read House was built on the site, visited by **Hayes, McKinley, FDR, Nixon, Reagan**, and Winston Churchill in 1932.

Grant limped or was carried into town with a sprained ankle on October 23, 1863, to rescue floundering Union forces hemmed in by Confederates recently victorious at nearby Chickamauga. He went immediately to General George Thomas's headquarters, the Richardson House at 316 Walnut, where the two with General William Sherman discussed options. **Grant** is claimed to have stayed in what became known as the Grant House at 110 E. First, visited officers at 407 E. Fifth, the Brabson House, and also stayed at Fort Wood, Fort Wood Street and Ft. Wood Place, the high point at the end of Vine. His field headquarters were moved to Orchard Knob,* between McCallie Avenue and E. Third, now a seven-acre reservation.

Garfield's headquarters were on the NE corner of Fourth and Walnut when he was chief of staff for General Rosecrans. He stayed at the SE corner. Both sites are now parking lots. While at his headquarters a strong-willed Confederate mother sought him out to describe her family's plight with no food. **Garfield** told her to take courage as he could do nothing, but did give her part of his hardtack and a piece of meat.

Grant and Thomas watched the Battle of Missionary Ridge from part of Orchard Knob on Orchard Avenue between Ivy and Fifth. When his soldiers charged up the hill without his orders he demanded to know who gave the order. No one knew; someone would pay! But the men were in a dangerous open position at the bottom and thought they could improve their chances of survival by moving up toward the Confederate line. The Southerners were so shocked that they retreated, ensuring a victory for **Grant**. Actually the Yankees charging up the hill had a limited view themselves, but could all be seen by the defenders, who could not see their own lines, and did not know how well off they were. The victory prompted **Grant's** promotion to commanding general as the first permanent three-star general since George Washington.

Grant was photographed near the Craven House* on the road going up to the National Historical Park on Lookout Mountain. In 1891 **Benjamin Harrison** visited, pointing out sites he commanded during the war. **McKinley** toured that year also and later while president. **Theodore Roosevelt** came to the National Park in 1902, via the incline, as did **FDR** in 1938. **Hayes** visited battlefields in the area in 1877 and stayed at the Stanton House, 301 Market. **McKinley** stayed at the Evans House on East Terrace at Cameron Hill. **Cleveland** and **Harding**, among other presidents, also toured the multiple Civil War sites in the area.

COLUMBIA • This small town is full of sites associated with its most famous resident, **Polk**. In 1806 the 11-year-old moved to a site marked six miles north on the east side of U.S. 31 and lived there until going to the University of North Carolina in 1816. During this time he went to Zion Church and school marked at the Zion community between Ashwood and Poplar Top, six miles west of Columbia. A marker on Route 412 at Zion Road directs you south to the present church and school. His father built the home in 1816 at 301 West Seventh* in Columbia, at the SW corner of Seventh and High, when James was 21. It now serves as a museum of the president's life. **Jackson** was here several times and probably at the home north of town. **Polk** lived here after returning from college with his seven younger siblings, and returned later to practice law. This is the only home still standing, other than the White House, where he lived. Many home and White House furnishings can be seen, including law office items and his inaugural Bible.

He later lived across the street at 318 W. Seventh with his wife until inaugurated as president. There he entertained **Jackson** and **Van Buren** during the 1844 campaign. **Polk** practiced law in the courthouse, rebuilt on site in 1905. His law office is marked on the NW corner of Seventh and Garden. A sister and brother-in-law, a political ally, lived at 305 W. Seventh,* next to his father in a home the father had built for her, now the visitor center. He visited sisters at Rally Hill, 319 W. Eighth, and another who was given a home at the SE corner of High and Seventh, now a church site.

A story is told that **Polk's** parents brought him as a young boy to be baptized at First Presbyterian, SE corner of North Garden and West Sixth, but because the father was not a member, the minister refused. The story is also told in North Carolina, but could have happened at both places. His mother continued to bring him after first worshipping in the courthouse. He purchased a pew in the new church after his marriage. The building burned in 1847.

First Methodist, at the NE corner across the street from the **Polk** House on West Seventh, is also on the site of a Methodist church that he attended with his wife, but never joined. **Polk** evidently subscribed to that faith, but attended with his Presbyterian wife and mother at their churches. The church contains a controversial window to the "tenth president." Actually **Polk** is the eleventh, but then Tyler was not considered president by some since he was not elected and not "a president on his own." Giving **Polk** a window was controversial also because he had not been a member, but the popular minister spoke for it. At **Polk's** request he baptized him on his deathbed even though his mother and wife had brought in two Presbyterian ministers.

Polk visited the Athenaeum Rectory at 808 Athenaeum, built for his nephew, although he never moved in. The nephew went to Washington when **Polk** was elected to Congress. **Polk** often visited his father's grave at Greenwood Cemetery at the corner of North Garden and West Fifth. The Nelson House, where **Jackson**, **Van Buren**, and **Polk** were entertained, still stands on North Main about a half block from the courthouse. They also greeted citizens in the square.

He visited his cousin at Rattle and Snap,* called "the most monumental house in Tennessee." It is seven and a half miles west on U.S. Highway 243, 1522 North Main Street in Mt. Pleasant. Hamilton Place* is adjacent and also in the **Polk** family. It was the home of a relative, Lucius Polk, and Rachel Jackson's niece.

Andrew Johnson worked for a tailor at the NE corner of the public square about six months in 1825 and 1826 upon first coming to Tennessee, and lived at 207 W. Sixth.

CUMBERLAND GAP • **Monroe** passed on a western trip in 1785 as far as Illinois (maybe) and Indiana. Unionist Senator **Johnson** was fired upon as he fled through in June 1861.

DANDRIDGE • **Jackson**, **Polk**, and **Andrew Johnson** stayed at the Shepard's Inn, 136 E. Main, in their travels through the state.

DOVER • **Grant** won a major victory here early in 1862 when he captured Ft. Donelson. During the first part of the battle, he was at the Crisp House, site marked on a country road just outside the park's western boundary, north of U.S. 79. He was at the Dover Inn* north of State 49, west of U.S. 79 on Perry Street at the river, when the last Confederate commander who had not fled, General Simon Buckner, asked for terms. He might have expected liberal ones since he had loaned **Grant** money in New York so **Grant** could get home years earlier. But **Grant** thrilled the victory-hungry North by responding, "No terms but Unconditional Surrender." This gave U.S. **Grant** a new nickname, as he became famous and known as "Unconditional Surrender" **Grant**. When the public learned he smoked cigars, thousands began to be sent that he smoked continually, leading to his death from cancer. **Grant** offered Buckner funds, and they became friends again after the war. Buckner visited **Grant** during his last illness and was a pallbearer.

FAYETTEVILLE • Just south of the U.S. 64 junction with U.S. 241 is the site of **Jackson's** camp in October 1813 where he mobilized troops for a punitive expedition after the massacre at Fort Mims. They marched back here to be mustered out and then assembled again in October 1814, to march against the British near New Orleans.

FRANKLIN • As prosecuting attorney for the area, **Jackson** was often at the Eaton House, 125 N. Third. He and **Polk** visited Carnton Mansion,* clearly marked south of town off Route 431, Lewiston Avenue, where he helped the owner's wife plan her garden. During the Civil War Battle of Franklin, five Confederate generals were said to have lain dead on the porch.

In 1830 **Jackson**, as president, met with 21 Chickasaw chiefs in the Presbyterian church.* The Choctaws were supposed to be here, but refused to come. The president was trying to convince them to remove west of the Mississippi River to preserve their tribal identity or submit to the white man's laws and culture, abhorrent to the Indian. After conferring among themselves for several days the chiefs met with the president back at the Masonic Lodge on Second Avenue North. The chiefs then informed the man they called "Sharp Knife" that they would comply and move to an unknown wilderness in the west, leaving their ancestral lands.

GALLATIN • **Houston** visited the Allen house for five years, courted Eliza, and married her there in January 1829. Her home, three miles south on the Cumberland River overlooking Coles Bend, is gone, but the courthouse where **Houston** practiced law remains. The future for the major general of Tennessee militia and governor then could not have been more promising. He had been elected twice to Congress and then ran for governor to help **Jackson's** political agenda. When **Jackson** was elected to the presidency, the Senate was offered to **Houston**, but **Jackson** wanted him to continue as governor. So **Houston** ran again, and it was felt he might be pushed into the nation's highest office after his mentor, **Jackson**, left it. (Another **Jackson** protégé, **Polk**, was so elevated from Congress.) The **Jacksons** also stopped at the Allen home "many times."

After a month's marriage, **Houston's** wife mysteriously left him in spite of his plea here for her to return to him. (Speculation as to the cause of the marital problems is that an old battle wound was repulsive to her; she married against her will; or that she could not adjust to life with the hard-drinking, swashbuckling, older man. Maybe he was insanely jealous as to some supposed or real indiscretion.) His marital breakdown eventually led him to Texas, where his ragtag army defeated the Mexican dictator at San Jacinto, changing the course of history. It is claimed that he came here to see her disguised after living with the Indians in Oklahoma for several years. **Houston** filed for divorce in Texas in 1833, but the petition was lost, then found in 1837 and granted. She remarried, had three children, and ordered all correspondence and portraits destroyed when she died in 1862 so that no one today even knows what she looked like.

GREENEVILLE • **Jackson** and **Polk** visited friends at the Dickson-Williams Mansion,* Church and Irish Streets, a showplace of East Tennessee for years. **Jackson** was also honored at the home of John Dickson in 1835, still at the SE corner of Main and Sumner.

Johnson had never gone to school for even a day. The young drifter wandered into town penniless in the mid 1820s and was seen by his future wife, probably in front of her house near the courthouse on Main. He asked her where he and his mother could stay and then told his mother that he would marry that girl some day. At the same time, the girl's friends kidded her for talking to such a tramp, but she replied that she was stricken by the poor boy, and exclaimed that she would one day marry him. They married at probably 18 and 16, although ages shown in various sources vary, usually younger. He later became the richest man in town.

The **Andrew Johnson** National Historic Site* at Depot and College contains his home from the 1830s until 1851 and adjacent tailor shop. He probably lived in part of a tailor shop first on Main Street, location unknown, and then at the present location until 1831, now enclosed as part of the visitor center.* Another modest home was located just behind the visitor's center at the water fountains, generally toward the house now preserved across the street. The enclosed shop may have been moved from Main Street and was active until 1843, when he began a full-time political career in Congress and as governor. **Johnson** employed young men to read to him in the shop, as did his wife. His shop became the local forum for poorer citizens speaking out to organize and control the town over richer ones. Even after he became mayor and was in the legislature, he was considered a bumpkin. As a laborer he had limited time to practice intellectual skills and acquire knowledge. After a few years he was able to purchase a house on Water Street. He traded this house later for his house on Main, but never parted with the tailor shop. The town council met here often while he was alderman and mayor, and the tailor shop became active in political meet-

Andrew Johnson home in Greeneville, Tenn., used as a brothel by Union troops in the Civil War.

ings. A replica of his North Carolina birthplace is across the street.

Three branches of the Lincoln family were located in Greenville when **Johnson** settled there. Lincoln's grandfather, Abraham, had a brother whose son, Mordecai, became prominent in the area, and as justice of the peace, performed the marriage ceremony for **Johnson** in nearby Warrensburg, where his wife was teaching. The site is unknown. Slaveholder Mordecai Lincoln and **Johnson** served on the town counsel and were members of a debating society together. **Johnson's** youngest daughter married Isaac Lincoln's adopted son. **Johnson** died at his daughter's house on land that had belonged to Isaac, known as the Lincoln Plantation, seven miles from Carter's Station near Elizabethtown. The home was moved in the 1960s to an area known as Fudd Town on W. Elk Ave. in Elizabethton and still stands. It is known that **Johnson's** friendship with Abraham **Lincoln's** distant relatives was a source of conversation between the two, probably in the old Library of Congress in the Capitol, when they were in Congress.

In 1851 **Andrew** moved a few blocks away to McKee and Main,* his homestead until 1875. The rear of the property reaches to College Street and still contains the spring where he camped his first night in town. During the Civil War, the home was used by Confederates as a hospital and by Union forces, who knew whose house it was, as a brothel. The oldest house still standing in town, now known as the Sevier-Lowry House, was given by **Johnson** to his daughter and is marked across and just north. His funeral was in the courthouse, Depot and Main, the center of political activity for the town. His grave* is at the **Andrew Johnson** National Cemetery, south on Monument Avenue. He had requested that this site, his property, be used as such as he went here to relax and meditate during life. Many of his family members are also buried here.

JACKSON • **Grant's** command post was at 518 E. Main prior to the Battle of Shiloh in 1862.

JONESBOROUGH • All three Tennessee presidents made frequent trips to this once important town still containing 18th century structures. It is the oldest town in Tennessee, and was on the Great State Route from Washington, D.C. **Jackson** stopped here in 1788 for five months waiting for enough of a caravan to move westward to Nashville through dangerous Indian territory.

While here he fought a duel with Colonel Waighstill Avery after the latter had made sarcastic statements in court about **Jackson's** legal deficiencies. Crowds followed the pair from the courthouse to a hill just south of town in Duncan's Meadow, now a park on Boone Street. Both were poor shots, and missed or fired purposely in the air, but honor was satisfied. This was the first of several **Jackson** duels. He stayed most of the time in the Taylor House now at 124 Main by the church, but then one mile west (marked) on Route 353. He made such an impression on the town that folks here believed the rumor circulated after the Battle of New Orleans that he had killed the whole British army and sailed for England.

The courthouse was on the same site as now, 100 E. Main and Cherokee. **Jackson** was admitted to the local bar on the site with his law office across the street, where he was later honored as president in 1836. After moving west he returned as judge of the Superior Court and stayed most of the time in the Chester Inn at Main and Cherokee. **Jackson** is credited with saving it from fire, fighting it in his nightshirt. Political enemies threatened to tar and feather him when in town for court in 1803. As he stayed here he sent word that "...my door is open to receive him and his regiment whenever they choose to wait upon me, and I hope the Colonel's chivalry will induce him to lead his men, not follow them." **Jackson** returned many times as he traveled back and forth to Nashville. In 1832 he came as president and spoke from the front porch at a large reception; he stayed again in 1836. Other guests included **Van Buren**, **Polk**, **Johnson**, and Charles Dickens, called the greatest novelist of the English language.

In 1861, Tennessee was greatly divided over secession. **Johnson** tried to rally the crowds for the Union from a platform in front of **Jackson's** old law office and was threatened to be shot until a local doctor jumped in front and yelled that he would have to be killed first. **Johnson** was forced to sit down, and rain then put a damper on the crowd; they moved to the basement of the courthouse, where **Johnson** tried to speak for the Union until yelled down. He was harassed all the way back to his lodgings at the Buckhorn House, 613 E. Main, and accused of being a traitor.

Jackson was entertained at a friend's, 119 West Main, stayed at Mansion (May) House at 200 W. Main, and visited the Washington (or Blair) House,* now a bed and breakfast, marked at 201

W. Main. Others there include **Van Buren**, **Davis** in 1873, and **Grant**, who had supper in 1865 when he got off the train that then ran across the street. The Eureka Hotel* at 127 Main claims the Tennessee presidents were entertained there. The then and now prominent DeVault Tavern, now a private home marked off Stagecoach Road, south of the first stop sign on the Leesburg Road, east of Route 11E, was frequented by **Johnson**, who attended the Methodist church at 211 W. Main and visited homes at 115 College, 210 W. Main, and the Mansion House. **Van Buren** visited the Gammon House opposite the courthouse, 204 E. Main, and a home at the SE corner of Main and Spring.

KINGSPORT • All three **Tennessee presidents** were guests at the Netherland Inn,* 2144 Netherland Inn Road.

KNOXVILLE • **Jackson** was a member of the First Constitutional Convention of Tennessee, meeting at the SW corner of Gay and Church and in the governor's office, serving as the Capitol, behind the William Blount Mansion,* 200 West Hill between Gay and State. Blount was **Jackson's** political mentor. **Jackson** took little part in the proceedings, although tradition credits him with suggesting the name "Tennessee," derived from the name of a Cherokee chief. Here he fell in with the Blount faction and was elected with their support to Congress. After resigning from the Senate, he served as a visiting judge and stayed in the Chisholm Tavern at Gay and West Hill. The other political faction in the state was controlled by war hero John Sevier. In 1802 **Jackson** ran against him for major general of the militia and won mainly on the basis of political organization. Sevier was incensed that a young upstart with no military experience could whip him and then ran for governor. During a political speech here, he saw **Jackson** and yelled that this man had done no service except to take a trip to Natchez with another man's wife. Shouts, shots, general mayhem, and the inevitable challenge to a duel resulted.

The Lamar Hotel on the SW corner of Cumberland and Gay, still standing as the Bijou Theatre,* hosted **Polk**, **Jackson**, **Andrew Johnson**, **Grant**, and **Hayes**.

FDR called Church Street Methodist* at 900 Henley "the most beautiful church I have ever seen."

LEBANON • **Houston** opened a law office in a log hut marked at 107 E. Main, just east of the square in 1818. The courthouse was in the square although it is now to the east. He made frequent trips to Nashville, generally staying at the Hermitage, where he was a favorite of Rachel **Jackson**. The capital then was in Murfreesboro, and **Houston** made numerous trips there as prosecuting attorney for Nashville district.

Jackson met his wife, Rachel Donelson, while boarding at the home of the Donelsons near Lebanon. The area is now a residential development, not marked, and hard to place exactly. When the **Jacksons** moved back after their 1791 marriage in Natchez they acquired their own home, Poplar Grove, across the Cumberland River in the hairpin curve of the now dammed river at Gallatin Road, northeast of Nashville on Route 45, now under the town of Old Hickory.

LEWISBURG • **Polk's** law office when he was elected occupied the SE corner of the square.

MARYVILLE • **Houston** hated farming more than he hated school, and wasn't much good at either. He lived with his widowed mother and siblings on a farm about six miles SW of town, west of Morgantown Road on Salem Road, about midway around its loop. (The state marker is nearby, three miles south on U.S. 129 & 411, two miles east of the county line.) He went to Porter Academy just off Main, worked in his brother's store in town, and had a blacksmith shop at the crossroads. But he then ran away at age 16 to live almost three years with the Indians. The site of the Indian village was Hiwassee Island, on the Tennessee-Hiwassee Rivers junction two miles from Dayton on Blythe Ferry Road. His Indian "father" was the chief, Oo-loo-te-ka, also known as John Jolly. He said he preferred living with the red man rather than the tyranny of his brothers. They came to get him and found him reading the *Iliad*. He promised to return, but did not for a year, then clerked, and wound up back with the Indians. When he returned to Maryville he opened a school and charged more than the other local teachers. The school was in a church that he had attended, and he had to pay off debts he had incurred to buy gifts for his Indian friends. To the surprise of many, he had a full house and paid the debts. He later said that this experience gave him more satisfaction and a higher degree of dignity than any of his other accomplishments. The rebuilt school* is six miles north on Sam Houston Schoolhouse Road, off TN 33. A spring nearby, used by the teacher and his pupils, still flows.

When he was just past his 20th birthday the army came to recruit on the square. Silver dollars were put on a drumhead. **Houston** picked up one and thus joined the army at a spot marked at the NW corner of Cusick and Broadway, where the courthouse then was located. After being wounded at Horseshoe Bend he returned home to be nursed by his mother. Then as an army officer he was able to convince his foster Indian father and other Cherokees to abide by a treaty and move to Oklahoma, then known as Indian Territory.

MEMPHIS • Fort Pickering was founded before the city at the Fourth Chickasaw Bluff on the north side of Crump Boulevard near the eastern end of the Memphis-Arkansas Bridge, south of the Interstate 40 Bridge. **Taylor** commanded here in 1809, a year after his brother was killed on the site. He, **Jackson**, and **Houston** were claimed to be at the Bell Tavern on the west side of Front Street, opposite and slightly south of the end of the east-west alley between Overton and N. Parkway Ave. **Jackson** was supposed to have planned the city that he founded there, but probably did the planning in absentia.

Andrew Johnson, Taylor, Polk, TR, and **Davis** stayed at the Gayoso Hotel, marked on Front between McCall and Gayoso. **Grant** visited the hotel, where later General William T. Sherman's admittedly favorite son Willy died in October 1863, in a tragedy reminiscent of the death of Lincoln's favorite son Willie in 1862. The boys, nine and eleven, probably died of the same disease, typhoid fever. General Nathan Bedford Forrest's brother, on a mission for his famous brother, once rode into the lobby on his horse to capture Union General Hurlbut. The general was somewhere else and thus did not flee, as per the legend, in his nightclothes.

Grant's summer 1862 headquarters were at the Hunt Phelan Home, 533 Beale,* now a bed and breakfast. He slept in a tent in the yard, and inside when his family visited. He used the library, which **Davis** had visited, as his office, and spent time reading in the excellent collection of books. **Jackson** and **Andrew Johnson** were also guests. **Grant** made his officers and men take off their boots to save the carpet. Later the home was used as a Union soldiers' center and hospital, where 2500 died. It is claimed that 100,000 soldiers were here at one time or the other.

Davis moved to Memphis in 1869 to be president of an insurance company with offices at 42 Madison. This was his only regular job after the war. After a two-year imprisonment and then a year and a half awaiting trial he had no job or support except charity. He lived some in Quebec and traveled to England, France, Switzerland, and Scotland. Federal charges against him were not dismissed until December 1868. He first lived in the Peabody Hotel, NW corner of Main and Monroe, until he went to England, where he had left his family in late 1870. Senator-elect **Johnson** stayed at the Peabody in 1875. **McKinley** stayed there before it burned down in 1928. But another Peabody* was built in 1925 at 149 Union and claims that every sitting president through **George W. Bush** has stayed there.

In December 1871, **Jefferson Davis** moved to 129 Court, where his family was together for the first time since the Civil War. His eleven-year-old son, another Willie, died the next year. He went to St. Lazarus Episcopal, 41 Madison, between Third and Fourth, and Calvary Episcopal on the SE corner of Adams and Second. **Jefferson Davis** resigned from the failed insurance company in August 1873 and traveled back to England, and then was here about a year before his family left England to rejoin him. The family moved in 1875 to 98 Court. Because of marital problems, his volatile wife continued to live here when he moved to the Gulf Coast, although she joined him later. **Davis** was at the bedside during the last illness of General Forrest in 1877 at 693 Union, and was a pallbearer at the Court Street Methodist Church at his funeral.

Grover Cleveland was entertained at the Fontaine House, 680 Adams.* **Theodore Roosevelt** spoke at the Beale Street Baptist Church* in the auditorium and adjacent park in 1902. It is located at Fourth and Beale. **Gerald Ford** dedicated the Commercial Square Fountain in 1976 and stayed at the Holiday Inn at the Riverfront. **George W. Bush** brought the Japanese prime minister to Elvis Presley's Graceland* in June 2006.

MURFREESBORO • **Polk** went to the Samuel Black Institution from 1814 to 1816, at a site on the NE corner of the Bradley School on South Academy Street, and got his political start as clerk of the Tennessee Senate when the town was the capital. The legislature was meeting in the courthouse at the square from 1819 until 1822 when **Monroe** passed through on his tour. Then the courthouse burned, and **Polk** served in the legislature in the Presbyterian church. This site is now a locked cemetery at 300 Vine, with a marker visible from the street. **Jackson** attended legislative sessions there. **Polk** met and married his wife at her home, Childress Place on East Main (destroyed), and attended many receptions in the other fine homes still on East Main.

Davis spent a night during the Civil War at Outlands at 900 North Maney Avenue, off U.S. 41, a mile north of town. **Jackson** was there often. In 1837, Van Buren stayed on the east side of the square at the site of today's Commerce Union Bank. **Andrew Johnson** debated at large gatherings in the square during political campaigns. **Garfield's** 1863 headquarters during the war were at Robert Wendell's House on East College. While here he conducted services at the Church of Christ on E. Main where a later building is marked.

NASHVILLE • **Jackson** arrived in late 1788 to live in the small community with only a courthouse and a few stores and taverns. Indians were still in the area, so the widow of one of the town's founders asked **Jackson** to stay with her large family several miles out of town to protect them. He was also able to provide a match to the widow's married daughter, Rachel, who was also fun-loving and could add spice to a wild side. Unfortunately her pathologically suspicious husband was not amused and took her to Kentucky, where marital conflicts continued. Soon Rachel had enough and begged her family to escort her home. They would not or could not, but Andy was available and did. This laid the grounds for her husband to file for divorce, and he did. But Rachel was still apprehensive about her husband, so the family arranged for her to flee to Mississippi. Fortunately **Andrew** was available again to be an escort. As explained in more detail in the entry on Natchez, the two were married there after a false assumption that the divorce had been granted. After they returned as husband and wife, they learned otherwise and were remarried. This led to lifelong slander and gossip, probably contributing to Rachel's death as she faced the prospect of moving to Washington as the president's wife.

Jackson's law office from 1789 to 1796 was at 333 Union, south side, midway between Third and Fourth. At this time the capital was Knoxville. He also was Tennessee District Attorney at the courthouse, 1791–6, at the same site as present, where he was honored with a big celebration after the Battle of New Orleans. He was also on the Superior Court from 1798 to 1804 after resigning as U.S. Senator. Since he had no military experience at age 35 before being elected major general of the state militia, a post leading to national prominence during the Indian Wars and War of 1812, he probably had the fastest rise in military rank and opportunity in history. When the U.S. Army was reorganized in 1814, he was given the rank of major general vacated by William Henry Harrison and command of the Southern Division. Part of his staff lived at the Hermitage, including **Houston**.

From 1796 until 1804 the **Jacksons** lived at their second home, Hunter's Hill plantation, 13 miles east of Nashville on what is now Saundersville Road and marked two miles south of the site on U.S. 70 near Shute Lane. They then moved nearby to what is now known as the Hermitage,* off U.S. 70N, 10 miles from Nashville. The affectionate couple called each other "Mrs. **Jackson**" or "wife," never "Rachel," and "Mr. **Jackson**," not "General," and especially not "Andy," never used by anyone until after his death. Their log cabin is now down a short path north of the present mansion, where they moved about 1821. The mansion was extensively rebuilt after an 1834 fire at the same spot that had been picked by Rachel. At the early original cabin he was nursed back to health after his duel when he killed Charles Dickinson, and he greeted guests **Monroe** and former Vice President Aaron Burr. The duel left **Jackson** with a bullet near his heart that continued to hemorrhage for the rest of his life. (In fact he was frequently confined during his presidency to his bedroom due to its complications.) The duel cost the former senator and judge much of his reputation until he was visited several times by the former vice president.

The **Jacksons** had no children of their own, but adopted one of twins when the mother could only care for one. The boy was given the name of Andrew Jackson Jr. The general had a soft spot for children and spoiled his son, who grew up to be irresponsible, to **Jackson's** sorrow. An Indian brought an Indian boy to him after a battle in the Creek War. The defeated enemy told **Jackson** to kill the infant since all of his family had been killed during the battle. Instead **Jackson** sent him home, adopted him, and raised him as his own. The boy, Lyncoya (also Lincoyer), never fully accepted his white environment, and frequently tried to run away until "pulmonary complications" (pneumonia or tuberculosis) killed him at about age 16 in June 1828. He was greatly mourned as "a favorite son" by both **Jacksons**. **Jackson** had planned to send him to West Point. The boy liked to paint himself up as a hostile, hide in the bushes, and jump out yelling and waving a tomahawk at unsuspecting strangers. Several other children were also raised by the **Jacksons**, including John and Andrew Jackson Donelson and Andrew Jackson Hutchings. At one time there were four "**Andrew Jacksons**" living here. In 1815 seven-year-old **Davis** was a guest for two weeks on the way to school in Kentucky, and played with the Andrews. Returning home after the presidency, the old man had six young children in the home, three from Andrew Jr. and three nieces and nephews.

Indian chiefs frequently traveled to see the Indian fighter and former governor of Florida to discuss treaties and grievances with **Jackson**, whom they thought would be fair. **Jackson** opened a store, tavern, and racecourse at Clover Bottom, on the Lebanon Road, U.S. 70, and Stone's River, noted by a marker at the northwest end of the bridge, west of the Hermitage. After various buildings were added, it became a local meeting place. **Jackson** won several horse races here, significant to his financial well-being.

Shortly before **Jackson** left as the first president elected outside of the capital since **Washington**, much of the zeal of life left him when his greatest treasure, his beloved Rachel, died of a heart attack. "Aunt Rachel" was a sweet-tempered, pious, generous woman, and virtual saint to her husband, but simple and "backwoodsy." She dreaded trying to live in snobbish Washington. It was felt that she could not bear the pressure of Washington society and gossiping tongues. She is described as suffering a "frightful blow," as being "grief stricken," and to have never recovered from the death of her son Lyncoya. She was kept as much as possible from the political name-calling during the dirty campaign, but it is thought that she overheard a conversation and saw critical slanderous campaign literature about her marriage while shopping in Nashville. This caused several further emotional distresses, from which she never recovered. Ten thousand attended her Christmas Eve funeral. **Houston** led the pallbearers. She was buried in her rose garden, where **Jackson** now also lies. It was **Jackson's** habit to visit her grave alone every day at sunset, and asking any companion to wait at the garden gate. He always asked that guests visit her to shed a tear and offer a prayer. **Jackson's** funeral on the back porch was interrupted when his old parrot, Polly, began an outburst of profanities and had to be removed.

A spark from the chimney caught the roof on fire during his presidency and damaged or destroyed much of the house, which was quickly rebuilt. Unlike other presidents' homes where furnishings were largely dispersed, here they are mostly original after the 1830s rebuilding, including the wallpaper, a copy of Rachel's favorite. His deathbed and a medicine chest still containing mercury and lead used by his doctors remain in the bedroom where he died. Like Washington, he liked to be bled, saying he "felt better after a pint." Incidentally, it took 28 days to reach Washington when **Jackson** left in 1824.

Jackson reportedly believed the world was flat and had unique ways of spelling. He believed if "urope" didn't spell the continent, "what the hell did it spell?" And he felt a man must be pretty stupid if he could only spell a word one way. **Fillmore**, **Andrew Johnson**, **Polk**, and **Van Buren** visited here during his lifetime. **Jackson** met **Monroe** in Georgia and accompanied him across Tennessee to Kentucky, by way of his home. **Pierce**, **Reagan**, and "a number of presidents" have visited. **TR** was at the Hermitage in 1907, as was **Taft** in 1911. **FDR** had a big breakfast sitting at the head of **Jackson's** table in 1934. **LBJ** also ate there. **Truman** came while presiding county judge in Missouri to measure **Jackson's** clothes for a statue of his hero that he wanted no larger or smaller than real life.

Houston was a frequent visitor, and stopped off on the way to Washington with his Indian friends to show them where the Great White Father lived. Earlier he had practiced shooting in the yard for an upcoming duel. At about the moment of **Jackson's** death, **Houston** was rushing up to the home to see his old friend and mentor. Arriving too late, he pleaded for his young son to look and always remember that he had seen the face of **Andrew Jackson**.

The 1836 mansion Tulip Grove* was built by **Jackson** nearby for his ward, Andrew Jackson Donelson, who probably had the best relationship with the patriarch of any child raised at the Hermitage. It was originally called Poplar Grove, but **Van Buren** suggested the change while visiting. Donelson married his cousin, who served as White House hostess. **Houston** stayed here for **Jackson's** funeral; Donelson was then in Texas as U.S. charge d'affaires.

Opposite the entrance to the Hermitage is Rachel's Hermitage Church,* built in 1823 and still in use. When it once needed to new roof, the clergyman called on **Jackson** and bet a church roof on one of the fighting cocks **Jackson** was watching. **Jackson** accepted, and as the clergyman's cock appeared to be losing, the parson yelled an appeal, "Remember the church needs a new roof! Fight, boys, fight!" The clergyman won, and **Jackson** paid for the roof. The president kept his long-standing promise to Rachel when he joined the church in 1838 and remained devout the rest of his life.

Jackson often came to the home of this longtime roommate Judge Overton at Travelers' Rest,* 636 Farwell Parkway, General Hood's headquarters during the Battle of Nashville. **Jackson** was often at Belle Meade,* 110 Leake, where **Polk, Houston, Benjamin Harrison, Teddy Roosevelt, Cleveland,** and **Taft** also visited.

The Nashville Inn (also Winn's Inn), NE corner of the Public Square and Second (Market), hosted **Monroe, Van Buren, Fillmore, Jackson,** and **Andrew Johnson. Jackson, Houston,** and **Polk** were lawyers who served in the courthouse on the square. The City Hotel on the Square south of the Nashville Inn was the scene of a fight in 1813 between **Jackson,** his friend John Coffee, and Jesse and Thomas Hart Benton. This resulted from a challenge to a duel between friends of each and an attempt by **Jackson** to soothe feelings. Jesse shot **Jackson** at least twice. He was carried to the Nashville Inn, almost bled to death, and could not move for three weeks. Doctors wanted to remove his arm, but **Jackson** kept the arm and the bullet; the latter was removed in 1832. The Bentons moved to Missouri, and later when Senator **Jackson** took his seat in Congress, he found himself next to Senator Thomas Hart Benton. The two became friends and political allies. **Johnson** lived at the Nashville Inn as governor in 1856 when it was destroyed by fire. He then moved to the Verandah Hotel on Second (Market) Street. He was in his room when the fire broke out, left it to see what was happening, and helped a lady move to safety. The noble act prevented him from saving the $1200 he had hidden under his pillow.

William Carroll had been governor of Tennessee, but was prohibited by constitutional term limit provisions from seeking another consecutive term. **Houston** was then elected, and **Jackson** wanted him to run for reelection after his term, contrary to Carroll's wish to then run again. Carroll promised **Houston** a Senate seat if he would not run. He followed **Jackson's** wishes and won a hotly contested election. The popular governor lived at Nashville Inn when he was married in January 1829 to 18-year-old Eliza Allen. (See the Gallatin entry.) He returned from his second election campaign on April 16 to find that the first lady of Tennessee had left him to seclude herself in her father's home in Gallatin, and would not return. No one ever revealed any information as to what had gone wrong, not **Houston**, not the Allens. The public assumed it was **Houston**'s fault, and he had ruined her honor. Crowds threatened him at the hotel, and he had to lock himself in. He abruptly left the office and the state, giving up his promising career to go live with the Indians in Oklahoma. Historians have argued ever since why she left and why he fled.

The capital was moved here from Murfreesboro in 1827 while **Houston** was governor. Congress first met in the Masonic Temple, where **Houston** was a member, located on the north side of Church Street between Fourth and Fifth, noted by a marker. Tradition backed by substantial evidence says that Mexican President and General Santa Anna owed his life to the fact that he was a Mason and gave the secret distress sign to his captor and to General **Houston** at San Jacinto. **Polk** served there as governor, and **Johnson** was in the lower house of the legislature there from 1835 until 1841. The new Capitol opened in 1843, but was replaced again by the current building before the Civil War. **Johnson** served in the earlier building in the State Senate and the present building as governor and later as military governor with dictatorial powers when the state acquired the Hermitage. He went to Washington to try to get the federal government to put a "West Point of the West" there.

The **Jacksons** attended Downtown (First) Presbyterian,* SE corner, Fifth Avenue North and Church, as did the **Polks.** (The present building dates to 1851.) **Jackson** had been presented a sword here from the state for his New Orleans victory. **Jackson** and **Van Buren** visited the Nashville Female Academy at Church and McLemore.

Polk is buried on the east side of the Capitol.* His last home, Polk Place, was set back a hundred feet or so south of Union between Seventh and Eighth, marked at the SW corner of Seventh and Union and also in the middle of the block closer to the actual site. He died there three months after leaving office, his health diminished by extremely hard work. This had been the home of his former associate and mentor, Senator Felix Grundy. His wife continued there for 42 years. **Grant** gave her a 100-man bodyguard and visited her there, as did **Hayes** in 1877.

Polk practiced law in Nashville at the begin-

The Capitol in Nashville: Polk is buried on this east side, where Andrew Johnson worked as the Union governor of Tennessee during the Civil War.

ning of his career and rented a house while governor. He worked in Grundy's office from 1818 until 1820 on the SW corner of Union and Vine. His 1849 funeral was at his and **Johnson's** McKendree Methodist,* 523 Church, where he had been inaugurated as governor in 1839 and **Johnson** was to be in 1853. **Polk** did not want to leave his position in the U.S. House, where he was speaker, but he dutifully ran for governor at the behest of **Jackson**, the party leader. After being buried at Old City Cemetery on South Fourth, between Central and Poplar, **Polk's** body was moved in 1850 to a garden at Polk Place, later the site of the city library, and then moved to the Capitol lawn in 1893 with his wife. Several presidents have visited the site, including **FDR** and **LBJ**.

Johnson stayed at the Maxwell House, at the NW corner of Fourth and Church, after he left the presidential office. **Cleveland, Hayes, Jackson, McKinley, TR, Taft,** and **Wilson** also stayed, as noted by the marker. The impeached **Johnson** at last felt vindication as the city went wild in 1875 with a reception here as the former president was elected to the Senate. The famous hotel gave its name to a coffee brand, given a slogan when **Theodore Roosevelt** remarked here, "It tasted good until the last drop." The hotel burned down in 1961.

Johnson served Tennessee as an elected governor and a military governor appointed by Lincoln. He served in the present governor's office in the Capitol,* and slept there many nights. As military governor **Johnson** confiscated the Neill Brown House directly in front of the Capitol on Charlotte Avenue, marked by a tablet on Legislative Plaza near the top of the stairs in front of the War Memorial Building. Brown was an old rival who found himself jailed for not taking an oath to support the Union government. **Johnson's** firm measures to his home state further alienated Union support. He stayed in the St. Cloud Hotel, NW corner of Church and Fifth, from 1862 to 1865 and often visited the Union headquarters, the Cunningham House, marked at 221 Sixth between Church and Union, that served **Grant** and other generals including **Hayes** and **Garfield**.

Grant laid the cornerstone of a building at Broadway and Eighth, still standing. He was here when he learned of his appointment as general-in-chief and issued his first orders. In 1877, **Hayes** laid the cornerstone for the Custom House* at Eighth and Broadway, made a speech at a reception in the Capitol, and lodged at the Hermitage Hotel, SW corner of Sixth and Union. **Taft** was there in 1911. **TR** made a speech at the Ryman Auditorium* in 1907, as did **Taft** in 1911, later the site of the "Grand Ole Opry" radio broadcast. **Wilson** visited his brother at 1012 S. 15th in 1905, 1907, and 1912 when he came to the Capitol. **George W. Bush** defended his State of the Union speech on February 1, 2006, at the new Grand Ole Opry at Opryland.*

ROCKY MOUNT • **Jackson** lived for six weeks four miles northeast of Johnson City, now on U.S. 11E, while he was waiting to get his law license. The two-story log house has been restored and noted with a marker. In 1790 William Blount, Governor of the Territory South of the River Ohio, selected Rocky Mount for the seat of the new territorial government, making this the capital of the first recognized government west of the Alleghenies.

ROGERSVILLE • All three Tennessee U.S. presidents, **Jackson**, **Polk**, and **Johnson**, are claimed to have stayed in the Hale Springs Inn, also called the McKinley Tavern, at 110 W. Main. **Jackson** was also at the Rogers Tavern at 205 S. Rogers

RUTLEDGE • In 1826, **Johnson** heard about a lawyer who was vacating a small shop that he could use as a tailor shop. So he came for about six months and then heard that a tailor in Greeneville had closed his shop. He remembered that town and a girl named Eliza and moved on. Markers are at the SW corner of the courthouse and at a replica tailor shop on Court Street.

SAVANNAH AND SHILOH NATIONAL MILITARY PARK • General **Grant** was taking it easy in the Cherry House* on April 6, 1862, when he heard the sound of cannon coming from the south, where his troops had paused on their way to find the Confederate army. He had not fortified his troop positions since he was concerned only with offense. And he did not suspect that the Confederates camped in Corinth, Mississippi, would actually attack him. He left on a boat at the landing below the home to join the Battle of Shiloh. Two generals died in the home: C.F. Smith, from a foot infection received leaping from one boat to another early in the battle; and W.H.L. Wallace, mortally wounded at Shiloh. The home is a block or so north of the marker at the northeast end of the U.S. 64 bridge and reached by going about a quarter mile farther east and turning back west from a block north.

Confederate General Albert Sidney Johnston attacked Union forces advancing toward Mississippi at a little country church called Shiloh,* meaning "place of peace." Johnston was trying to surprise **Grant** before he merged with Union General Buell's army. The Union was driven back, but held by a small force at the Hornet's Nest* until the day ended. During the night **Grant** tried to rest at a hospital* at a site marked at the visitor center, but could not due to the noise and confusion of severely wounded and dying men. He finally rested under a nearby tree in spite of heavy rain. The tree* is marked in the cemetery next to the bookstore. **Garfield** also fought here. The National Park Guide Map marks all sites mentioned and several other sites associated with General **Grant**.

TEXAS

ANDERSON • The Fanthorp Inn* on Main claims that **Taylor**, **Grant**, **Davis**, and **Houston** stayed.

AUSTIN • This new capital was on the frontier with its Capitol Building within a well-needed stockade when **Houston** was inaugurated as president of the Republic of Texas for the second time in December 1841. It was, like Washington, D.C., one of the few cities in the world founded to be a capital. **Houston** thought it "the most unfortunate site upon Earth." He had been the first president. The second, Mirabeau Lamar, had grandiose plans including extending the borders to at least the Rio Grande in today's New Mexico and Colorado, and maybe to the West Coast, of course after conquering the Indians and Mexicans in between.

President again, **Houston** took the oath at the first Capitol Building on a hill at the NE corner of Colorado and Eighth. Markers at both ends of the site extending down Eighth toward Congress Avenue say that every Texas president performed some function inside. When Texas joined the Union, **Houston** caught the flag as it was lowered here, and the Republic of Texas was declared to be no more. His offices were at 801 Congress. The presidential mansion, or "palace" as it was called, the only two-story building in town, was in the center of a block surrounded by Brazos, San Jacinto, Seventh, and Eighth, and marked inside the hotel there now. He frequented the Bullock Inn at the NW corner of Sixth and Congress, but did not like the town and at first refused to stay in the mansion, saying that the roof leaked and it was too run-down. The two other Texas presidents, Lamar and Anson Jones, did live there. A young **Hayes** visited the Capitol and mansion in his month-long trip to here and San Antonio in 1849 and thought Austin was an "inconsiderable village" with "large expectations."

Albert Sidney Johnston, the army commander, challenged **Houston** to a duel for some petty disagreement, but **Houston** told him he would have to wait his turn. (Johnston became the highest ranked officer in the Civil War to be killed in action, and is buried near Stephen F. Austin at the State Cemetery east of downtown.) While the Republic of Texas was recognized by several foreign nations, only France established an embassy, still existing as the French Legation* at Seventh and San Marcos. **Houston** matched wits with diplomats there. When the pompous French ambassador showed his medals to the president of the Republic, **Houston** bared his chest to show his battle wounds and said that a humble Republican soldier wears his medals there.

Mexico had never recognized President, or more correctly Dictator, Santa Anna's Texas peace treaty or the boundaries that the young republic had set, and a watchful eye was always kept south for another invasion. When a Mexican army did attack San Antonio in 1842 and Santa Anna became president again threatening to reconquer Texas, **Houston** moved the capital back to his more secure namesake city of Houston. Soon afterwards, Indians raided and carried off children in the vicinity of the old Capitol in Austin. The Republic became a state in 1845 with **Houston** one of the senators, and he became governor just before the Civil War. The first state constitution had moved the capital back to Austin.

The Governor's Mansion* at 11th and Colorado was completed in 1856, across from a new Capitol at the present site at the head of Congress Ave. on 11th. Street. Governor **Houston** and his family of eight children, including one born here when the governor was 67 — still the largest brood ever to live there — occupied it as the Civil War began. His inauguration occurred in front of the Capitol,* where he futilely argued against secession. He was a popular Texas figure, but lost favor in the state after failing to take an oath to support the Confederacy in 1861, and warned of the horrors of a civil war. Actually he lost the governor's race in 1857, while senator, because he opposed the Kansas-Nebraska Bill, but was elected in 1859 for the same reason.

As the nation drifted toward war, **Houston** felt that a United States or Texas invasion of Mexico would unite the Union. **Houston** could not pull this off and then received a letter from Lincoln offering to maintain him in office. The governor conferred in the mansion with advisors and then burned the letter in the fireplace. His supporters, Unionists opposed to secession, felt that he should not resist the decision of the Texas Secession Convention to secede. He told them that if he were ten years younger he would have accepted Lincoln's offer. Lincoln resubmitted the offer, but it was too late. He was finally told to pledge allegiance to the new Confederate government or leave office. In a dramatic scene comparable to Robert E. Lee's in Virginia, the family could hear him pace the floor of the mansion all night deciding what course to take. Unlike Lee he could not support the Confederacy and was forced out of office despite efforts of an armed group to maintain him. He did not feel that maintaining a "poor old man" in office a few days longer was worth the cost in blood. **Houston** then visited his friend and fellow Union supporter at Woodlawn Mansion* at Six Niles Road, the home of former Governor E.M. Pease.

George W. Bush lived in the Governor's Mansion* when he was elected president. He and his brother Jeb were the only sons of a president elected as governor of any state. **McKinley** ate there in 1901. Other visiting presidents include **LBJ**, **George H.W. Bush**, **Clinton**, and **Reagan**. Mrs. **Kennedy** was to be the first, first lady to visit on the evening of November 22, 1963. **McKinley** and **TR** both spoke at Old Main on the University of Texas campus. The original building was destroyed in 1930 to build the U.T. Tower.*

Speakers at the Capitol* include **McKinley**, **Theodore Roosevelt**, **Kennedy**, and both **Bushes**. All had parades down Congress Avenue. **TR** was photographed in 1905 on a stand in front facing downtown and was honored in the Governor's Public Reception Room, as was **McKinley**. The room is on the second floor under the great arch, room number 2S.1A. Mrs. **McKinley** reportedly was not feeling well and had to lie down on a sofa where there was no pillow. **McKinley** later sent one to the Capitol. **Coolidge** was here in 1934, and **George H.W. Bush** was made an honorary captain of the Texas Rangers in 1989 in the House chamber. **Clinton** honored former governor Ann Richards as she lay in state in the rotunda on September 17, 2006.

Young **Lyndon Johnson** came with his father to legislative sessions in the Capitol* and explored every corner of the building. He sometimes sat in the House Chamber* with his father, who was a member, and ran errands for other members. In 1935 he lived at Four Happy Hollow Lane in half of a two-family house and was the director of the National Youth Administration for Texas. His office then was on the sixth floor of the Littlefield Building at the NE corner of Sixth and Congress. He ran for Congress in 1936 with headquarters in the Stephen F. Austin Hotel at 701 Congress. In 1943 he lived in an apartment at 1901A Dillman. The Driskill Hotel* at 117 E. Seventh, called Texas's third legislative house, became his headquarters from 1934 until his 1964 election. He first saw his future wife walking down the street from inside here, went outside and stopped her, had a whirlwind courtship and married her shortly thereafter. During his Austin residency he also owned or rented 2808 San Pedro (1935–6), Four Happy Hollow Lane again (1937, 1939, 1941), and 3119 Tom Green Street (1938–9). One of his wife's shrewd financial decisions was the 1942 purchase of radio station KTCB at 119 E. Tenth, where he sometimes worked. The station and its FM sister have operated since 1973 under the call letters KLBJ.

Nixon dedicated the **LBJ** Library* west of I-35, north of downtown, where **Johnson** had his last public appearances, in 1971. He had an office on the top floor of the Federal Building downtown, 126 W. Sixth, and at the library, just north of the Texas Longhorns Stadium, where **LBJ** regularly attended. A block west of the library on the UT campus is the Texas Memorial Museum* dedicated by **FDR** in 1936. He is pictured at a train stop about a quarter mile from the location. **Carter, Clinton**, and five first ladies sat together at Lady Bird Johnson's funeral on July 14, 2007, at the Riverbend Centre, 4214 N. Capital of Texas Highway.

BONHAM • Four presidents (**Truman**, **Eisenhower**, **Kennedy**, and **Johnson**) were photographed sitting together in 1961 at the First Baptist Church,* 710 N. Center, during the funeral of Sam Rayburn, former Speaker of the U.S. House. **Truman** had visited the home and the football stadium during the 1948 election. They all visited the Rayburn Library* (dedicated by **Truman** in 1957) and home,* both on U.S. 82 just west of town.

BROWNSVILLE • General **Taylor** moved troops here in March 1846, as his country and Mexico contested the strip of land between the Rio Grande and the Nueces River. **Grant** saw his first battle action and hostile fire at the first battles of Mexican War, Palo Alto* and Resaca de la Palma,* both marked north on State Route 1847. These were the first large battles commanded by **Taylor**, who had never seen cavalry in action before Palo Alto. He planned an infantry charge, saw the Mexican cavalry, retreated, and then let his artillery company win the battle. **Grant** wrote that he slept on the ground "like it was a palace."

At Resaca de la Palma **Taylor** committed a series of uncoordinated small unit attacks. **Grant** wrote in his *Memoirs* that the army commanded by **Taylor** was the most efficient he ever saw, although historians question how much credit is due **Taylor**. Both battles were fought over a large area, and neither is marked other than by monuments and cannon located at documented general areas. Palo Alto ("tall trees") is marked at the NE corner of Highways 511 and 1847. Resaca ("small lakes that were once in the river bed") is marked on the east side of Route 1847 about two miles north of State 48. (A good map is provided by the local visitor center.)

Davis arrived at Brazos Island, in the Gulf southeast of Port Isabel, in August 1846 at the beginning of the war. United States troops arrived and departed at a site now inaccessible. **Taylor's** first headquarters was at the northeastern end of the University of Texas campus and later at Fort Brown, marked toward the river east of the international crossing opposite Matamoros, Mexico. **Davis, Grant**, and 20 future Civil War generals were at the site. It is also claimed that **Grant** and several future Civil War generals (McClelland, Lee, and Sheridan) stayed at the Miller Hotel at one time or the other, although the present building was built after the war. The Miller Building now occupies the hotel site at Elizabeth and 13th Streets.

When **Taylor** heard that war had been declared he moved the army to the Mexican town of Matamoras, and it became the "Army of Invasion." His headquarters were on a deep bend in the Rio Grande at the present international bridge. Since the river has shifted, it is impossible to determine an exact site. The Mexican War is probably our least known, although the percentage of soldiers killed was the highest in any war fought by the United States.

In the 1920s **Harding** stayed at the R.B. Creger home, now a retirement center at the NW corner of Fifth and Washington. He was paraded down Levee, Palm, and Elizabeth to the fort grounds for a speech.

COLLEGE STATION • **Carter**, **Ford**, and **Clinton** helped dedicate the **George H.W. Bush** Library, visited several times by **George W. Bush**. The first **Bush** frequently visits his office in the facility on the Texas A&M campus. **Davis** was offered the first presidency of the school in the 1870s, but turned it down after he visited since his wife did not want to move and he felt his that his presence would hurt the fundraising potential of the new school. **LBJ** and **Ike** visited A&M in 1937.

COTULLA • **Johnson** got his first teaching job with impoverished children at the Welhausen School at 804 Lane. No one seemed to care about them before he came, and he learned about the needs of the hungry and underprivileged. He lived in a shabby house on stilts next to the railroad tracks, at 202 S. Neal, and went to the Church of Christ at Medina and Kerr.

CORPUS CHRISTI • General **Taylor**'s established headquarters for his troops known as the "Army of Observation" here as the Republic of Texas and the United States were negotiating annexation. Mexico claimed the disputed territory south of the Nueces River. Four thousand troops, including **Grant**, camped along what are now Mesquite, Chaparral, and Water Streets from July 1845 until March 1846, on both sides of the Nueces, now a ship channel. Water Street then fronted the Gulf of Mexico. Officers included a "who's who" of later Civil War leaders including Longstreet, Hooker, Meade, Bragg, Hardee, Buell, Albert Sidney Johnston, Reynolds, Thomas, Sherman, E.K. Smith, Van Dorn, Kearney, Buckner, Hancock, and A.P. Hill. Many histories of Corpus and newspaper articles down through the years contained in the local library and elsewhere erroneously show Robert E. Lee, **Pierce**, and **Davis** here also at this time with **Taylor**, but they did not arrive with the army until it was in Mexico. **Davis** was still in Congress until mid–1846, and did not leave Washington until that summer. **Pierce** sailed directly from Rhode Island to Vera Cruz during May and June 1846.

Taylor ordered a well dug at 800 Chaparral, marked by a monument in Artesian Park, but it was abandoned due to mineral properties. Later it was found to be healthful and still provides water. A monument near the present visitor center at 1823 Chaparral marks the spot where the first U.S. flag was raised south of the Nueces River. **Taylor**'s headquarters are listed at various places, but were at a stucco house on Water Street between Pearl and Bennet, north of the river. Only Pearl Street remains north of the ship channel, and the site is now in the parking lot of the Texas State Aquarium, just south of Pearl. **Taylor** established the Bayview Cemetery at Broadway, Padre, Waco, and Ramirez Streets.

Taylor was a gifted veteran, but his legendary dislike for military formality was evident in his habit of wearing blue denim pants, a long linen duster, and a big palmetto hat. Various future Civil War personalities got to know one another very well here and perceived insights into their respective personalities and capacities, affecting future relationships and planning in Civil War battles. All recognized that **Taylor** was **Grant**'s role model, as Robert E. Lee seemed be the model of Winfield Scott, who later commanded at Mexico City, where **Grant** also served.

Expert horseman **Grant** broke many wild horses, including one delivered by boat by Mexicans that no one wanted because it was so ferocious. His expertise and methods were said to be the talk of every campfire in the U.S. Army, according to later Confederate General James

Longstreet. **Grant** did well at numerous horse races, and made his acting debut in Shakespeare's *Othello*, in which he played the feminine lead, complete with fan and hooped bell dress. But his friend Longstreet wrote that he was such a failure that they had to send to New Orleans for a professional actress to play the part in future productions. In December, **Grant** accompanied a paymaster's train to San Antonio and Austin as described in his *Memoirs*, going through New Braunfels, with nights at Goliad and Bastrop. He liked Corpus so much he thought about getting his fiancée, Julia, to join him. Once on the beach when he could not get the men to properly clear an underwater obstruction, he jumped in to show them how while "dandy officers," in **Taylor's** words, made fun of him. **Taylor** witnessed the scene and said he wished all of his officer would show such ingenuity. The army, becoming known as the "Army of Occupation," marched south to Mexico beginning in March 1846, roughly following today's U.S. Highway 77.

The Naval Air Station at the southern end of Ocean Avenue was the largest in the world when the elder **Bush** trained there during World War II.

DALLAS • **Houston** came to Bird's Fort and Grape Vine Springs (see Ft. Worth) west of here in mid–1843, coming through Dallas with various commissioners, including John H. Reagan, later U.S. Senator and Confederate postmaster general. **Houston** saw Dallas's founder, John Neely Bryan, then and later in 1851 at his cabin,* now on the lawn of the courthouse, Main and Houston. (Bryan had named the city after "a friend" in the early 1840s, but he could not have known George Dallas, later vice president under Polk, as popularly supposed. So no one knows who this "Dallas" was for whom the city was named. Dallas County was later named after the vice president when the state was admitted the Union in 1845.) The cabin was then at the Triple Underpass Bridge, a few blocks west of the courthouse, at the west end of Dealy Plaza.

Davis came on May 20, 1875, from Houston and Austin and got off at the depot still on the west side of Houston south of Commerce. He first rested at the San Jacinto Hotel at the NE corner of Austin and Commerce. **Coolidge** was there in 1930. **Davis** was treated to a parade down Commerce Street with arches at "Buckhorn Corner" and Tooley's Hall. After speeches at the Fair Grounds (same location as now), he came back to the hotel, rested shortly, and left for Memphis via Marshall, Jefferson, and Texarkana on the Texas and Pacific Railroad.

Recent presidents have made innumerable visits, matched in other cities throughout the country. A few visits are noted in this paragraph. **FDR** spoke at the Fair Grounds in 1936 and dedicated the Robert E. Lee statue in Lee Park at Hall and Turtle Creek. (I witnessed the remaining visits mentioned in this paragraph.) **Truman** drove down Jefferson Street in the Oak Cliff section in 1948 on the way to speak at Burnet Field, now a vacant lot at the SW corner of Colorado and I-35. **Eisenhower** was honored in a 1952 parade down Main and Commerce Streets, going to the Baker Hotel then on the south side of Commerce at Akard Street. **Johnson** introduced **Kennedy** in November 1957 at the Memorial Auditorium* on Akard. **Nixon** was at the Apparel Mart on North I-35 in 1970, near **Kennedy**'s general destination when he was assassinated. Georgia Governor **Carter** introduced Vice President **Ford** at the Sheridan Hotel,* Commerce Street east of Ervay, in 1974. Later **Carter** was at the Fairmount,* NW corner of Akard and Ross. **Reagan** was welcomed at Moody Coliseum* on the SMU campus in 1980 and later at a rally in Lowe's Anatole Hotel,* NW corner of I-35W and Market Central, in 1984 with **George H.W. Bush** and **George W.** during the Republican Nominating Convention at the Convention Center* on Griffin south of Young Street.

Johnson was assaulted by protesters at the Adolphus Hotel,* NW corner of Commerce and Akard, in 1960, helping him with sympathy votes. **Truman** stayed at the hotel several times including 1915 and 1941. His visit with an uncle about 1901 was the first Dallas visit by a person who became or was a U.S. president.

After spending the night in the Texas Hotel* in Ft. Worth on November 21–22, 1963, **Kennedy** flew to Love Field Airport* at mid-morning about an hour after **Nixon** flew out. His parade route was down Main Street west to Houston Street, then north one block to Elm, then west on Elm toward the Stemmons Freeway to the Dallas Trade Mart, where he was to make a speech. Lee Harvey Oswald fired from the sixth-floor southeast window of the Texas Schoolbook Depository* at the NW corner of Elm and Houston on Dealy Plaza. The Warren Commission and conclusive evidence shows that Oswald acted alone in assassinating the president. The Depository now houses a museum* on the sixth floor about the tragic event, and is about a block from the original site of the city founder's cabin.

George W. Bush's daughters were born in Baylor Hospital on Gaston Avenue, near downtown, although the family lived in Midland at the time. They shortly moved to Dallas at 6029 Northwood where the daughters attended public school, then Hockaday School for Girls, 11600 Welch Road. His Presidential Library will be built at Southern Methodist University on the west side of U.S. 75 and Mockingbird, north of downtown.

DENISON • **Eisenhower** was born in 1890 at Lamar Street and 208 East Day Street* as "David Dwight." His names were reversed later. His family lived here for about three years, and moved back to Kansas the next spring after Dwight was born. He always thought that he had been born in Tyler until someone remembered the baby named David (Dwight), which led to recognition and preservation of the site. He came back for a visit in 1946.

EL PASO • **Benjamin Harrison** traveled through on the train in 1891 and made a speech at the courthouse and depot at San Francisco and Davis. **McKinley** attended the Station Street Methodist Church in 1901, San Jacinto Plaza surrounded by Oregon, Main, Mills and Mesa, and walked the International Bridge, now U.S. 54. On October 16, 1909, **Taft** met the president of Mexico at the Custom House at the SE corner of Calle 16 de Septembre and Juarez. This was the first time that the presidents from each country had met, and they traveled across the border for a state dinner called the most important diplomatic event in the history of the two countries. The dinner cost the Mexican government $750,000, and the U.S. moved 3000 troops here for the event. Earlier in the day **Taft** spoke at the St. Regis on North Oregon Street.

FREDERICKSBURG • **Grant** and **Hayes** stayed at the Nimitz Hotel* where World War II Admiral Chester Nimitz grew up. This is now the National Museum of the Pacific War at 340 Main.

FT. WORTH • **Houston** came to Bird's Fort in July 1843 to negotiate a treaty with the Indians. He had first camped a little north in the vicinity of present Grape Vine Springs (marker in Irving, north side service road of I-635 and a mile west of McArthur Road), waiting for chiefs to appear. The Indians agreed to bring their white prisoners to Bird's Fort, further south. The chiefs never appeared, but the large council lingered for several weeks in August, listened to **Houston's** pledge that the white man would not venture past a certain line to the west, which embodied **Houston's** peace policy producing conditions ensuring peace for a generation. A marker is located in the Arlington city limits on FM 157 a mile north of the Trinity River mentioning the fort east of that point, now inaccessible on private land about a mile east of FM 157, between Green Oaks Blvd. and Calloway Lake Cemetery Road near a crescent-shaped lake.

Kennedy spent his last night in the Texas Hotel (now Radisson*) at Main and Eighth. A rally with **Johnson** at the west side was held on the morning of November 22, 1963, with a breakfast and speech inside. **George H.W. Bush** stayed there in 1981. **Wilson** and **Harding** had been to town before they became president, and **Taft** came afterward. **T. Roosevelt** came in 1905 and was photographed in a Main Street parade and making a speech on the square in the 100 block of Lancaster, now under the Interstate 30 overpass. He later planted a tree at the library, then at the NW corner of Houston and Ninth Streets, and in 1907 and 1912 went to the White Elephant Saloon,* Coliseum,* and 123 E. Exchange,* all still at the Stockyards on North Main.

TR, Truman, Ike, and **FDR** used the train station on Lancaster Street, now under the I-30 overpass. **FDR** came here five times, generally to see his grandchildren and his son Elliot, who lived at his Dutch Branch Ranch on the southern edge of Benbrook, and once made a fireside chat from a local radio station. **Truman** and **Johnson** had been frequent visitors at the Buck Oaks Farm, at 6312 White Settlement Road, known as the Tarrant County White House, torn down in 2004. **FDR's** helicopter landed on the lawn near the Naval Air Station. **Ford** spoke to various bar associations at the Convention Center, 1201 Houston Street, on April 28, 1976.

GALVESTON • **Houston** often stayed at the Menard House at 1603 33rd Street. He spoke against secession as Texas was preparing to vote on the question, from the balcony of the Tremont House, north side of Mechanic between 23rd and 24th, since he was locked out of the courthouse. Friends begged him not to appear before the ugly mob, but he proclaimed that they were headed for a course of "fire and rivers of blood." Someone shouted that he would be glad to drink all the blood that would be spilled in his predicted war.

Hayes stayed at the Tremont with his benefactor, Uncle Sardis, when he came to Texas in December 1848, for his health and to see a Texas school friend nearby at Gulf Prairie on the Brazos River. While on his trip around the world, **Grant** stayed in a later Tremont* on the same site at 2300 Ship's Mechanic Row in the popular Stand District. The Galvez Hotel,* still facing the ocean at 21st Street, claims that six presidents including **FDR** and **Eisenhower** stayed.

GEORGETOWN • **Houston** frequently spoke in San Gabriel Park and stayed with Elias Talbot at 209 Church Street, northeast of the courthouse, and just south of the river. Talbot's daughter told of his meeting with representatives of Lincoln in the house before the war started. He was here, or maybe the J.T. Coffee home at 1401 James, when he received Lincoln's letter offering to maintain him in the governor's office by force at the start of the Civil War. (He was probably at both houses that day.) Both homes have been destroyed.

HOUSTON AND VICINITY • The Mexican colony of Texas, with its white population of 30,000, mostly fleeing the Mexican army under orders to clear the area of Anglos, won its independence on April 21, 1836, at San Jacinto Battlefield* east of Houston. Mexican president, dictator, and commander in chief, Santa Anna, had lost maybe 1600 of his 8,000 men and valuable time to the force of about 187 men and boys at the Alamo. The only real Texas army existing then, about 400, was captured and executed at La Bahia. There Santa Anna's massacre lost him the public image-propaganda war. He then ordered Anglo Texas destroyed and divided his 6000 remaining forces to drive out the remaining colonists. All settlers fled in panic, except for a small army under **Houston** which proceeded as follows:

January and February, 1836: Commander in chief **Houston** is at La Bahia fortress* south of Goliad to order the colony's various forces to desist from invading Mexico and orders the Alamo abandoned and destroyed. This is ignored as three other commanders in chief are established and government and order become nonexistent. **Houston** resigns to go to meet Indians in Nacogdoches to prevent attacks on fleeing settlers.

March 2: **Houston** officially named commander in chief while at a convention at Washington-on-the-Brazos after Texas independence is declared on this date. The Alamo is under siege; General Fannin's army, the largest Texas force, is at La Bahia waiting for detachments to return and refuses **Houston's** orders to retreat. **Houston** leaves to join the army.

March 11: **Houston** arrives in Gonzales, one mile south of town on the river, via Burnham's Crossing on the Colorado River, then establishes headquarters in the Braches House, marked on U.S. 90A between Shiner and Gonzales. He receives word that the Alamo has fallen, orders Gonzales burned, and retreats on March 13. An oak tree is marked ten miles east on U.S. 90A where **Houston** rested with the army. He has fewer than 400 poorly supplied, undisciplined volunteers to face 6000 or more professionals.

March 17: Crosses with army at Burnham's Crossing between Columbus and Weimar, just north of Interstate Highway 10. Santa Anna later used the same site.

March 20: Begins camp on the east side of the Colorado at Beason's Crossing for eight days to organize. This is two miles south of Columbus a short distance from I-10. Solders are deserting after hearing atrocity stories concerning the Mexican army. Almost 400 Texans who surrendered under General Fannin are executed at Goliad on March 28 in addition to 30 executed in front of Refugio Mission. But other volunteers are arriving.

March 29: Passes through San Felipe, camps at Groce's Plantation beginning March 31 until April 14, near Raccoon Bend on the west side of the Brazos River. This is south of Hempstead and SE of Cochran, west of Route 1887 where it is marked. Texas is in panic; all settlers are fleeing. **Houston** attempts to establish some semblance of military order among volunteers eager to fight. Mexican soldiers are split into several wings with the location of Santa Anna unknown. **Houston** may have been trying to draw the Mexican army into heavily wooded East Texas or Louisiana where United States forces under General Gaines were stationed. A large force of Indians may be preparing to attack near Nacogdoches. Gaines eventually crosses the international border to Nacogdoches. But **Houston's** men, indignant about the atrocities at the Alamo and Goliad, will not wait much longer to fight in spite of odds.

April 16: Reaches "Which-way" tree, marked eight miles west of Tomball in New Kentucky Park, where **Houston** dramatically decides to go toward Harrisburg rather toward Nacogdoches and the United States border. This ensures a showdown battle. His spies had determined, maybe by infiltrating the enemy camp, Santa Anna's route and presence there with one wing of the army.

April 19: Marches through Harrisburg (present site of **Houston**) to arrive at San Jacinto River at Lynch's Ferry* (the present Lynchburg Ferry). A captured Mexican courier using Alamo commander Travis's saddlebags confirms that Mexicans forces are split with Santa Anna headed to the spot at the ferry, controlling escape where thousands had fled. Santa Anna plans to take a German ship out into the Gulf where a Mexican ship will take him to Mexico—his acting president has died—but the small Texas navy burned it this day, forcing him to stay.

By April 20, the armies knew where each other were. Santa Anna expected an early morning attack and worked all night to prepare defensive works. His brother-in-law joined him at 9:00 A.M. on April 21 with 500 more troops after marching all night. When no attack came, he ordered the exhausted men to sleep until after lunch. In theory, even though Santa Anna lost the battle, he still had other armies and the resources of a powerful nation of eight million behind him. **Houston** had only about 918 (plus maybe 250 left behind with measles) facing 1330 of the 6000 Mexican soldiers in Texas with the rest nearby. The fragile, broke Texas government and population were disorganized and in flight. **Houston** ordered Vince's Bridge, offering escape to both sides, cut down. (This may have been near the Ramada Inn on Route 225 a few miles west.) When the troops learned of this they knew both armies were surrounded by water and their fate was victory or death.

Houston could have attacked on the 20th or early on the 21st, but by afternoon the troops would wait no longer. (Why he waited has been debated ever since.) They marched across an open grass field in a ten-minute walk at 4:30 P.M. and surprised the enemy in broad daylight behind defensive works. In eighteen minutes the Mexican army was annihilated in the only battle in North America where the losing side had 100 per cent casualties (630 killed, 700 prisoners). Santa Anna got himself captured, leaving no leadership to continue the war. As the dictator was brought before **Houston** at his headquarters (marker number 20) on the battlefield south of the Battleship *Texas* and west of De Zavala Plaza, he congratulated the Texas commander for capturing the "Napoleon of the West." A portion of the tree trunk under which **Houston** rested is preserved. As Santa Anna was military dictator of eight million, and commander in chief of the army, this was maybe the Texas equivalent of capturing Hitler in early World War II. Thus the war, not just a battle, ended and everything from Texas west eventually fell into the hands of the United States (within the next decade) as Mexico never seriously threatened again. As author T.R. Fehrenbach says, "The American West was won."

The battlefield is well preserved, probably too much so, as it is now so park-like that the grounds look little like the original setting. The country's second tallest monument—only the St. Louis Arch is taller—marks the area with markers at the spot of **Houston's** camp, wounding, and various battle events. (The monument was completed partially with funds Senator Andrew Jackson Houston, Sam's 87-year-old son, helped pass through Congress in 1942. The fact that it is taller than the Washington Monument was not disclosed until after completion as Texans thought there would be objections to outdoing **George Washington**.)

Houston was so severely wounded in the ankle that he resigned his position of commander in chief and was taken to New Orleans for treatment. The serious wound was likely to cause lockjaw or some other serious complication, but the Texas provisional president, David Burnet, a political enemy, refused him a place on the only means of transportation, a small steamship that had brought the president and government to the battlefield. President Burnet claimed that since **Houston** was no longer a government official he had no right on the ship. The captain refused to move until he was placed on board. (While **Houston** was president, former President Burnet challenged him to a duel that **Houston** refused.)

In 1836 the new city of Houston was organized near the town of Harrisburg burned by Santa Anna. The promoters wanted to bring the capital there to promote the town and built a Capitol at the site of the Rice Hotel (now loft apartments),* NW corner of Texas and 518 Main Street. **Kennedy** stayed at the Rice in 1960 when he met Protestant pastors in the ballroom to discuss his religion, a major step towards his election. It was felt that this appearance might make or break his presidential hopes. The audience was generally favorably impressed with his arguments that he was an American above all and felt that the country would suffer if 40 million were excluded from presidential consideration because of their Catholic faith. And he argued that if Catholics could be excluded in 1960, anyone could be in the future.

The Houston city promotion worked temporarily, and the Texas Congress, meeting in Columbus, set the city of Houston as the capital of the Texas Republic in January 1837. But when **Houston** and Congress arrived in April and May, there was no roof on the Capitol Building. President **Houston's** office and home had two beds, for the president and surgeon general, and little else. The so-called Texas White House is marked at the Scanlan Building, 405 Main at the NE corner with Preston, where **Houston** and later President Lamar lived during their administrations. When **Houston** was here the ground floor was mud and Indians occasionally camped in the yard. Yellow fever epidemics and alligators killed several. **Houston** also lived just north of the NE corner of Prairie and Caroline. After the capital moved to Austin, the building became the Capitol Hotel, where **Houston** stayed many times. In 1858, the last president of the Republic, Anson Jones, told a friend in front that his career started here and might as well end as well. He then went to his room and killed himself.

The second president, Lamar, hated **Houston**, man and city, and did not want to honor the man by having the capital in his city. Lamar was easily elected after two candidates supported by **Houston** both committed suicide. (Note that the author of the Texas Declaration of Independence, the first U.S. Senator and secretary of war, and the last president also committed suicide.) So in 1840 Lamar got the capital transferred to the new city of Austin closer to the western territories. When **Houston** was reelected and new Mexican and Indian raids loomed near Austin, the capital was moved temporarily back to Houston, where Congress declared a war that **Houston** vetoed. Austin citizens refused to allow government papers to be removed so the capital wound up back there.

When **Houston** became governor, he had to sell his house in Huntsville to pay campaign expenses. After leaving the office in 1861, he moved back to nearby Cedar Point to a site now in the Bay, at the end of Cedar Point Road, seven miles east of Baytown, east off Route 2354, just east of the Route 1405 junction. There is an almost hidden marker at the northeast intersection of 2354 and Cedar Point Road. He had purchased the land in 1838 and lived there after first leaving the presidential office until he was elected again in 1841. Sam Houston Jr. joined the Confederate army, was wounded seriously at Shiloh, and was reported dead. An army doctor and admirer of this father put forth extra effort to save him after noting his name in a dedication in his Bible from his mother, and he returned home to parents who thought that he was dead.

Houston stayed many times at the Cherry-Rice House,* then on the north side of Court Square on Congress between Fannin and San Jacinto Streets and now in Sam Houston Historical Park. He came down with a fever after moving to Cedar Point, and William Marsh Rice, who later endowed the university with the same name, brought the old general here to recover.

FDR attended the 1928 Democratic convention at 810 Bagby Street at the Sam Houston Coliseum. This was his political reemergence after seven years of recovery from his polio attack in 1921. He could not walk, but had to appear as if he could. Heavy braces kept his legs straight. He had to lean on someone to shift his weight from one leg to the other and drag himself a short distance to a microphone, giving the appearance of walking. If he fell or appeared to be an invalid, he would have no political career. His walk and talk were successful, and he appeared to be healthy in nominating Governor Al Smith, who then sponsored **Roosevelt** for his old governor's job. When someone suggested that he should not support such a potentially popular rival, Smith said **Roosevelt** would be dead within a year.

Johnson lived with several cousins, two aunts, and an uncle at 435 Hawthorne and taught school at 1304 Capitol, now a vacant lot. He worked hard to make the debate team as exciting as the football team, and instilled great respect for knowledge as well as his own abilities.

George Bush lived at 5525 Briar from 1960 to 1967. The lot was so large that the house was torn down to build five new ones. The flagpole remains. His church remains St. Martin's Episcopal, 717 Sage Road. His offices were 1701 Houston Club Building, 1960–1967, and later at 1000 Memorial Dr. He lived at 5838 Indian Trail from 1977 to 1980 and 710 North Post Road, 1980–1981. Then his legal address was 111 N. Post Oak Lane, the Houstonian Hotel and Condominium, room 271 in 1985 and from 1989 to 1992. His residence from 1993 to the present is 9 SW Oak. Favorite restaurants include Molina's Mexican, 7933 Westheimer, and Otto's Bar-B-Q, 5502 Memorial. He was renominated in 1992 in the Astrodome,*

Kirby and Fannin. He along with **Nixon, Ford, Carter,** and **Reagan** have stayed at the Hyatt Regency, 1200 Louisiana.

HUNTSVILLE • In 1844 **Houston** lived 21 miles north of Liberty at Grand Cane, on the east side of Route 146. The next year he moved to Raven Hill, fourteen miles to the east of Huntsville in the woods, marked about three miles south of Oakhurst off County Road 3018 in the Hoby Community. His first daughter was born here, and his wife had breast surgery without any anesthesia. Knowing that his U.S. Senate duties would keep him away for long periods, that the country house was too far from civilization, and wanting the family to be near the Baptist church, he moved the family in 1847 to a log cabin as the Huntsville home, Woodland,* was being built. This and his log cabin law office* and inner sanctum remain adjacent to Sam Houston University, where there is also an excellent **Houston** museum. The complex is a few blocks south of the town square on TX 75 Business Route, a favorite whittling spot where he entertained numerous children with stories who gathered around him.

Four of his eight children were born at Woodland, and his mother-in-law moved in from Alabama. A later church building occupies the site of his church, First Baptist, at 1229 Avenue J at 13th Street. His Masonic Lodge was at 1030 12th, and he frequented the Gibbs Store at 1118 11th Street at Sam Houston Avenue. Store records there indicate the large amount of goods bought to supply his large family and the many visitors who spent the night. His home was also a favorite spot for visiting Indians to make campfires and visit their friend. **Houston** ran unsuccessfully for governor in 1857 and ran up such debts that he had to sell the house in 1858.

He was elected governor in 1859. After leaving the governor's mansion in Austin because of his refusal to support the Confederacy, he moved to Cedar Point and then back to Huntsville to the rented Steamboat House,* where he died in 1863. The location then is marked at the high point in the cemetery at the NE corner of Ninth and Martin Luther King Jr. Street, a block east of his prominent burial site at Ninth and J. The Steamboat House has been moved onto the grounds of Woodland. The state prison, where he visited Union prisoners, was nearby then as it is now.

INDEPENDENCE • This was another of the several homes of **Houston** in Texas. He came here in 1853 because of the higher elevation that he hoped would benefit his wife's asthma and because of the educational opportunities of Baylor University, the first university in the state. Sam Houston Jr. entered the preparatory school at age ten, as did eventually two of his brothers. A daughter attended the female department, as did eventually her three sisters. The college president baptized **Houston** in chilly Rocky Creek in November 1854. **Houston** often said that both he and his pocketbook were baptized into the Baptist church. When the preacher told him his sins were washed away, he said he hoped the Lord would help the fish. A later church building is marked at the site, the intersection of FM 50 and FM 390. The home site is marked across the road at the intersection of Spur 390 and Farm Road 390, three-tenths of a mile west of the intersection with FM 50 and FM 390. After two years the family moved back to Huntsville. His wife lived here with their eight children after his death. She is buried across from the church. Her death of yellow fever made it impractical to bury her next to her husband in Huntsville.

JEFFERSON • **Grant** and **Hayes** stayed at the Excelsior House,* still open for business on Austin between Vale and Market. Their names are on the displayed register and their bedrooms and original beds are still rented. **Houston** also stayed and spoke here as well as at the Presbyterian Manse at the NE corner of Alley and Delta. **LBJ** also visited the hotel several miles from his wife's childhood home in Karnack, marked on SR 43, two miles southwest.

JOHNSON CITY AND STONEWALL • **Johnson's** reconstructed birthplace* is the only presidential birthplace rebuilt during the president's time in office. His grandparents, the Sam **Johnsons**, had lived from 1867 to 1872 in a frontier log cabin* a few blocks west of the boyhood home, preserved as part of the National Historic Park in Johnson City. Visitors can see where his grandmother and aunt hid from Comanches in the cellar in 1869 as they ransacked the home Johnson later knew while the grandfather was on a cattle drive. They moved away and then back to Stonewall, fourteen miles west of Johnson City on U.S. 290, as it was said, "to be in sight of Sam's beloved mountains." Sam was so disgusted at having so many girls that he named one Frank, then finally had a boy, Lyndon's father, Sam Jr., who lived here when Lyndon was born in 1908. The family moved to Johnson City in 1913. The birthplace fell down in the 1930s, but **Johnson** bought the property from Aunt Frank in 1957 and built a replica in 1964 with some of the same stone and lumber. He enjoyed giving personal tours of the home, used as an overflow guest cottage until 1966. It occupies the same site on Park Road 49, northeast of the State Historical Park Visitor's Center on U.S. 290 and the National Historic Park or LBJ Ranch.

He wandered over or ran off to play with his cousins at recess at the Junction School* just east of the birthplace, and the teacher was persuaded to take in one more pupil, even though he was just four, to keep him from running away. The president came back in 1965 to sign an important education bill here, with his old teacher by his side. As a boy he had a crush on her, telling her he did not like her one bit; he just loved her. He thought the act of signing the bill in the old school illustrated how far an American could go. Later he went to school then about four miles away down the Lower Albert Road, due south of the cemetery, on the north side about one quarter of a mile east of the intersection of Road 1623.

The family moved to Johnson City when Lyndon was five, to Elm (Ninth) and G Streets,* one block south of Main Street, U.S. 290. It was one of the nicest houses in town, with running well water, but had no electricity or indoor plumbing. The restored home presents a deceivingly better picture of their living conditions with better furniture displayed in a now painted and repaired, more presentable home than the boy knew. Few original pieces are there, although their expensive old radio is still in the kitchen, where it was turned up loud during important broadcasts for the neighbors to gather outside and listen to. The family slept in summer on the back porch, where his father cut hair on weekends to make ends meet. **Lyndon** shared a small bedroom with his brother and was known to have high feelings about everything. At age ten he jumped off the barn and broke his arm (or leg, as various versions go). He yelled bloody murder until the old doctor hobbled up and started to treat him. He kept screaming that he was going to die. When the doctor told him he was going to give him a shot, **Lyndon** pleaded, "Please don't shoot me. I want to live a while longer."

With his father in the legislature, important people from all over came to discuss politics. **Lyndon** liked listen on the porch or in the living room. If he was excluded, he would stay in the bedroom and listen with the door slightly open. He also loved going on the campaign trail with his father, visiting constituents, and being given ice cream or warm tea, depending on the season.

After his grandparents died, the family moved back to their farmhouse* in 1920, just west of the birthplace house, to try to make a living in cotton. **Johnson** remembered sitting on his grandfather's porch listening to stories of trail drives, Indians, and the Civil War. Lyndon also tried to help his uncle on the ranch. In 1921 he stayed with an aunt and uncle at 507 E. Pecan (Seventh) Street. In 1922 when floods and drought financially ruined his father, the family moved back to Johnson City and the boyhood home. His father stayed in debt the rest of his life. He graduated from high school at age fifteen at the City High School, Cypress (Sixth) and D Avenue, in 1924. He was the youngest to graduate from the unaccredited school, although he was a poor student. He delivered the commencement address in 1964.

At the boyhood home in town, a marker notes that his first campaign speech for national office occurred on the front porch. When Lyndon was a boy, his father and uncle sat on the porch at least one night with a loaded shotgun because of threats by the KKK over Mr. **Johnson's** support for German Americans in the legislature during World War I. The National Visitor Center is located a block away. His home church throughout his life was the First Christian* at 401 E. Cypress (Sixth), a few blocks north near the schools. His father's office is now a bed and breakfast (The Pearl*) on the square.

The LBJ Ranch* on Highway 290 at Stonewall, called the Texas White House, was purchased from Aunt Frank in 1952. **JFK** visited in 1960, and was "reluctantly taken on a deer hunt." **Nixon** conferred shortly after his election. **Ford** visited, and Representative **George Bush** was advised there that he should aim higher than the lower house of Congress. The president came here for "serenity," but kept dozens of secretaries and advisors busy in a frenzy of activity. He loved driving his car fast, then hollering that the brakes had failed just before plunging into the deep river, showing that it was amphibious. **LBJ** had his fourth and fatal heart attack in the home on January 22, 1973, and is buried with his wife in the cemetery* between the birthplace and his grandparents' home. The Stonewall sites are at the National Historic Park, where most can only be reached on a private park road by the bus tour from the State Park Visitor Center across the road from the ranch. Trinity Lutheran and the Stonewall Head Start School next door were both visited by the **Johnsons** and are accessible just north of U.S. 90 due south of the cemetery.

MIDLAND • **George** and **George W. Bush** moved to the George's Court Motel, at 500 W. Wall Street, when they moved back to Texas in 1950 from California, then later to three other houses here until moving to **Houston** in late August 1959. He worked at 300 W. Texas. The first "cookie cutter," 847-square-foot, $7,500 house (1950–51) was at 405 E. Maple, and looked like all others in the neighborhood known as Easter Egg Row. **Bush** teamed up with a neighbor, who had baby-sat Little George, to form their own oil company. They then moved to their "dream house" at 1412 W. Ohio* in 1951, staying until 1956. It was restored at the cost of $1.8 million and dedicated by the senior **Bushes** in April 2006. Mrs. Bush then stated that she thought the 1500-square-foot house seemed "enormous" back then. It and a neighbor's home are museums. Here they claimed to have the first swimming pool in town. **W.** even wore his trunks to school under his jeans to show off. The family lived here when his little sister died of leukemia. The illness had been kept from him, and her death was a shock. Soon after, he told his father at a ball game that he wished that he was his sister. "She has a better seat from up there," he explained. His mother became very depressed, but snapped out of it when she heard her son tell a friend, "I can't come over to play because I have to play with mother. She's lonely."

The family lived a *Leave It to Beaver* existence, frequenting the Ritz Theatre at 207 Main and Agnes's Café at 109 S. Baird. He met **LBJ** at the Scarborough Hotel,* in the center of downtown at Routes 349 and 158, in 1953 and told him that he was Prescott Bush's son. The Democratic senator so praised the Republican Connecticut senator that **Bush** expressed surprise. **Johnson** said he just thought of his friend and himself as "good Americans." **Bush** wrote that he felt like humming a few verses of the "Star Spangled Banner." Later in 1956, they moved to 2703 Sentinel, backing up to Cowden Park* where the boys could run out the back gate to play baseball while their mother watched. **W.** loved to catch toads here after infrequent rains. Little George walked every day for six years to Sam Houston Elementary,* 2000 W. Louisiana, where he once felt that the spanking he got from his principal for drawing an ink beard and sideburns was worth it for the laughs he got from his classmates. He went to San Jacinto Jr. High,* 1400 North N (east side of Garfield between Cuthbert and Golf Course Road), where he was seventh-grade president and football quarterback. **George W.** is the only president to play Little League baseball, which he says was the happiest time in his life. (As former owner of the Texas Rangers Baseball Team, he built a little league diamond on White House grounds.) One coach was his father and another said that he felt he was coaching one of the richest little league catchers in the world. He came back to the elementary school in 1997 to announce that he would run for a second term as governor.

The elder **Bush** and his wife, Barbara, taught in First Presbyterian,* 800 W. Texas. Their last child, Dorothy, was born while here just before they moved to Houston in August 1959 to be closer to his offshore drilling operations. His offices as a partner in Zapata Petroleum Company were in Midland National Bank Building,* at 500 W. Texas, 1953–59.

After **George W.** graduated from Harvard Business School, he came back to what he considered his hometown in 1976 to the roots of his childhood, and lived at 2008A Bedford and then another apartment at the back of a house at 2006A Harvard. He went into the oil business like his father and worked at the Midland National Bank Building that his father had helped form, then the Petroleum (now Bank United) Building,* 214 W. Texas, and also the Permian Building, also downtown. He also taught Sunday school at First Presbyterian. When Laura came back to visit her parents, the two met and married at her church, First Methodist* (305 N. Baird), where they both later taught. She had vaguely known him at San Jacinto Jr. High.

The couple lived at 1405 W. Golf Course Road from 1978 until 1984, and later at 910 Harvard, where his parents visited their granddaughters. **George W.** lost his bid for Congress in 1978, although he got most of Midland's vote and won the respect of his opponent, who supported him politically later. Barbara told her daughter-in-law not to criticize her husband's speeches, but Laura made the mistake of doing so as they were driving into the garage. When he asked her what she felt on the way from a speech, she told him. As she told Jay Leno on national TV, George then crashed into the back wall. The Midland Country Club* on the Lamesa Highway started the **George W. Bush** award for the worst-dressed golfer. His favorite restaurant was Dona Anita's Mexican Restaurant, 305 W. Florida. A **Bush** Driving Tour

Map is available from the Chamber of Commerce, 109 N. Main.

NACOGDOCHES • When **Houston** first came to Texas on December 2, 1832, it was by Jonesboro Crossing on the Red River, marked 17 miles northwest of Clarksville on FM 410, and then down Trammel's Trace, marked near Texarkana on U.S. 59, 13.5 miles east of Henderson on U.S. 79, and in Tatum on State 149, among other places. He stopped here and then continued on to Stephen F. Austin's capital at San Felipe via the King's Highway, roughly Route 21. He made his way back to Natchitoches, Louisiana, to make a report to United States authorities there and claim expenses, indicating some agreement with President Jackson. He then moved back here and was elected as a delegate to a convention at San Felipe to meet on April 1, 1833. Under Spanish law only Catholics could practice law, so he was baptized at the well still in the yard of the Adolphus Sterne House,* Pilar and Lanana, where he lived. Mrs. Stern became a sort-of godmother, and he sent her a diamond ring after the Battle of San Jacinto with the provision that she wear it only on March 2, both his birthday and the date of the Texas Declaration of Independence, and April 21, the date of the victory of San Jacinto. Indian Chief Bowles signed a treaty in the house promising that his braves would not join the Mexicans during the Texas Revolution. (**Houston** had met Bowles at a site on now private property marked 6.2 miles southwest of Henderson near U.S. 79. The marker states that the treaty was signed at that spot.)

He then set up law practice in 1833 and lived at the SE corner of Pilar and Pecan on the Public Square. A major Texas landmark, the Old Stone Fort,* was also on the square, but now is on the campus of Stephen F. Austin University, a mile north of the original site at the NW corner of Fredonia and Main (State 21). This structure saw pioneers and filibusters coming to Texas for a half-century before the Battle of Nacogdoches was fought around the fort in August 1832, said to be the opening gun of the Texas Revolution, occurring after Mexico barred further immigration.

Houston fell in love with 14-year-old Anna Raguet and wanted to marry her. She had given him Spanish lessons in her home, the finest in town, located on what is now the north side of State 21, Main Street, surrounded by Main, Pilar, Walker, and Mound. But there had been no divorce in Tennessee where he had left his first wife, and he could not divorce under Mexican law before the Revolution. His second (Indian) common-law wife later died, but the girl insisted on legalities and eventually lost interest. **Houston** continued to send her love messages for several years until she married **Houston's** messenger.

ODESSA • **George H.W. Bush** moved here the day after he graduated from Yale, with his wife and newly born **George W.**, and lived at 1519 E. Seventh in a small "cracker-box" house shared with a mother-daughter prostitute team in 1947 and 1948. It was described as "just a bunch of boards nailed together with no insulation," one bathroom that they were sometimes locked out of, and the only refrigerator on the block. They later moved to 1523 E. Seventh and then 916 E. 17th in 1948 before moving to California.

PEARSALL • **Johnson** lived at 120 S. Oak, Spur 581, the town's main street, and taught at the high school for a short time. His lodging was a self-service hotel where you selected your room and then put a dollar in the slot.

REFUGIO • Texas General **Houston** was at the old mission in January 1836 and made an impassioned speech trying to dissuade soldiers of an independent Texas army from invading Mexico. Mexican dictator Santa Anna's agents were stirring up trouble and independent factions of the army were off on wild goose chases after they stripped the Alamo of much-needed supplies, men, and guns. **Houston's** eloquence and persuasive powers were partially successful. Many of the volunteer soldiers refused to go on the ill-fated campaign. While here he learned that he and Governor Smith had been deposed by the Texas Congress and that Santa Anna was on the way with an invasion to drive Anglos completely out of Texas. **Houston** went to San Felipe to meet with Smith and then to the Indians to try to keep them out of the conflict. Before leaving here, citizens promised to elect him as their delegate to the Congress in Washington-on-the-Brazos on March 1 to organize a government out of chaos. The mission site is marked at the Catholic church on the NW side of U.S. 77 and the Mission River, south of town.

SAN ANTONIO • The Spanish Governor's Palace,* 105 Military Plaza, was where Moses Austin convinced the Mexican governor to allow him to bring Anglo colonists into Texas as a buffer to the Indians, and also to develop the area, which Mexico had not been able to do. He died before he could, but his son did so and became "The Father of Texas." In 1832 **Houston** came to the Palace and also to the Veramendi House, 130 Soledad, at the invitation of Veramendi's son-in-law, Jim Bowie. Veramendi was the vice-governor of the dual state of Coahuila and Texas. The house is now gone, but the doors are preserved inside the Alamo. The location is marked on the downtown River Walk. (Texas hero Ben Milam was killed in front of the home during the 1835 Battle of San Antonio that drove out the Mexican army commanded by Santa Anna's brother-in-law.) **Houston** explained that he was Jackson's envoy to the Comanches. Then they met with various chiefs, although the purpose of his visit was unknown.

Houston, Hayes (1849), **Grant** (four days in 1880), **B. Harrison** (1891), **McKinley, TR** (1892, 1898, 1905), **Taft, Wilson, Eisenhower** (1916, 1917), **Truman, Nixon, Reagan, George H.W. Bush**, and **Clinton** have stayed at the Menger Hotel, 104 Alamo Plaza, adjacent to the Alamo. **Clinton** praised the house specialty, mango ice cream. **Grant** rode as an escort on supply wagons in February 1846, between here and Austin.

Hayes was surprised to find California travelers cooking in the room where Crockett was thought to have fallen in the Alamo. All presidents since **McKinley**, in addition to the above, have been to the Alamo. **LBJ** was here many times as a boy, with **JFK** on the 1960 campaign, and in retirement. Here about 187 settlers and immigrants held off Santa Anna's forces of 4000 for 13 days, giving **Houston** time to reorganize the Texas army and citizen's time to flee. The fight here on March 6, 1836, decimated the Mexican army, which lost maybe 600–1600 men plus many wounded who died from lack of proper medical care. (All numbers mentioned in this paragraph vary greatly in various sources.) The delay gave Texian families time to flee the area as dictator Santa Anna had decreed that all Anglo families were to leave. This loss of troops and maybe Santa Anna's overconfidence allowed **Houston** to surprise him later at San Jacinto, win that battle, and capture the dictator. This led to an uneasy freedom until Texas joined the Union in 1845, leading to the Mexican War and acquisition of one-third of the present United States.

Just before the Civil War, **Houston** had spoken for the Union on the north side of Main Plaza. **TR** trained the Rough Riders at the International Exposition grounds, south of downtown in Roosevelt Park on Mission Road, and recruited in the Menger Hotel Bar.*

Eisenhower was at Fort Sam Houston from 1915 to 1917. There he met Mamie Doud, whose family had a winter home at 1216 McCullough. He generally walked the two miles to take Mamie on dates. Then **Eisenhower** lived at 906 Easley, near the entrance to the infantry post, in Building 617, and then Building 688, Apt. E, following his marriage. While here he coached football at Peacock School and St. Mary's University. In their first thirty-five years of marriage, they moved thirty-five times. They were back here at 177 Artillery Post Road and then Number 179, where he was napping when awoken with news of the Dec. 7, 1941, attack on Pearl Harbor. Within hours he was ordered to Washington, D.C.

Johnson married at St. Mark's Episcopal, 315 East Pecan on the NW corner with Jefferson. The cornerstone was laid in 1859 with founding member Robert E. Lee attending. **Johnson's** wedding reception was across the street at the St. Anthony Hotel, 300 E. Travis at Navarro, across from the Plaza Hotel, where he spent his honeymoon. **Taft** (1909, when visiting his brother's nearby ranch) and **Truman** (1939) also stayed at the St. Anthony. **Truman** was also at the Gunter, 205 E. Houston.

San Augustine • **Houston** had many friends in the town and stayed with several. The marker at his law office site on the SW corner of Columbia and Montgomery claims he did business there for thirty years. The Halfway House in Chireno where **Houston** stayed, a few miles west on Highway 21, still stands, as do several homes he visited in San Augustine, including the Blount House on the NE corner of Columbia and Ayish Streets. After being wounded in the Battle of San Jacinto, **Houston** went to New Orleans, and then returned to Philip Sublett's home to recover. He stayed many times at this home, located east of town on the north side of Highway 21, at a bend in the road seven-tenths of a mile west of the marker to Elisha Roberts, and four miles east of the courthouse. A two-story later house is on the site with a Texas historical medallion on the front. He was here in 1833, having arrived late, somewhat drunk, but talkative. Sublett thought this was his opportunity to ask why he had left his Tennessee wife. He thought wrongly; **Houston** stormed out and rode away.

San Felipe de Austin • The capital of Stephen F. Austin's Colony is a state park off what is now U.S. 90 and I-10, at the junction of State 36, six miles from Sealy and 48 miles west of Houston. **Houston** came here to the political hub of Texas to meet Austin, who was largely responsible for the Anglo colonization of Texas. Austin was gone, but **Houston** did meet adventurer Jim Bowie, had Christmas dinner with him, and was invited to his father-in-law's home in San Antonio. He returned here on the way back to discuss plans with Austin, and returned again in 1833 as a delegate for a convention. The site of conventions in 1832, 1833, and 1835 are marked, as is a replica of Austin's home and office.

The 1833 convention voted to separate Texas from the Mexican state of Coahuila to which it was joined and sent Austin to Mexico to argue the point. Actually he had been to Mexico several times to renew colonization agreements with new governments after various revolutions. Any public meeting was illegal under Mexican law, and the highly respected Austin wound up in jail. In November 1835 a council met here to elect Henry Smith governor and **Houston** commander in chief of the army, but voted to remain part of Mexico and fight for its rights under the 1824 constitution abolished by Santa Anna. Then within a few weeks three others were given command of independent armies. **Houston** and the government lost control, and Texas descended into chaos with a Mexican army of thousands invading. A March 1836 convention restored **Houston** to sole command and declared independence from Mexico. The Mexican dictator chased **Houston's** army through here on the way to destiny at San Jacinto, and the town was then burned, never to recover. Austin's cabin is one mile west of the park on Bollinger Creek. The convention hall is nearby. The old well is still present where **Houston's** men and Santa Anna got water. All sites are marked.

SAN MARCOS • **Johnson's** grandmother frequently said that Lyndon was going to wind up in prison. College seemed a better alternative, and he went to Southwest State Teachers College, now Texas State, then considered a third-class institution. He also worked as a trash collector, assistant janitor, and the assistant to the president. He could not come after high school, as his school was unaccredited; so he went out to California at age sixteen with several friends and began here at age nineteen. He was so hard-working and enthusiastic that his boss once told him, "Lyndon, I declare you hadn't been in my office a month before I could hardly tell who was president of the school—you or me." He roomed in the home of the president, now the alumni center at 400 N. LBJ Drive. Later he roomed at Mrs. Gates's on Edward Gary Street; Pirtle House, 609 N. Austin, in 1927; 222 Talbot in 1928 and 1929; and at Mrs. Miller's on N. Comanche in 1929. He once gave a toast in the White House, saying, "It is gratifying to see at this table tonight the most superbly educated men in the world, for in this room there are three Rhodes Scholars, four graduates of Harvard, three of Yale, and one from Southwest State Teachers College."

UVALDE • **LBJ** (1952 and 1958) and **Truman** (1948) visited former Vice President John Nance Garner at his home 333 N. Park. **FDR** visited him at the train station in 1942.

WACO • **Eisenhower**, **Truman**, **Carter**, and **Ford** all have spoken on the Baylor University campus at Waco Hall.* **George W. Bush**'s Prairie Chapel Ranch is nearby at Crawford. In August 2002, he hosted the Economic Forum at Baylor's Umphrey Law Center* overlooking the Brazos River, and was back with the president of Mexico and Canadian prime minister in March 2005. The world's largest active military post is nearby at Ft. Hood, where both Presidents **Bush** attended Easter services in the chapel in 2007.

WASHINGTON • The Texas Independence Hall* is where **Houston** and other delegates met in 33-degree weather in an unheated shed to pass the Texas Declaration of Independence on March 2, 1836. The Texas Revolution was probably inevitable by the mid–1830s as "Texians" felt more and more misused by the tyrannical Mexican dictator Santa Anna, who was becoming more oppressive and was violating the Mexican Constitution. Santa Anna then ordered all Anglos out of Texas and came expecting to burn out and execute those who did not flee. As soon as the Declaration was passed and **Houston** named commander in chief, he left to find the army. The other delegates hurriedly wrote the Constitution, and then fled for their lives as Santa Anna was reported on the way.

After Texas became a republic, Washington was the capital for a short time beginning in 1842. **Houston** lived here as president, and his first child was born here in 1843. This is now in a state park east of Brenham off U.S. 290 on Farm Road 1155. All sites are marked. Texas president Anson Jones's house has been moved here from nearby where he was living when he lowered the Texas flag and ceremoniously raised the United States flag after Texas' admission to the Union.

WEST COLUMBIA AREA • The Republic of Texas Congress first met in this small town, then called "Columbia," known as the first capital of the Republic although it was never officially the capital. Provisional President David Burnet selected it for the meeting place since it was just one of two towns where there were enough buildings to support any meeting and had a printing press. (The press was from Gail Borden's newspaper. He later invented condensed milk and formed the Borden Company.) **Houston** consented to run for president eleven days before the first Texas presidential election and won. On October 22, 1836, he was sworn in at the House of Representatives building, marked on the NE corner of 17th and Brazos, Route 35. At the end of his inaugural address, he dramatically gave his San Jacinto sword to the speaker of the house, saying he would reclaim it if danger loomed in the future.

The senate building was across the street. **Houston** stayed at Josiah Bell's Hotel, mentioned below, then about a block east of Route 36 at County Road 247, a half-mile south of the above. The Texas Congress set ambitious boundaries to the Rio Grande, including Santa Fe and Albuquerque in present-day New Mexico, causing such animosity with Mexico that war was inevitable when Texas was admitted to the Union. Congress also selected the newly created Houston City as the capital and adjourned to there.

The army had wanted to execute captured Mexican dictator Santa Anna for the massacre at Goliad, among other reasons, but the government and **Houston** wanted him spared. **Houston** visited him in captivity at the Varner-Hogg Plantation,* one and a half miles north of town on Route 2582, and also at Orozimba, the plantation of Dr. James Phelps. The site is further up the same road to CR 255 on the Brazos River, now inaccessible on private property. It is marked on local maps, but the home is gone. Santa Anna was there when he tried to take his own life three times, pleaded for **Houston** to visit him, and wept on **Houston's** shoulder for release in return for his influence for recognition. One of **Houston's** first acts was to push for the dictator's release to go to Washington, D.C., to convince officials to recognize the Republic. That recognition finally came on November 25, 1836. Santa Anna was transferred to the United States, met President Jackson, and then regained power in Mexico several times, being overthrown each time. During one of his reigns, Texans invaded Mexico because of a Mexican raid on San Antonio, and the son of his West Columbia host Dr. Phelps and others were captured. The dictator executed or cruelly treated the prisoners but pardoned the boy, gave him money, and saw that he reached safety.

The facilities in town were terrible, and Secretary of State Stephen F. Austin, who labored long hours in fireless rooms in the Capitol, caught pneumonia and died December 27, 1836, at his lodging marked north of town, a few blocks east of Route 36 on CR 467. **Houston** visited there, declared, "The father of Texas is no more," and escorted the body for burial at Gulf Prairie Church,* marked just west of Route 36 on Gulf Prairie Road, about eight miles south of Brazoria. (The body was moved in 1910 to the State Cemetery in Austin.) Earlier **Houston** and Congress had honored the "Father of Texas" in Jane Long's Inn in "Old" Brazoria at Main and China Streets. She is called the "Mother of Texas." The inn was at the ferry landing used by **Houston** a few blocks north of the current Route 322 bridge over the Brazos River and about a mile northeast of the modern Brazoria business district. Only a few scattered houses are at the historical site. There are no historical markers, and only a few street signs to guide you to the location. It can be reached by Market or Marion Streets.

About two miles east of West Columbia is East Columbia, where the sites of the ferry landing and Bell's Hotel used by **Houston** are at Front and Austin. Many congressmen thought the fifty cents per night was so outrageous that they slept under trees. **Houston** escorted Austin's body here to go downriver for burial.

Houston spoke and stayed at places still in existence and open, including these not listed above:

Bastrop: Nicholson Stage Stop
Crockett: Rice Stage Coach Inn, five miles east on Route 121
Hempstead: Liendo Plantation
Henderson: Flanagan House
La Grange: Dedicated in January 1849 the cemetery at Monument Hill where Meir Expedition and Dawson Massacre victims are buried. (Now a state park south of town off U.S. 77 at Spur 92.)
Marshall: Two speeches (1849 and 1857) under the Houston Campaign Oak at the NE corner of Franklin and Burleson.

Montgomery: Arnold House
Navasota: Freeman Inn
Salado: Stagecoach Inn, still a restaurant and hotel on I-35, 1861 anti-secession speech
Seguin: Hollaman House
Sugar Land: Nibbs Home
Victoria: Ball and reception at the Phillips House, 705 N. Craig, on August 1, 1857.
Wheelock: Volney Cavitt House

UTAH

SALT LAKE CITY • Virtually every president since **TR** (plus **Grant, Benjamin Harrison**, and **Hayes**) has been to the Mormon Tabernacle on Temple Square. This includes **Wilson** in 1919, **Harding** in 1923, **Truman** in 1948, **Kennedy** in 1963, **Johnson** in 1964, **Nixon** in 1970, and **Carter** in 1978. During the early visits, city hall at First South near State served as the Territorial Capitol. **Grant** (1879) and **Hayes** (1880) stayed at the Walker Hotel at 246 S. Main before it was destroyed. **Grant** visited the Capitol then in the old courthouse, and **TR** visited the Capitol, then in the County Building at Fourth and S. State. **Harrison** made a speech at Liberty Park.

Kennedy and **Truman** stayed at the Hotel Utah at 15 E. S. Temple near Main. **Kennedy** was campaigning as early as January 1960 and attended a luncheon at the Newhouse Hotel and a ball in the Terrace Room. This was at the SW of Main and 400 South. **Reagan** was at the Little American Hotel at 500 S. Main in 1984 and attended the Salt Palace Convention Center in 1982 and 1984. It was at the same location as the present center where **George W. Bush** spoke on August 31, 2006. **Taft** visited the Unitarian church at 569 S. 1300 in 1909. The first President **Bush** stayed at the Marriott at 220 S. State. **Ford** spoke at the University of Utah in 1974.

VERMONT

BENNINGTON • The Walloomsac Inn, marked in Old Bennington, hosted **Jefferson** and **Madison** in 1791. (**Hayes** held a reception in the Inn during 1877.) They had to delay their journey here for a day because of a law prohibiting travel on Sunday. While lingering they wandered through the still quaint town and attended services in the Old Congregational Church* across the street on Highway 7, one of the most beautiful old churches in New England. When asked if they liked the music, they responded that they had no basis of comparison, as they had not been to church in years. This is on Monument Street leading to the Bennington Battle Monument, once the tallest in the world; the street is lined with many historical sites and colonial homes. This has been visited by **Hayes** (1877), **Benjamin Harrison** (1891), and **Coolidge** (1891). Included is the site of the meeting place of Ethan Allen's Green Mountain Boys. **Jefferson** and **Madison** also visited Bennington Battlefield* nearby in New York State.

BRATTLEBORO • In 1877 and 1889 **Hayes** visited the tavern (Bigelow House) that was owned by his ancestors and stayed at the Brooks Hotel on Main.

BURLINGTON • **Monroe** visited the academy in 1817. His Vermont tour included the State House,* Middlebury College, Woodstock, and Durham. **McKinley, TR**, and **Taft** have visited the Moore–Woodbury Home at 416 Pearl. **Coolidge** married at his in-laws' home at 312 Maple.

FAIRFIELD • **Arthur** was born here in 1830, probably about five miles east and northwest of the State 36/108 junction. The cabin eventually decayed and disappeared. A replica* is now probably on the correct site. There is a controversy as to the date—he evidently signed a family Bible with a more recent date to appear younger—and the exact site of his birth. Some believed during his lifetime that he was born in nearby Quebec, Canada, but a recent biographer does not believe there is any doubt and accepts the above replica site. His father was a roving Baptist minister and soon moved the family to North Fairfield, where the Reverend Arthur became pastor of the Old Brick Church, just north of the Chester Arthur Historic Site birthplace. They then lived in Williston (1832–4, Mountain View Road) and Hinesburg (1834–5) on Main Street, Route 116 two doors from the library, before moving to western New York.

GRAFTON • **Grant, Theodore Roosevelt,** and **Wilson** were among many celebrities honored at the 1801 Old Tavern* still operating at 92 Main.

MANCHESTER • **Grant, Taft,** and **TR** have stayed in the Equinox Hotel* on Main, where Mary Lincoln and her sons also stayed in 1863 and 1864 to escape the summer heat in Washington. It is claimed that **Lincoln** was scheduled to come here later in 1865. Robert Lincoln's beautiful mansion,* where he destroyed **Lincoln** papers shortly before his death, is nearby.

MONTPELIER • The State House has been visited by **B. Harrison** (1891), **TR, Taft** (1912), and claims most others since **Coolidge**.

NORTH POWNAL • **Arthur** was a principal of a school here in 1851, and his running mate **Garfield** taught at the same academy three years later.

PLYMOUTH NOTCH • **Coolidge** was born on July 4, 1872, in a small house attached to the general store, the only president born on this important date. A passage connected the residence and his father's store. The family moved in 1876 across and up the road to a home, now known as the **Coolidge** Homestead,* from where his father sent him at 13 a few miles south to Black River Academy in Ludlow, still in the center of that town.

He was home visiting when he was awakened by his father at 2:27 A.M. on August 3, 1923, with the news that President Harding had died. **Coolidge's** first thought was, "I believe I can swing it." The new president and his wife immediately dressed, prayed, and then assembled in the sitting room with a kerosene lamp he described as "the most modern form of lighting that had reached the neighborhood." **Coolidge** considered whether any additional oath was necessary other than the vice-presidential oath. It was decided that the father should administer the presidential oath, the only time a presidential father has done so. His authority as a notary public was questioned. The home was modernized over the years, and has been restored using old photographs. The upstairs of the store was used as a summer White House in 1924. The bed and other original furnishing are still inside as they appeared in 1923.

Coolidge returned home several times during his presidency, and stayed several weeks after burying his 16-year-old son, who died as **Coolidge** ran for president in 1924. The church* where several generations of family worshipped is also open. He also liked to travel back after he left office. A friend once remarked that he must be proud to see so many people driving by to see his home. "It's not so good as yesterday," he replied. "There were 60 of them then." The **Coolidges** are buried about a mile away at a clearly marked cemetery,* also on Vt. 100A. The entire small, serene mountain town is restored as an outdoor museum. **Coolidge's** school site is north of the home and marked by a rebuilt one-room schoolhouse.*

Virginia

Appomattox Court House • Union General **Grant** accepted the surrender of Confederate Robert E. Lee here on April 9, 1865. Lee's forces had fled from Petersburg trying to escape **Grant's** vise in the dim hope that they could join with General Joseph Johnston, commander of one of the other armies still in the field. The hope failed, leaving the starving, shoeless Confederates no choice. **Davis** was on the run with what was left of the Confederate government, still vowing to fight until the last Southern male could no longer stand. **Grant** could have proposed harsh terms to Lee, who now led starving scarecrows, but they could have taken to the hills and fought guerrilla style for years. The generous terms, with no chains, prison camps, or trials, no doubt largely agreed upon in recent conferences with **Lincoln**, helped the beginnings of reunification.

Several of the buildings in the outdoor museum town are original and open by the National Park Service. The McLean House, where the surrender occurred, was torn down in 1893 to be exhibited in Washington. The materials were left and mostly lost to souvenir hunters, and later used to rebuild **Grant's** headquarters and campsites. The park tour notes these, where **Grant** sent the note to Lee suggesting the surrender meeting, and the site of another **Grant**-Lee meeting on April 10, where they sat on horseback for about thirty minutes to discuss paroles and chances of further resistance. **Grant** suggested that Lee visit **Lincoln**, but he refused. He did not feel it was his duty as a soldier to meet with the civilian government. Lee's aide Colonel Marshall felt that this was a lost opportunity to restore peace and brotherhood. (The proposed meeting might also have changed Booth's mind about the assassination.) On April 12, 28,000 Confederates were paroled before 80,000 silent Federals.

Arlington, Alexandria, Fairfax County • Seventeen-year-old **Washington** surveyed and laid out the streets of Alexandria in 1749 as an apprentice. Several streets retain the original cobblestones. His home, Mount Vernon,* is south on the Washington and Mount Vernon Memorial Parkways. He lived here from age three until about seven, and then from 16 for almost a half century, although he was here barely half the time. The property had been in the family since 1674. **George**'s father deeded the land to his son Lawrence, who renamed the plantation in honor of his Navy commander, Admiral Edward Vernon. **George** then spent much time with his half-brother during his later childhood, leased, and then bought the property from the widow after Lawrence's death in 1752.

A close neighbor, William Fairfax, was Lawrence's father-in-law and lived at Belvoir at the mouth of Hunting Creek on the Potomac, a center of **Washington's** life. He wrote that the happiest moments of his life were here, and "I can not trace a room in the house that did not bring to mind the recollection of pleasing scenes." Maps of Fort Belvoir generally direct you to the outline of the mansion, burned in 1785, and the family graveyard, down a well-marked trail on the river from Fairfax and Forney Streets. (Fairfax is southeast of the Belvoir/23rd Street intersection. Enter the installation at Tulley Gate on Route One. A driver's license and car registration are necessary to tour the post.) This was also the center of the powerful Fairfax family in America that owned much of Virginia. Thomas, Lord Fairfax, had inherited five million acres in Virginia and to the west. He moved from England in 1747 to live for several years with his cousin William, also his agent, and one of the most important men in the Colonies. While here the English nobleman began a life-long friendship with **Washington**. The families shared much time together as Belvoir was only about two miles by water, although seven or eight by land.

One of the first indications of young **George**'s unusual qualities was the way he was taken in by the prominent family. He found his father's surveying instruments, taught himself how to use them, and was selected by Fairfax to go with him to survey his western wilderness lands. This led to a toughening and familiarity with the frontier, then to subsequent military assignments and adventures, helping to shape his life and career. William's son George was his close friend and only assistant. (See Winchester.) George Fairfax, aged 23, married 18-year-old Sally Cary in 1748, when **Washington** was 16. From that time until they moved to England in 1773 to handle family business, it is thought that **Washington** was in love with her, or at least had a life-long infatuation. In any event this did not seem to interfere with his friendship with Fairfax or his own later marriage to Martha as he wrote letters to Sally expressing his feelings, that Martha read. One letter, saved by Sally for the rest of her life, written when he was 66, recalled that the happiest moments in his life were in her company. It is not known what Martha, who read the letter, thought about such statements. He eagerly visited her as much as possible, but never saw her after the move. **Washington** acted as power of attorney for the Fairfaxes, who remained in England although sympathizing with America in the Revolution. He toured Belvoir after it burned and had to inform his friends of the loss of their home.

In 1759, he brought home his five-foot bride, Martha, maybe the richest widow in the Colonies, and her two children, six and four. Some have suggested that the marriage was at Mt. Vernon, but apparently it was at Martha's home, known as the "White House." He left to fight several wars— in fact he was not here between 1775 and 1781— and to assume various civilian duties, returning 15 times while president. He rode out at age 43 in 1775 to go to the Philadelphia Continental Congress and did not return to live until he was 51, the most famous man in the world. The plantation was his greatest joy, and he treasured the spectacular view of the river, still preserved into the 21st century. In 1785 he summoned **Madison** and other representatives to discuss commerce among the states, resulting in the Mt. Vernon Convention, one of several meetings leading to the Constitutional Convention in Philadelphia. Of course famous people visited during **Washington's** lifetime and ever since. **Madison**, a close confidant for several years, visited often before and after the Convention to confer with the nation's first citizen about how to engineer the Constitution's passage among hesitant states. He preformed a great service by convincing **Washington** on his visits to attend the convention where the Constitution was drafted and then to be president. He is said to have "always stopped at Mount Vernon" on his frequent trips in the area. Later he was back to help draft **Washington's** first inaugural address. Another visit resulted in collaboration with Hamilton on the *Federalist Papers*, without which the Constitution may not have been approved. **Jefferson** was there in September 1790 with **Madison** to discuss the site of the national capital and stopped at Gunston Hall for the same purpose. They stopped again in October 1791 to leave **Jefferson's** daughter with Martha, who would bring her to the capital. **Jefferson** breakfasted with the first president here on October 1, 1792, on the way to Philadelphia to urge him to accept his resignation as secretary of state and also for **Washington** to run again for reelection. **Madison** was a chief advisor who came for several days at a time until he had a falling out during **Washington's** last year or so in office over Jay's Treaty. **Monroe** also visited. **John Adams**, **Jefferson**, and **Madison** visited widowed Martha in 1800 as the government moved to the new capital.

With his wife's fortune, **Washington** was perhaps the richest man in the young republic, at least on paper, owning 60,000 acres, 8,000 of which were at Mt. Vernon, barely supporting about 240 people. But his enormous land holdings produced relatively little income, and he had few liquid assets. The land was poor and grew exhausted, and the inefficiency of the slave system and the large number of dependent slaves drained his resources. He described the estate as a tavern with its constant stream of visitors, both the distinguished and anyone else who showed up, who had to be fed and accommodated. In 1785 he counted 423 overnight guests, and stated once that he had not had dinner alone with his wife for over 20 years. He always dressed formally and required everyone else to do so. He kept his cantankerous mother from visiting by telling her that since the home was so much like a tavern, she would have to dress up all the time. His teenage step-granddaughter once refused, as did her guest, Martha's niece. **Washington** said nothing. But when rich Charles Carroll Jr. arrived with some French officers, and the girls asked to be excused to change, Martha sternly refused, telling them, "What is good enough for General **Washington** is good enough for any guest of his."

In December 1799, he caught a cold in bad weather on his daily ride, and was weakened by the practice of bleeding, supposedly to relieve the pressure caused by too much blood. No one knows what he died of, but it was probably diphtheria or a virulent streptococcus infection of the throat, either one fatal regardless of treatment then. Martha burned their personal letters after his death, depriving us of much knowledge, history, and many personal feelings between the two,

Washington's Mount Vernon had been visited by all presidents by the turn of the 21st century. Madison and Jefferson spent time here on their way to and from their homes.

as also happened with the **Jeffersons** and **Lincolns**. The room and bed where he died can still be seen.

The Prince of Wales (later Edward VII) and **Buchanan** laid a wreath on the tomb in 1860. Thirteen trees planted by **Washington** still stand on the property. He was the only one of the eleven slave-owning presidents to free all his slaves at his death. (Of the first 18 presidents, through **Grant**, all owned slaves at one time or the other, except the **Adamses, Van Buren, Fillmore, Pierce, Lincoln,** and **Buchanan**, although his "servants" are sometimes referred to as slaves. **Grant** briefly had a slave from his father-in-law, although his wife owned them.) His present tomb is not far from the house, as is the first tomb used until 1831. The Mount Vernon Association believes that every past president has visited during his term, as of the bicentennial of **Washington's** death in 1799. On February 19, 2007, **George W. Bush** here compared **Washington's** struggle to give birth to the nation with the war on global terrorism. Many presidents enjoyed sailing or steaming down the river and visiting here, especially **Jackson**, who enjoyed doing this with his family during this term. **Lincoln** visited Mt. Vernon in February 1848, and Mary came on March 27, 1861. On April 2, 1862, the president and his wife brought Mary's sister and Springfield friends. There is some question whether **Lincoln** came ashore then, although biographer Benjamin Thomas suggests that he did.

Washington's Grist Mill* is nearby, south on Route 235, Mount Vernon Memorial Highway, leading to U.S. 1. This follows the road used by **Washington** on many trips south down U.S. 1, U.S. 301, through Hanover, and U.S. 60 to victory at Yorktown in 1781.

Washington's stepson Jacky lived at Mt. Vernon until he married and moved to his own home at Abingdon, where **Washington** visited. He had three daughters and a son, George Washington Parke Custis, known as "Little Wash," born in 1780. When **Washington** passed by after being gone six years, on the way to Yorktown in mid–September 1781, Jacky, spoiled, indolent, self-indulgent, and rich, who had sat out the war, saw a chance for some excitement and the opportunity to mingle with aristocratic French officers. He joined as a voluntary aide and came down with some camp disease. Unaccustomed to camp life, food, unsanitary conditions, and water, he died November 5, near Yorktown at Eltham. Little Wash and an older sister then grew up at Mount Vernon and treated as **Washington's** children although never officially adopted. (This was of some advantage for Jacky's wife as she kept the oldest two daughters, remarried, and had 16 more children.) The ruins of Abingdon,* burned in 1930, are located by signs and marked at the Reagan Airport, between the terminal and the path to the rent-a-car offices, just west of the Metro tracks. (After the Confederate officer who owned Abingdon during the Civil War lost title, **Garfield** was successful in fighting to reestablish his ownership.) Little Wash grew up to build Arlington House in what is now Arlington National Cemetery.

Part of the Mount Vernon plantation is now maintained north of Mount Vernon at River Farm,* 7931 E. Boulevard Drive, off Washington Memorial Parkway, with its 1757 house purchased by **Washington** in 1760 and many walnut trees that he planted.

South of Mt. Vernon is George Mason's Gunston Hall,* four miles east of U.S. 1 on Route 242, north of Woodbridge. Mason was a colonial and Revolutionary War leader who influenced **Washington**, **Jefferson**, and others. He preferred to live here with his wife and nine children, but was called on repeatedly to serve Virginia. Among other accomplishments, he was the author of the Virginia Declaration of Rights and the first Bill of Rights and Constitution of Virginia, used as a basis for their federal counterparts. His great friend **Washington** frequently visited. **Jefferson** and **Madison** came here in 1784 to confer with Mason in September 1790. **Jefferson** was his last official visitor about a week before Mason died in October 1792. A guest room is pointed out as his. Mason would have had more impact on the early country if he had not had to stay home with his nine children since his wife died. If **Washington** visited and did not stay at Gunston Hall, he stayed with other friends at Rippon Lodge, still on Potomac and Neabsco Creek, also near Woodbridge, marked east of I-95 down Rippon Road and near Rippon Park.

The old colonial town of Alexandria, still with many early structures, predates the national capital. The Alexandria Academy (marked) was founded by **Washington**, who sent his stepson and two nephews there. It still sits back of the SE corner Washington and Wolfe Streets. **Madison** sent his ten-year-old stepson there, probably eagerly, since the boy had reportedly continued to insist, with Dolley's acquiescence, that he sleep with his mother after **Madison's** marriage. (Some experts question this oft-repeated claim.) **Washington** attended Christ Church,* at 118 North Washington just north of King Street, where you can sit in his pews. He was actually a member of the Pohick Church, but found it convenient to purchase a pew, number 60, in town. Other presidents attended Christ Church, including **Coolidge**, **Hoover**, **Eisenhower**, **FDR** with Churchill, and **Wilson** with David Lloyd George.

Washington came to Old Presbyterian Meeting House,* on Fairfax just north of Wolfe Street, in 1798 when war with France seemed imminent. His funeral service was held here, as the town could not easily get to Christ Church in a snowstorm.

The Carlyle House* is on the east side of Fairfax between King and Cameron, next to **Washington's** bank* on the SE corner of Cameron. Part of the bank building was also probably used as Arwell's Tavern, mentioned in **Washington's** diaries from 1768 to 1774. The Carlyle was the 1755 meeting place between English General Braddock and five royal governors. Young **Washington** was presented to the governors and offered a commission to aid Braddock, who stayed here to plan funding and strategy for the French and Indian War before his fatal march to Pittsburgh. While here Braddock sent a letter suggesting that a tax be imposed on the Colonies to help support the war, and thus this is sometimes called the Birthplace of the Revolution. **Jefferson** later stayed. The structure is advertised as original. By 1970 it was falling down and was dismantled. Two rooms and the flooring are mostly reconstructed with original materials, but the exterior is new. **Davis** was honored in an apartment building in front on the street in 1870 and 1871, but that was sacrificed in the reconstruction to allow it to have its original front yard.

Washington was entertained on the opposite (NW) corner from the Carlyle at the home of Charles Lee and was first addressed as "Mr. President" at the Wise Tavern on the NE corner of Cameron at 201 Fairfax. He celebrated his last July

Christ Church, Alexandria, was attended regularly by Washington. Coolidge, Hoover, Eisenhower with Churchill, and Wilson with David Lloyd George attended also.

4 here in 1799, when it was known as Kemp's. (**Jefferson** stayed at Wise's Fountain Tavern on Royal Street where he was honored upon his return from France.) **Washington** had been there often, as well as the Ramsey House,* moved to Fairfax and King in 1751. Ramsey was a friend of **Washington**, who ate and made many purchases at his store here. The house burned, sat for years in ruin, but was never condemned, and has been restored to become the town visitor center. All of these are marked.

Washington stayed at least two nights at 607 Oronoco,* the home of Robert E. Lee's grandfather-in-law, when William Henry Fitzhugh, the son of William Fitzhugh of Chatham, had the home, now known as Lee's boyhood home. Fitzhugh's daughter, Mary, married **Washington's** step-grandson here on July 7, 1804.

Washington's diary showed that he dined with Ludwell Lee on Shooters Hill, a site just SE of the George Washington Masonic National Memorial, on King west of the Old Town. **Jefferson** is said to have suggested the site of the memorial, the present one dedicated much later by **Harding. Monroe** met on site with defenders of the capital in 1814 to plan countermeasures for attacking the British fleet as it descended the Potomac River.

Washington spent many nights in his town house where a replica is marked at 508 Cameron, a block east of the "Light Horse Harry Lee" House. It is the second from the corner on the north side of Cameron, marked just east of Washington, where Robert E. moved at age four. **Madison** and **Monroe** visited him there. Young Lee got his name in print for the first time when it was reported that **Madison** told him to let his father's honor and gallantry set an example.

Gadsby's Tavern* at 134 North Royal Street, still open as a restaurant, is one of the most famous inns of **Washington's** era. He was a regular and loved the mallard duck. He used it as headquarters in 1754 and was hosted many times, including several birthday balls and at his last public appearance. He was born when the Julian calendar then in use read February 11. Even though the Gregorian calendar, still in use today, had been adopted, his birthday was still generally celebrated there during his lifetime on February 11, as it was in big celebrations during his retirement for 1798 and 1799. **John** and **John Q. Adams**, **Jefferson**, **Madison**, and **Truman** were also entertained. (*Historic Alexandria* says **Monroe** also, but this is not in other sources.)

The city hall to the south on Royal and Cameron was the site of many **Washington** meetings on official business and with his Masonic Lodge. This was the center of town, where he was when his diary frequently noted trips "to court." He and George Mason met here to draw up the celebrated Fairfax County Resolution protesting British tyranny. The city hall was also **Washington's** headquarters for the militia. He drilled in front and stopped on the way to his inauguration. From here he issued his last military order on November 1799.

The first president used the Stabler-Leadbeater Apothecary Shop* at 107 South Fairfax, as did **Monroe**. **Washington** enjoyed chatting with the owner and got his mail there. **Jefferson** was here and at Gadsby's on January 3, 1801, on the way to visit Martha at Mount Vernon.

Woodlawn,* completed after **Washington's** death, was built on land presented as a 1799 wedding present by **Washington** to his granddaughter. This is on U.S. 1 and Mt. Vernon Parkway, just south of Mount Vernon. Just south on U.S. 1, six miles from Mt. Vernon, is the still active Pohick Church* on a site selected by vestrymen **Washington**, George Mason, and George William Fairfax. **Washington** kept two pews here in his home church. An earlier unknown site nearby southwest of the church was attended before the erection of this one in 1769. The walls are original, but the interior was destroyed by successive occupations of Confederates and Federals in the Civil War. **Truman** attended in 1947.

The three **George**s were also vestrymen of the Falls Church at 115 E. Fairfax at Washington Street in the city of Falls Church,* built about the same time. Falls Church was a recruiting station during the Revolution, and **Washington** was on the building committee. He also occupied a pew, now preserved, in St. John's Church, across the river from Mt. Vernon in Piscataway, Maryland, on Broad Creek.

Between Alexandria and Mt. Vernon is Walnut Tree Farm,* the home of Tobias Lear, **Washington's** private secretary. Once part of Mt. Vernon, it is on Wellington Road east of the George Washington Memorial Parkway. Another original home visited by **Washington** in the area was Towlston Grange on Towlston Road, NE of Leesburg Pike, Route 7, west of the Dulles Airport Access, the home of his friend Bryan Fairfax, the Eighth Lord Fairfax. **Washington's** personal attorney and attorney general was Charles Lee, who lived at 407 N. Washington. **Adams** visited Lee, also his attorney general, here in 1800 and wrote that he was pleased with the town.

Washington was well traveled, as shown in a 1932 ***George Washington*** *Atlas* outlining over 1000 sites associated with him. Other homes and buildings still existing here known to have been visited by **Washington** include:

Duvall's Tavern, 305 Cameron Street, December 31, 1783

George William Fairfax's townhouse at 207 Prince Street (His sister married **Washington's** brother, Lawrence, and was first mistress of Mt. Vernon.)

Lee-Fendall House at the SE corner of Washington and Oronoco Streets, where his funeral was planned

NW corner Duke and St. Asaph, and frequently at Dr. James Craik's, 210 Duke

Tobias Lear home, 501 Duke, dined September 1795

Benjamin Dulany home, 601 Duke, 1785

405 Prince

Spring Gardens Tavern, 414 Franklin, July 4, 1798

125 S. Pitt, owned by **Washington** from 1765 until his death

Lomax Tavern (destroyed), south side of Princess between Lee and Fairfax Streets, dined and presided over the Potomac Company meetings

George Coryell, guide at Coryell's Ferry, Pa., 206 Duke (present home is c. 1850)

On trips back and forth from Monticello, **Jefferson** stayed with William Henry Fitzhugh at Wren's Station and Ravensworth, 312 Broad (Leesburg Pike) in Falls Church. It is now a shopping mall on Braddock Road. He also was entertained at Ossian Hall on the north side of Braddock Road, two miles west of Annandale. **Madison** visited friends at Sully,* another Lee family home, 3610 Sully Road, in Chantilly. **Washington** might have visited his friends the Lees, who, especially "Light Horse Harry," visited him at Mt. Vernon. They lived at Leesylvania on Va. 610, east of U.S. 1, between Woodbridge and

Dumfries in what is now Leesylvania State Park, where the home site and graves can be seen near the Potomac and Neabsco Bay.

When **Madison** fled as the British burned the capital in August 1814, he stayed a night in Salona, south of Dolley Madison Blvd., Highway 123, at 1214 Buchanan Street in McLean and NE of the Chain Bridge Road and Old Dominion intersection. He then came to Wiley's Tavern near Great Falls where Dolley had fled, and the two were reunited. Dolley stayed there while the president went to the Bentley House in Brookeville, Maryland.

The first assault on a president occurred at the dock in Alexandria when a man who had been dismissed on **Jackson's** orders came on board his ship and slugged or slapped him, drawing blood. Fortunately for the assailant, **Jackson** had trouble rising and the man was grabbed and thrown off the boat before the ferocious president could further react.

One of the nation's tragic events happened in the river at Mt. Vernon in 1844 when a huge cannon blew up during a demonstration aboard the *Princeton,* carrying President **Tyler** and his cabinet. Several including the secretaries of state and war were killed, as was the father of **Tyler's** fiancée. **Tyler** carried her ashore unhurt at the Navy Yard, and they soon married.

Lincoln often came past Alexandria on the Potomac River relaxing or to review troops. He boarded a steamer in Alexandria on October 19, 1861, on the way to Fort Washington* across the river in Maryland, and met with General McClellan in Alexandria on March 21 and April 1, 1862. **Washington** visited a friend who lived on the fort site and selected it for the fort in 1795, clearly visible from the Virginia side. **Monroe** and other presidents visited.

Lincoln visited Great Falls* on the Potomac on May 19, 1861, where various presidents came, including **Washington**. While president, **Jefferson** crossed the Potomac where the Chain Bridge is now, and came up the Virginia bank to Great Falls. **Lincoln** made several reviews of the army near Centerville including on October 22, 1862. On November 20, 1862, he visited Fort Albany, a site now under I-395, about a mile from the Long Bridge, near the present Potomac bridges. The site can be seen from an overlook at Nash and Arlington Ridge Road.

A marker notes that **Lincoln** and his entire cabinet attended a grand review on November 20, 1861, at Bailey's Crossroads on Route 7, 2.48 miles west of I-395. The 50,000 troops involved were "the largest and most magnificent military review ever held on this continent," at least up until then. This is just west of Fort Munson, Munson Drive and Apex Circle, five miles due west of Reagan Airport. **Davis** met with his Generals Johnston and Beauregard in the Fairfax Court House. **Lincoln** met General McDowell in June 1862 at Liberia or Weir Place, 8740 Mathis, in Manassas, now owned by the city. This is set back from the road on the west side, almost due west from the IHOP Restaurant on Rte. 28 on the eastern edge of town.

Truman visited his friend Supreme Court Justice Hugo Black at 619 Lee in Alexandria after Black joined the majority in ruling against **Truman's** government seizure of the steel mills in 1951. **Truman** told him he did not like his law, but his bourbon was good.

Eisenhower was ordered to the capital when World War II started and lived with his brother Milton at 708 E. Broad in Falls Church. He had stayed here before in Washington. While in office, the **Kennedys** rented at Glen Ora and later Wexford or Atoka, in Middleburg. **Reagan** stayed at the latter in 1980.

The **Fords** lived at 3426 and then 3538 Gunston Road before moving to 1521 Mount Eagle Place, all in the Parkfairfax section of northwest Alexandria, in June 1951, and then to 514 Crown View Drive where the children grew up. **Nixon** telephoned in 1973 to ask him to be his vice president. **Ford** requested that the president call back on his other line that had an extension, so Mrs. Ford could listen. She then fretted over what the constant presence of reporters would do to property values. The property was sold when he became president, and they never went back.

Charles City Area • Some of the country's oldest and most historical mansions are along Route 5 and clearly marked with many Revolutionary and Civil War markers. Their owners, including fathers of **William Henry Harrison** and **Tyler**, were some of the most influential men in the colony and friends and hosts of leaders including **Washington** and **Jefferson**. Route 5 traces the old colonial highway and main route from the 1600s until modern times. Actually the James River was the watery main street of the colony, and the mansions opened to it.

Berkeley Plantation* is 22 miles east of Richmond. **W. Harrison** was born here in 1773, the last president born an Englishman, and was later presented as the "Log Cabin Candidate" with log cabin ribbons, songs, buttons, and shaving soap. But this was then and still is one of the grandest plantations in Tidewater Virginia. As an eight-year-old he saw the traitor Benedict Arnold arrive with his Redcoats to devastate the plantation and burn all family portraits on the lawn. These were acquired at great cost by having painters sent over from England, and their destruction deprived the future of likenesses of the great family. All of the first 16 presidents are claimed to have visited, although this cannot be documented. **Washington** and **Jefferson** were clearly here. **William**'s father signed the Declaration of Independence and was a three-time governor. The future president was tutored in the house with his siblings until about age 14, and returned as president-elect in February 1841 to escape Washington City and wander through his birth room, examine old family books he had read as a youth, and write his lengthy inaugural address. **Tyler** visited at the time. Grandson **Benjamin Harrison** visited in 1889. **William** had 48 grandchildren, one more than **Benjamin**, and 106 great-grandchildren. This is more remarkable considering he outlived six of his children, and three more died shortly after he did.

Lincoln visited General McClellan here on July 8, 1862, as Union troops camped for miles along the James River. On the way, his steamer ran aground in the mud, giving him time to swim in the river as it was freed. After arriving late he reviewed of thousands of waiting troops in the moonlight. The next day **Lincoln** again inspected troops nearby and at another nearby colonial mansion, Westover,* the main area river landing since it is on the river and not set back like Berkeley. A former drummer boy of McClellan bought the 1,400-acre plantation for lumber in 1907. The historic house, being used as a barn, was included at no cost.

The first floor was used as a Civil War hospital. Guides and some books for sale on site claimed that **Lincoln** came inside to confer with "Little Mac" and visit the wounded. This would have followed **Lincoln's** pattern, and if so this would make this the only other private house (in addition to Chatham at Fredericksburg) visited by both him and **Washington.** But **Lincoln** is documented only as conferring with McClellan on his river steamer, and the general's headquarters were in the woods nearby, not the second floor as claimed on site.

Westover* is also one of the great river plantations claiming to have been visited by most if not all of the first 16 presidents, again a claim questioned. Westover Church,* visited by **Washington, Jefferson, W. Harrison**, and **Tyler**, among others, is nearby, easily accessible on Route 5. It was originally built on the river near Westover, but was moved brick by brick. Both the **Tyler** and **Harrison** families went to the church, where probably both future presidents were baptized. The early presidents mentioned are thought to have visited Belle Air on Rte. 5, the oldest James River plantation, and would have been familiar with the 1732 Charles City Courthouse* on Route 5 and the New Kent Courthouse* on Route 249 where **Tyler** practiced law.

Tyler was born in 1790 at Greenway, marked on the north side of VA. 5, 30 miles east of Richmond, near **Harrison**'s birthplace. They were the only president and vice president elected at the same time who grew up in the same neighborhood. The so-called fertility ticket had a total of 18 children, 11 still living by the 1840 election. **Tyler** had seven more later, making the combination 25, a record for running mates. (All but one each of **Harrison**'s ten and **Tyler**'s 15 children lived to adulthood. One **Tyler** child, born when he was 70 in 1860, survived World War II, and five lived into the twentieth century.) **Tyler** stayed here until entering William and Mary College in 1802, and returned after his marriage to live on part of the plantation in a house he called Mons Sacer, at the northwest corner of Greenway. The law office used by him and his father is still on the privately owned estate. His first marriage was at Cedar Grove a few miles north in New Kent County, west side of Va. 106, a mile north of U.S. 60, the northern section of Greenway. His wife is buried in the cemetery behind the house.

A few miles east, on the south side of Route 5 is "Sherwood Forest,"* where **Tyler** retired. **W. Harrison** once owned it, the only house owned by two presidents outside the **Adams** family. At 54 **Tyler** had married his second wife, who was 24. Her mother fussed that they spent so much time kissing that the president was leaving important matters undone. This was then and still is the longest frame house in America, 300 feet long. **Tyler** named it after Robin Hood's domain as he considered himself, a former Democrat elected on the Whig ticket, a political outlaw. (He was a Whig after **Jackson**'s administration, but was soon drummed out of the party as president.) But his young wife had so many balls that he could fi-

Tyler's home, Sherwood Forest, was when he lived here and still is the longest frame home in America.

nally say he was no longer a "president without a party." Senator Henry Clay also called him Robin Hood because of **Tyler's** social programs helping the poor. The **Tylers** planted about 80 varieties of trees, some still here. He followed his father's example and played the fiddle for the plantation children and slaves. Because **Tyler** and five of his sons (including 15- and 16-year-old privates) served the Confederacy, the house was devastated by federal solders during the Civil War, but is restored and still lived in by one of **Tyler's** 32 grandchildren as of the early 21st century, the only presidential home still occupied and owned by descendants.

Tyler and **Harrison** were at Brandon Plantation* nearby on Va. 611. **Polk** was honored there in 1845. **Jefferson**, a friend of and groomsman for the owner, either designed it or suggested architectural changes, and visited. **Davis** stopped here on the way to Richmond and his expected trial in 1867. Just east is Claremont Manor, c. 1756, in Claremont, that is sometimes claimed to have hosted **Washington** and even all presidents up to **Buchanan**, but no evidence is found for any president there. The inaccessible home is west of Va. 642 on the water.

Several **Washington** sites are west of the confluence of the Mattaponi and Pamunkey Rivers that form the York River. The White House was the home of Martha before she married **George**. It is possible that they first met here as **Washington** journeyed to Williamsburg to treat an illness. She had four children by her deceased first husband although two died before her second marriage. It is probably the site of her wedding to **George** on January 6, 1759. They did honeymoon here where they lived for the first three months of marriage. (**Washington** also is claimed to have stayed in the tavern in New Kent, the seat of this county.) The White House was later owned by Robert E. Lee's second son and was where the Lee family fled at the beginning of the Civil War. Union General McClellan used it as his headquarters. It was preserved for a time by a note left on the house when the Lee family fled, requesting that it be spared in honor of **Washington**, but it was burned by federal soldiers in spite of orders by McClellan to protect it. The site is marked and located on the Pamunkey River, Route 614, north of Route 608, due east of Richmond. The nearest exit (211) on I-64 is Route 106 north running near the c. 1701 St. Peter's Church* located north of

Tallysville, off Route 106 to 609 and then 642 on St. Peter's Lane. This church is about four miles south of the White House and known as the "First Church of the First First Lady." The church is also a possible **Washington** wedding site and is often so claimed to be, as in the *Virginia Travel Guide*. But churches were not heated, and it was probably too cold to have a January wedding there. It was not the custom for widows to be married in the church. The ceremony was said to be by candlelight, and home weddings were the custom because no church was then ever lighted by candle at night. Also, law prohibited church meetings of any kind after sundown. Reverend David Mossom, who officiated at the wedding, is buried beneath the chancel. **Washington** attended the church with Martha and was entertained by the rector, who married his parents at the Glebe, near Bushfield and St. Peter's. It faced New Kent Stage Road.

Also along the river, about a mile northwest of the White House, is Poplar Grove, off Route 608. In May 1758 **Washington** crossed the ferry here on the way to take important dispatches to Williamsburg. The owner invited him to dine and then to stay, but **Washington** said he could not delay the mission. He was told if he stayed he would be introduced to the prettiest and richest widow in Virginia. He did, was delayed, and returned to spend more time with Martha. In July he wrote that he embraced the opportunity "to send a few words to one whose life is now inseperable [*sic*] from mine. Since that happy hour when we made our pledges to each other, my thoughts have been continually going to you as to another self."

Martha was born in 1731 at Chestnut Grove. The site is about two miles northeast of the junction of Routes 249, 30, and 33, east of New Kent and Richmond. Just north of that spot are the remains of Eltham, one of the largest and finest colonial homes in Virginia, burned in 1875, frequently visited by **Washington**. These two sites are noted by markers on Va. 33, just west of the Rte. 273 junction, but are inaccessible. Eltham was the home of **Washington's** intimate friend Colonel Bassett and his wife, a sister of Martha. **Washington** probably spent more time in this home than any other outside of Mt. Vernon. **W. Harrison's** mother was born here, and he frequently visited in the 1770s and 1780s. **Washington** came here just to visit, check his property in the area, and on travels to and from Williamsburg, generally through Villboro and Bowling Green on Route 2, and King and Queen Courthouse on Rte. 14. He would have known the nearby King William Courthouse* on the other side of the Mattaponi, now on Rte. 30, the oldest continually operating courthouse in the country, dating to 1725. Martha's mother lived there. **Washington** was "disconsolate," by the side of his stepson Jacky, when he died there after the Yorktown surrender in 1781. Jacky is buried in Eltham Garden. It is just south of the Pamunkey River from West Point, opposite the mouth of the Mattaponi River. **Washington** also visited nearby Chelsea* several times, about six miles west of West Point on the Mattaponi River, north of Route 30 on Route 635, 874, and the single-lane, gravel Chelsea Plantation Lane, to the east of the historical marker noting the home on Rte. 30 at the Mattaponi River.

One of the largest Tidewater mansions is Shirley,* west of Route 5 on 608 at the county border on the James River. **Washington** was a regular visitor, but sent a gift to compensate for not being able to attend the wedding of "Light Horse Harry" Lee to his second wife in 1793. They became the parents of Robert E., who frequently visited. **Jefferson** visited on his honeymoon and had his carriage repaired. **Tyler** and both **Roosevelts** also visited.

Jefferson married Martha Wayles on New Year's Day, 1772, at the Forest (destroyed), north of Route 607 a little over one mile north on 605, between Routes 5 and 106, north of Berkeley and Shirley. He is first known here on October 6, 1770, and courted over a year at the home of her father. Once suitors came and heard a violin playing in the parlor. Knowing that **Jefferson** was the only player in the area, they looked resignedly at one another, and one said, "We are wasting our time; we might as well go home." Martha had a three-year-old son by her first marriage to a friend of **Jefferson's,** but the boy died before the wedding. The **Jeffersons** then traveled in the snow to his half-finished home, Monticello.

CHARLOTTESVILLE • As of the early 21st century, there are three structures classified as World Heritage Sites in the United States, other than prehistoric ruins. These are Independence Hall, Monticello, and the University of Virginia, the latter two in Charlottesville and attributed to **Jefferson**. He was born in 1743 at his father's home, Shadwell, site marked three miles east on U.S. 250. When he was two his father's close friend, who owned Tuckahoe Plantation,* died and commanded, in effect, rather than requested, that the senior **Jefferson** manage his estate and be the guardian of his four-year-old son and three daughters. No one really knows why, but the **Jeffersons** packed up in 1745 and moved there near Richmond, then returned in 1752. Shadwell was no mansion, just a house and group of buildings, although Tuckahoe was one of the finest.

Shortly after returning home, nine-year-old Tom was packed off for school five miles away from Tuckahoe at the Dover Church School, site unknown. Here the young student stayed for about eight months yearly for five years until his father died. Then he went to Reverend James Maury's school and home at the foot of Peter's Mountain, 14 miles from Shadwell, with close friends Dabney Carr, James Madison (cousin of the president), and Jack Walker. This was near Fredericksville, where he also attended church. Marker JE-6 on Va. 231, north of Castle Hill, four and a half miles from Gordonville, notes the site, close enough to go home on weekends. He had a good teacher who was the first to find fossils of sea creatures in the crest of the Blue Ridge Mountains, coloring **Jefferson's** religious and scientific thinking.

Indians camped in Shadwell's yard on journeys to and from Williamsburg. **Jefferson** remembered their conversations although he understood not a word, and looked with awe and veneration at a chief who always stopped. Nothing remains at the birthplace, which burned in 1771 with all family books and records, depriving us of much knowledge of **Jefferson's** early years. At the time he expressed great grief over the loss of his books, notes, and journals, but nothing over his mother's loss of her home and personal affects. His relationship with her was somewhat formal, maybe strained, and maybe similar to **Washington's** claimed relationship with his mother and **Lincoln's** with his father. **Jefferson** studied law for five years, much of the time here, before being admitted to the bar. By 1773 he had collected 1254 new books.

After Shadwell burned the family lived in various outbuildings until Monticello* was completed. **Jefferson** had already begun his new home, first called the Hermitage, in 1769, now on State 53, three miles southwest, one of the great houses of America. Being built on the top of a somewhat leveled mountain did not make much sense except for aesthetic or psychological reasons. It was away from town, materials, and workers, and water had to be constantly hauled.

The **Jeffersons** are said to have gone to church at St. Paul's (site unknown) between Shadwell and Charlottesville, although the claim that young Tom was baptized there is doubted by the local historical society. All records and the church have burned. There was no architectural school in America, so **Jefferson** had to train himself to build his estate, the center of his life after 1771. Monticello was not completed until about 1781 and then was remodeled for about 15 years, and indeed, for much of the rest of his life. He constantly tore down and rebuilt the house, helping to break him financially. The small brick south pavilion,* where he lived with his bride while the main house was being finished, is still adjacent. He brought her there on this honeymoon in one of the worst snowstorms in Virginia history, and they spent their first few days in this cold, dreary structure before going to Elk Hill, described later, near Richmond. He brought home 86 crates of furniture, furnishings, and art from Paris in 1789.

When he practiced law from ages 24 until 31, he had to ride long distances over wretched roads in bad weather. Few paid in cash, so his practice was not very productive. But he lived with the grace and elegance of a British lord with 25 house slaves. His joy was marred by the deaths of his wife's young son, three of his children, his wife, and his mother in just a few years. When his wife died, some reports show that he considered suicide and destroyed her letters. We know less about her than the wife of any other great man in our history.

One of **Jefferson's** guardians when his father died was the discoverer of Cumberland Gap, Dr. Thomas Walker, who lived at Castle Hill,* north of Shadwell on Route 231, just north of the junction with Route 22. **Washington** was a guest, and **Jefferson** and **Madison** frequently visited when they traveled to see each other. Young **Madison**, the future president, took dancing lessons in the home. When British Colonel Tarleton raided Charlottesville and stopped to capture Dr. Walker on the way to capture Governor **Jefferson** at Monticello, legend has it that Walker so beguiled the enemy with lavish hospitality that **Jefferson** had time to be warned and flee. In later years, **Monroe, Jackson, Van Buren, Tyler, Buchanan**, and Lafayette visited.

Jack Walker was a close friend of **Jefferson** from childhood who was an attendant in his wedding. In 1768 Jack went off with his father for about four months as a member of the Virginia delegation to Fort Stanwix to negotiate an Indian treaty. Before leaving he asked his friend to take care of his

Madison and Monroe visited for long periods at Jefferson's Monticello, and many more recent presidents have also visited.

family at his home, Belvoir, five and a half miles from Shadwell and three southwest of Castle Hill. **Jefferson** then made "inappropriate advances" to Mrs. Walker at Belvoir that Jack did not find out about until 1784. A scandal arose when **Jefferson** was president. Walker made a provocative statement written out, maybe inaccurately, by Henry Lee and probably exaggerated. **Jefferson** admitted to one inappropriate offer, before his marriage. Belvoir is still standing although moved twice, now east of Va. 231 at the intersection of Va. 647 and 22, first driveway across the railroad tracks, where the Kinlock House is now.

Jefferson came home as governor of Virginia, the largest state, during the Revolutionary War when the British approached Richmond. His term ended June 1, 1781, as the legislature also retreated to Charlottesville. No successor was appointed, so he was still considered governor when almost captured a few days later. Captain Jack Joulet overheard British plans to capture the governor and legislature and made a desperate ride to Charlottesville while the British were delayed at Castle Hill. **Jefferson** was warned a little after sunrise, sent his family off, viewed the area with his telescope, and saw nothing. He then breakfasted at leisure, worked on a few papers, and finally decided to flee with the two speakers of the two Virginia Assemblies, who were guests. He soon noticed that he had dropped his sword and went to get it, gathered some papers, was warned again, and then almost captured as he rode down one hill as the British rode up the other. One biographer (Randle) says that a detail sent to capture **Jefferson** was actually inside the house at the time **Jefferson** went back to get his sword. The fathers of two future presidents (**Harrison** and **Tyler**) were in the legislature and also fled. Patrick Henry escaped, but frontiersman Daniel Boone, representing Kentucky County, was captured.

Jefferson fled over Carter's Mountain to Colonel Carter's nearby Blenheim, where he stopped on his honeymoon, then to Cole's Place or Enniscorthy where his wife and children had fled, and continued to Poplar Forest. These estates still stand, although Poplar Forest has been rebuilt. (See Lynchburg.) Blenheim is six miles south of **Monroe's** Ash Lawn, and eight miles due south of Charlottesville at the junctions of Routes 708, 795 and 727. Enniscorthy is to the west, two miles west of Keene on Route 20, one mile southwest of the Va. 712 and 627 junction, on the west side of 627. **Madison** and **Monroe** were later there. The home burned in 1839, and the replacement mainly dates to 1850. He visited his close friend William Short that he wrote of as almost "an adopted son," at his home, Morven, just north of Blenheim, southwest of Ash Lawn. An 1820 replacement home is on the same site west at 791 Morven Drive, just northwest of the sharp turn on James Monroe Road/Va. 795. The site now belongs to the university.

British Captain McLeod stayed 18 hours at Monticello, but took and destroyed nothing, unlike General Cornwallis, who burned crops and barns and took slaves at **Jefferson's** Edge Hill, marked one mile east of Shadwell, north of the Routes 231 and 250 intersection and just north of Interstate 64. Most of these slaves soon died of smallpox. **Jefferson** often visited his daughter Martha, who later lived at Edge Hill. An 1828 brick house covered with clapboarding is at the site of a 1790 home moved to the rear. **Jefferson's** boyhood friend from Tuckahoe, Colonel Thomas Mann Randolph, and his second wife lived here with his son Thomas Jr., who married Martha. Thomas Jr.'s mother was from Ampthill Estate in Chesterfield County, mentioned in the Richmond entry. **Jefferson** enjoyed having his grandchildren and both Randolphs nearby. In fact they spent most of their time at Monticello. **Jefferson** was especially attached to his grandson, Thomas Jefferson Randolph, who managed his estate and was close to the president. He sometimes exhibited emotional problems and was governor of Virginia from 1819 to 1822.

During his youth **Jefferson** came alone or with his friend Dabney Carr, to study, write his thoughts, and think at a peaceful site he called "Tom's Mountain." The two friends promised to bury the other there when the first died. Monticello was built nearby. Carr, who married **Jefferson's** sister, was the first to be buried in the cemetery now holding the **Jefferson** family. All of the 3000 or so **Jefferson** descendants have the right to be buried here. Some 800 descendants of slave Sally Hemmings, who may or may not be related, also claim the right. Modern scientific DNA tests can trace a **Jefferson** family connection (maybe the president's brother or nephews) to one Hemmings child, but DNA tracing from the president is not possible unless his body is exhumed. Some leading scholars and the Thomas Jefferson Foundation do believe that **Jefferson** did father Sally's children, but this is passionately denied by others.

Even though he considered slavery "an abominable crime," **Jefferson** felt that freeing slaves was like abandoning innocent children. He had as many as 135 slaves working his farms, building his houses, and carrying out all chores. An extensive part of the current Monticello tour covers the slave culture, and the visitor center orientation film repeats his famous quote, "We have the wolf by the ears. We can neither hold him, nor safely let him go. Justice is on one scale, and self-preservation in the other." Virginia, like many other states, tried to alleviate their problem somewhat by passing a law that forced a freed slave to leave the state. By 1815, **Jefferson** was $100,000 in debt. He could have emancipated his slaves, but he kept them and his lifestyle until death. He also wrote, "I tremble for my country when I reflect that God is just: that his justice cannot sleep forever."

Jefferson used Monticello as summer White House, and spent 831 days here during his presidency, as shown in his *Memo Book*. He also spent more than 875 days here as vice president and almost 200 as secretary of state. After his presidency he stayed on his 5000-acre plantation with his daughter Martha, twelve grandchildren, and various nieces and nephews, in varying numbers. Many of his inventions, furniture, and personal items are still here. His furniture was scattered after his death, but only items clearly his are shown here. Monticello, like Mount Vernon, became like a tavern as long as he lived, with a constant stream of visitors coming to see one of the most interesting and attractive houses in America and one of the most engaging personalities, eating him out of house and home. He served as many as twelve friends dining with him at any one time. Visitors also avoided a tavern fee, and this fame strained the household economy and left him bankrupt. At one time four generations were living here when a great-granddaughter was born in 1817. By **Jefferson's** death at least eleven great-grandchildren were here. But like **Washington**, **Madison**, and **Monroe**, he left no son to carry on his name.

Van Buren visited in 1823. **Houston** came for a day in 1823 to converse with the learned sage after a letter of introduction was sent by **Jackson**. **Jefferson** and **Jackson** feuded politically, but became friends even though **Jefferson** did not think him qualified for the presidency. **Monroe** and **Madison** were frequent guests, and Lafayette visited for six weeks in 1825, although he only spent a day with **Adams** in Massachusetts. In fact **Madison** would stay two months at a time in the home, twice a year before, during and after his presidency. After **Jefferson** died he stayed here when came on university business as rector until 1834. **Jefferson** tried to get **Monroe** and **Madison** to move nearby, but only succeeded in persuading **Monroe**. The historical society believes that he visited his favorite nephew, Peter Carr, at Carrbrook, marked and still at the NE corner of Gloucester and Gloucester Court in the Carrbrook Addition just south of the Ravenna River. (Turn right off U.S. 29 north, just south of Sam's and Wal-Mart, onto Carrbrook, then left at Marlboro and right onto Gloucester.)

Some of **Jefferson's** 6,707 books were sold to the new Library of Congress, where many can be seen now, after the British burned the old library during the War of 1812. The price paid to **Jefferson** of about $24,000 was half their cost, but he needed the money. He died here on the 50th anniversary of the signing of the Declaration of Independence, July 4, 1826. He had been invited to Washington to celebrate the nation's fiftieth anniversary, but could not because of diabetes, urinary infection, and possible colon cancer. The estate had to be sold in 1831 due to the debt. He knew he was a financial failure even though one of the most admired and accomplished men in world history. Several presidents have delivered addresses from the steps of Monticello, including **Truman**, **Ford**, and **FDR**. **Clinton** toured the home, as shown in a nationally televised special, on the way to his first inaugural.

The courthouse at the NW corner of Jefferson and Park has always been a political center in the town of two presidents. The prior 1762 structure served briefly as the Capitol of Virginia when the legislature fled here. The present building may incorporate some of the old structure where Jack Joulet warned members of the Virginia Assembly that the British were coming. **Jefferson** was a magistrate and vestryman at church meetings there, where **Madison** and **Monroe** also worshipped. **Jefferson** called it "the common temple."

The three presidents also came to the Swan Tavern, at the NE corner of **Jefferson** and Parke Streets, to eat before gawking listeners. After years of **Jefferson's** urging him to move closer, **Monroe** decided to move here upon hearing that **Jefferson** was leaving France. In 1789 **Monroe** bought 402–414 E. Market, the block between Market, Main, Fourth, and Fifth, noted by a marker where the City Parking Garage now is. He lived there at what became the Central Hotel, which also hosted **Jefferson**, **Madison**, Lafayette in 1824, and Meriwether Lewis on his return from his western exploration, and served as a Civil War hospital until burned in 1862. **Monroe** is also claimed to have stayed at the Eagle Tavern, a town house, on the south side of Court Square at number 300. It is unclear exactly when or if **Monroe** lived on Market Street as some biographers show him moving to Monroe Hill House* from Fredericksburg, and the Albemarle Historical Society records are unclear. But he apparently lived there in town before building or reconstructing a home on what is now the campus of the University of Virginia and used some small outbuildings as a law office. He made frequent trips back to Fredericksburg, where his family stayed until the house was ready, maybe 1792. He lived at Monroe Hill in the early 1790s (exact dates unclear) and 1796–99. (In 1795 he was in France as ambassador.) **Jefferson** hoped to convert the house into an observatory. The university purchased it in 1817, and it is still used and marked south of the Alderman Library on the west side of McCormick.

Monroe then lived at Highland (renamed Ash Lawn,* as it is now known, after his death) from 1799 to 1819, two miles beyond Monticello on State 53 and County Road 795. It is sometimes claimed to have been planned or built by **Jefferson**, which is evidently not true, although **Jefferson** selected the site. Many houses in the area are claimed to have been at least partially planned by the well-known amateur architect, with many still standing. The land was poor and produced little, but **Monroe** made this his main home until he left to become president in 1817. Of course his close friends **Jefferson** and **Madison** visited both houses. The part completed during **Monroe's** residency is only the small rear part. **Jefferson** rode over in 1809 to get **Monroe** back into government after the former president had supported **Madison** and not **Monroe** as his successor. **FDR** (1940) and **Truman** (1947) visited the home and grounds.

Jefferson is considered the founder of the University of Virginia. In August 1818 he and **Madison** stayed at Farmington,* now a country club on U.S. 250 just west of town, on the way to Rockfish Gap to organize a university. Continuing, they met at Leake's Tavern or Old Mountain Top Tavern at Rockfish Gap, about where Route 250 now crosses the Blue Ridge Parkway, with other commissioners to determine where to select a site. (See Waynesboro.) **Jefferson** argued for the Charlottesville site over Lexington and Staunton and designed and supervised the construction of the first buildings, some of which survive. President **Monroe** laid the cornerstone of Pavilion VII with former presidents **Jefferson** and **Madison** present. It is now the Colonnade Club* on the west lawn.

Jefferson set up a telescope at Monticello with which he watched progress on the construction that he helped plan and that is still preserved, principally in the serpentine walls, pavilions, and Rotunda. The Rotunda's Dome Room was one of his favorite views, where he could sit and look down the Lawn towards the mountains in what he felt symbolized the limitless freedom of the mind. In the fall of 1825, undisciplined students rioted and attacked professors. The day afterward, the Board of Visitors, **Jefferson, Madison,** and **Monroe**, met students in the Rotunda. When **Jefferson** tried to speak he declared that the riot "was one of the most painful events of his life." He could not speak further, burst into tears, and sank back into his chair. The shock was electric, and his tears were said to have "melted their stubborn purpose." In 1824 **Jefferson** hosted a dinner for Lafayette in the unfinished Rotunda with **Madison** and 400 others. *The Life of James Monroe* says that he was here for the occasion, but had to leave for state business before the dinner. Lafayette returned the next year for a tour of the campus with **Monroe** and met with the three presidents at Monticello. The Rotunda was severely damaged by fire in 1895 and rebuilt. **Truman** and **George H.W. Bush** (1981, 1989) have spoken there, and **FDR** made his "stab in the back" speech nearby in 1940. Queen Elizabeth II visited in 1976. **JFK** visited with his brothers in 1958 and was introduced as "the next president."

The Michie Tavern* is now on the road to Monticello and catered to **Jefferson, Madison,** and **Monroe. Jackson's** biographer Marquis James claimed that **Jefferson** and **Jackson** met in the keeping room. Area history claims that it was a "haunt" of the four presidents. It has been moved from about nine miles north of Charlottesville, between Earlyville and Free Union, on the east side of Buck Mountain Creek and Va. 665 and 667 junction.

Madison's second cousin, **Taylor**, was probably born at Montebello, marked three miles west of Gordonsville. The site may have been a guest house on the property in 1784, about 15 miles northeast on Highway 33 between Barboursville and Gordonsville, twelve miles from his father's estate, Hare Forest, where he may have been born. The latter is northeast of Orange, on Va. 700, 1.4 miles north of Route 615. His parents had lived near Culpeper and had set out to find a new home near the Falls of the Ohio (Louisville, Ky.), where his father had been awarded land for his war service. Measles broke out in the party, and the **Taylors** were quarantined. His father left the family here to establish their home in Kentucky.

While **Wilson** was in the Law School he stayed in room 158, House F, Dawson's Row, facing the street in front of New Cabell Hall, south of the Rotunda. He was later at 31 West Range, east of Monroe Hall. He entered the school twice and had to leave both times due to ill health. **Harding** was serenaded at the university in 1921. **Truman** visited the area historic sites in 1947, including the Stanley Woodward House, Colle, on land that had belonged to **Jefferson**. The German officer Baron von Riedesel and his family had stayed there after being captured at Saratoga, and had visited with **Jefferson**. The home was at the SE intersection of Routes 53 and 732 between Ash Lawn and Monticello, and opposite a church and Simeon Vineyards.

From 1905 until 1908, **TR** came with his family to Pine Knot,* 17 miles south on Va. 712, two miles east of Va. 20, near Scottsville and Keene. He visited eight times while president for two to six days per visit, during which time no business was conducted. The family spent Christmas in 1905 there. They walked each Sunday morning to Christ Church at 900 Glendower Road, about a half-mile from the cottage. He visited Cabell Hall at the university in 1903.

In 1936, **FDR** spoke at Monticello and stayed in a former slave's house, now a part of Farmington, the country club mentioned above. He liked to come to nearby Kenwood,* where he generally stayed in an adjacent cottage, and was there at least once a year for the last six years of his life. *Life Magazine* dubbed it "The Little White House." The home, four-tenths of a mile from Monticello's gatehouse on Route 53, is open as a research library. **Lyndon Johnson**'s daughter lived in Charlottesville, and the former president once had a heart "spell" there and was taken to University Hospital. The elder **Bush** and **Clinton** debated at the University in 1992.

City Point (Hopewell) and Petersburg Battlefield • General **Grant's** Civil War headquarters during the last months were at the junction of the James and Appomattox Rivers. It was then one of the world's largest supply bases, and the largest of the Civil War. **Lincoln** and his son Tad visited June 21–22, 1864, and went to the Petersburg front to inspect the lines. **Lincoln** and **Grant** steamed up the river as far as it was considered safe and visited Fort Darling* at Drewry's Bluff, now part of the Richmond Battlefield Park. It can be reached about one mile east of I-95 off Bellwood Road at the Routes 145 and 656 junction on the James, south of Richmond.

Lincoln came back on March 23, 1865, for two of his last three weeks aboard the steamer *River Queen*, a sort of floating hotel. **Grant** and the president conferred in one cabin while their wives began a difficult relationship. **Lincoln** was at the Jordan House, now a depression in the ground adjacent to the visitor's center, Stop 1 on the Battlefield Tour map. The president requested and was taken to the front by a special train to Patrick Station* south of Petersburg and rode from there along the Halifax Road past Fort Dushane* and Fort Wadsworth* (Stop 10 on the Petersburg Battlefield tour map). Here the president, Tad, and General Meade witnessed a two-hour attack occurring north of Patrick Station over the current National Park Flank Road at Forts Urmston,* Conahey* (Stop 12), and Fisher* (Stop 13) over Virginia Routes 613, 676, and 672. All are clearly marked on the Park Service tour map, off Route 604.

On March 26 the party went to Malvern Hill* to review General Ord's Army of the James. This well-marked major battlefield site is on the Richmond Battlefield tour, Route 156, just north of the Rte. 5 junction. **Grant's** steamship docked at Aiken's Landing, where he and **Lincoln** went to the parade ground about two miles ahead and the women proceeded in an ambulance. Mrs. Lincoln, upset at not being at the parade on time and that her husband innocently rode beside Mrs. Ord instead of her, had her most celebrated tantrum, to everyone's embarrassment, and soon left for Washington, to everyone's relief. Aiken's landing and home, built in 1853, are privately owned but accessible from Kingsland Road and Varina Road off Route 5. Kingsland Road intersects Route 5 about two miles east of its interchange with I-295. The old home and site can be seen from the I-295 bridge just to the east.

On the third and fourth, **Lincoln** and Tad visited Petersburg and Richmond. Much of the president's time was spent at the cabin of Colonel Bowers, serving as the telegraph office, adjacent to the south side of Appomattox Manor,* the quartermaster general's headquarters and now Park Headquarters for City Point. The 1763 mansion is the largest structure in a small town of several pre–Civil War homes. There is no record that he went inside. **Lincoln** returned to Petersburg on the seventh and then left for **Washington** on the eighth after visiting wounded at the Depot Field Hospital about a mile away to the southwest, where the John Randolph Hospital is now. This visit lasted five hours in an effort to meet many of the 10,000 there, including Confederates. The president asked the band to play the Marseillaise for a visiting Frenchman, and then asked the surprised director to play "Dixie" as "the tune was now Federal property," and it is "good to show the rebels that, with us in power, they will be free to hear it again."

This landing area is now a unit of the Petersburg National Battlefield that maintains the site of **Grant's** headquarters, the ship landing sites, Appomattox Manor, and other historical structures and sites of the period. **Grant's** cabin* was and is in the yard to the east. It was moved to Philadelphia's Fairmount Park until 1981, when it was put back at its original site. Only a few logs on the east side are original.

COVINGTON • In 1756, **Washington** inspected Fort Breckenridge, three miles northwest on Falling Spring Creek, ten miles west of Roanoke on U.S. 11. The commander of Virginia forces barely escaped after being ambushed by Shawnees. He also inspected Forts William, three miles south of Fincastle; Young, in Covington on Route 154; Dinwiddie on Route 39, five miles west of Warm Springs; and Dickinson on Route 42 near Millsboro Springs, all marked.

CULPEPER • **Grant's** headquarters were at the Virginia Hotel in April 1864, at the corner of North Main and West Cameron. **Clinton** attended the First Baptist Church at West and Scanlon on the way to his first inaugural.

DANVILLE • Sometimes called the "last Capital of the Confederacy," this is where **Davis** met with his full cabinet for the last time from April 3 to 10, 1865, at 975 Main in the Sutherlin Mansion,* now the Museum of Fine Arts and History. He occupied a bedroom now restored upstairs and wrote his last proclamation. The last executive offices were set up also in the Benedict House at 703 Wilson Street, where he and his cabinet also met as frequently as they did at Sutherlin's. On April 8, a soldier arrived from General Lee with the shocking news that Lee could not make it to Danville. Then the next day, a rumor circulated that he had surrendered, and the government decided to move to Greensboro, North Carolina.

FARMVILLE • **Grant** used the Robinson or Prince Edward Hotel (sometimes called the Planters) on April 7, 1865, as the armies marched toward Appomattox. The site is now a parking lot at the NE corner of Main and Second, and is marked. The tradition that Lee also spent a night here is not valid. **Grant** sent from here his first correspondence to Lee about surrender and held a grand review of troops marching through town.

Five and a half miles south on Route 15 is the site of the colonial town and courthouse at Worsham, where **Washington** stayed on his Southern tour, June 7, 1791. A little further southwest is the small community of Charlotte Court House, where he breakfasted and was delayed getting shoes for his horses. Both towns were crowded to see what one diarist described as "...the Savior of their Country and object of their love." He then proceeded north to eat in Cumberland and stayed in what became Cartersville.

FREDERICKSBURG AREA • Fredericksburg calls itself the most historic town in America, not without reason. Many sites are open, but often inaccurately described, as is much of the history in decades of literature. This entry hopes to correct this information based on current research by Historic Fredericksburg and other authentic historic sources who have approved this section.

The colonial town is located on U.S. Highway 1, originally an Indian trail and later a post road used by **Washington**, **Jefferson**, and early leaders. **Washington** was born 38 miles east off State Route 3, at what is now George Washington's Birthplace National Monument* or Wakefield, on the south side of the Potomac River. Known as Popes Creek Plantation, it is located on the namesake creek, which is one and a half miles wide here within sight of the Potomac, five miles wide. The family settled in the area at Mattox Creek in the 1650s, bought the adjacent Bridges Creek Farm in 1664, but did not acquire the Popes Creek site until 1717.

The memorial house known as Wakefield* was built in 1930 on the site believed then to be the birthplace home that burned on Christmas Day 1779. Later archeological searches have revealed several other adjacent structures, one of which is now believed to have been the birth site. But historians simply do not know for sure where it was even though the rebuilt structure was called the birthplace spot through the 1960s. In the 1970s, the marked site of "Building X" was mentioned as a possible site of the original house, and now is believed to be the actual site. This is marked with outlines near the reconstructed Wakefield. After the home burned the family (including **George**'s half-brother) stayed in Blenheim, still on the north side of the road going into the park. **Washington** would have known the home, now private and difficult to see behind thick trees, but noted with a small sign in front.

The **Washington** family burying ground* nearby, with some original tombstones, is where many family members are buried, including his father, grandfather, and great-grandfather, who settled here. The Bridges Creek Farm of his brother is marked by the cemetery, where young **George** often visited and made his first surveys at age 15. His grandfather had lived here after being born at Mattox Creek Farm, north of Oak Grove on the east side of Mattox Creek and Rte. 205. **Washington's** father was also born at Mattox Creek, lost his father at age four, and moved to England as a young boy with his stepfather and family. He then came back to the area to spend his teenage years with an older cousin at Chotank, now inaccessible on the Potomac River, northeast of Fredericksburg, north of the Routes 218 and 206 intersection. This would have been north of St. Paul's Church mentioned below, and opposite Nanjenoy Creek in Maryland.

Virginia marker J-67 notes the site of a school probably attended by **Washington** and a brother at Oak Grove, while at Wakefield, on Route 3, a few miles west of the birthplace site, although there appears to be no direct evidence of this. Marker J-69a, 4.8 miles southeast of Oak Grove on Route 3, notes the site of Popes Creek Church (destroyed), attended by the **Washingtons**. It is possible that he was baptized at the Yeocominco Church* on the northwest side of the river of the same name, noted by marker JT-7 on Route 202, 8.1 miles northwest of Callao. It is down Yeocominco Road east of 202 off Va. 604 and marked on the grounds. There is also some speculation that he might have been baptized at Mattox Creek Church, a little over two miles from Popes Creek and about a mile west of Bridges Creek at Church Point.

In this area also is Nominy Church,* attended

by **Washington** at least twice, as noted by marker JT-2 on Route 202, 3.7 miles east of Templemans Cross Roads on the northeast side of the bridge. This was burned by the British in 1814. The present church was built in 1852. While visiting his cousins at Chotank he attended St. Paul's* at the SE intersection of Routes 218 and 206 west of Route 301 and the Potomac River Bridge. The present church was built in 1831 on the foundations of the original. He visited many nearby homes, including the Glebe on Glebe Road at the head and to the west of Sandy Point Road, north of the Glebe Harbor Country Club House in Glebe Harbor, north of Route 202 off Va. 628. It is also speculated but not documented that he visited Stratford Hall, nearby on Route 3, the home of the prominent Lee family, since all prominent landowners knew and visited each other. **Ike** visited there on May 4, 1958. **FDR** wrote the foreword to a book on Stratford history, saying that he had been there many times, and described his first trip when he landed at the riverside as giving him the thrill that Balboa felt "upon a peak in Darion." **Washington** also visited Lamb's Creek Plantation (including August 7, 1752, and January 15, 1760), Eagle's Nest, and Cleve Plantations. Lamb's Creek was on Routes 3 and 694, on Lamb's Creek at Grave's Corner, about ten miles east of Fredericksburg. Eagle's Nest was on the Potomac east of Fairview Beach.

Mary Ball, **Washington's** mother, is said to have been born at Epping Forest* on Route 3, twelve miles east of Warsaw, but this has been disproved. The actual site is the Joseph Ball home on Morrattico Creek, now on Va. Route 622 west of Route 354 on the Rappahannock, as shown in Paula Felder's *Fielding Lewis and the* ***Washington*** *Family*. Mary grew up at Cherry Point, south of the Westmoreland-Northumberland County line and south of Sandy Point, reached by Routes 3, 202 and 604, on the Potomac, just north of the county line. Cherry Point was the home of her stepfather, who died when she was about six. Her mother died when Mary was about 12, and she continued to live with her sister. A close family friend, George Eskridge, lived at Sandy Point, where she visited and was married. She named her oldest son after him, but did not live there as claimed by Virginia markers JT-4 and JT-16 nearby. Her supposed eccentric personality was not helped when she was here pregnant with **George** and lightning came down the chimney and killed her friend sitting next to her. The intense heat fused together her knife and fork. This traumatic event might have intensified her possessive feelings towards her son. **Washington** frequently visited his brother John at Bushfield, marker JT-5 on 202, 4.4 miles east of Templetons Cross Roads, down Bushfield Road off 202.

When **George** was three, his father moved the family to Little Hunting Creek, later known as Mount Vernon. In 1738 they moved to what has become known as **Washington's** Boyhood Home,* now a park on the north side of the river from Fredericksburg about a mile east of Chatham Estate, on Route 3. Here he lived much of the time from age six until adulthood. The name "Ferry Farm" is misleading since it was not called that during his lifetime. The ferry there now was not authorized until 1763, long after **Washington** and his siblings were grown, although an old ferry was at the southern end of the tract where Hazel Run joins the river on the west side. If **George** threw the coin (or rock, as claimed by a cousin) across the river or chopped down a cherry tree, it was here. Note that the river was wider prior to being rechanneled in 1870. The area has retained a pastoral setting reminiscent of **Washington's** early days, maintaining the sights, sounds, and smells of the plantation. While the family lived here they used the Willis Ferry at Wolfe Street to cross the river, as did **Jefferson** and **Madison**.

George inherited the Ferry Farm from his father, whose death at about age 49 ended the plan for the boy to go to England for schooling like his half-brothers. (Actually the age of his father at death was above average for men of the day.) **George**, at Chotank when his father died, was haunted by this disappointment for years and further hurt when his possessive mother would not allow him a career in the British Navy. Although it is believed that he did go to several unnamed schools near Mt. Vernon, maybe while he was with his cousins at Chotank and here, he is said to have had less education than any president, including **Jackson** and **Lincoln**, except maybe **Andrew Johnson**. There is evidence that he crossed the Willis Ferry every morning for many months to attend to Reverend James Marye's school on the NW corner of Charlotte and Princess Anne Streets. It is possible that he went to John Hobby's school, discussed later, as mentioned by Parson Weems, an early biographer.

The boy moved around between the various family homes, including Chotank and Popes Creek, his birthplace, then owned by half-brother Augustine. Here he first studied surveying, which later helped launch a career. A shed on the premises may date to **Washington's** era. Tradition holds that he found his father's surveying instruments and began to develop the skills that took him west. When **George** was not there, he was generally with his half-brother Lawrence at his home, Mount Vernon. Actually he spent as much time as he could with his half-brothers, as he probably did not get along well with his mother. Mary had five other children, none of whom amounted to much, and she supposedly doted on and tried to dominate **George** all her life. She is generally reported to have been quick-tempered, strong-willed, domineering, and constantly complaining. When her son had the weight of the Republic on his back during his war campaigns, she is described as bothering him over simple complaints. Or at least that is her reputation. Historian Douglas Southall Freeman relates that the strangest mystery of his life is his lack of affection for her. But recent research challenges this. (See local historian Paula Felder's works on **Washington** and his family.) Mary Washington did make one major contribution to history: she refused to allow him his desire to go to sea at a young age to be a British sailor.

The original home at the Ferry Farm burned when **George** was eight and has been located. Probably the second home was located at the same spot, but no structure existed there during the Civil War, and no house is here now. The **Washington** ferry site* was only used after 1763. **Washington** bought his mother a house in town and used it to transport her belongings in 1772 when she finally left the farm. Later it was the site of pontoon bridges used by Union troops until the Overland Campaign of May 1864. The home site battled becoming a Wal-Mart until the late 20th century, when it was saved as a National Historic Landmark. **Lincoln** was familiar with the **Washington** stories and would have passed near the boyhood home several times, although there is no documentation that **Lincoln** came to the home site.

Fredericksburg was the largest town **George** saw until his teens. As a young boy he is claimed, without proof, to have attended the Brunswick Parish Church in Falmouth across the river, marked with only a medallion one block east of the junction of U.S. 17 and 1. The ruins of one wall remain one block east of a car dealership, NE of the bridge and at the head of Carter Street, a block north of River Park on the River Road. He also is claimed to have attended Mr. Hobby's School near the ruins of the church, maybe kept by William Grove. A log building so identified exists at Carter and Butler Road within a block of the church wall, but this is evidently a reconstruction in the 1930s of a nineteenth-century barn. Old houses border these sites and are just north of the park on the river and south of the ruins. **Washington** probably knew some of these, but direct associations are unknown, and there are no documentations that can make any claims more than highly speculative. If **Washington** went to Hobby's School, it probably would have been near Little Falls Run, near the intersection of Route 3 and Forest Lane Road, about two miles south of the Ferry Farm, not in Falmouth. **Lincoln** is claimed to have crossed the river near the present U.S. 1 bridge near the Brunswick Church, although it is believed that the correct site was nearer Chatham, shown below.

Washington attended St. George's Episcopal* at Princess Anne and George, using the ferry to get there. **Monroe** was a later vestryman. The current 1849 building was used by soldiers to fire from during the Civil War. Martha **Washington's** father is buried in the churchyard.

In 1752 **Washington** was initiated into the Masonic Lodge, then at the Town Hall near the SW corner of William and Caroline. The new Masonic building containing **Washington** artifacts is at Princess Anne and Hanover. **Washington** is claimed in several sources to have attended a ball at the Mortimer House, 216 Caroline, but this is not documented and doubted. He was also frequently at the oldest house in town, now a bed and breakfast, the home of his close friend Charles Dick at 1107 Princess Anne.* (**Coolidge** and **Cleveland** later visited.) He also visited the Willis House on Marye's Heights where the Montfort Academy was later located, northeast of the Park Visitor Center and Kirkland Statue, and visited Julian's Coffee House at the NE corner of Princess Anne and Amelia. He also visited his friend John Spotswood, who lived near the river south of town, about where Ruffin Pond now is, north of the Routes 2/17 intersection. His Fredericksburg residence ended in 1748, but he continued to visit throughout his life.

In 1781 **Washington** and French ally General Rochambeau were moving toward the showdown with the British at Yorktown, as marked just north of both Stafford and Dumfries, and stopped at a favorite of **Washington's**, Peyton's Ordinary, 1.8 miles north of Stafford.

Washington's only sister married at "the advanced age" of 19 to Fielding Lewis, and lived at the imposing Kenmore Mansion,* 1200 block of Washington at Lewis Street, where his bed can still be seen. He generally stayed here rather than with his mother when he visited the area, and was closer to both his sister and brother-in-law than his own brothers. He last stayed here on his way to and from his 1791 Southern tour and was then honored in a large gathering at the Town Hall. The first home of the Lewis family was 1201 Princess Anne, where **Washington's** eleven nieces and nephews were born. (The present house there is built on the foundation of the home burned in 1807.) Fielding was guardian to **Washington's** brother Charles and involved in various business dealings with **Washington.** Across the street near Kenmore in the 1500 block of Washington is his mother's meditation rock,* where she is buried. **Jackson** laid the cornerstone for her monument there in 1833, but it was so damaged in the Civil War that **Cleveland** had to dedicate another in 1894. **Eisenhower** laid a memorial wreath on the grave in 1954.

Fielding Lewis's original store, c. 1750, where **Washington,** his mother, and **Madison's** father shopped, is restored across from the city library on the SW corner of Lewis and Caroline. Previously Lewis's father had a store begun about 1743 across the street at the present library.

Washington visited his mother as often as he could at 1200 Charles,* the last time in 1789 just before his inauguration. Her boxwoods and sundial are still in her yard. Presidential visits to Mary's home include **Monroe** and **Cleveland.** Although there is no proof or documentation, tradition says **Washington** bought St. James* at 1300 Charles for her, but she refused to live there. He dined at St. James on August 7, 1770.

Several sites on the interesting local tour are now thought to be in error. **Washington** used the office, pharmacy, and library at Hugh Mercer's Apothecary Shop, but not the shop* now open at Caroline and Amelia. That structure was a merchant's house and store, not Mercer's, which was actually one-half block north on same side of Caroline, near the NW corner with Amelia. An outstanding general and close friend to the first president, Mercer died at the Battle of Princeton.

Washington's diary shows that he frequently ate at the home of his brother Charles, now called the Rising Sun Tavern,* 1306 Caroline between Fauquier and Hawke. Charles's son converted it to a tavern about 1792. **Washington, Monroe,** and others are said to have met here to dine, drink, gamble, and discuss politics, but if so it would have been in a home here, not a tavern. Authors confuse this site with Weedon's Tavern or another tavern on Liberty with the same name. Thus modern footnotes in **Jefferson's** *Memo Book* and other references to 1306 Caroline being the Rising Sun are wrong. **Jefferson** passed through town several times from 1775 through his presidency and stayed at Smith's or Benson's, as Weedon's, the favorite of **Washington,** was variously called. It was recently marked with a sign at the southwest corner showing it was across on the NE corner of William and Caroline. The tavern was also called the Rising Sun, and it would have been here that **Jefferson** stayed. He stayed at Weedon's in January 1777, at the only meeting of the full committee to revise the laws of the Commonwealth. His task on the committee was to write the Virginia Statute of Religious Freedom that he considered one of his three major accomplishments. (The other two were the Declaration of Independence and the establishment of the University of Virginia.) **Jefferson** frequently got his hair cut in town and took the ferry at the foot of Wolfe, established in 1734. He was honored at a public dinner on March 19, 1798, and later July 1, when he was criticized for violating the Sabbath.

Washington, Jefferson, and **Monroe** were frequently at the courthouse. The building is newer, but the location is still on the east side of Princess Anne between George and Hanover. **Jefferson** stayed at Long's Ordinary opposite the courthouse on Caroline.

Washington is sometimes claimed to have been a guest at Federal Hill, Prince Edward, Charlotte, and Hanover (private), claimed to have been scarred in the Revolutionary and Civil Wars and used as a hospital in each. But probably this was constructed after the Revolution and has only Civil War damage from 135 cannon ball hits. The weight of bullets in the plaster of the ceiling almost caused it to fall, and when it was redone 25 baskets full of bullets were found in the attic and walls. Cannon balls are still embedded in the walls, and dried blood can be seen where a Civil War soldier cut himself while breaking a glass frame to steal a picture.

Monroe was born in 1758 about 30 miles east on Va. 205, north of Va. 3 between Oak Grove and Colonial Beach at the head of Monroe Creek. There is a monument on the site with boards nearby marking off the supposed site of the home, near **Washington's** Wakefield. He studied here until age 12, then tramped every day for several

Weedon's tavern site is shown in the background. This was a favorite meeting place for Washington and Monroe and where Jefferson served on a committee to draft the Virginia Statute of Religious Freedom.

miles to nearby Archibald Campbell's school with future Chief Justice John Marshall. It is claimed **Washington** and **Madison** may have attended there, but this does not seem likely.

While practicing law from 1786 to 1790, **Monroe** lived at 301 Caroline (private and not marked), a still imposing home that belonged to his uncle. His first daughter was born here, and **Madison** evidently visited as he passed through town on many occasions to his grandfather's plantation, Williamsburg, and elsewhere. Also on Caroline near **Monroe's** home is a house called the Sentry Box where all presidents from **Washington** through **Buchanan** are claimed to have been honored, but this is in doubt as none, including **Washington**, are documented there.

Monroe's law office* was at 908 Charles. The structure there was open until recent years as "his office," but is now known to date to the nineteenth century. The entrance stone is possibly original. Even though he lived in Charlottesville in the early 1790s he was still working some here when he met **Madison** to go to Congress in 1792. His legal work in the county continued until 1822, and more legal documents were recorded in the courthouse with his signature after he left than while living here. The site is a **Monroe** memorial with memorabilia and the desk where he wrote his inaugural address and other important papers. A young descendant once accidentally knocked it over and discovered a secret compartment with about 250 pieces of correspondence to **Monroe** from many important personalities. **FDR** visited this and other historical sites in 1933.

All presidents mentioned would have known naval hero John Paul Jones's residence on the NE corner of Caroline and Lafayette, dating to 1758. He visited his uncle here as an apprentice to a ship owner and celebrated four birthdays (ages 13, 14, 15, and 27), according to the present owner, an expert on Jones and the house.

The area around Fredericksburg is the most

fought-over on the continent, where 100,000 casualties occurred during the Civil War. The Battle of Fredericksburg in December 1862 was maybe the largest ever fought in the Western Hemisphere in terms of the number of men involved. **Lincoln** made six trips to these areas, visiting hospitals, troops, and various army headquarters by way of nearby Aquia Creek Landing,* marked near the end of Route 630 east of Stafford and located at the end of Virginia Route 608/628 on the Potomac. It can be reached by following signs from I-95 south of Stafford. This was the head of the railroad terminus used earlier by **Taylor** and later by **Grant**. A marker on U.S. 1 just north of Stafford notes the site of the Union Depot. They used the Falmouth Station (site) at Cool Springs Road and Route 218, approximately the site of the Eagles Lodge. **Lincoln's** visits to Falmouth included May 23, 1862, and April 4–10, 1863, and May 7, after the Union defeat at Chancellorsville. He was also at the Aquia Creek Landing to confer with his generals on April 19–20 and November 26–7, 1862, April 19 and May 7, 1863, the site of the longest encampment in our history.

Just across the river from Fredericksburg in Stafford County, west of the Route 3 bridge from downtown, is Chatham* or the Lacy House, dating to 1768, probably the only private house visited by both **Lincoln** and **Washington**. (But see Berkeley above.) A chair here has a silver plaque that says it was used by **Washington**, **Monroe**, **Madison**, and others. The magnificent structure now serves as the headquarters of the National Historical Park. On May 23, 1862, **Lincoln** met here in the morning and returned for dinner in the dining room east of the center hall with General McDowell, several cabinet members, and other generals, one of the largest assemblages of officers in the Civil War. A myth persists that **Washington** courted Martha here, although they were married in 1759. The builder, William Fitzhugh, was a close friend of **Washington**, and they visited each other many times. **Washington** wrote Colonel Fitzhugh: "I have put my legs oftener under your mahogany at Chatham ... and have enjoyed your good dinners, good wines, and good company more than any other." Fitzhugh's daughter married **Washington's** step-grandson, whose daughter married Robert E. Lee. **Jefferson's** *Memorandum Book* notes that he spent all day here on October 27, 1793.

On May 23, 1862, **Lincoln** crossed the river near **Washington's** home at the middle pontoon bridge and rode into Fredericksburg to visit Union headquarters at the Farmer's Bank on the NW corner of Princess Anne and George, pictured at the George Street door on the marker nearby. The mayor declined to communicate with **Lincoln** because he felt the town would not approve. **Davis** is also pictured in a painting inside the bank, passing by on March 22, 1862, on the way to make a speech at the Doswell House, SW corner of 1108 Princess Anne and Lewis. Fredericksburg was the only town visited by both presidents during the Civil War. **Lincoln** took a tour of the town and crossed back probably at the same pontoon site, maybe near the Belmont Mansion,* on Washington Street across the street from Carlton, 501 Melcher Drive, the headquarters of **Hayes**. **Lincoln** is claimed to have stopped at 404 Hanover.

The April 1863 visit was **Lincoln's** longest stay with the army until 1865 and improved troop morale and public confidence by the publicity and mutual devotion shown. The president, Mary, and Tad toured the army near Falmouth beginning April 5, 1863. The Union army camped north of Rte. 218 and west of Route 606 (Ringgold Rd.) at Myers Rd. and Jenny Lynn Road, now a residential addition. A historical marker on the south side of Rte. 218 at Kendalwood Street notes the general area. The **Lincolns** stayed in a tent during the cold weather.

Grant camped at various places around the area to the south and west. One campsite was at Guinea Station near the house,* which **Grant** visited, where Stonewall Jackson died after being shot by his own men during the Battle of Chancellorsville. (The site of his wounding is marked at the visitor's center on Route 3 west of Fredericksburg.) Guinea Station is east of exit 118 off I-95, NW of the Route 606 and Route 2 intersection, and marked as the "Jackson Shrine." Just east at the Route 609/606 intersection is the Motley House, where **Grant** was scolded for allowing his cigar to burn the porch. He and his officers were photographed at the Massaponax Church* at the NW corner of U.S. 1 and 608 directly east of Spotsylvania. Also marked on U.S. 1 is the Mount Carmel Church* in Carmel Church, exit 104, where **Grant** had his headquarters on May 24, 1864. The Wilderness and Spotsylvania Battlefields just west mark the first encounters between Lee and **Grant** with well-marked fields. **Grant** was also photographed at Bethesda Church,* 4.9 miles east on Route 360 from Mechanicsville, seated on a bench outside with his staff.

Other presidential visits to Fredericksburg include **Arthur** at the home of a friend, 623 Caro-

Above and opposite: **Three views of Chatham, the only private home where it can be proved both Washington and Lincoln were entertained. Jefferson and Madison also were here.**

line, now a restaurant known as The Chimneys. **McKinley** was at 401 Hanover when he came to dedicate a monument at the National Cemetery, and at the train station on Caroline in 1899 with former Confederate General Fitzhugh Lee. **Coolidge** dedicated the Battlefield Park, and **FDR** was at the George Washington Inn at 904 Princess Anne, now an office building. **Washington's** brother Samuel had lived on the site.

GORDONVILLE • **Washington**, **Madison**, and **Monroe** were served at the Toliver House, 209 N. Main. **Jefferson** often lodged at the Exchange Hotel* on the eastern end of downtown, on U.S. 33 and 15, as did **Madison** and **Monroe**. **Jefferson** was also at Gordon's Tavern on October 25, 1793. This is on the railroad track at the east side of town. Boswell's Tavern still stands in the town of the same name, five miles south and just east of Route 15 on Route 22, clearly marked and now a private residence on the Spotswood Trail. It hosted **Washington**, **Jefferson**, **Madison**, **Monroe** and a host of British trying to capture Governor **Jefferson**. **Taylor**'s birthplace site is marked three miles west on U.S. 33, as shown above.

HAMPTON ROADS–NORFOLK–FT. MONROE • **Monroe** visited while president in 1819 and dined at 323 Freemason* at Bank Street with Moses Myers and at the Exchange Coffee House. He also visited Portsmouth. **Jackson** visited the Murbaugh home, NW corner of Crawford and London, in 1829, and the Ball House at Crawford and Glasgow in 1833, now moved to 213 Middle Street. **Theodore Roosevelt** was also there. A leading hotel in Portsmouth was the Crawford House, at the NW corner of High and Crawford, where **Van Buren**, **Tyler**, and **Fillmore** were entertained. The National Hotel stood on St. Paul's Blvd. in Norfolk opposite the Courts Building, and hosted **Tyler** in 1859, one of many famous guests.

Lincoln arrived at Fort Monroe* on May 5, 1862. General McClellan was advancing toward Richmond, leaving 78-year-old General John

NATIONAL BANK

HISTORIC DISTRICT
NATIONAL BANK
War Comes to Fredericksburg

Wool in charge here with the army stalled 20 miles away at Yorktown. The Union fleet could not supply it because it would not challenge the Confederate ironclad *Merrimack*, renamed *Virginia*, lurking around Sewell's Point. The Union fleet was immobilized and prevented from using the James River, one of the greatest stalemates in American history. (The U.S. Naval Base is at Sewell's Point now, directly south of Fort Monroe and Fort Wool at the NW point of land.) While here, **Lincoln** stayed in Quarters No. 1,* an imposing building still opposite the East Gate on Bernard Road. The marker there shows that later Presidents **Grant**, **Hayes**, **Garfield**, and **Arthur** were entertained. **Hayes** stayed at the Princess Anne Hotel in Virginia Beach in 1892 near where the senior **Bush** lived in 1945.

On the first morning of the visit, **Lincoln** and cabinet secretaries Chase and Stanton rowed to Old Point Comfort Wharf (no longer there) near the lighthouse in constant use since 1802, east of the fort. (The Jamestown settlers landed here in 1607.) They then toured Ft. Wool and inspected the Sawyer gun. The fort was built on an artificial island after the War of 1812. During his eight-year term **Jackson** considered this, then called Rip Raps and used as a sort of informal summer White House, his favorite vacation spot. He stayed weeks at a time and went every day to the highest point of the rock overlooking the ocean to review mail and discuss matters of state. It is now north of the I-64 tunnel in Chesapeake Bay between Norfolk and Hampton. It is accessible only by water, but easily seen from the ramparts of Ft. Monroe. **Tyler** came here for solitude after his first wife died while he was in office in 1842.

Lincoln took a horseback ride through the ruins of Hampton, and reviewed troops at Camp Hamilton north of Ft. Monroe in Phoebus. The only building **Lincoln** passed that is still standing is St. John's,* dating to 1728 at 100 W. Queen. Hampton, the oldest English-speaking city in the country, was almost totally destroyed by Confederate orders on August 7, 1861, to prevent Union reoccupation. Meeting at Quarters No. 1 on May 8, the president planned Norfolk's liberation.

Lincoln stopped at Fort Monroe on the way to Harrison's Landing* on July 8, 1862, and came to meet **Grant** on July 30 and 31, 1864. On February 3, 1865, **Lincoln** met three Confederate representatives at Fort Monroe aboard the *River Queen* in an effort to establish peace. This Hampton Roads Peace Conference included Confederate Vice President Stephens, a former friend of the president. All three Confederates had opposed secession, but joined their states after they left the Union. No notes were taken, so we have only the recollections to reveal what went on. The *River Queen* was used after the Civil War as an excursion boat, proud of her Lincoln Room, before being destroyed by fire in Washington in 1911.

Fort Monroe was known as the "Gibraltar of Chesapeake Bay." Robert E. Lee was the chief engineer during the construction. His quarters are marked across the road from the Casement Museum.* **Jackson** stayed at the Captain House at Number 47, a part of the same house later occupied by Lee. **Davis** was imprisoned here for five months in what is now part of the museum* on Bernard Road on the west side of the interior of the fort. He was later moved a short distance to Carroll Hall, which stood in the Northwest Bastion, and remained a prisoner for 720 days, without trial. His wife was not allowed to see him for almost a year, and he did not see his four young children, aged ten and younger. Here he was visited by his old friend **Pierce**.

HANOVER • **Washington** passed through on the way to the Yorktown siege and many other times as this was on the stage route from Alexandria to Richmond. He and Lafayette stayed in the Hanover Inn* across from the 1735 Courthouse on current U.S. 301. Patrick Henry had married the owner's daughter and lived there. **Jefferson** also stayed on other occasions. The present inn may incorporate part of the 1733 structure, but dates mostly from the late 1700s and later. **Madison** as a baby went to Hanover Parish Church, off 301 at 9415 Kings Highway in King George's County, and later campaigned at the Courthouse.

HARRISONBURG AREA • The red brick house on the north side of Route 782 across a short bridge to the west of Route 42 is the site of the Bryan Cabin used by **Washington** in 1784 as he was returning from the Ohio Valley. The site lies on the road from Brock's Gap and the crossing of Linville Creek. **Lincoln's** ancestors lived and are

***Opposite:* Lincoln tried to meet the mayor of Fredericksburg, Virginia, at the Farmer's Bank where he met the Union Commander, but the mayor refused. Davis is pictured here riding in front later in the only city visited by both presidents during the war.**

buried north at Edom and his father was born nearby. **Polk** and **Van Buren** stayed at the Lincoln Inn in Lacey Springs on U.S. 11 in 1848.

Hot Springs/Warm Springs • These communities are in the center of an area of various warm springs where early resorts still continue to be popular. The Jefferson Pools are marked in Warm Springs, southeast of the Routes 39 and 220 junction, where **Jefferson** visited various times, as did **W. Harrison** and **Monroe**. The Falling Spring Branch Waterfall ten miles west may be the westernmost spot that **Jefferson** visited. He stayed three weeks in 1818 and was at first relieved of his rheumatism, but then developed painful boils attributed to the water, maybe due to other causes such as his rough ride up Warm Springs Mountain to Flat Rock. His portrait is prominently displayed at the Homestead Hotel in Hot Springs with a description of his visits to the area. Also shown in the President's Lounge are portraits of the 22 presidents associated with the hotel, with many photographs. The list includes **Washington, Madison, Van Buren, Tyler, Fillmore, Pierce, McKinley**, and every president since **Taft** (who came to lose 30 pounds for the 1908 election) except the second **Bush** as of 2004. **Wilson** honeymooned here. The hotel dates to 1766 although the structure is more recent.

Leesburg • **Washington** was hosted at a 1761 "ordinary" known by various names at 4 Loudoun Street. He also noted in his journal about staying at Roper's Tavern,* 20 South King, midway between Loudoun and Market, a block south of the courthouse. Drawings on the attic walls are said to have been done by Hessian soldiers imprisoned during the Revolution, but maybe date to the mid–nineteenth century. He is also thought to have made his headquarters during the French and Indian War in the oldest structure in town at 106 S. Loudoun. **Jefferson** stayed at McEntire's (not located) on September 7, 1776, and later as president at Raspberry Plain,* just north on Route 15 near the modern sign of Raspberry Falls residential area.

In 1794 **Monroe** inherited land 12 miles south of here on Route 15. Beginning in 1811 he stayed in a small frame house known as Monroe Cottage, now privately owned, until Oak Hill (private) was built in 1819. This became his principal residence in 1823 for much of his later life. Oak Hill is about a mile north of the U.S. 50 junction, on the west side of U.S. 15, and south of the Little River. He presided as a justice in the prior courthouse* on the present site. It is believed that he drafted speeches at Oak Hill that became known as the Monroe Doctrine. He attended St. James Episcopal * at 14 Cornwall, NW. After his term he retired here, where his wife died in 1830, leaving the home a virtual prison until he moved to New York to be with his daughter. **Quincy Adams's** diary mentions several visits including one with Lafayette on August 6, 1825, when they spent the day in conversation. **Jefferson** and **Madison** would not come then because of the heat. During the visit, Lafayette was honored at a courthouse banquet with **Adams**, who made the famous toast, "To the patriots of the Revolution, like the Sibylline leaves, the fewer they become, the more precious they are." (A popular story is probably not true that the Declaration of Independence and Constitution were hidden from the British in 1814 at 11 Cornwall NW.)

Just southwest of Oak Hill is the town of Middleburg, where **Kennedy** attended church in the community center in 1961 and 1962 while staying at his nearby Atoka farm. He was here during his last weekend, when John Jr. was filmed learning to salute. **Washington** frequently stopped at Chinn's Ordinary, now called the Red Fox Inn at the NE corner of U.S. 50 and Route 626. The building dates to 1728 as part of Lord Fairfax's proprietary. Hickory Hill was once General McClellan's headquarters across the Potomac from McLean, 1147 Chain Bridge Road. JFK owned it from 1953 until his wife lost her baby in 1956, and she convinced her husband to sell to his brother Robert. It is south of Middleburg off Route 58 down 776 to the first crossroads, right to the first estate on the left, to Glen Ora.

Monroe and **John Quincy Adams** shared a room in 1817 at Ludwell Lee's home, Belmont,* now a country club and marked on Route 7, south side about four miles east of Leesburg. **Madison** is said to have taken refuge here when the British burned Washington, although the historical sign does not mention any president. **Harding** was also here.

While Eleanor was away, **FDR** drove several times with her secretary, Lucy Mercer, to see friends at Outlands,* six miles south on U.S. 15 at 20850 Outlands Plantation Lane Road. **Truman** visited General Marshall at his home, Dodonna Manor,* northeast of downtown.

Lexington • A few miles north on Route 11 is the little town of Fairfield that has several eighteenth century houses, including the Albright

Tavern where **Washington** was a guest. While he was here, rain poured through the roof and ruined his new painting as it was being carried home. Natural Bridge* is now a park nearby, from which Rockbridge County gets its name. **Jefferson** bought it in 1774, built a tourist cabin, came frequently including several times in his old age (1815, 1817, and 1821 at least), and called the spot "the most sublime of Nature's works." **Washington** surveyed nearby, and is claimed to have been able to throw a stone from the base to the top, and to have carved his still visible initials twenty-three feet up here and on other rocks in the area. Young **Houston** played here when he visited his cousin nearby. **Davis** brought his children. Also nearby is Steele's Tavern in the town of that name, visited by **Jefferson** in 1767, who also explored numerous caverns in the Blue Ridge. **Houston** was born nearby in 1793, five miles north of Lexington on U.S. 11 opposite the 1756 Timber Ridge Church.*

LYNCHBURG • **Jefferson** crossed the ferry at the foot of Ninth Street as early as 1767. Later he designed and built Poplar Forest* six and a half miles southwest between Routes Bus. 460 and 221, off 661. He inherited the property from his wife and lived here intermittently until his death, moving his furniture back and forth from Monticello. He retreated here after almost being captured by the British at Monticello in 1781. During that visit he was injured falling from a horse and while recuperating wrote his famous *Notes on Virginia* that became one of the most important early books on American history. Later he sought solitude after his wife died. His *Memorandum Book* lists over 700 days here enjoying solitude that he could not get at Monticello. Several rooms were designed for the grandchildren when they visited. The present house was begun in 1806, but was damaged by fire in 1845 and rebuilt slightly altered in appearance.

Jefferson was frequently at the Nickols Tavern* at the SE corner of Eighth and Church (now a B&B) and visited the Miller-Claytor House* on the NE corner. The latter is now in Riverside Park, Ash Street entrance, where it was moved in 1930. Here he demonstrated to the owner's children that the tomato was not poisonous as was popularly believed. The owner of Brown's store, at the NE corner of Seventh and Main, had to write **Jefferson** about his delinquent account. **Jefferson's** *Memorandum Book* shows he ate at Towles Tavern, Main and 12th.

At Poplar Forest on November 4, 1815, **Jefferson** wrote that, "I am at this moment interrupted by a crowd of curious people come to see the house.... I was most agreeably surprised to find that the party whom I thought to be merely curious visitants were General **Jackson** [and company] ... passing on to Lynchburg...." This was after the Battle of New Orleans, fought earlier in the year, and many hoped **Jackson** would be the next president. But the party leadership wanted **Monroe**. **Jackson** and his wife had been staying for several days at the Reid House in Poplar Grove, west of New London and a few miles south of Poplar Forest. Reid was working on a biography of **Jackson**. **Jefferson** and **Jackson** had not met since 1798 and had been estranged since **Jackson**'s 1807 speech on the Richmond State House Green.

Three days later they rode into town together and attended a gathering of about 300. The two presidents were at the courthouse at the same site as now, and came to Bell's Tavern, NE corner across from St. Paul's at Seventh and Main. (**Jefferson** also visited when the tavern moved to Eighth and Madison.) Two seven-year-old boys were almost crushed trying to peer in the window when someone yelled, "What do you want?" They responded that they wanted to see **Jefferson** and **Jackson**. **Jefferson** insisted that they get inside, where they were warmly greeted.

The tavern was not big enough for a large gathering, so the banquet was held at Martin's Warehouse at the NW corner Tenth and Commerce, torn down in 1948. The former president made a toast: "Honor and gratitude to those who have filled the measure of their country's honor." **Jackson** answered with, "**James Monroe**, late Secretary of War." This ended the estrangement. **Jefferson** left before another reception at Bell's.

Jackson also visited his friend Dr. John Cabell on the NE side of Main between Fifth and Sixth, and returned through Lynchburg after visiting **Washington's** tomb. He visited once again his aide Reid, who stayed behind to tend a sick sister. Both the sister and Reid died within a few days, and **Jackson** vowed to find someone to finish the biography and give the proceeds to the Reid family. It was done, and **Jefferson** read the "valuable" book "with great pleasure" in 1817.

During the Civil War, Sandusky, a home on Sandusky Drive, served as headquarters for **Hayes**, **Garfield**, and **McKinley**. They were also at Fort Early, NE Fort and Vermont on Bus. 20.

ORANGE • **Madison's** home was Montpelier,* four miles west and one mile off Va. 20. His first home was a modest wooden house built by his grandfather next to or maybe 200 feet toward the later mansion from the family cemetery on the grounds, where he is buried. During his childhood in the 1750s, Indian attacks were still a real threat. James was the oldest of twelve children who lived in a rugged, utilitarian cabin as the mansion, where he moved at about age ten, was laboriously constructed nearby beginning about 1760. It was continually built in stages until after his death, when the home was lost to the family due to debts incurred by his compulsive gambler stepson, who was in and out of debtors' prison.

Madison's grandmother tutored the future president and taught him to read. From ages 11 to about 15 he boarded with Reverend Robert Innis and attended the Donald Robertson School, where he learned to love the school and teacher. The unmarked spot is believed to be near Newtown, north of the Mattaponi River in King and Queen County, at about where County Roads 625 and 628 meet. Later a graduate of Princeton schooled him at the home. For this reason and the fact that **Madison** did not like the authority of the Anglican Church and felt that the president of William and Mary hoped to be the first American Bishop, he went to Princeton. He returned afterward to tutor his siblings, but was limited by a physical problem, maybe an emotional illness with symptoms resembling epilepsy. Prior to the Constitutional Convention in 1787, he spent many hours in his large library on the second floor studying the history of government and took hundreds of pages of notes in order to learn from past governments' successes and failures. This enabled him to be a leader in the formation of the new government so that he was called the "Father of the Constitution," although many of his ideas were rejected.

Jefferson, a frequent visitor on the way to Monticello, suggested the portico, met **Madison** here so that they could travel to Philadelphia together, came by as vice president to complain about President **Adams,** and stopped as president. **Madison** came home intending to stay after **Jefferson** became vice president, but **Jefferson** came as president-elect to get him back into government and offered him the post of secretary of state.

At 43, the short, shy, and formal **Madison** had married the beautiful, vivacious, and tall 26-year-old, Dolley Payne, "the greatest blessing of my life." **Madison** also used his home as a summer White House. The **Madisons** raced one another on horseback on rainy days when they could not take their long walks around the property. **Monroe** frequently visited. After leaving office **Jefferson** came to Montpelier annually for many years, and liked to eat at Verdier's Ordinary in Orange. It is unclear where that was, as there was a tavern owned by Verdier in the town of the same name a few miles east and also a home in Orange where Verdier lived, Pelisco. That house is still west of Pelisco Street, at the end of Morton. The present courthouse is on the site of Bell's Tavern on Bus. 20, at the NW corner of Madison and Main, which was owned by Verdier. In 1802, **Jefferson** recommended Spring Garden Tavern, now opposite McDonald's Restaurant on the west side of Madison Road near Washington, although the present structure may be c. 1819. **Jackson** visited **Madison** in his sickbed as he ran for president in 1832.

The 20th century Montpelier was an expansion of the home, but it was returned to a more original-like state by "deconstructing" it, beginning in 2004, to its size in **Madison's** era. Having no children of his own he doted over various nieces and nephews who stayed there. Like the homes of the other plantation presidents, this became almost like a tavern, where Dolley sometimes fed as many as 90 at a time. Lafayette spent four days in 1824 and drew plans for the formal garden.

In **Madison's** childhood the big event of the week was attending the Brick Church in the area to the south side of U.S. 20 between Co. 612, 631, and 629, three miles southeast of the courthouse. The courthouse that **Madison** knew was just west of the present train station, converted into a visitor center, as shown on the historical marker on Main Street, east of the present courthouse. Lawyers **Jefferson** and **Monroe** were on the Courthouse site. It was here that **Madison** spoke when he ran for various offices. In 1788 he ran for the first Congress against his friend **Monroe,** who was strongly sponsored by Virginia's greatest orator, Patrick Henry. **Monroe** and Henry opposed the new Federal Constitution. **Madison** barely won, due to a large majority in his home county, and ensured by his standing at the courthouse greeting voters in such bitterly cold weather that he reportedly got frostbite. He visited his favorite brother, Ambrose, and favorite niece at Woodley, three miles south on the west side of U.S. 15 at the eastern edge of his property. The 1783 mansion is several hundred yards west of the highway and marked by a white sign. **Madison's** Oak, where the president tied his horse, is still in front. Ambrose was **Washington's** paymaster.

James and his mother were both hypochondriacs, and he refused some possible political appointments, thinking his life was limited. His mother lived here until age 98, and he inherited the property from her in 1801. After his presidency, **Madison** never ventured beyond his "neighborhood," here and Charlottesville, except to go to Richmond once in 1829. He died here at 85 on June 28, 1836, the last of the Founding Fathers, and his tomb is on the grounds. He refused stimulants to preserve his life until July 4, so as to die on this important date, as had **Adams**, **Jefferson**, and **Monroe**. His important notes on the Constitutional Convention were not to be released until the last signer died; that turned out to be him. Crop failure and an extravagant, irresponsible stepson ruined the plantation. The land and much of the furnishings were sold, but it is now furnished with some of his possessions and opened by the National Trust for Historic Preservation. Behind the house is a large, virgin forest claimed the largest in the east, and with over 100 trees dated to **Madison's** residency. **Hayes** made a speech at the grave in 1878.

Taylor went to his grandfather's church, St. Thomas Episcopal, at 119 Caroline, when he visited. He and **Madison** had the same great-grandfather. Lee camped on site during the Civil War, and **Davis** worshipped inside. The church is now next to the Madison Museum.* **Hoover**'s retreat, Camp Rapidan, was northwest, now in Shenandoah National Park, west of Criglersville.

PETERSBURG • The town brochure shows **Taft** dedicating the Pennsylvania Monument and states that he is the fifth president in town, following **Washington**, **Jefferson**, **W.H. Harrison**, and **Lincoln**. But they are not the only ones to come here. **Washington** was never documented at Golden Ball Tavern, SE Grove and North Market Streets, as claimed, or at the brother's tavern across the street, where he was supposed to have eaten during his 1791 visit. He was in town once, and maybe no more. The mayor is said to have coined the title "father of his country" at a public dinner for **Washington** in 1791 at the Armistead Tavern on Sycamore Street, west side just south of Tabb near the Civil War — era City Hall, although the term had been used many times before. He was also honored then at Mason's Hall in Blandford on Old River Street, now NW corner of Miller and Old Church (formally River) Streets, and noted in his diary that 60–70 ladies were present. He was back to Armistead's overnight and was asked when he would leave the next morning so that he could receive a cavalry escort. His diary admits that he purposely misled when he told them "before 8:00," although he actually left at 5:00 to avoid the annoying escort and dust they created. So much for **Washington** never telling a lie.

Nothing documents **Jefferson** in town, but he is thought to have visited the theater then on Grove Street, midway between Market and Cross Streets, as he wrote that he was coming. He also signed some important personal papers concerning Richard Hanson in March 1791, maybe in Petersburg, as he visited Eppington and Richmond on the way to assume his duties as secretary of state. When Lafayette toured the country in 1824 he was received at Niblo's Tavern at the NE corner of Second and Bollingbrook. He had battled the traitor Benedict Arnold here in 1781 and then Cornwallis on the way to Yorktown. **Washington** and **Jefferson** were both at Halfway House,* still a restaurant halfway between Richmond and Petersburg on U.S. 1 and 301, 10301 Jefferson Davis Highway. **Grant** and others were known to have been there. Another famous tavern is marked at the southwest corner of Washington and Union, known at various times as Moss's, the Railroad Tavern, or Albemarle. **Polk** (May 28, 1847) and **Grant** stayed there. **Davis** accompanied John C. Calhoun's body to St. Paul's at 110 N. Union, where Lee worshipped during the Civil War siege and where his son was later married in 1867.

Petersburg was a major railroad and supply center and was the headquarters of Robert E. Lee's army for more than nine months as **Grant** laid siege, surrounded, and cut off the town. When **Grant** captured the last supply line feeding Petersburg and Richmond, Lee evacuated on April 2, 1865. The next day **Lincoln**, Tad, and party came by way of Hancock Station, the Jerusalem Plank Road, and Fort Mahone,* where they stopped and observed many dead bodies on the recent battlefield. (This fort is on the park tour, just southwest of the junction of Routes 301-A and 301, South Boulevard and Sycamore Street.) The Union flag was seen on the old courthouse* on the way to **Grant's** temporary headquarters at the Wallace House, 204 S. Market Street, on the SW corner with Brown Street, still standing, as are many homes from the period. There is some question as to whether they entered the home or just stayed on the porch where **Lincoln** remained an hour and a half, and then went on a tour of the devastated city.

He returned with Mary and Tad on April 7, and stopped at headquarters in Center Hill,* a brick mansion on the north side of Franklin between Jefferson and Adams. **Taft** was photographed on the front porch. **Tyler** was probably here and maybe **W. Harrison. Grant** ate at Jarratt's Hotel after the war, SW corner of Union and Washington, at the Southern Depot. **Davis** passed through to assume his presidency. The city hall, c. 1859, was Confederate headquarters.

The Petersburg National Battlefield surrounds the town on the east and south. All of the forts mentioned above are on the National Park Tour map. **Lincoln's** presence on the battlefield is mainly described in the entry on nearby City Point.

Port Conway, Port Royal • **Madison** was born in 1751 just northwest of the Port Conway bridge in the home of his paternal grandfather, Belle Grove or Conway House (private, marked on the highway), about 400 yards down a tree-lined dirt road. He was the oldest of twelve children. **Washington** crossed the ferry here at least eleven times. (Dates of **Washington's** eleven crossings are in *Historic Northern Neck of Virginia*, page 13, which also lists **Washington's** visits to the Conway House.) John Wilkes Booth crossed during his escape. Just across the bridge, Port Royal has several marked colonial-era homes including the Fox Tavern, near the NW corner of Water and King Streets, where **Washington** stayed twice. The town had been earlier considered for the site of the national capital.

Richmond and Area • All presidents have been to Richmond except possibly the **Adamses, Arthur, Pierce**, and **Buchanan. Jefferson** lived and was educated with his Randolph cousins from 1745 to 1752 at Tuckahoe,* 13 miles west and just south of Va. 650, River Road, in Goochland County. It is at the Henrico County boundary on the north side of the James River, just west of Tuckahoe Creek, the county line. A marker on the south side of Va. 650 directs you down a straight road to the old home at the first turn, about a mile south. The little schoolhouse in the east front yard is marked as the building

Grant and Lincoln met on the porch of this Petersburg home when the president visited his general after the Confederate army fled.

where **Jefferson** attended school from 1748 to 1752. He did not like school and sometimes skipped. **Washington** also visited Tuckahoe, one of the best-preserved Virginia plantations, as did British Lord Cornwallis during the Revolution.

Jefferson's father had promised his close friend William Randolph that he would move to the large estate with his family if Randolph died with young children. He died at age 33, so **Jefferson's** family then lived in his house, and Peter Jefferson raised Randolph's kids as well as his own. Since Peter's mother was a Randolph, the children were cousins. Fortunately the "H"-shaped house could accommodate separate families. There were hundreds of slaves, and blacks outnumbered whites by at least ten to one. It is taken for granted that black children of both sexes were among Jefferson's youngest friends, but everyone knew they obeyed and were not schooled.

When Thomas was nine, his father felt that the Randolph children were old enough to be on their own more and moved back to the family home near Charlottesville. Shortly the boy was sent to Dover Church five miles away from Tuckahoe for a classical education with Reverend William Douglass in Northam. We know nothing of the next five years, mostly because letters and records were lost in the fire that destroyed their home. It is assumed that he returned home for three or four months each year. **Jefferson** revisited Tuckahoe all of his life, including on trips to and from Williamsburg and Richmond, his honeymoon, and in 1790 to try to convince his boyhood friend and brother-in-law, Thomas Mann Randolph, to sell Edge Hill to his son and **Jefferson's** son-in-law. In 1781 he sent his family to Tuckahoe in relative safety as traitor Benedict Arnold was ravishing the area, and fled here himself as the British neared Richmond.

Jefferson is thought to have been familiar with Richmond from an early age when he came while living nearby. He later owned property on the south side of Cary between 14th and 15th Streets and on the north side of Broad between 29th and 30th Streets. In 1767 he dined at Cowley's near the courthouse, then at the SW corner of Main and 23rd, and Vaughn's on the NW corner of Main and 19th. This had been Benedict Arnold's headquarters when he invaded.

On March 23, 1775, the Virginia Convention met in St. John's Church,* Broad Street and 24th Streets, Richmond's largest building, to discuss problems and approve measures of the Continental Congress. It had convened away from the capital in Williamsburg without the consent of the royal governor, who frequently dissolved the House of Burgesses or legislature when he did not like their uppity attitude. The royal governor had just harangued them when he learned of their plan to boycott British goods. **Jefferson** made his first public speeches here. One of the few he ever made supported Patrick Henry, who stood before **Washington**, **Jefferson**, and most of the leading figures in Virginia to make his famous challenge, "Give me liberty or give me death." There was disagreement as to whether to put the colony in a state of defense. Henry won over the leadership stating, "The war is actually begun! The next gale that sweeps from the north will bring to our ears the clash of resounding arms! Our brethren are already in the field! Why stand we here idle?" The first shots of the Revolution actually occurred less than a month later on April 19, in Massachusetts.

Jefferson's teacher and **Washington's** host, George Wythe, is buried in the churchyard, a probable victim of poisoning by his grandnephew upset at seeing Wythe change his will to leave property to a mulatto, possibly Wythe's son. (Wythe lived long enough to disinherit the nephew.) A slave witness probably could have secured a criminal conviction, but blacks were forbidden to testify in court. Wythe had lived at 503 E. Grace, where he was visited by **Madison**, **Jefferson**, and probably **Monroe**. **Madison** attended St. John's later as a member of the legislature, as did **Monroe** in 1782.

Jefferson was familiar with Richmond Hill House at the SW corner of 22nd and Grace. The owner believed that **Jefferson** would use his influence to put the Capitol Building there or in the vicinity, but it was built on the site of the home of another friend of **Jefferson's**, James Gunn, where **Jefferson** had stayed in earlier years. In early 1778 **Jefferson** stayed with his friend James Currie opposite the present city hall on Broad near Tenth.

After the capital was moved inland to Richmond in 1780 during the Revolution, **Jefferson** lived as governor on the brow of Capitol Hill, probably northeast or southeast of the present Governor's Mansion on Governor (12th) Street, south of (old) Capitol Street. The former marker at the mansion, listing **Jefferson** as having lived on the spot, is probably an error, but his rented residence was close, as were the homes of all governors before the present brick mansion in Capitol Square was authorized in 1811 and occupied in 1813. (The private house occupied by **Jefferson** was probably south of the present mansion, at the

Several presidents have lived in the Governor's Mansion in Richmond, Virginia, on or near the site of the current 1813 Mansion (Jefferson, Monroe, William Henry Harrison, Tyler), and many others have visited.

imaginary intersection of Franklin and 12th Streets if they reached that far. There is a possibility it was on a corner of Broad and Governor.) Eight-year-old **William Henry Harrison** lived in the "Governor's Mansion," an unpretentious wooden structure that was rented when his father was governor six months after **Jefferson**. The dwelling was soon purchased by the state for a governor's residence. When the senior Harrison left the governor's office, he ran for the legislature and was defeated by the senior John Tyler. **Washington** ate at this wooden mansion in 1791. Future president **John Tyler Jr.** was with his father in the old mansion from 1809 until 1811 and later in the present brick mansion when he himself was governor from 1825 to 1827. In 1809, Governor **Tyler** honored **Jefferson** at the dilapidated "mansion" with the 19-year-old future president making the arrangements. The senior Tyler resigned to accept a federal judgeship, and **Monroe** was selected as governor. So four occupants of the various mansions in a fairly short time were future presidents, two as governor and two as sons of the governor.

The old wooden mansion was rapidly deteriorating so that Governor **Monroe** in his second term refused to stay, moving probably to Ninth and Marshall. **Monroe** was governor twice, from 1799 to 1802 and in 1811, when he resigned to become secretary of state, leading to his election as president. The marker shows that England's Edward VII, Winston Churchill, **Hayes, Cleveland, McKinley, Theodore Roosevelt**, and **Taft** have been entertained in the current mansion on the same site.

The temporary Capitol Buildings were at the foot of Council Hill on 14th at the NW corner of Cary, where a marker on the corner and a large sign on a building by the parking lot note the site. Recent research shows that the government met in two adjacent buildings on this corner facing 14th. The House of Delegates (**Madison, Mon-**

roe) and Governor's Council (**Monroe**) met in a warehouse there. **Monroe** and **Madison** were opposing leaders in the 1788 Virginia Ratification Convention in the Quesnay Academy on Academy Square, 12th Street between Broad and Marshall. This is said to have been the most distinguished body ever to meet in Virginia. Those opposed to ratification of the proposed Federal Constitution included a future president, **Monroe**, and the fathers of two others, **Harrison** and **Tyler**. **Monroe** had been hurt not to have been chosen to attend the Constitutional Convention in Philadelphia, but many thought he was too poor to be able to afford to pay his way. He and others feared that the proposed government would destroy their newly found freedoms. **Madison** argued for it against such Virginia giants as George Mason and Patrick Henry. The new federal government would not be a lasting entity without the critical support of the largest and most populous state. Those against the Constitution wanted another to be drafted and with added amendments. **Madison's** side won, and he ran for the first Congress with his friend **Monroe** opposing him, debating different sides of the ratification issue in various counties. **Madison** won, but the state Senate later elected **Monroe** to the United States Senate in 1790. **Monroe** wanted to run for president in 1808, but did not out of respect for his friend **Madison,** supported by **Jefferson**. He then practiced law in Richmond.

In the 1770s **Jefferson** frequented Hogg's Tavern, on the SW corner of 15th and Main, to plan the new capital. In 1780 he was at Formicola's Tavern on the south side of Main between 15th and 17th Streets. **Madison** and **Monroe** boarded there from 1782 to 1784 when they were in the House of Delegates, and **Monroe** was on the Governor's Council which had to approve every act of the governor, who was powerless otherwise. At that time the council met in a rented brick building at the top of Council Hill, east of the wooden Governor's Mansion.

Madison served here in the legislature from 1784 until 1788. **Jefferson** met Lafayette for the first time in the spring of 1781 as the general met the governor to protect the capital. Traitor Benedict Arnold occupied Richmond in January. When another British force was threatening in April the Assembly voted on May 10, 1781, to go to Charlottesville with the governor having expanded powers before the arrival of an even larger army under General Cornwallis. But **Jefferson's** term officially ended June 1. He resigned and then left town, but was still considered governor when almost captured at Monticello a few days later. **Jefferson** probably hid property at Belvedere, near Belvedere and China Streets. Since the government had no permanent buildings, Arnold had earlier missed the temporary structures used by the assembly and council as well as **Jefferson's** rented quarters. **Jefferson** was later elected to the House of Delegates in 1782, but declined to serve due to the illness of his wife, who died in September.

In 1788 the new State Capitol* on Shockoe Hill was occupied although uncompleted. This was the first building designed for a modern republican government and had to have a monumental setting. **Jefferson** recommended a Classical design based on the Maison Carree in Nimes, France. He believed that the intact Roman temple he had admired was "Unsurpassed among monuments of Greece and Rome." He had earlier seen the original in France and an exact replica on his English tour to Stowe Gardens with **Adams.** **Washington** visited the Capitol in 1791, his last visit to Richmond. His life-size statue, placed in the rotunda in 1796, maybe America's most valuable art object, is the only one of the first president modeled from life as the artist spent two weeks at Mt. Vernon. Jefferson saw the still incomplete Capitol for the first time in 1799. **Madison, Monroe**, and **Tyler** served in the legislature in the present building. The office where **Monroe** and **Tyler** met with their Governor's Council was on the third floor above and to the left of main front entrance. Governor **Tyler** was speaking at the Capitol eulogizing **Jefferson** when, as he concluded, a note about **Adams's** death arrived. He paused, composed himself, and eulogized **Adams** extemporaneously before the stunned audience.

The Old House Chamber has always been in the same place and is now a museum. Former vice president Aaron Burr was tried for treason here in 1807 with supporter **Jackson** in attendance. Robert E. Lee's statute dominates the room at the position where he accepted command of Virginia's troops at the beginning of the Civil War. The State Constitutional Convention, meeting here in 1829 and 1830, with **Madison**, **Monroe**, and **Tyler** in attendance, was called the "last meeting of the giants." The convention shifted to the First African Church at Broad and College, where **Davis**, on February 6, 1865, rejected **Lincoln's** demands to restore the Union and predicted Confederate victory. The Confederate vice president thought the speech was "brilliant," but

The Virginia Capitol has been visited by most presidents beginning with Washington, including Lincoln. It was designed by Jefferson, and was the Confederate Capitol.

"demented." The Supreme Court met in the front hall of the Capitol until about 1840, when they switched with the Senate, which had been meeting over the House. That room is now inaccessible to the public tours. **Monroe** alternated Episcopal and Presbyterian services in the Old Hall of Delegates from 1799 until 1802 and in 1811 when he was governor.

From 1809 to 1811, **Tyler** studied law at 1002 Capitol under Edmund Randolph. He was in the legislature starting at age 21 from 1811 to 1816, 1823 to 1825, and 1838 to 1840, and served as governor, meeting with the council in an office on the third floor of the Capitol, from 1825 to 1827. He later served as a member of the Confederate Congress here. Other presidents to visit the Capitol include **Van Buren** (1822), **Taylor, Polk, Fillmore**, both **Johnsons, Grant**, and **Reagan**. Van Buren wanted to see the famous Natural Bridge, but had such a good time in town that he did not make other visits. **Wilson** and **Eisenhower** gave speeches before their presidential terms.

In 1784 **Jefferson** and Lafayette had dinner in Bell's Tavern, later called City Hotel, East Main in Shockoe District below 15th. **Washington** was often there and visited the state buildings at 14th and Cary. **Jefferson** also stayed at Richmond Tavern, SW corner of Main and 23rd, and at the Swan Tavern. **Washington** stayed at the Swan, NW corner of Broad and Ninth, and visited the old State House, and also the Old Stone House,* 1914 E. Main, now Edgar Allan Poe's shrine. It was claimed to be a tavern at one time, visited by **Jefferson. Monroe** boarded there while attending the 1788 Virginia Convention. **TR** visited it in 1905.

Washington addressed the city council at city hall. He attended a ball at the Masonic Hall* at 1805 Franklin and noted in his diary "60 or 70 ladies," but did not mention any men. In his 1791 southern tour, he stayed with Colonel Edward Carrington at NW Marshall and 11th and ate at the Eagle Tavern at the SE corner of Main and 12th. **Jefferson** was entertained there June 5, 1794;

March 4, 1805; and October 21, 1809. In 1794 **Jefferson** took the only journey of consequence between his cabinet days and vice presidency and came to the Eagle and City Taverns. On October 9, 1809, **Jefferson** was entertained at Swan's and Vaughn's or City Tavern at the NE corner of Main and 19th, also called Galt's. **Washington** and **Tyler** also stayed here.

Jefferson visited the half-sister of his wife at Eppington, west of Tuckahoe on Route 664, four and a half miles from the Chesterfield-Amelia County line, Appomattox River at Winterpock Creek, near Lake Cheslin. **Jefferson's** daughter, Lucy, died in here in 1785 and is probably buried here. **Jefferson** visited upon his return from France, when he probably learned that **Washington** wanted him as the first secretary of state.

Washington and **Jefferson** stayed at Wilton,* now at the end of Wilton Road off 5400 Cary Road, having been moved in 1934 from the north side of the James southeast from Richmond. The original location is noted by Virginia marker V-1 on Route 5, two miles south of Richmond, five miles away. **Washington** was a guest during the March 1775 Virginia Convention. His presumed bedroom is called the "Washington Room." Ampthill is nearby and marked in the 5100 block of Cary Road, at Ampthill Road that forks several blocks south where the left or east extension dead-ends into the home. **Washington** stayed when it was located downstream in Chesterfield County on the south side of the James in the village of Warwick. It was moved in 1929. A marker (S-3) on U.S. 1 less than a mile south of Richmond notes the original site. **Jefferson** visited several times and took his children for a smallpox vaccination in late 1782.

Forty-five miles west of Richmond is another pre-revolutionary Ampthill, also associated with **Jefferson**, sometimes spelled without the "t," on a road with the same name at the James and Willis Rivers, three miles north of Route 45 on Route 602 west of Carterville, Cumberland County. That original house was begun in 1732 with Jeffersonian additions. On the opposite side of the James River on a bluff nearby was another house owned by **Jefferson** known as Elk Hill, southwest of George's Tavern, 1.7 miles south of Route 6, on 608 or Elk Hill Road, and west of the Routes 6/45 intersection on the James River and Byrd Creek opposite Elk Island. He had purchased this second home and hunting lodge in 1778, and was here on his honeymoon. In June 1781, Cornwallis set out west of Richmond with units led by Colonel Tarleton to capture the Virginia Assembly and Governor **Jefferson**. Cornwallis made his headquarters in the home, tore it up, destroyed the barns, and took all the corn and livestock, except horses that were killed as too young for service. **Jefferson** visited soon thereafter and lamented over the thirty slaves carried off, not that he lost them, but that most if not all died. Nothing is here now.

Jefferson may have visited John Marshall at his house 818 E. Marshall Street* as claimed, but this is doubted as the president and chief justice hated each another. Marshall's cousin **Madison** and **Monroe** visited in 1784. Marshall has been called the most important American never president.

Former governors and presidents **Monroe** and **Tyler** are buried a few feet apart in Hollywood Cemetery,* just west of downtown at Cherry and Albemarle Streets. Their graves are high on the southern side on Hillside Avenue where President's Circle is formed with Oak Avenue. **Davis** is buried at the far western end where Waterview Avenue forms Davis Circle.

W.H. Harrison was an apprentice in 1790 for a physician at 18th and Franklin, and later in 1836 stayed on the SE corner of Broad and 11th at the Powhatan House, as did **Fillmore** in 1851. It was later known as Ford's Hotel and was east of the present city hall and north of the Governor's Mansion. President **Tyler** brought his first wife's body here, where he stayed often. He was frequently at the Union Hotel at the SE corner of 19th and Main. **Taylor** and **Fillmore** stayed here when **Taylor** came to dedicate the cornerstone of the equestrian Washington statue on the Capitol grounds in 1850. **Jackson** was here in 1807 for Aaron Burr's trial as a witness and stayed at the Eagle Tavern. He denounced **Jefferson** from the Capitol steps as not being forceful enough on British "outrages" on America.

The Union occupied the capital of the Confederacy on April 3, 1865. **Lincoln** was visiting General **Grant** nearby at City Point, and came to see the city with son Tad on his twelfth birthday, April 4. At Drewry's Bluff* below the city, a line of obstructions prevented the passage of their ships. This is just east of the Turnpike and accessible from Routes 1 and 301 via State 656, Bellwood Street, about four miles south of Route 150. They then proceeded by a shallow-draft barge pulled by a tug that ran aground at Rocketts Landing, about where 31st and Main meet the James River. (**Davis** landed here in 1867 on the way from prison at Fort Monroe to trial.) From there the oars were used to drive the barge, which landed about a hundred yards from Libby Prison. The infamous prison was at the SE corner of Cary and 20th Streets. **Lincoln** recognized it from many pictures he had observed. (After the war Libby was torn down and rebuilt for the World Fair in Chicago. A facade is now in the Chicago Historical Society.)

Lincoln walked up 19th, Main, 17th and Broad to the railroad station, and climbed the hill into the main business section. The crowd included some whites, including a lady draped in an American flag at the Spotswood Hotel, SW corner of Eighth and Main. **Davis** had stayed and made speeches from the balcony of Richmond's finest hotel. **Grant** and **Johnson** stayed in 1867 when it was one of the few hotels operating. **Davis** had headquarters and private rooms when he moved to Richmond as Confederate president for his first two months, and stayed in the same rooms when he returned during his incarceration while his trial for treason was being considered. **Lincoln** is also stated to have been by the Exchange Hotel at the SE corner of 14th and Franklin, where **Tyler** had lived. **Taylor** came there in 1850, as did **Hayes** in 1877. **Lincoln** passed by the Ballard House on the NE corner, where **Tyler** died during the war waiting to take his seat in the Confederate Congress. (It is sometimes stated that **Tyler** died at the Exchange, but this is not believed correct. The confusion may be because the Ballard and Exchange Hotels were connected by a second-floor passage over the street.)

After about an hour of chaos and potential disaster, a squad of Union horsemen cleared the streets, and **Lincoln** proceeded, with Tad clinging, up 12th, past the Capitol and Governor's Mansion to **Davis's** home, now occupied by Union General Godfrey Weitzel. They entered the Confederate White House,* 12th and Clay, now adjacent to the Confederate Museum,* and turned right from the hallway into a reception room on the west corner. He did not know that on the east side was the site of the balcony from which **Davis's** favorite son, Joseph, age five, fell to his death less than a year before. **Davis's** grief had equaled **Lincoln's** at the death of his favorite, Willie. Joe is buried with his father in Hollywood Cemetery shown above. **Davis** removed the balcony a few months afterwards. **Van Buren** had visited the former owner in 1822.

Lincoln met with Federal officers in the far right-hand corner room, sat in **Davis's** armchair still here, and correctly stated that the chair must have been "President **Davis's**," the only known time he referred to **Davis** as "president." A few days later **Johnson** and then Mary Lincoln toured the residence where her seamstress and friend, Elizabeth Keckley, enjoyed sitting in Mr. **Davis's** chair. A former slave, she had previously been seamstress for Mrs. **Davis**. About 80 percent of the original furniture remains. They toured the house and ate in the reception room. It is possible that **Lincoln** went above the first floor, but upper stories were generally private, although **Davis** did have an office there since he worked at home due to poor health. Here still is the oval table where **Davis** met with Lee, Jackson, and others. Afterward **Lincoln** received several prominent Confederate leaders including Judge John A. Campbell, the Confederate assistant secretary of war, now pale and haggard. He had appeared dignified and tall when he met with **Lincoln** a few weeks before at Hampton Roads to discuss a possible end to the war.

From there the party rode in an army hack through the city past St. Paul's Episcopal,* SW corner of Ninth and Grace, where **Davis** and Lee worshipped, and **Tyler's** funeral was held. **Davis** was confirmed here at age 53 and had to leave during the middle of the last Sunday's service upon getting an urgent message from Lee that he could no longer hold the Union troops. His pew, number 63, not quite midway down the center aisle, right side, can still be seen and used. Robert E. Lee and family used number 111, one row in front and to the left of **Davis. Andrew Johnson** came as president later. **Eisenhower** attended in 1954.

Lincoln then entered the Capitol grounds opposite the church, and stopped before the bronze equestrian statute of George Washington under which **Davis** had been sworn in as president of the Confederate States. President **Taylor** had dedicated the cornerstone with former President **Tyler**, Vice President **Fillmore**, Lee, and Stonewall Jackson present. **Davis** had walked by it every day on his way to and from his office. **Lincoln** then briefly toured the abandoned and desecrated State House, also the Confederate Capitol, without any recorded comment. He walked past the famous **Washington** statue in the rotunda at the north end of the hall where Virginia delegates met to consider secession and the Confederate Provisional Congress met in 1861. Generals Jackson and Jeb Stuart had lain in state in the Hall of Congress at the south end of the Capitol. **Davis** would later lie in state in the rotunda.

When Lincoln toured the Richmond Capitol after the Confederate evacuation, he saw what is now considered America's most valuable art object, Washington's statue from life.

The legislative chamber then extended into the present hallway since the building had no side wings, front door, or steps as now.

Lincoln also visited **Davis's** office in the government offices directly across on Bank Street, the current Federal Courthouse and post office, across from the front of the Capitol. This 1858 structure was one of the few that escaped the Evacuation Fire of 1865 that destroyed over 900 buildings in the business district. Before the war it was the U.S. Customhouse, and listed on Main between 10th and 11th Streets. **Davis's** second-floor office faced Eleventh on the east side. He was later brought back here in 1867 and 1868 to face charges of treason. A marker is on the north side of the building, which has been subsequently enlarged many times. **Lincoln** then proceeded through fashionable residential districts and part of the business section to Castle Thunder Prison (north side of Cary Street between 18th and 19th Streets) and Libby Prison, boarded tugs that carried them to the *Malvern,* Admiral Porter's ship, which had made its way past the obstructions and was now anchored at Rocketts.

Davis's first public speech after the Civil War was at the First Presbyterian Church where he received "a Storm of applause." **Grant** did not make it to Richmond until 1867 when he came with **Johnson.** Both visited the city hall on Broad Street and 12th, which was torn down in 1874. The Jefferson Hotel* at 101 W. Franklin hosted **Benjamin Harrison**, **McKinley**, **Wilson**, **Coolidge**, **Taft**, **Truman**, **Carter**, and **Reagan**, as well as both **Roosevelts**. **Bush** and **Clinton** debated at the Robins Center at the University of Richmond in 1992. **TR** spoke to Confederate veterans by the statue as well as Lee's statue on Monument Avenue.

SPERRYVILLE • Two **Washington** sites are located here on the eastern side of Thornton Gap. The young surveyor stayed in Thornton Hill, now on Route 522, and then later when it was owned by his aunt. Relatives also owned another property built by Thornton, Montpelier, off Route 231.

Stanton • **Jefferson** practiced law, attended court, and conferred with attorneys and clients in the seat of the nation's then largest county, extending to North Carolina and the Mississippi River. The present courthouse* is at the same site as then, Johnson and Augusta Streets. About the only known story of his circuit-riding days involves John Madison, who nurtured **Jefferson** and went with him on his trips. One night they were near the courthouse watching several men play cards by torchlight. Madison and **Jefferson** used two powder horns to secretly drop powder around the players, making a trail they lit, causing some amount of surprise and panic.

Pierce made a speech in August 1854 and a year later at the Virginia Hotel at the railroad tracks on S. New Street. He was on the way through with his wife, who was finally able to take a vacation, having recovered from sickness and depression after their last son died just before his inauguration. The Washington House was on this site earlier and is said to have hosted **Jefferson**, **Madison**, and **Fillmore**. In one of **Jefferson's** last trips he stayed with Archibald Stuart on Church Street.

Wilson was born in 1856 at Presbyterian Manse* at 24 North Coalter (Highway 11) and Frederick. The family moved about a year later, but **Wilson** came back after his election in 1912. The site of their church, where his father was pastor, is on the north side of Frederick about 200 feet west of Coalter. It can be seen out the back portico of the Manse marked in red bricks on the campus of Mary Baldwin College, where **Ike** visited in 1960. The church fell down as it was bringing expanded. **Coolidge** visited it in 1928, and **FDR** dedicated the birthplace site in 1941.

Tappahannock • **Washington** stopped between Mt. Vernon and Williamsburg, at Webb's Tavern. In his youth and manhood, he frequently visited Naylor's Hole directly north across the Rappahannock River at what is now Naylor's Beach at Routes 634 and 636. He is claimed to have visited sweetheart Betsy Fauntleroy at the home.

Waynesboro • **Jefferson** and **Madison** met in 1818 at the Old Mountaintop Tavern to decide the location of the University of Virginia. (Some sources falsely claim **Monroe** was also here.) This is now at about the site of the Howard Johnson Hotel at I-64 and the Blue Ridge Parkway. The exact site of the much-bulldozed area cannot be specifically identified. **Jefferson's** *Memo Book* shows that he came through Rockfish Gap here several times and was entertained at various taverns on both sides of the Gap. **Coolidge** liked to come to the Swannanoa Country Club nearby and stayed at the Swannanoa Mansion* also just off the Parkway.

Williamsburg • Almost every building in the vast historic area, including 88 original colonial structures and numerous other reconstructions, has associations with our colonial heritage and the early Virginia presidents. And virtually all presidents have been there, at least since **TR**. **Jefferson** called it "Devilsburg," but lived, studied, and worked here for fifteen years. **FDR** opened the restored historical street and town in 1934.

At the west end of Duke of Gloucester Street is the c. 1699 Wren Building* of William and Mary College, the oldest college building in America, where **Jefferson**, **Monroe**, and **Tyler** went to school and **Jefferson** may have lived as a student. **Washington** was chancellor for eleven years. **Jefferson** worked on plans to extend the building, but work stopped when the capital moved to Richmond. The early presidents listed were familiar with and visited the two colonial homes still on the front lawn. One is the Indian School dating to 1723, established to teach Indian boys the ways of the white man. The identical 1732 President's House, Cornwallis's Revolutionary War headquarters, was damaged by French officers before the Yorktown siege. The French commander ordered damages reimbursed by his government. While in the legislature, **Madison** lived in the President's House from 1778 to 1779, the home of a cousin with his same name, the college president. **Jefferson** also visited with the senior **Madison**, his former schoolmate and close friend. The legislature met in the Wren Building while **Jefferson** was governor as work was being done on the Capitol at the other end of the street, a mile away. **Monroe** left school at age 18 to join Washington's army, and returned later to study law with George Wythe. Queen Elizabeth II was photographed at the building in 1957.

Washington's diary places him at almost every location in the area. **Jefferson's** *Memorandum Book* shows him here over 1400 days between September 1767 and April 1780 at virtually every site now open, including locations now reconstructed or used for other purposes, such as an apothecary and merchant at the site of the King's Arms Tavern, Dixon's Store on the site of Chowning's, Brammer's Store on site of the reconstructed Blue Bell Inn, and Vobe's Tavern at the site of Christina Campbell's. **Jefferson** practiced in the General Courts that met here. It is unknown where he lived most of the time, but a favorite tavern was Ayscough's on site of the reconstructed Ayscough's House on Francis Street. Part of the time he shared a study room with John Tyler Sr., four years younger, later college president, governor, and the father of the president. **Jefferson** rented rooms in the Market Square Tavern, at the SW corner of Queen and Duke of Gloucester, for much of the time he studied law. Peyton Randolph's home* is still at the NW corner of Nicholson and England Streets. He was **Jefferson's** relative, wanted **Jefferson** to live there rather than the Wren building, and hosted him and **Washington** frequently. **Jefferson** suggested books for Randolph's library that **Jefferson** bought when Randolph died.

Jefferson graduated from William and Mary in two years but then stayed another five to study law with George Wythe, the country's first law professor. He referred to Wythe as his second father. Most of his studies were in Wythe's imposing house* near the Governor's Palace. After he wrote the Declaration of Independence, **Jefferson** and his family came back to Williamsburg and lived in the home beginning in October 1776, for him to attend the Virginia Assembly when Wythe was in Congress in Philadelphia. He was not pleased at how the Declaration was revised by others, had no idea that it would be immortal, and felt that the assembly in Virginia was more important that the Philadelphia Continental Congress. **Washington** expressed disgust that so many important Virginians, including George Mason, Benjamin Harrison, George Wythe, Edmond Pendleton, Thomas Nelson, and others, were more concerned with their state than the whole of the Colonies. **Madison** began serving in the Assembly in May 1776, soon first met **Jefferson**, and continued later in the year as his aide, a great man serving a greater. They became best friends, and **Madison** became his protégé when later meeting with Governor **Jefferson** as a member of the Council.

It was in the October session that **Jefferson** proposed a codification of the laws of the new state of Virginia "adapted to our republican form of government." **Washington** later made the Wythe House his headquarters before the 1781 Yorktown siege; he joined Lafayette, who was already quartered there when the commander arrived. Nearby **Washington** also was a guest of the Carter House,* southwest of the Governor's Palace, with Carter's 17 children.

Washington appeared at the Palace* at age 21 to seek and get the important duty of being a royal emissary to scout the wilderness in Pennsylvania for a fort site and determine French intentions. No other Virginian had frontier experience and social standing. He met again with Governor Fauquier at the Palace after the French and Indian War seeking relief for his men. Fauquier became a close friend of **Jefferson** through two mentors, Wythe and Dr. William Small, and was glad to have the young student play the violin at his parties in the Palace. (For the twelve years before the Revolution, **Jefferson** practiced three hours a day.) **Jefferson** ate at the Palace often with the governor and Wythe, and wrote, "I have heard more good sense, more rational and philosophical conversations [at the Palace with Fauquier, Wythe, and Small] than in all my life besides." He called the dining room table here "his university." Probably **Jefferson's** Deist philosophy was nurtured here, as was his lifelong habit of living beyond his means.

He and Patrick Henry occupied the Palace as governors before the capital was moved to Richmond on Governor **Jefferson's** urging in late 1779 because it was inland from the danger of British attack. The building was occupied by French troops after the British surrender at Yorktown, burned in 1781, and then rebuilt in the 1930s, partly from plans drawn by **Jefferson** when he lived there. At the beginning of the war in 1775, **Monroe**, who was staying in the Wren Building and attending the college, raided the Palace with 23 others to get 200 guns and 300 swords for the militia, beating **Madison's** group to the punch. He joined the Virginia Infantry here and came back to be commissioned second lieutenant in 1779. But the area could not then raise the troops, and he stayed to study law with Governor **Jefferson** until the capital moved. Given the choice of following **Jefferson** or staying to study with Wythe, **Monroe** followed his uncle's advice that association with **Jefferson** offered more promise. He became another **Jefferson** protégé and was sent to tour North Carolina with American troops.

Green Spring, the first great house in the New World, was built three miles north of Jamestown in 1650 by Governor Berkeley and demolished in 1796 after **Jefferson** visited. John Smith had built

Washington made his headquarters before Yorktown in the Wythe House, where Jefferson lived with his family while attending the legislature, and where Madison, Monroe, and Tyler visited, among others more recently.

a glass plant there in 1608. Virginia marker W-36 on U.S. 60, 4.3 miles southeast of Toano, notes that it was five miles south. The ruins are on Va. 614.

At the east end of Duke of Gloucester is the rebuilt Capitol.* As **Jefferson** listened outside of the chamber, Patrick Henry denounced the British with his inflammatory "Caesar had his Brutus" speech. **Washington** served 14 years as a member of the House and was so nervous trying to make his first speech that the speaker mercifully asked him to sit down. (In his first election at age 27 he served up 160 gallons of liquor to win over the 397 voters. This would average 64 shots each.) **Jefferson** served in the House, and **Madison** worked in the Council Room when he helped write the State Constitution. **Madison** was defeated the next year, probably because he refused to buy whiskey, but learned his lesson and was returned the next year. **Jefferson** used the law library as a student and received there, as governor, Clark's report on the capture of Vincennes and the hated British General Henry Hamilton. Elizabeth II of England and Japanese Emperor Hirohito are among the visiting foreign rulers where **Ike** spoke in 1953.

The British governor dismissed the Virginia House of Burgesses (with **Washington** and **Jefferson**) several times when it was getting too rebellious to suit him. So they adjourned to the Apollo Room in the Raleigh Tavern,* where **Washington** once introduced a resolution to boycott English goods that **Jefferson** signed. Then they drank a toast to the king, but this was a step toward revolution. The Raleigh was the center of town business, inside and outside its doors, and has been called the most famous tavern in the Colonies and the "unofficial Capitol of Virginia." **Madison** is known to have frequented, and **Washington's** diary documents many times that he danced and engaged in games of chance here. At age 19, **Jefferson** thought he had fallen in love with Rebecca Burwell, nicknamed by him Belinda. (It was customary to nickname a wife or girlfriend. Both **Washington** and **Jefferson** nicknamed their wives "Patsy," although both given names were Martha.) The romance was mostly in his mind, but he practiced and rehearsed a proposal, delivered while dancing in the Apollo Room. He was so nervous that he could not speak and wrote, "When I had the opportunity of venting [my thoughts] a few broken sentences, uttered in great disorder, and interrupted with pauses of uncommon length, were the too visible marks of my strange confusion." He asked her to wait until he went on a proposed trip, but she evidently did not take him seriously and married someone else, to his chagrin. (Her daughter married John Marshall, who became Chief Justice and swore in President **Jefferson**.)

In 1773 **Jefferson**, Patrick Henry, the talented Lee brothers, and other indignant burgesses organized the Virginia Committee of Correspondence in the tavern, the first extra-legal representative body to discuss growing grievances. They felt that the older members did not have the zeal needed for the problems of the times and the need for the colonies to be unified. **Jefferson** and Henry were close friends and lived together in Williamsburg for a while. A year later, representatives met at the Raleigh to call for the first Continental Congress. Inside, Lafayette was honored in 1825, as was **Tyler** in 1859, the year it burned to the ground.

Washington, **Jefferson**, **Madison**, **Monroe**, and **Tyler** attended the c. 1715 Bruton Parish Church.* All except **Washington** sat in the south half allotted to students, and **Jefferson** was later a vestryman. Two of Martha Custis Washington's children by her first husband are buried outside the north door facing the Wythe home, and Jefferson's friend, Royal Governor Fauquier, is buried in the floor at the front. **Washington** stood as godfather for at least 14 slaves baptized at the altar. He missed only eight meetings in 12 years as vestryman. **Franklin. Roosevelt** attended in 1934. **Ike** attended with Winston Churchill in 1946.

Original taverns open to the public include Christiana Campbell's,* c. 1741, east across from the Capitol, a favorite stopping point for **Washington**. She also ran the inn at the James Anderson House on the south side of Duke of Gloucester, the second lot west of Botetourt toward Colonial Street, where **Washington** in his diary shows that he generally stayed. The King's Arms Tavern,* midway on Duke of Gloucester, is another spot where **Washington** frequently ate, as did probably the others mentioned. It is still open for dining. Other taverns hosting presidents include the Charlton (mostly **Washington**), south and just east of the Raleigh, where **Jefferson** stayed while practicing law, and Wetherburn's,* west of the Charlton.

Martha Washington's first husband left his Williamsburg town house, Six Chimneys, on four acres, to his son. It was on the south side of Francis Street, east of Nassau, south of Bruton Parish Church, now Custis Square. Martha had lived there before her husband's death, and it is believed that **Washington** later spent time there, possibly part of their honeymoon or first winter. **Washington** administered the property for his wife and stepson for twenty years. Remains of a small brick building known as "Martha Washington's Kitchen" are said to still be near the reconstructed hospital, but no one seems to know where they are, and I can not find them.

Jefferson, with close friends John Page and Dabney Carr, often sat on steps of Blair House* on the Duke of Gloucester Street and sang, at least once joined by the royal governor. The home is still on the north side of the street halfway between Nassau and Henry, between the church and the college. John Blair signed the Constitution and was a close friend of **Washington**, who probably visited and later appointed him to the Supreme Court. **Madison** was also a close friend of Blair and Page and surely visited both.

Tyler began studies at William and Mary in the Preparation Division, equivalent to a grammar school, when he was 12. He entered the college at 14 and graduated at 17. During some of this time he boarded with his brother-in-law on Francis Street near Walker. **Tyler** was living at his law office* (reconstructed), on the SW corner of England and Francis Streets, when elected vice president. The building is now an overnight accommodation of Colonial Williamsburg. One prominent Virginian wrote that **Tyler** was on his knees playing marbles with his boys here when word reached him that President **Harrison** had died, making him the first "acting president." But his sons were married except for one, so more probably, he was awakened early in the morning by Senator Daniel Webster's son sent to fetch him. He had not been told that the president was sick and expected to have few official duties as vice president while he reestablished his legal practice in Williamsburg. At 51, **Tyler** became the youngest president up to that time. The Consti-

Above and opposite: The reconstructed Capitol in Williamsburg is where Washington, Madison, Monroe and others served before the capital was moved to Richmond. Modern presidents including Eisenhower spoke there.

tution, prior to the 25th Amendment in 1967, only states that the vice president shall discharge the duties and powers of the office, and it is unclear if he actually becomes president if the president dies. Former president **John Quincy Adams** felt that the vice president remained as such and his proper title should be "Vice President acting as President." **Tyler** disagreed with the interpretation of the Constitution limiting his authority and set the precedent that a succeeding vice president becomes full president with all Constitutional powers. If he had decided otherwise as Congress wanted, he would have only acted while another was chosen president. One of **Tyler**'s sons became president of the college and welcomed **Wilson** at Bassett Hall in 1916. He wrote a book about the school, but did not describe his father's presidential notification or time here.

Confederate General Joseph Johnston's and then Union General McClellan's Civil War headquarters were in the Kerr or Palmer House, c. 1707, on the southwest corner across from the Capitol. The jail just northwest once held Blackbeard's pirates and the notorious "Hair Buyer," British General Henry Hamilton of the Northwest Territory, who allegedly paid for white scalps. Governor **Jefferson** received Hamilton at the Palace.

Carter's Grove Plantation* is about six miles southeast on U.S. 60, and is part of Colonial Williamsburg. For years the story was told here and in print about the "refusal room" where both **Washington** and **Jefferson** were turned down in marriage proposals. This is to the left of the main entrance. The stories are now thought not to be true although some current books still repeat them. But they were both frequently here, and the home is one of the most beautiful in America's heritage. **Reagan** and **FDR** both visited, among probably many other presidents. **FDR** came in 1936 to lunch after cruising the James River and touring Jamestown.

Jefferson frequently visited close friend John Page at Rosewell,* about six miles north of Williamsburg, as the crow flies, across the York River. They were said to be like brothers for 50 years. The route then was by water via Queen's Creek, the York River, and Carter's Creek. The four-story mansion, begun in 1725, outdid the Governor's Palace, and had 23 rooms and three

Many presidents attended Bruton Parish Church in Williamsburg, including those associated with the then capital of Virginia, plus Eisenhower and FDR later. Martha Washington's children by her first husband are buried on the opposite side.

wide halls. It was called the largest and finest colonial mansion in Virginia, and even in America, until destroyed by fire in 1916. The proximity and style of the home made it a social center and surely must have been visited by **Washington** and other founding fathers. Page no doubt needed all the rooms for his 20 children. **Jefferson** came for days at a time, spent hours observing stars from the wide roof, and wrote of the pleasure of his "philosophical evenings" there. When **Jefferson** was governor, Page was lieutenant governor and president of the Virginia Council. During that election for governor by the Assembly, **Jefferson** received 67 votes and Page 61. Page served in Congress from 1789 until 1797 when **Jefferson** was secretary of state, and succeeded **Monroe** as governor from 1802 to 1805. The Virginia Constitution had placed most of the power in the legislature and little in the governor, who was an arm of the legislature and supposed to follow the Council. The romantic ruins are served by a visitor center and are northeast, about midway between Gloucester and Williamsburg, south of Co. 614, right to 632 at the Virginia marker, south and east on the east side of York River at Carter's Creek. Fairfield, home of **Jefferson's** old flame Rebecca Burwell, was excavated in 2003 on the other side of Carter's Creek.

Ford and **Carter** debated in Phi Beta Kappa Memorial Hall on October 22, 1976. This is on the campus on Jamestown Road near Griffin Street. **George W. Bush** helped celebrate nearby Jamestown's 400th anniversary with Queen Elizabeth II in May 2007.

WINCHESTER • **Washington** spent a substantial portion of ten years here serving in the Virginia militia and as an aide to rich English landowner Lord Fairfax. He probably spent more nights here than any other place away from home except New York City and Philadelphia. A Virginia historical marker about 20 miles southeast, just south of Paris, notes that he traveled this way at age 16 in 1748 to survey Fairfax's land beyond the Blue Ridge and in the area around Winchester for about three years. **Washington** also supported himself by surveying for several years, bought 2300 acres in the Shenandoah Valley nearby, and represented the town in the legislature. A detailed route developed by local historian Patricia Gochenour and others shows his path from:

Belvoir on the Potomac near Mt. Vernon along Routes 1 to Woodbridge,
Route 253 to Occoquan,
Routes 640 (Davis Ford Road) and 234 (Dumfries Road), to Independent Hill,
Routes 646 (Aden Road), 607, 606 (Warrenton Road), and 28 to Catlett,
Routes 667 and 670 to Neavil's Ordinary, marked at Auburn,
Routes 602 and 605 to Route 17 past Airlie,
Route 17 through Marshall and Ashby's Gap to Route 50,
To Lord Fairfax's Quarters south of Route 50 down 638 and 603 to about where 603 meets Route 643 near the Shenandoah River.

He and his friend George Fairfax ate and stayed at Hite's, six miles south on the east side of Route 11, on April 11, 1748. Hite's 1753 home, marked there, was visited by **Madison**, whose sister married into the family. **Madison** traveled through many times on the way to Berkeley Springs. Another marker on **Washington's** route is 2.6 miles east of Warrenton on Route 211. In 1749, Fairfax established a home at Greenway Court, about eleven miles southeast, and three miles south of a historical marker on Route 340, two miles northwest of Millwood, southeast of Winchester. It is southeast of the intersection of U.S. 340, U.S. 522, and Va. 277, one mile south of White Post. White Post is named for the post erected by **Washington** in 1750 at what is now White Post Road and Berry Ferry Road, to point the way to Greenway Court. A replica made from Mt. Vernon timber stands in the center of town that **Washington** visited for many years.

Fairfax inherited five million acres in Northern Virginia from his mother while in England, and is said to have hated all women because of being betrayed on his wedding day. He abandoned London and came here to bury his grief in a new, mostly unknown country, by setting up the almost solitary manor of 10,000 acres where no woman except servants crossed his threshold. He had taken a paternal interest in 16-year-old **Washington**, after meeting him at Belvoir (see Alexandria). **Washington** was frequently at Greenway Court and Winchester between 1749 and 1752 for a time totaling about 15 weeks. Fairfax remained a loyalist but was not molested like many. It was a known blow to him that the boy he had loved as a son was named colonial commander. He was buried at an old church at Loudoun and Boscawen, but later moved to the churchyard of Christ Episcopal at Boscawen and Washington Streets.

Washington is claimed to have used the log structure on the NE corner of Braddock and Cork as a survey office* in 1748. This date is found in town literature and on the plaque here, but he probably used the building only later. Garland Quarles, in *George Washington and Winchester, Virginia, 1748–1758*, makes a strong argument that he did not use the office until later military duties, and worked only at Greenway Court when not in the field surveying. The structure actually dates largely to the Civil War era with only parts of the middle room, including the low door, dating to **Washington's** time. His surveys then included the Point Pleasant and Berkeley Springs areas of present-day West Virginia. During the next several years he made surveying trips back to the area and came on the way to Maryland and Pennsylvania several times.

English General Braddock and **Washington** led forces up what is now Route 7, another colonial highway, and spent several days at Cock's Inn, 21 S. Loudoun, hoping to meet various Indian chiefs who might be allies against the French, but the chiefs did not show up. **Washington** also stayed at Cock's, replaced by a 1797 structure, and several other times.

After Braddock's defeat in Pennsylvania in July 1755, Virginians became concerned about Indians crossing the Blue Ridge and invading settlements. In August **Washington**, then age 23, was appointed commander-in-chief of Virginia forces, with offices in Winchester, to repel the French and Indians. He then spent from September 1755 until the end of 1758 staying probably at Hite's, Cock's, and at the fort. During this time he oversaw the building of many forts on the frontier, and used the same office mentioned above that he might have used as a surveyor at Braddock and Cork, Routes 11 and 7. Cannon in the yard are from the fort and Braddock's march. He also occupied an office at 204 S. Loudoun in 1755 while the fort was built, the first of a series along the mountain barrier to North Carolina.

He used the area north of the office as a drilling ground. This was probably used from the fall of 1755 while he built Fort Loudoun on Loudoun Street between Clark and Peyton. Part of the southwest bastion is still at the NW corner of Peyton and Loudoun. He moved in December 1756 to the highest hill in town at the fort. "Washington's Well" is still nearby, unmarked except by vines visible from the street covering an enclosed area in a private yard at 419 N. Loudoun.

After the French evacuated the site of Pittsburgh in 1758, **Washington** ended his continuous relationship with Winchester, but was here at various times in later years. While here he ran for the House of Burgesses in 1755, 1758, and 1761, winning the last two. The 1840 Courthouse is on site of the 1751 log building where **Washington** started his political career. **Washington's** lot and blacksmith shop are marked at the SE corner of Fairfax and Braddock. He did business at some time at the site of the Red Lion Tavern* at the SE corner of Cork and Loudoun. After the war he was at the Golden Buck Inn on Cameron. **Washington** also visited a friend and political associate at Glen Bernie (private and reconstructed in 1794), on the south side of Amherst, Highway 50, west of town about a half mile west of Stewart Street.

Madison honeymooned at Belle Grove,* eleven miles southwest on Route 11 near Middletown, site of the 1864 Battle of Cedar Creek. His brother-in-law's home is now owned and shown by the National Trust for Historic Preservation. The **Madisons** had intended to go to their home, but Dolley became ill and recovered here for two weeks.

Jefferson came through several times and spent four days just south of town with Isaac Zane. His *Memorandum Book* shows that he stayed at McGuire's in 1784. The location later became the Taylor Hotel. This prominent downtown landmark, pictured in many Civil War paintings, was built at 225 N. Loudoun (Main) Street 1836. It still claims **Washington** stayed, not possible unless this refers to the earlier McGuire's at the same site. During the Civil War it was Stonewall Jackson's headquarters, and **Hayes** and **McKinley** stayed at the time of one of the many battles here, the Battle of Kernstown. A plaque at the SE corner of Piccadilly and Loudoun marks where young **McKinley** took his Masonic Oath on May 3, 1865. **FDR** dedicated the restoration of the fort and town historical structures in 1934.

YORKTOWN • This is the site of one of the most decisive operations and momentous events in world history. The town is much like it was during the Revolution. The visitor center is on the siege line. British General Lord Cornwallis had chased Lafayette's army around Virginia in 1781 for about two months after deciding to abandon his frustrating attempts to defeat General Nathaniel Greene in North Carolina. The neurotic British commander Sir Henry Clinton in New York had ordered him north to relieve the pressure that he felt he faced under **Washington.** So Cornwallis brought his whole army to Yorktown on the way to New York and then sat to await developments and transport ships.

French General Rochambeau and **Washington** saw an opportunity. They convinced French Admiral de Grasse, fighting in the Caribbean, to come north and cut off British help, and then quickly slipped their allied armies from New York State and Rhode Island. The French fleet sealed off the end of the bay and defeated the British in a sea battle so that no ships could rescue the British Army. Now **Washington**, arriving via present Routes 235, 1, 301, 605, 60, trapped Cornwallis. As it turned out, the British surrender on October 19, 1781, virtually guaranteed freedom for the Colonies, whereas a few months before it looked again like they would lose the war. No one knew this at the time as **Washington** captured only about a quarter of the British army in America that still outnumbered the Continental army several times over. But Clinton's 12,000 could not aid here, and the British were becoming less willing to put forth the effort necessary to win the final victory against a people united more and more against the British, a unity that **Washington,** the non-soldier and civilian in arms, had done much to foster.

The Thomas Nelson's House* hosted **Washington** and **Jefferson,** is now a visitor center, and is still the dominant landmark of the historic area. Nelson had been governor of Virginia during the war. He told **Washington** to bombard it during the siege to drive out the occupying British, and offered a reward for those who hit his house. Several cannon balls are embedded in the home, but generally date to a later owner. Cornwallis had to flee to a cave* to escape the shelling. **Washington** stayed at the Shield (Sessions) House* on Nelson Street, where at least five other presidents are claimed to have been guests, and the Swan Tavern,* now reconstructed.

Two stops on the battlefield include **Washington's** headquarters* and the spot where he fired the first cannon ball. His tent is in the visitor's center, one of three still preserved. (The other two are on display at Valley Forge and the Smithsonian History Museum.) He signed the surrender terms at Redoubt Number 10* after subordinates worked out the terms in the Moore House.* Cornwallis pleaded sickness in order not to have to appear at the ceremonies, so **Washington** designated General Lincoln to accept surrender at the site marked on the battlefield tour. The dream of creating a new country now was almost a reality, not an historic footnote.

WASHINGTON

OLYMPIA • On May 23, 1903, **TR** visited the Old Capitol at 600 S. Washington, now the Thurston County courthouse. As shown later, **FDR** visited the forest areas on the Olympic Peninsula, including Lake Crescent, and commented he hoped that the SOB who had cut so much "was rotting in hell." On June 9, 1948, **Truman** was greeted by 200 at 2:00 A.M. upon arrival at the Olympia Station. In the morning he strolled the gardens and Capitol grounds before going to Tacoma and other towns and returned for a speech in Sylvester Park.

SEATTLE • **Hayes** arrived at Yesler Wharf at the foot of Mill Street on October 11, 1880, where he was greeted with an arch across the street. He later spoke at the Occidental Hotel at Mill and James. On the next day, after visits to coal mines in Newcastle and Renton, he shook hands with over 2000 at Squire's Opera House, east side of Commercial and First Avenue.

Benjamin Harrison saw most of the town's 43,000 in a rainy parade on May 6, 1891. **TR** sailed into the harbor on May 23, 1903, and got off his ship at Arlington Dock, foot of University Street, to participate in "the greatest Naval parade in the history of Puget Sound." The Great White Fleet had just returned from **Roosevelt's** world-wide show of New World power that he wanted to display. He took an excursion to Everett and came back to Arlington Dock before helping open the grand Washington (Denny) Hotel on Denny Hill surrounded by Second, Fourth, Stewart, and Virginia Streets. The hotel and hill are now gone. The assembly at the Grand Opera House at 217 Cherry was called the largest in the state's history. He also watched a baseball game at Ft. Lawton, present-day Discovery Park.

Taft visited the Alaska-Yukon-Pacific Exposition (a world's fair held on the university campus) in September 1909. He arrived from Spokane at the King Street Station,* 303 S. Jackson, as did **Wilson** when he came in September 1919 to review the Pacific Fleet in Elliot Bay. **Taft** saw a livestock parade at the University of Washington Stadium, spoke at the Rainier Club on Fourth between Marion and Columbia, and stayed at the New Washington (Josephinum) Hotel at 1902 Second Ave. **Wilson**, standing in an open car, paraded down Second Avenue, Stewart, First and Yesler before attending dinner at the Hippodrome, 500 University. His main purpose was to defend his peace treaty and League of Nations at the Arena on Fifth Avenue between Seneca and University. On Sunday he attended First Presbyterian at Spring and Seventh before touring Seattle and leaving at the station, whose tower, modeled after the Campanile of Saint Mark's in Venice, was the tallest building in Seattle when completed in 1906.

Harding made his last speech of his 40-day western tour on July 27, 1923, at University Stadium. He died in San Francisco on August 2. It is suggested that he had fallen ill here. The transport carrying him and Secretary of Commerce **Hoover** rammed a destroyer in the fog in Elliot Bay before he viewed the fleet in the harbor and the Bell Street Pier. After a downtown parade he greeted children at Volunteer Park and then heard 50,000 children and Boy Scouts recite the Pledge of Allegiance in Woodlawn Park. (A 1925 memorial at the site was buried in the 1970s under what is now the central knoll in the Woodland Park Zoo African Savannah.) Afterwards he visited Children's Orthopedic Hospital on Queen Anne's Hill.

On August 3, 1934, **FDR** visited the Bonneville and Grand Coulee Dam sites on the Columbia River. He came back on September 30, 1937, from Victoria and Port Angeles, and was greeted by hundreds of school children with a sign pleading, "Mr. President we want Olympus National Park." In fact he came in order make a tour of the Olympic Peninsula loop from Lake Crescent, where he spent the night. His route included Lake Quinault on October 1, where he ate lunch at the Inn, Aberdeen and Hoquiam. He made his first commitment to establish the park, accomplished nine months later when he returned for the dedication. He came in August 12, 1944, on the *Indianapolis* coming back from Hawaii and made a speech at Bremerton Ship Yard to thank workers for their war effort. The speech was timed to be between work shifts so that two crews could hear him. He also thanked the press for voluntary censorship in not revealing his movements as the enemy was close by on the trip. During the speech he is believed to have suffered an angina attack, but cardiograms afterward could find nothing wrong.

Truman made a "non-political" tour on June 9, 1948, "fighting two wars, with the Communists abroad and Republicans at home," and lambasted the Republican Congress at every opportunity. He urged voters to vote out the present Congress and told one reporter in Spokane that his paper and the *Chicago Tribune* were the worst in the country. He went by Grand Coulee Dam, Ephrata, Columbia River flood damage, and Wenatchee, and spoke to 5000 in Everett. During a speech in front of the Elks Club at Bremerton on Pacific Avenue, someone yelled, "Given 'em Hell, Harry!" He said he intended to do just that. A plaque claims that this was the first time that famous phrase was used. He also attended the first commencement of Olympia College, where he got an honorary degree. He spoke to only 7000 in half-filled Memorial Stadium in Seattle, but saw 100,000 in his downtown parade. Afterwards he visited the Washington State Rehabilitation Center near Fourth and Cherry, where he was presented with a pair of boxing gloves to properly handle Congress.

JFK made a major speech at the University of Washington on November 16, 1961, after arriving at Boeing Field and traveling via a 15-block "Welcome Lane" down Fourth, Jefferson, and Stewart with the music of 26 bands, before about 30,000. He made a brief stop at the Olympic Hotel, where **Truman, Eisenhower, LBJ, Ford,** and **Carter** also stayed, 411 University. He then spoke at the Edmundsen Pavilion, traveling along Aurora Ave. N. and N. 40th past "Fair Play for Cuba" signs. He referred to the 1861 founding of the university when the territory had only the simplest element of civilization and it was not known if the country would survive. He came back to the Olympus to honor a local senator and also spoke to the overflow crowd across the street at 410 University. Several sources, including the "Online Encyclopedia of Washington State History," report that two ladies of ill repute came at night to his 11th-floor suite under dire threats not to reveal their presence.

On November 20, 1993, **Clinton** convened a summit of 13 leaders of Pacific Rim nations attending a conference held at Black Island State Park in Puget Sound in Kitsap County.

TACOMA • **B. Harrison** came on May 6, 1891, when virtually all of the city's 36,006 inhabitants saw him in driving rain. After leaving the station at 17th and Pacific, he rode under a number of arches through the "mud lagoon known as Pacific Street." Factories and schools were let out, and he expressed fear for the children mostly amassed between Ninth and Eleventh in such weather. The major reassured him that they were used to it. But he refused to stop for children to greet him as requested and would not listen to the many children, including 119 Indian School choir members, who had prepared a serenade at 11th Street. He did make a brief speech at the Five Corners platform in front of the Tacoma Theater. **TR** stayed in the Sheraton Tacoma, 1320 Broadway Plaza in 1903. **JFK** later stayed and the hotel's current publicity quotes him praising the service.

VANCOUVER • In 1852 **Grant** served at Fort Vancouver on the Columbia River in charge of supplying surveying parties to the mountains. The commanding officer's residence then is now known as the Grant House,* open as a restaurant on Officer's Row, 1106 Evergreen, east of Interstate 5. **Grant** was present there many times, but did not live there. It was renamed for him as the town wanted to honor the former president when he revisited on October 13, 1879. Future general George McClellan once passed through in charge of an expedition to explore the Cascades and observed **Grant** drinking. He did not drink much, but a drink or two affected him noticeably. This evidently made a negative impression on McClellan, who refused to see him in Ohio at the beginning of the Civil War when **Grant** came to request a position.

Grant tried hard to make money while here, cutting ice to ship to San Francisco, raising potatoes, sending chickens to San Francisco, and cutting cord wood for steamboats. All failed, as did all of **Grant's** other projects prior to the Civil War. His potato farm was about First and Grand, marked at the triangle of streets at Fifth, R, and Davis. He lived at Quarter Master's Ranch at a site now under I-5 at the Route 14 northeast ramp just west of the restored fort. The long-gone prefab house was built in New York, and carried by ship to San Francisco and then here. **Grant** did not return until 1879, when he came with great fanfare to stay with General Howard, greet hundreds in the public park, and visit the old fort. Howard lived in the present information center, still known as the Howard House,* just southwest of the circle at the north entrance, Evergreen and Fort Vancouver Way. **Hayes** came on October 2, 1880, with General Sherman and stayed two nights, probably at the Howard House, before going up the Columbia River.

Carter visited the area in front of Officer's Row during his first campaign, but did not enter any of the restored homes. **Eisenhower** dedicated the McNary Dam on the Columbia in September 23, 1954.

WEST VIRGINIA

BECKLEY AREA • **Hayes** and **McKinley** were stationed in Beckley and in the area during the Civil War. **Hayes** wrote that Gauley Bridge had the "grandest mountain scenery that he had ever beheld." Miller Tavern on Main Street was their headquarters there. They also had headquarters in Fayetteville on WV 16 and at the Old Stone House in Clifftop, two miles south of the U.S. 60 and WV 41 junction. **Jackson** was there. **Hayes** wrote many letters from the area describing the plight and suffering of women during the war.

BERKELEY SPRINGS • **Washington** came to what is claimed to be America's first spa, surveying at age sixteen in 1748 for Lord Fairfax. The area claims to be known as a resort because of

Washington's enthusiasm for the waters and later visits with his terminally ill brother Lawrence, hoping to find a cure or ease from pain. Later he brought his stepdaughter to find relief from her epileptic seizures. Fairfax granted the springs to the Virginia Colony, "to be forever free to the publick [*sic*] for the welfare of humanity." It is still known by the name of "Bath," and a modern resort still uses the historic springs in the center of town (SE corner of Fairfax and Washington), with markers telling of the **Washington** connection. He owned lots 58 and 59, marked on the SE corner of at Fairfax and Mercer ("Montgomery" on earlier maps), drew plans for 134 lots, and incorporated the town.

The **Washingtons** were here several times. Once they were served tea at the home of their friends George and Sally Fairfax, NE corner of Washington and Liberty. This was across from where they probably stayed several times, including 1784 and his last visit in 1794, at a Sign of the Flagg House, west of Washington St., Route 522, at Market Street. The exact site is in the parking lot of the Inn and Spa, 1 Market Street. A bathhouse at Wilkes and Fairfax is on another site used by **Washington** near the springs. The Washington Elm, on the NW corner of Washington and Liberty, is marked with a claim to have been planted by **Washington**.

Madison (many times), **Polk** (1848), **Fillmore**, and **Pierce** (1853) also used the waters. **Franklin Roosevelt** is pictured at the corner of Washington and Fairfax on one of his several trips here.

BETHANY • **Davis** and **Garfield** were among the many famous visitors to the Campbell Mansion* just east on SR 67.

CHARLESTON • Presidential visits include **Jackson** at 1710 Kanawha Blvd., and **Kennedy** at the Kanawha Hotel at Summers and Virginia in 1960 and 1963 when he visited the Capitol. **Theodore Roosevelt** was at the Old Capitol in 1900 and **Carter** visited the Governor's Mansion in 1977 at 1716 Kanawha and Charleston Civic Center, 200 Civic Center Dr. in 1978.

CHARLES TOWN • **Washington** surveyed the land here at age sixteen and urged his older half-brother to purchase tracts in the area. Lawrence did, then died, leaving parcels to George's younger brother Charles, who moved here and laid out the town, naming streets for his brothers. Another brother, Samuel, lived nearby at Harewood (private), where George visited, as did Lafayette later. **Madison** married Dolley at this home of her sister on Route 51, three miles west of town. The then lifelong bachelor was seventeen years older than the once-married sociable Quaker, who learned to smoke and dip snuff. Of the first four presidents, three were from Virginia and all married widows. None, including the fifth, Virginian **Monroe**, had surviving sons to carry on their name.

Washington frequently visited Charles at Happy Retreat at the end of Blakeley Place on Mordington Avenue, an extension of West Street, and at his office on the east side of Lawrence between Liberty and Washington Streets. The private home is a block west of the main north-south street, George Street, south of the courthouse where abolitionist John Brown was tried in 1859. **Washington's'** farm is marked on Summit Point Road four miles west. **Washington's** Masonic Cave east of U.S. 340 on Old Cave Road is claimed to be where Masons gathered in 1753, presided over by Worshipful Master **George Washington**, but this is questioned.

During the Civil War, Generals **Grant** and Sheridan met at the Carriage Inn* at 417 E. Washington in 1864.

FORT ASHBY • Of the 69 forts built by **Washington** in the 1750s, only Fort Ashby survives, with help from the WPA. The reconstruction is at the intersection of Routes 46 and 28.

HARPERS FERRY • **Washington** was known to have been here several times because of his surveying duties and later land speculation searches. These included trips to Charles Town and Wheeling, and through much of the then uncharted wilderness west of the Blue Ridge. **Jefferson** stopped on the way to Philadelphia as a delegate to the Continental Congress on October 25, 1783, his first time here. A rock above the town is marked as the place where he observed that "the view was worth a trip across the Atlantic." He referred to it as "perhaps one of the most stupendous scenes in nature." But it is believed that he was up higher where he could see the rivers' junction when he made the observation, maybe near the McMahon House, where **Cleveland** stayed. **Madison** climbed a hill overlooking the town at the confluence of the rivers in the mid–1780s. A popular excursion from Washington, D.C., for many years was to come up the C and O Canal to here and climb the trail to Jefferson's Rock.* **Pierce** was here in 1834, as were **Polk**, **John Quincy Adams**, **Carter**, and other presidents at various times.

Lincoln visited on October 1, 1862, on the way

Many presidents have visited Harpers Ferry, where Jefferson thought the scene was "worth a trip across the Atlantic" to see. Many came here in the early days on an excursion up the Potomac. Lincoln visited John Brown's fort in the distance.

to see General McClellan at Antietam Battlefield. He arrived by train over the pontoon bridge near the ruined bridge, still visible where the rivers join. The president was taken to General Edwin V. Sumner's headquarters, now the left side as you face the front of the Mather Training Center, and prominently located on a hill between Rte. 340 and Fillmore Street, between Jackson and McDowell Streets. (**Wilson** once used the building as his retreat.) **Lincoln** met briefly with McClellan, reviewed troops on Bolivar Heights, and inspected the ruins of the railroad bridge and engine house that John Brown used for a fort during his fatal 1859 raid. That building has now been relocated a short distance from the original site, as noted in the marker at the new location and the obelisk on the original site. **Lincoln** returned to Sumner's headquarters and spent the night. The president also reviewed troops at Loudoun and Maryland Heights on the next morning.

LEVI • **Washington** patented 125 acres of the Burning Spring, a well containing gas that burned.

PARKERSBURG • In 1770 **Washington** stopped at the Point, the south side of the confluence of the Ohio and Little Kanawha Rivers, now Murphy Park* in downtown. He was here locating lands given to him by Governor Dinwiddie for military service. He later was granted 7276 acres between Black Betsey and Red House on U.S. 35 and on the Great Kanawha River between Charleston and the Ohio border. **Hayes** stayed at the Swan House Hotel in 1863.

WHEELING • The McClure House at 1200 Market dates to when Wheeling was the state capital and claims to have hosted **Grant, Garfield, Arthur, B. Harrison, McKinley, TR, Taft, Truman, Ike, JFK,** and **Nixon.**

WHITE SULPHUR SPRINGS • A marker at the old hotel site shows where **Monroe, Van Buren, Tyler, Pierce, William Henry Harrison, Fillmore,** and **Buchanan** stayed. **Tyler** honeymooned at Greenbrier Cottage while president and greeted **Pierce**. Fourteen presidents including **Van Buren,**

Fillmore, Pierce, and **Buchanan** summered at President's Cottage. It was torn down in 1913 to build the Greenbriar Hotel,* where **Coolidge, Wilson** (on his second honeymoon), **Ford, Kennedy, Nixon,** and **Eisenhower** were guests. **TR** visited as a child for his chronic asthma. Robert E. Lee and his family spent summers for three years beginning in 1867 at the Lee Cottage in Baltimore Row.

Just south of the State Route 63 and U.S. 219 is Organ Cave,* claimed to have been visited by **Jefferson** in 1791 when a member of his party discovered the remains of a prehistoric three-toed sloth. However, I do not find credible evidence that **Jefferson** was in this area. The hotel and grounds are open to guests only. Also nearby is Sweet Springs, where **Monroe, Van Buren, William Henry Harrison, Tyler,** and **Pierce** stayed in resort hotels long since destroyed.

The underground Greenbrier Bunker here is an underground safe haven meant to safeguard 1000 top government officials, including Congress and the president, in case of nuclear threat. When the *Washington Post* revealed the secret in 1992, its usefulness was ruined.

WISCONSIN

BELOIT • On October 1, 1859, **Lincoln** met local Republicans at the depot located south of St. Paul Street between State and Pleasant and ate in the Bushell House, NE corner of Grand and State. Another hotel here earlier, the Rock River House, claimed to have entertained **Lincoln** and **Buchanan**. He may have visited the Cyrus Eames home on the NE corner of Mill and St. Paul.

Lincoln then came to Hanchett Hall, marked on the NE corner of Broad and State Streets, where he spoke on the packed third floor. After the presentation, he left for Janesville, retracing the old war trail, now Prairie Street, from his 1832 Black Hawk War march, when it is believed that he camped at Park and White Streets.

BRULE • This little town of less than 600 has hosted **Cleveland, Coolidge** (1928), **Hoover** (1928), **Grant, Truman,** and **Eisenhower** (1947) in its celebrated trout streams and rivers. It claims to be the preeminent spawning grounds for western Lake Superior. **Coolidge** stayed at Cedar Island Lodge, off U.S. 2 west of the Iron River, in 1928.

JANESVILLE • On October 1, 1859, **Lincoln** spoke at the Young American Hall then at the location of the drive-up teller windows at the Johnson Bank on Milwaukee Street, east of Main. The next day he attended services at the Congregational Church, SW corner of Dodge and Jackson. He stayed at the Tallman House,* 440 N. Jackson Street at Madison off U.S. 14 business route two blocks northeast of the U.S. 51 junction, believed to be the only standing private residence in the state where **Lincoln** slept and where his bed remains.

MADISON • **Davis** claimed to have led the first white men to this area in the late 1820s. **Lincoln's** law partner, John T. Stuart, wrote that he and **Lincoln** came to Four Lakes (Madison) while serving as privates in the Black Hawk War. Virtually all presidents beginning with **Grant** have visited the Capitol. **Cleveland** visited the Vilas home at 521 N. Henry in 1887. **TR** was at Lafollette's home at 314 S. Broom in 1893, and **Taft** was at the Executive Mansion, 130 E. Gilman, in 1917. **TR** was at the Mansion in 1893 and 1903 and addressed the legislature in 1911.

MILWAUKEE • **Lincoln** stopped on the way back from New England on October 4, 1848, and toured the city. It is thought that he saw the present cathedral,* c. 1847, on the east side of Jackson at Cathedral Square, as this was the center of town where the customhouse and courthouse were. On September 30, 1859, he spoke at the exhibition of the Wisconsin Agricultural Society, or State Fair. He arrived at the depot at Second and St. Paul. His host had arranged for **Lincoln** to stay in the best hotel in town, the Newhall House, NW corner of Broadway and E. Michigan. He arrived earlier than expected, found no room, and slept on a cot.

The spot where he spoke was marked with a

boulder on W. 13th between N. Wells and W. Kilbourn, although the marker has been removed during recent construction. He toured the grounds and amazed his escorts when he seized and held straight "an enormous sledge with a handle long and strong," used to pound tent stakes. Later in the day friends persuaded him to make an address at the Newhall House.

While running for president on a third-party ticket in 1912, **Theodore Roosevelt** was shot while coming out of the Hotel Gilpatrick at the current site of the Hyatt Regency, west side of Third between Wells and Kilbourn, marked just inside the door. The bullet broke a rib, barely missing his heart, but hit his glasses case and folded speech, lessening the impact. (These relics are on display in the birthplace museum in New York City.) He insisted that he continue to the Milwaukee Auditorium at 500 W. Kilbourn to make his hour and a half speech anyway, more remarkable because the speech was insignificant and the effort was life-threatening. He began by telling the audience to be very quiet, as he had been shot. They laughed, thinking that he was joking, but he opened his coat, revealing a bloody shirt. It may be that he wanted to die, thinking this would be the grandest exit in history. The shooter was an anti–third term fanatic who was declared insane and died in confinement in 1940, the year FDR was elected for the third term. After the speech **Roosevelt** was taken to the Mercy Hospital in Chicago.

The Pfister Hotel,* NW corner Wisconsin and Jefferson Streets, dating to 1893, claims to have been the host of every president from **McKinley** through **George W. Bush**.

PRAIRIE DU CHIEN • **Davis**, at Fort Crawford with his slave and while serving under **Taylor**, met his future wife, Taylor's sixteen-year-old daughter. **Davis** served here from 1829 to 1833, as did **Taylor** from 1832 to 1836. **Davis** left in 1833 and did not see his fiancée for two years until his marriage in Louisville, Kentucky, with **Taylor** still protesting, but acquiescing. He objected to his daughter's marrying a solder and being subject to camp life, although an older daughter had already married an army surgeon at Ft. Snelling, Minnesota. The fort was built by **Davis** and **Taylor** at Beaumont Road and Dunn Street, where **Taylor** lived with his family in a large house at 717 S. Beaumont,* now open as medical museum.

SUPERIOR • **Coolidge** used the Central High School at 1015 Belknap as summer White House in 1928 and fished near Brule.

WYOMING

CHEYENNE • The 1886 Union Pacific Depot,* now the Cheyenne Visitor Center, has seen various presidents riding the railroad west. The tracks still used follow the first transcontinental route. The museum there claims that all presidents since the construction of the tracks until Reagan were there. It is at the head of Capitol Street with the Capitol seen at the far end.

Grant came through in 1868 and also in 1875 on his way to and from Salt Lake City. The former president was given an impromptu reception on the way to Denver in 1880. **Arthur** stopped for 25 minutes in 1883 with Secretary of War Robert Lincoln and others on the way to hunt in the western part of the state and visit Yellowstone. Security was high due to threats of horse thieves in the area to kidnap the president. The group stopped at Fort Washakie off U.S. 287 to meet the famous chief of that name whose statue is inside the Capitol, but not Sacagawea, the famous female interpreter of Lewis and Clark, said to be still alive at the fort. Afterwards they moved over Robert Lincoln Pass (now Union Pass) to see the Tetons and Gros Ventre Valley. **Hayes** and General Sherman spoke here in 1880. **McKinley** came through with a sick wife in 1901, and did not make any appearances.

TR came to town at least three times. He visited First Methodist, 18th and Central, in May 1903 and was back at First Congregational, 3501 Forest Drive, in 1910. He also visited the Capitol and came from Laramie in his first visit, riding all the 53 miles on horseback after an invitation that he could not pass up. He is pictured on Sherman Hill and 16th in front of the now restored Atlas Theater, riding to the Capitol. **Taft** was here in October 1911, when he went to Frontier Park to review troops, see a rodeo, and make an address at the Capitol. **Wilson** spoke for the League of Nations on September 24, 1919, the day before his tragic effort at Pueblo, Colorado, where he had a physical breakdown. **Hoover** came in 1928. **FDR** came in 1932 and visited St. Mark's Episcopal in 1936 at 1908 Central. **Truman** ate the Old Governor's Mansion* at 300 E. 21st with his family in June 1948. **Ike** passed through in 1952 and then went to Casper.

Nixon visited the Capitol in 1956, as did **George H.W. Bush** in 1989. **Nixon** spent the night in the guest bedroom of the Old Governor's Mansion in 1968. **JFK** attended a fundraiser at the Plains Hotel, NW corner of 16th and Central. The Frontier Days celebration has been attended by **TR** and **George H.W. Bush** while in office. **LBJ** was there in 1960.

EVANSTON • This entry is shown to illustrate a typical presidential visitation to many similar towns across the country. The "most notable day in the town's history," a phrase used over and over to describe the excitement over a presidential visit, was said to have occurred on May 30, 1903, when excursion trains brought hordes of visitors to see a president, presenting "the grandest opportunity of life." There was scarcely breathing room in the tightly packed audience that came from many miles away trying to hear **Teddy Roosevelt** at the triumphant arch just past the depot. He also attended a dance and concert at the Opera House on Front Street that became the Transcontinental Garage when the Lincoln Highway opened.

GRAND TETON NATIONAL PARK • **Arthur** camped by Jackson Lake with Robert Lincoln in 1883 after being amazed at the Tetons. **Hoover** fished in the lake. **Carter** stayed by it at the Brinkerhoff Lodge on U.S. 287 and Teton Park Drive in 1978, north of Signal Mountain, where **Nixon** stayed in 1971 and **G.H.W. Bush** and **JFK** also visited. **Carter** went to a rodeo in Jackson. **JFK** came in late September 1963 after greeting thousands at the Cheyenne airport fence. **Reagan** visited the park and nearby Lost Creek Ranch. **George W.** visited his vice president's home near the 18th hole of the Teton Village Golf Course.* In 1992, **G.H.W. Bush** was honored with a large barbecue at the airport after fishing west of Cody. He stayed with Secretary James Baker at his ranch near Boulder in the Wind River Range, and is pictured fishing at Ox Bow Bend on the Snake River and on Jackson Lake. He spent two days in Jackson in 1987 at the Spring Creek Ranch.

Clinton spent several weeks in the area in 1995 after purchasing a $25 Golden Eagle park pass, staying with Senator Jay Rockefeller at his home at the Jackson Hole Golf Course and Tennis Club.* He played there, shook hands on the 18th hole, and hit a ball through a window of a home next to the course. They also played the Teton Pines Golf Course,* ate at the Rancher Bar* on the square and at Jackson Lake Lodge. He attended the Church of the Transfiguration* in the park (as did **Carter**), hiked around Jenny Lake and five miles in and out of Cascade Canyon to Harlequin Pond near the mouth of the canyon, saw Menter's Ferry,* and ate at Dornan's Chuckwagon, among other places. (The Cascade Canyon hiking trail has been listed as the most scenic in the country, and I readily agree.) He also ate with actor Harrison Ford, who lives in the area, and at the home of the World Bank president. He dedicated the Wilson post office nearby. The publicity for the area was great, as was the police coverage bill: $7600 of the town's $60,000 annual police budget.

LARAMIE • Fort Sanders was on the southern edge of the city in 1868, one and three-quarters of a mile east of the Laramie River and one mile south of Lodge Pole Creek. Little is there now, but it was north of Kiowa Street on Route 287, now marked with a monument. **Grant** used the Union Pacific Railroad to visit it in 1868 and is pictured here with Generals Sheridan and Sherman. **Hayes** came for a reception with Sherman in 1880.

TR spoke in Maennerchor Hall and then Root's Opera House in September 1900. **JFK** spoke to 12,500 at the University's War Memorial Fieldhouse* on September 25, 1963. **Harding** stopped at the station for five minutes on his final trip.

SHERIDAN • The Sheridan Inn, SW corner of Broadway and 5th, was designed after an old Scottish country inn. It hosted **Taft, Hoover,** and **Truman**, among other famous Americans.

YELLOWSTONE NATIONAL PARK • **Arthur** (1883) camped at the site of Mammoth Springs Hotel,* where his carriage is displayed. The party came by train to Green River City, and then joined a 150-mule pack train with 300 cooks, packers, guides, and workers. A courier changed

Jackson Lake and the Grand Tetons were seen by many presidents beginning with Arthur. The visitors include Hoover, Kennedy, Nixon, Carter, Clinton, and the Bushes.

horses every 15 minutes to rush back to telegraph lines to check on any news for the president. They crossed the Continental Divide, probably at Sheridan Pass or Union Pass, 17 miles south of Togwotee Pass on today's Route 287. Their camps included the north shore of Lewis Lake, West Thumb of Yellowstone Lake, in the center of the present Old Faithful Lodge, the site of the Lake Hotel, and just west of Tower Falls.

TR came several times before and during his presidency, including 1890 with his wife and April 1903 with a small group trying to avoid the customary presidential fanfare and publicity so that he could study the wildlife in the park. Much of the area was then still deep in snow, and the president traveled by sled and skis. He came with a pack of dignitaries and elegant camp furnishings and even left his physician and the Secret Service behind so that he could camp two weeks in several spots with naturalist John Burroughs and a few others near Tower Falls and Yellowstone Canyon. He stayed in hotel cabins at Norris and the Canyon, camped at the site of Roosevelt Lodge, and laid the cornerstone for the arch at the northern entrance named for him. The president related during the 1903 trip that earlier on a hunting trip in the park, he climbed down to the river at the bottom of the Grand Canyon of the Yellowstone to catch trout for dinner. The trip through the West lasted over two months, and he arrived back at the White House fresh, even though he had made nearly 300 speeches. He claimed that the 52 miles between the park and Cody were the most scenic in the country. Among his prolific writings are long articles in 1903 praising the beauty of the Grand Canyons here and in Arizona, Yosemite (which he saw with naturalist John Muir), and the Tetons.

Coolidge came through Cody on the way here in 1927 for a week's tour in the park. He praised the Buffalo Bill Museum* still amazing visitors in Cody. **Harding** saw Yellowstone and Jackson Hole in 1923. He then went on to Canada, the first president to visit there while in office. **Taft** and **Ford** have both stayed in the Old Faithful Inn,* in 1907 and 1976. As the only president to have worked for the Park Service, **Ford** worked here as a ranger in 1936, getting the job with help from his estranged natural father. He was an armed guard on the bear-feeding truck and welcomed arriving dignitaries at Canyon Hotel and Lodge, although he thought it "undemocratic and un-American" to give them special attention. The football player kept in shape by running around from 5:00 until 7:00 A.M. listing guests' license plates. **FDR** stayed at the Nichols Cottage on U.S. 89 in 1937. **George H.W. Bush** celebrated his 65th birthday in the park. **Carter** took his own photographs of Old Faithful in 1978 while staying in the Tetons. He also fished in Yellowstone and Jackson Lakes. **Clinton** celebrated his 49th at Grand Teton and took a day to visit Old Faithful, the Upper Geyser Basin, and the Canyon, eating in a fire lookout tower on Mt. Washburn.

Appendix: England

John Adams, with ten-year-old **John Quincy Adams**, sailed for France in February 1778, at great personal and financial risk and sacrifice, to serve as a diplomat in France until the summer of 1779, when they returned home. Then the next November, the two, with John's younger son Charles, aged nine, came back to France as the senior **Adams** had been appointed to negotiate peace with Great Britain. Unfortunately Great Britain had no such idea, so they stayed in France and the Netherlands until after **Adams** and others finally successfully negotiated the peace treaty ending the Revolution there in 1783. (To celebrate his pride of accomplishment, **Adams** later named his home in Massachusetts "Peacefield.") In October 1783, a month after the treaty was signed, **John** and **John Quincy** went to London and then Bath. On their way to and from Paris they came through Dover, Canterbury (where they surely saw the magnificent cathedral), and Rochester, also with an outstanding cathedral and adjacent castle. Dover Castle, dating to the Roman era, is still prominent on a hill, visible from a great distance at sea.

In London they stayed at the Adelphi Hotel at Six Adam Street near the Strand, near the Thames River, between Westminster and Blackfriars Bridges. The 1770 building still stands east of the present Adelphi Hotel, a larger, more recent building. John Adam Street (named for the English developer of the area) runs into the site north of Savoy Place and the Embankment Gardens. (Benjamin Franklin had lived nearby at 36 Craven Street from 1757 until 1772 when he moved up the street a few doors until 1775.) **Adams's** diary notes that he visited John Jay at Number 30 Harley Street, Cavendish Square. (The site now has a new building.) Later **Thomas Jefferson** and **Adams** dined on Charles Street on the same square. **Adams** toured Buckingham House (Palace) with U.S. diplomat John Jay and artist Benjamin West on November 8, 1783, and was especially impressed with the king's large library. **Adams** brought **Jefferson** to see it during his later visit. The royal family was at Windsor Castle, and West had permission to show "the whole house" to the two diplomats as his paintings were exhibited. The **Adamses** also saw St. Paul's,* Westminster Abbey,* several museums, and Richmond,* now a park on the site of the palace of medieval kings where Henry VII and Elizabeth I died. Richmond is at the end of the District Underground Line, one stop beyond Kew Gardens* that **Adams** and **Jefferson** saw. **Adams** was based in France by now as a French minister and also lived in the Netherlands attempting to secure loans and recognition for the new United States government.

In July 1784, **John's** wife and daughter, Abigail and Nabby, expected to meet their family in London, after an absence of five years, but found they were in the Netherlands. (Young Charles had returned for Massachusetts, and was presumed for months to be lost at sea until he finally made it home.) Finding Low's Family Hotel at Number 43 King Street in Covent Garden too expensive, Abigail moved to the Adelphi, where **John** and **John Quincy** had stayed. Low's building, dating to 1716, is still north of the Strand. When the **Adams** men finally arrived in August, they were surprised to find Abigail, who was shocked at the mature appearance of her now seventeen-year-old son. She drew back, not believing her eyes, and exclaimed that the little boy she remembered

**Designates a site open to the public.*

was now "a Man." After being reunited, the family left for Paris, where **John** was stationed with his secretary, **John Quincy**. **Jefferson** was also in Paris and formed an almost father-son close relationship with the teenager.

In May of the next year, **Adams** returned to London as the first United States minister to the Court of St. James. **John Quincy** returned to the States as the family was leaving France, charged on his ship by Lafayette with feeding the seven dogs that he was sending to George Washington. Back in London, the **Adamses** (**John**, Abigail, and their daughter) first stayed at Number 62 Harley Street and then the Bath Hotel, Number 156 Piccadilly. Finally they took a house that Abigail found, still at Number 9 Grosvenor Square, Duke and Brook Streets at the NE corner, one of the two original houses on the Square to have survived from that period. The house is marked, one of the only two markers mentioning an American president found in London. The other is **Eisenhower's** headquarters. The American Embassy is now on the west side of this square. **Adams's** daughter married in the house in 1786. **Adams's** diary shows numerous addresses where he visited in London while here. The prime minister during the American Revolution, Lord North, lived across the square, to Abigail's amusement.

Adams first came to St. James Palace on June 1, 1785, to be presented to George III. The 16th century palace, built by King Henry VIII, is still on the Mall. Several kings and queens were born (Charles II, James II, Mary II, Anne, George IV), died (Mary I), and married (Anne, William III, Mary II, George III through V, Victoria) here and at the adjacent chapel. The meeting must have been awkward for the prime mover of the Declaration of Independence and the king called a "tyrant," but the diplomatic first between the two nations went as well as could be expected. **Adams** came to court often and presented **Jefferson** the next March. **Adams** visited the twenty-four-year-old prime minister, William Pitt, at 10 Downing Street, discussing evacuation of British forts on the American frontier and reimbursement for slaves set free by British forces. Britain was still impressing American seamen, even in the Port of London, and angry American sea captains paid frequent visits to see their minister. While the **Adams** family was here, **Jefferson**'s eight-year-old daughter Polly stayed for a time on the way to Paris, where her father was the French minister. She did not want to go to France. Abigail in particular was sympathetic and formed a close relationship with her, as she had been tricked into going on board the ship in Boston with her cousins, who left the vessel without her knowledge just before it sailed.

John and Abigail attended the theater frequently and enjoyed a performance of *Messiah* at Westminster Abbey, as did **Jefferson**. (The composer, Handel, was buried there in 1759.) Surely all presidents mentioned in this chapter have visited this magnificent and most historic structure in England, the traditional coronation site where many kings, queens, statesmen, military leaders, and artists are buried, dating back to Edward the Confessor in 1066.

Jefferson came to London from Paris at the urging of **Adams** in March 1786 as **Adams** wrote that as minister to France he should confer with him about paying bribes to the Barbary States. The two were at St. James Palace on March 17 and attended a levee by George III at Buckingham Palace on March 18. **Jefferson** felt that they very "ungraciously received." **Jefferson** still wrote angrily about the event late in life, although how much discourtesy was actually shown or intended by George III is disputed. It is probable that the only problem was **Jefferson's** misconception. **Jefferson's** rooms were at Number 14 Golden Square, but he was constantly at **Adams's** residence. (A later building is now on site at the southeast side of the square a few blocks north of Piccadilly Circus.) He was a frequent visitor to the theater at Drury Lane and Covent Garden, at the site of the Royal Opera House. **Jefferson's** *Memo Book* mentions numerous locations in London where he visited and made purchases, including a museum in the Leicester House in Leicester Square, 85 Cornhill, where he bought flintlock pistols now at Monticello; Dolly's Chop House in Paternastro Row, Number 10 Haymarket; a tavern at Number 3 Bishopgate; and shops at 136 Fleet Street and Numbers 5 and 6, Duke's Court on St. Martin's Lane.

Jefferson and **Adams** visited Woburn, Hampton Court* (which **Jefferson** thought "old fashioned"), Birmingham, Hagley, Worcester, Edge Hill Battlefield,* Buckingham, Blenheim Palace* (**Jefferson** admired the gardens more than the magnificent palace), and Oxford. They stayed at the Hop Pole Inn in Worcester, Antelope Inn in High Wycombe (northwest of Windsor), White Hart in Uxbridge (at exit 1, M-40, northeast of Windsor), and dined at the Swan Tavern in Birmingham. At Stratford-on-Avon they stayed in an inn three doors from Shakespeare's birthplace,* cut off a piece of Shakespeare's chair "as was the custom," and saw his grave and the garden on the site of the house where he died. **Adams** wrote that **Jefferson** was so overcome when he arrived at Shakespeare's town that he knelt and kissed the ground. **John** was likewise moved at the Edge Hill Battlefield just south of Worcester, where King Charles I fought Parliament. **Adams** sternly lectured an Englishman living on the site, ignorant of the significance, that "all Englishmen should come here in pilgrimage," as this was holy ground where liberty was fought for, more so than at their churches. They especially liked the English gardens such as Chiswick, Kew,* and Twickenham (accessible on the London subway), and also Hagley House, Stowe Gardens,* Stourbridge* and Wotton, northeast of Oxford about fifteen miles, west of Aylesbury. Wotten was built in 1704, the only historic house with the same plan as Buckingham Palace.

Many structures, pavilions,* and temples* seen in Kew Gardens—"the most famous gardens in the world"—still survive, including the Kew Palace* of George III, all of which they would have seen. This is also true of Stowe Gardens* including the mansion, now a school,* several pavilions,* temples,* bridges,* and the pillar (Cobham Monument*) climbed by **Adams** and **Jefferson**. Stowe, the most celebrated garden in Georgian England, is between Oxford and Northampton. The 1748 Temple of Concord and Victory* there is based on the Roman temple Maison Carree in Nimes, France, used by **Jefferson** to plan the Virginia Capitol Building. He would have seen this before the French original.

Jefferson sat for a portrait at Mather Brown's Studio either at Number 1, Wells Street or his home in Cavendish Square. **John**, Abigail, and **Jefferson** also visited the Vauxhall Gardens, on the south side of the Thames opposite the Tate Gallery,* Tower of London,* Osterley House* and Park, and Sion* (also "Syon") House, and observed a steam machine on the south side of Blackfriars Bridge. The Syon House is clearly visible from Kew Gardens, across the Thames River. Going and coming to London, **Jefferson** traveled through Rochester, Sillingborne, Canterbury, and Dover, where he visited the castle.*

(In Europe, **Jefferson** visited Cologne, Frankfort, Bonn, Avignon, Lyon, Fontainebleau Palace,* Dijon, Vienne, Aix, Nice, Arles, Menton, Monaco, Amsterdam, Haarlem, Milan, Pavia, Nimes, Blois, Tours, Aix-en-Province, Marseilles, Genoa, Orange, Heidelberg, and Strasbourg, and cruised the Rhine River while on his five-year assignment living in Paris and Versailles. He left in late 1789 thinking he would soon return, but found that President Washington wanted him for secretary of state and never came back.)

In later travels around England with Abigail, the **Adamses** saw Winchester Cathedral,* Dorchester, Maiden Castle,* Weymouth, Exeter, and Plymouth, and passed through Salisbury, but did not stay as they could not find a room. Exeter and Salisbury have particularly magnificent cathedrals that would have been admired. **Adams's** diary notes that he saw the sights in Bath including the Royal Crescent.

Monroe was sent to London from July 1803 until October 1804 and in July 1805 until October 1807, to negotiate a treaty to restore trade and end impressment of sailors, among other things. When he first arrived he moved into the former minister's home and office at One Great Cumberland across from the Marble Arch on the NW corner where Oxford Street meets Bayswater. He, like the other presidents, evidently saw the tourist sites frequented today. The latter assignment was a difficult task, and he signed a treaty without settling the impressment issue. It was thought that a favorable treaty could make the negotiator the next president. He and William Pinckney could get little concession from the British and thought they got the best treaty they could. But the terms angered President **Jefferson**, who already was angry with **Adams**, **Washington**, Chief Justice Marshall, and many others. Maybe **Monroe** just wanted to hurry back to politic for president, but **Jefferson** and Secretary of State **Madison** were furious, the treaty was rejected, and **Jefferson** picked **Madison** to succeed him as president. **Monroe** hated London's coal smoke and its high cost of living that he claimed was more than his salary. At his first state dinner at St. James Palace, he was put between representatives of "two little principalities no bigger than my farm in Albemarle." He was so angry that he would not join the toast to the King and insulted all present. The Russian minister came to his rescue, toasted the health of the U.S. President, and honored him as the newest minister.

John Quincy Adams lived in Europe from age ten in 1778, until age seventeen, except for one brief trip home. He had been secretary first to his father and then at fourteen to the American minister to Russia because of his ability to speak the language of the court, French. In 1794 he was minister to the Dutch Republic (Netherlands) and was back in London in 1795 to help with Jay's Treaty. In 1797 he was still minister at The Hague when **Washington** named him minister to Portugal. On the way, while **John Quincy** in London, the new president, **Adams**, named him the first United States minister to Prussia, but he objected to getting an appointment from his father. The senior **Adams** wrote that he too had scruples, and quoted **Washington** in saying that he was "the most valuable public character we have abroad," and argued that he should "not withhold merited promotion ... because he is your son." **Quincy** was then married in 1797 at All Hallows Barking-by-the-Tower,* just west of the Tower of London. (William Penn had been baptized there in 1644. The bombed shell was restored after World War II.) His wife was the only foreign-born first lady and grew up in London and Nantes, France, where she met twelve-year-old **John Quincy** when she was four. After the wedding, the couple proceeded to Prussia. In 1809 he was appointed minister to Russia to go again to St. Petersburg and then served in Ghent, Belgium, to negotiate the treaty ending the War of 1812. In 1815 he was minister to Great Britain (as his father and son also were) and lived at 67 Harley Street, several blocks north of Cavendish Square, and later in Ealing about eight miles from Hyde Park. When he was unable to make it home in the evening, his London offices became his headquarters. These were located at 25 Charles, 13 Craven, the Strand, and 28 Craven Street.

Van Buren came to the Thomas Hotel, 25 Berkeley Square (near Charing Cross Station), when he arrived in 1831 to serve as American minister-delegate, and soon moved to permanent quarters at Number 7 Stratford Place. (This is east of the present Selfridges Store off Oxford Street, north of the Bond Street Station.) He lived with his secretary, author Washington Irving, who here completed his work, *The Alhambra*. But **Van Buren**'s residency was premature as he learned a few months later that his nomination had been defeated in the Senate by one vote. The tiebreaker, Vice President John C. Calhoun, was proud that he had ruined a minister but then made a vice president as **Van Buren** was soon to be. Even before he left, he ousted Calhoun as the vice presidential nominee in **Andrew Jackson's** reelection, due somewhat to sympathy votes. The British deemed this fiasco as proof of the incompetence of the American political machinery. **Van Buren** had been a guest at Windsor Castle for two days where King William IV showed him his gardens, saying he loved this more than any other palace. **Van Buren**, a gardening enthusiast, is thought to have received inspiration for White House gardens back home. The king and public liked the future president and went out of their way to be kind to him in the few months longer that he resided in town. In 1853, he became the first ex-president to visit England, where he was greatly honored, and he was back in 1855 at the same time as **Millard Fillmore**. The two visited several places together including the House of Commons, where they were officially recognized. **Fillmore** visited Westminster Abbey and was presented at the Court of St. James, where Queen Victoria supposedly pronounced that he was the handsomest man she had ever seen.

Buchanan was minister to Great Britain from 1853 until 1855, and lived at 56 Harley Street. He was presented to Queen Victoria at Buckingham Palace. He wore a plain black suit rather than silk stockings and gold lace in accordance with directives from the secretary of state, but this was seen as a lack of respect. He had also toured London in 1833. Because of his time here as his country was in turmoil over the infamous Kansas-Nebraska Act, **Buchanan** was able to return home unscathed by the fuss, with few enemies, and secure the 1856 presidential nomination.

Pierce toured the country in 1858. Confederate President **Davis** came to Europe five times after the Civil War to live in various places, including 18 Upper Gloucester Place, Dorset Square, in London and Leamington, as did Mary and Tad Lincoln. **Davis** also lived in Paris and nearby Chantilly. While in Great Britain, he visited Chester Cathedral,* Scotland's Dryburgh* and Melrose Abbeys,* Rob Roy and Robert Burns sites, most of the tourist sites of London and many in Scotland. (**Abraham Lincoln** was never here, but Mary and Tad **Lincoln** lived for a while at Number 9 Woburn Place on the east side of Russell Square, diagonally across from the Russell Hotel in what is now a post office. **Lincoln's** grandson and namesake died at age seventeen in his parents' home, Number 2, Cromwell House, Kensington. The former president's son Robert was then the American ambassador.)

Grant took one of the grandest tours of the world ever taken by an American, 28 months, surely the grandest of any American president. He began with a visit to England and Scotland, arriving at St. Pancras Station,* and stayed at Number 17 on the NW corner of Cavendish Square (north of Oxford Circus Station) with his wife and nineteen-year-old son, Jesse. He heard himself referred to in a sermon in Westminster Abbey,* was honored at the Guildhall,* and ate at Kensington Palace* and Marlborough House* with entertainer Lily Langtry and writer Julia Ward Howe. (Prince Charles and Princess Diana lived in Kensington, where Queen Victoria was born and William III, Mary II, and Queen Anne died.) He discussed military history with the Duke of Wellington's son in the Waterloo Chamber of the Duke's Apsley House* and was received at the American Embassy. They left from Paddington Station* where they were received by Queen Victoria at Windsor Castle* to stay an evening and have dinner. Jesse was brought uninvited, coaxed into coming by his mother, did not want to come as he wanted to attend a ball in London, and then was not invited to eat at the Queen's table. He pouted like a spoiled ten-year-old, finally got an invitation, but acted so immature that the queen later pronounced him "a very ill-mannered young Yankee." During the night a cable from Army of the Potomac veterans arrived for **Grant**. A messenger boy arrived at the gate of the Castle and rang the bell. Her austere Majesty called out the window, "Who is it?" The boy hollered back, "Cable for General **Grant**. Is he staying in this house?" **Grant**'s daughter later lived in London.

Both **Theodore** and **Franklin Roosevelt** traveled extensively in Europe as children and visited all of the attractions in London normally seen today by tourists, including Westminster Abbey,* St. Paul's,* Hampton Court,* the British Museum,* etc. **Theodore** loved the Rembrandts at the National Gallery,* but hated and was shocked by the Rubens nudes. One of the places he visited as a child was Liverpool, where he admired his Confederate-leaning uncle and argued politics with Confederate **Davis's** son, who was in school there.

Theodore Roosevelt had come here as part of a year's trip in Europe at age eleven and also at age fourteen. One favorite London tavern in later life was Ye Olde Cheshire Cheese, 145 Fleet Street, also a favorite of Voltaire, Alexander Pope, Dickens, Thackeray, Mark Twain, Longfellow, and Conan Doyle. Before and after his second marriage, **TR** stayed at Brown's Hotel,* still at Number 21 Dover and running east to Albemarle Street, northwest of the Royal Academy of Arts on Piccadilly Street. In 1881 he came with his bride and continued to Switzerland, where he climbed the Jungfrau and Matterhorn. His 1886 second marriage occurred at St. George's Church,* a block south of Hanover Square at the SE corner of Maddox and St. George. The great musician George Handel had been the organist here in the 18th century. In 1910, returning from an African safari, **TR** came back as U.S. representative to the funeral of King Edward VII. **Roosevelt** was on a year's trip abroad and was here when the crowned heads of Europe last met, and may have then been the most famous man in the world. Kaiser Wilhelm told him, "Call upon me at 2:00; I have just forty-five minutes to give you." **Roosevelt** answered, "I will be there at two, Your Majesty, but unfortunately, I have but twenty minutes to give you."

Franklin Roosevelt came to Europe eight times in his first fourteen years. He and his new wife also stayed at Brown's on their honeymoon in 1905. (Author Mark Twain also had lived there.) **Roosevelt** was delighted to be given the Royal Suite because he was thought to be **Theodore's** son, but Eleanor was appalled at the $1000 per day cost. They lunched at the American Embassy and visited Allenwoods School at Southfields near Wimbledon, where Eleanor had gone to school. They dined at the Dorchester House on the east side of Hyde Park. In 1918 **Franklin**, as assistant secretary of the Navy, dined with George V in Buckingham Palace, met Winston Churchill at another dinner, and spent the weekend at Cliveden on the Thames north of Eton.

In 1886 **Taft** honeymooned for three months in France, England, and Scotland. The couple visited Hampton Court,* Lincoln* and York Cathedrals,* Holyrood Palace* and the castle* in Edinburgh, Wordsworth and Coleridge sites in the Lake Country, and stayed at the Royal Hotel, Blackfriars in London.

Wilson and his wife were the first non–royal overnight guests at Buckingham Palace in 1918 and also attended a luncheon at the Guildhall.* The trip was a success in spite of Mrs. **Wilson's** refusal to curtsy to the queen and **Wilson's** use of "sir" rather than "Your Majesty." In 1896 and 1899 he had stayed in the Covent Garden Hotel, Number 22–25 Southampton Street, and also visited several other times, seeing Cambridge, Oxford, Edinburgh, Glasgow, Stratford-on-Avon, and Tintern Abbey.*

Beginning in 1902, **Hoover** lived at a house called the White House on Ashley Drive, Walton-on-Thames near London. Later he was at the end and east side of Hyde Park Gate, Number 39 just south of Kensington Gardens until 1907. Their two sons were born here and both traveled halfway around the world within their first five weeks. He later moved to the Red House on Hornton Street West, Kensington, in 1907, where he stayed until 1914. While here he worked at his counseling firm at 1 London Wall in the City. In August 1914 as the war was beginning, he got a call from the U.S. consulate that stranded Americans were flocking to his office trying to get back. **Hoover** left his office to help, and for the rest of his life dedicated his life to public service, accepting no compensation even as president. He also donated his compensation from writing and speaking to charity. He headed a World War I relief committee at the Savoy Hotel in the Strand, just west of Waterloo Bridge. **Truman** was honored at the Savoy in 1956, with British Lord Halifax remarking that all there "would be quite happy to go tiger hunting [with him]." During a World War I German bombing raid, the **Hoovers** frantically searched for their missing sons, who were found calmly watching the destruction from a roof. At that they moved back to California.

Eisenhower's headquarters when he arrived in June 1942 were Suite 408, Claridge's Hotel,* still at Number 51 Brook Street, about two blocks from the American Embassy. **Ike** did not like the hotel, trimmed in black and gold, as he felt it looked like a Hollywood set. After about two weeks he moved to the Dorchester Hotel* on Brook Street across Park Lane from Hyde Park. His bedroom was described as "whorehouse pink." He shook so many hands at the American Embassy* on the west side of Grosvenor Square on July 4, he could not even initial memos. He visited Buckingham Palace as a tourist, and Churchill as a guest at Chequers, saying that he found the house cold and cheerless. He visited Windsor Castle* in 1942 with several other officers. His guide had agreed with the king that if he, the king, were seen, the tour would end. The king and his family forgot about the tour and came out to the garden to have tea when they saw the group coming. Not wishing them to be embarrassed and have the group leave, the king, queen, and Princess Elizabeth got on all fours and crawled beyond a wall to exit the area. The king and later Queen Elizabeth II laughed when they told the story to **Ike**.

Ike was later a guest of the king and queen back at Buckingham, and established headquarters at Number 20 Grosvenor Square and then Number 47 as Supreme Commander of the Allied Expeditionary Forces in January 1944. The planning for the D-Day Normandy landings was done here. In the springtime he had preferred to live in Telegraph Cottage on Comb Hill, Kingston-on-Thames. He was also at Norfolk House, Number 31 St. James Square, and the Dendreton on Park Lane. King George III's 1738 birthplace at the site of the Norfolk House was demolished in 1938. So many buildings on Grosvenor Square were occupied by high American military command that it was called "Eisenhowerplatz." After the war he spoke in the Guildhall.* As president he met in 1959 with the prime minister at 10 Downing Street, where he had frequently met with Churchill during the war. British commander Montgomery once parked in **Ike's** parking place, designated for the Allied commander. That's probably forgivable as Monty had a problem remembering who was who, but **Ike** did not press the matter. His driver did secure an agreement not to do so again. After the war he was given use for life of an apartment on the top floor of Culzean Castle in Ayrshire, Scotland, that can be rented today. He stayed here four times, once as president.

Kennedy lived with his family at Number 14 Princes Gate overlooking Kensington Gardens, just south of Hyde Park, and north of the Victoria and Albert Museum* that he surely saw. J.P. Morgan had given the house to the U.S. government for use as an embassy residence. **Kennedy's** father was the American ambassador from March 1938 until October 1940 and worked in the American Embassy. **JFK** met Churchill and the king and queen, thought Princess Elizabeth "had eyes for him," and attended a reception at 10 Downing. His father immediately embarrassed the American press by referring to the queen as "a cute trick." The British Foreign Office felt that he was a great publicity seeker who yearned to be the first Catholic president, but the country would have to wait a few years for one. (**Roosevelt** may have appointed Joseph Kennedy to the post here to get him out of the country, also sensing his presidential office aspirations.) The ambassador met many times here with the aviator Charles Lindbergh, who tried to convince him that England must greatly accelerate aircraft production or appease Hitler. King George VI and Queen Mary were guests in the house at Princes Gate, and watched Disney cartoons and *Goodbye Mr. Chips*. The future president attended the London School of Economics and witnessed the formal declaration of war with Germany in 1939. He was given a state dinner at Buckingham Palace in 1961 and attended the baptism of his niece at Westminster Cathedral.*

Truman made an extended tour of Europe in 1956, during which he received an honorary degree at Oxford's Sheldonian Theatre.* The ceremony was in Latin, and the students cheered, "Give 'em hell, Harricum!" The ex-president visited the House of Commons, Churchill's home, Chartwell,* south of London, and ate with Elizabeth II at Buckingham Palace.

In 1958 **Nixon** attended the American Memorial Chapel at St. Paul's and spoke in the Guildhall.

Carter had dinner at Buckingham Palace in 1977 and worshipped at Westminster Abbey. He was pleased to find a bust of American Henry Wadsworth Longfellow in the Poet's Corner, but complained that his favorite poet, Welshman Dylan Thomas, was not honored. A stone was soon installed. At this time he ate with the prime minister at 10 Downing, Lancaster House (next to St. James Palace), and White Hall Banqueting House.* **George H.W. Bush** was at Number 10 Downing and Buckingham Palace in 1989, 1990, and 1991, and Chequers House in 1984.

Movie star **Reagan** was at Savoy Hotel (mentioned above) in November 1948 until March 1949 for filming and visited many landmarks in 1984, including the Guildhall and St. James Palace. In 1982 he became the only president ever to address the Houses of Parliament and implored the free world to seize the initiative to end the cold war and put Marxism on the ash heap of history. He ate at Buckingham Palace in 1989, getting the Most Honorable Order of Bath. Eisenhower got it in 1943.

Clinton was the first president who had been a Rhodes Scholar at Oxford University in Oxford. In 1968 and 1969 he stayed in an almshouse on the right rear of Helen's Court. Later he moved to Holywell Manor and then 46 Leckford Road. Turf Tavern and Porter's Lodge saw him frequently. He was so active in demonstrations against the Vietnam War that he did not earn a degree. He came back to England several times before, during, and after the presidency, had tea with Elizabeth II at Buckingham Palace, and visited two prime ministers at their retreat, Chequers. He also visited the beautiful American Cemetery near Cambridge with its Wall of Missing.

George W. Bush stayed three days at Buckingham Palace in November 2003, and discussed policy at the Whitehall Royal Banqueting House. (Charles I had his head chopped off in 1649 at a location marked outside.) This was during the turmoil of the Iraq War. One British writer commented, "Perhaps never before in [history] has a state visit seemed so like an exercise in public humiliation, for the host and guest involved."

Bibliography

Many libraries supplied vertical files with old newspaper clippings of presidential presence outlined, more or less, some without specific dates. State and city WPA Guides of various editions, brochures and leaflets from most of the towns, parks and historical sites are not generally listed separately, but were also considered. Exact dates are believed to be as accurate as possible; dates were often not readily available from the sources consulted. Brochures and pamphlets are available for many of the sites.

Abraham Lincoln at the Hampton Roads Peace Conference. Norfolk: Fort Monroe Museum, 1968.

Adams papers, Series 1: Diaries. Cambridge: Belknap Press of Harvard University, 1961.

Adams, Arthur G. *Hudson River Guidebook.* Bronx, New York: Fordham University Press, 1996.

Adams, George Rollie, and Ralph Jerry Christian. *Nashville: A Pictorial History.* Virginia Beach: Donning, 1981.

Adams, William Howard. *The Paris Years of Thomas Jefferson.* New Haven: Yale University, 1997.

Allensworth, Ben C. *History of Tazewell County.* Published locally, 1905.

Alper, M. Victor. *America's Freedom Trail.* New York: Collier Macmillan, 1976.

Alsop, Joseph. *FDR.* New York: Thames and Hudson, 1982.

Alton General City Directory for 1858. Alton, Illinois.

The American Heritage Book of the Presidents. New York: Simon and Schuster, 1968.

Ammon, Harry. *James Monroe: The Quest for National Identity.* New York: McGraw-Hill, 1971, 1981.

Anderson, Elizabeth B. *Annapolis: A Walk Through History*, third printing. Centreville, Maryland: Tidewater Publishers, 1995.

Anderson, James W. "The Real Issue: An Analysis of the Final Lincoln-Douglas Debate." *Lincoln Herald*, Lincoln Memorial University Press, Spring 1967.

Angle, Paul M. *Here I Have Lived.* Chicago: Abraham Lincoln Book Shop, 1971.

_____. *Lincoln in Springfield.* Springfield, IL: Lincoln Centennial Association, 1925.

_____, ed. *Lincoln Reader.* Piscataway, NJ: Rutgers University Press, 1947.

Anthony, Carl Sferrazza. *America's First Families.* New York: Simon and Schuster, 2000.

_____. *America's First Ladies.* New York: Touchstone, 2000.

_____. *First Ladies.* New York: William Morrow, 1990.

Archer, Bill. *Columbus Vignettes II.* Nida-Eckstrein Printing, 1967.

Ardery, W.B. "The Other Ride of the Revolution." *American History Illustrated*, October 1971.

Armes, Ethel. *Stratford Hall.* Richmond, VA: Garrett and Massie, 1936.

Arnett, Earl. *Maryland: A New Guide to the Old Line State.* Baltimore: Johns Hopkins Press, 1999.

Ashbury, John W. *...And All Our Yesterdays: A Chronicle of Frederick County, Maryland.* Essex, England: M&B Printing, 1997.

Ashenhurst, John M. *All About Chicago.* Rolling Springs, IL: Riverside Press, 1933.

Ashland, Home of Henry Clay. Members of the Board of the Henry Clay Memorial Foundation, undated.

Austin, Texas, History Center newspaper files.

Baber, Adin, and Mary E. Lobb. "The Lincoln Log Cabins." *Lincoln Herald*, Spring 1969.

Baer, Christopher. *Canals and Railroads of the Mid-Atlantic States 1800–1860.* Wilmington, DE: Eleutherian Mills-Hagley Foundation, 1981.

Baertich, Frank. *History of Troy, Indiana.* Utica, KY: McDowell Publications, 1983.

Bailey, James H. *Pictures of the Past.* Virginia Antiquities, 1989.

Bak, Richard. *The Day Lincoln Was Shot.* Dallas: Taylor, 1998.

Baker, Jean. *Mary Todd Lincoln.* New York: W.W. Norton, 1987.

Ballard, Michael B. "Cheers for Jefferson Davis." *American History Illustrated*, May 1981.

Banton, O.T. *History of Macon County*. Macon County Historical Society, 1976.

Barefoot, Daniel W. *Touring North Carolina's Revolutionary War Sites*. Winston-Salem, NC: John F. Blair, 1999.

_____. *Touring South Carolina's Revolutionary War Sites*. Winston-Salem, NC: John F. Blair, 1999.

Baringer, William E. *Lincoln's Vandalia*. Abraham Lincoln Association, Piscataway, NJ: Rutgers University Press, 1949.

Barnard, Harry. *Rutherford B. Hayes and His America*. Newtown, CN: American Political Biography Press, 1992.

Barringer, Floyd S. *Historic Homes of Springfield*. Self-published, 1966.

_____, M.D. *Tour of Historic Springfield*. Self-published, 1971.

Barton, William E. *The Life of Abraham Lincoln*. Indianapolis: Bobbs-Merrill, 1925.

_____. *Lincoln at Gettysburg*. Indianapolis: Bobbs-Merrill, 1930.

_____. *Lincoln at Gettysburg*. Peter Smith, 1930 (1950 reprint).

Basler, Roy P., ed. *Collected Works of Abraham Lincoln*. Piscataway, NJ: Rutgers University Press, 1953.

Bassett, William B. *Historic American Buildings Survey of New Jersey*. Newark: New Jersey Historical Society, 1977.

Bassuk, Daniel. "Lincoln in Trenton, N.J.— A Sequel." *Lincoln Herald*, Spring 1995.

Battaile, Connie Hopkins. *The Oregon Book*. Ashland, OR: Saddle Mountain Press, 1998.

Bauer, K. Jack. *Zachary Taylor: Soldier, Planter, Statesman of the Old Southwest*. Newtown, CT: American Political Biography Press, 1985.

Bayne, Julia Taft. *Tad Lincoln's Father*. Lincoln, NE: University of Nebraska, 2001.

Bear, James A, Jr., and Lucia C. Stanton, eds. *Jefferson's Memorandum Books*. Princeton: Princeton University Press, 1997.

Bearss, Edwin C. *Historic Resource Study and Historic Structure Report, Lincoln's Neighborhood*. U.S. Dept. of the Interior, 1977.

Beeson, Helen, et. al. *Places and People in Old Decatur*. Decatur, IL: Zonta Club of Decatur, 1975.

Benbow, Nancy D. Myers, and Christopher H. Benbow. *Cabins, Cottages, and Mansions*. Gettysburg, PA.: Thomas Publications, 1993.

Bergheim, Laura. *The Washington Historical Atlas*. Bethesda, MD: Woodbine House, 1992.

Berton, Pierre. *Niagara: A Brief History of the Falls*. Tokyo: Kodansha International, 1997.

Bill, Alfred Hoyt. *The Beleaguered City: Richmond, 1861–1865*. New York: Alfred A. Knopf, 1946.

_____. *A House Called Morven: Its Role in American History*. Princeton, NJ: Princeton University Press, 1954.

Bishop, Arthur, ed. *Thomas Jefferson, 1743–1826: Chronology, Documents, Bibliographical Aids*. New York: Oceana Publishing, 1971.

Bishop, Jim. *FDR's Last Year*. New York: Pocket Book Editions, 1975.

Black, Mary. *Old New York in Early Photographs*. Mineola, NY: Dover Publishing, 1973.

Blair, Edward. *Leadville, Colorado's Magic City*. Fred Prewett Publishers, 1980.

Blankmeyer, Helen Van Cleave. *The Sangamon Country*. Springfield, IL: Philips Bros., 1965.

Blodgett, Bonnie, and D.J. Tice. *At Home With the Presidents*. New York: Overlook Press, 1988.

Boatner, Mark M. III. *The Civil War Dictionary*. New York: David McKay, 1976.

_____. *Landmarks of the American Revolution*. Mechanicsburg, PA: Stackpole Books, 1973.

Bodenhamer, David J., and Robert G. Barrows, eds. *The Encyclopedia of Indianapolis*. Bloomington, IN: University of Indiana Press, 1994.

Boller, Paul F., Jr. *Congressional Anecdotes*. New York: Oxford University Press, 1991.

_____. *Presidential Anecdotes*. New York: Penguin Book, 1981.

_____. *Presidential Campaigns*. New York: Oxford University Press, 2004.

_____. *Presidential Inaugurations*. San Diego: Harcourt, 2001.

_____. *Presidential Wives*. New York: New York: Oxford University Press, 1988.

Bond, Frederic William. *A Little History of a Great City*. Winnetka, IL: Book and Print Guild, 1934.

Bourte, Miriam Anne. *First Family*. New York: W.W. Norton, 1982.

Boyd, Julian P., ed. *The Papers of Thomas Jefferson 1785–1786*. Princeton: Princeton University Press, 1954.

Boye, Alan. *Complete Roadside Guide to Nebraska*. St. Johnsbury, VT: Saltillo Press, 1993.

Braden, Waldo W. "Lincoln's Western Travel, 1859." *Lincoln Herald*, Summer 1988.

Brands, H.W. *T.R.: The Last Romantic*. New York: Basic Books, 1997.

Brandywine Story, Brandywine Battlefield Park Commission, 1975.

Brawley, James S. *Rowan County: A Brief History*. Salisbury, NC: Historic Salisbury Foundation, 1984.

_____. *The Rowan Story*. Salisbury, NC: Rowan Printing, 1953.

Breck, Lt. George. *Rochester Union and Advertiser*. Several articles from the collection at Fredericksburg Battlefield Visitors Center.

Bremer, Howard F., ed. *John Adams, 1735–1826* (Chronology-Documents-Bibliographical Aids). New York: Oceana Publishing, 1967.

Brevet's Illinois Historical Markers and Sites. Sioux Falls, SD: Brevet Press, 1976.

Brodie, Fawn M. *Thomas Jefferson: An Intimate History*. New York: Bantam Books, 1975.

Brooks, Chester L., and Mattison, Ray H. *Theodore Roosevelt and the Dakota Badlands*. Washington, D.C.: National Park Service, 1958.

Brooks, Gertrude Zeth. *First Ladies of the White House*. Chicago: Chas. Hallberg, 1970.

Brooks, Noah. *Washington in Lincoln's Time*. New York: Quadrangle Books, 1871.
Brown, Abram English. *Faneuil Hall and Faneuil Hall Market*. Boston: Lee and Shepard, 1900.
Brown, Richard C. *Buffalo, Lake City in Niagara Land*. Brightwaters, NY: Windsor Publications, 1981.
Browning, Judith H. *New York, Yesterday and Today*. Stamford, CT: Corsair Publications, 1990.
Bruce, Philip Alexander. *History of University of Virginia*. Charlottesville: General Alumni Association, 1920.
Bryant, Irving. *James Madison*. Indianapolis: Bobbs-Merrill, 1970.
Bryner, R.C. *Abraham Lincoln in Peoria*. Peoria, IL: Edward J. Jacob, 1926.
Burgwyn, Diana. *The 1776 Guide for Pennsylvania*. New York: Harper Colophon Books, Harper and Row, 1975.
Burlingame, Michael. *The Inner World of Abraham Lincoln*. Urbana: University of Illinois, 1994.
_____. *An Oral History of Abraham Lincoln*. John G. Nicolay's Interviews and Essays. Carbondale, IL: Southern Illinois University Press, 1996.
_____, and John R. Turner Ettlinger. *Inside Lincoln's White House*. Carbondale, IL: Southern Illinois University, 1997.
Burns, Ric, and James Sanders. *New York: An Illustrated History*. New York: Alfred A. Knopf, 1999.
Burr, Nelson R. "Abraham Lincoln: Western Star Over Connecticut." *Lincoln Herald*, Spring 1983.
Burtschi, Mary. *Vandalia: Wilderness Capital of Lincoln's Land*. Decatur, IL: Huston-Patterson Corporation, 1963.
Bush, George. *All the Best*. New York: Scribner's, 1999.
Bushong, Millard K. *Historic Jefferson County* [West Virginia]. Boyce, VA: Carr Publishing, 1972.
Cable, Mary. *The Avenue of the Presidents*. Boston: Houghton Mifflin, 1969.
Caemmerer, H. Paul. *Historic Washington*. Washington, D.C.: Columbia Historical Society, 1954.
Cagle, Eldon, Jr. *Fort Sam: The Story of Fort Sam Houston, Texas*. San Antonio: Maverick Publishing, 2003.
Calkins, Chris. *Civil War Petersburg, 1861–1865*. City of Petersburg, 2003.
Calkins, Earnest Elmo. *They Broke The Prairies*. Champaign, IL: University of Illinois Press, 1937, 1989.
Callahan, H.M. Augusta, *A Pictorial History of Richmond*. Richmond: Richmond County Historical Society, 1980.
Cannon, Timothy, et. al. *Pictorial History of Frederick, Maryland*. Frederick, MD: Key Publishing, 1995.
Carnegie, Dale. *Lincoln the Unknown*. East Cleveland, OH: Forest Hills Publishing, 1932.
Caro, Robert A. *The Years of Lyndon Johnson*. New York: Alfred A. Knopf, 1990.
Caroli, Betty Boyd. *First Ladies*. New York: Oxford University Press, 1987.
Carr, Clark E. *Lincoln at Gettysburg*. Chicago: A.C. McClurg, 1906.
Carson, Will C. *Historical Souvenir of Greenville, Illinois*. LeCrone Press, 1905.
Carter, Kathryn. *Stagecoach Inns of Texas*. Waco, TX: Texian Press, 1977.
Cashman, George I. *Little Known Facts ...Abraham Lincoln and the Civil War*. Lincoln Center, 1963.
Cass County Historian. June 1988.
Castel, Albert. "Sam Houston's Last Fight." *American Heritage Magazine*, December 1965.
Cathcart, Charlotte. *Indianapolis From Our Old Corner*. Indianapolis: Indiana Historical Society, 1965.
Catton, Bruce. *The Centennial History of the Civil War*. New York: Doubleday, 1961.
Cawthorne, Nigel. *Sex Lives of the Presidents*. New York: St. Martin's Paperbacks, 1996.
Century 1, Notes on Sullivan, Illinois. Moultrie County Historical Society.
Chadwick, Bruce. *Two American Presidents*. Secaucus, NJ: Carol Publishing Group, 1999.
Chambers, S. Allen, Jr. *Lynchburg: An Architectural History*. Charlottesville, VA: University Press of Virginia, 1981.
Chicago City Directories, 1855–1873.
Chitwood, Oliver Perry. *John Tyler: Champion of the Old South*. New York: Russell and Russell, 1964.
Christ, Elwood M. *We Are Met on a Great Battlefield: American Presidential Performance at Gettysburg, 1863–1938*. Unpublished manuscript, 1995.
Christian, W. Asbury. *Lynchburg and Its People*. Lynchburg, VA: J.P. Bell, 1935.
_____. *Richmond, Her Past and Present*. Richmond, VA: L.H. Jenkins, 1912.
City Directories for many cities, including: Albany, Alton, Boston, Buffalo, Cincinnati, Columbus, Chicago (many years), Concord, Dayton, Hartford (1860), Leavenworth, Lowell, Manchester, Memphis, New Bedford, New Haven, New London, Norwich, Providence, Richmond, Springfield, Taunton, Trenton, Worcester, Washington, D.C. (1860, 1862–5).
"Civil War at West Point." *Blue and Gray Magazine*, December 1991.
Clark, Anne. *Historic Homes of San Augustine*. Austin: Encino Press, 1973.
Clarke, James W. *American Assassins*. Princeton: Princeton University Press, 1982.
Clinton, Bill. *My Life*. New York: Alfred A. Knopf, 2004.
Clotworthy, William G. *In the Footsteps of George Washington*. Granville, OH: McDonald & Woodward Publishing, 2002.
_____. *Presidential Sites*. Granville, OH: McDonald & Woodward Publishing, 1998.
Cohen, Stan B. *A Pictorial Guide to West Virginia's Civil War Sites*. Forest Park, IL: Pictorial Histories Pub., 1990.
Colbert, Judy. *Off the Beaten Path in Maryland and Delaware*. Guildford, CT: Globe Pequot Press, 2005.
_____. *Off the Beaten Path in Virginia*. Guildford, CT: Globe Pequot Press, 2007.
Coleman, Charles Hubert. *Abraham Lincoln and Coles County, Illinois*. Lanham, MD: Scarecrow Press, 1955.

Coleman, J. Winston. Jr. *Kentucky: A Pictorial History.* Lexington, KY: University Press of Kentucky, 1971.

_____. "Mary Todd Lincoln's Birthplace." *Lincoln Herald,* Spring 1963.

_____. *The Squire's Sketches of Lexington.* Lexington, KY: Henry Clay Press, 1972.

Collections of the Illinois State Historical Library, Vol. III, Lincoln Series, *Vol. I, The Lincoln-Douglas Debates of 1858.* Springfield.

Collier, Christopher. *Decision in Philadelphia.* New York: Ballantine Books, 1987.

Collier, Peter. *The Roosevelts.* New York: Simon and Schuster, 1994.

Collier's Magazine, Lincoln Centennial Issue. Reprint. Original date February 13, 1909.

Collins, Tom. *The Search for Jimmy Carter.* Waco, TX: Word Books, 1976.

Columbia Historical Society, Reprints from the Records, Vol. 21. Gist Blair, 1921.

Community Guide and Business Directory. Greater Silver Spring Chamber of Commerce, 1998.

Condon, George E. *Yesterday's Cleveland.* Miami: E.A. Seemann Publishers, 1976.

_____. *Yesterday's Columbus.* Miami: E.A. Seemann Publishing, 1977.

_____. *Yesterday's Philadelphia.* Miami: E.A. Seemann Publishing, 1976.

Conner, Jane Hollenbeck. *Lincoln in Stafford.* Stafford, VA: Parker Pub., LLC, 2006.

Conway, W. Fred. *Young Abe Lincoln.* New Albany, IN: FBH Publishers, 1997.

Cooling, Benjamin F. III, and Walton H. Owen II. *Mr. Lincoln's Forts: A Guide to the Civil War Defenses of Washington.* Shippensburg, PA: White Mane Pub., 1988.

Cooper, William J. *Jefferson Davis, American.* New York: Alfred A. Knopf, 2000.

Coski, John M. *The Army of the Potomac at Berkeley Landing.* Richmond, VA: Berkeley Plantation, 1989.

Cox, Ethelyn. *Historic Alexandria, Virginia, Street by Street.* Alexandria: Historic Alexandria, 1976.

Crady, Wilson. "Incident of Destiny." *Lincoln Herald,* Fall 1981.

Cramer, John Henry. *Lincoln Under Fire.* Baton Rouge: LSU Press, 1948.

Crawford, Charles W. *Yesterday's Memphis.* Miami: E.A. Seemann Publishing, 1976.

Cresson, W.P. *James Monroe.* Chapel Hill: U. of North Carolina, 1946.

Cromie, Alice Hamilton. *A Tour Guide to the Civil War.* Nashville, TN.: Rutledge Hill Press, 1990.

Crooks City Directories (Chicago), 1855–1875 (CHS).

Cullen, Joseph P. "Brandywine Creek." *American History Illustrated,* August 1980.

Cuquox, Rene. *The Leadville Story.* Johnson Publishers, 1994.

Current, Richard N. *The Lincoln Nobody Knows.* New York: Hill and Wang, 1958.

Currier, John J. *History of Newburyport, Mass.* New Haven: New Haven Printing, 1909.

Curry, J. Seymour. *Abraham Lincoln's Visit to Evanston in 1860.* Evanston, IL: City National Bank, 1914.

Dabney, Virginius. *Richmond: The Story of a City.* New York: Doubleday, 1990.

Dallas Weekly Herald, May 22, 1875.

D'Amato, Donald J. *Springfield* [Mass.], *350 Years: A Pictorial History.* Virginia Beach, VA.: Donning, 1985.

Daniels, Josephus. *The Life of Woodrow Wilson, 1856–1924.* Will H. Johnston, 1924.

Darter, Oscar H. *Colonial Fredericksburg and Neighborhood in Perspective.* New York: Twayne, 1957.

Davenport (Iowa) Sunday Times-Democrat, February 10, 1963.

Davenport, Don. *In Lincoln's Footsteps.* Maryville, MO: Prairie Oak Press, 1991.

Davis, Deering, Stephen P. Dorsey, and Ralph Cole Hall. *Alexandria Houses.* New York: Bonanza Books, 1956.

Davis, Edwin. "Lincoln and Macon County, Illinois." *Journal of Illinois State Historical Society,* April-July.

Davis, John H. *The Kennedys.* New York: McGraw-Hill, 1984.

Davis, Kenneth S. *Invincible Summer: An Intimate Portrait of the Roosevelts.* New York: Athenaeum, 1974.

Davis, William C. *Jefferson Davis: The Man and His Hour.* Baton Rouge: LSU Press, 1996.

Day, Richard. *Vincennes: A Pictorial History.* St. Louis, MO: G. Bradley Publishing, 1994.

DeBolt, Margaret Wayt. *A Historical Portrait of Savannah.* Virginia Beach, VA.: Donning Pub., 1976.

De Chambrun, Clara (Longworth). *Cincinnati: The Story of the Queen City.* New York: Chas. Scribner's, 1939.

DeGregorio, William A. *The Complete Book of U.S. Presidents.* New York: Dembner Books, 1984.

De La Hunt, Thomas James. *Perry County, A History.* W.K. Stewart, 1916.

Delaplaine, Edward S. *The Life of Thomas Johnson.* Westminster, MD: Willow Bend Books, 1927.

Delaware's Heritage Trail. State publication, undated.

Denault, Patricia. *The Little Giant,* American History Illustrated, October 1970

Di Ionno, Mark. A *Guide to New Jersey's Revolutionary War Trail.* New Brunswick: Rutgers University, 2000.

Dodge, Daniel Kilham. "Lincoln in Champaign County." *Illinois Magazine.*

Donald, David Herbert. *Lincoln.* London: Jonathan Cape Random House, 1995.

_____. *Lincoln Reconsidered.* New York: Random House, 1961.

_____. "This Damned Old House: The Lincolns in the White House." In *The White House: The First 200 Years.* Boston: Northeastern University Press, 1994.

Dooley, Claude and Betty. *Why Stop? A guide to Texas Historical Roadside Markers.* Houston: Lone Star Books, 1985.

Dorchester ...Old and New. Dorchester, Massachusetts, Tercentenary Committee, Chapple Pub., 1930.

Dover's Heritage Trails. Greater Dover Chamber of Commerce.

Dowdey, Clifford. "The Harrisons of Berkeley Hundred." *American Heritage Magazine*, April 1957.
Dows, Olin. *Franklin Roosevelt at Hyde Park*. New York: American Artists Group, 1949.
Drake, Samuel Adams. *Old Landmarks and Historic Personages of Boston*. Rutland, VT: Charles E. Tuttle, revised 1975.
Drury, John. *Old Illinois Homes*. Springfield: Illinois State Historical Society, 1948.
Dulaney, Paul S. The *Architecture of Historic Richmond*. Charlottesville, VA: University Press of Virginia, 1992.
Dumbauld, Edward. *Thomas Jefferson, American Tourist*. Norman, OK: University of Oklahoma, 1946.
Dumych, Daniel M. *Niagara Falls (Images of America Series)*. Mt. Pleasant, SC: Arcadia, 1996.
Duncan, Kunigunde, and D.F. Nickols. *Mentor Graham: The Man Who Taught Lincoln*. Chicago: University of Chicago Press, 1944.
Dunlap, David W. *On Broadway: A Journey Uptown Over Time*. New York: Rizzoli, 1990.
Dunshee, Kenneth Holcomb. *As You Pass By*. New York: Hastings House, 1952.
Durant, John. *The Sports of the Presidents*. New York: Hastings House, 1964.
Durant, John and Alice. *Pictorial History of American Presidents*. New York: A.S. Barnes, 1955.
Durfee, David A., ed. *William Henry Harrison, 1773–1841; John Tyler, 1790–1862: Chronology, Documents, Bibliographical Aids*. New York: Oceana Publishing, 1970.
Dyba, Thomas J., and George L. Painter. *Seventeen Years at Eighth and Jackson*. Lisle, IL: IBC Publications, 1985.
Dyer, Brainerd. *Zachary Taylor*. Baton Rouge: LSU Press, 1946.
East, Ernest E. *Abraham Lincoln Sees Peoria*. Chicago: Record Publishing, 1939.
_____. *Story of Peoria*. Chicago: Record Publishing, 1939.
Eastman, John. *Who Lived Here*. New York: Facts on File, 1983.
Eberlein, Harold D., et al., *Historic Homes in Georgetown-Town of Washington City*. Petersburg, VA: Dietz Press, 1958.
Eckenrode, H.J., ed. *Richmond, Capital of Virginia*. Richmond, VA: Whittet and Shepperson, 1938.
Eckley, Robert S. "Lincoln's Intimate Friend, Leonard Swett." *Journal of Illinois State Historical Society*, Autumn 1999 (and similar article in Spring 2000).
Edgington, Frank E. *History of the New York Avenue Presbyterian Church*. Washington, D.C.: New York Avenue Presbyterian Church, 1961.
Edwards City Directories (Chicago), 1855–1876.
Ehrmann, Bess V. *The Missing Chapter in the Life of Abraham Lincoln*. Chicago: Walter M. Hill, 1938 (reprinted 1990).
Eisenhower, Dwight D. *At Ease: Stories I Tell To Friends*. New York: Doubleday, 1967.
Elliot, Ian, ed. *James Madison, 1751–1836: Chronology, Documents, Bibliographical Aids*. New York: Oceana Publishing, 1969.
_____. *James Monroe, 1758–1831: Chronology, Documents, Bibliographical Aids*. New York: Oceana Publishing, 1969.
Elwood, Mary Ann. *Charlottesville and the University of Virginia*. Virginia Beach, VA: Donning, 1982.
Embrey, Alvin T. *History of Fredericksburg, Virginia*. Richmond, VA: Old Dominion Press, 1937 (reprinted 1994).
Engle, Morey. *Denver Comes of Age*. Boulder, CO: Johnson Books, 1994.
Erickson, Gary. "The Graves of Ann Rutledge and the Old Concord Burial Ground." *Lincoln Herald*, Fall 1969.
Evelyn, Douglas E., and Paul Dickson. *On This Spot: Pinpointing the Past in Washington, D.C.* Washington, D.C.: Farragut Pub., 1992.
Ewing, Charles. *Yesterday's Washington, D.C.* Miami: E.A. Seemann Publishing, 1976.
Farrar, Emmie Ferguson. *Old Virginia Houses Along the James*. New York: Bonanza Books, 1957.
_____, and Emilee Hinds. *Old Virginia Houses Along the Fall Line*. New York: Hastings House, 1971.
_____, and _____. *Old Virginia Houses: The Heart of Virginia*. Hale Pub., 1974.
_____, and _____. *Old Virginia Houses: The Northern Peninsulas*. New York: Hastings House, 1972.
Farrell, John J., ed. *James Polk, 1795–1849: Chronology, Documents, Bibliographical Aids*. New York: Oceana Publishing, 1970.
_____., ed. *Zachary Taylor, 1784–1845: Chronology, Documents, Bibliographical Aids*. New York: Oceana Publishing, 1971.
Faule, Wilson H. *Great Hartford Picture Book*. Virginia Beach, VA.: Donning, 1985.
Fay, Jim. "Lincoln and Douglas at the Bryant Cottage." *Lincoln Herald*, Winter 1998.
Federal Writers Project. *Our Washington*. Chicago: A.C. McClurg, 1939.
_____. *Philadelphia: A Guide to the Nation's Birthplace*. Philadelphia: William Penn Association of Philadelphia, 1937.
_____. *U.S. One*. U.S. No. One Highway Association, Inc. New York: Modern Age Books, 1938.
_____. *WPA Guidebooks*, all states and many cities.
Fehrenbach, T.R. *Lone Star*. New York: Macmillan. Third Printing, 1974.
Fehrenbacher, Don E. *Prelude to Greatness*. Palo Alto, CA: Stanford University Press, 1962.
_____. *Recollected Words of Abraham Lincoln*. Palo Alto, CA: Stanford University Press, 1996.
Felder, Paula S. *Forgotten Companions*. Fredericksburg, VA: Historic Publications of Fredericksburg, 1982.
_____. *George Washington's Fredericksburg*. American History Commission, 1998.
Felsenthal, Carol. *Alice Roosevelt Longworth*. New York: Putnam's, 1988.
Fenson, Rod, and Julie Foreman. *Illinois: Off the*

Beaten Path. Guilford, CT: Globe Pequot Press, 1987 and 1999.

Ferling, John. *John Adams: A Life.* Knoxville: University of Tenn., 1992.

Ferrell, Robert H. *Harry S. Truman.* Boston: Little, Brown, 1983.

_____. *Off The Record.* New York: Penguin Books, 1980.

_____. *Truman: A Century of Remembrance.* New York: Viking Press, 1984.

Ferris, Gary. *Presidential Places.* Winston-Salem, NC: John F. Blair Publisher, 1999.

Ferris, Robert G., ed. *The Presidents.* Washington, D.C.: U.S. Dept. of the Interior, National Park Service, 1976.

_____. *Signers of the Declaration.* Washington, D.C.: U.S. Dept. of the Interior, National Park Service, 1973.

Final Report of the Boston National Historic Sites Commission. Washington, D.C.: U.S. Government Printing Office, 1961.

Findley, Paul. *A. Lincoln: The Crucible of Congress.* New York: Crown, 1979.

Fite, Gilbert C. *Mount Rushmore.* Norman, OK: University of Oklahoma Press, 1952.

Fitzpatrick, John C., ed. *The Diaries of George Washington 1748–1799.* 4 vols. Boston: Houghton Mifflin, 1925.

Fleming, Thomas. *The Living Land of Lincoln.* New York: Reader's Digest Press, 1980.

Flexner, James Thomas. *George Washington in the American Revolution.* New York: Little, Brown, 1967, 1968.

_____. *Washington: The Indispensable Man.* New York: Signet, 1984.

Floyd, Viola C. *Lancaster County Tours.* Lancaster, PA: Lancaster County Historical Society, 1956.

Fogelman, Marguerite Flint. *Historical Markers of Richmond Co. Ga.* Richmond County Historical Society, 1986.

Forman, Stephen M. *A Guide to Civil War Washington.* Roseland, NJ: Elliot and Clark Pub., 1995.

Fort Monroe Guide Book. The Casement Museum, Fort Monroe, 1993.

Foster, Genevieve. *Abraham Lincoln's World.* New York: Scribner's, 1944.

Fox, Elise Scharf. *Hotel Gettysburg.* Downtown Gettysburg, 1988.

Frank, Sid, and Arden Davis Melick. *Presidential Tidbits and Trivia.* New York: Greenwich House, 1984.

Franklin Pierce of New Hampshire. Lloyd Hills Press, undated.

Frassanito, William A. *Antietam: The Photographic Legacy of American's Bloodiest Day.* New York: Scribner's, 1978.

_____. *Gettysburg: A Journey in Time.* New York: Scribner's, 1975.

_____. *Grant and Lee: The Virginia Campaigns, 1864–1865.* New York: Scribner's, 1983.

Frazier, Carl, and Rosalie Frazier. *The Lincoln Country in Pictures.* Fern Park, FL: Hastings House, 1963.

Free Lance-Star (Fredericksburg, Virginia), Feb. 12, 1999, June 11, 1999.

Freeman, Andrew A. *Abraham Lincoln Goes to New York.* New York: Coward-McCann, 1960.

Freeman, Douglas Southall. *Washington.* New York: Simon and Schuster, 1968.

Fricke, Chuck, ed. *Mount Pulaski 1836–1986.* S. J. Clarke Pub., 1986.

Froncek, Thomas. *The City of Washington.* New York: Alfred Knopf, 1985.

Frost, Lawrence A. *U.S. Grant Album.* Seattle: Superior Publishing, 1966.

Gady, Anita. "Lincoln's Interests in Jacksonville." Thesis, Jacksonville Library.

Garrett, Jill, and Claudia Jack. *A Walk with James K. Polk.* Columbia, TN: Columbia Historical Society, undated.

Garrett, Wendell. *Our Changing White House.* Boston: Northeastern University Press, 1995.

Garrison, Webb. *The Amazing Civil War.* New York: MJF Books, 1998.

_____. *The Lincoln No One Knows.* Nashville: Rutledge Hill Press, 1993.

_____. *A Treasury of White House Tales.* Nashville: Rutledge Hill Press, 1989.

_____. *Unusual Personages of the Civil War.* Fredericksburg, VA: Sergeant Kirkland's, 1996.

Gary, Ralph. *Following in Lincoln's Footsteps.* New York: Carroll and Graf, 2001.

Geddes, Jean. *Fairfax County.* Middleburg, VA: Denlinger's, 1967.

Gelbert, Douglas. *American Revolutionary War Sites, Memorials, Museums, and Library Collections.* Jefferson, NC: McFarland, 1998.

George Washington in New York. Normal, IL: Masonic Book Club, 1987.

Georgetown (Ohio) News Democrat, April 27, 1972.

Georgia Historic Quarterlies, Number 33 (1), p. 27, and Vol. 55, Number 3.

Gerlach, Don R. *Philip Schuyler's Saratoga.* West Nyack, NY: Dexter Press, undated.

Gernon, Blain Brooks. *The Lincolns in Chicago.* Chicago: Ancarthe Publishers, 1934.

Gies, Joseph. *FDR: Portrait of a President.* New York: Doubleday, 1971.

_____. *Harry S. Truman: A Pictorial Biography.* New York: Doubleday, 1968.

Gilman, Arthur. *The Story of Boston.* New York: Putnam's, 1902.

Gilman, Daniel C. *James Monroe.* Boston: Houghton Mifflin, 1911.

Gleason, Paul E. *Lincoln (Illinois), A Pictorial History.* St. Louis: G. Bradley Publishing, 1998.

Godrick, John T. *Historic Fredericksburg: The Story of an Old Town.* Whittet and Shepperson, 1922.

Goff, John S. *Robert Todd Lincoln: A Man in His Own Right.* Norman, OK: University of Oklahoma, 1969.

Gordon, Paul P., and Rita Gordon. *A Textbook History of Frederick County.* Board of Education of Frederick County, MD, 1975.

Gordon, William A. *The Ultimate Hollywood Tour Book.* El Toro, CA: North Ridge Books, 1998.

Graham, Otis L., and Meghan Robinson Wander, eds. *Franklin D. Roosevelt, His Life and Times*. G.K. Hall, 1985.

Grant, Jessie R. *In the Days of My Father, General Grant*. New York: Harper and Row, 1925.

Grant, Marian Hepburn, and Ellsworth Strong Grant. *City of Hartford 1784–1984*. Hartford: Connecticut Historical Society, 1986.

Green, John B., III. *A New Bern Album*. New Bern, NC: Tryon Palace Commission, 1985.

Green, Constance McLoughlin. *The Church on Lafayette Square*. Dulles, VA: Potomac Books, 1970.

Greiff, Constance, and Wanda S. Gunning. *Morven, Memory, Myth, and Reality*. Princeton: Historic Morven, 2004.

Grizzard, Frank E., Jr. *George Washington: A Biographical Companion*. ABC-Clio, 2002.

Groden, Robert J. *The Killing of a President*. New York: Viking Studio Books, 1994.

Groff, Sibyl. *Guide to New Jersey Homes*. New York: A.S. Barnes, 1971.

Groton School 1884–1985. Groton, MA: Trustees of Groton School, 1986.

Guide to Historic Alton, Illinois on the Mississippi. Alton Area Landmarks Association.

Guide to Historical Markers of Pennsylvania. Harrisburg, PA: Pennsylvania Historical and Museum Commission.

Guide to North Carolina Historical Markers. Raleigh: State Department of Archives and History, 2001.

Gullan, Harold I. *First Fathers*. Emeryville, CA: John Wiley, 2004.

Gurney, C.S. *Portsmouth, Historic and Picturesque*. Portsmouth, NH: Strawberry Bank Pub., 1981.

Gurney, Gene, and Nick Apple. *The Library of Congress*. New York: Crown, 1981.

Hagedorn, Hermann. *The Roosevelt Family of Sagamore Hill*. New York: Macmillan, 1954.

Hagedorn, Hermann, and Gary G. Roth. *Sagamore Hill: An Historical Guide*. Oyster Bay, NY: Theodore Roosevelt Association, 1977.

Hall, Ralph Cole, Deering Davis, and Stephen P. Dorsey. *Georgetown Houses of the Federal Period*. New York: Bonanza Books, 1954.

Hallwas, John E. *Macomb: A Pictorial History*. St. Louis: G. Bradley Pub., 1990.

Hamberger, Eric. *Historical Atlas of New York City*. New York: Henry Holt, 1994.

Hamilton, Charles, and Lloyd Ostendorf. *Lincoln in Photographs*. Norman, OK: University of Oklahoma, 1963.

Hamilton, Holman. *Zachary Taylor, Soldier of the Republic*. Indianapolis: Bobbs-Merrill, 1941.

Hanchett, William. *The Lincoln Murder Conspiracies*. Urbana, IL. University of Illinois Press, 1983.

Hann, William F. III. "Abraham Lincoln's 1860 Visit to Rhode Island." *Lincoln Herald*, Winter 1978.

Hanna, William F. *Abraham Among the Yankees*. Taunton, MA: Dedham Historical Soc., 1983.

Happel, Ralph. *Chatham: The Life of a House*. Eastern National Park and Monument Association, 1984.

Harden, William. *History of Savannah and Southern Georgia*. Chicago: Lewis Publishing, 1913.

Harkins, John E. *Metropolis of the American Nile: A History of Memphis and Shelby County, Tennessee*. Memphis, TN: E F W Commercial Ventures, 1995.

Harris, Bill. *The History of New York City*. New York: Crown, 1989.

_____. *Homes of the Presidents*. New York: Crescent, 1987.

Harris, John. *Historic Walks in Old Boston*. 4th ed. Guilford, CT: Globe Pequot Press, 2000.

Harrison, Noel G. *Fredericksburg Civil War Sites*. Vols. 1 and 2. Lynchburg, VA: H.E. Howard, 1995.

Hart, Richard E. *Lincoln's Springfield: The Public Square*. Springfield, IL: Elijah Iles House Foundation, 2004.

Hartford Landmarks. Curriculum Research Project, 1966.

Harvey, Karen G. *A Pictorial History of Alexandria*. Virginia Beach, VA.: Donning, 1977.

Hass, Irvin. *Historic Homes of the American Presidents*. Mineola, NY: Dover Publications, 1991.

Hatfield, J.H. *Fortunate Son: George W. Bush and the Making of an American President:* New York: Soft Skull Press, 2000.

Hatter, Russell. *Historic Frankfort: A Walking Tour*. Pub. by author, 2003.

Haycraft, Samuel. *Haycraft's History of Elizabethtown, Kentucky and Its Surroundings*. Elizabethtown, KY: Hardin County Historical Society, 1960 (reprint of 1869 original).

Heathcote, Charles Williams, and John H. Cramer. "Lincoln in Philadelphia." *Lincoln Herald*, December 1944.

Helm, Katherine. *Mary, Wife of Lincoln*. Manchester, VT: Academy Books, 1999.

Henderson, Archibald. *Washington's Southern Tour*. Boston: Houghton Mifflin, 1923.

Henderson, William D. *Petersburg in the Civil War*. Lynchburg, VA: H.E. Howard, 1998.

Herrick, Clay, Jr. *Cleveland Landmarks*. Cleveland Restoration Soc., 1986.

Herron, Paul. *The Story of Capitol Hill*. New York: Coward-McCann, 1963.

Hertz, Emanuel. *Lincoln Talks*. New York: Crown, 1986.

Heymann, C. David. *A Woman Named Jackie*. Carol Communications, 1989.

Hickey, James T. *Lincoln Sites in Springfield*. Illinois State Hist. Lib., undated but probably mid–1960s.

_____. "The Lincoln's Globe Tavern." *Journal of Illinois State Historical Society*, Winter 1863.

_____, and King V. Hostick. *The Lincoln Home*. Self-published, 1964.

Hicks, Dave. *Denver History*. Denver: ATP Publishers, 1980.

Hill, Michael. *Guide to North Carolina Markers*. Raleigh: Department of Archives and History, 2001.

Historians of the Independence National Historical Park. *1787: The Day-to-Day Story of the Constitutional Convention*. New York: Exeter Books, 1987.

Historic Philadelphia. Philadelphia: American Philosophical Society, 1953.
Historic Places and Events in Northern Virginia. Alexandria, VA: United Virginia Bank, 1974.
Historical and Descriptive Sketches of Edwardsville, Alton, Etc. 1866.
Historical Guide to the United States. American Association for State and Local History. New York: Penguin Books, 1986.
Historical Scrapbook of West Columbia, Texas. First Capitol Replica Board, 1986.
History of Coles County, Illinois. Windmill Publications, 1990 reprint.
History of DeWitt County, Illinois 1839–1968. Board of Supervisors, Dewitt County, 1968.
History of Edgar County. Chicago: William Baron, 1879.
History of Knox and Daviess Counties, Indiana. Vincennes, IN: Vincennes Historical and Antiquarian Society, 1973.
History of Leadville and Lake County, Colorado. Leadville, CO: Colorado History Society, 1996.
History of Macoupin County, Illinois. Philadelphia: Brink, McDonough, 1971 (reprint of 1879 original).
History of Madison County, Illinois.
History of Presidential Tours. Fredericksburg, VA: Monroe Center, Mary Washington College, 2003.
History of Sangamon County. Chicago: Inter-State Publishing, 1881
History of Shelby and Moultrie Counties. Philadelphia: Brink, McDonough, 1997 (reprint of 1881 original).
History of Tazewell County, Illinois. Chicago: Charles C. Chapman, 1975 (reprint of 1879 original).
History of Warrick, Spencer and Perry Counties, Indiana. Chicago: Goodspeed, 1885.
Historylink.org/essays/output.cfm?file_id=882 (Hayes visit to Washington State), 5067 (Harrison), 883 (TR), 880 (Taft), 879 (Wilson), 878 Harding), 7269 (FDR), 5434 (FDR), 5466 (Truman), 5673 (Eisenhower), 968 (Kennedy), 5333 (Clinton).
Hobson, J.T. *Footprints of Abraham Lincoln.* Dayton, OH: Otterbein Press, 1909.
Hoch, Bradley R. *The Lincoln Trail in Pennsylvania.* University Park, PA: Pennsylvania State University Press, 2001.
Hochsteller, Nancy, ed. *Illinois Historical Markers, A Guide.* Guide Press, 1986.
Hogarth, Paul. *Walking Tours of Old Philadelphia.* Barre, MA: Barre Publishing, 1976.
Holmes, Fred L. *Abraham Lincoln Traveled This Way.* Boston: L.C. Page, 1930.
_____. *George Washington Traveled This Way.* L.C. Page, 1935.
Holsinger, Rufus W., Cecile Wendover Clover, and F.T. Heblich. *Holsinger's Charlottesville: A Collection of Photographs by Rufus W. Holsinger.* Charlottesville, VA: Art Restoration Services, 1995.
Holt, Col. John R. *Historic Frederick.* Frederick, MD: Marken and Bielfeld, 1949.
Holzer, Harold. *Lincoln As I Knew Him.* Chapel Hill, NC: Algonquin Books, 1999.
_____. *Lincoln at Cooper Union.* New York: Simon and Schuster, 2004.
_____, ed. *The Lincoln-Douglas Debates.* New York: Harper Collins, 1993.
_____. "Lincoln's New Home." *Americana Magazine,* February 1989.
_____. "Philadelphia/1787." *American History Illustrated,* May 1981.
"Homestead of Irish-American President." *Colonial Homes Magazine,* July-August 1986.
Hooper, Anne B. *Braddock Heights.* French-Bray Printing, 1974.
Horan, James D. *Mathew Brady.* New York: Bonanza Books, 1955.
Horgan, Paul. *Citizen of New Salem.* New York: Farrar, Straus and Cudahy, 1961.
Hostelry, Dorothy Holcombe. *The Story of Gadsby's Tavern.* Alexandria, VA: Newell-Cole, 1952.
"How Chicago Influenced the Career of Lincoln." *Chicago Sun Times.* February 6, 1955.
Howard, Robert P. "The Illinois Campaign of 1856." *Lincoln Herald,* Summer 1985.
Howells, William Dean. *Life of Abraham Lincoln.* Springfield, IL: Abraham Lincoln Association, 1938 (reprint of 1860 original version corrected by Lincoln and with Lincoln's notes).
Huber, Leonard, *New Orleans: A Pictorial History.* New York: Crown, 1971.
Huntley, Elizabeth Valentine. *Peninsula Pilgrimage.* Princeton: Pyne Press, 1941.
Huson, Hobart. *Refugio.* Rooke Foundation, 1953.
Huss, Wayne A. *Whitpain Township: A Tricentennial Reflection, 1701–2001.* Philadelphia: National Pub., 2001.
Idaho Daily Statesman, October 29, 1976; August 19, 1978; October 30, 1982; January 14, 2001; August 5, 2005; June 25, 2003.
Idaho State Journal, September 7, 1960; June 29, 1974.
Illinois Department of Conservation Publications. *Illinois History,* Various issues including February 1961, 1963, 1965, 1966, 1968, 1979, 1987, 1989, 1993, 1995, April 1998, March 1979, and October 1987.
Illinois State Historical Library: All file folders pertaining to Lincoln, Lincoln Memorial Highway.
Illustrated Encyclopedia and Atlas of Madison County, Illinois. 1873.
Images of the Past: A Photographic Review of Winchester and Frederick County, Virginia. Frederick Co. Historical Society, 1980.
Jackson, Donald, and Dorothy Twohig. *George Washington's Diaries.* Richmond: University of Virginia Press, 1999. (Also 1925, 1976 editions.)
Jackson, Kenneth T., ed. *The Encyclopedia of New York.* New Haven: Yale University Press, 1995. Jacques, Kelly. *Bygone Baltimore.* Virginia Beach, VA.: Donning, 1982
Jaffeson, Richard C. *Silver Spring Success.* Philadelphia: Xlibris Corporation, 1996.
James, Marquis. *The Raven: A Biography of Sam Hous-*

ton. Indianapolis: Bobbs-Merrill, 1929; reprint, Garden City, NY: Halcyon House, 1949.
Jefferson County, Facts and Figures. Jefferson Co. Historical Society, Taylor.
Jefferson's Albemarle. American Guide Series, WPA, 1941.
Jennings, Dana Close. *A Century of Worship: Emmanuel Episcopal Church of Rapid City.* Pub. by the church, 1988.
Jenson, Amy Lafollette. *The White House.* New York: McGraw-Hill, 1962.
Jillson, William R. *Pioneer Kentucky.* Frankfort, KY: State Journal, 1934.
Johannsen, Robert W. "America's Little Giant." *Civil War Times Illustrated,* April 1974.
Johns, Jane Martin. *Personal Recollections, 1849–1865, of Early Decatur, Abraham Lincoln, Richard J. Oglesby, and the Civil War.* Decatur, IL: Decatur Chapter Daughters of the American Revolution, 1912.
Johnson, Clint. *Touring Virginia's and West Virginia's Civil War Sites.* Winston-Salem: John F. Blair, 1999.
Johnson, Mark, et al. *Lincoln Herndon Law Offices Volunteer Manual.* Illinois Historic Preservation Agency, January 1986.
Johnson, Ronald W. *Chatham, Preliminary Historic Resource Study.* Fredericksburg and Spotsylvania County Battlefields Memorial, U.S. Dept. of the Interior.
Johnson, William J. *Abraham Lincoln The Christian.* New York: Abingdon Press, 1913.
Johnston, Elizabeth Bryant. *George Washington Day by Day.* New York: Baker and Taylor, 1894.
Johnston, Jean. *Mattoon: A Pictorial History.* St. Louis: G. Bradley Pub., 1988.
Johnston, William Davison. *TR: Champion of the Strenuous Life.* New York: Theodore Roosevelt Assoc., 1981.
Jones, Charles C., Jr. *Memorial History of Augusta, Georgia.* Spartanburg, SC: Reprint, 1980.
Jones, Kenneth. *John Quincy Adams, 1767–1848: Chronology, Documents, Bibliographical Aids.* New York: Oceana Publishing, 1970.
Jones, William C., and Kenton Jones. *Denver: A Pictorial History.* Boulder, CO: Pruett Publishers, 1973.
Kane, Joseph Nathan. *Facts About the Presidents.* New York: H.W. Wilson, 1981.
Kaufman, Michael W. *American Brutus.* New York: Random House, 2004.
Kay, Jane Holtz. *Lost Boston.* Boston: Houghton-Mifflin, 1980.
Keller, Allan. "Battles for New York." *American History Illustrated,* July 1971.
Kelly, C. Brian. *Best Little Stories from the White House.* Nashville: Cumberland House, 1999.
Kempf, Gary. *The Land Before Fort Knox.* Charleston, SC: Arcadia, 2004.
Kennedy, William. *O Albany.* New York: Viking Press, 1983.
Kennell, Brian A. *Beyond the Gatehouse.* Evergreen Cemetery Association, 2000.
Kerr, Bettie L., and John D. Wright, Jr. *Lexington: A Century in Photographs.* Lexington, KY: Lexington-Fayette Co. Historic Commission, 1984.
Kerwood, John R. "The Plot to Rob Lincoln's Tomb." *American History Illustrated,* January 1971.
Ketcham, Ralph. *James Madison: A Biography.* New York: Macmillan, 1971.
Ketchum, Richard M. *The World of George Washington.* New York: American Heritage Publishing, 1974.
Kimball, David A. "The Lincoln Boyhood National Memorial." *Lincoln Herald,* Spring 1964.
Kimbell, Fiske. *The Capitol of Virginia.* Richmond: Virginia State Library and Archives, 1796.
Kimmel, Stanley. *Mr. Davis's Richmond.* New York: Bramhall House, 1958.
_____. *Mr. Lincoln's Washington.* New York: Bramhall House, 1957.
Kinnaird, Clark. *George Washington: The Pictorial Biography.* Fern Park, FL: Hastings House, 1967.
Kiper Hon. Roscoe. *Abraham Lincoln in Indiana.* New York: Kiwanis Magazine, 1927.
Kirkman, Kay. *Wichita, A Pictorial History.* Western Century, 1981.
Kitman, Marvin. *George Washington's Expense Account.* New York: Simon and Schuster, 1970.
Kleber, John E., editor. *The Encyclopedia of Louisville.* Lexington: University of Kentucky Press, 2000.
_____, editor in chief. *The Kentucky Encyclopedia.* Lexington: University of Kentucky Press, 1992.
_____. *Kentucky's Abraham Lincoln.* Kentucky Historical Society, 1997.
Klein, Frederic Shriver. *Old Lancaster.* New York: Early American Series, 1964.
Klein, Jerry. *Peoria.* Peoria Historical Society, 1985.
Klement, Frank L. *The Gettysburg Soldier's Cemetery and Lincoln's Address.* Shippensburg, PA: White Maine Pub., 1993.
Knepper, George W. *An Ohio Portrait.* Columbus: Ohio Historical Society, 1976.
Kochmann, Rachel M. *Presidents Birthplaces, Homes, and Burial Sites.* Lemoyne, PA: Haas Printing, 1989.
Kogan, Herman, and Lloyd Wendt. *Chicago: A Pictorial History.* New York: Bonanza Books, 1958.
Kostyal, K.M. *Virginia.* New York: Compass American Guides, 1994.
Kouwenhoven, John A. *Columbia Historical Portrait of New York.* New York: Harper and Row, 1972. Kramer, Carl E. *Capital on the Kentucky.* Frankfort, KY: Historic Frankfort, 1986.
Kruh, David, and Louis Kruh. *Presidential Landmarks.* New York: Hippocrene Books, 1994.
Kunhardt, Dorothy Meserve. "Strange History Brought to Light...And His Face Was Chalky White." *Life Magazine,* February 15, 1963.
Kunhardt, Dorothy Meserve, and Philip B. Kunhardt Jr. *Mathew Brady and His World.* Des Moines, IA: Time-Life Books, 1977.
Kunhardt, Philip, and Dorothy Meserve Kunhardt. *Twenty Days.* New York: Harper and Row, 1965.
Kunhardt, Philip B., Jr., Philip B. Kunhardt, and Peter

W. Kunhardt. *Lincoln.* New York: Alfred A. Knopf, 1992.

Laman, Ward Hill. *Recollections of Abraham Lincoln.* Lincoln, NE: University of Nebraska, 1994.

Lamb, George. *Dixon: A Pictorial History.* St. Louis: G. Bradley Publishing, 1987.

"Land of Lincoln." *Historic Traveler Magazine,* April 1998.

Landrum, Carl A. *Historical Sketches of Quincy.* (undated about 1960)

Lane, Mills. *Savannah Revisited.* 3rd ed. Bronx, NY: Beehive Press, 1977.

Langguth, A.J. *Patriots.* New York: Simon and Schuster, 1988.

Lanning, Lt. Col. (Ret.) Michael Lee. *The Military 100.* Secaucus, NJ: Citadel Press, 1996.

Lattimer, John K. *Kennedy and Lincoln.* New York: Harcourt Brace Jovanovich, 1980.

Lawing, Hugh A. *Andrew Johnson National Historic Site.* Revised reprint from the Tennessee Historical Quarterly.

Lawson, Evald Benjamin. "When Lincoln Visited New Jersey." *Contemporary Life,* February 1943.

Lay, K. Edward. *Architecture of Jefferson Country.* Charlottesville, VA: University of Virginia Press, 2000.

Leamer, Laurence. *The Kennedy Men.* New York: William Morrow, 2001.

Leavell, Alfred, Jr. *An Early History of Alton.* Thesis, Carbondale, IL: Southern Illinois University.

Lee, Richard M. *Mr. Lincoln's City.* McLean, VA: EPM Publications, 1981.

Leish, Kenneth W. *The White House.* New York: Newsweek Book Division, 1972.

Leland, Jack. *60 famous Houses of Charleston, South Carolina.* Charleston: Evening Post, 1979.

Lexington Kentucky Cemetery. Hisle's Headstones, 1986.

Liberty Hall. Historical Activities Commission, 1989.

Lincoln and Douglas Debate Festival Booklet, 1994.

"Lincoln as a Lecturer." *Jacksonville Journal Courier.*

Lincoln Herald, 1941–present. (Many articles and notes in addition to those listed.)

Lincoln Heritage Trail Tour Guide Magazine, various dates.

Lincoln: His Words and His World. Country Beautiful Foundation, 1965.

"Lincoln History Tour of Chicago." *Chicago Daily News,* February 9, 1957

Liberty Hall, Hickey and Hostick.

Lincoln in Chicago. Chicago Historical Society, undated.

"Lincoln in Danville." Supplement to the *Commercial News of Danville,* 2/12/93.

"Lincoln in Massachusetts." *Lincoln Herald,* Summer 1978.

Lincoln Lore. Ft. Wayne, IN: Lincoln National Life (numerous bulletins).

Lincoln National Memorial Highway: Hearings before the Special Commission, September 30, 1930; Report to Governor, July 7, 1929; Report of Route Recommended, August 11, 1932.

Lincoln Trail Association (files), Illinois State Historical Library.

Lincoln Visits Beloit and Janesville, Wisconsin. Lincoln Fellowship of Wisconsin, 1949.

Lincoln Way, Report of the Board of Trustees of the Illinois State Historical Library, 1913.

Lincoln's Springfield: A Guidebook and Brief History. Springfield: Abraham Lincoln Association, 1938.

Lindsey, Mary. *Historic Houses and Landmarks of Alexandria, Virginia.* Alexandria: Newell-Cole, 1947.

Lipscomb, Terry W. *South Carolina in 1791.* Columbia: South Carolina Department of Archives and History, 1993.

Listokin, Barbara C. *The Architectural History of New Brunswick, New Jersey.* University Microfilms International, 1984.

Livingston, E.A. *President Lincoln's Third Largest City: Brooklyn and the Civil War.* London: Budd Press, 1994.

Lloyd, John A. "Lincoln in Ohio." Address to Queen City Optimists Club, February 9, 1980.

Lodge, Henry Cabot. *Boston.* London: Longmans, Green, 1891.

Long, David E. *The Jewel of Liberty.* Mechanicsburg, PA: Stackpole Books, 1994.

Long, E.B. *The Civil War Day by Day.* New York: Doubleday, 1971.

Long, R.L. *Dinwiddie Co.* Board of Surveyors, 1976.

Looney, Robert F. *Old Philadelphia in Early Photographs, 1839–1914.* Mineola, NY: Dover Publications, 1976.

Lorant, Stefan. *FDR: A Pictorial Portrait.* New York: Simon and Schuster, 1950.

_____. *The Glorious Burden.* Crawfordsville, IN: R.R Donnelley, 1968.

_____. *Lincoln: A Picture Story of His Life.* New York: Harper Brothers, 1957.

_____. *Pittsburgh: The Story of an American City.* 4th ed. Lenox, MS: Authors Ed., 1988.

Louisiana Plantation Homes. Baton Rouge: Louisiana Department of Commerce and Industry Tourist Bureau, undated.

Louisville, Kentucky City Directory, 1843. G. Collins.

Lyman, Susan Elizabeth. *The Story of New York.* New York: Crown, 1975.

Lynchburg (Virginia) Journal of Local History. Various articles, Fall 1988, Fall–Winter 1992–3.

Lynn, Ruth Wallace. *Prelude to Progress: The History of Macon County, Illinois.* Mason County Board of Supervisors, 1968.

Lynn, Stuart. *New Orleans.* New York: Bonanza Books, 1949.

Malone, Dumas. *The Story of the Declaration of Independence.* New York: Oxford University Press, 1954.

Manbeck, John B., consulting editor. *The Neighborhoods of Brooklyn.* New Haven: Yale University Press, 1998.

Mansfield, James Roger. *A History of Early Spotsylvania.* Green Publishers, 1977.

Mapp, Alf J., Jr. *Thomas Jefferson: A Strange Case of*

Mistaken Identity. Lanham, MD: Madison Books, 1987.
Marian, John Francis. *The Charleston Story*. Harrisburg, PA: Stackpole Books, 1978.
Mayo, Edith P., general ed. *The Smithsonian Book of the First Ladies*. New York: Henry Holt, 1996.
McClure, Daniel Elmo, Jr. *Two Centuries in Elizabethtown and Hardin County, Kentucky*. Hardin County Historical Society, 1977.
McClure, J.B. *Abraham Lincoln's Stories and Speeches*. Chicago: Rhodes and McClure Pub., 1896.
McCullough, David. *Mornings on Horseback*. New York: Simon and Schuster, 1981.
_____. *1776*. New York: Simon and Schuster, 2005.
_____. *Truman*. New York: Simon and Schuster, 1992.
McCullough, Noah. *The Essential Book of Presidential Trivia*. New York: Random House, 2006.
McElroy, Richard L. *James A. Garfield, His Life and Times*. Canton, OH: Daring Books, 1986.
McFeely, Mary D., and William S. McFeely, eds. *U.S. Grant: Memoirs and Selected Letters*. New York: Library of America, 1990.
McFeely, William S. *Grant*. New York: W.W. Norton, 1982.
McHale, John E. *Dr. Samuel A. Mudd and the Lincoln Assassination*. Parsippany, NJ: Dillon Press, 1995.
McKay, Ernest A. *The Civil War and New York City*. Syracuse, NY: Syracuse University Press, 1990.
McMeekin, Isabel McLennan. *Louisville: The Gateway City*. New York: Julian Messner, 1946.
McMurtry, R. Gerald. *Lincoln Highlights in Indiana History*. Ft. Wayne, IN: Lincoln Nat. Life Ins., 1971.
_____. "Rediscovering the Supposed Grave of Lincoln's Brother." *Lincoln Herald*, February 1946.
McPherson, James M. *Battle Cry of Freedom*. New York: Oxford Press, 1988.
_____. *Crossroads of Freedom: Antietam*. New York: Oxford Press, 2002.
Mead, William B., and Paul Dickson. *Baseball: The President's Game*. Washington, D.C.: Farragut Publishing, 1993.
Melick, Arden Davis. *Wives of the Presidents*. Maplewood, NJ: Hammond, 1972.
Memoirs of Abraham Lincoln in Edgar County, Illinois. Edgar County Historical Society, 1925.
Menard County, Illinois. Dallas: Taylor, 1988.
Merrill, Nancy C. *Four Walking Tours of Exeter, New Hampshire*. Exeter Historical Society, 1980.
Miers, Ear, editor-in-chief. *Lincoln Day By Day*. Dayton, OH: Morningside, 1991.
Miller, Paul W. *Atlanta, Capital of the South*. New York: Oliver Durrell, 1949.
Miller, Merle. *Lyndon: An Oral Biography*. Toronto: Academic Press, 1980.
Miller, Nathan. *The Roosevelt Chronicles*. New York: Doubleday, 1979.
Miller, Walter H. *Lincoln Lived Here*. Williamsburg, VA: Walter H. Miller, 1971.
Mills, W. Jay. *Historic Houses of New Jersey*. Philadelphia: J.B. Lippincott, 1902.
Minutaglio, Bill. *First Son: George W. Bush and the Bush Family Dynasty*. New York: Time Books, 1999.
Mr. Lincoln's White House. Website: www.mrlincon-swhitehouse.org. The Lehrman Institute, 2000.
Mitchell, Alexander D. *Washington, D.C. Then and Now*. San Diego: Thunder Bay Press, 2000.
Mitchell, Mary H. *Hollywood Cemetery: The History of a Southern Shrine*. Richmond: Virginia State Library, 1985.
Mongan, Charles W., ed. *Story of Oregon, Illinois*. Oregon, IL: Oregon Sesquicentennial, 1988.
Montgomery, Rachel. *Camden Heritage, Yesterday and Today*. Columbia, SC: R.L. Bryan, 1971.
Monticello, A Celebration. Monticello Celebrations, 1987.
Moore, John Hammond. *Albemarle, Jefferson's County, 1727–1976*. Charlottesville: University Press of Virginia, 1976.
_____. *Columbia and Richland County*. Columbia: University of South Carolina Press, 1993.
Moore, Samuel J.T., Jr. *Moore's Complete Civil War Guide to Richmond*. Rev. ed. Printed by author, 1978.
Morgan, George. *The Life of James Madison*. Boston: Small, Maynard, 1921.
_____. *The Life of James Monroe*. Boston: Small, Maynard, 1923.
Morgan, H. Wayne. *William McKinley and His America*. Syracuse, NY: Syracuse U. Press, 1964.
Morgan, James. *Theodore Roosevelt: The Boy and the Man*. New York: Macmillan, 1919.
Morgantown, West Virginia and Its People. Morgan County History and Genealogical Society, Taylor, 1981.
Morris, Charles. *The Authentic Life of William McKinley*. Washington, D.C.: W.E Scull, 1901.
Morris, Lloyd. *Incredible New York*. New York: Bonanza Books, 1960.
Morris, Richard. *Seven Who Shaped Our Destiny*. New York: Harper and Row, 1973.
Morton, Frederic. *The Story of Winchester in Virginia*. Strasburg, VA: Shenandoah Pub., 1925.
Mounts, Willard. *The Pioneer and the Prairie Lawyer*. Denver: Ginwill Publishing, 1994.
Muir, Dorothy Troth. *Mount Vernon: The Civil War Years*: Mount Vernon Ladies Assoc., 1993.
Murray, Robert K. *The Harding Era*. Minneapolis: University of Minn. Press, 1969.
Mylod, John. *Biography of a River*. New York: Bonanza Books, 1964.
Nagel, Paul C. *John Quincy Adams*. New York: Alfred A. Knopf, 1997.
National Park Service Maps and Guides for Richmond, City Point, Gettysburg, Antietam, Abraham Lincoln Birthplace, Fredericksburg, Gettysburg, George Washington Birthplace, Jefferson Barracks, Martin Van Buren's Home, Petersburg, Yorktown, Shiloh Battlefield, Theodore Roosevelt Birthplace, Franklin Roosevelt's Hyde Park, Fort Vancouver, and virtually all sites listed in the text.
Neely, Mark, Jr. *The Abraham Lincoln Encyclopedia*. New York: McGraw-Hill, 1982.

Netherton, Ross, and Nan Netherton. *Fairfax County in Virginia: A Pictorial History*. Virginia Beach, VA:

Nevins, Allan. "He Did Hold Lincoln's Hat?" *American Heritage*, February 1959.

New Hampshire Historical Markers. State Historical Commission, 1974.

"New York City During the Civil War." *Blue and Gray Magazine*, December 1996.

Newbraugh, Frederic T. *Warm Springs Echoes*. Automated Systems Corp., 1967.

Newcomb, Rexford. *In the Lincoln Country*. Philadelphia: J.B. Lillincott, 1928.

Niagara, River of Fame. Kiwanis Clubs of Niagara Falls and Stamford, Ontario: Ryerson Press, 1970.

Nichols, Roy Franklin. *Franklin Piece*. Newtown, CT: American Political Biography Press, 1993.

Nightengale, Joseph R. "Shapers of Lincoln's Religious Image." Springfield, IL: *Journal of Illinois State Historical Soc.*, Autumn 1999.

Niles, Blair. *Martha's Husband*. New York: McGraw-Hill, 1951.

Niven, Penelope. *Old Salem: The Official Guidebook*. Winston-Salem, NC: Old Salem, 2000.

Nixon, John. *Martin Van Buren*. Oxford: Oxford Press, 1983.

Nofi, Albert A. *The Civil War Notebook*. Conshohocken, PA: Combined Publishing, 1993.

Norton, W.T. *Centennial History of Madison County*. Albany, GA: Lewis Publishing, 1912.

Norwood, Frank C. *A Brief Review of the City Hotel*. 1916.

Nutt, Charles. *History of Worcester and Its People*. New York: Lewis Historical Publishing, 1919.

Nye, W.S., ed. *The Valiant Hours*. Mechanicsburg, PA: The Stackpole Company, 1961.

Oates, Stephen B. *Abraham Lincoln: The Man Behind the Myths*. New York: New American Library, 1984.

_____. *With Malice Toward None*. New York: Harper and Row, 1977.

O'Brien, Dr. Terrance E. *Lincoln's New Salem: Guidebook of the Record of the Historic Site*. New Salem Lincoln League, 1984.

Official Guidebook and Map. Colonial Williamsburg, 1965.

Olmert, Michael. *Official Guide to Colonial Williamsburg*. Colonial Williamsburg Foundation, 1985.

Olson, Gary D., and Erik L. Olson. *Sioux Falls, South Dakota: A Pictorial History*. Virginia Beach, VA.: Donning Pub., 1985.

Olszewski, George J. *Restoration of Ford's Theatre*. Washington, D.C.: National Park Service, 1963.

Onstot, T.G. *Pioneers of Menard and Mason County, Illinois*. Forest City, IL: 1902; reprinted 1986.

Ostendorf, Lloyd. "Lincoln's Ohio Tour." *Lincoln Herald*, Spring 1960.

_____. "Lincoln Made His Mark in Ohio." *Lincoln Herald*, Spring 1997.

Osterweis, Rollin G. *Three Centuries of New Haven, 1638–1938*. New Haven: Yale University Press, 1964.

Owen, Lewis. *Washington's Final Victory*. Saddle River, NJ: K/S Historical Publications, 1967.

Paige, Lucius R. *History of Cambridge, Massachusetts*. Boston: H.O. Houghton, 1877.

Painter, George. *Mr. Lincoln's Neighborhood*. Eastern National Park and Monument Assoc., 1985.

Paletta, Lu Ann, and Fred Worth. *The World Almanac of Presidential Facts*. New York: Pharos Books, 1988.

Panaggio, Leonard J. *Portrait of Newport*. Providence, RI: Mowbray, 1969.

Parks, George E. *History of Union County*. Self-published, 1987.

Parmet, Herbert S. *George Bush: The Life of a Lone Star Yankee*. New York: Scribner's, 1997.

Patch, Joseph Dorst. *The Concentration of General Zachary Taylor's Army at Corpus Christi, Texas*. Undated pamphlet in Corpus Christi Library.

Patterson, Carolyn Bennett. "Our Land Through Lincoln's Eyes." *National Geographic*, 1978.

Patterson, Jerry E. *The City of New York*. New York: Harry N. Abrams, 1978.

Paulmier, Hilah. *Abe Lincoln*. New York: Alfred A. Knopf, 1953.

Pemberton, William E. *The Life and Presidency of Ronald Reagan*. Armonk, NY: M.E. Sharpe, 1997.

Perrin, William Henry. *History of Jefferson County, Illinois*. South St. Paul, MN: Globe Publishing, 1883.

Peterson, Henry J. "Lincoln at the Wisconsin State Fair As Recalled by John W. Hoyt." *Lincoln Herald*, December 1949.

Peterson, Merrill D., ed. *James Madison: A Biography in His Own Words*. New York: Newsweek, 1974.

Pfanz, Donald. *The Petersburg Campaign: Abraham Lincoln at City Point, March 20–April 9, 1865*. Lynchburg, VA: H.E. Howard, 1989.

"Philadelphia Guide." *Philadelphia Magazine*, 1968.

"Philadelphia Houses a Proud Past." *National Geographic*, August 1960.

Pictorial History of Edgar County. Paris, IL: Beacon Publications, 1997.

Piersel, W.G. *First Methodist Church (of Springfield)*. January 1947.

Pinckney, Charles. *National Historic Site*. Washington, D.C.: National Park Service.

Plowden, David. *Lincoln and His America*. New York: Viking Press, 1970.

Podmore, Harry J. *Trenton Old and New*. Trenton, NJ: MacCrellish and Quigley, 1964 (reprint of 1927 original, Mary J. Messler, ed).

Pohl, James W. *The Battle of San Jacinto*. Austin: Texas State Historical Association, 1989.

Portland Oregonian, December 12, 1950.

Powell, Lymon P., ed. *Historic Towns of the Middle States*. New York: Putnam's, 1899.

Prairie Progress. Dallas: Taylor, 1976.

Pratt, Harry E. *Lincoln 1840–1846*. Springfield, IL: Abraham Lincoln Association, 1939.

_____. *Lincoln's Springfield*. Springfield: Illinois State Historical Society, 1955.

_____. *The Personal Finances of Abraham Lincoln*. Madison, WI: Lakeside Press, 1943.

_____. "Springfield's Public Square in Lincoln's Day." *Illinois Bar Journal*, May 1952.
Pratt, Richard. *Houses, History, and People*. New York: M. Evans, 1965.
Preston, Daniel, and Marlena C. DeLong, eds. *Papers of James Monroe: A Documentary History of the Presidential Tours of James Monroe, 1817, 1818, 1819*. Westport, CT: Greenwood Press, 2003.
Pryor, Mrs. Roger A. *Reminiscences of Peace and War*. New York: Macmillan, 1904.
Puhala, Bob. *Illinois Off The Beaten Path*. 5th ed. Guilford, CT: Globe Pequot Press, 1999.
Quarles, Garland R. *George Washington and Winchester, Virginia*. Winchester, VA: Frederick County Historical Soc., 1974.
Quirk, Lawrence J. *The Kennedys in Hollywood*. Dallas: Taylor, 1996.
"Rally Day in Carmi." *Illinois History Magazine*, February 1962.
Randall, Ruth Painter. *I, Mary*. New York: Little, Brown, 1959.
_____. *Lincoln's Sons*. New York: Little, Brown, 1955.
_____. *Mary Lincoln: Biography of a Marriage*. New York: Little, Brown, 1953.
Randall, Willard Sterne. *George Washington: A Life*. New York: Henry Holt, 1997.
_____. *Thomas Jefferson: A Life*. New York: Henry Holt, 1993.
Rawlings, Mary. *The Albemarle of Other Days*. Charlottesville, VA: Michie, 1925.
_____. *Ante-bellum Albemarle*. Peoples National Bank of Charlottesville, 1982.
Rayback, Robert J. *Millard Fillmore*. Newtown, CT: American Political Biography Press, 1959.
Redway, Maurice W., and Dorothy Kendall Bracken. *Marks of Lincoln On Our Land*. Fern Park, FL: Hastings House, 1957.
Reinking, Donna. *Lincoln in Bloomington-Normal*. Bloomington, IL: McLean County Historical Society, 1998.
Remini, Robert V. *Andrew Jackson*. New York: Twain Publishers, 1966.
_____. *Andrew Jackson and His Indian Wars*. New York: Viking, 2001.
_____. *Andrew Jackson*. Vol. 2, *The Course of American Empire*. Baltimore: Johns Hopkins University Press, 1998.
Reminiscences of General Herman Haupt. In files at Fredericksburg National Military Park.
Renehan, Edward J., Jr. *The Lion's Pride*. New York: Oxford University Press, 1998.
Report of the Boston National Historic Sites Commission. Washington, D.C.: U.S. Govt. Printing Office, 1961.
Richmond, Robert W. *Kansas: A Pictorial History*. Lawrence, KS: University Press of Kansas, 1992.
Riddle, Donald W. *Congressman Abraham Lincoln*. Urbana, IL: University of Illinois, 1957.
Riley, Edward M. *Independence National Historical Park*. Washington, D.C.: National Park Service Historical Handbook Series, 1956.
Roberts, John B. *Rating the First Ladies*. New York: Kensington Publishers Group, 2003.
Roberts, Octavia. *Lincoln in Illinois*. Boston: Houghton Mifflin, 1918.
Robinson, James I., Jr. *Civil War Sites in Virginia*. Charlottesville, VA: University Press of Virginia, 1982.
Rock Island Argus and Union, February 11, 1922.
Rockford Morning Star, February 10, 1952.
Rockport-Spencer County Sesquicentennial, 1968.
Roosevelt, Eleanor. *Franklin D. Roosevelt and Hyde Park*. Hyde Park Association, undated.
_____. *This I Remember*. New York: Harper and Brothers, 1949.
_____. *This Is My Story*. New York: Harper and Brothers, 1937.
Roosevelt, Elliot. *As He Saw It*. New York: Duell, Sloan, and Pearce, 1946.
_____, and James Brough. *The Roosevelts of Hyde Park*. New York: Putnam's, 1973.
Roosevelt, James. *My Parents: A Differing View*. Chicago: Playboy Press, 1976.
_____, and Sidney Shalett. *Affectionately, F.D.R.* New York: Harcourt, Brace, 1959.
Rose, William G. *Cleveland: The Making of a City*. New York: World Pub., 1950.
Ross, Ishbel. *An American Family: The Tafts, 1678 to 1964*. Westport CT: Greenwood Press, 1977.
_____. *The General's Wife*. New York: Dodd Mead, 1959,
Rossiter, Clinton. "The Two Greatest Presidents." *American Heritage*, February 1959.
Round, Harold F. "Aquia Creek." *Virginia Cavalcade*, Summer 1963.
Rouse, Parke, Jr. *Remembering Williamsburg*. Richmond: Dietz Press, 1989.
_____. *Virginia: A Pictorial History*. New York: Scribner's, 1975.
Routes Traveled By George Washington in Maryland. Maryland Commission on Roads, 1932.
Ruehrwein, Richard L. *Grouseland*. Lawrenceburg, IN: Creative Company, 1998.
_____. *Historic Homes of Lexington*. Lawrenceburg, IN: Creative Company, 1996.
Rumple, Rev. Jethro. *A History of Rowan County, North Carolina*. Baltimore: Regional Publishing, 1974 (reprint of 1881 original).
Russell, Frances. "The Four Mysteries of Warren Harding." *American Heritage*, April 1963.
Ryan, William. *The White House: An Architectural History*. New York: McGraw-Hill, 1980.
St. Louis District Historic Properties Management Report No. 36. U.S. Army Corps of Engineers, November 1988.
St. Louis Post-Dispatch, February 12, 1997.
Sandburg, Carl. *Abraham Lincoln*. New York: Harcourt, Brace, reprint 1959.
Sangamon Valley Library, various newspaper files on Springfield, Illinois, sites.
Sarles, Frank B., Jr., and Charles E. Shedd. *Colonials and Patriots*. Washington, D.C.: National Park Service, 1964.

Scenic and Historic Tours of New Jersey. New Jersey Department of Transportation (undated).

Scheller, William, and Kay Scheller. *New Jersey Off the Beaten Path.* Guilford, CT: Globe Pequot Press, 2006.

Schessler, Ken. *This is Hollywood.* LeVern, CA: Ken Schessler Publishing, 1989.

Schildt, John W. *Drums Along the Antietam.* Parsons, WV: McClain Printing, 1972.

_____. *Four Days in October.* Self-published, 1978.

_____. *Hail to the Chief: Presidential Visits to Antietam.* Brunswick, MD: E Graphic, 2002.

Schrifthiesser, Karl. *The Amazing Roosevelt Family.* New York: Wilfred Funk, 1942.

Schroeder, Rev. John E. *Pioneer Days in Troy.* 1966.

Scott, De'Onne C. *James Monroe Living in Fredericksburg.* Senior Research Project in Historic Preservation. Fredericksburg, VA: Mary Washington College, 1999.

Seager, Robert II. *And Tyler Too.* New York: McGraw-Hill, 1963.

Seale, William. *The President's House.* Washington, D.C.: White House Historical Assoc., 1986.

_____. *Virginia's Executive Mansion.* Richmond: Virginia State Library and Archives, 1988.

Searcher, Victor. *Lincoln's Journey to Greatness.* Chicago: John C. Winston, 1960.

Sears, Stephen W. *Fire on the Mountain.* Ticknor & Fields, 1983. (Also article and Antietam site descriptions in *Blue and Gray Magazine,* December–January1986–7.)

_____. *Landscape Turned Red.* New York: Ticknor and Fields, 1983.

Selected Menard County, Illinois, Cemetery Inscriptions. No date or author listed.

Sellers, Charles. *James K. Polk, Jacksonian.* Princeton, NJ: Princeton University Press, 1957.

Shaw, Archer H., comp. *Abraham Lincoln Encyclopedia.* New York: Macmillan, 1950.

Sheads, Scott Sumpter. *Baltimore During the Civil War.* Silver Springs, MD: Toomey Press, 1967.

Shelbyville Past and Present. Chautauqua History Book Committee, 1991.

Shibley, Ronald E. *Fredericksburg.* Fredericksburg, VA: Historic Fredericksburg Foundation, 1977.

Shick, Nancy Easter, and Douglas K. Meyer. *Pictorial Landscape History of Charleston, Illinois.* Charleston, IL: Rardin Graphics, 1985.

Silver, Nathan. *Lost New York.* Boston: Houghton Mifflin, 1968.

Simpson, Brooks D. *Ulysses S. Grant: Triumph Over Adversity, 1822–1865.* Boston: Houghton Mifflin, 2000.

Sloan, Irving J., ed. *James Buchanan,* 1791–1868*: Chronology, Documents, Bibliographical Aids.* New York: Oceana Publishing, 1968.

Smith, Bessie White. *Boyhood of the Presidents.* New York: Lothrop, Lee and Shepard, 1929.

Smith, Mrs. E. Vale. *History of Newburyport.* Newburyport, MA: Privately published, 1854.

Smith, Harvey H. *Lincoln and the Lincolns.* Lacoste Printing, 1931.

Smith, Jean Edward. *Grant.* New York: Simon and Schuster, 2001.

Smith, Page. *Jefferson: A Revealing Biography.* New York: American Heritage Publishing, 1976.

Smith, Richard Norton. *Who is Buried in Grant's Tomb?* Washington, D.C.: National Cable Satellite Corp., 2000.

Smith, Sarah B. *Historic Nelson County.* Louisville, KY: Gateway Press, 1971.

Soderberg, Susan Cooke. *A Tour Guide to Civil War Sites in Maryland.* Shippensburg, PA: White Mane Books, 1998.

Soltis, Stephen, and Stacy Soltis. *West Virginia Off the Beaten Path.* Guilford, CT: Globe Pequot Press, 2003.

Somerville, Mollie. *Washington Walked Here: Alexandria on the Potomac.* Camarillo, CA: Acropolis Books, 1970.

South Carolina Historical Markers Guide. Columbia: Department of Archives and History, 1992.

Sprague, Stuart, and Elizabeth Perkins. *Frankfort: A Pictorial History.* Virginia Beach, VA: Donning Publishers, 1980.

Staudenraus, P.J. *Mr. Lincoln's Washington: The Civil War Dispatches of Noah Brooks.* New York: Thomas Yoseloff, 1967.

Steadman, Melvin Lee, Jr. *Historic Leesburg, Virginia.* Loudoun County Chamber of Commerce, 1968.

Steers, Edward Jr. *Blood on the Moon.* Lexington: University of Kentucky, 2001.

_____. *The Escape and Capture of John Wilkes Booth.* Gettysburg, PA: Thomas Pub., 1992.

_____. *Lincoln: A Pictorial History.* Gettysburg, PA: Thomas Publications, 1993.

_____. "A Question of Faith." *North and South Magazine,* September 1999.

Steinburg, Sheila, and Cathleen McGuigan. *Rhode Island: A Historic Guide.* Providence, RI: Rhode Island Centennial Foundation, 1976.

Steinmetz, Rollin C., ed. *History Trails of Lancaster.* Lititz, PA: Entertain, 1976.

Stember, Sol. *The Bicentennial Guide to the American Revolution.* 3 vols. New York: E.P. Dutton, 1974.

Stephens, Greg, et al. *Traveler's Guide to Well Known and Little Known Presidential Sites.* Public Schools of Independence, Mo., 1980.

Sterling, Col. James T. "How Lincoln 'Lost' His Inaugural Address." *Lincoln Herald,* December 1943.

Stevens, Maud Lyman. *Washington and Newport.* Bulletin of the Newport Historical Society, Number 84, July 1932.

Stoddard, William O. *Inside the White House in War Times.* Ed. by Michael Burlingame. Lincoln: University of Nebraska, 2000.

Story of Farmington. Farmington Historic Home, 1997.

Stringer, Lawrence B. *History of Logan County, Illinois.* Chicago: Pioneer Publishing, 1911.

Strode, Hudson. *Jefferson Davis.* New York: Harcourt, Brace, 1955.

Strozier, Charles B. "Lincoln's Quest for Union." In *The Historian's Lincoln.*" Edited by Gabor Boritt. Champaign, IL: University of Illinois, 1988.

_____. *Lincoln's Quest for Union*. New York: Basic Books, 1982.
Stryker, Roy, and Mel Serdenberg. *A Pittsburgh Album, 1758–1958*. Pittsburgh: Pittsburgh Post Gazette, 1959.
Styple, William B. *The Little Bugler*. Kearny, NJ: Belle Grove Publishing, 1998.
Sundstrom, Jessie Y. *Pioneers and Custer State Park*. Custer, SD: Self pub., 1994.
Suppiger, Joseph E. "The Intimate Lincoln." *Lincoln Herald*, various issues beginning 1981.
Survey of Historic Sites, Lancaster County. Central Piedmont Regional Planning Commission, 1971.
Swanson, Stevenson, ed. *Chicago Days*. Chicago: Chicago Tribune, 1997.
Sween, Jane C. *Montgomery County: Two Centuries of Change*. Woodland Hills, CA: Windsor Publications, 1984.
Taft, William Howard, and James Bryce. *Washington, the Nation's Capital*. Washington, D.C.: National Geographic, 1915.
Tails and Shrines of Abraham Lincoln. Lincoln Memorial Publishing, 1934.
Tarbell, Ida M. *The Early Life of Abraham Lincoln*. New York: A.S. Barnes, 1974.
_____. *In the Footsteps of the Lincolns*. New York: Harper and Row, 1924.
Taylor, Frank H. *Philadelphia in the Civil War*. City of Philadelphia, 1913.
Taylor, John M. "Willards of Washington." *American History Illustrated*, October 1979.
Taylor, Robert M., et al. *Indiana: A New Historical Guide*. Indianapolis: Indiana Historical Society, 1989.
Taylor, Tim. *The Book of Presidents*. New York: Arno Press, 1972.
Taylorville, Illinois newspaper clippings, Feb. 9, 1985.
Teague, Michael. *Mrs. L.: Conversations with Alive Roosevelt Longworth*. New York: Doubleday, 1981.
Temple, Sunderine (Wilson), and Wayne C. Temple. *Illinois' Fifth Capitol*. Springfield, IL: Philips Brothers, 1982.
Temple, Wayne C. *Abraham Lincoln and Others at the St. Nicholas*. Springfield, IL: St. Nicholas Corporation, 1968.
_____. *Abraham Lincoln: From Skeptic to Prophet*. Mohamet, IL: Mayhaven Publishing, 1995.
_____. *By Square and Compass: The Building of Lincoln's Home and Its Saga*. Mill Valley, CA: Ashlar Press, 1984.
_____. "Lincoln and the Burners at New Salem." *Lincoln Herald*, Summer 1965.
_____. "Lincoln in the Governor's Chambers of the Illinois State House." *Lincoln Herald*, Winter 1982.
_____. "Lincoln in Trenton, N.J." *Lincoln Herald*, Fall 1993.
_____. *Lincoln's Connections with the Illinois and Michigan Canal*. Springfield, IL: Illinois Bell, 1968.
_____. "Location of the Rural Hotel in Springfield Where Abraham Lincoln Drank a Toast." *Lincoln Herald*, Fall 1979.
_____. "When Lincoln Left Town With Another Woman." *Lincoln Herald*, Winter 1966.
Tennessee Historical Markers. 6th ed. Tennessee Historical Commission, 1972.
Thane, Elswyth. *Dolley Madison: Her Life and Times*. New York: Crowell-Collier Press, 1970.
Theobald, Mary Miley. *Colonial Williamsburg*. Williamsburg, VA: The Colonial Williamsburg Foundation, 2001.
"This Side of the Mountains: Abraham Lincoln's 1848 Visit to Massachusetts." *Lincoln Herald*, Summer 1978.
Thomas, Benjamin P. *Abraham Lincoln*. New York: Alfred A. Knopf, 1952 (1994).
_____. *Lincoln's New Salem*. Springfield, IL: Abraham Lincoln Association, 1934.
Thomas, E.H. Gwynne. *The Presidential Families*. New York: Hippocrene Books, 1989.
Thomson, David S. *A Pictorial Biography: HST*. New York: Grosset and Dunlap, 1973.
Thurheimer, David C. *Landmarks of the American Revolution in New York State*. Albany, NY: New York State American Bicentennial Commission, 1976.
Tilberg, Frederick. *Historic Adams County, Pennsylvania*. Gettysburg: Hancock Handbook Committee, Times and News Publishing, 1950.
Tisler, C.C., and Aleita G. Tisler. *Lincoln Was Here (For Another Go at Douglas)*. Jackson, TN: McCowat–Mercer Press, 1958.
Toole, Robert M. *A Look at Metroland*. R.M. Toole, 1976.
Toomey, Daniel Carroll. *The Civil War in Maryland*. Baltimore, MD: Toomey Press, 1983.
Townsend, Timothy P. *The Site Adrift in the City: The Evolution of the Lincoln home Neighborhood*. Thesis by Park historian.
Townsend, William H. *Lincoln and the Bluegrass*. Lexington: University of Kentucky Press, 1955.
_____. *Lincoln in His Wife's Home Town*. Indianapolis: Bobbs-Merrill, 1929.
Trefousse, Hans L. *Andrew Johnson*. New York: W.W. Norton, 1989.
Tregillis, Helen Cox. *Lincoln and Shelbyville*. Private printing, 1979.
Trenton Historical Society. *A History of Trenton 1679–1929*. Princeton, NJ: Princeton University Press, 1929.
Trudell, Clyde. *Colonial Williamsburg*. New York: Viking Press, 1971.
Truman, Margaret. *First Ladies*. New York: Fawcett Columbine, 1995.
_____. *Harry S. Truman*. New York: William Morrow, 1972.
Trussell, John B.B., Jr. *Pennsylvania Landmarks of the Revolution*. Harrisburg: Pennsylvania Department of Transportation, undated.
Tuckerman, Arthur. *When Rochambeau Stepped Ashore*. Preservation Society of Newport County, 1955.
Tupper, Chris. "On the Plains of San Jacinto." *Texas Highways Magazine*. Austin: April 1986.

Tursi, Frank V. *Winston-Salem: A History.* Charlotte, NC: R.R. Donnelley, 1994.

U.S. Grant Sesquicentennial Souvenir Program, 1972.

Vacationlands, New York State. Published by the Department of Commerce for New York.

Van Arsdol, Ted. *Northwest Bastion.* Vancouver, WA: Heritage Trust of Clark, 1991.

Van Natter, Francis Marion. *Lincoln's Boyhood: A Chronicle of His Indiana Years.* Washington, D.C.: Public Affairs Press, 1963.

Villard, Henry. *Lincoln on the Eve of '61.* Edited by Harold G. Villard and Oswald Garrison Villard. Westport, CT: Greenwood Press, 1974 reprint.

Virginia Landmarks Register. Richmond: Virginia Historical Landmarks Commission, 1976.

Voges, Nettie Allen. *Old Alexandria.* Marshall, VA: EPM Pub., 1975.

Waldron, Larry. *Lincoln Parks: The Story Behind the Scenery.* Las Vegas, NV: Eastern National Parks, KC Publications, 1986.

Walk Around Leesburg. Loudoun Museum, 1995.

Walker, Carroll. *Pictorial History of Norfolk.* Virginia Beach, VA.: Donning, 1975.

Walker, Hon. Charles A. *History of Macoupin County, Illinois.* Chicago: S.J. Clark Publishing, 1911.

Walker's Brief History of Illinois.

Walking Tour of Historic Georgetown. Foundation for the Preservation of Historic Georgetown, 1971.

Walking Tour of Historic Winchester. Preservation of Historic Winchester, revised 1981.

Walking Tour of North and South Streets, Litchfield, Connecticut. Litchfield Historical Soc., My Country Society.

Walking Tour of Virginia's Historic Petersburg. Chamber of Commerce of Petersburg, 1969.

Wall, Bernardt. *Following Abraham Lincoln.* New York: Algonquin Publishing, 1943.

_____. *Following General Sam Houston.* Austin: Steck, 1935.

Wall, Charles Cecil. *George Washington Citizen Soldier.* Charlottesville: University of Virginia, 1980.

Wallace, Mike, and Edwin G. Burrows. *Gotham: A History of New York City to 1898.* New York: Oxford University Press, 1999.

Ward, Geoffrey C. *Before the Trumpet.* New York: Harper & Row, 1985.

_____. "The House at Eighth and Jackson." *American Heritage,* April 1989.

_____. "The House at Hyde Park." *American Heritage,* April 1987.

Ward, Harry M., and Harold E. Greer, Jr. *Richmond During the Revolution.* Charlottesville, VA: University Press of Virginia, 1977.

Warren, Louis A. *Lincoln's Youth.* Indianapolis: Indiana Historical Society, 1991.

_____. *Louisville Lincoln Loop.* Standard Printing, 1922.

Warwick, Jack. *Growing Up With Warren Harding.* Marion, OH: 1938.

Washington County Historical Association, Inc. *History of Washington County, Tennessee.* Johnson City, TN: Overmountain Press, 2001.

Watson, Alan D. *A History of New Bern and Craven Count.* New Bern, NC: New Bern Palace Commission, 1987.

Waugh, Ely Culbertson. *North Carolina Capital, Raleigh.* Chapel hill, NC: University of North Carolina Press, 1967.

Waugh, John C. *Reelecting Lincoln.* New York: Crown, 1997.

Wayland, John W. *The Lincolns in Virginia.* Harrisburg, VA: C.J. Carrier, reprinted 1987.

We the People: The Story of the United States Capitol. Washington D.C., *National Geographic,* 1964.

We, the People. The United States Capitol Historical Society, 1976.

Wead, Doug. *All the Presidents' Children.* New York: Atria Books, 2005.

_____. *The Raising of a President.* New York: Atria Books, 2005.

Weigley, Russell F., ed. *Philadelphia: A 300–Year History.* New York: W.W. Norton, 1982.

Weil, Tom. *Civil War Sites.* New York: Hippocrene Books, 1994.

Wells, Damon. *Stephen Douglas: The Last Years, 1857–1861.* Austin: University of Texas, 1971.

Wells, Mertle, and Arthur A. Hart. *Boise: An Illustrated History.* Sun Valley, CA: American Historical Press, 2000.

Westerguard, Barbara. *New Jersey: A Guide to the State.* Piscataway, NJ: Rutgers University Press, 1987, 1998.

Wheeler, Roy. *Historic Virginia.* Charlottesville, VA: Self-published, 1927.

Wheeless, Carl. *Landmarks of the American Presidents.* New York: Gale Research, 1996.

Whiffen, Marcus. *The Eighteenth-Century Homes of Williamsburg.* Williamsburg: Colonial Williamsburg, 1950.

White, Noral, and Elliot Willenski. *AIA Guide to New York City.* New York: Crown, 2000.

White House Historical Association. *The White House: An Historic Guide.* Washington, D.C., 1962.

Whitehill, Walter M., and Norman Kotker. *Massachusetts: A Pictorial History.* New York: Scribner's, 1976.

Whitelaw, Robert N.S., and Alice E. Levkoff. *Charleston, Come Hell or High Water.* Charleston: self- published, 1976.

Whitmore, Nancy, and T. Cannon. *Fredrick: A Pictorial History.* Toronto: Key Pub., 1981, 1995.

Whitney, Henry Clay. *Life on the Circuit With Lincoln.* Caldwell, ID: Caxton Printers, 1940.

Willets, Gibson. *Inside History of the White House.* New York: The Christian Herald, 1908.

Williams, Amelia. *Following General Sam Houston.* Austin: Steck, 1935.

Williams, Samuel C. *The Lincolns and Tennessee.* Lincoln Memorial University, 1942.

_____. "The Lincolns in Tennessee." *Lincoln Herald,* October 1941.

Williams, Thomas J.C., et al. *History of Frederick County, Maryland.* Baltimore: Regional Pub., reprint 1979.

_____. *History of Washington County, Maryland*. Baltimore: Regional Publishing, 1968.

Willingham, Robert M. Jr. *History of Washington, Georgia*. Washington Historical Soc., 1992.

Wills, Garry. *Lincoln at Gettysburg*. New York: Simon and Schuster, 1992.

Wilmington Walking and Driving Tour. Historical Society of Delaware, 1980.

Wilson, D. Ray. *Greater Chicago Historical Tour Guide*. Carpentersville, IL: Crossroads Communications, 1989.

Wilson, Douglas L. *Honor's Voice*. New York: Alfred A. Knopf, 1998.

_____. *Lincoln Before Washington*. Champaign, IL: University of Illinois Press, 1997.

_____, and Rodney O. Davis. *Herndon's Informants*. Urbana: University of Illinois, 1998.

Wilson, Everett. *Early Southern Towns*. New York: Castle Books, 1967.

_____. *Fifty Early American Towns*. South Brunswick, NJ: A.S. Barnes, 1966.

_____. *Maryland's Colonial Mansions*. New York: A.S. Barnes, 1965.

Wilson, John. *Chattanooga: A Story*. Published by author, 1980.

_____. *Lookout: The Story of an Amazing Mountain*. Published by the author, 1977.

Wilson, Robert H., ed. *Philadelphia*. Maplewood, NJ: Hammond Incorporated, 1968.

Winkelmann, Judith. *Restoring Mr. Lincoln's Home*. Dallas: Taylor, 1989.

Winstead, Guy. *Elizabethtown and Hardin County, Kentucky*. Virginia Beach, VA.: Donning, 1989.

Winter, William C. *The Civil War in St. Louis*. St. Louis: Historical Society Press, 1994.

Wisehart, M.K. *Sam Houston, American Giant*. Washington, D.C.: Robert B. Luce, 1962.

Woerner, H. Ray. "Taverns of Early Lancaster and Pennsylvania." *Journal of Lancaster County History*, 1973.

Woodall, Charles L. "Lincoln's Religion and the Denominations." *Lincoln Herald*, Fall 1982.

Woodbridge, George. "George Washington and Newport." *Bulletin of the Newport Historical Society*, Summer 220, Vol. 64, Pt. 3.

Woodward, W.E. *Meet General Grant*. New York: Literary Guild of America, 1928.

Wooldridge, Ruby A. *Brownsville: A Pictorial History*. Virginia Beach, VA.: Donning, 1982.

Wright, John D., Jr. *Lexington: Heart of the Blue Grass*. Lexington-Fayette County Historic Commission, 1982.

Wyatt, Edward A., and James G. Scott. *Petersburg's Story*. Richmond: Dietz, 1960.

Yancy, Rosa Faulkner. *Lynchburg and Its Neighbors*. Richmond: J.W. Fergusson, 1935.

Yater, George H. *Two Hundred Years at the Falls of the Ohio: A History of Louisville and Jefferson County*. Louisville, KY: Heritage, 1979.

Ziegler, Philip. *William IV, The First English King in America*. New York: Harper and Row, 1973.

Index to Sites by President

All presidents are discussed in the District of Columbia, Philadelphia, and New York City sections.

General Index